MICROWAVES

Introduction to
Circuits, Devices and Antennas

MICROWAVES

Introduction to Circuits, Devices and Antennas

Prof. M.L. Sisodia
Advisor
ECE, Global Institute of Technology
Sitapur, Jaipur, Rajasthan

Vijay Laxmi Gupta
Ex-Associate Professor
Department of Electronic Science
University of Delhi, New Delhi

PUBLISHING FOR ONE WORLD

NEW AGE INTERNATIONAL (P) LIMITED, PUBLISHERS
New Delhi • Bangalore • Chennai • Cochin • Guwahati • Hyderabad
Jalandhar • Kolkata • Lucknow • Mumbai • Ranchi
Visit us at **www.newagepublishers.com**

Published by New Age International (P) Ltd., Publishers
First Edition: 2001
Reprint: 2014

BRANCHES

- **Bangalore** 37/10, 8th Cross (Near Hanuman Temple), Azad Nagar, Chamarajpet Bangalore-560 018, Tel.: (080) 26756823, Telefax: 26756820 **E-mail: bangalore@newagepublishers.com**
- **Chennai** 26, Damodaran Street, T. Nagar, Chennai-600 017, Tel.: (044) 24353401 Telefax: 24351463, **E-mail: chennai@newagepublishers.com**
- **Cochin** CC-39/1016, Carrier Station Road, Ernakulam South, Cochin-682 016 Tel.: (0484) 2377004, Telefax: 4051303 **E-mail: cochin@newagepublishers.com**
- **Guwahati** Hemsen Complex, Mohd. Shah Road, Paltan Bazar, Near Starline Hotel Guwahati-781 008, Tel.: (0361) 2513881, Telefax: 2543669 **E-mail: guwahati@newagepublishers.com**
- **Hyderabad** 105, 1st Floor, Madhiray Kaveri Tower, 3-2-19, Azam Jahi Road Nimboliadda, Hyderabad-500 027, Tel.: (040) 24652456 Telefax: 24652457, **E-mail: hyderabad@newagepublishers.com**
- **Kolkata** RDB Chambers (Formerly Lotus Cinema) 106A, 1st Floor S.N. Banerjee Road, Kolkata-700 014, Tel.: (033) 22273773 Telefax: 22275247, **E-mail: kolkata@newagepublishers.com**
- **Lucknow** 16-A, Jopling Road, Lucknow-226 001, Tel.: (0522) 2209578, 4045297 Telefax: 2204098, **E-mail: lucknow@newagepublishers.com**
- **Mumbai** 142C, Victor House, Ground Floor, N.M. Joshi Marg, Lower Parel Mumbai-400 013, Tel.: (022) 24927869, Telefax: 24915415 **E-mail: mumbai@newagepublishers.com**
- **New Delhi** 22, Golden House, Daryaganj, New Delhi-110 002, Tel.: (011) 23262368, 23262370, Telefax: 43551305, **E-mail: sales@newagepublishers.com**

ISBN: 978-81-224-1338-0

₹ 195.00

C-13-06-7014

Printed in Ramprintograph, Delhi.

PUBLISHING FOR ONE WORLD

NEW AGE INTERNATIONAL (P) LIMITED, PUBLISHERS
7/30 A, Daryaganj, New Delhi - 110002
Visit us at **www.newagepublishers.com**

PREFACE

This book is intended as an introductory text on microwave circuits, devices and antennas. It can be used not only by the students of physics and engineering at the graduate and the postgraduate levels, but also by practising engineers, technicians and research workers in the area of microwaves. It contains comprehensive up-to-date text for a standard course on transmission lines, guided waves, passive components (including ferrite devices), periodic structures and filters, microwave vacuum tubes, solid state devices and their applications, strip-lines, MICs and antennas. It also includes microwave measurements at length. To limit the book to a manageable size, we assume that the reader is familiar with electromagnetics, solid state physics and electronics. The material has been used by us while teaching at I.T. BHU (MLS), University of Rajasthan [MLS] and Delhi University [VLG].

The written text is supplemented with a large number of suitable diagrams and a good number of solved examples for reinforcing the key aspects. Each chapter has a select bibliography/references and good number of problems and review questions at the end. This will help the students, research workers and practising engineers and technicians to widen the horizons of the knowledge who want to go into more details, or test their grasp of the subject matter.

The preparation of this book owes much to the work of other authors, including many referenced in the text; our indebtendness to all of them is gratefully acknowledged. Errors in the text are inevitable, however, special care has been taken in the reproduction of all equations. Suggestions for corrections and for further improvement of the text from the readers will be greatly appreciated.

We acknowledge with thanks the contribution of Prof. R.C. Bhandari and Prof. G.S. Raghuvanshi in preparing this text.

Authors

Contents

☐☐☐

1
Introduction

In this chapter we shall discuss briefly the subject matter of microwave electronics which is treated in greater detail later on in the text.

1.1 Microwave Frequency Bands in Radio-Spectrum

The whole electromagnetic-spectrum that extends from d.c to γ- rays is broadly divided into two regions, namely, the radio- spectrum from d.c. to 300 GHz and the optical spectrum extending from 300 GHz to infinity. The term microwaves is commonly used to designate for those frequencies ranging from 300 MHz to 300 GHz or with wave lengths ranging from 100 cm. to 1 mm. in radio-spectrum. The microwave region has been further divided into three bands, namely, ultrashort wave (Ultra high frequency – UHF), Supershort wave (Super high frequency – SHF) and Extreme short wave (Extreme high frequency – EHF) according to recommendations of the International Radio consultative committee. The position of microwave bands in entire ratio-spectrum is shown in Table 1.1. The region of microwaves has been pushed into wavelengths lower than 1 mm and are known as submillimetre waves (> 300 GHz)

TABLE 1.1 Position of Microwave Bands in the Entire Radio-Spectrum

S. No.	Frequency band	Wave length band	Designation (I.R.C.C. band)	Remarks
1.	0 to 30 KHz	infinity to 10^4 m	Very low frequency (VLF)/ Very long waves	–
2.	30 to 300 KHz	10^4 to 10^3 m	Low frequency (LF)/Long waves	–

3.	300 to 3000 KHz	10^3 to 10^2 m	Medium frequency (MF)/ Medium waves	–
4.	3 to 30 MHz	100 to 10 m	High frequency (HF)/ Short waves	–
5.	30 to 300 MHz	10 to 1m	Very high frequency (VHF)/ Very short waves.	–
6.	0.3 to 3 GHz	1 to 0.1 m	Ultra high frequency (UHF)/ Ultra short waves	micro-waves
7.	3 to 30 GHz	10 to 1 cm	Super high frequency (SHF)/ Super short waves	micro-waves
8.	30 to 300 GHz	10 to 1 mm	Extreme high frequency (EHF)/ Extreme short waves	micro-waves
9.	300 to 3000 GHz	1 to 0.1 mm	Submillimetre waves	

The Institute of Electrical and Electronics Engineers (IEEE) recommended microwave band designations as listed in Table 1.2.

TABLE 1.2 IEEE Microwave Frequency Bands

Frequency range (GHz)	Designation
0.003 to 0.030	HF
0.030 to 0.300	VHF
0.300 to 1.000	UHF
1.000 to 2.000	L band
2.000 to 4.000	S band
4.000 to 8.000	C band
8.000 to 12.000	X band
12.000 to 18.000	Ku band
18.000 to 26.000	K band
26.000 to 40.000	Ka band
40.000 to 300.000	Millimeter
>300.000	Submillimetre

The radar band classification, as listed in Table 1.3, came into use during world war II and is still in use to-day even though the new military band designation, as listed in Table 1.4 has been adopted by the U.S. Department of Defence since 1970.

TABLE 1.3 U.S. Military Microwave Bands (Radar Bands)

Frequency rangs (GHz)	Designation
0.225 to 0.390	P band
0.390 to 1.550	L band
1.550 to 3.900	S band
3.900 to 6.200	C band
6.200 to 10.900	X band
10.900 to 36.000	K band
36.000 to 46.000	Q band
46.000 to 56.000	V band
56.000 to 100.000	W band

TABLE 1.4 U.S New Miltary Microwave Bands (New Radar Bands)

Frequency range (GHz)	Designation	Frequency range (GHz)	Designation
0.100 to 0.250	A band	6.000 to 8.000	H band
0.250 to 0.500	B band	8.000 to 10.000	I band
0.500 to 1.000	C band	10.000 to 20.000	J band
1.000 to 2.000	D band	20.000 to 40.000	K band
2.000 to 3.000	E band	40.000 to 60.000	L band
3.000 to 4.000	F band	60.000 to 100.000	M band
4.000 to 6.000	G band		

1.2 Microwave Applications

Microwaves are characterized by small size of wave lengths, large bandwidth, propagation along the line-of-sight paths, transmission through ionosphere with negligible absorption and reflection, small antenna size and reflection from metallic surfaces, microwave heating and microwave resonance in molecular, atomic and nuclearsystems. These features have opened up new vistas of applications in communication, in radar, in astronomy and remote sensing, in basic and applied research, in industry, in domestic sphear and in biomedical fields. Below, we basically enumerate the various applications of microwaves without much account of them. The list is far from complete but does give an idea to the reader of the wide variety of uses to which this portion of radio-spectrum is put.

Communication and radar systems

Microwave band is widely used for telephone networks, in broadcast, in television systems, in long distance communication, for microwave links, for space communication, in satallite communication and in several other communication applications by police, civil aviation, railways and services, etc.

Microwaves are extensively used for Radar (Radio detection and ranging) systems. Beside, high-resolution radar capable of detecting and locating enemy planes and ships there are varied forms of radars such as missile-tracking radar, early warning radar, air-port, traffic-control radar, fire-control radar, weather-detecting radar, missile-guidance radar and doppler radar.

The sub-nanosecond pulse (major portion of these pulse spectrum lies in microwave region) are useful in several special purpose radars for docking the pre-collision sensing, etc. These pulses are being used in high speed logic circuits. Thus microwaves techniques are being introduced in extremely fast computer operations.

Recently (1999-2000) Jeffrey Danials of Ohio State University reported in Geophysical Research Letters that ground penetrating radar (GPA) could be used in detecting subsurface hazardous waste.

Satellite as microwave relay station have been deployed for communication as well as for surveillance and collecting data on atmospheric and weather conditions.

The list is far from complete but represents a major use of microwave band for communication and radar systems.

Radio-astronomy and remote-sensing application

Sensitive microwave receivers are used in radio-astronomy to detect and study the electromagnetic radiation, which lie in microwave region of radio spectrum, orgninating from the sun and other astronomical objects. The microwave radiometers are used to map atmospheric temperature profiles, moisture conditions in soils and crops, and for other remote-sensing applications.

Basic and applied research

It is observed that the molecular, atomic and nuclear systems display various resonance phenomena when subjected to electromagnetic fields and many of these resonances occur in the microwave frequency range, hence microwaves have provided an experimental tool to study the basic properties of materials which led to the development of microwave spectroscopy. Later it also led to the development of non-reciprocal ferrite devices and solid-state microwave generators, e.g., masers and lasers.

Microwaves are used in linear accelarators to produce high- energy beams of charged particles for use in atomic and nuclear research.

Industrial and domestic applications

1. Microwaves are used extensively for non-destructive testing of materials, process controls such as moisture and thickness detectors, etc.

It is used to measure the concentration of different gases e.g. in exhaust chimneys, in order to control the emission of pollutants or in chemical processes in order to record continuously the concentration of gases evolved in the process.

2. It is used for several industrial applications involving heating. This is used for industrial processing in Food, Plastic, Rubber, Chemicals and Forest products industries. In mining it is used for breaking rocks and coal seams and in tunnel boring. It is also used for drying/breaking up concrete. It is also used for drying inks, textiles, leather, tobacco, grains etc.

3. Microwave ovens are being increasingly used in domestic sphere for cooking and roasting. The microwave frequency used for this application is 2450 MHz with a power output of 500 – 1000 W.

Biomedical applications

Microwave radiation has also been found useful for cancer therapy – hyperthermia. Electromagnetic techniques are used for medical diagnosis such as monitoring of heart-beat, lung water detection, etc.

It has a potential application in the field of Energy

Satellite power stations have been proposed to harness solar energy. From these power station energy would be transported in form of microwaves.

Table 1.5 summarises the typical and unique applications of microwaves. The scope of microwave applications in communication industry and basic and applied research is ever increasing. The extension of microwave techniques into the field of development of optical communication system is one such example.

TABLE 1.5

S. No.	Applications	Frequency Band
1.	Television, satellite communicaton, Surveillance radar, navigational aids, food industry (microwave-ovens) point to point communication.	0.3 to 3 GHz
2.	Altimeter, air and ship borne radar, microwave links, common-carrier land mobile communication, satellite communication, navigation, basic research-microwave spectroscopy.	3 to 30 GHz
3.	Radar, radio-astronomy, radio-meteorology, space research, nuclear physics, nucleonics.	30 to 300 GHz

Therefore, it is a fascinating field of study and research, which has vast opportunities in varied applications. As such large number of postgraduate students in Physics and Engineering as well as undergraduate students opt for specializing in microwave electronics/ engineering.

Figure 1.1 shows a typical microwave system. It has a transmitter subsystem, which normally consists of microwave generator, waveguides, wavemeter, attenuator and transmitting antenna, and a receiver subsystem, which normally consists of receiving antenna, waveguides, a microwave amplifier, detector. Another typical radar system is shown in Fig. 1.2. which uses single antenna for transmission and receiption.

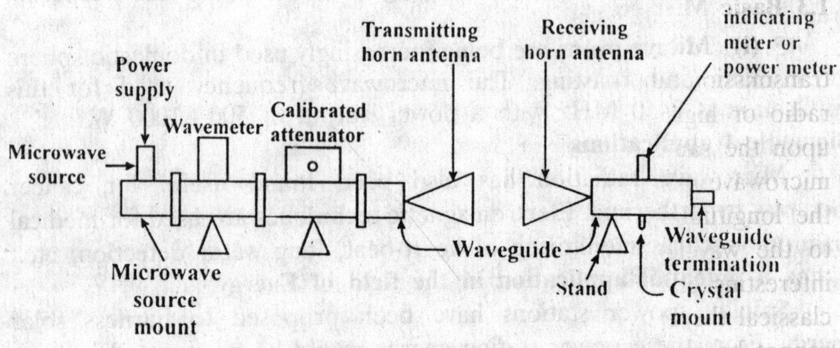

Fig. 1.1. Typical microwave system

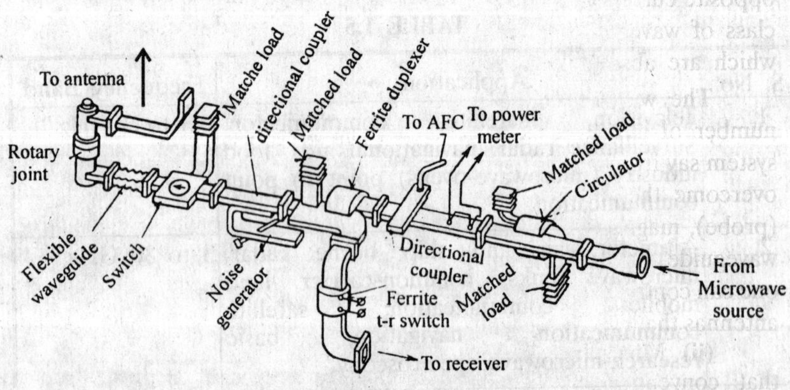

Fig. 1.2. Typical radar system

Therefore, a first course on microwave should include three major areas of study, namely (i) microwave transmission lines and waveguides, (ii) microwave circuit elements and (iii) microwave sources, amplifiers and detector. In addition to these the course should also include microwave measurements which provided the link between theory and practice, microwave radiating antennas, microwave striplines and integrated circuit.

These topics are discussed in the text keeping a balance between mathematical and physical approach. However, inbrief few basic concepts of microwaves are presented below to provide an overview of microwaves to the reader.

1.3 Basic Microwave Concepts

(i) Microwave Transmission : The principles of microwave transmission cannot be derived by mere extensions of either low frequency radio or high frequency optical concepts, although they are all based upon the same fundamental laws of electromagnetism. For instance, if microwave power is fed in a conventional two conductor line where the longitudinal and transverse dimensions of the line are comparable to the wavelength of the propagating signal, it leads to a series of interesting effects that fall outside the scope of problems examined by classical theory of long transmission lines. It turns out that such a line cannot be used for microwave transmission. One has, therefore, to use hollow metal tubes called waveguides. The energy propagation in these structures is basically a reflection phenomena. Conversely, a hollow-pipe waveguide cannot be treated by the rules of low-frequency electricity, for by these rules opposite currents cannot flow in the same metallic conductor without coalescing into one net current, yet we see that opposite currents can flow in the same conductor in waveguides. Another class of waveguides of most recent origin is called surface waveguides which are absolutely uncommon to low frequency transmission.

The waveguide transmission of microwaves is associated with a number of interesting problems such as coupling of power to another system say from generator to line, exciting of waves in a waveguide, etc. To overcome these, three basic coupling methods, viz. electrical coupling (probe), magnetic coupling (loop), and aperture coupling (waveguide to waveguide) have been evolved. The basic feature of these methods is that one can control the amount of coupling because these structures have small antennas that radiate into the waveguide to be coupled.

(ii) Microwave Circuit Elements : It is a well-established fact that conventional circuit elements such as resistors, inductors and capacitors do not respond well at microwave frequencies. For instance, a coil of wire may be an excellent inductor at 1 MHz, but at 500 MHz it may be an equally good capacitor because of the predominating effect of inter-turn capacitance. However, this does not mean that energy dissipating (resistors) and storing (capacitors and inductors) elements cannot be constructed at microwave frequencies but their geometrical shape will be quite different. As will be seen, a section of a microwave line (distributed parameters), offers reactances varying form $-\infty$ to $+\infty$ if its length is suitably chosen.

Similarly, conventional resonant and anti-resonant circuits are replaced by resonant microwave line sections known as resonant cavities. Often resonant cavities are used as circuit elements with varying properties.

When a number of such microwave circuit elements are connected together, we have a microwave circuit. The analysis of a microwave circuit can be carried out either in terms of equivalent transmission line, voltage and current waves or in terms of amplitudes of the incident and reflected waves. The first approach is called the conventional equivalent impedance description approach while the second is known as the scattering matrix approach. The latter approach being closely related to the wave nature of fields.

(iii) Generation and Amplification of Microwaves : The operation of conventional vacuum tubes and solid state devices is limited by transit time effects. However, the frequency range of operation of these devices can be extended to the lower edge of the microwave spectrum at the cost of power output and noise characteristics. Therefore, the development of new devices was essential to exploit this frequency region. Fortunately, number of new principles of operation such as velocity modulation, interaction of space charge waves with electromagnetic fields were proposed. It involves transfer of power from a source of direct voltage to a source of alternating voltage by means of a density-modulated stream of electrons resulting in the development of klystron (in 1939 by R.H. Varian and S.F. Varian[1]), magnetron (in 1921 by Hull and an improved model in 1940 by Boot and Randal [2]) and travelling-wave tube (TWT) (in 1944 by R.Komfner [3]).

The interaction of the impact ionization avalanche and the transit time of charge carriers was used to develop Reed diode in 1958 [5], IMPATT by Johnston et al. in 1965 [6], TRAPATT by Prager et al. in 1967 [7]. Quantum mechanical tunneling was used to develop Tunnel Diode by Esaki in 1958 [8]. Transferred electron techniques were used to develop transfer electron devices by Ridley el al. in 1961 [9] and Hilsum in 1962 [10]. Gunn oscillator was developed in 1963 [11] which operate simply by the application of a dc voltage to a bulk. In all solid-state devices the negative resistance characteristies is exploited for microwave generation and amplification.

1.4 Format of the Book–The book is organized into ten chapters.

Chapter 1 gives introduction to field of microwaves.

Chapter 2 treats microwave transmission lines.

Chapter 3 deals with waveguides and cavities.

Chapter 4 describes circut components (including ferrite devices).

Chapter 5 treats microwave filters and periodic structures.

Chapter 6 studies beam dynamics, O-type tubes and M-type tubes.

Chapter 7 deals with microwave solid state devices-parameteric. devices, Avalanche transit time devices, Transferred electron devices (TEDs), microwave transistor's, tunnel diodes and microwave field-effect transistors.

Chapter 8 deals with microwave striplines and microwave integrated circuits.

Chapter 9 discusses the microwave antennas

Chapter 10 describes microwave measurements.

Selected titles and references are listed below.

Select Titles

1. Collin, R.E., **Foundations for Microwave Engineering**, McGraw-Hill Book company, NewYork, 1966.
2. Gandhi, O.P., **Microwave Engineering and Applications**, Pergamon Press, New York, 1981
3. Liao, S.Y., **Microwave Devices and Circuits,** Prentice-Hall Inc, Englewood cliffs, N.J., U.S.A. 1995 [Indian reprint]
4. Soohoo, R.F., **Microwave Electronics,** Addison-wesley publishing company, Reading, Mass., 1971.
5. Reich, H.J., et al, **Microwave Principles,** D. Van Nostrand Reinhold company New York 1957 (an East-West Edition)
6. Reich, H.J., et, al, **Microwave Theory and Techniques,** D. Van Nostrand Reinhold Company, New York, 1953.
7. Brownwell, A.B., AND R.E. Beam, **Theory and Application of Microwaves**, McGraw-Hill Book Co., New York 1947.
8. Chatterjee, R., **Elements of Microwave Engineering**, East-West Press, New Delhi, 1984.

Microwave Circuits and Passive Devices

1. Jordan, E, and K.G. Balmain, **Electromagnetic Waves and Radiating Systems,** Prentice – Hall, Inc. Englewood cliffs, N.J., 1968
2. Liao, S.Y., **Engineering Application of Electromagnetic Theory**, West Publishing company, St. Paul, Minn., 1988
3. Rizzi, P.A., **Microwave Engineering : Passive circuits,** Prentice-Hall, Inc., Englwood cliffs., N.J., 1988

4. Sisodia, M.L. and G.S. Raghuvanshi, **Microwave circuits and Passive Devices,** John Wiley & Sons, New York 1987 (Wiley Eastern Limited, New Delhi 1987)
5. Dworsty, L.N., **Modern Transmission Line Theory and Applications.,** John wiley & Sons, New York, 1979
6. Southworth, G.E., **Principles and Applications of Waveguide Transmission,** D. Van Nostrand company, Princeton N.J. 1950.
7. Soohoo, R.F., **Therory and Applications of Ferrites,** Prentice-Hall, Inc., Englewood cliffs, N.J. 1960.

Microwave Tubes

1. Hamilton, R.D., et al, **Klystrons and Microwave Triodes,** Radiation Lab. Series, McGraw-Hill Book Co., New York 1948
2. Hutter, R.G.E., **Beam and Wave Electronics in Microwave Tubes,** D.Van Nostrand Company, Princeton., N.J., 1960
3. Pierce, J.R., **Travelling-wave Tubes,** D. Van Nostrand Company Princeton, N.J., 1950
4. Beck, A. H.W., **Space-charge Waves and Slow Electromagnetic waves,** Pergamon Press, New York, 1958
5. Gewartowski, J.V., and H.A, Watson, **Principles of Electron Tubes**, D.Van Nostrand Company Princeton, N.J. 1965.
6. Liao S.Y., **Microwave Electron Tubes**, Prentice. Hall Inc, Englewood cliffs, N.J. 1988
7. Chatterjee, R., **Vacuum Electron Devices**, Affiliated East-West Press Private Limited New Delhi, 1999.
8. Chodorow, M., and C. Susskind **Fundamentals of Microwave Electronics**, McGraw–Hill Book Company, New York, 1964.
9. Gilmour, A.S., Jr., **Microwave Tubes,** Artech House, Dedham, Mass., 1986
10. Sisodia, M.L. **Microwave Active Devices,** in Press.

Microwave Solid State Devices

1. Liao, S.Y., **Semiconductor Electronic Devices,** Prentice-Hall, Inc., Englewood cliffs, N. J., 1990
2. Sze, S.M., **Semiconductor Devices : Physcs and Technology,** John wiley & sons, New york, 1985

3. Hess, K., **Advanced Theory of Semiconductor Devices,** Prentice-Hall, Ins., Englewood cliffs, N.J., 1988
4. Mines, A.G., **Semiconductor Devices and Integrated Electronics, D.** Van Nostrand Rehinhold company, New York, 1980.
5. Chang, K.K.N., **Parametric and Tunnel Diodes,** Prentice-Hall, Engle wood cliffs, N.J., 1964.
6. Watson, H.A., (ed) **Microwave Semiconductor Devices and their circuit Applications**, McGraw-Hill Book company, New york, 1969.
7. Vander Zil, A., **Solid state Physical Electronics,** Prentice- Hall of India Pvt. Ltd., 1971.
8. Bahl, I., ed. **Solid. – State Circuits Design.**, John Wiley & sons, New York, 1988.
9. Streetman, B.G., **solid-state-Electronic Devices,** Prentice-Hall Inc., Englewood cliffs, N.J., 1989
10. Chattarjee, R., **Microwave and Millimeter-wave Semiconductor Devices,** Affiliated East-West press (P) Limited, New Delhi.

Microwave Measurement

1. Sucher, M. and J. Fox., **Handbook of Microwave Measurements**, Vol I, II, III, John Wiley & Sons Inc., New York, 1963.
2. Gintzton E.L., **Microwave Measurements** McGraw – Hill Book Company, 1957
3. Sisodia, M.L. and G.S. Raghuvanshi, **Basic Microwave Techniques and Laboratory Mannual,** John Wiley & Sons, 1987. (Wiley Eastern Limited 2000, New Delhi.)

References

1. Warnecke. R.R., et al., **Velocity Modulated Tubes**. In Advances in Electronics, vol. 3. Academic Press, New York, 1951.
2. Hull, A.W., Phys. Rev. **18,** 31 (1921)
3. Okress, E., Editor, **Crossed Field Microwave Devices,** Academic press, New York, vols, I and II, 1961.
4. Kompfner, R., **The travelling wave tube as amplifier at microwaves,** proc. IRE **35**, 124-127, February 1947
5. Read, W.T., **A proposed high frequency negative-resistance diode,** Bell System tech. J., **37**, 401-446 (1958)

6. Johnston, R.L., B.C. Deloach, and G.B. Cohen, **A silicon diode microwave oscillator,** Bell System Tech., J., **44** 369-372, February 1965.
7. Prager, H.J., et al., **High-power, high-efficiency silicon avalanche diodes at ultra high frequencies,** Proc. IEEE (letters), **55,** 586-587, April 1967.
8. Esaki, L., **New phenomenon in Narrow Ge p-n junctions**, Phys. Rev., **109,** 603 (1958)
9. Ridley, B.K., and T.B. Watkins, **The Possibility of negative resistance effect in semiconductors**, Proc. Phys. Soc., **78** 293- 304, August 1961
10. Hilsum, C., **Transferred electron amplifirs and oscillators, Proc. IEEE., 50,** 185-189 February 1962
11. Gunn, J. B., **Instabilities of current in III-V semiconductors,** IBM J. Res. Develop., **8** 141-159, April 1964

■■■

2

Transmission Lines

2.1. Introduction

Any structure used to guide the flow of electrical energy or electromagnetic field energy from one point to the other or from the source to the load is called *Transmission Line*. Wave propagation in unbounded media, that is in the media of infinite extent is unguided. Since in such medium the uniform plane wave exists throughout all space and the em energy associated with the wave spreads over a wide area. Wave propagation in unbounded media is used in radio and T.V. broadcasting, where the information being transmitted is meant for multiple users. But in telephony or data communication the information is used by single person. So this type of propagation will not be of much use.

Another means of information propagation is by the guided structures. They guide the propagation of energy from source to load. Examples of such structures are transmission lines and waveguide. There are four general types of transmission lines :

(i) parallel two wire lines

(ii) the twisted pair

(iii) the shielded pair

(iv) the Coaxial line

The use of particular type of transmission line depends upon the frequency, the power to be transmitted and the type of insulation. However, at microwave frequencies, waveguides are normally used. The two wire lines are used at radio-frequencies, for low frequency transmission the twisted pair transmission line is used. The shielded pair shown in Fig. 2.1 consists of two parallel conductors separated from each other and surrounded by solid dielectric. The principal advantage of shielded pair is that the two conductors are balanced with respect to ground, that is, the capacitance between each conductor and ground is uniform around the entire length of the line and the wires are shielded against any pick up from stray field.

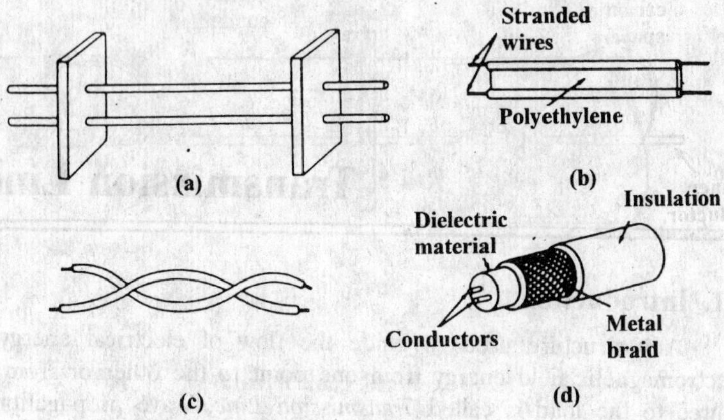

Fig. 2.1. Various types of transmission lines (a) two-wire air dielectric (b) two-wire ribbon type (c) twisted pair (d) shielded pair

The coaxial cables are the most widely used type of transmission line. Figure 2.2 shows the flexible and rigid coaxial cables. They consist of an inner conductor held in place, exactly at the centre of the other conductor. The outer conductor completely shields the inner. Hence no radiation loss takes place. The coaxial line is sometimes referred to as an unbalanced line since the inner conductor does not have the same electrical capacitance to ground as the outer conductor.

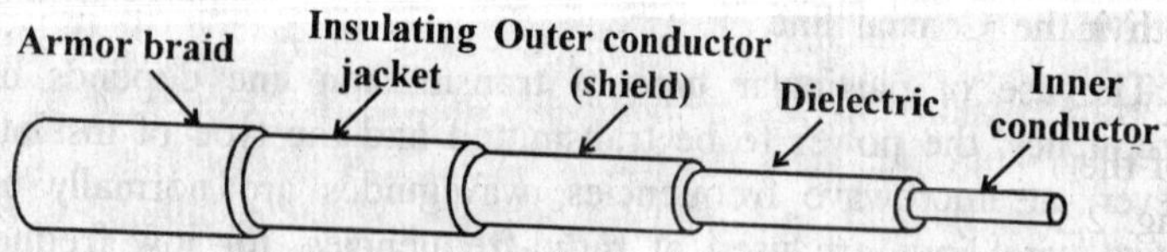

Fig. 2.2. (a) Flexible

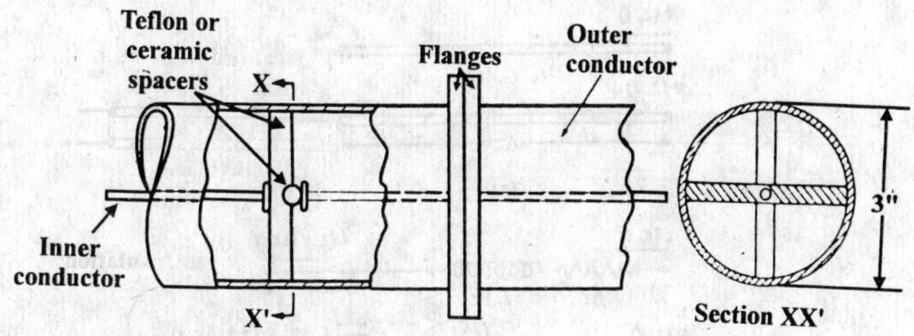

Fig. 2.2. (b) Rigid coaxial cables.

The desired characteristics of the transmission lines are :

(i) small attenuation

(ii) low radiation

(iii) single mode propagation over wide band of frequencies

(iv) maximum power transfer

2.2. Distributed Constants of Transmission Lines

At low frequencies circuit analysis assumes that circuits consist of lumped elements. It is assumed that the current at every point of series circuit has the same value and also the voltage between all pairs of opposite points on connecting leads are identical. Also circuit analysis assumes that physical dimensions of network components are much smaller than the electrical wavelength. However, in the frequency region where this condition does not hold the transmission line to be considered has distributed parameters where current and voltages can vary both in magnitude and phase.

A transmission line is schematically shown as a two wire line. Some of the results obtained can be used for all types of transmission lines. Fig. 2.3(a, b) shows a schematic diagram of a transmission line. The short piece of line length 'Δz' can be modelled as a lumped element circuit. A finite length line can be viewed as a cascade of sections of the form shown in Fig. 2.4. The four parameters – Inductance (L), Resistance (R), Capacitance (C) and Conductance (G) are all expressed in their respective units per unit length.

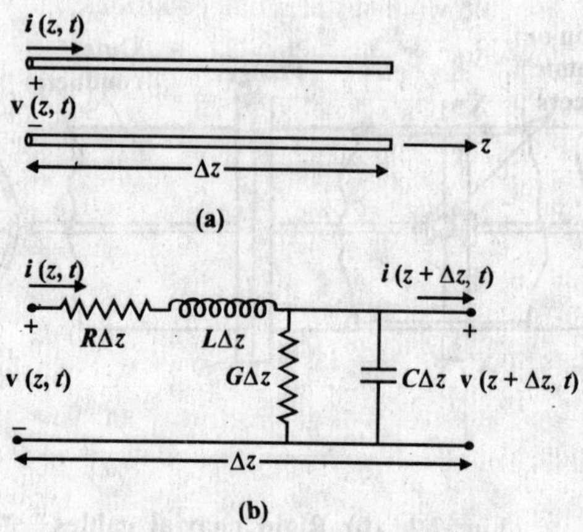

Fig. 2.3. (a) Voltage and current on the transmission line (b) Lumped-element equivalent circuit.

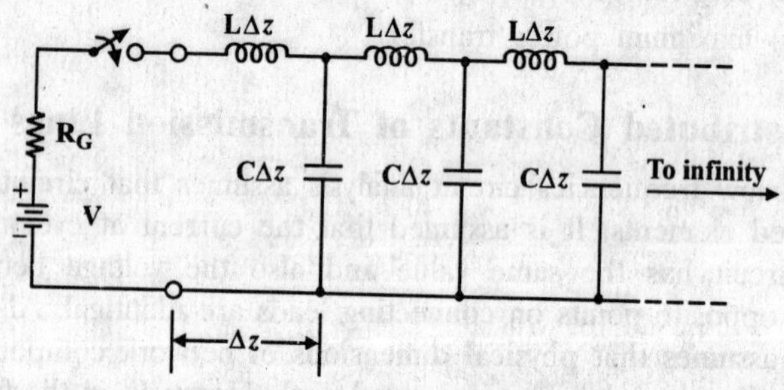

Fig. 2.4 Lumped equivalent circuit representation of an infinitely long loss less line

Applying Kirchoff's voltage law to Fig. 2.3b, we get

$$v(z, t) - R\Delta z\, i(z, t) - L\Delta z \frac{\partial(z, t)}{\partial t} - v\,(z + \Delta z\,, t) = 0 \quad \text{....(2.1a)}$$

Kirchoff's Current law leads to

$$i(z, t) - G\Delta z\, v(z + \Delta z, t) - C\Delta z \frac{\partial v(z + \Delta z, t)}{\partial t} - i(z + \Delta z, t) = 0$$

....(2.1b)

Dividing Eq. 2.1a and Eq. 2.1b by Δz and taking the limit $\Delta z \to 0$ gives the following differential equations :

$$\lim_{\Delta z \to 0} \left[\frac{v(z + \Delta z, t) - v(z, t)}{\Delta z} \right] = Ri\,(z, t) + L\,\frac{\partial i\,(z, t)}{\partial t}$$

or
$$\frac{-\partial v(z, t)}{\partial z} = Ri\,(z, t) + L\,\frac{\partial i(z, t)}{\partial t} \quad \text{....(2.2a)}$$

$$\frac{-\partial i(z, t)}{\partial z} = Gv\,(z, t) + C\,\frac{\partial i(z, t)}{\partial t} \quad \text{....(2.2b)}$$

These are the time domain forms of the transmission line equations, also called the telegrapher equations.

For the sinusoidal steady-state condition, with cosine-based phasors, Eq. 2.2 simplify to

$$\frac{dV(z)}{dz} = -\,(R + j\omega L)\,I\,(z) \quad \text{....(2.3a)}$$

$$\frac{dI(z)}{dz} = -\,(G + j\omega C)\,V\,(z) \quad \text{....(2.3b)}$$

Solving the two equations 2.3a and 2.3b simultaneously, we get the wave equation in $V(z)$ and $I(z)$

$$\frac{d^2V(z)}{dz^2} - \gamma^2 v\,(z) = 0 \quad \text{....(2.4a)}$$

$$\frac{d^2I(z)}{dz^2} - \gamma^2 I\,(z) = 0 \quad \text{....(2.4b)}$$

where $\gamma = \alpha + j\beta = \sqrt{(R + j\omega L)\,(G + j\omega C)}$ ....(2.5)

,
is the complex propagation constant, which is a function of frequency. The travelling wave solution to Eq 2.4 are

$$V(z) = V_s\,e^{-\gamma z} + V_r\,e^{\gamma z} \quad \text{....(2.6a)}$$

$$I(z) = I_s\,e^{-\gamma z} + I_r\,e^{\gamma z} \quad \text{....(2.6b)}$$

where, V_s, I_s = sending end voltage and current at $z = 0$

V_r, I_r = receiving end voltage and current at $z = z$

$e^{-\gamma z}$ = term represents the wave propagation in $+z$ direction

$e^{\gamma z}$ = term represents wave propagation in $-z$ direction.

Substitute for $V(z)$ in Eq. 2.3a from Eq. 2.6a, we get

$$I(z) = \frac{\gamma}{(R + j\omega L)} [V_s e^{-\gamma z} - V_r e^{\gamma z}] \quad \text{....(2.6c)}$$

Equating coefficients of $e^{-\gamma z}$, $e^{\gamma z}$ from Eqs. 2.6b and 2.6c we define the characteristic impedance Z_o as

$$Z_0 = \frac{V_s}{I_s} = \frac{-V_r}{I_r} = \frac{R + j\omega L}{\gamma} = \sqrt{\frac{R + j\omega L}{G + j\omega C}} \quad \text{....(2.7)}$$

We can write Eq. 2.6b in the following form :

$$I(z) = \frac{V_s}{Z_0} e^{-\gamma z} - \frac{V_r}{Z_0} e^{\gamma z} \quad \text{....(2.8)}$$

Converting back to time domain, voltage waveform can be expressed as :

$$V(z, t) = |V_s| \cos(\omega t - \beta z) e^{-\alpha z} + |V_r| \cos(\omega t - \beta z) e^{\alpha z} \quad \text{....(2.9)}$$

We can define the wavelength on the line as the distance between two successive maxima or minima on the wave at a fixed instant of time, thus

$$(\omega t - \beta z) - (\omega t - \beta\{z + \lambda\}) = 2\pi$$

or

$$\lambda = \frac{2\pi}{\beta} \quad \text{....(2.10)}$$

The phase velocity is the velocity of a fixed phase point on a travelling wave and is obtained by keeping the argument of cos in Eq. 2.9. as a constant. That is,

$$\omega t - \beta z = k = \text{constant}$$

$$v_p = \frac{dz}{dt} = \frac{\omega}{\beta} = \lambda f \quad \text{....(2.11)}$$

2.3. Types of Transmission Lines

For attenuation considerations, transmission lines can be divided into three types :

(i) Ideal or lossless lines

(ii) Lines with small losses

(iii) Distortionless lines

Out of these three lines the only line which is of practical importance is the line with low losses.

(A) Ideal or loss less line

A transmission line is said to be lossless if the conductors of the line are perfect ($\sigma_C \approx \infty$) and the dielectric media seperating the two conductors is lossless ($\sigma \approx 0$).

For such a line

$$R = G = 0$$

Hence the line propagation constant can be given as

$$\gamma = \alpha + j\beta = j\omega\sqrt{LC}$$

$$\beta = \omega\sqrt{LC}$$

$$\alpha = 0 \text{ and } Z_0 = \sqrt{\frac{L}{C}} \qquad \text{....(2.12)}$$

It should be noted that the characteristic impedance is purely resistive and is real. It also means that the current and voltage in this case for a travelling wave are in phase, *i.e.*

$$V(z) = V_s e^{-\gamma z} \qquad \text{....(2.13a)}$$

and

$$I(z) = \frac{V_s}{Z_0} e^{-\gamma z} \qquad \text{....(2.13b)}$$

Wavelength and phase velocity for lossless transmission line is

$$\lambda = \frac{2\pi}{\omega\sqrt{LC}} \qquad \text{....(2.14a)}$$

$$v_p = \frac{1}{\sqrt{LC}} \qquad \text{....(2.14b)}$$

(B) Line with small losses

When long lines with appreciable attenuation have to be considered, the simplifying assumption considered in the earlier case are no longer valid. Still in many practical lines, it is true that $R << \omega L$ and $G << \omega C$. For such cases the expressions for γ and Z_0 can be simplified to

$$\gamma = \alpha + j\beta = j\omega\sqrt{LC}\left(1 + \frac{R}{j\omega L}\right)^{1/2}\left(1 + \frac{G}{j\omega C}\right)^{1/2} \qquad \text{....(2.15)}$$

Expanding by binomial theorem and neglecting terms higher than second order,

$$\gamma = \alpha + j\beta \approx j\omega\sqrt{LC}\left(1 + \frac{R}{2j\omega L} - \frac{R^2}{8j^2\omega^2L^2} + \dots\dots\right) \times \left(1 + \frac{G}{2j\omega C} - \frac{G^2}{8j^2\omega^2C^2} + \dots\dots\right)$$

$$\cong j\omega\sqrt{LC}\left[\left(1 + \frac{R}{2j\omega L} + \frac{G}{2j\omega C}\right) + \frac{1}{2}\left(\frac{R}{2\omega L} - \frac{G}{2\omega C}\right)^2\right] \quad \text{....(2.16)}$$

$$\therefore \quad \beta = \beta'\left[1 + \frac{1}{2}\left(\frac{\alpha_c}{\beta_0} - \frac{\alpha_d}{\beta_0}\right)^2\right] \quad \text{....(2.17a)}$$

where $\beta' = \omega\sqrt{LC} = \frac{2\pi}{\lambda'}$ (β' and λ' are quantities for lossless line)

$\alpha_c = \frac{R}{2Z_0'}$ and $\alpha_d = \frac{G}{2Y_0'}$ (Z_0' is characteristic impedance for lossless line)

The wavelength relation is

$$\lambda = \lambda'\left[1 - \frac{1}{2}\left(\frac{\alpha_c}{\beta_0} - \frac{\alpha_d}{\beta_0}\right)^2\right] \quad \text{.....(2.17b)}$$

Here α_c and α_d represent conductor and dielectric attenuation constant.

It may be noted that when $\alpha_c = \alpha_d$, β and λ have same value as for the ideal case.

Writing the real part of Eq. 2.16, α can be written as

$$\alpha = \frac{R}{2}\sqrt{\frac{C}{L}} + \frac{G}{2}\sqrt{\frac{L}{C}} = \frac{R}{2Z_0'} + \frac{G}{2Y_0'} \text{ (Nepers/m).}$$

It is easily recognised that the first term is due to conductor loss and the second term due to dielectric loss.

$$\alpha = \alpha_c + \alpha_d \quad \text{....(2.18)}$$

Characteristic impedance is

$$Z = \sqrt{\frac{L}{C}}\left(1 + \frac{R}{j\omega L}\right)^{1/2}\left(1 + \frac{G}{j\omega C}\right)^{1/2}$$

Applying binomial expansion and retaining terms up to second order,

$$Z_0 = \sqrt{\frac{L}{C}}\left[1+\frac{1}{2}\left(\frac{R^2}{4\omega^2L^2}+\frac{RG}{2\omega^2LC}-\frac{3G^2}{4\omega^2C}\right)+j\left(\frac{G}{2\omega C}-\frac{R}{2\omega C}\right)\right]$$

Simplifying as earlier, we get

$$Z_0' = Z_0'\left[1+\frac{1}{2}\left(\frac{\alpha_c}{\beta'}+\frac{3\alpha_d}{\beta'}\right)\left(\frac{\alpha_c}{\beta'}-\frac{\alpha_d}{\beta'}\right)-j\left(\frac{\alpha_c}{\beta'}-\frac{\alpha_d}{\beta'}\right)\right] \quad \text{...(2.19)}$$

It can be seen from the above equation that if α_c can be made equal to α_d, characteristic impedance is equal to Z_0' of a lossless line which is purely resistive. This is very important result since a line terminated in its characteristic impedance gives real or resistive impedance, such as when the line is connected to a generator having internal impedance purely resistive with value equal to characteristic impedance of the line, this will transfer maximum energy to the transmission line. The transmission line has generally reactive elements which will neither absorb nor dissipate energy and will transmit practically all energy to the terminating impedance.

Thus we note that the dielectric and conductor losses add in case of α but both β and Z_0 remain equal to their ideal line values of β_0' and Z_0'.

(C) Distortionless line (R/L = G/C)

A signal normally consists of a band of frequencies. Wave amplitude of different frequency components will be attenuated differently in a lossy line as α is frequency dependent. This results in distortion. A distortionless line is one in which the attenuation constant α is frequency independent while the phase constant β is linearly dependent on frequency. From the general expression for α and β in Eq. 2.5, it is evident that a distortionless line results if the line parameters are such that

$$(R/L = G/C) \quad \text{....(2.20)}$$

Thus for a distortionless line

$$\gamma = \sqrt{RG\left(1+\frac{j\omega L}{R}\right)\left(1+\frac{j\omega C}{G}\right)}$$

$$= \sqrt{RG}\left(\frac{1+j\omega C}{G}\right) = \alpha + j\beta$$

or $\alpha = \sqrt{RG}\,, \beta = \omega\sqrt{LC}$ ....(2.21)

This shows that α does not depend on frequency whereas β is a linear function of frequency.

Also, $Z_0 = \sqrt{\dfrac{R(1+j\omega L/R)}{G\,(1+j\omega C/G)}} \approx \sqrt{\dfrac{R}{G}} = \sqrt{\dfrac{L}{C}} = R_0 + jX_0$

....(2.22a)

or $R_0 = \sqrt{\dfrac{R}{G}} = \sqrt{\dfrac{L}{C}}$ and $X_0 = 0$ ....(2.22b)

$$u_p = \frac{\omega}{\beta} = \frac{1}{\sqrt{LC}} = f\lambda \quad ....(2.22c)$$

We conclude, that a lossless line is also a distortionless line, but a distortionless line is not necessarily lossless. Lossless lines are desirable in power transmission, while telephone lines are required to be distortion- less.

2.4. The Terminated Lossless Transmission line

Figure 2.5 shows a lossless transmission line terminated in an arbitrary load impedance Z_L. Assume that an incident wave of the form $V_i\, e^{-j\beta z}$ is generated from a source $Z < 0$. The ratio of voltage to current for such a travelling wave is Z_0, the characteristic impedance. But in the case when line is terminated in an arbitrary load $Z_L \neq Z_0$, the ratio of voltage to current at the load must be Z_L. Thus a reflected wave is excited with the appropriate amplitude to satisfy this condition. The total voltage on the line can be written as

$$V(z) = V_s\, e^{-j\beta z} + V_r\, e^{+j\beta z} \quad ....(2.23a)$$

The load current on the line is given as

$$I(z) = \frac{V_s}{Z_0}\, e^{-j\beta z} - \frac{V_r}{z_0}\, e^{j\beta z} \quad ....(2.23b)$$

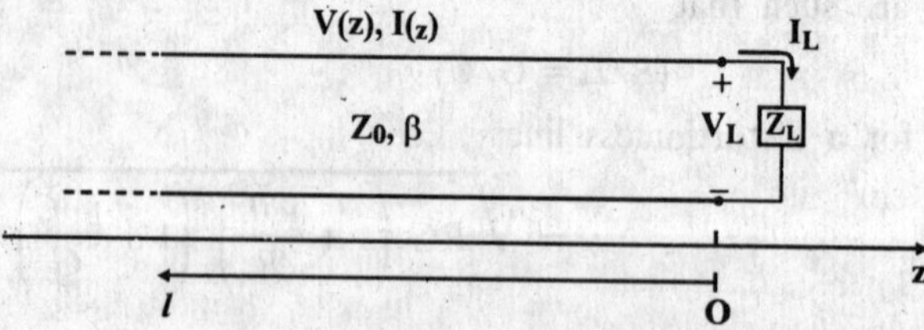

Fig. 2.5. A transmission line terminated in an arbitarary load Z_L

The total voltage and the current at the load are related by load impedance, so at $Z = 0$, we must have

$$Z_L = \frac{V(0)}{I(0)} = \frac{V_s + V_r}{V_s - V_r} Z_0 \qquad \text{....(2.24)}$$

Solving for V_r, we get

$$V_r = \frac{Z_L - Z_0}{Z_L + Z_0} V_s$$

We define the voltage reflection coefficient, Γ as the ratio of the reflected voltage to the amplitude of the incident voltage wave.

$$\Gamma = \frac{V_r}{V_s} = \frac{Z_L - Z_0}{Z_L + Z_0} \qquad \text{....(2.25)}$$

A current reflection coefficient can also be defined. It is just negative of voltage reflection coefficient. In this chapter we will use only the voltage reflection coefficient to avoid confusion.

The total voltage and current waves on the line then can be written as :

$$V(z) = V_s\,[e^{-j\beta z} + \Gamma\, e^{j\beta z}] \qquad \text{....(2.26a)}$$

$$I(z) = \frac{V_s}{Z_0}\,[e^{-j\beta z} - \Gamma\, e^{j\beta z}] \qquad \text{....(2.26b)}$$

From these equations, it is seen that the voltage and current on the line consists of superposition of an incident and reflected waves, such waves are called standing waves. When $\Gamma = 0$, then there is no reflected wave. The condition $\Gamma = 0$ is obtained if the load impedance $Z_L = Z_0$. Such a load is said to be matched to the line, since there is no reflection of the incident wave.

Using equations 2.26a and 2.26b we write the time average power flow along the line z

$$P_{av} = \frac{1}{2} \text{Re}\,[V(z)\, I\,(z)^*] = \frac{1}{2} \frac{|V_s|^2}{Z_0} \text{Re}[1 - \Gamma^* e^{-2j\beta z} + \Gamma\, e^{2j\beta z} - |\Gamma|^2]$$

....(2.27a)

The two terms in the middle are of the form $A - A^* = 2jI_m\,(A)$, and so are purely imaginary.

This simplifies the P_{av} expression to

$$P_{av} = \frac{1}{2}\frac{|V_s|^2}{Z_0}(1 - |\Gamma|^2) \quad ....(2.27b)$$

The total power delivered to the load is equal to incident power $(|V_s|^2/2Z_0)$ minus the reflected power $\{|V_s|^2 |\Gamma|^2/2Z_0\}$. If $\Gamma = 0$, maximum power is delivered to the load, while no power is delivered to the load when $\Gamma = 1$. We have assumed that the generator is matched, so that there is no reflection of the reflected wave from $Z < 0$.

When the load is mismatched $(Z_L \neq Z_0)$, then all the power from the generator is not delivered to the load. This 'loss' is called return loss (R_L) and is defined ir (dB) as

$$R_L = -20 \log |\Gamma| \text{ dB} \quad ....(2.28)$$

The Return "loss" is a loss, hence it is a negative value. The higher the negative value is, the better the match, that is for a perfect match, the return loss ideally is ∞ dB. That is not possible, but a return loss of 35 to 45 dB shows an excellent match. Return loss for a short circuit and open circuit where all the energy is reflected back is 0 dB$(|\Gamma| = 0)$.

If the load is matched $(\Gamma = \theta)$, the magnitude of the voltage on the line is $|v(z)| = |V_s|$, which is a constant. When the load is mismatched, reflected waves occur and give rise to standing waves, where the voltage on the line are not constant. Thus from Eq. 2.26a

$$|V(z)| = |V_s|\ |1 + \Gamma e^{2j\beta z}|$$

$l = -z$ is the positive distance measured from the load at $z = 0$, if θ is the phase of the reflection coefficient $(\Gamma = |\Gamma| e^{j\theta})$

$$|V(-l)| = |V_s|\ |1 + \Gamma e^{j(\theta - 2\beta l)}| \quad ....(2.29)$$

The maximum value occurs when the phase term $e^{j(\theta - 2\beta l)} = 1$ and Minimum value when $e^{j(\theta - 2\beta l)} = -1$. Thus,

$$V_{max} = |V_s|\ (1 + |\Gamma|) \quad ....(2.30a)$$

$$V_{min} = |V_s|\ (1 - |\Gamma|) \quad ....(2.30b)$$

The ratio of V_{max} to V_{min}, is a measure of mismatch of the lines and is called voltage standing wave ratio (*VSWR*)

$$VSWR = S = \frac{V_{max}}{V_{min}} = \frac{1 + |\Gamma|}{1 - |\Gamma|} \quad ....(2.31)$$

VSWR is a real number and has value from 1 to ∞ depending on the value of $|\Gamma|$.

For a mismatched line the voltage amplitude oscillates with position on the line, hence the impedance looking into line varies with position. At a distance $l = -z$ from the load, the input impedance seen looking towards the load is

$$Z_{in} = \frac{V(-l)}{I(-l)} = \frac{V_s\,[e^{j\beta l} + \Gamma e^{-j\beta l}]}{V_s\,[e^{j\beta l} - \Gamma e^{-j\beta l}]} = \frac{1 + \Gamma e^{-2j\beta l}}{1 - \Gamma e^{-2j\beta l}} \quad \text{....(2.32)}$$

Using the relation 2.25 for Γ we get a more usable form

$$Z_{in} = Z_0 \frac{(Z_L + Z_0)\,e^{j\beta l} + (Z_L - Z_0)\,e^{-j\beta l}}{(Z_L + Z_0)e^{j\beta l} - (Z_L - Z_0)e^{-j\beta l}}$$

$$= Z_0 \frac{Z_L \cos\beta l + jZ_0 \sin\beta l}{Z_0 \cos\beta l + jZ_L \sin\beta l}$$

$$= Z_0 \frac{Z_L + j\,Z_0 \tan\beta l}{Z_0 + jZ_L \tan\beta l} \quad \text{....(2.33)}$$

This is an important result giving the input impedance of a length of transmission line with an arbitrary load impedance. This equation is also referred as the transmission line impedance equation.

2.4.1. Special cases of lossless terminated lines :

(A) Shorted line ($Z_L = 0$)

Fig. 2.6 shows a line terminated in a short circuit $Z_L = 0$. The reflection coefficient from Eq. 2.25 for a short circuit line is $\Gamma = -1$, from Eq. 2.31 the VSWR ratio for this case is infinite. From Eq. 2.26 the voltage and current on the line are

$$V(z) = V_s\,[e^{-j\beta z} - e^{j\beta z}] = -\,2j\,V_s \sin\beta z \quad \text{....(2.34a)}$$

$$I(z) = \frac{V_s}{Z_0}\,[e^{-j\beta z} + e^{j\beta z}] = \frac{jV_s}{Z_0} \cos\beta z \quad \text{....(2.34b)}$$

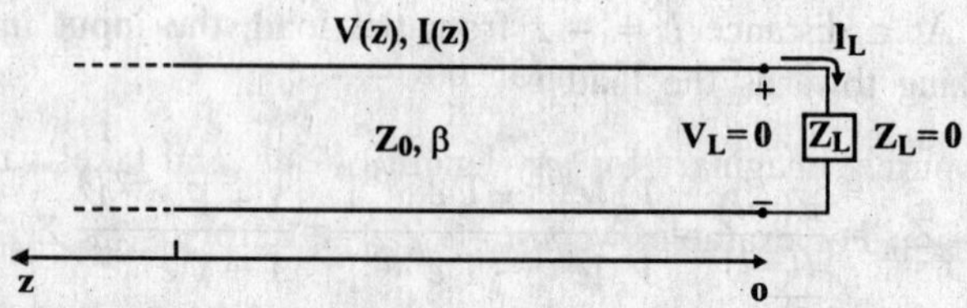

Fig. 2.6 A transmission line terminated in a short circuit.

which shows that $V = 0$ at the load (short circuit), while the current is maximum there. Input impedance from Eq. 2.33 is

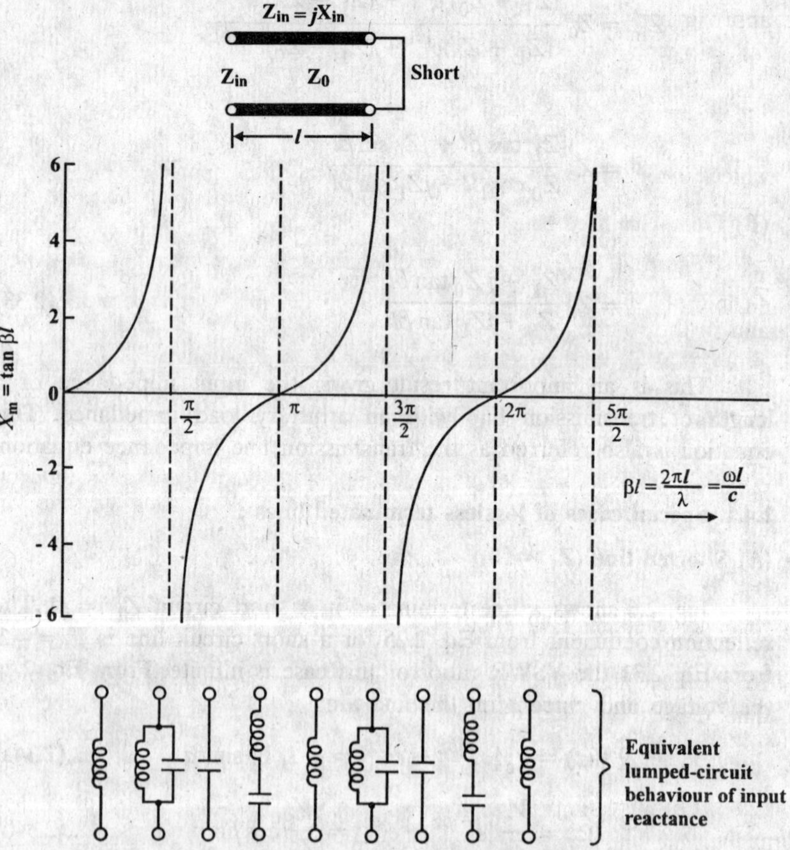

Fig. 2.7. Normalized input reactance versus βl for a short-circuited, lossless transmission line.

$$Z_{is} = +jZ_0 \tan\beta l \qquad \text{....(2.35a)}$$

$$\Gamma = -1 \text{ and } VSWR = \infty$$

which is purely imaginary for any length of line, and takes values from $+j\infty$ to $-j\infty$. For example, when $l=0$ $Z_{is} = 0$, for $l = \frac{\lambda}{4}$, $Z_{is} = \infty$. Eq. 2.35a shows that line impedance is periodic in l, repeating for multiple of $\lambda/2$.

The input reactance for the short-circuited line are plotted in Fig. 2.7. When the length of short-circuited line is very short in comparison to wave length, that is $\beta l << 1$. Eq. 2.35a becomes approximately

$$Z_{is} = jZ_0\beta l = j\sqrt{\frac{L}{C}}\,\omega\sqrt{LC}\,l = j\omega Ll \qquad \text{....(2.35b)}$$

which is the impedance of an inductance of L henries.

(B) Open-circuited line

Figure 2.8a shows an open circuited transmission line where $Z_L = \infty$. Dividing the numerator and denominator in Eq. 2.19 by Z_L and in the limiting case when $Z_L \to \infty$ we get $\Gamma = 1$ and the VSWR $= \infty$. The input impedance from Eq. 2.33 is

$$Z_{i0} = -j\,Z_0 \cot\beta l \qquad \text{....(2.36a)}$$

The input admittance is

$$Y_{i0} = jB_{i0} = jY_0 \tan\beta l \qquad \text{....(2.36b)}$$

When $l = \lambda/2$, $Z_{in} = Z_L$ ....(2.37)

This shows that when the line is open circuited and of length to $\lambda/2$ equal (or any multiple of $\lambda/2$) the input impedance is equal to the load impedance, regardless of the characteristic impedance. The reactance of open circuited line is shown in Fig. 2.8b.

From Eq. 2.35 and 2.36, we have

$$Z_0 = \sqrt{Z_{io}\,.\,Z_{is}} \qquad \text{....(2.40)}$$

and

$$\gamma = \frac{1}{l}\tan^{-1}\sqrt{\frac{Z_{is}}{Z_{io}}} \qquad \text{....(2.41)}$$

V(z), I(z)
I_L
+
Z₀, β
V_L = 0
Z_L = 0
z
o

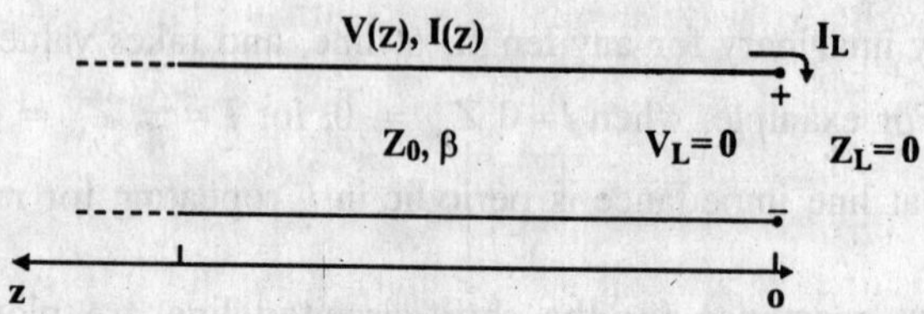

Fig. 2.8a. A Transmission line terminated in open circuit.

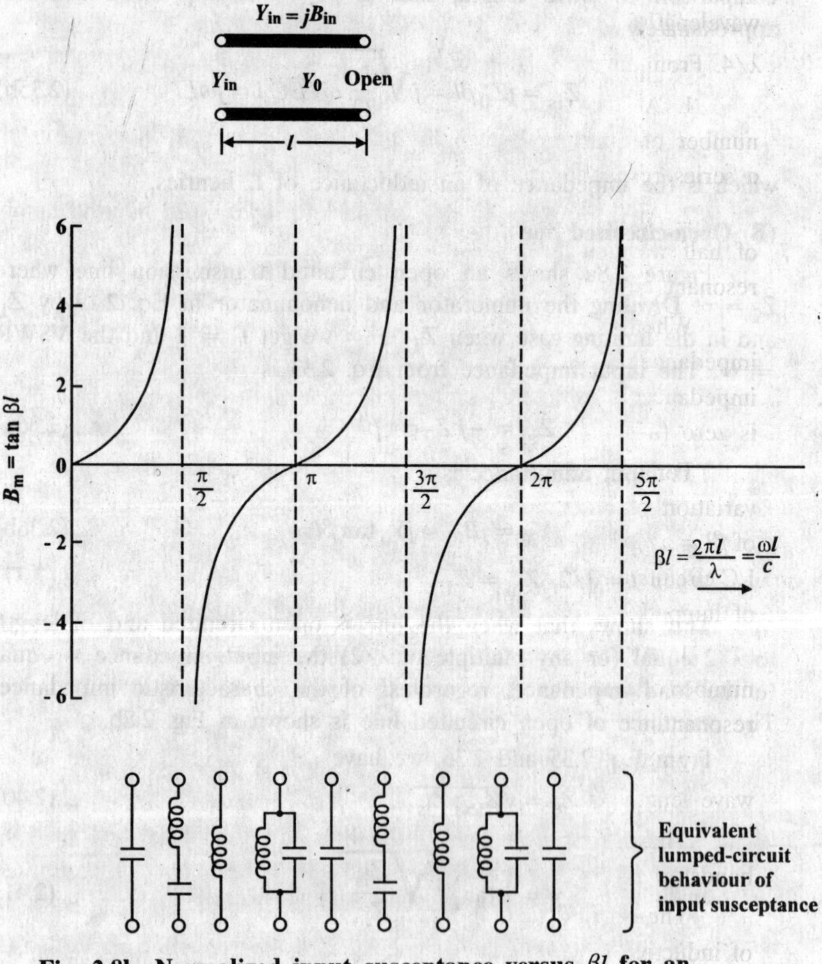

Y_in = jB_in
Y_in
Y₀
Open
l
B_m = tan βl
6
4
2
0
- 2
- 4
- 6
π/2
π
3π/2
2π
5π/2
βl = 2πl/λ = ωl/c
Equivalent
lumped-circuit
behaviour of
input susceptance

Fig. 2.8b. Normalized input susceptance versus βl for an open circuited, lossless transmission line.

When the length of an open circuited line is very short in comparison with a wavelength, $\beta l << 1$ than $\tan \beta l = \beta l$. From Eq. 2.33, we have

$$Z_{io} = jX_{io} \cong \frac{-jZ_0}{\beta l} = \frac{-j\sqrt{L/C}}{\omega\sqrt{LC}l} = -j\frac{1}{\beta Cl}$$

which is the impedance of a capacitance of Cl farads. In the region $\pi/2 < \beta l < \pi$, the input susceptance is inductive since B_{i0} is inductive. Also Y_{io} is 0 (Open Circuit) when l is multiple of half wavelength, $Y_{io} = \infty$ (a short circuit) when l is an odd multiple of $\lambda/4$. From Fig. 2.8b the following equivalences can be stated :

1. At frequencies in the vicinity of $\beta l = (2n-1)\pi/2$ (an odd number of quarter wavelengths), the open circuited line behaves like a series resonant circuit.

2. At frequencies in the vicinity of $\beta l = n\pi$ (an integral number of half wavelengths), the open-circuited line behaves like a parallel resonant circuit.

When $\pi/2 < \beta l < \pi$, X_{is} is negative and hence the input impedance is capacitive. Also when $l = \lambda/4\,(\beta l = \pi/2)$, the input impedance is infinite (an open circuit), while for $l = \lambda/2\,(\beta l = \pi)$, it is zero (a short circuit).

For a fixed length l, the characteristics of Fig. 2.7 represent the variation of reactance with frequency since $\beta l = \omega l/c$. In the vicinity of $\beta l = \pi/2$ and π, the shorted line behaves similar to that of resonant LC circuits. If the shorted line is compared with frequency characteristics of lumped L-C circuits, it leads to the following equivalences :

1. At frequencies in the vicinity of $\beta l = (2n-1)\pi/2$ (on odd number of quarter wavelengths) the shorted line behaves like a parallel resonant circuit.

2. At frequencies near $\beta l = n\pi$ (an integrated number of half wave lengths), the shorted line behaves like a series resonant circuit.

These properties are utilized in the design of bandpass and bandstop filters at microwave frequencies.

The shorted line for length $l < \lambda/4$ is purely inductive. Any value of inductive reactance can be realized by mearly choosing βl, so that $Z_0 \tan \beta l$ yields the desired value. Note that the inductive reactance achieved this way has no resistive part.

(c) Quarter wave section ($l = \lambda/4, \beta l = \pi/2$)

When the length of line is an odd multiple of $\lambda/4, l = (2n - 1)\,\lambda/4$ where $n = 1, 2, 3.....$

$$\beta l = \frac{2\pi}{\lambda}(2n - 1)\,\lambda/4 = (2n - 1)\,\pi/2$$

$$\tan \beta l = \tan [(2n - 1)\,\pi/2] \rightarrow \pm\,\infty$$

and Eq. 2.33 becomes

$$Z_{in} = \frac{Z_0^2}{Z_L} \qquad ....(2.40)$$

Hence, a quarter wave lossless line transforms the load impedance to the input terminals as its inverse multiplied by the square of the characteristic resistance; it is often referred to as quarter wave transformer. An open circuit quarter wave line appears as short circuit at the input terminals, and the short circuited quarter length line appears as an open circuit.

(D) Half wave sections ($l = \lambda/2, \beta l = \pi$)

When the length of the line is an integral multiple of $\lambda/2, l = n\lambda/2$ ($n = 1, 2, 3......$),

$$\beta l = n\pi$$

$$\tan \beta l = 0$$

Eq. 2.33 reduces to

$$Z_{in} = Z_L \qquad ....(2.41)$$

Eq. 2.39 states that a half wave lossless line transfers the load impedance to the input terminals without change.

2.4.2 Lines with resistive termination

When a transmission line is terminated in a load impedance Z_L different from the characteristics impedance Z_0, both an incident wave (from the generator) and a reflected wave (from the load) exist. Eq. 2.29 reveals that $|V_{max}|$ and $|I_{min}|$ occurs together when $|e^{j\beta z}| = 1$, independent of Z.

i.e. when $\theta - 2\beta z_m = -2n\pi \quad n = 0, 1, 2, ...$ ....(2.42)

On the other hand $|V_{min}|$ and $|I_{max}|$ occurs together when

$$\theta - 2\beta z_m = -(2n + 1)\,\pi \quad n = 0, 1, 2, ... \qquad ....(2.43)$$

For resistive termination on a lossless line $Z_L = R_L$, Z_0 is equal to R_0 then the reflection coefficient simplifies to

$$\Gamma = \frac{R_L - R_0}{R_L + R_0} \qquad \text{....(2.44)}$$

The voltage reflection coefficient is therefore purely real. Two cases are considered depending upon the values R_0 and R_L :

(i) $R_L > R_0$

In this case Γ is positive real and $\theta = 0$. At the line termination z=0, the condition from Eq. 2.42 is satisfied. This means a voltage is maximum and current is minimum at the termination resistance. The other voltage maxima occurs at

$$2\beta z = 2n\pi \text{ or } z = n\lambda/2 \qquad n = 1, 2, \ldots.. \text{ from the load.}$$

(ii) $R_L < R_0$

Equation 2.44 shows that in this case Γ will be negative real and $\theta_1 = -\pi$. At the line termination $z = 0$ the condition from Eq. 2.43 is satisfied (for $n = 0$). A voltage minimum (current maximum) will occur at the terminating resistance. Other minima will be located at $z = n\lambda/2$ (n=1, 2...) from the load. The ratio of voltage and current standing wave are interchanged from those for the case $R_L > R_0$, except that $|V(0)|$ and $|I(0)|$ curves are now magnitudes of sinusoidal functions of the distance l from the load. Fig. 2.9 illustrates some typical standing waves for a lossless line with resistive termination.

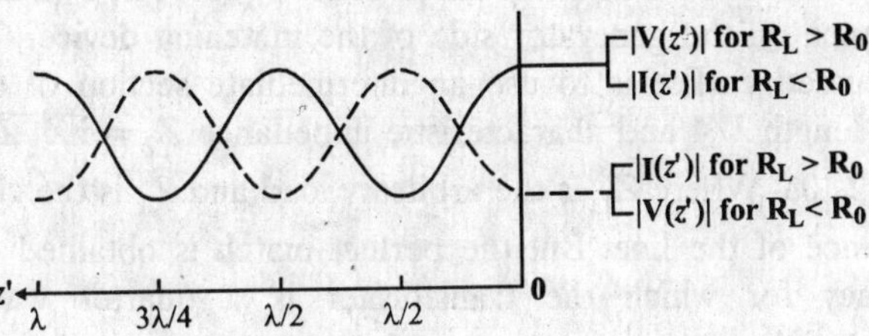

Fig. 2.9a. Voltage and Current standing waves on resistance terminated lossless line.

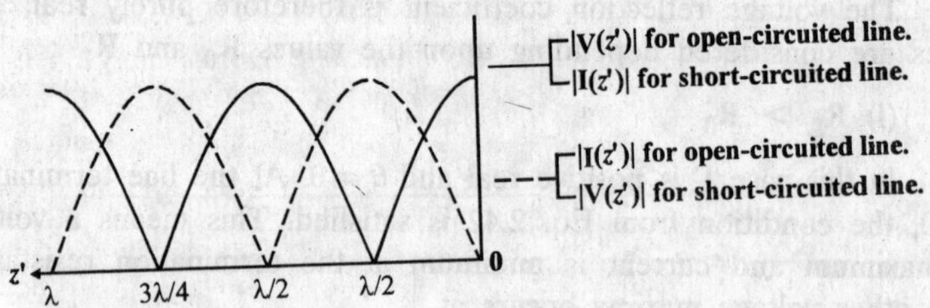

Fig. 2.9b. Shows voltage and current standing waves for open and short-circuited lossless lines.

2.5. Transmission Line Matching using Quarter Wave Transformer

When transmission line is terminated by an arbitrary load, there would be standing waves on the line. Also the input impedance of the line will vary with frequency since the electrical length of the line and hence $\Gamma(l) = \Gamma_R e^{-j\beta l}$ changes. The variation of input impedance with frequency deteriorates the performances of a transmission line. For maximum power flow consideration also, it is desirable to eliminate standing waves on line by connecting a matching device near the load such that line views an effective impedance equal to its own characteristic impedance on the generator side of the matching device. One method as discussed earlier is to use an intermediate section of transmission line of length $\lambda/4$ and characteristic impedance $Z_2 = \sqrt{Z_1 Z_L}$ as shown in Fig. 2.10a. Where Z_L is the arbitrary load and Z_1 is the characteristic impedance of the line. But the perfect match is obtained only at that frequency for which the transformer is a quarter wavelength or $(n\lambda/2 + \lambda/4)$ long.

We now show that the bandwidth of a quarter wave section is very narrow and can be determined by considering the electrical length $\beta l = \theta$ and finding the input reflection coefficient Γ.

At any frequency the input impedance at the main line is

$$Z_{in} = Z_2 \frac{Z_L + jZ_2 \tan\theta}{Z_2 + jZ_L \tan\theta} \quad \text{....(2.44a)}$$

Reflection coefficient is

$$\Gamma = \frac{Z_{in} - Z_1}{Z_{in} + Z_1} \quad ....(2.44b)$$

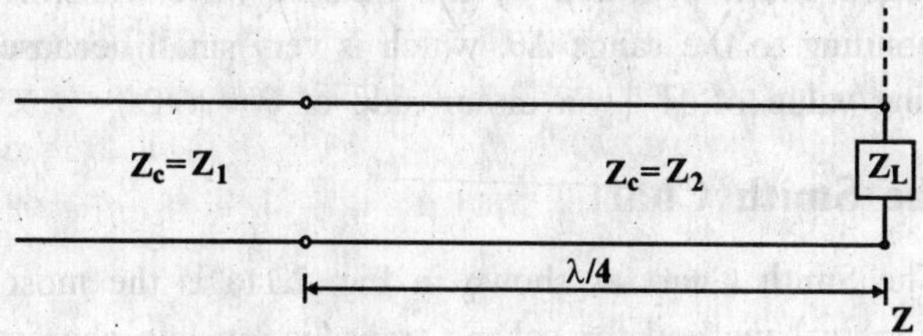

Fig. 2.10a. A quarter wave transformer

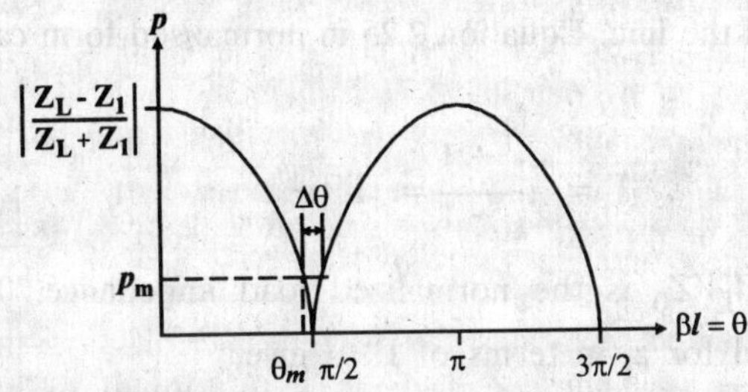

Fig. 2.10b. Bandwidth characteristic for a single- section quarter-wave transformer.

Substitude for Z_{in}, in Eq. 2.44(b) we get

$$\Gamma = \frac{Z_L - Z_1}{Z_L + Z_1 + 2j \tan\theta \sqrt{Z_1 Z_L}} \quad ....(2.45)$$

The magnitude of Γ is given as

$$|\Gamma| = \frac{1}{\left[1 + \left(\frac{2\sqrt{Z_1 Z_L}}{Z_L - Z_1} \sec\theta\right)^2\right]^{1/2}} \quad ....(2.46)$$

When θ is near $\pi/2$ this equation can be approximated by

$$|\Gamma| = \frac{|Z_L - Z_1|}{2(Z_L Z_1)^{1/2}} |\cos\theta| \quad \text{....(2.47)}$$

A plot of $|\Gamma|$ versus $\beta l = \theta$ is shown in Fig. 2.10b. It shows that $|\Gamma|$ has periodic variation with frequency (βl). If $|\Gamma|_m$ is the maximum value of reflection coefficient that can be tolerated, the useful band width provided by the quarter wave transformer is that corresponding to the range $\Delta\theta$, which is very small because of rapidly increasing value of $|\Gamma|$ on either side of $\theta = \pi/2$.

2.6 The Smith Chart

The Smith Chart as shown in Fig. 2.11a is the most commonly used graphical method for solving transmission line characteristics. In 1939, Philip H. Smith devised this technique to avoid tedious solution methods to calculate the impedance of a transmission line as one moves along the line. The chart is constructed from the normalized input and load impedance equations with respect to the characteristic impedance of the line. Equation 2.25 in normalised form can be written as

$$\Gamma = \frac{Z_L - 1}{Z_L + 1} = |\Gamma| e^{j\theta} \quad \text{....(2.48)}$$

where $z_L = Z_L/Z_0$ is the normalized load impedance. This relation can be solved for z_l in terms of Γ to give

$$z_l = \frac{1 + |\Gamma| e^{j\theta}}{1 - |\Gamma| e^{j\theta}} \quad \text{....(2.49)}$$

This complex equation can be reduced to two real equations by writing Γ and z_l in terms of their real and imaginary parts. Let $\Gamma = \Gamma_r + j\Gamma_i$ and $z_L = \overline{R}_L + j\overline{X}_L$. Then

$$\overline{R}_L + j\overline{X}_L = \frac{(1 + \Gamma_r) + j\Gamma_i}{(1 - \Gamma_r) - j\Gamma_i} \quad \text{....(2.50)}$$

On simplification, we get

$$\overline{R}_L = \frac{1 + \Gamma_r^2 - \Gamma_i^2}{(1 - \Gamma_r)^2 + \Gamma_i^2} \quad \text{....(2.51)}$$

$$\overline{X}_L = \frac{2\Gamma_i^2}{(1-\Gamma_r)^2 + \Gamma_i^2} \quad \text{....(2.51b)}$$

Rearranging Eq. 2.51, we get

$$\left(\Gamma_r - \frac{\overline{R}_L}{1+\overline{R}_L}\right)^2 + \Gamma_i^2 = \left(\frac{1}{1+\overline{R}_L}\right)^2 \quad \text{....(2.52a)}$$

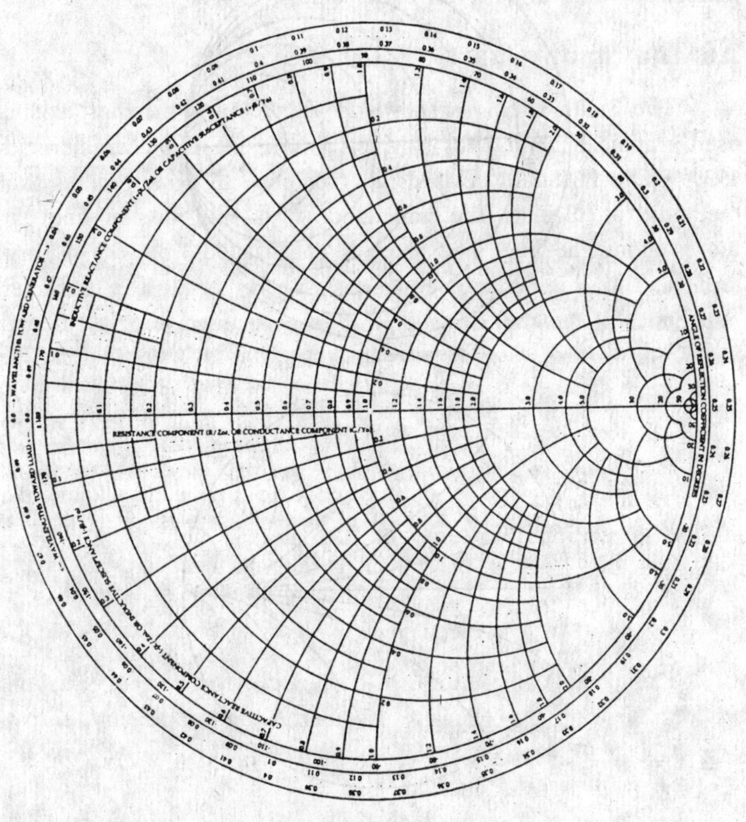

Fig. 2.11a. The Smith Chart

$$(\Gamma_r - 1)^2 + \left(\Gamma_i - \frac{1}{\overline{\overline{X}}_L}\right)^2 = \left(\frac{1}{\overline{\overline{X}}_L}\right)^2 \qquad \text{....(2.52b)}$$

which represent two families of circles in the Γ_r, Γ_i plane. Eq. 2.52a represents a circle with centre $[\overline{R}_L/(\overline{R}_L + 1), 0]$ and radius equal to $1/(1 + \overline{R}_L)$, while Eq. 2.52b represent a circle with centre at $\left(1, \frac{1}{\overline{\overline{X}}_L}\right)$ and radius equal to $1/|\overline{X}_L|$. These circles of constant resistance and constant reactance are shown in Fig. 2.11b.

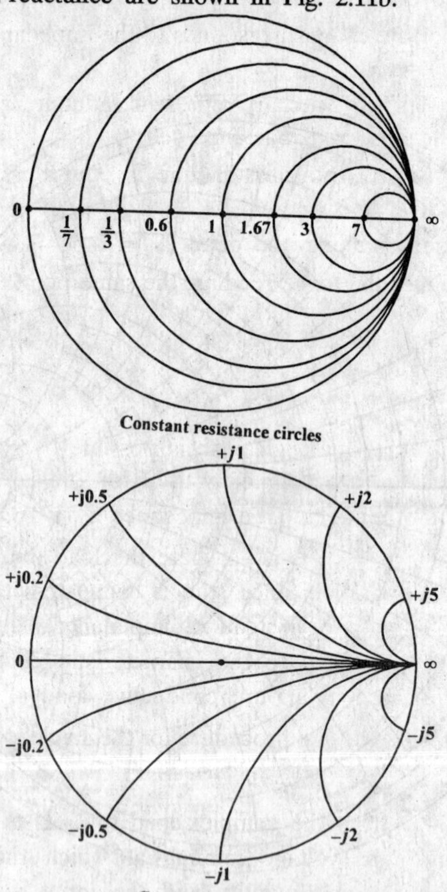

Fig. 2.11b Constant resistance circles and constant reactance lines. (Note : The reactance lines are portions of circles.)

The Smith Chart has the following features :

1. Impedance or admittance value read on the chart are normalized values.

2. Moving away from the load (toward generator) corresponds to moving in a clockwise direction.

3. The line impedance and the reflection coefficient change as we move towards the generator or towards the load. The distance along the line in terms of wavelength is given along the circumference of the chart ($|\Gamma| = 1$). Moving clockwise is going towards generator and anticlockwise is going towards the load. A complete revolution around the chart covers a distance $\lambda/2$ along the line.

4. The centre of the chart corresponds to the impedance matched condition since $\Gamma(z) = 0$.

5. The upper half of the chart represent inductive reactance ($j\chi$) while the lower half capacitive reactance ($-j\chi$).

6. Moving along the transmission line is equivalent to moving along constant $|\Gamma(z)|$ circle.

7. For impedance reading, the point ($\Gamma_r = 1, \Gamma_i = 0$) correspond to an open circuit. For admittance reading, the same point corresponds to a short circuit.

2.7. Impedance Matching

2.7.1. Shunt Stub

Impedance matching by single stub is possible by using parallel or series stub. The shunt stub is mostly used for coaxial lines.

Suppose a line of characteristic impedance Z_0 is to be matched to a complex load $Z_L = R_L + jX_L$, where the load impedance and stub-impedance are in parallel. Since stub is connected in parallel, it is advisable to use admittance instead of impedance. The generator end is assumed to be matched to the characteristic impedance. We consider a line terminated in a pure conductive load of normalized admittance $\overline{Y}_L = \overline{G}_L$. The design procedure for the single stub matching is explained below

If we move away from the complex load towards the generator along the line, there are voltage minima at which the reflection coefficient is a negative real quantity and the input admittance is purely conductive of value $Y_{in} = (1 - \Gamma)/(1 + \Gamma) = S$. Similarly, there are voltage maxima at which the admittance is purely conductive of value $Y_{in} = (1 + \Gamma)/(1 - \Gamma) = 1/S$. Hence in between two points, there must be a point at a certain distance from the first voltage minimum, where the real part of the normalized admittance is unity, so that $Y_{in} = 1 + jB - jB = 1$. The reactive component of this admittance can be cancelled by an equal and opposite susceptance $\pm jB$ of a parallel single stub of length l, located at the point and having characteristic impedance equal to that of the line *i.e.* Z_0.

To find the position d, we must solve the expression.

$$Y_{in} = 1 + j\overline{B} = \frac{\overline{Y}_L + jt}{1 + j\overline{Y}_L t}$$

If we assume that $Y_L = \overline{G}$ is pure real, we require

$$(1 + j\overline{B})(1 + j\overline{G}t) = \overline{G} + jt \qquad \text{....(2.53)}$$

where $t = \tan \beta d$

By equating real and imaginary part, we get two equations, which when solved for d gives,

$$d = \frac{\lambda}{2\pi} \cos^{-1} \sqrt{\frac{\overline{G} - 1}{\overline{G} + 1}} \qquad \text{....(2.54)}$$

and the value of input susceptance $j\overline{B}$ is given by

$$\overline{B} = \frac{1 - \overline{G}}{\sqrt{\overline{G}}} \qquad \text{....(2.55)}$$

The required length l_0 of the short circuited stub to give an input susceptance $-j\overline{B}$ shown in Fig. 2.12a is found from the relation,

$$\overline{Y}_{in} = -j\overline{B} = -j \cot \beta l_0 \qquad \text{....(2.56)}$$

From Eq. 2.55

$$\cot \beta l_0 = \frac{1 - \overline{G}}{\sqrt{\overline{G}}} \qquad \text{....(2.57)}$$

or $$l_0 = \frac{\lambda}{2\pi} \tan^{-1} \frac{\sqrt{\overline{G}}}{1 - \overline{G}}$$

The value of d (stub position) is given as,

$$d_o = \frac{\lambda}{4\pi} \cos^{-1} \frac{S - 1}{S + 1} \qquad \text{....(2.58)}$$

and stub length l_o is,

$$l_o = \frac{\lambda}{2\pi} \tan^{-1} \frac{\sqrt{S}}{S-1} \quad ....(2.59)$$

The position of the stub from the load is computed by finding the distance of V_{min} position from the load and adding this to d_0.

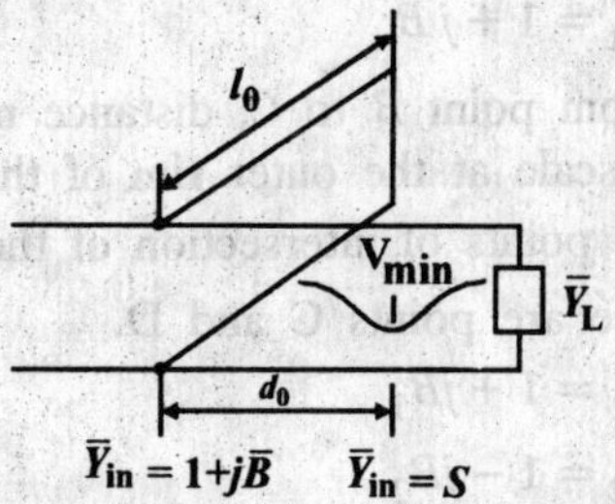

Fig. 2.12a Location of stub relative to a voltage minimum

The following steps are involved in the design of single shunt stub using Smith Chart illustrated in Fig. 2.12b.

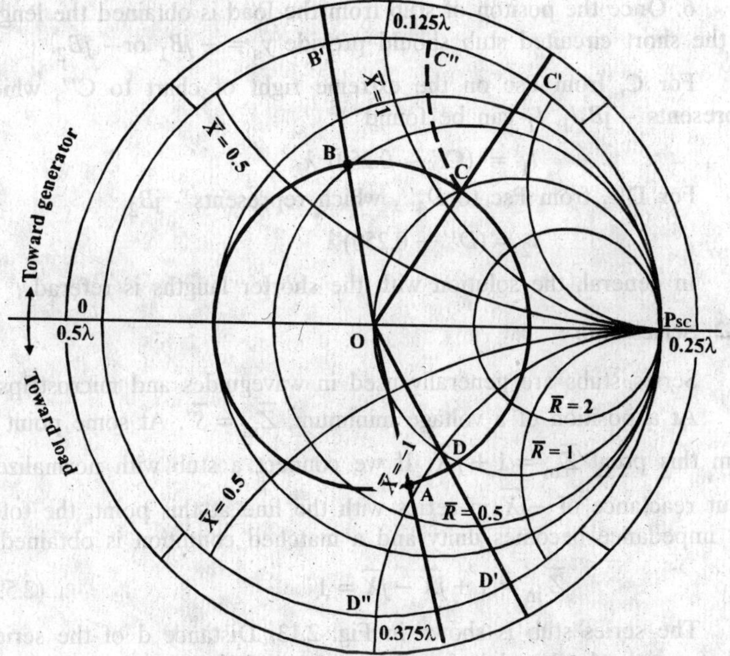

Fig. 2.12b Design of single shunt stub.

1. The load impedance point is located at point *A*. Then draw a constant VSWR circle passing through point A. Join the centre O with A, the line AO is extended to cut the circle at *B*, which represents Y_L.

2. Next move from the admittance point *B* on the constant VSWR circle to reach the point C on the unit conductance circle. At point C the admittance is

$$\overline{Y}_t = 1 + j\overline{B} \quad \text{....(2.58)}$$

3. In moving from point *B* to *C*, distance moved can be found from the wavelength scale at the outer rim of the Smith Chart.

4. Note the two points of intersection of the VSWR circle with the $\overline{G} = 1$ circle these are points C and D.

At C $\quad Y_{\theta 1} = 1 + jB_1$

At D $\quad Y_{\theta 2} = 1 - jB_2$

5. Solution for the position of the stub is obtained

For C (from B' to C') $= d_1\lambda$

For D (form B' to D') $= d_2\lambda$

6. Once the positon of stub from the load is obtained the length of the short circuited stub should provide $y_s = -jB_1$ or $-jB_2$.

For C, from Psc on the extreme right of chart to C″, which represents $-jB_1 l_1$, l_1 can be found

$$l_1 = (C'' - 0.250)\,\lambda$$

For D″, from Psc to D_4'', which represents - jB_2

$$l_2 = (D'' - 0.250)\,\lambda$$

In general, the solution with the shorter langths is referad.

2.7.2. Series stub :

Series stubs are generally used in waveguides and microstrips. At a position of a voltage minimum, $\overline{Z}_{in} = \overline{S}'$. At some point *d* from this point $\overline{Z}_{in} = 1 + j\overline{X}$. If we connect a stub with normalized input reactance of $-j\overline{X}$ in series with the line at this point, the total put impedance becomes unity and a matched condition is obtained.

$$\overline{Z}_{in} = 1 + j\overline{X} - j\overline{X} = 1 \quad \text{....(2.59)}$$

The series stub is shown in Fig. 2.13. Distance d of the series stub from the load end is found by solving the equation

$$\bar{Z}_{in} = 1 + j\bar{X} = \frac{S^{-1} + j\tan\beta d_o}{1 + jS^{-1}\tan\beta d_o} \qquad \text{....(2.60)}$$

The solution gives

$$d_o = \frac{\lambda}{4\lambda}\cos^{-1}\frac{1-S}{1+S} \qquad \text{....(2.61)}$$

$$= \pm\frac{\lambda}{2} + \frac{\lambda}{4\pi}\cos^{-1}\frac{S-1}{S+1} \qquad \text{....(2.62)}$$

The required stub length l_o is determined by the equation

$$j\tan\beta l_o = -j\bar{X} \qquad \text{....(2.63)}$$

Hence $$l_o = \frac{\lambda}{2\pi}\tan^{-1}\frac{1-S}{\sqrt{S}} \qquad \text{....(2.64)}$$

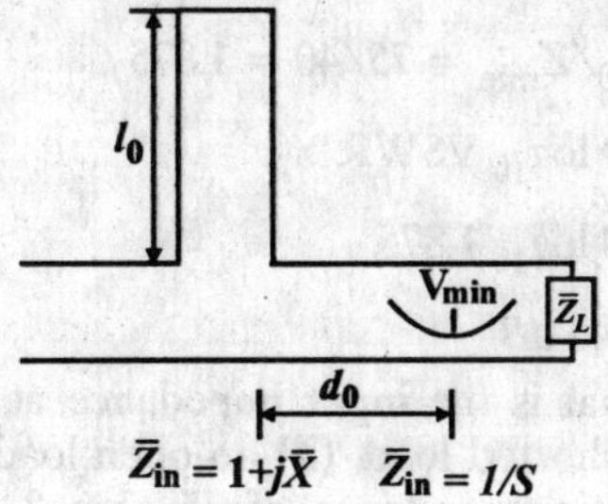

Fig. 2.13. The series stub.

The disadvantage of using single stub is that every load requires a new stub position. This can be avoided by using two stubs either in series or in parallel depending upon the type of transmission line. The two stubs are spaced by a fixed amount and are located at a fixed distance from the load. Hence it is more convenient to use two stubs as shown in Fig. 2.14.

The two stubs are generally placed at a separation of $\lambda/8, 3\lambda/8$.... The expressions for two stubs are not developed since they are quite involved. It is always better to use Smith Chart for finding out the length l_1 and l_2 for impedance matching. The illustration of double stub matching is shown in Fig. 2.14.

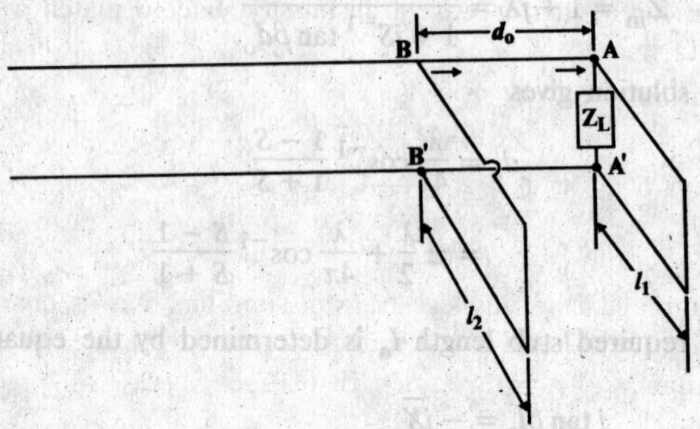

Fig. 2.14. Impedance matching by double-stub method.

Example 2.1. A transmission line with a characteristic impedance of 75 ohms has a minimum impedance 40Ω. What is the SWR in dB?

Solution :

$$VSWR = Z_0/Z_{min} = 75/40 = 1.875$$

$$SWR = 20 \log_{10} \text{VSWR}$$

$$= 20 \log_{10} 1.875$$

$$= 5.46\ dB$$

Example 2.2. What is the input impedance at a point one-eighth wavelength from (i) a shorted load, (ii) an open load for a transmission line with a characteristic impedance of 75 ohm ?

Solution :

(i) $$\beta l = \frac{2\pi}{\lambda} l = \frac{2\lambda}{\lambda} \frac{\lambda}{8} = 45°$$

$$Z_{in} = Z_0 \frac{Z_L + iZ_0 \tan \beta l}{Z_0 + jZ_1 \tan \beta l}$$

$$= 75 \frac{0 + j75}{75 + j(0)} = \frac{75(j\,75)}{75}$$

$$= j\,75\,\Omega \quad \text{(inductive reactance)}$$

(ii) Divide the numerator and denominator by Z_L, hence

$$Z_{in} = 75 \frac{1 + j(0)}{0 + j \tan 45} = \frac{75}{j1}$$

$$= -j\,75 \text{ (capacitive reactance)}$$

Example 2.3. What will be the value of the characteristic impedance for a quarter wave transmission line to match a **50Ω line** with a 75Ω line ?

Solution :

$$Z_0 = \sqrt{Z_{in}\, Z_{out}}$$

$$= \sqrt{50 \times 75}$$

$$= 61.2\ \Omega$$

Example 2.4. A lossless transmission line has a characteristic impedance of 50 Ω and a self inductance of 0.0921 μ H/m. Calculate the capacitance of a 5 meter length of line.

Solution :

As the line is lossless.

$$R = 0, G = \infty$$

$$Z_0 = \sqrt{L/C} \text{ or } C = L/Z_0^2$$

$$C = \frac{0.092 \times 10^{-6}}{50 \times 50} = 36.8\, pF/m$$

$$\text{Total capacitance } = 5 \times 36.8\, pF$$

$$= 184\, pF$$

This capacitance will limit the high frequency response of the cable.

Example 2.5. A coaxial line has the following characteristics at 1.0 GHz;

R = 4 ohms/m, L = 450 nH/m, G = 7×10^{-4} mhos/m and C = 50 pF/m.

(a) Calculate Z_0, α, β, v and λ at 1 GHz.

(b) With V_s = 10 ∠0 V and V_r = 0, calculate V and I at Z = 4 m.

Solution :

$$Z = R + j\,\omega L$$

$$= 4 + j\,(2\pi \times 10^9)\,(450 \times 10^{-9}) = 4 + j2827 \text{ ohms/m}$$

$$Y = G + j\omega C$$

$$= 7 \times 10^{-4} + j\,(2\pi \times 10^9)\,(50 \times 10^{-12})$$

$$= 10^{-4}\,(7 + j\,3142) \text{ mhos/m}$$

$$Z_0 = \sqrt{Z/Y} = 95\ \angle 0.023° \text{ ohms}$$

$$\gamma = \alpha + j\beta = \sqrt{ZY} = \sqrt{-888 + j\,3.24} = 0.054 + j\,29.8$$

Thus $\alpha = 0.054\,\omega_p/m$

or in $dB = 0.47\ dB/m$

and $\beta = 29.8\ rad/m$

Also $\beta = 2\pi/\lambda = \omega/v$

Hence $v = \omega/\beta = \dfrac{2\pi\ 10^9}{29.8} = 2.11 \times 10^8\ m/s$

and $\lambda = 2\pi/\beta = 0.21\ m$

(b) Since $V_r = 0$, only the forward wave exists, that is

$$V_i = V_{os}\, e^{-\alpha z} e^{-j\beta z}$$

$$= V_{os}\, e^{-\alpha z\ -\beta z}$$

For $z = 4\,m$

$$\alpha z = 0.054 \times 4 = 0.22\ Np$$

and $\beta z = 119.2$

Therefore, at $z = 4\,m$

$$V = 10\,e^{-0.22}\,e^{-j\,119.2}$$

$$V = 8.03\ \ -119.2 \text{ rad V}$$

$$I = \frac{V}{Z_0} = \frac{8.03\ -119.2 \text{ rad}}{95\ \ 0.023}$$

$$= 0.084\ \ -119 \text{ rad A.}$$

Example 2.6. A loss less line of characteristic impedance $R_0 = 50\Omega$ in terminated in a load $Z_L = 50 + j50\ \Omega$ and the operating wavelength $\lambda = 4$cm. Determine the first V_{max} and first V_{min} from the load and the VSWR ρ_L.

Solution :

1. Normalized load impedance

$$z_L = \frac{50 + j50}{50} = 1 + j1$$

2. Enter $z_L = 1 + j1$ on the smith chart at A, (shown in Fig. 2.15) the load point.
3. Draw a dashed line from the center of the chart through the load point and intersectiong the distance scale at B. It reads 0.162λ.
4. Move a distance from the point B (at 0.162λ) toward the generator and first slop at the voltage maximum on the right-hand real axis at 0.25λ.
   Then First V_{max} d_1 (V_{max}) = $(0.25 - 0.162)\ \lambda = (0.088)\ 4 = 0.352$ cm.
5. Similarly, move a distance from the point B (at 0.162λ) toward the generator and first stop at the voltage minimum on the left hand of the real axis at 0.5λ. Then
   First V_{min} $d_2(V_{min}) = (0.5 - 0.161)\lambda = 0.338 \times 4$
   $= 1.472$ cm.
6. Draw standing wave circle with the centre (see Fig. 2.15) with radius OA i.e. circle pass throw normalize load point A. This circle intersect the right portion of the real axis atc C which indicates the SWR. This is $\rho_L = 2.6$

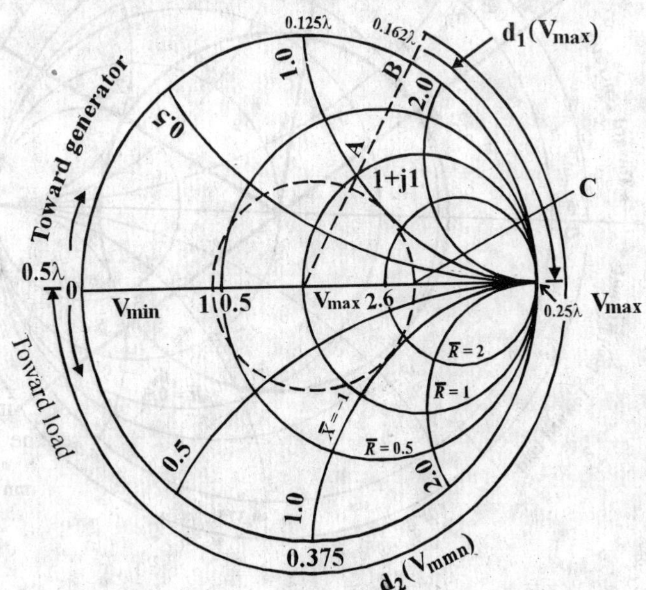

Fig. 2.15 Graphic solution for Example 2.6.

Example 2.7. A 4.5 cm length of lossless 100 ohm line is terminated in a load impedance $Z_L = 30 + j40$ ohms. Determine the load impedance at a point 1.5 cm from the load end. The signal frequency is 900 MHz and $\lambda = \lambda_0$

Solution :

Steps are

(1) Plot the normalized load impedance $z_L = Z_L/Z_0 = 0.3 + j0.4$ on the Smith Chart Fig. 2.16 as point A. This is done by starting from the 0.30 point on the resistance axis and moving up to 0.4 reactance arc. Draw a circle from centre of the chart through A. The VSWR is read as 4. $|\Gamma_L|$ from the bottom radially scaled parameter is read as 0.58.

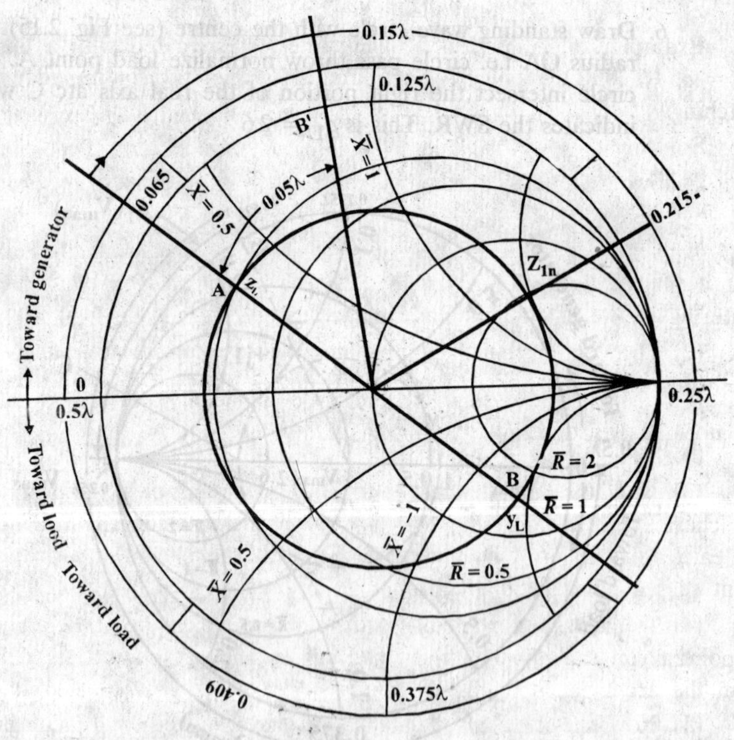

Fig. 2.16 Graphic solution for Example 2.7.

(2) A graphical method of obtaining Γ_{in} when Γ_L and βl are known is described as follows :

Draw a straight line from the center of the chart through z_L(point A). to the periphery. Read the value on the wavelength towards generator scale as 0.065.

3. Since λ_0 is 30 cm at 1GHz and the input is 4.5 cm from load, rotate clockwise from 0.065 a distance $l/\lambda = 4.5/30 = 0.150$. Draw a radial line from the centre of chart through the 0.215 point on the outer scale as shown in Fig. 2.16. The intersection of the radial line with the SWR circle represents Z_{in}. In this case $z_{in} = 2.38 + j1.8$ or $Z_{in} = 238 + j\ 180$ ohms.

(4) To obtain the impedance at $d = 1.5$ cm, start from z_L and rotate clockwise $1.5/30 = 0.050$ and draw a radial line therough the 0.115 point. Its intersection with the SWR circle yields,

$\bar{z} = 0.44 + 0.8$ or $Z = 44 + j\ 80$ ohms.

Example 2.8. A lossless 50 ohm line is terminated with a load $Z_L = 35 + j65\ \Omega$. Design a short circuited single stub for impedance matching.

Solution :

Following steps will occur in solving this problem :

(1) Find the normalized impedance $z_l = \dfrac{35 + j65}{50} = 0.7 + j\,1.3$.

Plot it on the Smith Chart in Fig. 2.17 as A. Draw a SWR circle, centering at the origin and passing through A.

(2) Draw point B which is diametrically opposite to point A. The value of B can be read directly from the Smith Chart and it is the normalized admittance $y_l = \dfrac{1}{z_l} = 0.32 - j\,0.6$.

(3) Now the line joining A to B is extended past the rim of the chart. This line intersects at 0.409, on the wavelength scale. In the earlier discussion it was mentioned that a stub placed at a proper point sees a normalized admittance of $1 + jb$ $(1 + j\,1.16)$.

(4) To arrive at this point, move clockwise from point B, arrive at point C on the $r = 1$ circle. The susceptance at point C is read from the arc from C to inner scale as $+ j1.6$.

(5) Now the clockwise distance we have moved to reach this point is calculated, the distance from B to horizontal line is $0.5 - 0.409 = 0.091$ wavelength. Also the distance from the horizontal line to C is 0.179 as read from the outermost scale. The total distance

moved is 0.091 + 0.179 = 0.27 wavelength. This is the distance from load where the stub will be placed.

(6) Now we have to calculate the length of the short circuited stub. We know at C the line has a normalized susceptance of 1 $+j1.6$. A susceptance of exactly $-$ $j1.6$ will cancel out this value, leaving a pure resistance value y = 1.0. Locate point D where susceptance is –j1.6 Draw a line from centre of the chart through this point and read the wavelength as 0.339. Since the stub has a short circuit at its end hence the admittance at that point will be infinity, which is located at the extreme right hand of the *r*-axis. The wavelength at this point is marked as 0.25. Therefore the length of the stub will be 0.339 – 0.25 = 0.089, as shown in Fig. 2.17.

Hence we conclude that a short circuited stub of length 0.089λ long located on the line 0.27λ away from the complex load Z_L = 35 $+j65$ ohms will make the SWR of the line as 1.0, resulting into maximum transfer of power from source to load.

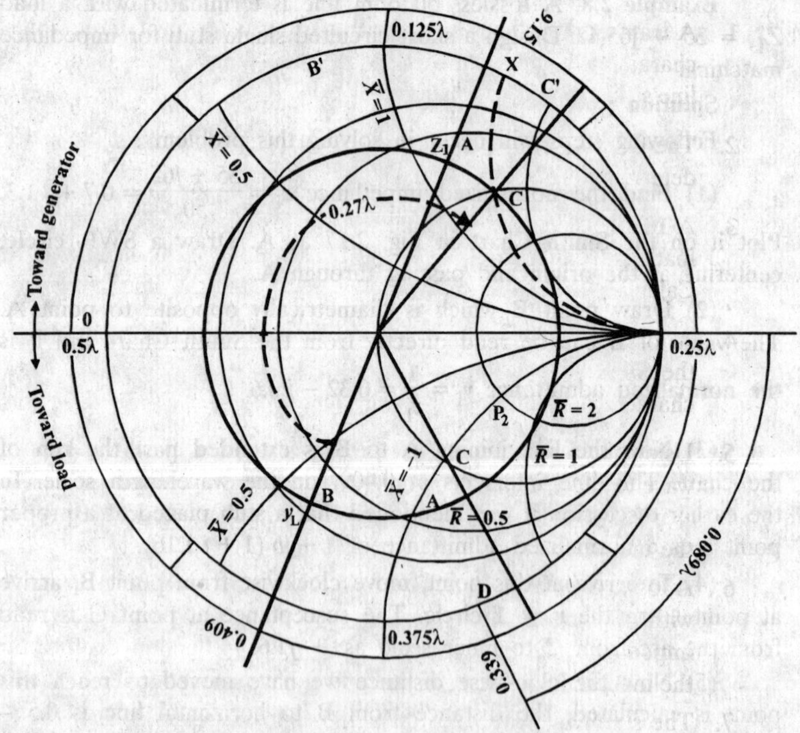

Fig. 2.17. Graphic solution for Example 2.8.

Select Bibliography

1. Collin, R.E., Foundation for Microwave Engineering, second Edition, McGraw-Hill, Inc., New York, 1992
2. Jordan, E.C., et al., Electromagnetic waves and Radiating Systems, Second Edition Prentice Hall Inc., 1978.
3. Gupta, K.C., Microwaves, New Age. International Publishers, New Delhi, Reprint 1997.
4. Sisodia, M.L. and G.S. Raghuvanshi, Microwave Circuits and Passive Devices, New Age International Publishers, New Delhi, Reprint 2001.
5. Ramo, S., et al., Fields and Waves in Communication Electronics, John Wiley, New York, 1965.

Problems and Review Questions

1. A transmission line has a distributed inductance of 11.3μH/m. Its characteristic impedance is 250 ohms. What is the value of the line's distributed capacitance?
2. The distance between adjacent nodes of a standing wave in air is determined to be 2.406 cm. What is the frequency of the generator?
3. A 10V source with an impedance of $Z_g = 50\Omega$ is connected to a load impedance $Z_L = 80 + j\,40\ \Omega$ with a 50 Ω transmission line. Calculate the power delivered to the load if the line is 0.6 λ ?
4. A lossless transmission line is terminated with a 100 ohm load. If the SWR on the line is 1.5, find the two possible values for the characteristic impedance of the line.
5. Using the Smith chart, find the nearest point at which a quarter wave transformer may be connected to a complex load, $Z_L = 255 + j\,255$ ohm in order to get a VSWR = 1.0, $Z_0 = 300$. What is the impedance (Z_o) of the transformer?
6. A lossless transmission line of electric length $l = 0.3\lambda$ is terminated with a complex load, $Z_L = 40 + j20\ \Omega$. The characteristic impedance of the line is 75 Ω. Find the reflection coefficient at the load, the SWR on the line and the input impedance to the line.
7. The standing wave ratio on a 100 Ω lossless line is 8. If the first voltage maxima is 0.3λ away from the load, calculate the load impedance and the voltage reflection coefficient.

8. Calculate the input impedance of a $\lambda/8$ section of a 50 Ω transmission line terminated with (a) 40 Ω (inductive reactance) (b) 30 – j 60 Ω.

9. A 50 Ω transmission line is terminated with an unknown load Z_L, the standing wave ratio is measured to be 2.5 and the distance between adjacent minima is 10 cm. Calculate Z_L given that when the load is replaced by a short, the positions of the minima are shifted by 4 cm (a) towards the load, (b) towards the generator.

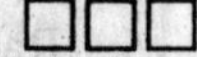

3
Waveguides

3.1. Introduction

Hollow waveguides are generally used as transmission lines at frequencies around 1GHz and above. Waveguides have certain advantages in comparison to coaxial lines. These are

(1) Higher power handling capability.

(2) Lower loss per unit length.

(3) A simpler, lower cost structure.

Moreover, the reflections caused by the flanges used in connecting waveguide sections is much less than that associated with coaxial connectors. It is precisely because of the low loss factor, that waveguides

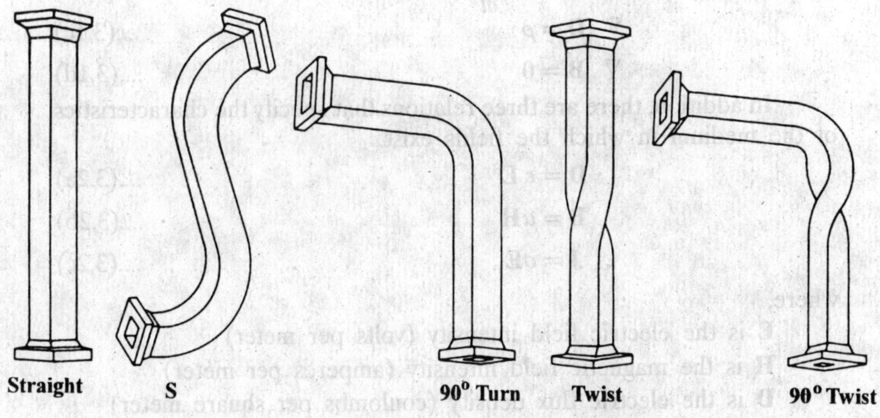

Fig. 3.1 : Typical wave guide shapes

have edge over other kinds of transmission lines at higher frequencies. By definition, a waveguide is simply a pipe of virtually any consistent cross-sectional shape through which an em wave travels by reflection, and not by conduction. It is because of this reason that we always speak of electric and magnetic fields rather than voltage and current as was the case with transmission lines. Since the method of propagation in a waveguide is by means of reflection, hence the interior surfaces should be smooth, often silvered, free of moisture and abrupt changes in shape or direction otherwise they will cause reflections to occur back towards the source. A few typical waveguide shapes are shown in Fig. 3.1.

In this chapter brief discussion of the boundary conditions is given, propagation in parallel plate guide, rectangular and cylindrical guides supporting both TE and TM modes is discussed. Attenuation in these guides is also considered. Finally rectangular and cylindrical cavities are described.

3.2. Maxwell's Equations

Maxwell's equations, sometimes called electromagnetic equations, express the fundamental relations between electromagnetic fields and their sources, *viz.* currents and charges.

The four Maxwell's equations are

$$\nabla \times \mathbf{H} = \frac{\partial \mathbf{D}}{\partial t} + \mathbf{J} \quad \text{....(3.1a)}$$

$$\nabla \times \mathbf{E} = -\frac{\partial \mathbf{B}}{\partial t} \quad \text{....(3.1b)}$$

$$\nabla . \mathbf{D} = \rho \quad \text{....(3.1c)}$$

$$\nabla . \mathbf{B} = 0 \quad \text{....(3.1d)}$$

In addition, there are three relations that specify the characteristics of the medium in which the fields exist.

$$\mathbf{D} = \varepsilon \, \mathbf{E} \quad \text{....(3.2a)}$$

$$\mathbf{B} = \mu \mathbf{H} \quad \text{....(3.2b)}$$

$$\mathbf{J} = \sigma \mathbf{E} \quad \text{....(3.2c)}$$

where,

E is the electric field intensity (volts per meter)

H is the magnetic field intensity (amperes per meter)

D is the electric flux density (coulombs per square meter)

B is the magnetic flux density (webers per square meter)

I is the electric current density (amperes per square meter)

ρ is the electric charge density (coulombs per cubic meter)

ε is the capacitivity (permittivity) of the medium

μ is the inductivity (permeability) of the medium

σ is the conductivity of the medium.

Matter is often classified according to the values of σ, ε and μ. Materials having very large values of σ are called conductors and those having small values of σ are called insulators or dielectrics. For analysis we generally approximate good conductors by perfect conductors having $\sigma = \infty$, and approximate perfect dielectrics by $\sigma = 0$. The permittivity of any material is never less than that of vacuum ε_0 which in MKS units has the value :

$$\varepsilon_0 = 8.854 \times 10^{-12} \cong \frac{1}{36\pi} \times 10^{-9} \text{ farads per meter}$$

The ratio $\varepsilon_r = \dfrac{\varepsilon}{\varepsilon_0}$ is called the dielectric constant or relative capacitivity. For most linear materials permeability is approximately that of free space μ_0. The ratio $\mu_r = \mu/\mu_0$, called the relative permeability is essentially unity for non-magnetic materials.

The value of μ_0 is

$$\mu_0 = 4\pi \times 10^{-7} \text{ henry per meter}$$

Corresponding to each of Eq. 3.1, there are the integral forms of Maxwell's equations

$$\oint \mathbf{H}.dl = \frac{d}{dt}\iint \mathbf{D}.ds + \iint \mathbf{J}.ds \qquad \text{....(3.3a)}$$

$$\oint \mathbf{E}.dl = -\frac{d}{dt}\iint \mathbf{B}.ds \qquad \text{....(3.3b)}$$

$$\iint \mathbf{B}.ds = 0 \qquad \text{....(3.3c)}$$

$$\iint \mathbf{D}.\text{ds} = \iiint q_v dt \qquad \text{....(3.3d)}$$

These relations are actually more general than Eq. 3.1 because it is no longer required that the various quantities be well-behaved. A quantity is called well-behaved whenever it is a continuous function and has continuous derivatives. Solution to any particular problem is determined by applying the boundary conditions of the problem and the solution thus obtained are called eigenvalues or characteristic values.

In order to determine the electromagnetic field configuration within the guide Maxwell's equations are solved subject to the appropriate boundary conditions at the walls of the guide.

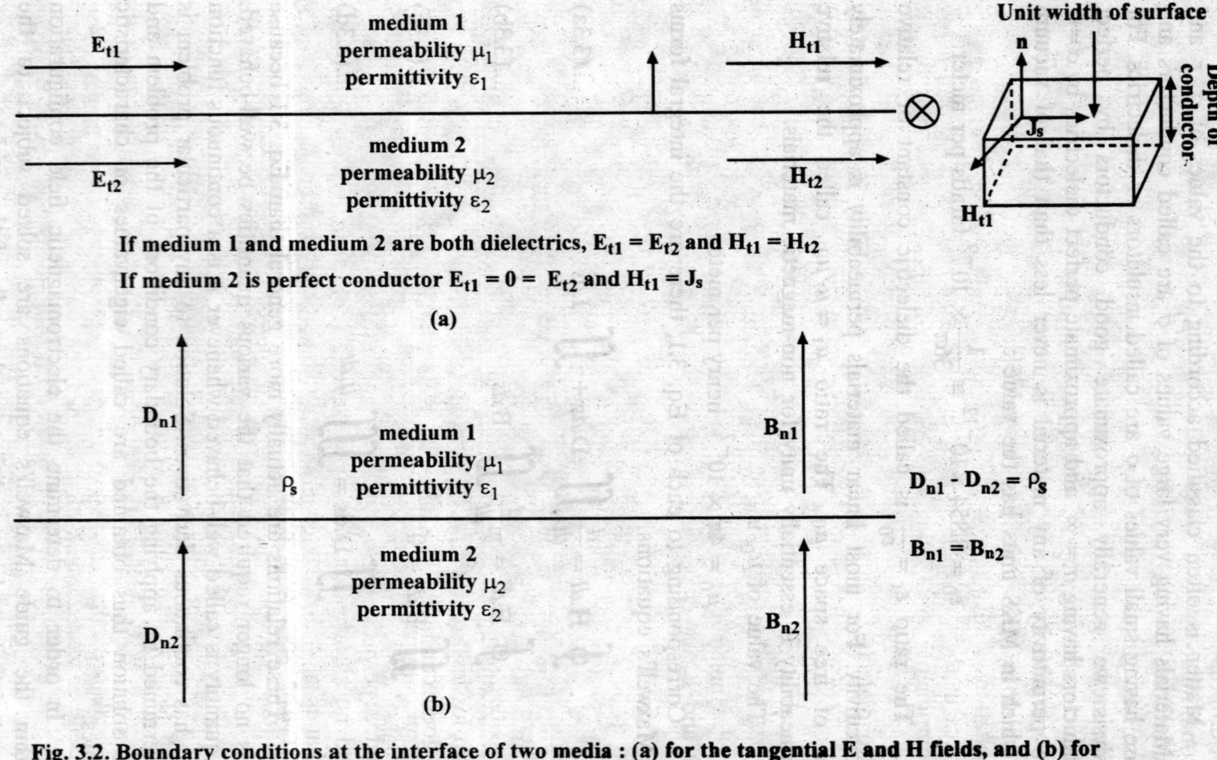

Fig. 3.2. Boundary conditions at the interface of two media : (a) for the tangential E and H fields, and (b) for the normal D and B fields.

3.3. Electromagnetic Boundary conditions

To solve electromagnetic problems involving continuous region of different constitutive parameters, it is necessary to know the boundary conditions that the field vectors E, D, B and H must satisfy at the interfaces. Boundary conditions are derived by applying the integral form of Maxwell's equations 3.3 to a small region at an interface of two media. The application of integral form of a curl equation to a flat closed path at the boundary with top and bottom sides in the two touching media yields the boundary conditions for the tangential components while the application of the integral form of divergence equations to a shallow pillbox at an interface with top and bottom faces in the two media gives the boundary conditions for the normal components. Fig. 3.2 gives the boundary surface between two media.

The boundary condition for the tangential components between two dielectric media are obtained from Eqs. 3.3a and 3.3b as

$$a_{n2} \times (H_1 - H_2) = J_s \quad (A/m) \qquad \text{....(3.4a)}$$

$$E_{1t} = E_{2t} \quad (V/m) \qquad \text{....(3.4b)}$$

Similarly the boundary conditions for the normal components of D and B are obtained from Eqs. 3.3c and 3.3d as

$$a_{n2} \cdot (D_1 - D_2) = \rho_s \quad (C/m^2) \qquad \text{....(3.4c)}$$

$$B_{1n} - B_{2n} = 0 \quad (T) \qquad \text{....(3.4d)}$$

where a_{n1}, a_{n2} are the outward normal unit vectors in medium 1 and 2.

Consider two important special cases of (1) a boundary between two lossless media, and (2) a boundary between a good dielectric and a good conductor.

A lossless linear medium can be specified by a permittivity ε and a permeability μ with $\sigma = 0$. There are usually no free charges and no surface currents at the interface between two lossless media. That is $\rho_s = 0$ and $J_s = 0$. Hence the boundary conditions are listed as

$$E_{1t} = E_{2t} \Rightarrow \frac{D_{1t}}{D_{2t}} = \frac{\varepsilon_1}{\varepsilon_2} \qquad \text{....(3.5a)}$$

$$H_{1t} = H_{2t} \Rightarrow \frac{B_{1t}}{B_{2t}} = \frac{\mu_1}{\mu_2} \qquad \text{....(3.5b)}$$

$$D_{1n} = D_{2n} \Rightarrow \varepsilon_1 E_{1n} = \varepsilon_2 E_{2n} \qquad \text{....(3.5c)}$$

$$B_{1n} = B_{2n} \Rightarrow \mu_1 H_{1n} = \mu_{2n} H_{2n} \qquad \text{....(3.5d)}$$

When interface between a dielectric and a perfect conductor is encountered the above mentioned boundary conditions are slightly modified. Practical cases will only have good conductors, for ease of solution of field problems good conductors are often considered as perfect conductors. For the boundary conditions if the second medium is conductor $E_2=0$, $H_2=0$, $D_2=0$ and $B_2=0$,

$$E_{1t} = 0, \quad E_{2t} = 0 \qquad ....(3.6a)$$

$$a_{n2} \times H_1 = J_s, \quad H_{2t} = 0 \qquad ....(3.6b)$$

$$a_{n2} . D_1 = \rho_s, \quad D_{2n} = 0 \qquad ....(3.6c)$$

$$B_{1n} = 0, \quad B_{2n} = 0 \qquad ....(3.6d)$$

In chapter two, we learned that transmission lines consist of two or more conductors and they support transverse electromagnetic (TEM) waves. This shows that they do not have longitudinal field components. TEM waves have a uniquely defined voltage, current and characteristic impedance. Waveguides, often consist of a single conductor and support transverse electric (TE) or Transverse Magnetic (TM) waves, they support ,one/or both the longitudinal field components. Also these guides do not have a unique definition for characteristic impedance.

We assume time harmonic fields with an $e^{j\omega t}$ dependence, and wave propagation along the *z*-axis. For understanding wave propagation in TE or TM mode we first discuss the case of wave propagation in parallel conducting planes.

3.3.1 Wave equation in source free region

The Maxwell's equations in source-free region become

$$\nabla \times \mathbf{H} = j\omega\varepsilon\mathbf{E} \qquad ....(3.1a)$$

$$\nabla \times \mathbf{E} = -j\omega\mu\mathbf{H} \qquad ....(3.1b)$$

$$\nabla . \mathbf{D} = 0 \qquad ....(3.1c)$$

$$\nabla . \mathbf{B} = 0 \qquad ....(3.1d)$$

Take the curl of Eq. 3.1b

$$\nabla \times \nabla \times \mathbf{E} = -\nabla \times (j\omega\mu\mathbf{H})$$

LHS from the vector identity is given as

$$\nabla \times \nabla \times \nabla . \mathbf{E} = \nabla \nabla \mathbf{E} - \nabla^2\mathbf{E}$$

Using 3.1a, we have

$$\nabla^2\mathbf{E} = -(j\omega\mu)(j\omega\varepsilon)\mathbf{E}$$

putting

$$\gamma = \sqrt{(j\omega\varepsilon)(j\omega\mu)}$$

$$\nabla^2\mathbf{E} - \gamma^2\mathbf{E} = 0 \qquad \text{....(3.7a)}$$

Similarly from Eq. 3.1a, we get

$$\nabla^2\mathbf{H} - \gamma^2\mathbf{H} = 0 \qquad \text{....(3.7b)}$$

Eq. 3.7 are the wave equations in **E** and **H**.

The two curl equations can be written in the rectangular coordinates as

$$\frac{\partial E_z}{\partial y} - \frac{\partial E_y}{\partial z} = -j\omega\mu H_x \qquad \text{....(3.8a)}$$

$$\frac{\partial E_x}{\partial z} - \frac{\partial E_z}{\partial x} = -j\omega\mu H_y \qquad \text{....(3.8)}$$

$$\frac{\partial E_y}{\partial x} - \frac{\partial E_x}{\partial y} = -j\omega\mu H_z \qquad \text{....(3.8c)}$$

and

$$\frac{\partial H_z}{\partial y} - \frac{\partial H_y}{\partial z} = j\omega\varepsilon E_x \qquad \text{....(3.9a)}$$

$$\frac{\partial H_x}{\partial z} - \frac{\partial H_z}{\partial x} = j\omega\varepsilon E_y \qquad \text{....(3.9b)}$$

$$\frac{\partial H_y}{\partial x} - \frac{\partial H_x}{\partial y} = j\omega\varepsilon E_z \qquad \text{....(3.9c)}$$

As mentioned earlier it is assumed that the propagation is in the *z*-direction and the variation of all field components in this direction will be expressed as $e^{-\bar{\gamma}z}$, where in general, propagation constant $\bar{\gamma} = \bar{\alpha} + j\bar{\beta}$ is a complex quantity. When the time variation factor is combined with the *z*-variation factor, it gives

$$e^{j\omega t}\, e^{-\bar{\gamma}z} = e^{(j\omega t - \bar{\gamma}z)} = e^{-\bar{\alpha}z}\, e^{j(\omega t - \bar{\beta}z)} \qquad \text{....(3.10)}$$

which represents a wave propagating in *z*-direction. If γ is an imaginary quantity, that is if $\bar{\alpha} = 0$, expression 3.10 represent a wave without attenuation. On the other hands if $\bar{\gamma}$ is real so that $\bar{\beta} = 0$, there is no wave motion but only an exponential decrease in amplitude.

The six components of Eq. 3.8 and 3.9 can be solved for the four transverse field components in terms of H_z and E_z as

$$H_x = -\frac{\bar{\gamma}}{h^2}\frac{\partial H_z}{\partial x} + j\frac{\omega\varepsilon}{h^2}\frac{\partial E_z}{\partial y} \quad \text{....(3.10a)}$$

$$H_y = -\frac{\bar{\gamma}}{h^2}\frac{\partial H_z}{\partial y} - \frac{j\omega\varepsilon}{h^2}\frac{\partial E_z}{\partial x} \quad \text{....(3.10b)}$$

$$E_x = -\frac{\bar{\gamma}}{h^2}\frac{\partial E_z}{\partial x} - j\frac{\omega\mu}{h^2}\frac{\partial H_z}{\partial y} \quad \text{....(3.10c)}$$

$$E_y = -\frac{\bar{\gamma}}{h^2}\frac{\partial E_z}{\partial y} + j\frac{\omega\mu}{h^2}\frac{\partial H_z}{\partial x} \quad \text{....(3.10d)}$$

where

$$h^2 = \bar{\gamma}^2 + \omega^2\mu\varepsilon \quad \text{....(3.11a)}$$

putting $k_0^2 = \omega^2\mu\varepsilon$, then $h^2 = \bar{\gamma}^2 + k_0^2$ ....(3.11b)

From 3.10 it is clear that there must be *a z* component of either E or H; otherwise all the components would be zero and there would be no field at all in the region considered. Wave propagation in parallel conducting planes is discussed below.

3.4. Parallel Conducting Planes

3.4.1. Transverse electric modes (TE, $E_z = 0$)

When we consider the case of parallel conducting plates shown in Fig 3.3 the space between the planes is of infinite extent in the *y* direction. Hence it can be assumed that the field is constant in the *y* direction. In other words, derivation with respect to *y* in Eqs. 3.8 and 3.9 can be equated

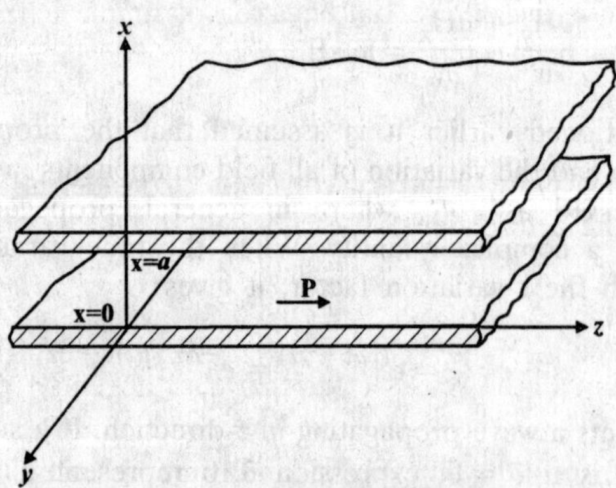

Fig. 3.3 Parallel plate guide

to zero. In the *x* direction the boundary conditions must be met, which put restrictions on the fields distribution in this direction.

When $E_z = 0$ and $H_z \neq 0$, also $\frac{\partial}{\partial y} = 0$, the field components H_y and E_x from Eq. 3.10 will also be zero. Components H_x and E_y will be non-zero. Hence the wave Eq. 3.7 in this particular case reduces to the following differential equation

$$\frac{\partial^2 E_y}{\partial x^2} + \bar{\gamma}^2 E_y = -\omega^2 \mu \varepsilon E_y \qquad \text{....(3.12a)}$$

This can be written as

$$\frac{\partial^2 E_y}{\partial x^2} + h^2 E_y = 0 \qquad \text{....(3.12b)}$$

Where E_y is of the form,

$$E_y = E_y^0(x)\, e^{-\bar{\gamma} z}$$

This shows that electric field is in y direction and has variation in the transverse *x* direction, and no variation in the y direction. Also the E field wave is propagating in the *z* direction with propagation constant γ. Substituting in Eq. 3.12b we get

$$\frac{d^2 E_y^{\,0}}{dx^2} = -h^2 E_y^{\,0} \qquad \text{....(3.12c)}$$

Eq. 3.12c is the differential equation of simple harmonic motion. Its solution can be written in the form

$$E_y^{\,0} = A_1 \sin hx + A_2 \cos hx \qquad \text{....(3.13a)}$$

where A_1 and A_2 are arbitrary constants. Considering the variation with time in the *z* direction the expression for E_y is

$$E_y = (A_1 \sin hx + A_2 \cos hx)\, e^{-\bar{\gamma} z} \qquad \text{....(3.13b)}$$

The arbitrary constants A_1 and A_2 can be found from boundary conditions. From Fig. 3.3 it is clear that the tangential component of E should be zero at the surface of the conductor (assumed perfect for simplicity) for all values of *z* and time. Hence, the boundary conditions will become

$$\left.\begin{aligned} E_y &= 0 \text{ at } x = 0 \\ E_y &= 0 \text{ at } x = a \end{aligned}\right\} \quad \text{for all values of } z$$

On applying first of these boundary conditions, it is evident that A_2 must be zero, the expression for E_y then becomes

$$E_y = A_1 \sin hx\, e^{-\bar{\gamma}z} \qquad ....(3.14)$$

Second boundary condition puts restriction on h when E_y is zero at $x = a$. For all values of z and t it is necessary that

$$h = \left(\frac{m\pi}{a}\right) \quad \text{where } (m = 1, 2, 3, ...)$$

therefore

$$E_y = A_1 \sin\left(\frac{m\pi}{a}x\right) e^{-\bar{\gamma}z} \qquad .....(3.15)$$

The other components of E and H can be obtained by substituting the value of E_y along with $E_z = 0$ and $\frac{\partial}{\partial y} = 0$ in Eq. 3.10, we get

$$\left.\begin{aligned} E_y &= A_1 \sin\left(\frac{m\pi}{a}x\right) e^{-\bar{\gamma}z} \\ H_z &= -\frac{m\pi}{j\omega\mu a} A_1 \cos\left(\frac{m\pi}{a}x\right) e^{-\bar{\gamma}z} \\ H_x &= -\frac{\bar{\gamma}}{j\omega\mu} A_1 \sin\left(\frac{m\pi}{a}x\right) e^{-\bar{\gamma}z} \end{aligned}\right\} \qquad .....(3.16)$$

Each value of m specifies a particular field configuration or mode, and the mode associated with the integer m is designated as the TEm_0 mode. The first subscript shows variation of field in the x direction. The second subscript which is zero in this case refers to variation in the y direction. The lowest value of m which can be used in the TE waves is $m = 1$. If $m = 0$ is chosen, all the field components become zero. Hence the lowest order mode in this case is TE_{10}.

The propagation constant $\bar{\gamma}$ can either be pure real or pure imaginary. For the case when it is real, *i.e.* $\bar{\alpha}$ has value but $\bar{\beta}$ is zero. In such a case there will be attenuation but no phase shift, and therefore, no wave propagation. On the other hand in the range of frequencies where $\bar{\gamma}$ is imaginary, $\bar{\alpha} = 0$ and $\bar{\beta}$ has a value, so there is a wave motion in the conducting planes. Writing $\bar{\gamma} = j\bar{\beta}$, Eq. 3.16 become

$$E_y = A_1 \sin\left(\frac{m\pi}{a}x\right) e^{-j\bar{\beta}z} \qquad \text{....(3.16a)}$$

$$H_z = \frac{jm\pi}{\omega\mu a} A_1 \cos\left(\frac{m\pi}{a}x\right) e^{-j\bar{\beta}z} \qquad \text{....(3.16b)}$$

$$H_x = -\frac{\bar{\beta}}{\omega\mu} A_1 \sin\left(\frac{m\pi}{a}x\right) e^{-j\bar{\beta}z} \qquad \text{....(3.16c)}$$

The TE wave impedance can be found to be

$$Z_{TE} = \left|\frac{E_y}{H_x}\right| \text{ or } \left|\frac{E_z}{H_x}\right| = \frac{\omega\mu}{\bar{\beta}} \qquad \text{....(3.16d)}$$

3.4.2. Transverse magnetic modes (TM, $H_z = 0$)

The case of TM waves in parallel planes can be solved in a manner similar to that used for TE waves. In this case since $H_z = 0$, the field components H_x and E_y will also be zero, while E_z, E_x and H_y will be present. Solving the wave equation in H_y we have the solution for H_y as

$$H_y = (B_1 \sin hx + B_2 \cos hx)\, e^{-\bar{\gamma}z} \qquad \text{....(3.17)}$$

For finding the constants B_1 and B_2 the boundary conditions can not be applied to H_y directly because H_y is not zero at the surface of the conductor plates. But from Maxwell's curl equation in component form of Eq. 3.8, we know

$$E_z = \frac{1}{j\omega\varepsilon}\frac{\partial H_y}{\partial x}$$

using Eq. 3.17, we have

$$E_z = \frac{h}{j\omega\varepsilon}\left[B_1 \cos hx - B_2 \sin hx\right] e^{-\bar{\gamma}z} \qquad \text{....(3.18)}$$

The boundary conditions that E_z should follow are

$$E_z = 0, \quad \text{at } x = 0$$
$$E_z = 0, \quad \text{at } x = a$$

The field components present in this case are written as

$$\left.\begin{aligned} E_z &= \frac{jm\pi}{\omega\varepsilon a} B_2 \sin\left(\frac{m\pi}{a}x\right) e^{-j\bar{\beta}z} \\ E_x &= \frac{\bar{\beta}}{\omega\varepsilon} B_2 \cos\left(\frac{m\pi}{a}x\right) e^{-j\bar{\beta}z} \\ H_y &= B_2 \cos\left(\frac{m\pi}{a}x\right) e^{-j\bar{\beta}z} \end{aligned}\right\} \quad ....(3.19)$$

As in the case of TE waves, there are an infinite number of modes corresponding to various values of m ($m = 1........\infty$). However in this case (TM mode), there is a possibility of putting $m = 0$ in the above Eq. 3.19 which show that when $m = 0$ all the fields will not vanish. This particular case of $m = 0$ will be discussed later.

3.4.3. Characteristics of TE and TM modes

Examination of Eq. 3.16 for TE waves and Eq. 3.19 for TM waves show that for each of the components of E or H there is a sinusoidal or cosinusoidal variation across the guide in x direction. That is, each of these component present vary in amplitude but not in phase in the x direction. By assumption there is no amplitude or phase variation in the y direction. Thus any x-y plane is a equiphase plane for each of the field components. Also these equiphase surfaces progress along the guide in the z-direction with a velocity $v = \omega/\bar{\beta}$; where $\bar{\beta}$ is the imaginary part of the propagation constant $\bar{\gamma}$. Now in the case of parallel conducting planes, $\bar{\gamma}$ can be expressed in terms of h, frequency and constants of the medium by

$$\bar{\gamma} = \sqrt{h^2 - \omega^2\mu\varepsilon} = \sqrt{\left(\frac{m\pi}{a}\right)^2 - \omega^2\mu\varepsilon} \quad ....(3.20)$$

Eq. 3.20 shows that at frequencies sufficiently high $\omega^2\mu\varepsilon >> \left(\frac{m\pi}{a}\right)^2$, γ will be pure imaginary equal to $j\bar{\beta}$, then

$$\bar{\beta} = \sqrt{\omega^2\mu\varepsilon - \left(\frac{m\pi}{a}\right)^2} \quad ....(3.21)$$

In this case, the fields will progress in the z direction as waves and the attenuation of these waves will be zero, provided the conducting planes are perfect. As the frequency is decreased, a critical frequency $f_c = \omega_c/2\pi$ will be reached at which

$$\omega_c^2 \mu\varepsilon = \left(\frac{m\pi}{a}\right)^2 \qquad \text{....(3.22)}$$

For all frequencies below f_c, $\bar{\gamma}$ will be a positive real number, that is, $\bar{\alpha}$ will have value and $\bar{\beta} = 0$. This means that the fields will be attenuated exponentially in the z direction, and that there will be no wave propagation in the z direction ($\bar{\beta} = 0$). The frequency f_c where wave motion ceases is called the cut-off frequency of the conducting plane guide and from Eq. 3.22 it can be written as

$$f_c = \frac{m}{2a\sqrt{\mu\varepsilon}} \qquad \text{....(3.23)}$$

Equation 3.23 shows that cut-off frequency depends on the mode number m; the separation between the conducting planes a, and the velocity in the medium. From Eq. 3.21 it is seen that β varies from zero at the cutoff frequency, upto the value $\omega\sqrt{\mu\varepsilon}$ as the frequency approaches infinity. The distance required for the phase to vary 2π radians is one wavelength. Hence, the wavelength λ is given in terms of $\bar{\beta}$, as

$$\bar{\lambda} = \frac{2\pi}{\bar{\beta}} \qquad \text{....(3.24)}$$

Also the phase velocity

$$\bar{v}_p = \bar{\lambda} f = \frac{2\pi f}{\bar{\beta}} = \frac{\omega}{\bar{\beta}} \qquad \text{....(3.25)}$$

Substituting for $\bar{\beta}$ in Eqs. 3.24 and 3.25, the wavelength and phase velocity are given as

$$\bar{\lambda} = \frac{2\pi}{\sqrt{\omega^2\mu\varepsilon - \left(\frac{m\pi}{a}\right)^2}} \qquad \text{....(3.26)}$$

$$\bar{v}_p = \frac{\omega}{\sqrt{\omega^2\mu\varepsilon - \left(\frac{m\pi}{a}\right)^2}} \qquad \text{....(3.27)}$$

We see from these relations that at cut-off frequency both $\bar{\lambda}$ and $\bar{v}_p$ are infinitely large. At higher frequencies the velocity decreases from this very large value to a limiting value of v.

$$\bar{v}_p \to v_o = \frac{1}{\sqrt{\mu\varepsilon}} \qquad \text{....(3.28)}$$

For very high frequencies $\left(\frac{m\pi}{a}\right)^2$ is negligible compared to $\omega^2\mu\varepsilon$. If the dielectric between the guides is air, then $\mu = \mu_0$ and $\varepsilon = \varepsilon_0$ the free space constants and v_o is equal to c, the free space velocity.

Hence it is concluded that the phase velocity of the wave varies from a value equal to the velocity of light in free space upto an infinitely large value as the frequency is decreased below the cut-off frequency. This phase velocity is different from the velocity with which the wave propagates.

3.4.4. Transverse electromagnetic waves

The lowest value of *m* that is possible for parallel plane TE mode was one, *i.e.,* the lowest order mode is TE_{10}, but in the case of TM waves, even when *m* was made equal to zero, all field components were not zero. Hence for TM propagation $m = 0$ can be used, and in this case the fields are

$$H_y = B_2 e^{-j\bar{\beta}z}$$

$$E_x = (\bar{\beta}/\omega\varepsilon)\, B_2 e^{-j\bar{\beta}z} \qquad \text{....(3.29)}$$

$$E_z = 0$$

For this special case of TM waves, the components E_z and H_z are both zero and the electromagnetic fields are entirely transverse. As already mentioned when fields are only transverse, this wave is called TEM wave. Althought it is a special case of guided wave propagation, it is very important concept because the waves at low frequencies propagate in this mode along all ordinary two-conductor transmission lines. It is generally called the principle wave.

Several interesting properties of TEM waves are obvious from the expressions in 3.29, that the fields are entirely transverse, they are constant in amplitude across a cross-section normal to the direction of propagation, and their ratio is also constant. For $m = 0$ and air as dielectric across the conducting planes, the expressions for $\bar{\gamma}, \bar{\beta}, \bar{v}_p$ and λ reduce to

$$\left.\begin{aligned} \bar{\gamma} &\rightarrow \gamma_0 = j\omega\sqrt{\mu_0\varepsilon_0} \\ \bar{\beta} &\rightarrow \beta_0 = \omega\sqrt{\mu_0\varepsilon_0} \\ \bar{v}_p &\rightarrow c = \frac{1}{\sqrt{\mu_0\varepsilon_0}} \\ \bar{\lambda} &\rightarrow \lambda_0 = \frac{2\lambda}{\omega\sqrt{\mu_0\varepsilon_0}} = \frac{c}{f} \end{aligned}\right\} \qquad \text{....(3.30)}$$

These expressions are same as for wave propagation in free space. Unlike the TE and TM waves, the velocity of the TEM wave is independent of frequency and has the value, $c \approx 3 \times 10^8$ m/s. Also the cutoff frequency of the TEM wave from Eq. 3.30 is zero, *i.e.*, all frequencies down to zero frequency can propagate along the line.

3.5. Rectangular Guides

Rectangular waveguides were one of the earliest types of transmission lines used to carry microwave signals. The hollow rectangular waveguides can propagate in TE or TM modes, but not in TEM mode, since only one conductor is present. As mentioned earlier the rectangular waveguides have cut-off frequencies below which propagation is not possible. The waveguide shown in Fig. 3.4a is filled with a source free lossless dielectric material ($\sigma_d = 0$) and its walls are perfectly conducting ($\sigma_c \approx \infty$).

Fig. 3.4b shows a parallel plate transmission line similar to that in Fig. 3.3. The width of the metal strip is w and their spacing is b. Power is delivered to the load via longitudinal current flow along the two plates. If now a pair of shorted stubs of lengths l_s are connected to the parallel strip as shown in the Fig. 3.4b, and the stubs are quarter wavelength long, they will have no effect on the transmission of power since they present an infinite impedance in shunt with the line. The current flow in the stub is reactive as no real power can be delivered to the shorts. Power can only be delivered by longitudinal currents, which is why they are called power currents. Note that the direction of power and reactive currents are perpendicular to each other. We can connect an infinite set of such quarter wavelength shorted stubs along the length of the parallel plate transmission line. The resultant configuration will be exactly similar to the rectangular waveguides shown in Fig. 3.4a, where $a = w + 2l_s$.

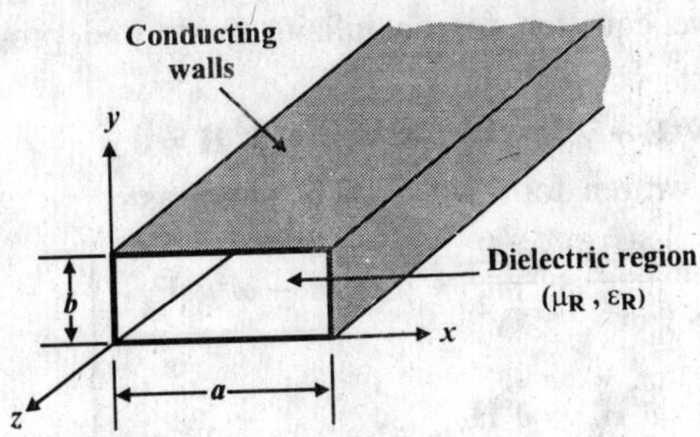

Fig. 3.4a. Rectangular waveguide.

Since $l_s = \lambda/4$ and the width w must be finite so that power currents can flow, the condition for power transmission is

$$a > \lambda/2$$

In other words, electromagnetic wave propagation in rectangular waveguides can only occur at frequencies high enough to satisfy this inequality. As the frequency decreases, λ increases and hence $\lambda/4$ stubs take up a greater portion of the guide width a, leaving less room for w the parallel-plate line. Decreasing the frequency to the point where $a = 2l_s = \lambda/2$ results in $w = 0$, which prevents the flow of power currents. The frequency at which this occurs is called the cutoff frequency (f_c) of the guide.

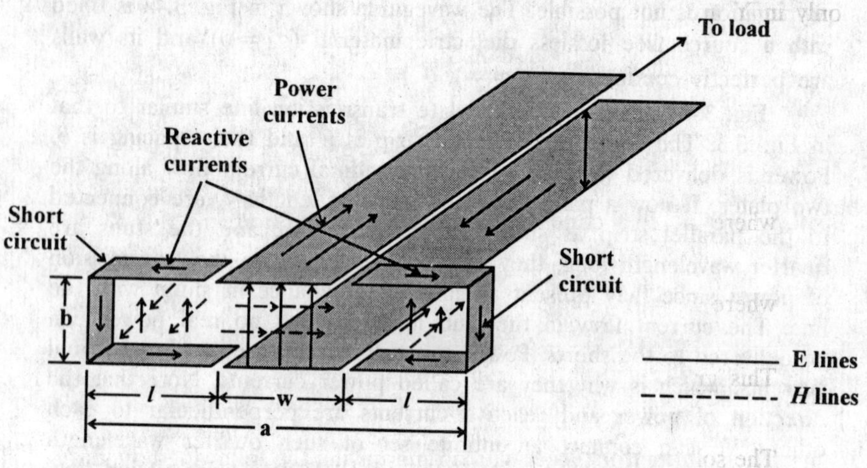

Fig. 3.4b. The development of rectangular waveguide from a paralled-plate transmission line.

The wave equation for an infinite guide and propagating in z direction are

$$\nabla^2 \mathbf{E} + \bar{\gamma}^2 \mathbf{E} = 0 \text{ and } \nabla^2 \mathbf{H} + \bar{\gamma}^2 \mathbf{H} = 0 \qquad ....(3.31)$$

which can be written for TM and TE waves as

$$\left.\begin{aligned} \frac{\partial^2 E_z}{\partial x^2} + \frac{\partial^2 E_z}{\partial y^2} + \bar{\gamma}^2 E_z &= -\omega^2 \mu\varepsilon E_z \\ \frac{\partial^2 H_z}{\partial x^2} + \frac{\partial^2 H_z}{\partial y^2} + \bar{\gamma}^2 H_z &= -\omega^2 \mu\varepsilon H_z \end{aligned}\right\} \qquad ....(3.32)$$

3.5.1. Transverse magnetic (TM) modes in rectangular guides

The wave equations in 3.32 are partial differential equations and can be solved by the method of separation of variables. For the case of TM modes $H_z = 0$ using the wave equation in E_z, we can write

$$E_z(x, y, z) = E_z^{\,0}(x, y)\, e^{-\bar{\gamma} z} \quad ....(3.33)$$

Let $$E_z^{\,0} = XY \quad ....(3.34)$$

where X is a function of x alone and Y is a function of y alone. Substituting Eq. 3.34 in Eq. 3.32, one obtains

$$Y\frac{d^2X}{dx^2} + X\frac{d^2Y}{dy^2} + \bar{\gamma}^2 XY = -\omega^2\mu\varepsilon XY$$

Using $h^2 = \bar{\gamma}^2 + \omega^2\mu\varepsilon$ two equations one only in X and other only in Y are obtained.

$$\frac{1}{X}\frac{d^2X}{dx^2} + h^2 = A^2$$

$$\frac{1}{Y}\frac{d^2Y}{dy^2} = -A^2$$

where A^2 is a constant solution in X and Y are

$$X = C_1 \cos Bx + C_2 \sin Bx$$

where $B^2 = h^2 - A^2$

$$Y = C_3 \cos A_y + C_4 \sin A_y$$

This gives

$$E_z^0 = XY$$

The solution for this equation on applying the following boundary conditions,

$$E_z = 0, \text{ when } x = 0, x = a, y = 0, y = b \text{ gives}$$

$$E_z^{\,0} = C \sin\left(\frac{m\pi}{a}\right) x \sin\left(\frac{n\pi}{b}\right) y \quad ....(3.35)$$

where C is a constant. The other field components are obtained from Eq. 3.10 as

$$E_x^{\,0} = -\frac{j\bar{\beta}C}{h^2}\left(\frac{m\pi}{a}\right) \cos\left(\frac{m\pi}{a}\right) x \,\sin\left(\frac{n\pi}{b}\right) y \quad ....(3.36a)$$

$$E_y^{\,0} = -\frac{j\bar{\beta}C}{h^2}\left(\frac{n\pi}{b}\right) \sin\left(\frac{m\pi}{a}\right) x \,\cos\left(\frac{n\pi}{b}\right) y \quad ....(3.36b)$$

$$H_x^0 = \frac{j\omega\varepsilon C}{h^2}\left(\frac{n\pi}{b}\right) \sin\left(\frac{m\pi}{a}\right)x \cos\left(\frac{n\pi}{b}\right)y \quad ....(3.36c)$$

$$H_y^0 = -\frac{j\omega\varepsilon C}{h^2}\left(\frac{m\pi}{a}\right) \cos\left(\frac{m\pi}{a}\right)x \sin\left(\frac{n\pi}{b}\right)y \quad ....(3.36d)$$

The propagation constant γ in this case is given by

$$\bar{\gamma} = \bar{\alpha} + j\bar{\beta} = \sqrt{\left(\frac{m\pi}{a}\right)^2 + \left(\frac{n\pi}{b}\right)^2 - \omega^2\mu\varepsilon} \quad ....(3.37)$$

When the attenuation constant $\bar{\alpha}$ is equal to zero, the phase constant $\bar{\beta}$ will have the value

$$\bar{\beta} = \sqrt{\omega^2\mu\varepsilon - \left(\frac{m\pi}{a}\right)^2 - \left(\frac{n\pi}{b}\right)^2} \quad ....(3.38)$$

The cut-off frequency ω_c is obtained when $\bar{\beta} = 0$

$$\omega_c = \frac{1}{\sqrt{\mu\varepsilon}}\sqrt{\left(\frac{m\pi}{a}\right)^2 + \left(\frac{n\pi}{b}\right)^2} \quad ....(3.39)$$

This is the frequency below which wave propagation will not occur.

$$f_c = \frac{1}{2\pi\sqrt{\mu\varepsilon}}\sqrt{\left(\frac{m\pi}{a}\right)^2 + \left(\frac{n\pi}{b}\right)^2} \quad ....(3.40)$$

The corresponding cut-off wavelength is

$$\lambda_c = \frac{2}{\sqrt{\left(\frac{m}{a}\right)^2 + \left(\frac{n}{b}\right)^2}} \quad ....(3.41)$$

from which it can be seen that

$$f_c\lambda_c = v_0$$

The phase velocity is given by

$$\bar{v}_p = \frac{\omega}{\bar{\beta}} = \frac{\omega}{\sqrt{\omega^2\mu\varepsilon - \left(\frac{m\pi}{a}\right)^2 - \left(\frac{n\pi}{b}\right)^2}} \quad ....(3.42)$$

This expression indicates that the velocity of propagation of the wave in the guide is greater than the phase velocity in the free space. As the value of frequency is increased above cut-off, the phase velocity decreases from an infinitely large value and approaches *c*, the velocity of free space. Since the wavelength in the guide is given by

$\bar{\lambda} = \bar{v}_p/f$, it will be longer than the corresponding free space wavelength. The lowest possible value for m and n for TM mode is 1. Substituting for $m = n = 1$ in Eq. 3.36 we get fields for the lowest particular mode called the TM_{11}. Higher-order modes require higher frequencies in order to be propagated along the guide of given dimensions.

The wave configuration for different TM modes in a waveguide are shown in Fig. 3.5. The subscripts indicate the number of half sine wave variations of the field components in the x and y directions respectively.

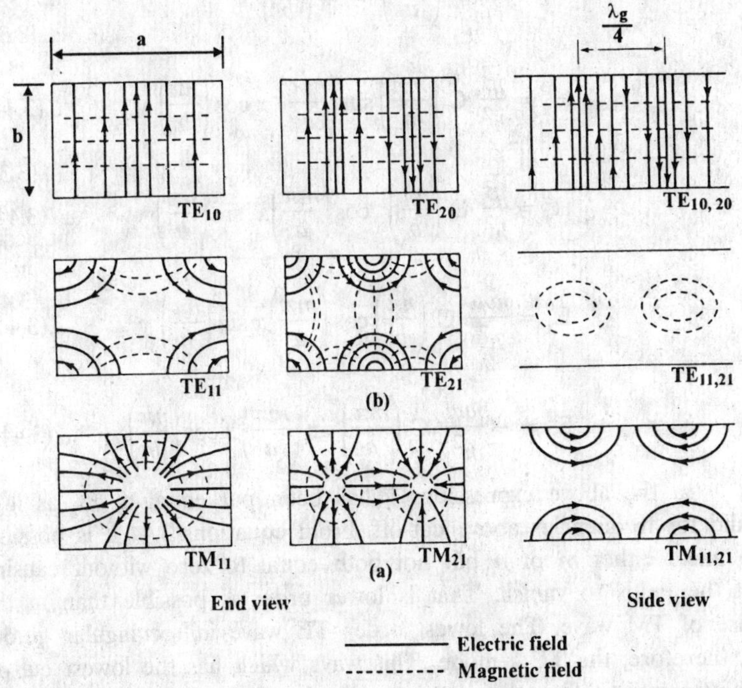

Fig. 3.5. Field patterns for the Lower order modes rectangular waveguide (TM and TE)

3.5.2. Transverse electric (TE) modes

The solutions for transverse electric waves are derived in similar manner to that for transverse magnetic waves. The H_z component will be given as

$$H_z(x,y,z) = H_z^{\,0}(x,y)\, e^{-\bar{\gamma} z}$$

Let $$H_z^{\,0} = XY$$

Boundary conditions cannot be applied to H_z directly. Hence it is differentiated with respect to x and y to obtain $E_x^{\,0}$, $E_y^{\,0}$, $H_x^{\,0}$ and $H_y^{\,0}$. The boundary conditions are then applied to these field components as

$$E_x^0 = 0 \text{ at } y = 0, b$$

$$E_y^0 = 0 \text{ at } x = 0, a$$

The field expressions result in the following relations :

$$H_z^0 = C \cos\left(\frac{m\pi}{a}\right) x \cos\left(\frac{n\pi}{b}\right) y \qquad \text{....(3.43)}$$

$$H_x^0 = \frac{j\bar{\beta}}{h^2}\, C \left(\frac{m\pi}{a}\right) \sin\left(\frac{m\pi}{a}\right) x \cos\left(\frac{n\pi}{b}\right) y \qquad \text{....(3.44a)}$$

$$H_y^0 = \frac{j\bar{\beta}}{h^2}\, C \left(\frac{n\pi}{b}\right) \cos\left(\frac{m\pi}{a}\right) x \sin\left(\frac{n\pi}{b}\right) y \qquad \text{....(3.44b)}$$

$$E_x^0 = \frac{j\omega\mu}{h^2}\, C \left(\frac{n\pi}{b}\right) \cos\left(\frac{m\pi}{a}\right) x \sin\left(\frac{n\pi}{b}\right) y \qquad \text{....(3.44c)}$$

$$E_y^0 = -\frac{j\omega\mu}{h^2}\, C \left(\frac{m\pi}{a}\right) \sin\left(\frac{m\pi}{a}\right) x \cos\left(\frac{n\pi}{b}\right) y \qquad \text{....(3.44d)}$$

In the above expressions $\bar{\gamma}$ has been put equal to $j\bar{\beta}$, as it is valid for frequencies above cut-off. From equations 3.44 it is possible to make either m or n but not both equal to zero without causing all the fields to vanish. That is lower order is possible than in the case of TM wave. The lowest order TE wave in rectangular guides is, therefore, the TE_{10} mode. This wave which has the lowest cut-off frequency is called the dominant mode. Because of the practical importance of the TE_{10} mode, the field components, when m = 1 and n = 0 case are given as follows

$$H_z = C \cos\frac{\pi x}{a} \qquad \text{....(3.45a)}$$

$$H_x^{\,0} = \frac{j\bar{\beta} a C}{\pi} \sin\frac{\pi x}{a} \qquad \text{....(3.45b)}$$

$$E_y^0 = -\frac{j\omega\mu a C}{\pi} \sin\frac{\pi x}{a} \quad ....(3.45c)$$

$$E_x^0 = H_y = 0$$

and $$\bar{\beta} = \sqrt{\omega^2\mu\varepsilon - \left(\frac{\pi}{a}\right)^2} \quad ....(3.47)$$

$$f_c = \frac{c}{2a}, \qquad \lambda_c = 2a \quad \text{and } h = \frac{\pi}{a}$$

For the TE_{10} mode the cutoff frequency is independent of the dimension *b*. Field configurations for some of the TE modes are shown in Fig. 3.5.

3.5.3. Degenerate modes

Some of the higher order modes, having the same cut-off frequency, are called degenerate modes. It can be seen that in a waveguide the possible TE_{mn} and TM_{mn} modes (both *m* and *n* cannot be zero) are always degenerate. The wave guide dimensions are always selected in such a way that only the desired mode (generally the dominant TE_{10} or TM_{11}) propagate and higher modes are not supported.

3.6. Excitation of Modes in Rectangular Waveguides

We present certain aspects of excitation of various modes in a guide using a typical coaxial line-waveguide probe coupling. In order to launch a particular mode, probe is chosen which will produce lines of E and H that are roughly parallel to the lines of E and H of the particular mode. Fig. 3.6 shows that the short circuit position and probe depth can be adjusted to achieve maximum power transfer from the coaxial line into the waveguides. The centre conductor of the coaxial line extends into the waveguides to form an electric probe. For maximum coupling of the dominant TE_{10} mode in a rectangular guide, the probe should extend into the guide through the centre of the broad face so that to coincide with the positions of maximum electric field for the TE_{10} mode. The evanescent modes that are also excited are localized fields that store reactive energy. These give the junction its reactive properties.

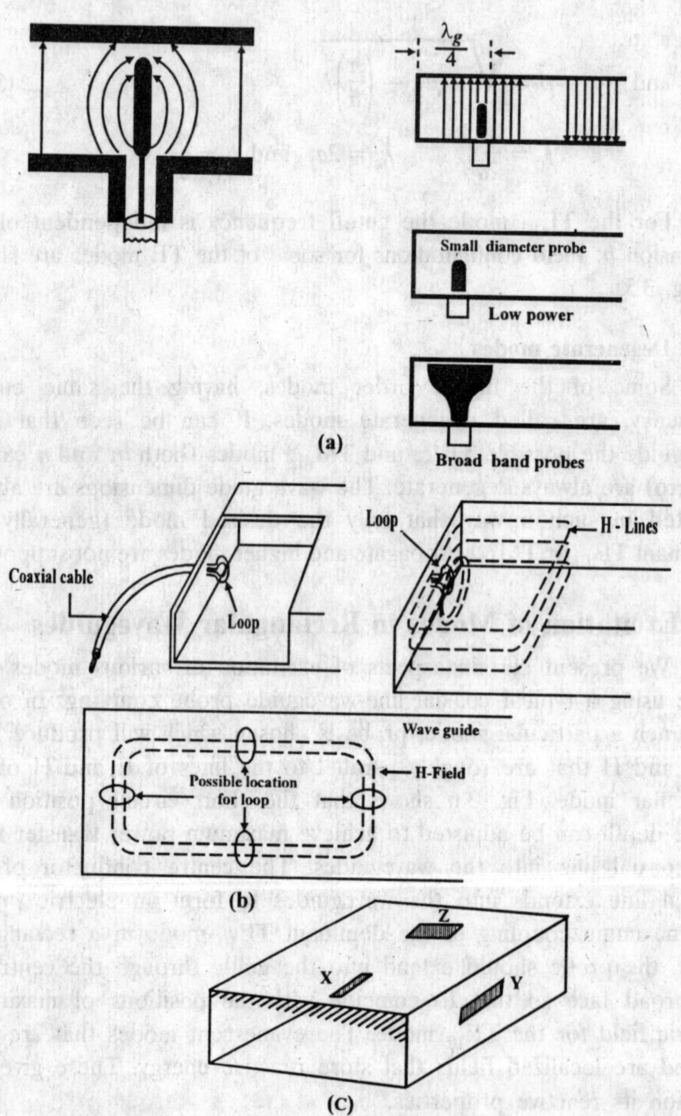

Fig. 3.6. Methods of coupling to and from a rectangular waveguide.

All TE_{m0} modes with m even has a zero field at the centre and field polarities reverse alternately in the transverse direction. These modes can be excited by two probes fed with opposite phase currents. Fig. 3.6b illustrates loop or inductive coupling. The loop is placed at a point where magnetic field (H) is maximum. There are a number of locations possible for H to be maximum. Aperture coupling is shown in Fig. 3.6c, slot X is at a position of maximum E field while slot Y is in a region of maximum H field density.

We have seen that only TE ($E_z = 0$) and TM ($H_z = 0$) modes can propagate in hollow rectangular and cylindrical waveguides. The familiar TEM mode for which there in no axial component of either E or H does not propagate. Suppose a TEM wave is assumed to exist within a hollow guide of any shape. Then lines of H must lie entirely in the transverse plane. In a non-magnetic material,

$$\nabla \cdot H = 0$$

which requires that lines of H should be closed loops. Hence, if a TEM wave exists in a hollow guide then the lines will be closed loops in the plane perpendicular to the axis. But by Maxwell's first equation the magnetomotive force around each of these closed loops must equal to the axial current through the loop. In the case of a coaxial transmission line, this axial current through the H loops is the conduction current in the inner conductor. But as the hollow waveguides do not have an inner conductor, this axial current must be a displacement current. But an axial displacement current requires an axial component of E field, which is not present in a TEM wave. Therefore the TEM wave does not exist in a single conductor waveguide.

3.7. Power Flow in Rectangular Waveguides

The power flown through the guide for the TE_{10} mode is calculated as

$$P_{10} = \frac{1}{2}\text{Re}\int_{x=0}^{a}\int_{y=0}^{b} E \times H \,.\, z.dy\,dx \qquad \text{....(3.48)}$$

$$= \frac{1}{2}\text{Re}\int_{x=0}^{a}\int_{y=0}^{b} E_y H_x^* \,dy\,dx$$

$$= \frac{\omega\mu a^2}{2\pi^2}\text{Re}(\bar{\beta})\left|C_{10}\right|^2\int_{x=0}^{a}\int_{y=0}^{b}\sin^2\frac{\pi x}{a}\,dx \qquad \text{....(3.49)}$$

$$= \frac{\omega\mu a^3\left|C_{10}\right|^2 b}{4\pi^2}\text{Re}(\bar{\beta})$$

3.8. Attenuation in Rectangular Waveguide

Attenuation in the waveguides occurs due to (1) dielectric loss (2) conductor loss.

The power lost per unit length due to finite wall conductivity is given as

$$P_l = \frac{R_s}{2} \int_C |J_s|^2 \, dl \quad \text{....(3.50)}$$

where R_s is the wall surface resistance, and the integration contour C encloses the perimeter of the guide walls. The surface current on all four walls contribute to losses. We compute the power lost in the walls at $x = 0$ and $y = 0$, and double their sum to get the contribution from other two walls. The surface current on the $x = 0$ (left) walls is

$$J_s = \hat{n} \times H\Big|_{x=0} = -\hat{y} H\Big|_{x=0} = -\hat{y} C e^{-\bar{\beta} z} \quad \text{....(3.51)}$$

The surface current on the bottom wall at $y = 0$ is

$$J_s = \hat{n} \times H\Big|_{y=0} = \hat{y} \times \left(\hat{x} H_x\Big|_{y=0} + \hat{z} H_z\Big|_{y=0}\right)$$

$$= \hat{z} \frac{j\bar{\beta} a}{\pi} C \sin\frac{\pi x}{a} e^{-j\beta z} + \hat{x} C \sin\frac{\pi x}{a} e^{-j\bar{\beta} z} \quad \text{....(3.52)}$$

On substituting Eq. 3.52 in Eq 3.50, we obtain power loss as

$$P_l = R_s \int_{y=0}^{b} |J_{sy}|^2 dy + R_s \int_{x=0}^{a} \left[|J_{sx}|^2 + |J_{sz}|^2 \right] dx$$

$$= R_s |C|^2 \left(b + \frac{a}{2} + \frac{\bar{\beta}^2 a^3}{2\pi^2} \right) \quad \text{......(3.53)}$$

The attenuation due to conductor loss is obtained by perturbation method. According to this method the field magnitude decreases as $e^{-\alpha z}$ and the power decreases as $P_0 e^{-2\alpha z}$, where P_0 is the power at the sending end $z = 0$.

The rate of decrease of power for any mode (TE_{mn} or TM_{mn}) is given by

$$-\frac{dP_{mn}}{dz} = 2\alpha_c P_{mn} = P_l \quad \text{....(3.53)}$$

where P_l is the power loss per unit length of the guide and P_{mn} is the power transmitted through the guide. Hence the attenuation constant is given by

$$\alpha_c = \frac{P_l}{2P_{mn}} \quad \text{....(3.54)}$$

We have already obtained P_1 and P_{10}, substituting these in Eq. 3.54 the attenuation for TE_{10} mode is given as

Attenuation versus frequency curves are drawn in Fig. 3.7.

$$\alpha_c = \frac{P_1}{2P_{10}} = \frac{2\pi^2 R_s \left[b + a/2 + (\beta^2 a^3/2\pi^2)\right]}{\omega\mu a^3 b\beta} \quad \text{....(3.55)}$$

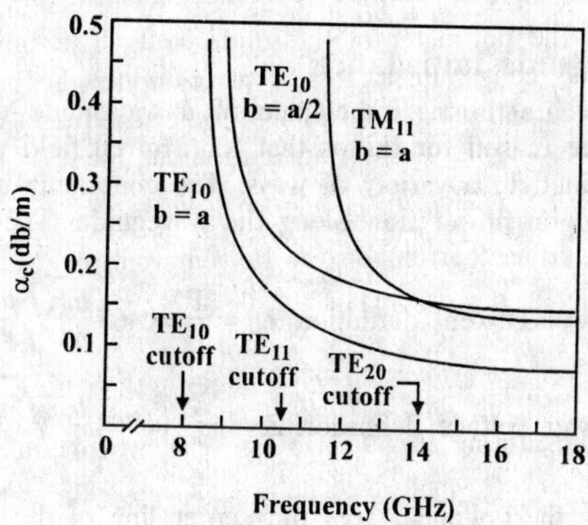

Fig. 3.7 Attenuation vs. frequency curves for various modes in a typical rectangular brass guide.

Attenuation due to dielectric loss is computed from the propagation constant, using complex dielectric constant

$$\bar{\gamma} = \bar{\alpha}_d + j\bar{\beta} = \sqrt{h^2 - \omega^2\mu\varepsilon}$$

$$= \sqrt{h^2 - \omega^2\mu\varepsilon\,(1 - j\tan\delta)} \quad \text{....(3.56)}$$

For most dielectric materials $\tan\delta << 1$, Eq. 3.56 can be written as

$$\bar{\gamma} = \sqrt{h^2 - \omega^2\mu\varepsilon + j\omega^2\mu\varepsilon\tan\delta}$$

$$= \sqrt{h^2 - \omega^2\mu\varepsilon}\left(1 + \frac{j\omega^2\mu\varepsilon\tan\delta}{\sqrt{h^2 - \omega^2\mu\varepsilon}}\right)^{1/2}$$

$$= \sqrt{h^2 - \omega^2\mu\varepsilon} + \frac{j\omega^2\mu\varepsilon\tan\delta}{2\sqrt{h^2 - \omega^2\mu\varepsilon}}$$

$$= \frac{\omega^2 \mu\varepsilon \tan\delta}{2/\bar{\beta}} + j\bar{\beta} \qquad \text{....(3.57)}$$

where $j\bar{\beta} = \sqrt{h^2 - \omega^2 \mu\varepsilon}$

From Eq. 3.57 it is observed that when the loss is small the phase constant $\bar{\beta}$ is unchanged, while the attenuation constant due to dielectric loss is given by

$$\bar{\alpha}_d = \frac{\omega^2 \mu\varepsilon \tan\delta}{2\bar{\beta}} \text{ Np/m} \quad \text{for both TE and TM modes.}$$

3.9. Waveguide Impedance

The characteristic impedance of a waveguide is not uniquely defined. The reason for this is that for a given field pattern, voltage can be defined in a variety of ways. The commonly used definitions are based upon power flow along the waveguide. These are

1. Power current definition $Z_0 = \frac{P}{I_z^2} = 465 \frac{b}{a} \sqrt{\frac{\mu}{\varepsilon}} \frac{\lambda_g}{\lambda}$ ohm

2. Power voltage definition $Z = \frac{V_{cl}^2}{P} = 754 \frac{b}{a} \sqrt{\frac{\mu}{\varepsilon}} \frac{\lambda_g}{\lambda}$ ohm

Here V_{cl} is the voltage across the center line of the waveguide and I_z is the longitudinal current.

3. Modified power voltage definition

$$Z_0 = 377 \frac{b}{a} \sqrt{\frac{\mu}{\varepsilon}} \frac{\lambda_g}{\lambda} \text{ ohms}$$

where $\lambda_g/\lambda = \frac{1}{\sqrt{1-(f_c/f)^2}}$

Note that all these definitions differ only by a constant. Most commonly used definition is the modified power-voltage one.

3.10. Circular Waveguide

A hollow metal tube of circular cross-section also supports TE and TM waveguide modes. Fig. 3.8 shows a circular waveguide of inner radius *a*. We employ cylindrical coordinates when dealing with cylindrical waveguide with circular cross-section. The wave equation for this geometry is written as

$$\frac{\partial^2 \psi}{\partial \rho^2} + \frac{1}{\rho}\frac{\partial \psi}{\partial \rho} + \frac{1}{\rho^2}\frac{\partial^2 \psi}{\partial \phi^2} + \frac{\partial^2 \psi}{\partial z^2} + \omega^2 \mu\varepsilon\psi = 0$$

For TM modes ψ stands for E_z and for TE modes as H_z.

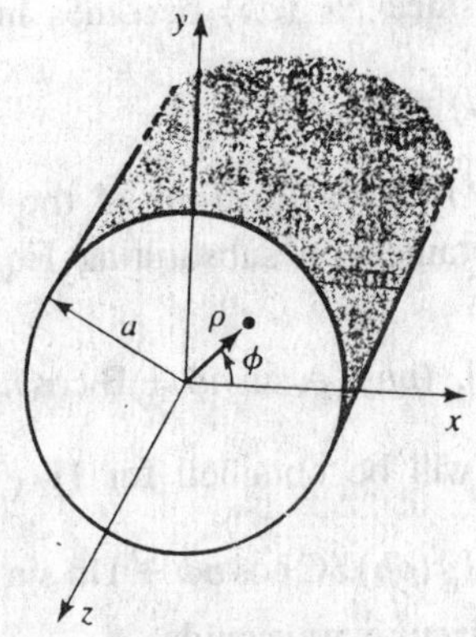

Fig. 3.8. Circular waveguide section

3.10.1. TM wave equations

In this case $H_z = 0$, the wave equation becomes

$$\frac{\partial^2 E_z}{\partial \rho^2} + \frac{1}{\rho^2}\frac{\partial^2 E_z}{\partial \phi^2} + \frac{\partial^2 E_z}{\partial z^2} + \frac{1}{\rho}\frac{\partial E_z}{\partial \phi} + \omega^2 \mu \varepsilon\, E_z = 0 \quad ....(3.60)$$

A solution can be derived using the method of separation of variables as used for rectangular waveguides.

Hence $\quad E_z = P(\rho)\, Q(\phi)\, e^{-\bar{\gamma} z} = E_z^{\,0}\, e^{-\bar{\gamma} z}$ ....(3.61)

We obtain

$$Q\frac{d^2 P}{d\rho^2} + \frac{1}{\rho P}\frac{dP}{d\rho} + \frac{1}{Q\rho^2}\frac{d^2 Q}{d\phi^2} + h^2 = 0 \quad ....(3.62)$$

Equation 3.62 can be broken up into two differential equations

$$\frac{d^2 Q}{d\phi^2} = -\,n^2 Q \quad ....(3.63)$$

$$\frac{d^2 P}{d(\rho h)} + \frac{1}{(\rho h)}\frac{dP}{d(\rho h)} + \left[1 - \frac{n^2}{(\rho h)^2}\right] P = 0 \quad ....(3.64)$$

Eq. 3.63 has a solution

$$Q = (A \sin n\phi + B \cos n\phi) \quad ....(3.65)$$

Equation 3.64 is a standard form of Bessel's equation in terms of (ρh). The second order equation as usual will have two solutions $J_n(\rho h)$ and $N_h\,(\rho h)$, called Bessel functions of first and second kind respectively. For the present problem solution that is finite at $(\rho h) = 0$ is only acceptable, since $N_h(\rho h)$ becomes infinite at $\rho = 0$.

Hence, $$P(\rho h) = J_n(\rho h) \quad \text{....(3.66)}$$

where $J_n(\rho h)$ is Bessel's function of the first kind of order n. The value of E_z is obtained on substituting Eq. 3.65 and 3.66 in Eq. 3.61 as

$$E_z = J_n(\rho h)(A \sin n\phi + B \cos n\phi)\, e^{-\bar{\gamma} z} \quad \text{....(3.67)}$$

Similar solution will be obtained for H_z (TE) mode.

$$H_z = J_n(\rho h)(C \cos n\phi + Dn \sin n\phi)\, e^{-\bar{\gamma} z} \quad \text{....(3.68)}$$

3.10.2. TM modes in circular waveguides

$$E_z(\rho, \phi) = (A \sin n\phi + B \cos n\phi)\, J_n(h\rho)$$

For the TM mode is that the boundary conditions can now be applied directly to E_z, since

$$E_z(\rho,\phi) = 0 \text{ at } \rho = a \quad \text{....(3.69a)}$$

Thus, we must have

$$J_n(ha) = 0 \quad \text{....(3.69b)}$$

or $$h_{nm} = \frac{P_{nm}}{a} \quad \text{....(3.70)}$$

where P_{nm} is the mth root of $J_n(x)$, that is $J_n(P_{nm}) = 0$. Table 3.1 gives first few values of P_{nm}.

Table 3.1.

Values of P_{nm} *for TM modes of a circular guide*

n	P_{n1}	P_{n2}	P_{n3}
0	2.405	5.520	8.654
1	3.832	7.016	10.174
2	5.135	8.417	11.620

The propagation constant of TM_{nm} mode is

$$\bar{\beta}_{nm} = \sqrt{k_0^2 - h_{nm}^2} = \sqrt{k_0^2 - (Pnm/a)^2} \quad \text{....(3.71a)}$$

The cut-off frequency is

$$\bar{f}_{cnm} = \frac{h_{nm}}{2\pi\sqrt{\omega\varepsilon}} = \frac{P_{nm}}{2\pi a\sqrt{\omega\varepsilon}} \quad \text{....(3.71b)}$$

The first TM mode to propagate is TM_{01} with $P_{01} = 2.405$.

This is greater than $P'_{11} = 1.81$. Hence TE_{11} is the dominant mode of circular waveguide.

The transverse field components for TM_{01} are given as

$$E_\rho = \frac{-j\bar{\beta}}{h_{nm}} A \sin n\phi\, J_1'(h\rho)\, e^{-j\bar{\beta}z} \quad \text{....(3.72a)}$$

$$E_\phi = \frac{-j\bar{\beta}n}{h_{nm}^2 \rho} A \cos n\phi\, J_1(h\rho)\, e^{-j\bar{\beta}z} \quad \text{....(3.72b)}$$

$$H_\rho = \frac{j\omega\varepsilon n}{h_{nm}^2 \rho} A \cos n\phi\, J_1(h\rho)\, e^{-j\bar{\beta}z} \quad \text{....(3.72c)}$$

$$H_\phi = \frac{-j\omega\varepsilon}{h_{nm}} A \sin n\phi\, J_1'(h\rho)\, e^{-j\bar{\beta}z} \quad \text{....(3.72d)}$$

3.10.3. TE modes in circular waveguides

The boundary conditions to be met for TE waves are that $E_\phi = 0$ at $\rho = a$. But E_ϕ is proportional to $\frac{\partial H_z}{\partial \rho}$, and therefore to $J'_n(h\rho)$, where the prime denotes the derivative with respect to $(h\rho)$. Hence, for TE modes the boundary conditions required are

$$\frac{\partial J_n(ha)}{\partial a} = 0 = J_n'(ha) = 0 \quad \text{....(3.73)}$$

3.10.4. TE modes

If the roots of $J_n'(x)$ are defined as P'_{nm}, so that $J_n'(P'_{nm}) = 0$, where $P'_{nm} = 0$ is the mth root of J'_n, then h_{nm} must have the value

$$h_{nm} = \frac{p'_{nm}}{a} \quad \text{....(3.74)}$$

First few values of P'_{nm} are given in table 3.2.

Table 3.2.

Values of P'_{nm} *for TE Modes of a circular waveguide*

n	P'_{n1}	P'_{n2}	P'_{n3}
0	3.832	7.016	10.174
1	1.841	5.331	8.536
2	3.054	6.706	9.970

The TE_{nm} modes are thus defined by the cutoff wave number $h_{nm} = P'_{nm}/a$ where n refers to number of full wave variation in the circumferential (Φ) direction and the second number (m) refers to the Bessel function variation in the radial direction. The propagation constant of the TE_{mn} mode is

$$\bar{\beta}_{nm} = \sqrt{\omega^2 \mu\varepsilon - h^2} = \sqrt{k_0^2 - h_{nm}^2}$$

$$= \sqrt{k_0^2 - \left(\frac{P'_{nm}}{a}\right)^2}$$

The cutoff frequency is

$$f_{cnm} = \frac{h_{nm}}{2\pi\sqrt{\mu\varepsilon}} = \frac{P'_{nm}}{2\pi a\sqrt{\mu\varepsilon}} \quad ....(3.75)$$

The first mode (dominant mode) to propagate is the mode with the smallest P'_{nm} which from the table is TE_{11} mode. There is no TE_{10} mode in the circular waveguide but there exists a TE_{01} mode.

The transverse field components for TE_{11} mode are

$$H_z = D \sin\phi\, J_1(h\rho)\, e^{-j\bar{\beta}z} \quad ....(3.76a)$$

$$E_\rho = \frac{-j\omega\mu}{h_{nm}^2 \rho} D \cos\phi\, J_1(h\rho)\, e^{-j\bar{\beta}z} \quad ....(3.76b)$$

$$E_\phi = \frac{j\omega\mu}{h_{nm}} D \sin\phi\, J'_1(h\rho)\, e^{-j\bar{\beta}z} \quad ....(3.76c)$$

$$H_\rho = \frac{-j\beta}{h_{nm}} D \sin\phi\, J'_1(h\rho)\, e^{-j\bar{\beta}z} \quad ....(3.76d)$$

$$H_\phi = \frac{-j\beta}{h_{nm}^2 \rho} D \cos\phi\, J_1(h\rho)\, e^{-j\bar{\beta}z} \quad ....(3.76e)$$

$$E_z = 0 \quad ....(3.76f)$$

Here we have assumed that the coordinate system has been rotated about z axis to give H_z a $\sin\phi$ variation hence, $\cos\phi$ variation is equated to zero.

The wave impedance is

$$Z_{TE} = \frac{H_\rho}{H_\phi} = \frac{-E_\phi}{H_\rho} = \frac{\eta k_0}{\bar{\beta}} = \frac{\eta}{\sqrt{1 - (f_c/f)^2}} \quad ....(3.77)$$

Field paterns for some low order modes in a circular waveguide are shown in Fig. 3.9a.

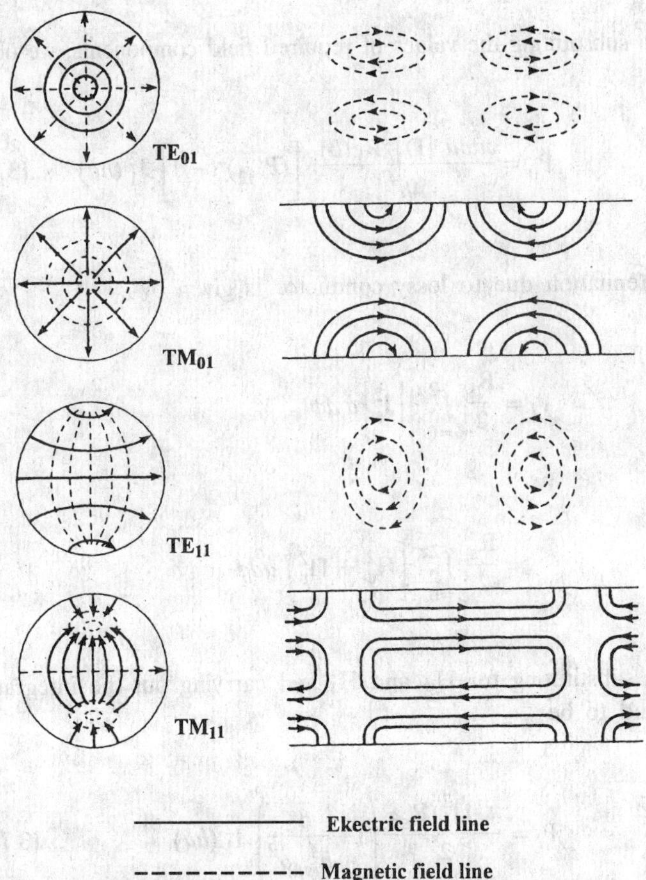

3.9a. Circular waveguide field patterns for lower order modes

3.11. Attenuation in Circular Guides

For TE modes the power flow down the guide can be computed as follows

$$P_0 = \frac{1}{2} \text{Re} \int_{\rho=0}^{a} \int_{\theta=0}^{2\pi} E \times H^* . \hat{z} \rho \, d\phi \, d\rho$$

$$= \frac{1}{2} \text{Re} \int_{\rho=0}^{a} \int_{\phi=0}^{2\pi} \left[E\rho H_{\phi}^{*} - E_{\phi} H_{\rho}^{*} \right] \rho d\phi \, d\rho$$

On substituting the values of required field components, we obtain

$$P_0 = \frac{\pi\omega\mu \; |D|^2 \text{Re}(\bar{\beta})}{4h^4} \left[(P'_{11})^2 - 1 \right] J_1^2 (ha) \quad \text{....(3.78a)}$$

Attenuation due to lossy conductor is given by

$$P_l = \frac{R_s}{2} \int_{\phi=0}^{2\pi} \left| J_s^2 \right| a \, d\phi$$

$$= \frac{R_s}{2} \int_{\phi=0}^{2\pi} \left[H_{\phi}^2 + H_{\rho}^2 \right] a d\phi$$

On substituting for H_ϕ and H_z and carrying out the integration P_l is found to be

$$P_l = \frac{\pi |D^2| R_s a}{2} \left(1 + \frac{\bar{\beta}^2}{h_{nm}^4 a^2} \right) J_1^2 (ha) \quad \text{....(3.78b)}$$

Substitute for P_l and P_0 to obtain α

$$\alpha_c = P_l / 2P_0$$

$$\alpha_c = \frac{R_s}{a\omega\mu\beta} \left(h_{nm}^2 + \frac{\omega^2 \mu\varepsilon}{(P'_{11})_{11}^2 - 1} \right) \text{Np}/m \quad \text{....(3.79)}$$

Attenuation for TM waves in circular waveguide can be obtained similarly. Figure 3.9b shows the attenuation due to conductor loss versus frequency for various modes of a circular waveguide. From the figure it is observed that the attenuation of the TE_{01} mode decreases to a very small value with increasing frequency. Because of this property of TE_{01} mode it is of interest for low loss transmission over long distance. Note this mode is not the dominant mode of the circular waveguide, hence when used for signal propagation power can be lost from this mode (TE_{01}) to the lower order mode (TE_{11} or TM_{01}) of propagation.

3.12. Dielectric Waveguides

In earlier sections we discussed the behaviour of electromagnetic waves propagating along waveguides with conducting walls. In this section, we show that dielectric slabs and rods without conducting walls can also support guided modes which are confined mostly within the dielectric medium. Fig. 3.10 shows a longitudinal cross section of

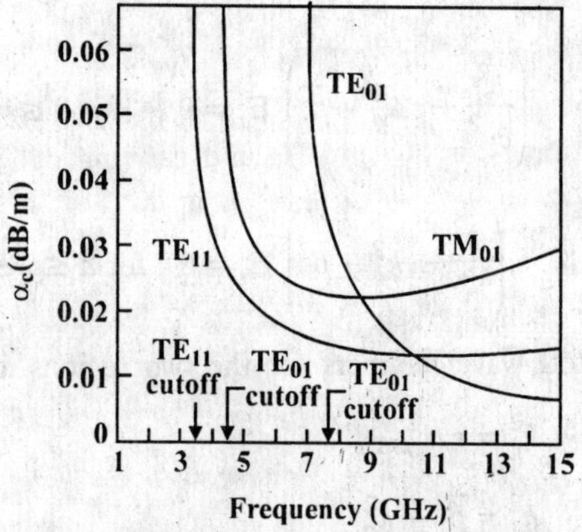

Fig.3.9b. Attenuation vs. frequency curves in a circular guide.

a dielectric slab waveguide of thickness d. We assume that, as in earlier cases, z is the direction of propagation. Also field variation does not depend on x direction, *i.e* $\frac{\partial}{\partial x} = 0$. We also assume that the dielectric is lossless.

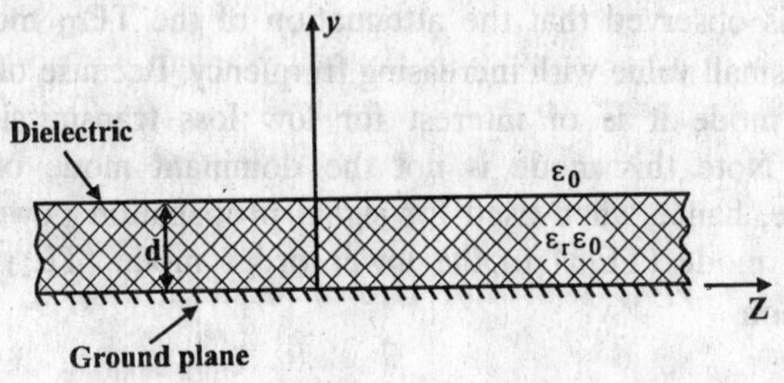

Fig. 3.10. Dielectric slab waveguide

The behaviour of TM and TE modes can be found as for other guided structures. One salient feature of dielectric rod waveguide is that because there are two distinct regions, with and without a dielectric, we must separately consider the fields in these regions, and then match tangential fields across the interface. For the TM mode the E_z field must satisfy the wave equation in each region. The wave equations can be written as

$$\left(\frac{\partial^2}{\partial y^2} + \varepsilon_r k_o^2 - \overline{\beta}^2\right) E_z = 0 \quad \text{for } 0 \le y \le d \quad \text{....(3.80a)}$$

$$\left(\frac{\partial^2}{\partial y^2} + k_o^2 - \overline{\beta}^2\right) E_z = 0 \quad \text{for } d \le y \le \infty \quad \text{....(3.80b)}$$

The cutoff wave numbers for the two regions are

$$k_c^2 = \varepsilon_r k_o^2 - \overline{\beta}^2 \quad \text{....(3.81a)}$$

$$h^2 = \overline{\beta}^2 - k_o^2 \quad \text{....(3.81b)}$$

The general solutions are then

$$E_z = A \sin k_c y + B \cos k_c y \quad \text{for } 0 \le y \le d \quad \text{....(3.82a)}$$

$$E_z = C\, e^{hy} + D\, e^{-hy} \quad \text{for } d \le y \le \infty \quad \text{....(3.82b)}$$

The boundary conditions to be satisfied are

$$E_z = 0 \quad \text{at } y = 0$$

$$E_z < \infty \quad \text{as } y \to \infty$$

E_Z and H_Z are continuous at $y = d$

The final solution is obtained as

$$k_c \tan k_c d = \varepsilon_r h \qquad \text{....(3.83a)}$$

This is a transcendental equation and, cannot be solved easily, but only by applying numerical techniques. Once k_c and h are found for a particular surface wave mode the other field expressions can be obtained easily.

For TM modes wave equation in H_z is written. The solution is obtained as for TE case and is expressed as

$$k_c \cot k_c d = h \qquad \text{....(3.84a)}$$

The surface wave propagation constants for various modes are plotted in Fig. 3.11.

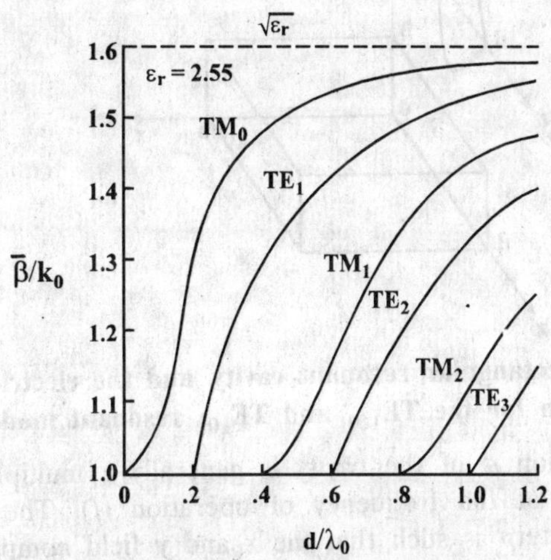

Fig. 3.11 Surface wave propagation constants for a grounded dielectric slab with $\varepsilon_r = 2.55$

3.13. Waveguide Cavities

Waveguide resonators (cavities) are short-circuited at both ends of the waveguide, this forms a closed box or cavity. Electric and magnetic energy is stored within the cavity, and power can be dissipated in the metallic walls of the cavity and the dielectric filling of the cavity. The resonant frequencies for a general TE or TM mode can be derived using the wave equation. The method of separation of variables is used to solve for the electric and magnetic fields that satisfy the boundary conditions of the cavity.

3.13.1. Rectangular waveguide cavity

The geometry of a rectangular cavity is shown in Fig. 3.12. It consists of a rectangular waveguide of length d which is shorted at both ends ($z = 0, d$).

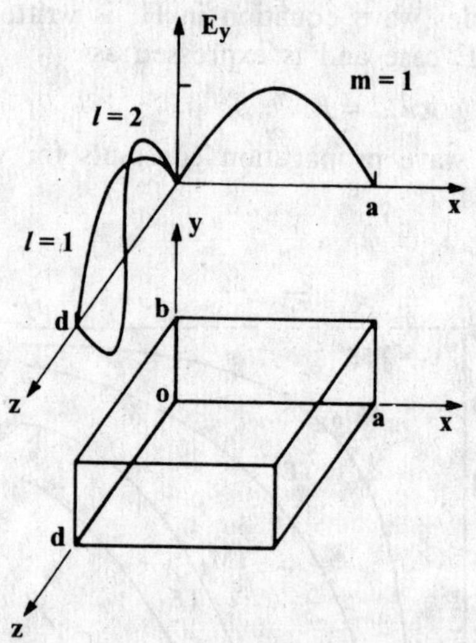

Fig. 3.12. A rectangular resonant cavity, and the electric field distribution for the TE_{101} and TE_{102} resonant modes.

The dimension d of the cavity is generally a multiple of half guide wavelength at the frequency of operation (f). The resulting standing wave pattern is such that the x and y field components of the electric field are zero at $z = 0$. The cavity geometry reveals that field solutions can be obtained directly from the corresponding waveguide solutions. For the TE_{mn} or TM_{mn} mode, the propagation constant is given by

$$\bar{\beta}_{mn}^2 = \omega^2 \mu \varepsilon - \left(\frac{m\pi}{a}\right)^2 - \left(\frac{n\pi}{b}\right)^2 \qquad \text{....(3.84b)}$$

We require $\bar{\beta}_{mn}\, d = l\,\pi$, where l is an integer, in order for cavity to be a multiple of half guide wavelength long. Thus when l is specified as

$$\bar{\beta}_{mn} = \frac{l\,\pi}{d} \quad l = 1, 2, \ldots.. \qquad \text{....(3.85a)}$$

If we put $k^2 = \omega^2 \mu \varepsilon$

and define a the cutoff wave number for the rectangular cavity as

$$k_{mnl} = \left[\left(\frac{l\pi}{d}\right)^2 + \left(\frac{m\pi}{a}\right)^2 + \left(\frac{n\pi}{b}\right)^2\right]^{1/2} \quad ....(3.85b)$$

Hence, the resonance frequency of the cavity is given by

$$f_{mnl} = \frac{ck_{mnl}}{2\pi} = c\left[\left(\frac{l}{2d}\right)^2 + \left(\frac{m}{2a}\right)^2 + \left(\frac{n}{2b}\right)^2\right]^{1/2} \quad ....(3.86)$$

where c is the velocity of light. It can be observed from Eq. 3.86 that there is a triply infinite number of resonant frequencies corresponding to different field distributions. Also note that there is more than one field distribution since Eq. 3.86 holds for both TE and TM modes.

For a TE_{101} resonant mode the field expression are given as follows

$$E_y = E_o \sin\left(\frac{\pi x}{a}\right) \sin\left(\frac{l\pi}{d} z\right) \quad ....(3.87a)$$

$$H_x = -j\frac{E_o}{Z_{TE}} \sin\left(\frac{\pi x}{a}\right) \cos\left(\frac{l\pi}{d} z\right) \quad ....(3.87b)$$

$$H_z = \frac{j\pi E_o}{k\eta a} \cos\frac{\pi x}{a} \sin\left(\frac{l\pi}{d} z\right) \quad ....(3.87c)$$

Note that the magnetic field is ± 90° out of phase relative to electric field. This is always the case in a lossless cavity and corresponds to voltage and current being ± 90° out of phase with each other in a lossless LC circuit. We can now compute the Q of this mode by finding the stored electric and magnetic energies, and the power lost in the conducting walls and the dielectric.

At resonance, the average stored electric energy is given by

$$W_e = \frac{\varepsilon_0}{4} \int_0^a \int_0^b \int_0^d E_y E_y^* \, dx\, dy\, dz$$

$$= \frac{\varepsilon_0 abd}{16} E_o^2 \quad ....(3.88)$$

$$W_m = \frac{\mu}{4} \int_v \left(H_x H_x^* + H_z H_z^*\right) dx\, dy\, dz = W_e$$

This shows that at resonance the stored electric and magnetic energies are equal, which is analogous to the LC resonant circuits.

For small losses we can find the power dissipated in the cavity walls by

$$P_c = \frac{R_s}{2} \int_{walls} J_s \cdot J_s^* \, ds = \frac{R_s}{2} \int_{walls} \left| H_t \right|^2 ds$$

where $R_s = \sqrt{\omega \mu / 2\sigma}$ is the surface resistivity of the metallic walls, and H_t is the tangential magnetic field at the surface of the walls. Substituting from 3.87b,c we get

$$P_c = \frac{R_s E_0^2 \lambda^2}{8\eta^2} \left(\frac{l^2 ab}{d^2} + \frac{bd}{a^2} + \frac{l^2 a}{2d} + \frac{d}{2a} \right) \qquad \text{....(3.89)}$$

For arriving to this result the symmetry property of the cavity has been used and the contributions from the walls at $x=0$, $y=0$ and $z=0$ doubled, to account for the contributions from $x=a$, $y=b$ and $z=d$ respectively. We can now find the Q of the cavity with lossy conducting walls but lossless dielectric as

$$Q_c = \frac{2\omega_0 W_c}{P_e}$$

$$= \frac{(kad)^3 b \eta}{2\pi^2 R_s} \frac{1}{\left[2 l^2 a^3 b + 2 b d^3 + l^2 a^3 d + a d^3 \right]}$$

....(3.90)

If we have to compute power loss in the dielectric, consider a lossy dielectric which is complex, and the imaginary part will contribute to power loss, i.e.

$$\varepsilon = \varepsilon' - j\varepsilon'' = \varepsilon_r \varepsilon_o \left(1 - j \tan \delta \right)$$

Then the power dissipated in the dielectric is

$$P_d = \frac{1}{2} \int_v J \cdot E^* dv = \frac{\omega \varepsilon''}{2} \int_v \left| E^2 \right| dv = \frac{abd\, \omega \varepsilon'' \left| E_o \right|^2}{8}$$

....(3.91)

Hence the Q of the cavity with a lossy dielectric inside the cavity, but with perfectly conducting walls is

$$Q_d = \frac{2\omega W_e}{P_d} = \frac{\varepsilon'}{\varepsilon''} = \frac{1}{\tan \delta} \qquad \text{....(3.92)}$$

When both wall losses and dielectric losses are present, the total power loss is

$$Q = \left(\frac{1}{Q_c} + \frac{1}{Q_d} \right)^{-1} \qquad \text{.....(3.93)}$$

3.13.2. Cylindrical cavity

The cylindrical cavity is obtained from a small section of circular waveguide of length *d* and radius *a*, whose ends are short-circuited. Since the dominant mode of a circular waveguide is TE_{11}, TE_{111} will be the dominant mode of cylindrical cavity. Fig. 3.13 shows the geometry of a cylindrical cavity. This type of cavity is generally used for wave

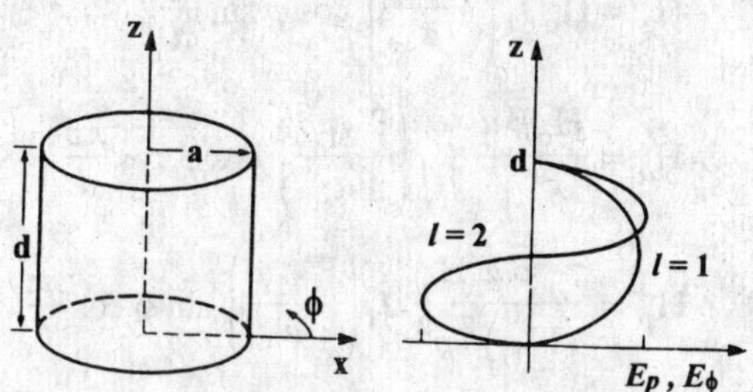

Fig. 3.13. A cylindrical resonant cavity, and the electric field distribution for resonant modes with l = 1 or l = 2

metres, used to measure frequency, because it provides very high Q and wide frequency range of operation. Having high Q cavity ensures high degree of resolution or accuracy in the measurement of an unknown frequency. When the cavity is tuned to the frequency of the unknown source, it absorbs a maximum power from the input waveguide. A detector coupled to the input line is used to indicate this dip in power at resonance.

The fields in the cylindrical cavity are determined from the corresponding waveguide fields. The resonant frequency for the TE_{nml} mode is obtained from the relation,

$$f_{nml} = \frac{c}{2\pi\sqrt{\mu\varepsilon}} \sqrt{\left(\frac{P'_{nm}}{a}\right)^2 + \left(\frac{l\pi}{d}\right)^2} \quad ....(3.94)$$

and the resonance frequency for the TM_{nml} mode is

$$f_{nml} = \frac{c}{2\pi\sqrt{\mu\varepsilon}} \sqrt{\left(\frac{P_{nm}}{a}\right)^2 + \left(\frac{l\pi}{d}\right)^2} \quad ....(3.95)$$

For the TE_{nml} mode

n = 0, 1, 2, is the number of field variation along the circumference (ϕ)

m = 1, 2, 3 ----, is the number of zeroes of the field in radial direction

l = 1, 2, 3-----, is the number of half wave in z direction.

The fields for the TE_{111} mode are

$$H_z = H_o J_1\left(\frac{P'_{11}\rho}{a}\right)\cos\phi \sin\frac{\pi z}{d} \quad \text{....(3.96a)}$$

$$H_\rho = \frac{H_o \bar{\beta} a}{P'_{11}} J'_1\left(\frac{P'_{11}\rho}{a}\right)\cos\phi \cos\frac{\pi z}{d} \quad \text{....(3.96b)}$$

$$H_\phi = \frac{-\bar{\beta} a^2 H_o}{(P'_{11})^2\rho^2} J_1\left(\frac{P'_{11}\rho}{a}\right)\sin\phi \cos\frac{\pi z}{d} \quad \text{....(3.96c)}$$

$$E_\rho = \frac{jk_o\eta\, a^2 H_o}{(P'_{11})^2\rho} J_1\left(\frac{P'_{11}\rho}{a}\right)\sin\phi \sin\frac{\pi z}{d} \quad \text{....(3.96d)}$$

$$E_\phi = \frac{jk_o\eta\, a H_o}{P'_{11}} J'_1\left(\frac{P'_{11}\rho}{a}\right)\cos\phi \sin\frac{\pi z}{d} \quad \text{....(3.96e)}$$

$$E_z = 0 \quad \text{....(3.96f)}$$

To find Q of the TE_{111} mode, the time average stored electric and magnetic energies are equal, and the total stored energy is given by

$$W = 2W_e = \frac{\varepsilon}{2}\int_{z=0}^{d}\int_{\phi=0}^{2\pi}\int_{\rho=0}^{a}\left[|E_\rho|^2 + |E_\phi|^2\right]\rho\, d\rho\, d\phi\, dz$$

$$P_c = \frac{R_s}{2}\int_s |H_t|^2 ds$$

Finally Q of the cavity is obtained as

$$\frac{Q\,\delta_s}{\lambda_o} = \frac{\left[1-\left(\frac{n}{P'_{nm}}\right)^2\right]\left[(P'^2_{nm}) + \left(\frac{\pi a l}{d}\right)^2\right]^{3/2}}{2\pi\left[(P'_{nm})^2 + \frac{2a}{d}\left(\frac{l\pi a}{d}\right)^2 + \left(1-\frac{2a}{d}\right)\left(\frac{\pi a n l}{(P'_{nm})\, d}\right)^2\right]}$$

where $l = n = m = 1$.

From above relation it can be noted that right hand side is independent of frequency, hence Q varies as λ_0/δ_s for any cavity and thus decreases as $f^{-1/2}$. For wave meters TE_{011} mode is significant because its Q is two to three times that of TE_{111} mode. Another advantage of the TE_{011} mode is that $H_\phi = 0$ and as such there are no axial currents present. Hence the end plates of the cavity can be freely moved to adjust the cavity length *d* for tuning purposes without introducing significant loss, since no currents flow across the gap, *i.e.* the gap between the circular end plate and the cylinder wall is parallel to the current flow lines. Care should be taken when working with TE_{011} mode, since TE_{011} mode is not the lowest order mode, other mode should not be excited within the tuning range of the cavity. A mode chart is shown in Fig 3.14 which shows what modes will resonate for a given value of (2a/d) and frequency.

Such a chart is very useful for the design of cavity resonators, as it shows which modes can be excited at a given frequency for a given cavity size. For example, for $(2a/d)^2$ between 3 and 4, only TE_{011} mode can resonate in the frequency range corresponding to $(2af)^2$ between 12.5 to 14.5×10^8.

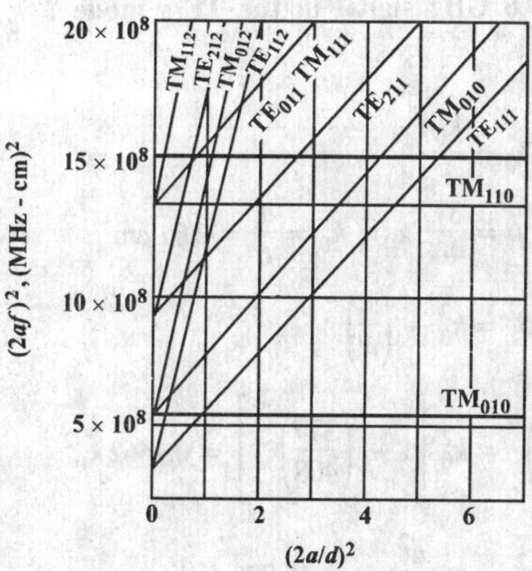

Fig. 3.14 Resonant frequencies for the first few modes of a circular cylinderical cavity.

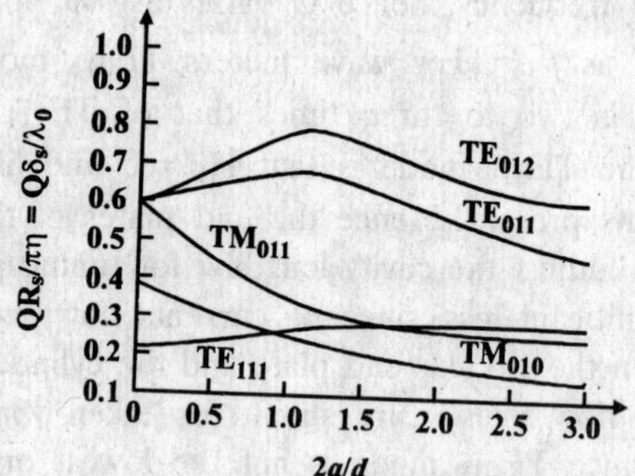

Fig. 3.15 Normalized Q for various cylinderical cavity modes.

Fig. 3.15 gives a plot of $Q\,\delta_s/\lambda_0$ versus $\left(\frac{2a}{d}\right)$ for several modes. It is evident from the figure that considerably higher value of Q is obtained for the TE_{011} mode compared to that for the TE_{111} mode. It is also clear that typical values of Q range from 10,000 to 40,000 or more.

Example 3.1. What is the width (*a*) of a rectangular waveguide whose characteristic impedance Z_0 is 408 ohms and which is required to propagate a 9.6 GHz signal in the TE_{10} mode ? **[4.09 cm.]**

Solution :

$$Z_0 = \frac{k_0 \eta}{\beta}$$

$$\beta = \frac{377}{408} k_0 \ ; \ k_0 = \frac{\omega}{c} = 2.01 \text{ cm}^{-1}$$

Also $$\beta^2 = k_0^2 - \left(\frac{\pi}{a}\right)^2$$

$$\left(\frac{\pi}{a}\right)^2 = k_0^2 \left[1 - \left(\frac{377}{408}\right)^2\right] = 0.1462\, k_0^2$$

$$a^2 = \frac{\pi^2}{0.1462\, k_0^2} = 16.728$$

$$a = 4.09 \text{ cm}$$

Example 3.2. A rectangular waveguide of cross-section 5 cm × 2 cm is used to propagate TM_{11} mode at 9GHz. Determine the cut-off wavelength and wave impedance.

Solution :

For TM_{11} mode, $m = 1$, $n = 1$ at $f = 9\times10^9$, $\lambda = 3.33$ cm.

$$\lambda_c = \frac{2}{\sqrt{(m/a)^2 + (n/b)^2}} = \frac{2ab}{\sqrt{a^2 + b^2}}$$

$$= \frac{2\times5\times2}{\sqrt{5^2 + 2^2}} = 3.714 \text{ cm}$$

$$Z_0 = 120\pi\sqrt{1 - (\lambda/\lambda_c)^2}$$

$$= 120\pi\sqrt{1 - \left(\frac{3.333}{3.714}\right)^2} = 325\Omega$$

Example 3.3. A waveguide operating in TE_{10} mode has dimensions $a = 2.26$ cm and b = 1 cm. The measured guide wave length is 4 cm. Find (a) the cut-off frequency of the propagating mode (b) the frequency of operation, (c) maximum frequency of propagation in this guide.

Solution :

(a) For TE_{10} mode, cut-off frequency f_c is

$$f_c = \frac{1}{2a\sqrt{\omega\varepsilon}} = \frac{c}{2a} = \frac{3\times10^{10}}{2\times2.26} = 6.64\text{GHz}$$

(b) $$\beta = \frac{2\pi}{\lambda_g} = \frac{2\pi}{4}$$

$$\beta_{10} = \sqrt{\omega^2\mu\varepsilon - \left(\frac{\pi}{a}\right)^2}$$

$$\beta_{10}^2 + \left(\frac{\pi}{a}\right)^2 = \left(\frac{2\pi f}{c}\right)^2$$

$$f = \frac{c^2}{4\pi^2}\left[\beta^2 + \left(\frac{\pi}{a}\right)^2\right]$$

$$= 10 \text{ GHz.}$$

(c) First higher order mode is TE_{20} mode

Here, $m = 2$, $n = 0$

$$f_{20} = \frac{c}{2\pi}\sqrt{\left(\frac{2\pi}{a}\right)^2} = \frac{c}{a} = 13.27\text{GHz}$$

Example 3.4. A rectangular waveguide with dimensions a =2.5 cm, b =1 cm is to operate below 15.2 GHz. How many TE and TM modes can be propagated in the waveguide if the guide has the medium parameters given by $\sigma = 0$, $\varepsilon = 4\varepsilon_0$, $\mu_r = \mu_0$. (a) Calculate the cut off frequencies of the modes (b) Also calculate the phase constant, phase velocity and the wave impedance for TE_{10} mode operating at 15 GHz.

Solution:

(a) the cut off frequency is given by

$$f_{c_{mn}} = \frac{c'}{2}\sqrt{\frac{m^2}{a^2} + \frac{n^2}{b^2}}$$

Given $a = 2.5$ cm, $b = 1$ cm, $\varepsilon_r = 4$

$$c' = \frac{1}{\sqrt{\mu\varepsilon}} = \frac{c}{\sqrt{\mu_r\varepsilon_r}} = \frac{c}{2}$$

Hence,

$$f_{cmn} = \frac{c}{4a}\sqrt{m^2 + \frac{a^2}{b^2}n^2}$$

$$= \frac{3 \times 10^8}{4(2.5 \times 10^{-2})}\sqrt{m^2 + 6.25\,n^2}$$

$$= 3\sqrt{m^2 + 6.25\,n^2} \quad \text{GHz}$$

To find all $f'_{cmn} < 15$ GHz, we fix $m = 0$ and vary n. We obtain

for TE_{01} mode (m =0, n =1) $f_{c_{01}} = 7.5$ GHz

TE_{02} mode (m =0, n =2) $f_{c_{02}} = 15$ GHz

$f_{cmn} < 15.2$ GHz the maximum n =2.

Now fix n and increase m till $f_{cmn} < 15.2$ GHz.

For TE_{10} mode (m =1, n =0) $f_{c_{10}} = 3$ GHz

TE_{20} mode, $f_{c_{20}} = 6$ GHz

TE_{30} mode, $f_{c_{30}} = 9$ GHz

TE_{40} mode, $f_{c_{40}} = 12$ GHz

TE_{50} mode, $f_{c_{50}} = 15$ GHz

TE_{60} mode, $f_{c_{60}} = 18$ GHz

That is for $f_{cmn} < 15.2$ GHz, the maximum m =5. We have found the maximum m and n, other possible combinations in between these values of m and n are.

For TE_{11}, TM_{11} (degenarate modes), $f_{c_{11}} = 8.078$ GHz

TE_{21}, TM_{21} $f_{c_{21}} = 9 \cdot 6\ GH_z$

TE_{31}, TM_{31} $f_{c_{31}} = 11.72$ GHz

TE_{41}, TM_{41} $f_{c_{41}} = 14.14\ GH_z$

TE_{12}, TM_{12} $f_{c_{12}} = 15.3$ GHz

Hence the modes for which the cut-off frequency is less than 15.2 GHz are eleven TE modes and four TM modes.

(b) For TE10 mode

$$\beta = \omega \sqrt{\mu\varepsilon} \sqrt{1 - \left(\frac{f_c}{f}\right)^2}$$

$$= \frac{2\pi \times 5 \times 10^9 \times 2}{3 \times 10^8} \sqrt{1 - \left(\frac{3}{15}\right)^2}$$

$$= 200\pi \sqrt{0.96} = 615.6 \text{ rad/m}$$

$$u_p = \frac{\omega}{\beta} = \frac{2\pi \times 15 \times 10^9}{615.6} = 1.531 \times 10^8\ m/s.$$

$$\eta_{TE} = \sqrt{\frac{\mu}{\varepsilon}} \sqrt{1 - \left(\frac{f_c}{f}\right)^2}$$

$$= 60\pi \sqrt{0.96} = 192.4\ \Omega$$

Example 3.5. A rectangular waveguide has $a = 3.0$ cm, $b = 1.5$ cm, $\mu = 1$ and $\varepsilon = 2.25$. Calculate (a) the cutoff wavelength and frequency for TE_{10}, TE_{20} and TM_{11} modes, (b) λ_g and Z_o and Z_o at 4.0 GHz.

Solution :

(a) $$\lambda_c = \frac{1}{\sqrt{\left(\frac{m}{2a}\right)^2 + \left(\frac{n}{2b}\right)^2}}$$

for TE_{10}, $m = 1$, $n = 0$ $\lambda_c = 2a$

TE_{20}, $m = 2$, $n = 0$ $\lambda_c = a$

TE_{11}, $m = 1$, $n = 1$ $\lambda_c = \dfrac{2ab}{\sqrt{a^2 + b^2}}$

Thus the cut-off wavelengths :
for

$$TE_{10} = 6 \text{ cm}$$
$$TE_{20} = 3 \text{ cm}$$
$$TM_{11} = 2.68 \text{ cm}$$

The cut-off frequencies are functions of the dielectric properties of the insulating material as well as the guide dimensions.

$$f_c = \frac{c}{\lambda_c\sqrt{\varepsilon\mu}}$$

substitute for $\varepsilon = 2.25$, $\mu = 1$ and different value of λ_c Then

$$f_{c_{10}} = 3.33 \text{ GHz}$$
$$f_{c_{20}} = 6.66 \text{ GHz}$$
$$f_{c_{11}} = 7.46 \text{ GHz}$$

(b) At 4.0 GH_Z, $\lambda_o = 7.5$ cm

$$\lambda_g = \frac{\lambda_o}{\sqrt{\mu\varepsilon - \left(\lambda_o/\lambda_c\right)^2}}$$

In this case $\varepsilon = 2.25$, $\mu = 1$ hence

$$\lambda_g = \frac{7.5}{\sqrt{2.25 - \left(\lambda_o/\lambda_c\right)^2}}$$

$$= 9.05 \text{ cm.}$$

λ_g for TE_{10} mode is 9.05 cm.

The characteristic impedance of the guide is calculated from the relation

$$Z_o = \frac{377b/a\sqrt{\frac{\mu}{\varepsilon}}}{\sqrt{1 - \left(\frac{f_c}{f_0}\right)^2}} = 377\frac{b}{a}\sqrt{\frac{\mu}{\varepsilon}}\,\frac{\lambda_g}{\lambda}$$

$$= 377 \times \frac{1.5}{3.0}\sqrt{\frac{1}{2.25}} \times \frac{9.05}{7.5/\sqrt{2.25}} = 227 \text{ ohms}$$

Example 3.6. A rectangular waveguide has a cross-section of 1.5 cm × 0.8 cm, $\sigma = 0$, $\mu = \mu_0$, and $\varepsilon = 4\,\varepsilon_0$. The magnetic field component is given as

$$\mathbf{H_x = 2 \sin\left(\frac{\pi x}{a}\right) \cos\left(\frac{3\pi y}{b}\right) \sin(\pi \times 10^{11}\, t - \beta z)\ A/m}$$

Determine :

(a) The mode of operation.

(b) The cut-off frequency.

(c) The phase constant β.

(d) The propagation constant γ.

(e) The intriasic wave impedance η .

Solution :

(a) From the expression for H_x, it is clear that $m = 1$, $n = 3$ that is the guide is operating in either TM_{13} or TE_{13} mode. We choose TE_{13} mode

(b) $$f_{c13} = \frac{1}{2\sqrt{\mu\varepsilon}} \sqrt{\left(\frac{1}{a}\right)^2 + \left(\frac{3}{b}\right)^2}$$

$$\frac{1}{\sqrt{\mu\varepsilon}} = \frac{c}{\sqrt{\mu_r \varepsilon_r}} = \frac{c}{2}$$

Hence $$f_{c_{13}} = \frac{c}{4} \sqrt{\left(\frac{1}{1.5\times 10^{-2}}\right)^2 + \left(\frac{3}{0.8\times 10^{-2}}\right)^2}$$

$$= \frac{3\times 10^8}{4} \left(\sqrt{0.444 + 14.03}\right) \times 10^2 = 28.57\ \text{GHz}$$

(c) Phase constant $\beta = \omega \sqrt{\mu\varepsilon} \sqrt{1 - \left(\frac{f_c}{f}\right)^2}$

Here, $\omega = \pi \times 10^{11}$ or $f = 50$ GHz

$$\text{or } \beta = \frac{\pi \times 10^{11} (2)}{3\times 10^8} \sqrt{1 - \left(\frac{28.57}{50}\right)^2} = 1718.81\ \text{rad/m}$$

(d) Propogation constant, $\gamma = j\beta = j1718.81/\text{m}$

$$\eta TE_{13} = \frac{\eta}{\sqrt{1 - (f_c/f)^2}} = \frac{377}{\sqrt{\varepsilon_r}} \left[1 - \left(\frac{28.57}{50}\right)^2\right]^{1/2}$$

$= 229.69\ \Omega$

Example 3.7. An air-filled rectangular wave with cross-section of 4 cm × 2 cm transports energy in the dominant mode (TE_{10}) at a rate of 2 mW. If the frequency of operations 10GHz, determine the peak value of the electric field in the waveguide.

Solution :

The field expressions corresponding to TE_{10} mode are

$$E_x = 0, \; E_y = -\frac{j\omega\mu ac}{\pi} \sin\left(\frac{\pi x}{a}\right) e^{-j\beta z}$$

$$f_c = \frac{c}{2a} = \frac{3\times10^8}{2\left(4\times10^{-2}\right)} = 3.75 \text{ GHz}$$

$$\eta = \frac{\eta_o}{\sqrt{1-\left(\frac{f_c}{f_0}\right)^2}} = 406.7\,\Omega$$

The average power transmitted is

$$P_{ave} = \int_{y=0}^{b} \int_{x=0}^{a} \frac{\left|E_y\right|^2}{2\eta} dx\, dy$$

$$= \frac{E_s^2}{2\eta} \int_0^b dy \int_0^a \sin^2\left(\frac{\pi x}{a}\right) dx$$

where $E_o = \frac{\omega\mu a}{\pi} c$

$\therefore \quad P_{ave} = \frac{E_o^2 ab}{4\eta}$

Therefore,

$$E_o^2 = \frac{4\eta P_{ave}}{ab} = 4\left(406.7\right)\times2\times\frac{10^{-3}}{8\times10^{-4}}$$

$$= 4067$$

or $\quad E_0 = 63.77$ V/m

Example 3.8. A copper waveguide has dimensions *a* = 2.286 cm, *b* = 1.016 cm and is operating at a frequency *f* = 10GHz in TE_{10} mode. For a guide of 1 m length, find the attenuation in dB.

Solution :

At 10GHz, the propagation constant of the TE_{10} mode is

$$\beta = \sqrt{k_o^2 - \left(\frac{\pi}{a}\right)^2}$$

$$k_o^2 = \omega^2 \mu \varepsilon = \left(\frac{2\pi f}{c}\right)^2 = 209.44\ m^{-1}$$

$$a = .02286\ m$$

$$\beta = 158.05\ \text{m}^{-1}$$

For copper walls ($\sigma = 5.8\times10^7$ s/m)

Hence $\quad R_s = \sqrt{\dfrac{\omega\mu}{2\sigma}} = 0.026\ \Omega$

So the attenuation constant from Eq. 3.55, is

$$\alpha_C = \frac{R_s}{a^3 b\,\beta\,k_o\,\eta}\left(2b\pi^2 + a^3 k_o^2\right) = 0.0125\ N_p/m$$

$$\alpha_C(\text{dB}) = -\ 20 \log e^{-\alpha_C} = 0.11\ \text{dB/m.}$$

Example 3.9. An air-filled resonant cavity with dimensions a = 5 cm, b = 4 cm, and c = 10 cm is made of copper $(\sigma_c = 5.8\times10^7 \text{mhos/m})$. It is filled with a lossless material $(\mu_r = 1)$, $(\varepsilon_r = 3)$. Find the resonant frequency f_r and the quality factor for TE_{101} mode.

Solution :

$$\text{Resonant frequency } f_r = \frac{1}{2\sqrt{\mu\varepsilon}}\sqrt{\left(\frac{m}{a}\right)^2 + \left(\frac{n}{b}\right)^2 + \left(\frac{l}{c}\right)^2}$$

$$\frac{1}{2\sqrt{\mu\varepsilon}} = \frac{c}{2\sqrt{3}} = \frac{1.5\times10^8}{1.732}$$

$$f_{r_{101}} = \frac{1.5\times10^8}{1.732}\left[\left(\frac{1}{5\times10^{-2}}\right)^2 + \left(\frac{1}{10\times10^{-2}}\right)^2\right]^{1/2}$$

$$= 1.936\text{GHz}$$

(b) The quality factor for TE_{101} mode is given as

$$Q_{TE101} = \frac{\left(a^2 + c^2\right) ab\, c}{\delta\left[2b\left(a^3 + c^3\right) + ac\left(a^2 + c^2\right)\right]}$$

$$= \frac{(25 + 100)\, 200 \times 10^{-2}}{\delta\left[\delta\left(125 + 1000\right) + 50\left(25 + 100\right)\right]}$$

$$= \frac{1}{61\delta} = \frac{\sqrt{\pi f_{101} \mu_o \sigma_c}}{61}$$

$$= 10.93 \times 10^3$$

Select Bibliography

1. Ramo, S., Whinnery, J.R. and Van Duzer, T.; **Fields and waves in communication Electronics,** John Wiley and Sons, 1965.
2. Jordan, E.C. and Balmain, K.G. **Electromagnetic waves and Radiating systems,** Prentice Hali Inc., 1968.
3. Collen, R.E., Foundations for **Microwave Engineering. McGraw-hill Inc. New York, 1992.**
4. Sisodia, M.L., Raghuvanshi, G.S. Microwave Circuits and passive Devices New Age Int. (P) Ltd., 2001

Review Questions and Problems

1. What is meant by a cut off frequency of a waveguide?
2. Explain why single conductor hollow or dielectric filled waveguide cannot support TEM waves.
3. Can a waveguide have more than one cuttoff frequency? On what factors does the cutoff frequency of a waveguide depend.
4. Is the guide wavelength of a propagating wave in a waveguide longer or shorter than the wavelength in the corresponding unbounded dielectric medium?
5. What is meant by the dominant mode of a waveguide? What is the dominant mode of a parallel plate waveguide?
6. Does the attenuation constant due to dielectric losses increase or decrease with frequency for TM and TE modes in a parallel plate waveguide?
7. Discuss the general attenuation behaviour caused by wall losses as a function of frequency for the TE_{10} mode in a rectangular waveguide.

8. What are cavity resonantors? What are their most desirable properties?
9. In terms of field patterns what does the TM_{110} and TE_{123} mode signify.
10. Define the quality factor Q of a resonator. Explain why the measured Q of a cavity resonator is lower than the calculated values.
11. Consider a circular waveguide with a = 0.7cm Determine the cutoff frequencies and identify the first four propagating modes.
12. Derive the expression for the attenuation of the TM_{nm} mode of a circular waveguide with finite conductivity.
13. An X band waveguide filled with teflon is operating at 9GHz. Calculate the phase and group velocities in the waveguide.
14. An air filled rectangular waveguide made of copper ($\sigma = 5.80 \times 10^7$ s/m) and having transverse dimensions a = 7.20 cm and b = 3.40 cm operates at a frequency of 3GHz in the dominant mode. Find (i) f_c (ii) λ_g (iii) λ_c and (iv) distance over which the field intensities of the propagating wave will be attenuated by 50%.
15. Find expressions for the electric surface density on the walls of a rectangular waveguide for a TE_{10} mode. Why can a narrow slot be cut along the center line of the broad wall of a rectangular waveguide without perturbing the operation of the guide?
16. An air filled rectangular cavity with brass walls ε_0, μ_0, $\sigma = 1.54 \times 10^7$ (S/m) has the following dimensions a = 4cm, b = 3cm and d = 5cm. Determine
    (a) The dominant mode and its resonant frequency for this cavity.
    (b) Find the Q and the time average stored electric and magnetic energies at the resonant frequency, assuming H_0 to be 0.1 A/m.

4.1. Introd

In chap

power from

guiding struc

rectangular

described in

coupling ene

stub-type ma

and capacitiv

to control the

structures are

most common

connectors

junctions, hyb

ferrite devices

Section

microwave ne

the microwave

4.2. Scatter

A wave

and one outpu

one-port netw

form three p

outgoing wave

network comp

is defined by)

We acknowl

this chapter.

4

Microwave Circuit Components*

4.1. Introduction

In chapters 2 and 3, we discussed the propagation of microwave power from one point to another point without radiation loss through guiding structures like transmission lines and hollow pipe guides. The rectangular waveguide is widely used guiding structure. We have also described the methods of existing fields in guides and methods of coupling energy out. Short circuited sections of guiding structures, stub-type reactive elements and waveguide windows are used as inductive and capacitive elements. Waveguide cavities are used as resonant circuits to control the frequency of oscillator. Microwave filters and slow-wave structures are discussed in chapter 5. In this chapter, we will describe most commonly used microwave circuit components such as wave guide connectors and fittings, terminations, attenuators, phase changers, junctions, hybrid junctions, directional couplers, reflectometers and ferrite devices such as isolators, gyrators and circulators.

Section 4.2 is devoted to the scattering matrix representation of microwave network. Other sections are devoted to the description of the microwave components mentioned earlier.

4.2. Scattering Matrix Representation of Microwave Network

A waveguide section is a two-port network *i.e.* it has one input and one output. The output port is terminated by some means it is one-port network. Similarly, tees (Fig. 4.20) and coupler (Fig. 4.37) form three port networks. The relationship between incoming and outgoing waves at various ports of a network describe the system or network completely. The input-output relationship (the wave approach) is defined by scattering matrix which is widely used to characterize

---

* We acknowledge with thanks the contribution of Prof. G.S. Raghuvanshi in developing this chapter.

multiports. However, there are other two types of matrices, namely, impedance matrix and admittances matrix, these two are based on Kirchhoff's laws for electrical networks. These two are not convenient since voltage currents and impedances cannot be measured precisely and directly at microwaves. On the other hand transmission coefficient, reflection coefficient, and standing wave ratio at microwaves are easily and precisely measurable. These form the basis of the scattering matrix formulation. **Scattering matrix is a linsar relationship between input and output that involves precisely measurable parameters.**

4.2.1. Scattering matrix formulation

Consider the n-post network as shown in Fig. 4.1.

Let us define a parameter a_n proportional to the incident wave at the nth port and parameter b_n proportional to the outgoing wave at n^{th} port in the following manner,

$$a_n = V_n^+ / \sqrt{Z_c} \quad \text{....(4.2.1)}$$

$$b_n = V_n^- / \sqrt{Z_c} \quad \text{....(4.2.2)}$$

where V_n^+ represents incident wave along the line connected to the nth port.

and V_n^- represents outgoing wave along the line connected to the nth port.

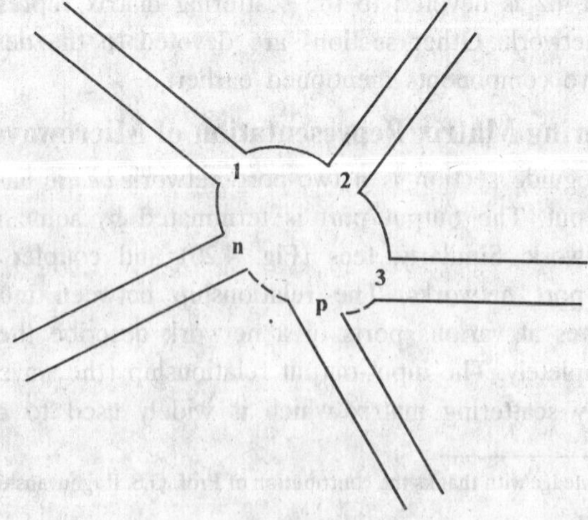

Fig. 4.1. N-Port Network.

and Z_c is the characteristic impedance of the line. For a two-port network the relationship between b_n's and a_n's may be written as

$$b_1 = S_{11}a_1 + S_{12}a_2$$

$$b_2 = S_{21}a_2 + S_{22}a_2 \quad \text{....(4.2.3)}$$

where S_{11} is a reflection coefficient at port 1

S_{22} is a reflection coefficient at port 2

S_{12} is a transmission coelticient from part 2 to port 1

S_{21} is a transmission coefficient from port 1 to port 2.

Figure 4.2a shows the S-Parameter of a two-port network.

Equation 4.2.3 can be put in the matrix form.

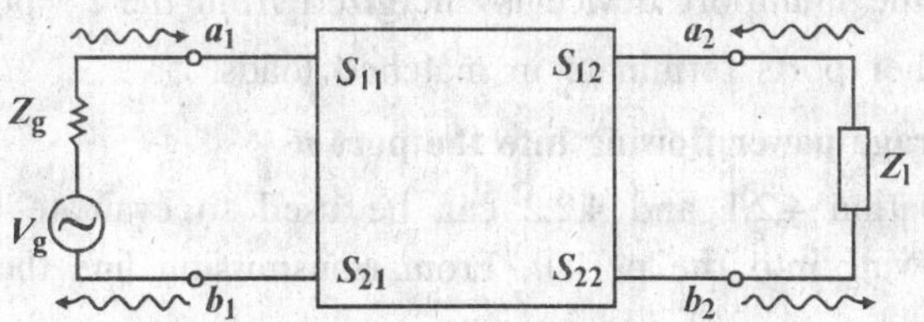

Fig. 4.2a. S-Parameters of two-port network.

$$\begin{bmatrix} b_1 \\ b_2 \end{bmatrix} = \begin{bmatrix} S_{11} & S_{12} \\ S_{21} & S_{22} \end{bmatrix} \begin{bmatrix} a_1 \\ a_2 \end{bmatrix} \quad \text{....(4.2.4)}$$

or $$[b] = [S]\ [a]$$

where S is known as the scattering matrix for the network. For n-port network the relationship between b_n's and a_n's may be written

$$b_1 = S_{11}a_1 + S_{12}a_2 + S_{13}a_3 + \text{.......}S_{1n}a_n$$

$$b_2 = S_{21}a_1 + S_{22}a_2 + S_{23}a_3 + \text{.......}S_{2n}a_n \quad \text{....(4.2.5)}$$

$$\dots\dots\dots\dots\dots\dots\dots\dots\dots\dots$$

$$\dots\dots\dots\dots\dots\dots\dots\dots\dots\dots$$

$$b_n = S_{n1}a_1 + S_{n2}a_2 + S_{n3}a_3 + \text{.......}S_{nn}a_n$$

as each incident wave will make a contribution to the total resultant wave from n^{th} port.

Eqation 4.2.5 can be put in the following matrix from :

$$\begin{bmatrix} b_1 \\ b_2 \\ \cdot \\ \cdot \\ \cdot \\ b_n \end{bmatrix} = \begin{bmatrix} S_{11} & S_{12} & S_{1n} \\ S_{21} & S_{22} & S_{2n} \\ \cdot & \cdot & \cdot \\ \cdot & \cdot & \cdot \\ \cdot & \cdot & \cdot \\ S_{n1} & S_{n2} & S_{nn} \end{bmatrix} \begin{bmatrix} a_1 \\ a_2 \\ \cdot \\ \cdot \\ \cdot \\ a_n \end{bmatrix} \quad \text{....(4.2.6)}$$

Equation 4.2.6 can be rewritten in matrix notations

$$[b] = [S] \; [a] \quad \text{....(4.2.7)}$$

where $[a]$ and $[b]$ are the respective matrices of the incident (input) and reflected (output) waves and $[S]$ by definition the **scattering matrix**.

Equation 4.2.7 resembles to relation $E_{\text{ref.}} = \rho E_{\text{inc}}$.

where ρ is the reflection coefficient. The scattering coefficients S_{11}, S_{22}, S_{33} carry the simple physical meaning of reflection coefficients ρ_i, when the multiport device is energized from the ith port provided all the other ports terminate in matched loads.

4.2.2. Average power flowing into the port n

Equation 4.2.1 and 4.2.2 can be used to evaluate the average power flowing into the port n. From transmission line theory we can write

$$V_n = V_n^+ + V_n^- = \sqrt{Z_c}\,(a_n + b_n) \quad \text{....(4.2.8)}$$

and

$$I_n = \frac{1}{\sqrt{Z_c}}(V_n^+ - V_n^-) = \frac{1}{\sqrt{Z_c}}(a_n - b_n) \quad \text{....(4.2.9)}$$

The average power flow into the port n is given by

$$W_n = \frac{1}{2}\,\text{Re}\,(V_n I_n^*)$$

$$= \frac{1}{2}\,\text{Re}\{(a_n\, a_n^* - b_n\, b_n^*) + (b_n\, a_n^* - b_n\, a_n^*)\}$$

$$= \frac{1}{2}\,(a_n\, a_n^* - b_n\, b_n^*) \quad \text{....(4.2.10)}$$

Equation 4.2.10 shows that W_n is equal to the power carried into the port n by the incident wave (which is given by $\frac{1}{2}\, a_n\, a_n^*$) less the power reflected back (given by $\frac{1}{2}\, b_n\, b_n^*$).

4.2.3. Insertion loss, transmission loss, reflection loss and return loss in terms of S-parameters when the ports are matched terminated :

Let us consider two port network in which

P_i is power fed at port 1,

P_r is power reflected from port 1

P_o is output power at port 2 then the following losses are defined in terms of S-parameters.

(i) Insertion loss (db) $= 10 \log \frac{P_i}{P_0} = 10 \log \frac{|a_1|^2}{|a_2|^2}$

$$= 20 \log \frac{1}{|S_{21}|}$$

$$= 20 \log \frac{1}{|S_{12}|}$$

(ii) Transmission loss or attenuation (db) $= 10 \log \frac{P_i - P_r}{P_0}$

$$= 10 \log \frac{1 - |S_{11}|^2}{|S_{12}|^2}$$

(iii) Reflection loss (db) $= 10 \log \frac{P_i}{P_i - P_r}$

$$= 10 \log \frac{1}{1 - |S_{11}|^2}$$

(iv) Return loss (db) $= 10 \log \frac{P_i}{P_r}$

$$= 20 \log \frac{1}{|P|}$$

$$= 20 \log \frac{1}{|S_{11}|}$$

4.2.4 Properties of S-Parameters

S-parameters are, in general, complex quantities having following properties : –

(i) Zero property of [S] matrix–The sum of the products of each term of any column (or row) multiplied by the complex conjugate of the corresponding terms of any other column (or row) is zero *i.e.*,

$$S_{11} S_{23}^* + S_{21} S_{22}^* + \ldots\ldots S_{N1} S_{N2}^* = 0$$

or
$$\sum_{n=1}^{N} S_{ns} S_{nr}^* = 0 \quad (\because s \neq r)$$

(ii) Unity property of [S] matrix—The sum of the products of each term of any one row (or column) multiplied by its complex conjugate is unity, that is

$$\sum_{n=1}^{N} S_{ni} S_{ni}^* = 1$$

(iii) Symmetric property of [S] matrix—For any lossless linear and reciprocal network (same transmission characteristics in either direction of a pair of ports) the scattering matrix is symmetrical, *i.e.* $S_{ij} = S_{ji}$ $(i \neq j)$.

(iv) Phase Shift property—Suppose the reference plane of 1 and 2 of two port network are shifted to 1′ and 2′ (shown in Fig. 4.2b) by electrical phase shift $\phi_1 = \beta_1 l_1$ and $\phi_2 = \beta_2 l_2$ respectively, the new wave variables are $a_1 e^{j\phi_1}$, $a_z e^{-j\phi_1}$, $b_1 e^{j\phi_2}$, $b_2 e^{-j\phi_2}$. The new S matrix S' is then given by

$$[S'] = \begin{bmatrix} e^{j\phi_1} & 0 \\ 0 & e^{j\phi_2} \end{bmatrix} \begin{bmatrix} S_{11} & S_{12} \\ S_{21} & S_{22} \end{bmatrix} \begin{bmatrix} e^{-j\phi_1} & 0 \\ 0 & e^{-j\phi_2} \end{bmatrix}$$

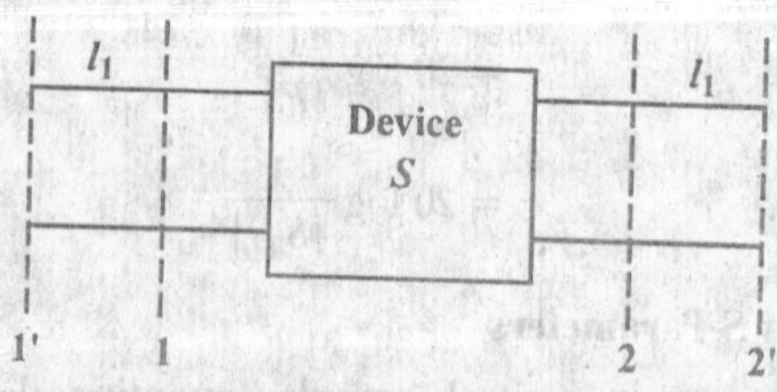

Fig. 4.2b. Reference plane shifted

This property is valid for any number of ports and is called phase shift property when reference planes are shifted.

4.3. Waveguide Connectors and Fittings

Regardless of the purpose for which waveguides may be used, some means must be available for connecting adjacent sections. The basic requirement is that the joint should offer no appreciable discontinuity to the flow of microwave power. Various joints are available. In this section we will describe few of these, such as waveguide flanges, bends, twists and corners, transitions, rotary joints etc., however, detailed information and discussion may be found in literature.*

4.3.1. Waveguide flanges

Rectangular waveguide sections are joined by means of flanges which may be of either the cover type or the choke type.

(i) Cover-flange coupling – Two wavegide sections with cover-flanges can be bolted together to form a contacting joint as shown in Fig. 4.3.

A cover flange connector has flat, smooth, clean and square contacting surfaces. It avoids reflections and resistive loss at this joint.

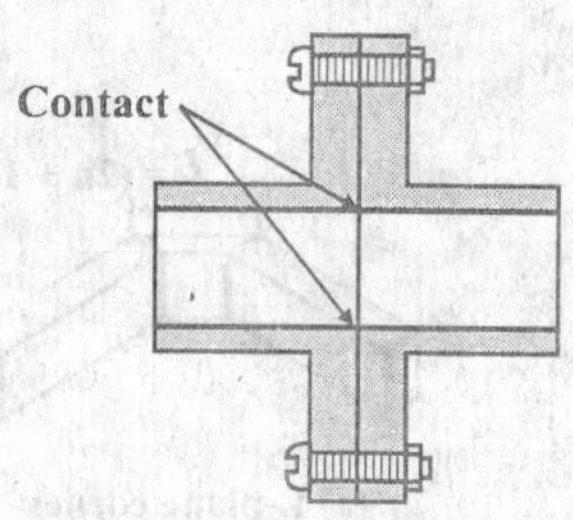

Fig. 4.3. Cover to cover coupling

In high power applications voltage breakdown may occur at this joint, however, these are widely used because of simplicity of the cover to-cover connection. In general, the VSWR from such a joint is of the order of 1.03 or less.

(ii) Choke flange – Figure 4.4 depicts the choke-type waveguide connectors. It utilizes the transmission line theory in a way that largely obviates the discontinuity due to a break in the conductivity of a waveguide wall. Two quarter-wave sections present a short circuit at the joint and electrical continuity is thus preserved.

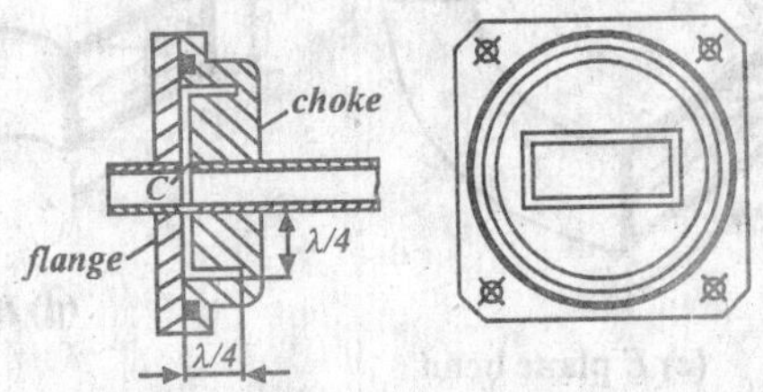

Fig. 4.4. Waveguide choke-flange coupling.

* [1] Stalter, J.C., **Microwave Electronics**, D. Van Noastrand Co. Inc., New York, 1950.
[2] Southworth G.C., **Principles and Applications of Waveguide Transmission**, D. Van Nostrand Co. Inc., New York, 1950.
[3] Sisodia, M.L. and G.S. Raghuvanshi, **Microwave Circuits and Passive Devices**, New Age, International (P) Limited Publishers, New Delhi-31, 3rd reprint 2000.

In this there is negligible voltage drop across the ohmic contact between the flanges as such voltage breakdown is avoided. Therefore cover-to-choke connections can be used for high power applications. In general, the VSWR for this joint is of the order of 1.05 or less but it is more frequency dependent than the cover to cover joint.

4.3.2. Waveguide corners, bends and twists

Waveguide corners (E and H Plane) and bends, which are shown in Fig. 4.5, are normally used to change the direction of the guide through a desired angle. Corners are also used to reduce the overall system of dimensions. These produce discontinuities and in order to minimize reflections from the discontinuities, the mean length (Fig. 4.5a, b),

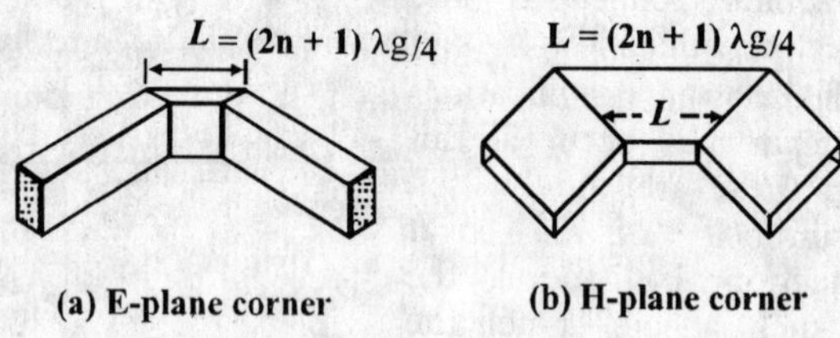

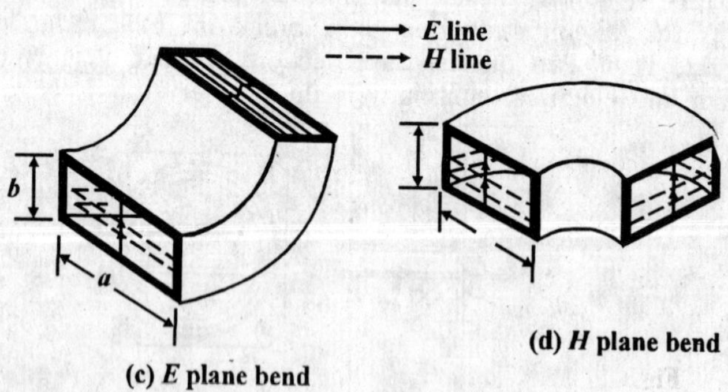

Fig. 4.5. Waveguide corners and bends.

L between the junction of the corners is kept equal to **an odd number of quarter-wave lengths.** That is

$$L = (2n + 1)\lambda_g/4 \quad ....(4.3.1)$$

where $n = 0, 1, 2, 3, ...$ and λ_g is the guide wavelength. In this situation the reflected waves from both ends of waveguide sections are completely cancelled.

In case of bends the radius of curvature for minimum reflection is given by Southworth [2 opt. cit.] as

$$R = 1.5b \text{ for an E–bend [Fig. 4.5d]}$$

and

$$R = 1.5a \text{ for a H–bend Fig. 4.5c]}$$

For a good quality of match, long radius bends should preferably be used or the length of a bend be made a multiple of a half of a guide wavelength.

Twists :

Waveguide twists are used to rotate the plane of polarization in a waveguide. In case of rectangular waveguides this may be done by filling the interior with a low melting point material and twisting the whole waveguide to the desired angle. The low melting point material is then removed. The circular waveguide rotator is made by placing a diametral septum with a progressive twist in the guide. The twists are shown in Fig. 4.6. These may also be electroformed.

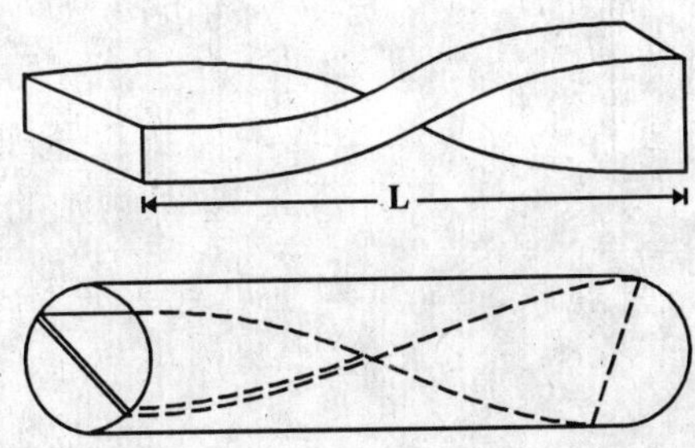

Fig. 4.6. Waveguide twists or rotators (used to rotate plane of polarization).

The length of the twist is kept equal to an odd multiple of the quarter guide wavelength ($\lambda_g/4$).

Bends and also other more complicated waveguide structures may be electroformed, *i.e.,* constructed by depositing electrolytically the required thickness of metal on a carefully made matrix.

4.3.3. Transitions

In a microwave system, it is often necessary to change frcm one form of waveguide to another or from waveguide to coaxial line or back. This is achieved by transitions, also known as adopters.

It is mostly desired to have a transition from a coaxial line to a waveguide and vice versa. Figure 4.7 illustrates such transitions. Discontinuities resulting from sudden termination of the dielectric or transformation of the radial electric wave into a coaxial to the dominant wave in the waveguide are turned out by varying either coaxial tuner settings or the length of the central conductor protruding into the guide.

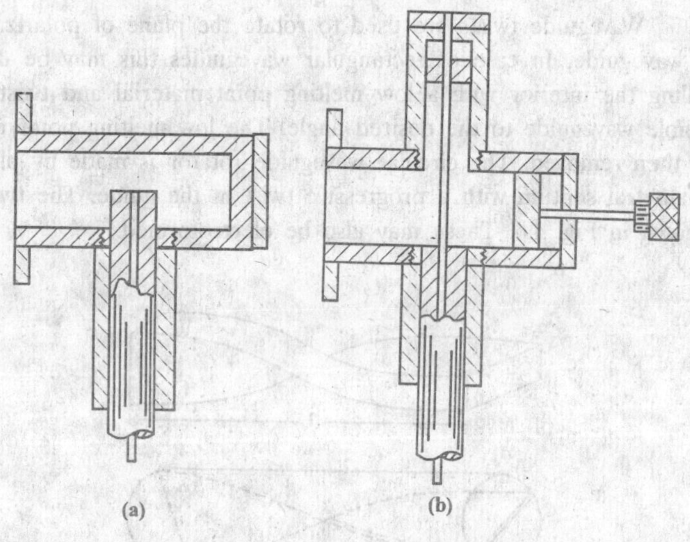

Fig. 4.7 (a) Transition from coaxial line to waveguide.
(b) Transition from one from of waveguide to another.

The transition from one form or shape of a waveguide to another may be achieved by waveguide transformers shown in Fig. 4.7b. The reader could find more information in literature [2, 3, opt. cit.]

4.3.4 Rotary Joints

A rotary joint allows one section of a waveguide to rotate with respect to the other, while passing microwave energy, and does with low reflection and negligible power leakage through it. Rotary joints are assembled from short sections of a coaxial line or a circular waveguide. In case of radar a fixed waveguide is connected to a horn

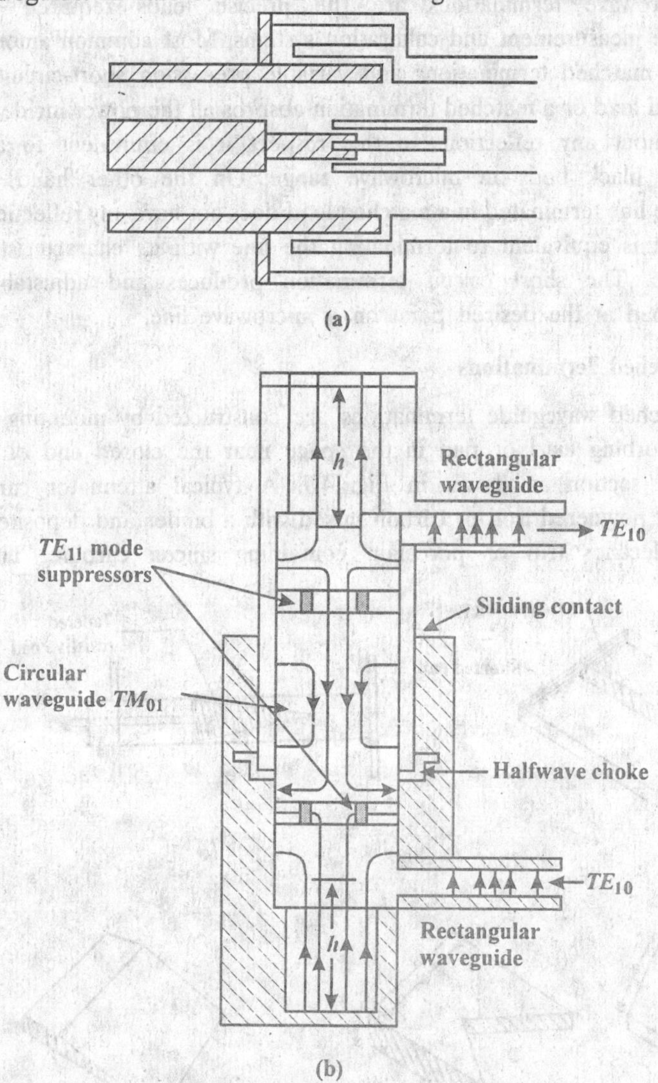

Fig 4.8. Rotary joints (a) Coaxial version (b) Circular waveguide version.

antenna by a rotary joint for feeding a paraboloid reflector which rotates for tracking. Coaxial and waveguide rotary joints are shown in Fig. 4.8 a, b. These joints produce a VSWR < 1.1.

4.4. Microwave Terminations

Microwave terminations are the precise loads required in microwave measurement and calibration systems. Most common among them are matched terminations and variable precession short-circuits. A matched load or a matched termination absorbs all the power incident on it without any reflection. In this respect it is equivalent to an absolutely black body in microwave range. On the other hand, a microwave line terminated in a matched load does not have any reflection and hence is equivalent to terminating the line with its characteristic impedance. The short circuit termination produces and adjustable reactive load at the desired point on a microwave line.

4.4.1. Matched Terminations

Matched waveguide terminations are constructed by mounting a power-absorbing card or pad in the space near the closed end of a waveguide section as shown in Fig. 4.9. A typical attenuator card consists of powdered iron or carbon mixed with a binder and deposited on a dielectric strip or porcelain containing silicon carbide. The

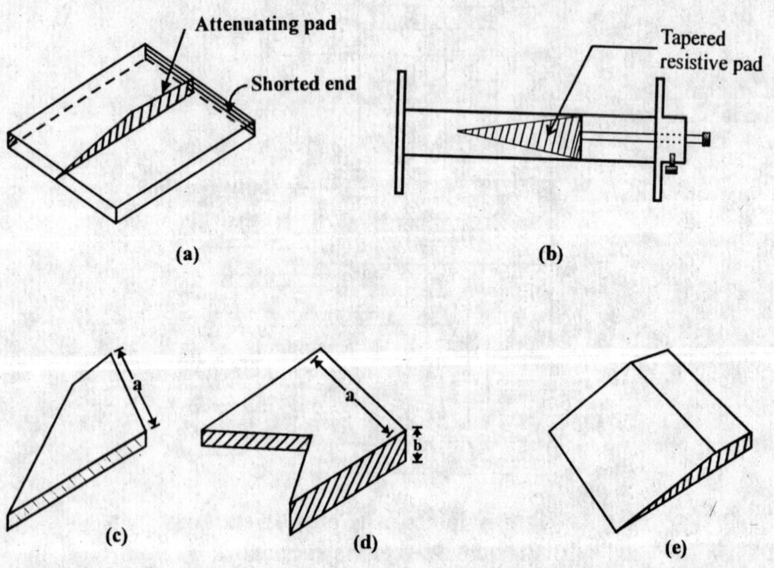

Fig. 4.9. Waveguide matched terminations (*a*) pad type (*b*) tunable (*c*), (*d*) and (*e*) lossy type.

reflections arising from the end are minimized by tapering the card. The card is placed parallel to the dominant TE_{10} mode at a place where the electric field is maximum to have maximum attenuation. As the card has finite thickness, the reflections arising from it cannot be ruled out. Moreover, it is located at E_{max} which will give maximum reflected power. To avoid this the pad is kept closer to the side wall and its length is increased. Tunable matched termination is shown in Fig. 4.9*b*.

Matched loads may also be designed by loading the whole of the waveguide with lossy materials such as powdered metal, lossy dielectric, wood, flowing water, sand, etc. as shown in Fig. 4.9 *c*, *d* and *e*.

4.4.2. Variable waveguide short-circuit termination

Waveguide short-circuit terminations provide standard reflection at desired, precisely measurable position. The basic idea behind it is to provide short-circuit by changing reactance of the termination.

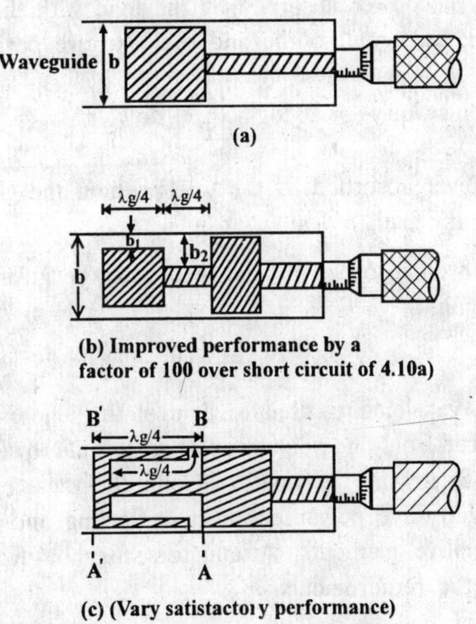

Fig. 4.10. Waveguide short-circuits a. Adjustable type, b. Choke type $b_2 \approx 10b_1$(improved performance by a factor of 100 over short-circuit of Fig. 4.10a).
c. Folded choke type (Very satisfactory performance.)

The simplest form of an adjustable waveguide short-circuit is shown in Fig. 4.10*a*. It consists of a sliding block of a good conductor (such as copper) which makes as snug fit in the waveguide. The position of the block is varied by means of a micrometer drive. However, the electrical short circuit position deviates from the physical short circuit position in a random manner owing to the erratic contact between the sliding block and the waveguide wall. Furthermore, some power leakage past the block may occur thereby making the reflection coefficient less than unity. This too is highly undesirable. These problems are overcomed in choke-type shorting plungers shown in Figs. 4.10, *b* and *c*.

4.5. Microwave Attenuators

Attenuation – The term attenuation, usually used in high frequency techniques, is defined as the ratio, expressed in decibels, of the power level or voltage level between two points in a circuit. Clearly, attenuation or (insertion loss) of a component under test will be the ratio, expressed in decibels, of the power absorbed by the load without the component in the line to the power absorbed by the load with the component in the line, when the signal source and the load are perfectly matched.

$$\text{Attenuation } A = 10 \log_{10} \left(\frac{P_1}{P_2}\right) \text{ db}$$

P_1 = Power absorbed by the load without the given component in the line;

P_2 = Power absorbed by the load with the given component in the line.

Attenuators :

The passive elements used to control the amount of microwave power transferred from one point to another on a microwave transmission line are called microwave attenuators. Generally, these elements control the flow of microwave power either by reflecting and/or absorbing it in some dissipative elements. Attenuators may be fixed or variable depending on the requirements.

An ideal attenuator when placed in a transmission line, must present a good impedance match at both the terminals, *i.e.* it should be a *well-matched reciprocal device*. The attenuation is a function of frequency and so due care should be taken if standard attenuation is desired.

In the following sections, we shall discuss some of the common waveguide attenuators. However, a brief reference to coaxial attenuators will also be made.

4.5.1. Flap or Card attenuators (Fixed Type)

The fixed type [Fig. 4.11] consists of a dissipative element (pad) placed in a section of the waveguide with its plane parallel to the electric field and at the position where the electric field of the dominant TE_{10} mode is maximum. The dissipating element is generally in the form of card or pad. One class of such pads consists of thin metallic films coated on a glass plate. A baked-on metallic film combining platinum and palladium and also an evaporated film of chromium or nichrome with a protective film of magnesium fluoride have been satisfactorily used. The base material, glass, is chosen because it does not react with the film, its surface is smooth, and it can maintain its original shape at the temperatures we come across. The card is held parallel to the electric field by means of two thin metal rods.

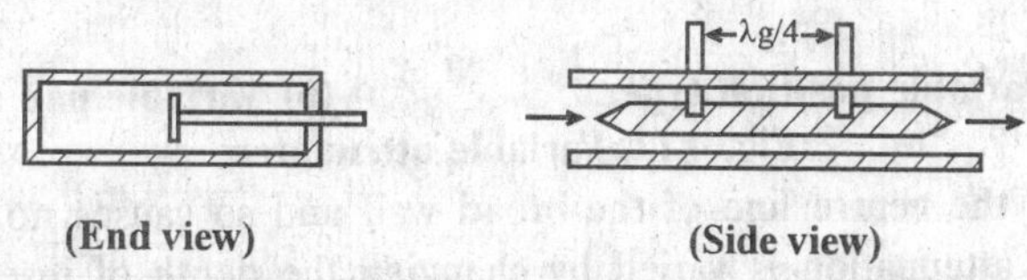

Fig. 4.11. Fixed type Flap or Card attenuators

To minimize reflections, the rods are held normal to the electric field and spaced quarter-wavelength apart, and the ends of the pad are tapered. When a dominant TE_{10} mode enters the waveguide attenuator, the electric field tangential to the pad causes a dissipative current and is thus absorbed. The amount of microwave power thus dissipated or the attenuation produced depends upon the strength of the electric field, *i.e.,* location of the pad within the waveguide, area of the pad intercepted by the electric field and the frequency.

4.5.2. Variable attenuators

The waveguide variable attenuators are shown in Fig. 4.12. In Fig. 4.12*a* variable position type attenuator is shown. A nob and gears (not shown in figure) control the movement of the card from the wall to the centre. The amount of attenuation introduced is controlled by changing the position occupied by the absorbing plate inside the waveguide, moving the plate from the narrow wall towards the waveguide axis thus producing an increase in attenuation, which becomes maximum when the plate is moved in the region of maximum electric field intensity, *i.e.*, along the axis.

The second type of waveguide variable attenuator is the variable pad area [Fig. 4.12*b*]. It consists of a slotted waveguide section. The

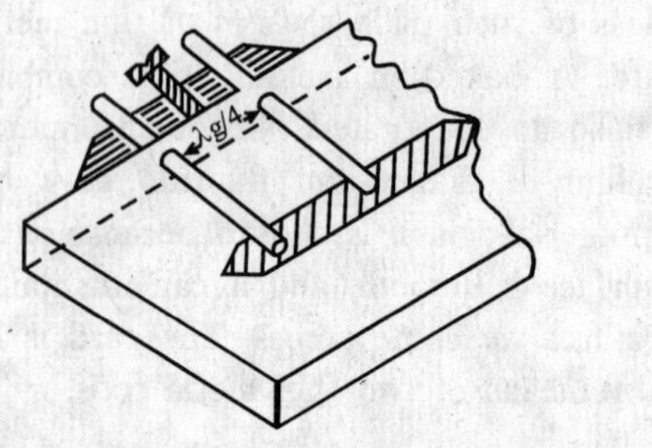

(a) Variable position type.

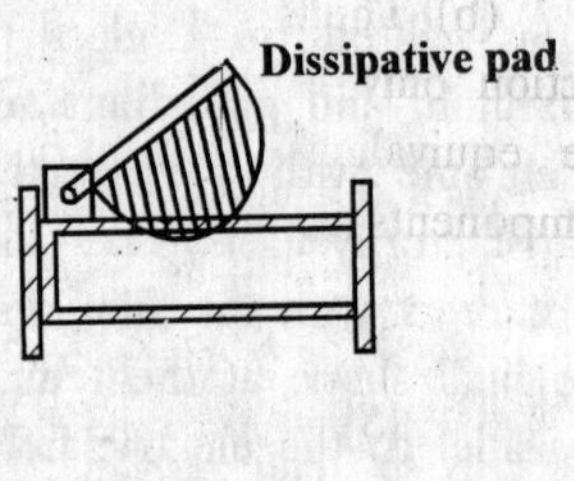

(b) Variable pad area.

Fig. 4.12. Variable attenuater

slot is on the centre line of the broad wall and so causes no radiation loss. The attenuation is varied by changing the depth of insertion and hence the intercepted pad area of an absorptive flap into the waveguide through the slot. The attenuation is maximum when the resistive pad or flap extends all the way across the guide and decreases continuously while the card is withdrawn. A suitable deriving mechanism and a dial may be attached to the flap in order to read and calibrate the attenuator.

4.5.3. Cut-off attenuators

It was pointed out in chapter 3 that if the dimensions of the waveguide are such that $\lambda >> \lambda_c$ (λ_c is the cut-off wavelength) the wave is exponentially attenuated. Therefore, a waveguide of cross-section sufficiently small to ensure $\lambda >> \lambda_c$ can be used as an attenuator. It has a great operating bandwidth. It has a substantial initial attenuation which seriously hampers their application.

4.5.4. Precision Variable Attenuators

The most satisfactory precision attenuator is the variable rotary attenuator depicted in Fig. 4.13. It comprises the following components :

(a) The first part is the tapered rectangular to circular waveguide transition having an attenuating pad placed parallel to the broad wall of the rectangular waveguide.

This component transforms with negligible reflections, the dominant TE_{10} mode in the rectangular waveguide to a TE_{11} mode in a cylindrical waveguide. The orthogonal polarization of the TE_{11} mode, having its electric field parallel to the plane of the attenuating pad is absorbed while the other polarization having electric field perpendicular to the plane of the pad passes unattenuated.

(b) The second part is a plane circular waveguide section. This section only changes the reference polarizations (ports) as shown in the equivalent circuit [Fig. 4.13(ii)]. The scattering matrix of the components is

$$[S] = \begin{bmatrix} 0 & 0 & \cos\theta & \sin\theta \\ 0 & 0 & \sin\theta & \cos\theta \\ \cos\theta & \sin\theta & 0 & 0 \\ -\sin\theta & \cos\theta & 0 & 0 \end{bmatrix} \quad \text{....(4.5.1)}$$

(c) The third and the main component of the instrument is a rotatable circular waveguide section having a tapered resistive pad. At the minimum attenuation condition, the plane of this pad is the same as that of the pad in component (a). If the plane of the pad in section (c) is rotated through an anble θ, the electric field component E sin θ, parallel to the resistive pad will be absorbed while the electric field perpendicular to the resistive pad, E cos θ passes unaffected.

(d) The fourth component is symmetrical with section (*b*).

(d) The fifth component is symmetrical with section (*a*).

The electric field E cos θ coming out of section (*d*) makes an angle (90 – θ) with the resistive pad of section (*e*); consequently, the normal component of this electric field, *i.e.* (E cos θ) cos θ = E $\cos^2\theta$ passes unattenuated while the tangential component (E cos θ) sin θ is absorbed. The power transmitted is, therefore, given by

$$P_{trans} = \frac{1}{R}|E\cos^2\theta|^2 = P_{incident}\cos^2\theta$$

Or the attenuation is

$$\begin{aligned} A &= -\ 20 \log_{10} \cos^2 \\ &= -\ 40 \log_{10} \cos\theta \ \text{ db} \end{aligned} \quad \text{....(4.5.2)}$$

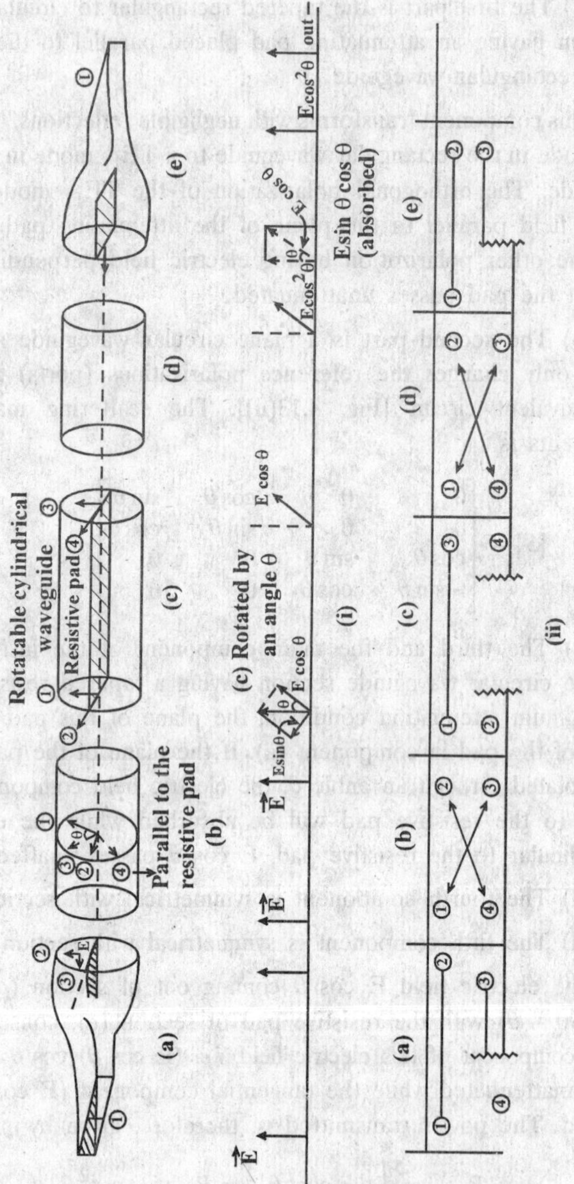

Fig. 4.13 Precision variable attenuator (i) Component form with working principle (ii) Equivalent circuit.

It is clear from Eq. 4.5.2 that the attenuation depends only on the angle of rotation θ. This suggests that the attenuator may be precisely calibrated. Note that the scale will not be linear.

4.5.5. High power attenuators

The attenuators discussed so far cannot be used at high powers because of high heat production when power is dissipated in the

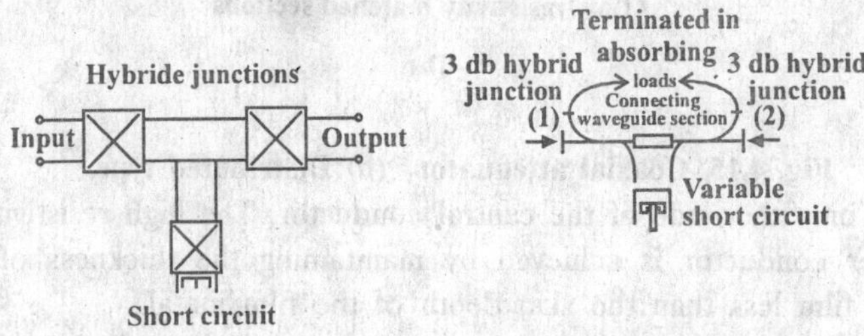

Fig. 6.14. High power microwave attenuator using 3 db hybrids.

attenuator pads. A typical high power microwave attenuator consisting of a waveguide hybrid junction is shown in Fig. 4.14. One port of the hybrid is terminated in a variable short circuit in series with one of the two connecting lines of a cascade arrangement of two hybrids. The high power signal is dissipated in a high power load such as circulating air or water.

4.5.5. Coaxial Attenuators

Typical coaxial attenuators are shown in Fig. 4.15. The T- section type attenuator consists of the "central conductor" made of glass tube having two resistive metalized film sections on either side of a metalized

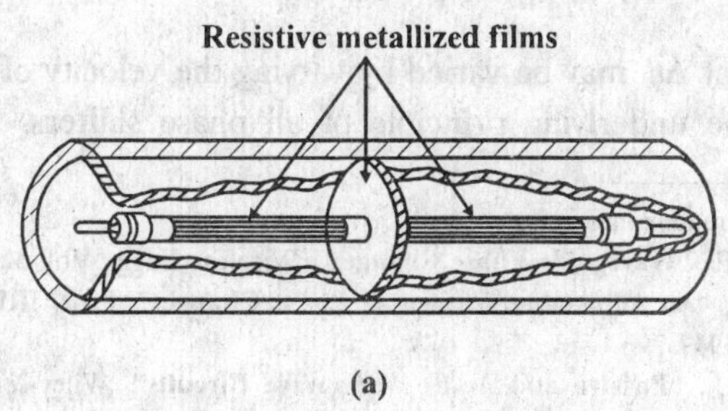

Fig. 4.15. Coaxial attenuator (a) T-sectiontype.

circular disc. The distributed type attenuator consists of higher resistive main attenuating section in the centre and lower resistive matching

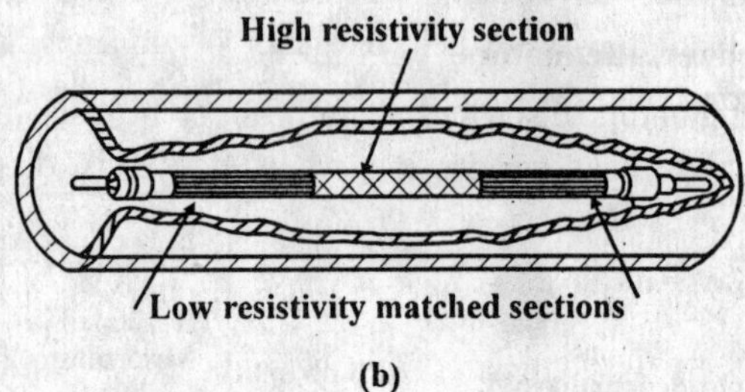

(b)

Fig. 4.15. Coaxial attenuator (b) Distributed type.

sections on either side of the central conductor. The high resistivity of the inner conductor is achieved by maintaining the thickness of the resistive film less than the skin depth of the film metal.

Variable type coaxial attenuators utilise cut off phenomenon as discussed in Sec. 4.5.3.

4.6. Microwave Phase Shifters*

These are the instruments or microwave circuit elements that produce the desired change in the phase of a propagating wave without any attenuation. The underlying principle of all types of phase shifters may be summarized as follows. When a wave propagates on a line, a phase difference prevails between any two arbitrary points along its path. Usually, it is constant and is determined by the velocity of propagation and hence a function of medium parameters. The phase difference between two points, l distance apart can be written as

$$\Delta\phi = \phi_2 - \phi_1 = \beta l = \frac{2\pi}{\lambda} l. \quad \text{....(4.61)}$$

Note that $\Delta\phi$ may be varied by varying the velocity of propagation and this is the underlying principle of all phase shifters.

---

* For details the reader may refer to :

1. Collin, R.E., **"Waveguide Phase Changer"**, Wireless Engg., Vol. **32**, March 1955.
2. Fox, A.G., **"An Adjustable Waveguide Phase Changer"**, Proc. IRE, Vol. **35**, No., 12, Dec., 1947.
3. Helszain, J.. **"Passive and Active Microwave Circuits"**, Wiley-Interscience, New York, 1978.
4. Altman, J.L., **"Microwave Circuits"**, Van Nostrand, New York, 1964.

4.6.1. Dielectric phase shifter

A simplest waveguide phase shifter consists of a rectangular waveguide loaded with a dielectric slab of thickness t, height h and dielectric constant ε in such a way that dimension h is parallel to the

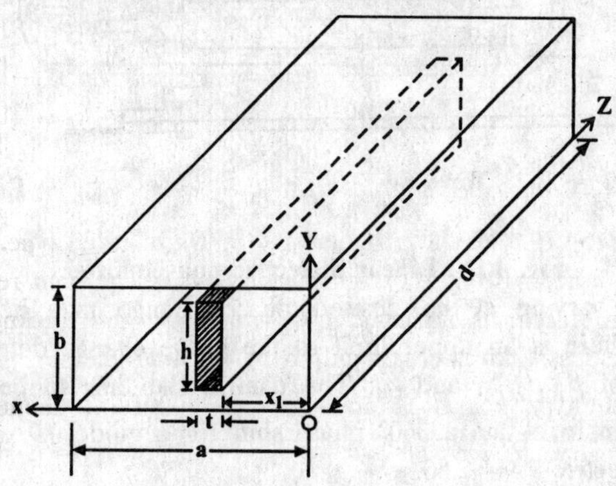

Fig. 4.16. Waveguide loaded with a dielectric slab.

electric field of the dominant TE_{10} mode as shown in Fig. 4.16. The dielectric inserted reduces the velocity of propagation of microwaves which results in an increased electrical path and hence a phase delay.*

4.6.2. Linear phase shifter

A typical linear dielectric phase shifter (Fig. 4.16) consists of three dielectric slabs placed in a rectangular waveguide such that the central slab is movable longitudinally by a suitable drive mechanism. A dielectric key protruded through a long centred slot cut in one broad face of the guide is attached to the central slab. The ends of the slabs are so cut that these constitute multisection broad band quarter-wave transformers that provide a match between unloaded and dielectric loaded waveguides. It is found that when the central slab is about 0.3 a times wide, $\beta_1 + \beta_2 > \beta_2 + \beta_4$. Therefore, referring to Fig. 4.17, the displacement of the central slab towards the right by a distance l amounts to an increase in the length of the lines. 1 and 3 by an amount l and to decrease in the length of the lines 2 and 4 by the same amount. Consequently, the wave propagating through the phase changer undergoes a phase change

$$\Delta\phi = \{(\beta_1 + \beta_3) - (\beta_2 + \beta_4)\}\, l \qquad \text{....(4.6.2)}$$

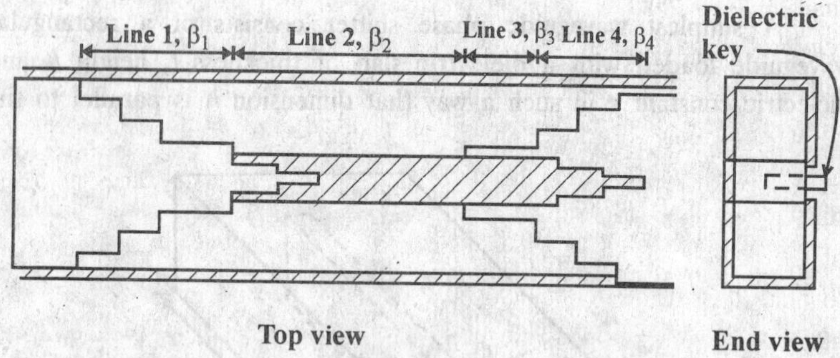

Fig. 4.1.7. Linear dielectric phase shifter.

Thus varying l, the desired phase change may be obtained. However, there is an upper limit to the phase change determined by the value of $\beta_1, \beta_2, \beta_3$ and β_4. The central slab has to be displaced about 16 cm to obtain a 360° phase shift for a guide 0.9 inch loaded with a dielectric $\varepsilon = 2.56$.

4.6.3. Differential phase shifter : Quarter and half-wave plates

Consider a circular waveguide diametrically loaded with a thin dielectric slab as shown in Fig. 4.18. Clearly the dominant TE_{11} mode will suffer maximum phase delay when its electric field lies in the principal dielectric plane and minimum (almost zero) when it lies perpendicular to it. Now a wave approaching the slab, polarized at some intermediate angle may be considered to be made up of two components, one lying in the plane of the slab and another perpendicular to it. Further, if both these degenerate TE_{11} modes are matched (by suitably tapering the slab), then while passing through such a section

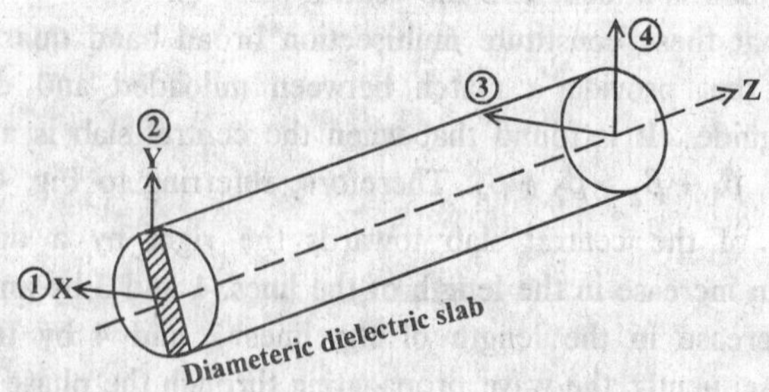

Fig. 4.18. Quarter-half-wave plate using dielectric slab in a circular waveguide.

the mode polarized paralled (||) to the slab will be retarded more than the one perpendicular (⊥) to it. After passing through the dielectric region the two degenerate modes combine but the wave suffers a net differential phase shift. Such a device is called a differential phase shifter.

The differential phase shift obtainable from the differential phase shifter depends upon the length, the dielectric constant and the thickness of the slab. If these parameters are suitably adjusted, it is not difficult to obtain a differential phase shift or $\pi/2$ or π and accordingly we can have quarter or half-wave sections. These are respectively designated as $\angle$ 90° and $\angle$ 180°.

4.6.4. Precision rotary phase changer

A precision rotary phase changer is shown in Fig. 4.19(a). The instrument consists of two rectangular to circular waveguide tapered transitions, together with two quarter-wave sections on both the sides of the free rotatable central half-wave section. The quarter-wave sections are oriented at an angle 45° relative to the broad wall of the rectangular waveguide. The incoming linearly polarized TE_{11} mode is decomposed into two modes polarized parallel and perpendicular to the quarter-wave section. When a half-wave section happens to be in its zero set position, the outgoing wave suffers a total phase of $90° + 180° = 270°$. Consequently, the wave going out of the second quarter-wave section suffers a total phase $270° + 90° = 360°$, *i.e.,* no phase change under ideal conditions. However, when the central half-wave section is rotated by an angle θ, the outgoing wave suffers a phase delay of 2θ.

The basic operation of the device can be understood with reference to Fig. 4.19(c) which explicitly shows all the components except transitions.

$E_i < 0$ represents the vertically polarized input wave in the input quarterwave section. It is decomposed into two transverse components, one E_1, polarised parallel and other, E_2 perpendicular to quarterwave plate (Fig. 4.19c(i)). After propagation through the quarter wave plate these two components are

$$E_1 = E_i \cos 45° \, e^{-j\beta_1 l} = E_0 e^{-j\beta_1 l}$$

$$E_2 = E_i \sin 45° \, e^{-j\beta_2 l} = E_0 e^{-j\beta_2 l} \quad \text{....(4.6.3)}$$

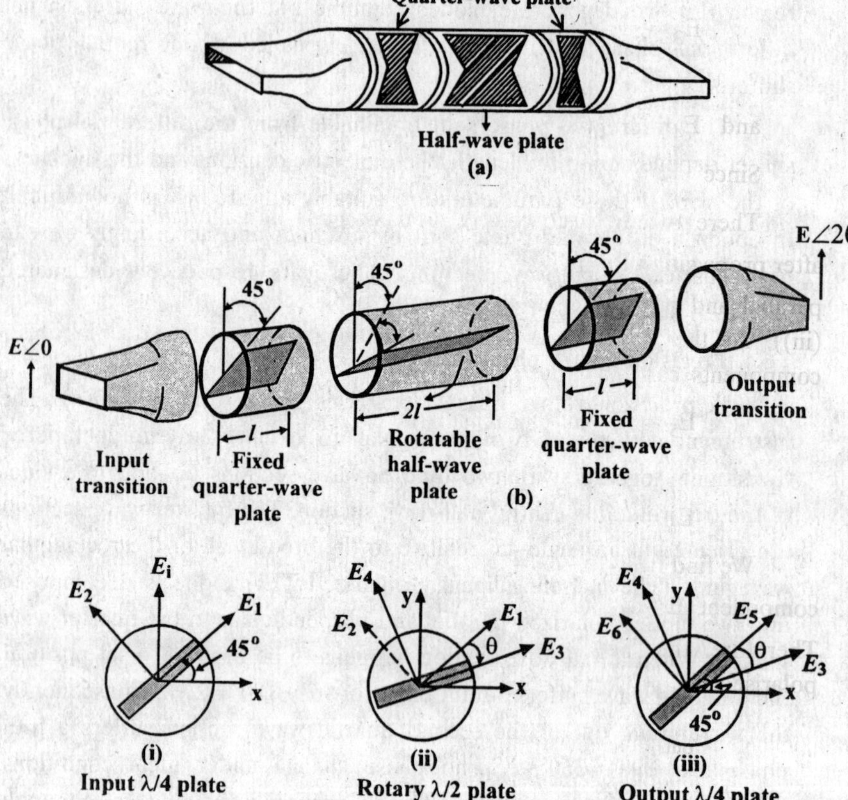

Fig. 4.19. Precision rotary phase shifter : (a) compact form; (b) component form (c) vector-phasor.

where $E_0 = \frac{E_1}{\sqrt{2}}$. The length l is adjusted such that these two components will have equal magnitude but a differential phase chang of $(\beta_1 - \beta_2)l = 90°$. Thus, after propagation through the quarterwave plate these two field components become

$$E_1 = E_0 e^{-j\beta_2 l}$$

$$E_2 = jE_0 e^{-j\beta_2 l} = -jE_1 = E_1 e^{j\pi/2} \quad ....(4.6.4)$$

We note that the quarterwave section convest a linearly polarized TE_{11} wave to a circularly polarised wave and vice-versa,

After propagation through half wave plate the field components parallel and perpendicular to the half wave plate are as (Fig. 4.19. c(ii)).

$$E_3 = (E_1 \cos\theta - E_2 \sin\theta)\, e^{-j2\beta_1 l} = E_0 e^{-j\theta} e^{-j3\beta_1 l} \quad ....(4.6.5)$$

and $E_4 = (E_2 \cos\theta + E_1 \sin\theta)\, e^{-j2\beta_2 l} = E_0 e^{-j\theta} e^{-3\beta_1 l}\, e^{-j\pi/2}$

Since $2(\beta_1 - \beta_2)\, l = \pi$ or $-2\beta_2 l = (\pi - 2\beta_1 l)$

There two field components (E_3 and E_4) are again decomposed after propagation through half-wave plate into two TE_{11} modes, polarised parallel and perpendicular to the output quarterwave plate (Fig. 4.19c (iii)). At the output end of this quarterwave plate, the decompose components can be written as

$$E_5 = (E_3 \cos\theta + E_4 \sin\theta)\, e^{-j\beta_1 l} = E_o\, e^{-j2\theta}\, e^{-j4\beta_1 l} \quad ....(4.6.6)$$

$$E_6 = (E_4 \cos\theta - E_3 \sin\theta)\, e^{-j\beta_2 l} = E_o\, e^{-j2\theta}\, e^{-j4\beta_1 l}$$

We find from Eq. 4.6.6 that parallel component E_5 = perpendicular component E_6 at the output end in magnitude as well as in phase. Therefore, these two will produce a resultant field which in liniarly polarised TE_{11} wave

$$E_{out} = \sqrt{2}\, E_0\, e^{-j2\theta}\, e^{-j4\beta_1 l}$$

$$= E_i e^{-j2\theta}\, e^{-j4\beta_1 l} \quad ....(4.6.7)$$

Which has the same direction of polarisation as the incident field E_1 with a phase charge of $(2\theta + 4\beta_1 l)$. At a given frequency and structure θ can be varied and $4\beta_1 l$ in fixed, a phase shift of 2θ can be obtained by rotating the halfwave plate precisely through an angle θ with respect to the quarter wave plate.

The simple dependence of the phase change on a mechanical rotation may be used to calibrate the phase changer precisely and is the chief advantage of the rotary phase changer.

4.7. Microwave Junctions – E and H Plane Waveguide Tees

Waveguide junctions play an important role in microwave techniques. Most commonly used are *E*-plane or series tee, *H*-plane or shunt tee, and combination of the two, that is hybrid or magic tee. These junctions are used to split the line power into two or combine

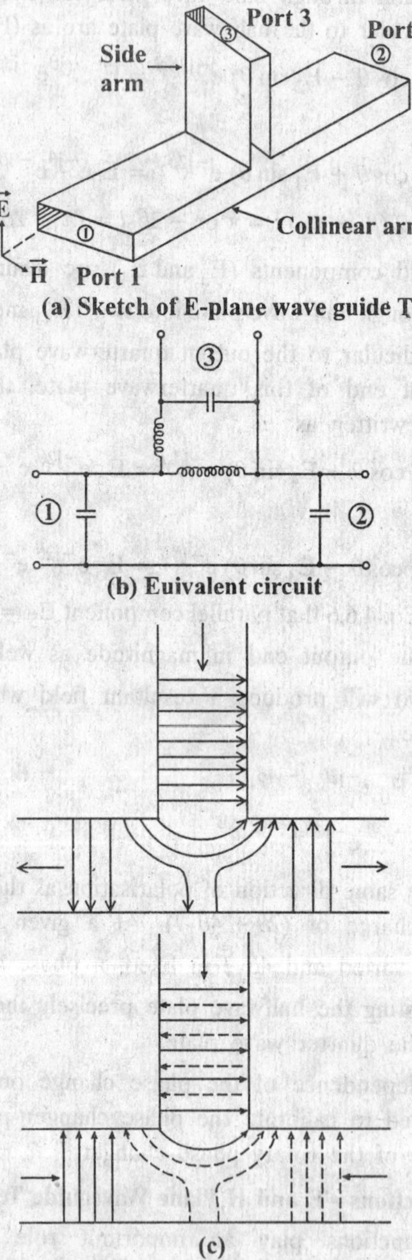

Fig. 4.20. E-plance waveguide T-junction (a) sketch (b) equialent circuit (c) coupling of power of fields.

In this section E and H-plane tees are described and their properties discussed.

4.7.1. Waveguide E-plane tee

Figures 4.20a and 4.20b respectively show the sketch of the E-plane tee and its equivalent circuit. It is clear from the sketch of the E-plane tee that an auxiliary waveguide arm (E-arm or arm 3) is fastened to the broader wall of the main guide (arms 1 and 2). Thus it is also a three-port device in which the auxiliary arm axis is parallel to the plane of the electric fields of the main guide and the coupling from the main guide to the auxiliary guide (E-arm) is by means of electric fields. Therefore, it is also known as E-plane tee. From Fig. 4.20(a) and 4.20(b), it is clear that it causes load connected to its branches to appear in series. So it is often referred to as a series tee.

As indicated in Fig. 4.20a, and 4.20b, the two main guide arms are symmetrical with respect to the auxiliary guide arm. As such if power is fed from the auxiliary arm (E-ram), it is equally distributed in the two arms 1 and 2 (Fig. 4.20c). when they are terminated in equal loads. However, as depicted in the field configuration (Fig. 4.20c), the power flowing out in arm 1 is 180° out of phase to the one in arm 2. As such this tee is known as 'subtracter' or 'differencer'.

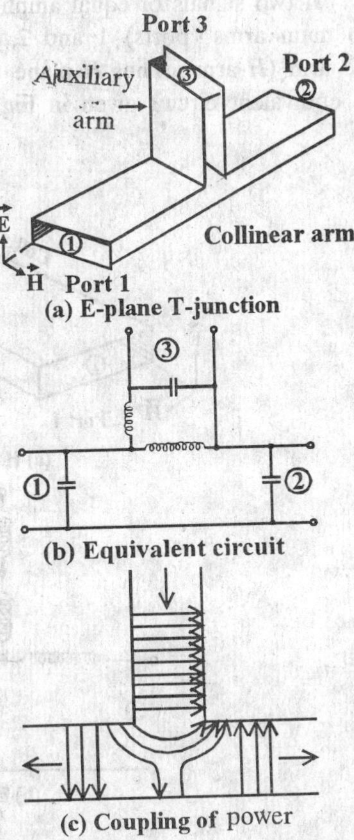

Fig. 4.20. E**-Plane** T**-junction**

4.7.2. Waveguide H-plane tee

Figure 4.21(a) shows the sketch of an H-plane tee. It is clear from the sketch that an auxiliary waveguide arm (H-arm or arm 3) is fastened perpendicular to the narrow wall of a main guide (arms 1 and 2), thus it is a three-port device in which axis of the auxiliary or side arm is parallel to the planes of the magnetic field of the mian guide and the coupling from the main guide to the branch guide (arm 3) is by means of magnetic fields. Therefore, it is also known as H-plane tee.

The perpendicular arm (H-arm) is generally taken as input and other two arms are in shunt to the input and hence it is also called as shunt tee. Because of symmetry of the tee [see Fig. 4.21(b); equivalent circuit of H-plane tee], when power enters the auxiliary arm (H-arm), and the two main arms 1 and 2 are terminated in identical loads, the power supplied to each load is equal and in phase with one another.

If two signals of equal amplitude and in same phase are fed into two main arms (ports) 1 and 2, they will be added together in the side arm (H-arm). Thus H-plane tee is an 'adder'. This is clear from the equivalent circuit given in Fig. 4.21(b).

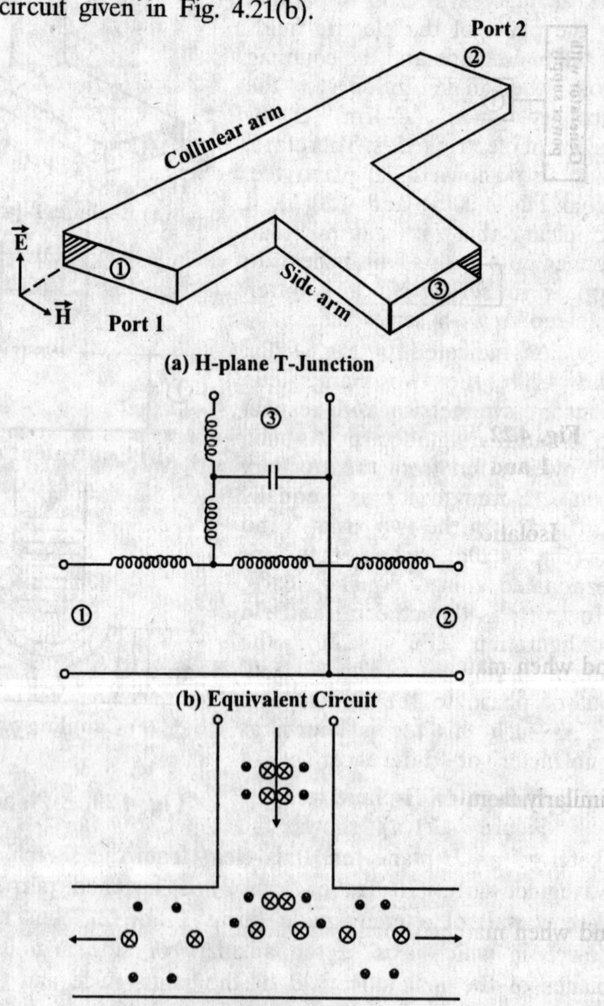

Fig. 4.21. ***H*-Plane waveguide *T*-junction :**

4.7.3. Characteristic parameters

(a) Isolation

The isolation of a *T*-junction is the ratio of power supplied from a matched generator to one of the arms, to the power coupled to a matched detector in any other arm when the remaining arm is terminated in a matched load.

From Fig. 4.22(a)

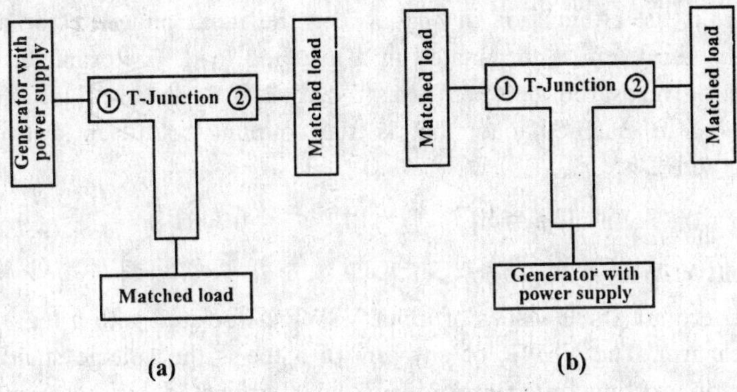

Fig. 4.22. Terminated *T*-junction (a) generator at the input port 1 and matched detector at the port 2; (b) generator at the coupled port 3 and matched detector at port 1.

Isolation between port 1 and 2 is

$$I_{12} = 10 \log_{10} \frac{P_1}{P_2} \text{ dB} \qquad \text{....(4.7.1,a)}$$

and when matched load and detector are interchanged,

$$I_{13} = 10 \log_{10} \frac{P_1}{P_2} \text{ dB} \qquad \text{....(4.7.1,b)}$$

Similarly from Fig. 4.22(b)

$$I_{31} = 10 \log_{10} \frac{P_3}{P_1} \text{ dB} \qquad \text{....(4.7.1,c)}$$

and when matched load and detector are interchanged,

$$I_{32} = 10 \log_{10} \frac{P_3}{P_2} \text{ dB} \qquad \text{....(4.7.1,c)}$$

When arm 2 becomes the input, we will have other two values of isolation, *i.e.*, I_{21} and I_{23}. Due to reciprocity property, I_{21} will be the same as I_{12}. Therefore, we shall measure only the first four isolation coefficients.

(b) Coupling coefficient

Corresponding to the values of isolation, we can compute the coupling coefficients by the formula

$$C = 10^{-\propto/20} \qquad \text{....(4.7.2,a)}$$

where α is the attenuation in *db* between the input and detector arm when the third arm is terminated in a matched load. For example, the attenuation measured between arms 1 and 2 is 2 db when arm 3 is terminated in matched load, that is, the coupling coefficient between arms 1 and 2,

$$C_{12} = 10^{-\alpha/20} = 10^{-3/20} = 0.708 \text{ dB} \qquad \text{....(4.7.2,b)}$$

(c) Input VSWR

There are three values of input VSWR associated with a tee, one for each arm. The VSWR of any arm of a tee is the voltage standing wave ratio existing on a transmission line terminated by that arm of the tee when the other two arms of the tee are terminated in matched loads.

For the experimental study of these parameters reader is referred to literature*.

4.7.4. Scattering matrix for tee junction

Tee is a three-port device, so the scattering matrix, in general, be written as

$$[S] = \begin{bmatrix} S_{11} & S_{12} & S_{13} \\ S_{21} & S_{22} & S_{23} \\ S_{31} & S_{32} & S_{33} \end{bmatrix} \qquad \text{....(4.7.3)}$$

Since $[S]$ is symmetric, we have

$$S_{12} = S_{21},\ S_{13} = S_{31},\ S_{23} = S_{32}$$

and more ever tee is symmetric about port 1 and 2 (symmetric arms)

Sisodia, M.L., and G.S. Reghuvansi : **Basic Microwave Technique and Laboratory Manual,** New Age International (P) Limited, Publishers, New Delhi, 2000.

$$S_{11} = S_{22}$$

Using these properties of Tee junction Eq. 4.7.3 would become

$$[S] = \begin{bmatrix} S_{11} & S_{12} & S_{13} \\ S_{12} & S_{11} & S_{23} \\ S_{13} & S_{23} & S_{33} \end{bmatrix} \quad \text{....(4.7.4)}$$

E-plane tee—When the input is fed from side arm (Port 3), the wave appearing at the two ports 1 and 2 of collinear arm will be opposite in phase and in the same magnitude, that is

$$S_{13} = -S_{23} \quad \text{....(4.7.5)}$$

However, it does not mean that S_{13} is always positive and S_{23} is always negative.

S-matrix will be

$$[S] = \begin{bmatrix} S_{11} & S_{12} & S_{13} \\ S_{12} & S_{11} & -S_{13} \\ S_{13} & -S_{13} & S_{33} \end{bmatrix} \quad \text{....(4.7.6)}$$

H-Plane Tee—When the input is fed from side arm (port 3), the wave appearing at the two ports 1 and 2 of collinear arm will be in phase and in the same magnitude, that

$$S_{13} = S_{23}$$

Thus its [S] matrix is written as

$$[S] = \begin{bmatrix} S_{11} & S_{12} & S_{13} \\ S_{12} & S_{11} & S_{13} \\ S_{13} & S_{13} & S_{33} \end{bmatrix} \quad \text{....(4.7.7)}$$

We note that (for both *E* and *H*-plane tees) from purely isotsrpy and symmetry properties, the number of unknown scattering coefficients reduced to four.

If we assume

$$S_{11} = \alpha, S_{13} = \gamma, S_{12} = \delta, S_{33} = \beta$$

Hence scattering matrix for E-plane tee (Eq. 4.7.6) can be written as

$$[S] = \begin{bmatrix} \alpha & \delta & \gamma \\ \delta & \alpha & -\gamma \\ \gamma & -\gamma & \beta \end{bmatrix} \quad \text{....(4.7.8)}$$

and for H-plane Tee (Eq. 4.7.7) can written as

$$[S] = \begin{bmatrix} \alpha & \delta & \gamma \\ \delta & \alpha & \gamma \\ \gamma & \gamma & \beta \end{bmatrix} \quad ....(4.7.9)$$

Further these devices are loss-less hence $[S]$ must be **unitary.**

4.8. Hybrid Tee (Magic Tee)

An interesting type of T-junction is the hybrid tee, commonly known as 'magic tee', which is shown in Fig. 4.23. The device, as can

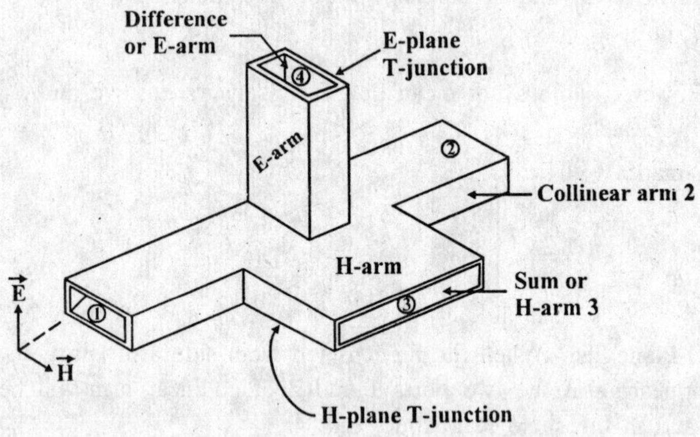

Fig. 4.23. E-H tee or magic tee.

be seen from Fig. 4.23, is a combination of the E-and H-plane tees. Arm 3, the H-arm, forms an H-plane tee and arm 4, the E-arm, forms an E-plane tee in combination with arms 1 and 2. The central lines of thet two tees coincide and define the plane of symmetry, that is, if arms 1 and 2 are of equal length, the part of structure on one side of the symmetry plane shown by shaded area in Fig. 4.24a is the mirror image of that on the other. Arms 1 and 2 are sometimes called as the side or collinear arms.

4.8.1. Magic of the magic tee

The name 'magic tee' is derived from the manner in which power divides among various arms. If power is fed into arm 3 (H-arm), the electric field divides equally between arms 1 and 2 as shown in Fig. 4.24b and the fields are in phase. Because of symmerty of the T-junction, no net electric field parallel to the narrow dimension of the waveguide is excited in arm 4. (Required to propagate power in the TE_{10} dominant mode). Thus no power is coupled in port 4. Reciprocity demands no coupling in port 3 (*H*-arm) if power is fed in 4 (*E*-arm).

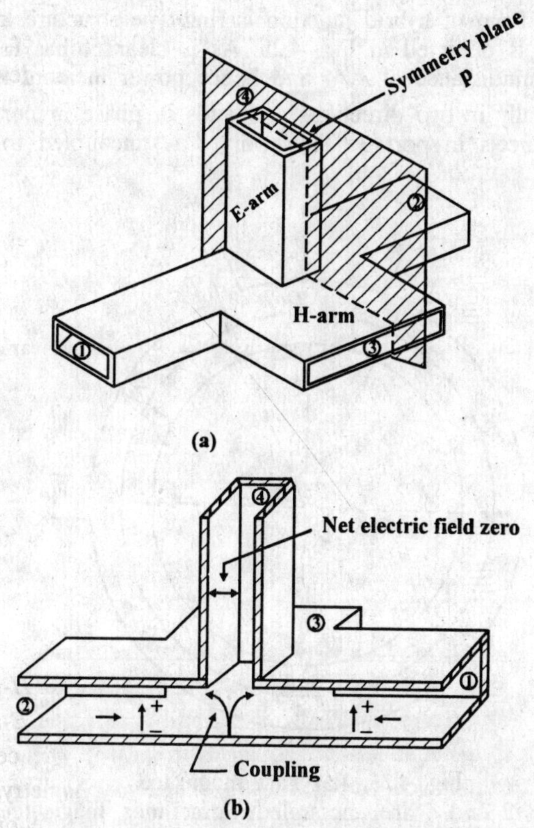

Fig. 4.24. (a) Symmetry plane shown by shaded area, (b) Cutway rear view of a waveguide E-H tee.

Another property that results from the symmetry of the junction is, if power is fed in *E*- or H-arm, it is equally divided between arms 1 and 2.

Further, magic tee being combination of *E*- and *H*-plane tees, if power is fed from arms 1 and 2, it is added in *H*-arm (3) while it is subtracted in *E*-arm (4).

A simple *E*-*H* tee has disadvantage of not being matched when seen from *E*- and *H*-arms when side arms are terminated in matched loads. The VSWR being > 2 (generally), the most commonly used method to reduce VSWR is to introduce discontinuity such as port iris in or near *T*-junction to cancel out reflections occurring therein.

4.8.2. Rat race

Another from of hybrid junction is ring-type structure known as 'rat race' and is depicted in Fig. 4.25. As is clear, it has four ports each at a circumdistance of $\lambda_g/4$ and hence power incident in port 1 is divided equally in two directions and adds in phase in ports 2 and 4, while it cancels in port 3. Thus port 3 is uncoupled to port 1.

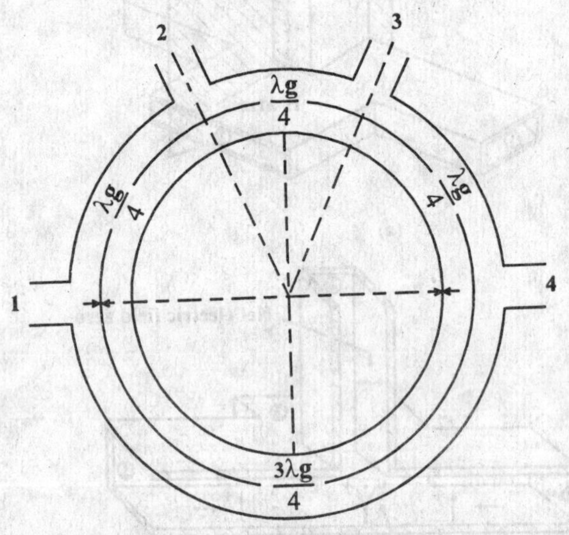

Fig. 4.25. Rat race magic tee.

Similarly, ports 2 and 4 are uncoupled. Sometimes, magic tee is used in mixer, frequency discriminator circuits, etc.

4.8.3. Magic tee parameters

The basic properties of a magic tee are defined as follows :

(a) Input VSWR

Corresponding to each port of a magic tee as load to the line, there is a value of VSWR. Thus there are four values of VSWR. As in Chapter 2, VSWR is defined as the ratio of maximum voltage to minimum voltage of the standing waves existing on the line when one port of the tee terminates the line while other three ports are terminated in matched loads.

(b) Isolation

The isolation between *E*- and *H*-arms is defined as the ratio of the power supplied by the matched generator connected to *E*-arm (port 4), to the power detected in *H*-arm (port 3) by a matched detector when collinear arms (1 and 2) are terminated in matched loads. It is expressed in db.

$$I_{34} = 10 \log_{10} \frac{P_4}{P_3}.$$

P_4 : Power incident in port 4 (*E*-arm)

P_3 : Power detected in port 3 (*H*-arm)

Similarly isolation between other ports may also be defined and measured.

(c) Coupling coefficient

The voltage coupling coefficient from *i* to arm *j* is defined as

$$C_{ij} = 10^{-\alpha/20}$$

where α is the attenuation in dB when *i* is the input and *j* the output arm.

Thus

$$\alpha \text{ (dB)} = 10 \log \frac{P_i}{P_j}$$

where P_i is the power delivered to *i*-arm by a matched generator and P_j is the power detected by a matched detector in arm *j*.

In the case of magic tee, there are 12 coupling constants, one for each of the arms as an input to each of the other three arms as an output. However, if we have a perfectly matched detector and generator, $C_{ij} = C_{ji}$ and also the reciprocity desires $C_{12} = C_{21}$, $C_{32} = C_{31}$ and $C_{41} = C_{42}$.

For the study of these parameters reader is referred to literature.*

*1. SISODIA, M.L., and G.S. Raghuvanshi, **Basic Microwave Techniques and Laboratory Manual**, New Age International (P) Limited, Publishers, New Delhi, 2000 (2nd reprint).

2. SISODIA, M.L., and G.S. Raghuvanshi, **Microwave Circuits and passive devies**, New Age International (P) Limited, Publisher, New Delhi, 2001 (4th reprint).

3. Altman, J.L., **Microwaves circuits**, D. Van Nostrand Company, Inc., 1964.

Applications :

A magic tee is frequently employed in various microwave circuits, such as impedance bridge, the *E-H* tuner for impedance matching, antenna duplexer, balance mixes in microwave super-heterodyne receiver to balance phase detector, frequency discriminator, modulator etc. Detail discussion may be found in the literature*. Few of these applications are described in section 4.8.5.

4.8.4. Scattering matrix for hybrid tee

A hybrid tee is a four-port device, so in general [*S*] matrix is

$$[S] = \begin{bmatrix} S_{11} & S_{12} & S_{13} & S_{14} \\ S_{21} & S_{22} & S_{23} & S_{24} \\ S_{31} & S_{32} & S_{33} & S_{34} \\ S_{41} & S_{42} & S_{43} & S_{44} \end{bmatrix} \qquad \text{....(4.8.1)}$$

Assuming the tee to be loss-less and medium inside to be isotropic, the symmetry of the tee requires

$$S_{12} = S_{21},\ S_{13} = S_{31},\ S_{14} = S_{41},$$
$$S_{23} = S_{32},\ S_{24} = S_{42},\ S_{34} = S_{43} \ldots\ldots\ldots$$

Thus,

$$[S] = \begin{bmatrix} S_{11} & S_{12} & S_{13} & S_{14} \\ S_{12} & S_{22} & S_{23} & S_{24} \\ S_{13} & S_{23} & S_{33} & S_{34} \\ S_{14} & S_{24} & S_{34} & S_{44} \end{bmatrix} \qquad \text{....(4.8.2)}$$

Since the magic tee is symmetrical about plane *P* as shown in Fig. 4.24a, arms 1 and 2 are mirror images of one another with respect to this plane. Moreover, the boundary conditions which are to be satisfied by the electric field are also the same. It, therefore, follows from the uniqueness theorem* that the electric field distribution in arms 1 and 2 must be identical. Hence, the electric coupling from arms 3 to arm 1 and from arm 3 to arm 2 must be identical.

$$S_{13} = S_{23} \qquad \text{....(4.8.3)}$$

If power is fed in port 4, *i.e.* *E*-arm, it divides antisymmetrically in arms 1 and 2, *i.e.* the electric field in these arms is equal in magnitude

---

* The solution of Maxwell's equations under given boundary conditions is unique
Montgomery, G.C., R.H. Dicke, E.M. Purcell : **Principles of Microwave Circuits,** McGraw-Hill Book Co. 1948.

but π radians or 180° is out of phase as illustrated in Fig. 4.26. It, therefore, follows that coupling coefficients from 1 to 4 and 2 to 4 are equal in magnitude and opposite in phase, that is

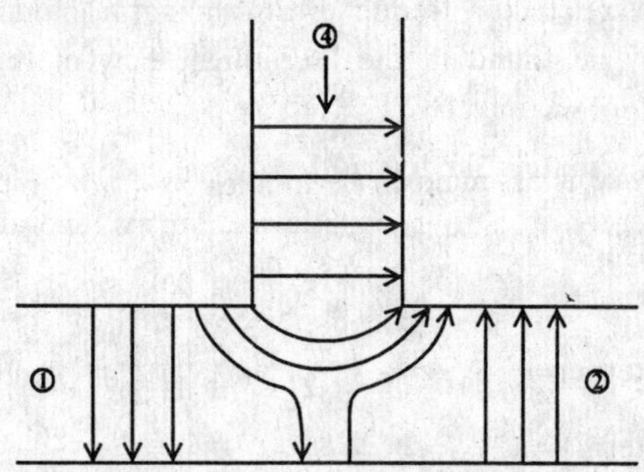

Fig. 4.26. Power incident in port 4 of magic tee is divided into equal and out of π phase powers in ports 1 and 2.

$$S_{14} = -S_{24} \quad \text{....(4.8.4)}$$

The symmetry of the magic tee, looking into port 1, with all other ports matched terminated, is equivalent to looking into port 2, with all other ports matched terminated. Hence

$$S_{11} = S_{22} \quad \text{....(4.8.4)}$$

Moreover, ports 3 and 4 are uncoupled because of cross-polarizations of the electric field.

$$S_{34} = 0 \quad \text{....(4.8.5)}$$

Using Eqs. 4.8.3 through 4.8.5, Eq. 4.8.2 can be reduced to

$$[S] = \begin{bmatrix} S_{11} & S_{12} & S_{13} & S_{14} \\ S_{12} & S_{11} & S_{13} & -S_{14} \\ S_{13} & S_{13} & S_{33} & 0 \\ S_{14} & -S_{14} & 0 & S_{44} \end{bmatrix} \quad \text{....(4.8.6)}$$

Equation 4.8.6 is the scattering matrix of any symmetrical, 4 port tee of the form shown in Fig. 4.24,a. It does not matter what is inside the junction provided it is symmetrical and propagates the TE_{10} mode. However, in practice, the device is made more useful by making ports 3 and 4 well-matched, *i.e.*

$$S_{33} = S_{44} = 0. \quad \text{....(4.8.7)}$$

This can be done by having a proper choice of the reference planes on ports 3 and 4. Using Eq. 4.8.7 in Eq. 4.8.6, we obtain

$$[S] = \begin{bmatrix} S_{11} & S_{12} & S_{13} & S_{14} \\ S_{12} & S_{11} & S_{13} & -S_{14} \\ S_{13} & S_{13} & 0 & 0 \\ S_{14} & -S_{14} & 0 & 0 \end{bmatrix} \qquad \text{....(4.8.8)}$$

Since the device is assumed to be loss-less,

$$[S]\,[S]^* = [1].$$

whose

$$(1,\ 1)\ \text{term} = |S_{11}|^2 + |S_{12}|^2 + |S_{13}|^2 + |S_{14}|^2 = 1 \qquad \text{....(4.8.9,a)}$$

$$(3,\ 3)\ \text{term} = 2\,|S_{13}|^2 = 1 \qquad \text{....(4.8.9,b)}$$

$$(4,\ 4)\ \text{term} = 2\,|S_{14}|^2 = 1. \qquad \text{....(4.8.9,c)}$$

From Eqs. 4.8.9b and 4.8.9c, we have respectively,

$$S_{13} = \frac{1}{\sqrt{2}}\, e^{j\phi} \text{ and } S_{14} = \frac{1}{\sqrt{2}}\, e^{j\phi} \qquad \text{....(4.8.10)}$$

Phases ϕ and ψ in Eq. 4.8.10 are the choices of the reference planes and can be made each equal to zero, *i.e.*, $\phi = \psi = 0$. It then follows from Eq. 4.8.9a and 4.8.10, that

$$S_{11} = S_{12} = 0 \qquad \text{....(4.8.11)}$$

because each of $|S_{11}|^2$ and $|S_{12}|^2$ is positive or zero.

Therefore, using Eqs. 4.8.10 and Eq. 4.8.11, Eq. 4.8.8 can be reduced to

$$[S] = \frac{1}{\sqrt{2}} \begin{bmatrix} 0 & 0 & 1 & 1 \\ 0 & 0 & 1 & -1 \\ 1 & 1 & 0 & 0 \\ 1 & -1 & 0 & 0 \end{bmatrix} \qquad \text{....(4.8.12)}$$

This equation is used to describe hybrid tee with various terminal conditions such as the ports of the tee are well matched, the ports of the tee are not necessarily matched etc.

4.8.5. APPLICATIONS OF THE MAGIC TEE

Impedance Bridges

A magic tee is frequently employed in microwave impedance measuring bridges. These bridges are similar to low frequency wheatstone bridges. Figure 4.27 depicts a typical microwave impedance bridge designed by utilizing a magic tee. Power from a matched source is fed in the *H*-arm (3) of the magic tee. A standard variable impedance is connected to port 1 as reference impedance and arm 2 is terminated in the impedance to be measured. A matched detector is connected to port 4 (*E*-arm) to receive power reflected from arms 1 and 2. These powers will be out of 180° phase.

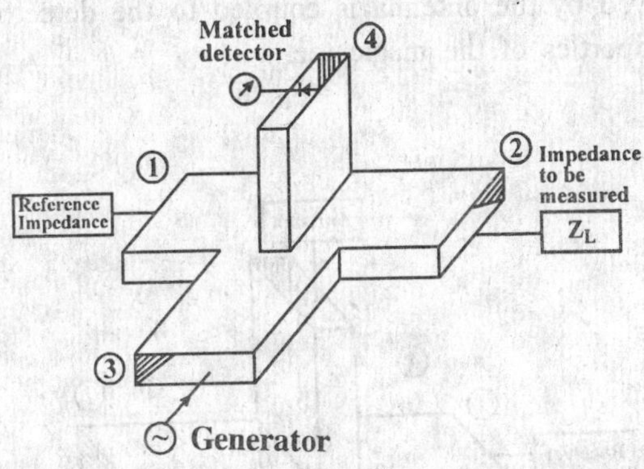

Fig. 4.27. Impedance bridge using magic tee

The reference impedance is adjusted so as to have no signal in the detector. Under this condition the power reflected from the reference impedance and reaching the detector (half of the reflected power) equals the power reflected from the unknown impedance reaching the detector. Because the two powers are out of 180° phase and the lengths of the two ports are equal (or in other words, when the bridge is balanced), then

$$\Gamma_P = \Gamma_\Lambda$$

or
$$\frac{Z_R - 1}{Z_R + 1} = \frac{Z_L - 1}{Z_L + 1}$$

Γ_P and Z_R are respectively the reflection coefficient and normalized impedance for the reference impedance whereas Γ_Λ and Z_L are the respective quantities for the given unknown impedance. The above equation may be used to determine Z_L in terms of Z_R.

Antenna Duplexer

A duplexer system couples two circuits to the same load but avoids mutual coupling. A typical duplexing system is depicted in Fig. 4.28. The same antenna is used for the transmitter as well as receiver but the transmitter power is kept out of the receiver and vice-versa. In this system the matched generator and matched detector are connected to arms 1 and 2 respectively. H-arm (3) is terminated in a matched load and E-arm (4) is connected to the matched antenna. In this case, power received by the antenna is coupled to the detector due to the coupling properties of the magic tee.

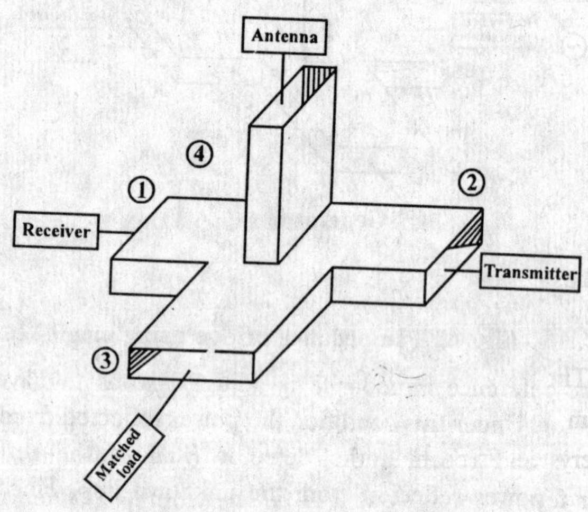

Fig. 4.28. Magic Tee-antenna duplexer system

In this *tee*, since half of the power is transmitted, it is useful at low power levels.

Balanced Mixer

A balanced microwave mixer is used in superhetrodyne receivers to balance out the local oscillator noise at the input of the intermediate frequency (*i.f.*) amplifier. Figure 4.29 depicts a typical arrangement for *i.f.* frequencies 1 to 100 MHz. The superhetrodyne mixer receives signals from both the antenna and the local oscillator of the receiver but the local oscillator power is prevented from reaching the antenna by the isolation properties of E and H-arms.

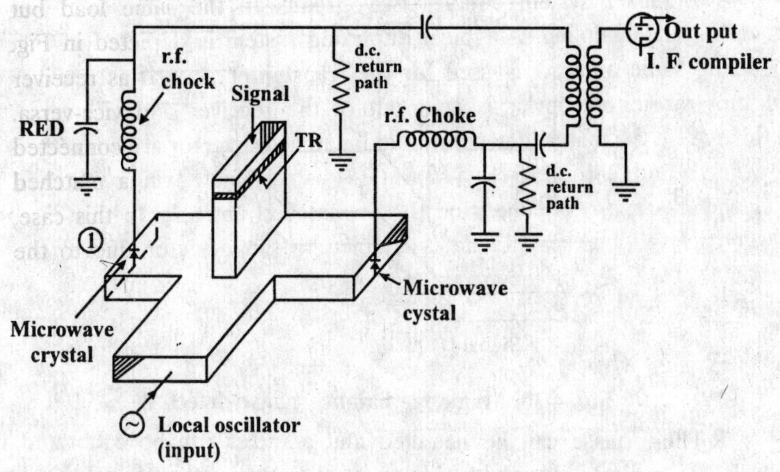

Fig. 4.29. Magic tee balanced mixer

Balanced Phase Detector

Figure 4.30 shows a balanced phase detection system utilizing a magic tee. The two signals whose relative phase has to be detected, are fed from the *E*- and *H*-arms. The powers detected by matched microwave crystals at ports 1 and 2 are fed to the differential amplifier. If the power fed at ports 1 and 2 is equal, *i.e.*, $a_3 = a_4$, then the output power recorded by the differential amplifier will be

$$P_{output} = G\left[\left\{\frac{1}{\sqrt{2}}(a_3 + a_4)\right\}^2 - \left\{\frac{1}{\sqrt{2}}(a_3 - a_4)\right\}^2\right]$$

G being the amplifier gain factor. Now, if there is a phase relation $a_4 = a_3 e^{j\theta}$, then

$$P_{output} = G\,(\cos^2\theta/2 - \sin^2\theta/2)$$

$$= G\cos\theta.$$

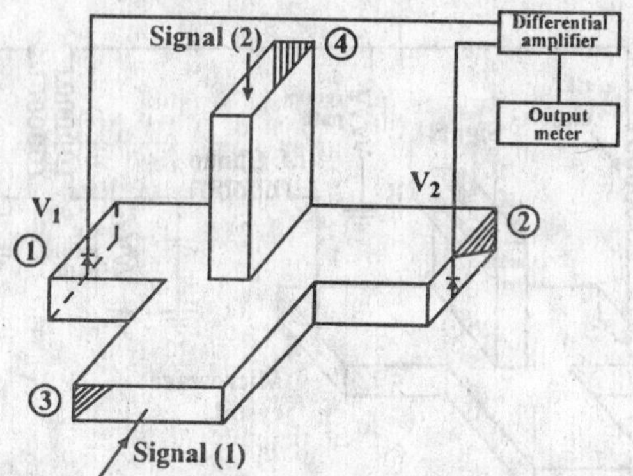

Fig. 4.30. Magic tee balance phase-detector.

Thus, phase can be detected and a meter can be calibrated in cos θ to indicate the phase difference directly on the scale.

4.9. Directional Coupler

A directional coupler is a useful hybrid waveguide joint which couples power in an auxiliary waveguide arm in one direction. It is a four-port device but one of the ports is terminated into a matched load. To understand its operation we consider the block diagram in Fig. 4.31.

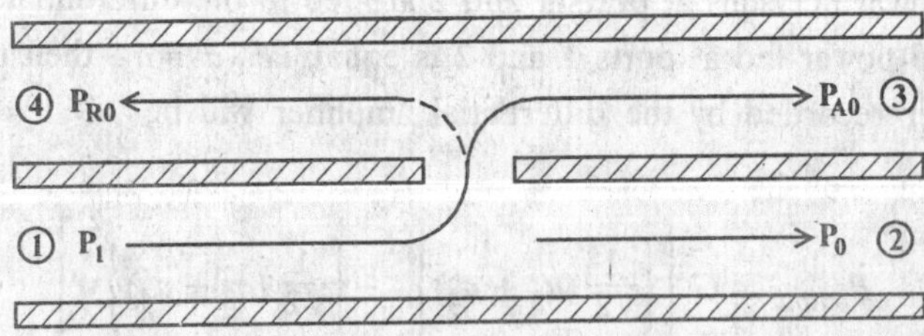

Fig. 4.31. Power coupling in a directional coupler.

(i) If power is fed into port (1), the power is coupled in ports (2) and (3), *i.e.*, power flows in the forward direction of the auxiliary arm port (3) but no power couples in port (4), *i.e.*, in backward direction. Similarly power fed in (2) couples into ports (1) and (4) and not in (3).

(ii) All the four ports are matched, *i.e.*, if three of them are terminated in matched loads, the fourth is automatically terminated in a matched load.

(iii) If power couples in reverse direction, *i.e.*, power fed in (1) appears in ports (2) and (4) and nothing in (3), then such type of coupler is known as backward *directional coupler*. The conclusion is that in the auxiliary section the power is coupled in only one direction.

4.9.1. Directivity and coupling of a directional coupler

The characteristics of directional couplers are expressed in two parameters namely *directivity* and *coupling* defined as follows :

(a) Directivity (D) of a directional coupler is defined as the ratio, expressed in decibels, of the power output in the coupled auxiliary arm to the power flowing in uncoupled auxiliary arm. Theoretically, D should be infinite because no power should couple in arm 4.

(b) Coupling factor or coupling (C) is defined as the ratio, expressed in decibels, of the power (entering) at input of the main line to the power coupled at the output in the auxiliary arm.

The high value of C is desired. Both the parameters are frequency-dependent. Hence, to have a wide-band directional coupler, ideal conditions cannot be achieved. However, total directivity of the signal, in addition to frequency, depends upon reflections from internal termination, intrinsic directivity and reflections from the output flange.

4.9.2. Types of couplers

There are a variety of ways in which auxiliary arm may be coupled to the main guide to have a directional coupler. The most common are the aperture-coupled besed on Bathe hole theory. We will discuss here some of them in brief.

(a) Bethe-hole coupler (Single hole)

This type of directional coupler consists of two rectangular waveguides coupled by means of a circular aperture located at the centre of the common broad wall. To achieve directional coupling, the axes of the two waveguides are inclined at an angle $\theta°$ (Fig. 4.32a), determined by frequency and the dimension of the hole. If θ is zero then the hole is to be taken offset and not at the centre. This construction may be understood by considering TE_{10} mode incident on port (1).

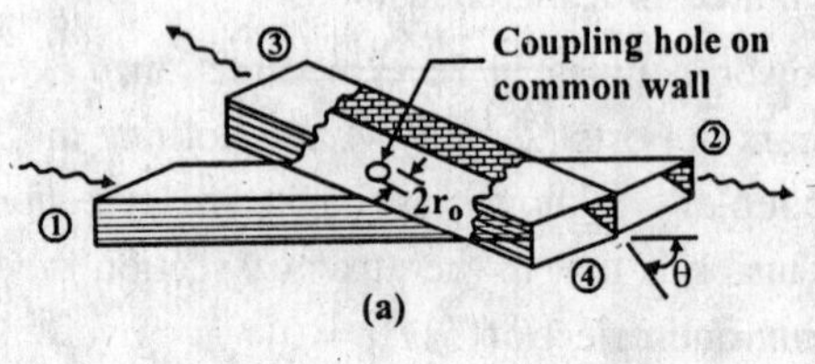

(a)

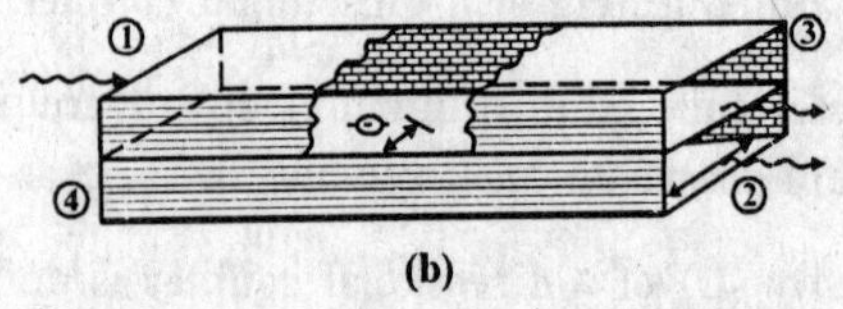

(b)

Fig. 4.32. Bethe single hole coupler
(a) cross-guide coupler (b) off set coupler

This produces a normal electrical dipole in the aperture plus a tangential magnetic dipole, whose direction is the same as that of the incident wave and magnitude is proportional to the incident wave strength. Now, in the auxiliary arm (upper waveguide) the normal electric dipole and axial component of magnetic dipole radiate symmetrically in both the directions but the transverse component of magnetic dipole radiates antisymmetrically, so proper adjustment of the axes of two waveguides at an angle θ causes the complete cancellation of backward power in the auxiliary arm. This cancellation may also be achieved by offsetting the hole as shown in Fig. 4.32b.

By varying the angle θ between the two waveguides or by changing the distance *d* powers in port 3 and port 4 can be controlled. When the transmission take place from port 1 to port 2, the uncoupled port is called *isolated port* (power coupled = 0), however practically it is not zero. Coupling and directivity of this Bethe-hole coupler (centre hole) are given by

$$C = -20 \log \frac{4}{3} \frac{\beta r_0^3}{ab} (\cos \theta + \lambda_g^2 / 2\lambda^2) \text{ db} \quad \text{....(4.9.1)}$$

$$D = 20 \log \frac{2\beta^2 \cos \theta + k_0^2}{2\beta^2 \cos \theta - k_0^2} (\cos \theta - \lambda_g^2 / 2\lambda^2) \, dy \quad \text{....(4.9.2)}$$

Where r_0 = Radius of hole

$a \times b$ = Wave guide-cross-sectional dimension

$$\beta = 2\pi/\lambda_g$$

$$\lambda_g = \frac{\lambda_0}{[\sqrt{1-(\lambda_0/2a)^2}]}$$

and $$k_0 = 2\pi/\lambda_0.$$

The optimum angle θ (for $P_4 = 0$) is given by the relation $\cos\theta = \lambda_g^2/2\lambda_0^2$.

For the off-set hole, the optimum forward coupling ($P_4 = 0$) is obtained for the off-set value '*d*' given by

$$\sin(\pi d/a) = \frac{\lambda_g}{\sqrt{6}a}$$

The maximum coupling and directivity are :

$$C = 20 \log [(1 + x^2)/x] \quad \text{....(4.9.3)}$$

$$D = 20 \log 1/x \quad \text{....(4.9.4)}$$

where $x = (16\pi r_0^3/3ab\lambda_g) \sin^2(\pi d/a)$

In these relations the guide wall thickness is assumed negligibly small. For the derivation the reader is referred to J.L. Altman, op. cit.

(b) Double-hole or multi-hole couplers

Two-hole couplers are constructed by coupling two identical rectangular waveguides by means of two identical apertures spaced by a distance of $\lambda_g/4$, **i.e.,** quarter guide wavelength apart. In this type of coupler, as shown in Fig. 4.33a, the signal which travels back to the first hole from the second hole is 180° out of phase and so the two signals tend to cancel in the backward direction. The signals in the forward direction are in phase and hence they add together. If the distance between the holes is other than $\lambda_g/4$, the said characteristics of coupling and directivity cannot be achieved and so this type of coupler is a narrow-band coupler. It is to be noted that directivity and coupling parameters are the sums of inherent property of the single Bethe-hole and the one associated with array (two-hole array in this case).

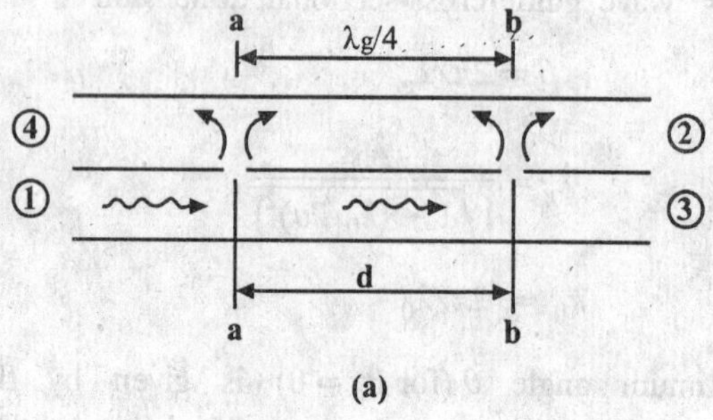

(a)

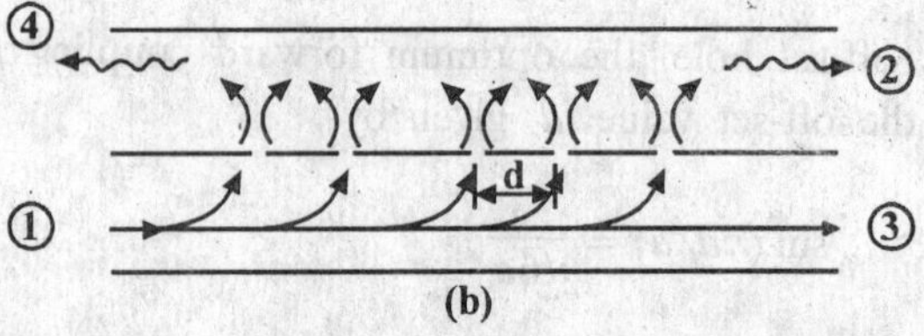

(b)

Fig. 4.33. Bethe hole coupler (a) two-hole type (b) multi-hole type.

Multi-hole couplers (Fig. 4.33b) operate on the same basic principles as two-hole coupler. The coupling array holes are each separated by a distance of $\lambda_g/4$. The hole dimensions are so varied that a wide frequency band is covered. Here coupling versus frequency variations are ±0.5 db over the entire waveguide range. The holes are drilled in the narrow side of the waveguides for high power operation.

(c) Schwinger reversed phase coupler

This coupler is designed to make directivity less dependent on frequency. To achieve this, one aperture is made to radiate a field which is in negative to the one radiated by another. This acts as a reverse coupler because fields in the auxiliary arm cancel in forward direction but are added together in the reverse direction (Fig. 4.34) Considering TE_{10} mode incident on port (1), the operation of this coupler may be explained as before.

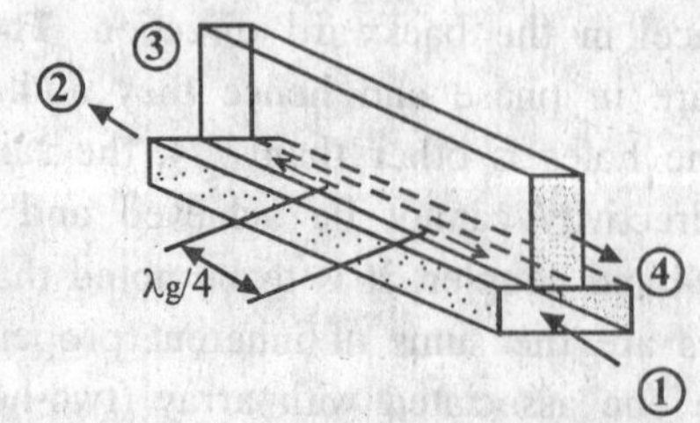

Fig. 4.34. Schwinger reversed phase coupler.

In applications where multi-hole coupler is not needed, we employ less expensive and more compact couplers as cross-guide coupler and *T*-slot coupler (Figs. 4.35 and 4.36). Although directional coupler is a four-port device, but as frequently stated earlier, one of its uncoupled arms is terminated and it is thus a three-port device as shown in Fig. 4.37.

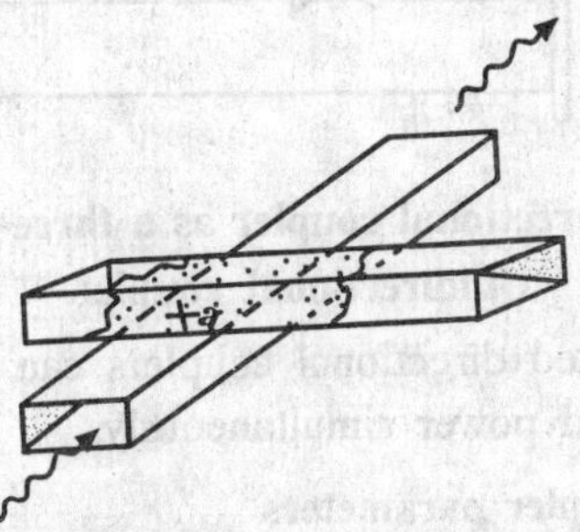

Fig. 4.35. Double aperture cross-guide coupler.

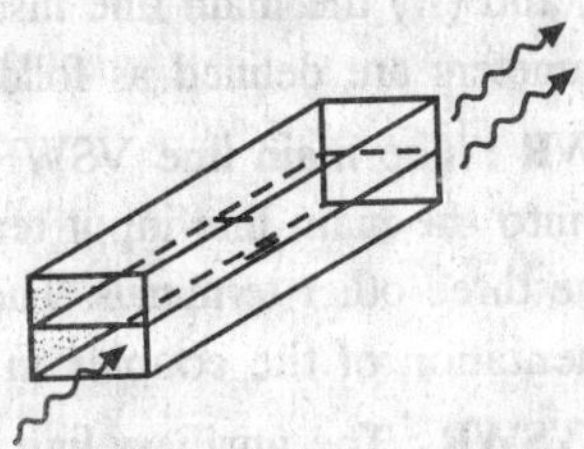

Fig. 4.36. Waveguide T-slot coupler.

Directional couplers are used in bench test set-ups in microwave systems. They are ideal for power monitoring, frequency, reflection coefficient, noise and pulse shape detection. They are also used for injecting local oscillator and coding signals into a transmission line as well as for the connection of subsidiary equipment to the line. Broad-band applications include measuring low level VSWR, tuning waveguide systems and measuring VSWR by refractometer set-ups. The cross-guide couplers find special applications in monitoring power in waveguide transmission lines, in measurement of reflections, in attenuation of power, in decoupling microwave instruments such as frequency meters, in mixing microwave signals and in measuring receiver sensitivity.

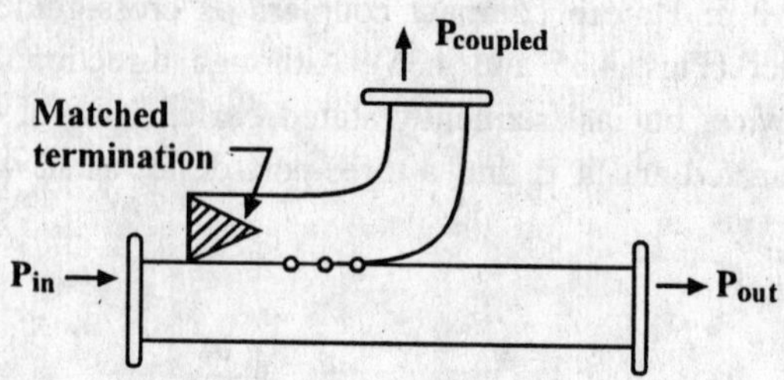

Fig. 4.37. Directional coupler as a three-port device : Unidirectional coupler.

The unterminated directional couplers can be utilized to sample incident and reflected power simultaneously.

4.9.4. Directional coupler parameters

We now study the characteristics of a directional coupler. We will measure (i) main line and auxiliary line VSWR as a function of frequency, (ii) coupling coefficient as a function of frequency, (iii) directivity as a function of frequency, and (iv) the main line insertion loss as a function of frequency. These parameters are defined as follows :

(i) Main line VSWR : The main line VSWR is the standing wave ratio measured looking into the main line input terminals when matched loads are placed at all the three other terminals. The main line VSWR will be the same for any orientation of the coupler in the transmission line.

(ii) Auxiliary line VSWR : The auxiliary line VSWR is the standing wave ratio measured in the auxiliary line looking into the output terminal to which the detector is normally connected when matched loads are placed at all the three other ports or terminals.

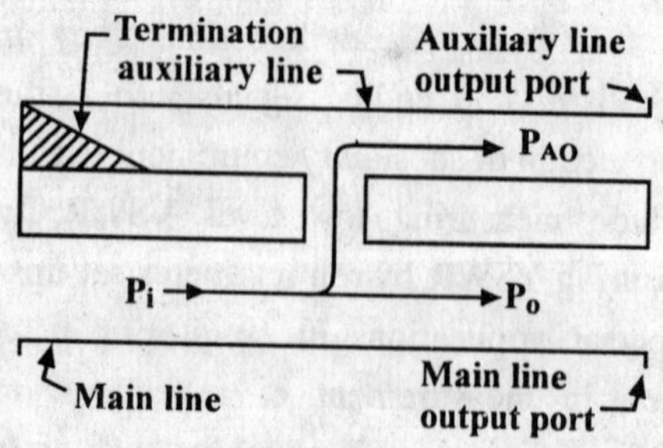

Fig. 4.38. Power coupling in a directional coupler.

(iii) Coupling : Coupling coefficient is the ratio of power supplied to the main line input (P_i) to the power outpu (P_{AO}) at the auxiliary output. The coupling coefficient C is usually expressed in decibels as a positive number. From Fig. 4.38.

$$C = 10 \log_{10} (P_i/P_{AO}) \text{dB} \quad \text{....(4.9.5)}$$

(iv) Main Line Insertion Loss : The main line insertion loss is the attenuation introduced in a transmission line by the insertion of the directional couper. The auxiliary line of the coupler is assumed to be properly terminated. Therefore, referring to Fig. 4.38, the main line insertion loss, L is given by

$$L = 10 \log_{10} \left(\frac{P_i}{P_0}\right) \text{dB} \quad \text{....(4.9.6)}$$

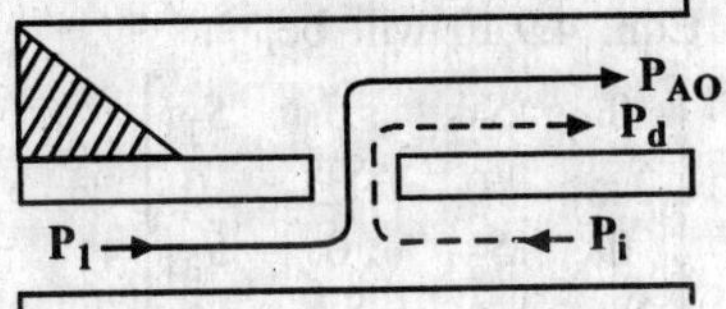

Fig. 4.39. Directivity of a directional coupler.

(v) Directivity : The directivity D is a measure of the discrimination property of a directional coupler between the waves travelling in the two directions in the main line. It is measured as the ratio of the two power outputs from the auxiliary line when a given amount of power is successively applied to each terminal of the main line. The other terminals or ports of the coupler not in use in the particular measurement are assumed to be terminated in matched loads. Referring to Fig. 4.39

$$D = 10 \log_{10} (P_{AO}/P_d) \quad (4.9.7)$$

4.9.5. S-Matrix of a directional coupler

Directional coupler is a four-port matched device so in general [S] matrices is a four by four matrix with diagonal element

$$S_{11} = S_{22} = S_{33} = S_{44} = 0$$

Thus

$$[S] = \begin{bmatrix} 0 & S_{12} & S_{13} & S_{14} \\ S_{21} & 0 & S_{23} & S_{24} \\ S_{31} & S_{32} & 0 & S_{34} \\ S_{41} & S_{42} & S_{43} & 0 \end{bmatrix} \quad \text{....(4.9.8)}$$

Morever, the device is symmetric, hence

$$S_{ij} = S_{ji} \; ; \; i \text{ and } j = 1, 2, 3, 4 \qquad \text{....(4.9.9)}$$

Using Eq. 4.9.9 in Eq. 4.9.8.

$$[S] = \begin{bmatrix} 0 & S_{12} & S_{13} & S_{14} \\ S_{12} & 0 & S_{23} & S_{24} \\ S_{13} & S_{23} & 0 & S_{34} \\ S_{14} & S_{24} & S_{34} & 0 \end{bmatrix} \qquad \text{....(4.9.10)}$$

As noted, there is no coupling between port 1 and port 4 and between port 2 and port 2 and port 3 *i.e.*, referring to Fig. 4.31, from the property of the directional coupler.

$$S_{13} = S_{31} = S_{24} = S_{42} = 0$$

Consequently Eqn. 4.9.10 will be,

$$[S] = \begin{bmatrix} 0 & S_{12} & 0 & S_{14} \\ S_{12} & 0 & S_{23} & 0 \\ 0 & S_{23} & 0 & S_{34} \\ S_{14} & 0 & S_{34} & 0 \end{bmatrix} \qquad \text{....(4.9.11)}$$

For a lossless network the S-matrix in unitary, hence

$$S_{12} S_{12}^{*} + S_{14} S_{14}^{*} = 1 \qquad \text{....(4.9.12)}$$

$$S_{12} S_{12}^{*} + S_{23} S_{23}^{*} = 1 \qquad \text{....(4.9.13)}$$

$$S_{23} S_{23}^{*} + S_{34} S_{34}^{*} = 1 \qquad \text{....(4.9.14)}$$

$$S_{14} S_{14}^{*} + S_{34} S_{34}^{*} = 1 \qquad \text{....(4.9.15)}$$

$$S_{12} S_{23}^{*} + S_{14} S_{34}^{*} = 0 \qquad \text{....(4.9.16)}$$

From the equations 4.9.12 and 4.9.13, we get

$$|S_{14}| = |S_{23}| \qquad \text{....(4.9.17)}$$

and from Eqs. 4.9.13 and 4.9.14, we get

$$|S_{12}| = |S_{34}| \qquad \text{....(4.9.18)}$$

By choosing reference plane of ports 1 with respect to that of port 2 and reference plane of port 3 with respect to that of 4, We can make S-parameters real,

$$S_{12} = S_{34} = \alpha \qquad \text{....(4.9.19)}$$

Where α is positive real number. Then from equation 4.9.16

$$\alpha\,(S_{23}^{*} + S_{14}) = 0$$

Since $\quad \alpha \neq 0, S_{23}^{*} + S_{14} = 0$ ....(4.9.20)

Now again selecting the reference plane of port 4 with respect to port 1, we can make S_{14} real, so that

$$S_{23} = -\,S_{23}^{*} = S_{14} = \beta \qquad \text{....(4.9.21)}$$

Thus $[S]$ matrix Eq. 4.9.11 may be written as

$$[S] = \begin{bmatrix} 0 & \alpha & 0 & \beta \\ \alpha & 0 & \beta & 0 \\ 0 & \beta & 0 & \alpha \\ \beta & 0 & \alpha & 0 \end{bmatrix} \qquad \text{....(4.9.22)}$$

where $\quad \alpha^2 + \beta^2 \;=\; 1$ for conservation of energy, α is called the transmission factor and β in called the coupling factor.

Coupling of such an ideal coupler is given by

$$C = -20 \log \beta \text{ dB}$$

If the coupler is not perfect the directivity is given to

$$D = 20 \log |\beta / S_{13}| \text{ dB}$$

Note that $S_{13} \;=\; 0$ for an ideal coupler.

The amount of coupling and the directivity depend upon the size and location of the hole in the common wall.

4.10. Reflectometer Techniques – Application of Directional Coupler

VSWR measurements, which indicate characteristics of termination or mismatch, play a determinant role in microwave circuitry. Point-to-point VSWR measuring systems are time-consuming even if low accuracy desired. To avoid this undesired waste of time, reflectometer techniques are used. Reflectometer is a special system which permits rapid measurement of VSWR of an unknown termination over wide frequency ranges in a few seconds.

4.10.1. Basic reflectometer technique

Since there is a direct relationship between the VSWR and the reflection coefficient of a waveguide, by measuring the ratio of relative amplitudes of reflected and incident signals, i.e., reflection coefficient,

VSWR can be measured. This constitutes the underlying principle of reflectometer techniques. The basicr eflectometer system, shown in Fig. 4.40 consists of components used to sample incident and reflected power by means of two directional couplers, connected in opposite directions. Auxiliary arms of the two directional couplers are respectively connected to the incident and reflected channels of a ratiometer via tuned identical detectors. Ratiometer directly computes the reflection coefficient and displays it on the recorder having long persistent screen. The ratiometer may also be calibrated to measure VSWR directly.

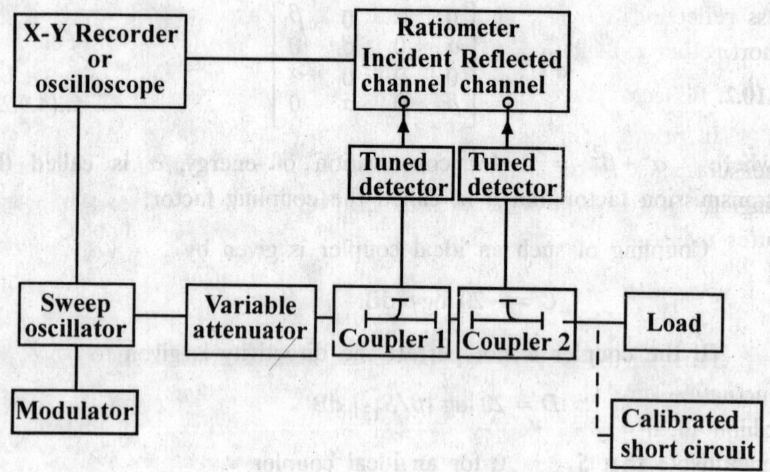

Fig. 4.40. Basic reflectometer set-up.

The sweep generator used as microwave power source is generally a 1000-cycle square wave modulated because the ratiometer is designed for operating at this frequency. The forward 20 db coupler (1) connected therein samples the incident power. The power coupled to the auxiliary arm is detected and applied to the incident channel of the ratiometer. The power coupled to the 10 db reverse coupler (2) is much small and is absorbed in the internal termination of the coupler and negligible power flows to the connected detector. The remaining power impinges on the load. If load is not a matched one, a portion of the incident power, proportional to the degree of mismatch, is reflected and travels towards the generator. The reverse 10 db coupler (2) samples the reflected power which is applied to the reflected channel of the ratiometer via tuned detector. The remaining reflected power faces 20 db coupler (1) connected in reverse direction and so power coupled is absorbed by its internal termination. A variable attenuator or a pad is generally provided to avoid overloading of the source due to reflected power. The ratiometer measures and displays the ratio of the magnitudes of reflected and incident power, which is nothing out the reflection coefficient. Since detectors follow square law in the specified range of power we are working in, so the ratiometer is calibrated to indicate square root of detected powers. dc. oscilloscope or *XY* recorder displays the power ratio, *i.e.*, power reflection coefficient. The calibration of the ratiometer is achieved by a waveguide short-circuit termination which corresponds to a 100 per cent reflecting load. Since any load will be less reflecting than the short, so taking reference level determined by short, other reflection coefficients can be obtained in db.

4.10.2. Reflectometer versus slotted line technique

In principle, the reflectometer method is superior to slotted line measurements because it measures the ratio of the two dissimilar magnitudes (incident voltage, reflected voltage) of voltages while the latter measures the ratio of nearly equal magnitudes :

$$\text{(incident voltage + reflected voltage)} \div \text{(incident voltage – reflected voltage)}.$$

Further, the slotted line measuring system is insensitive to power fluctuations and slot errors. However, because components used do not exhibit ideal characteristics, so two types of errors, *i.e.*, due to scalar quantities and vector quantities, are most common.

4.11. Microwave Ferrite Devices

4.11.1 Introduction

'Ferrite' is a generic name given to ferromagnetic (or ferrimagnetic) insulators with specific resistivity as high as 10^{14} times that of metals and with dielectric constants round 10 to 15 times or greater and relative permeabilities of several thousand. Ferrites are made by sintering a mixture of metallic oxides and have the general chemical composition M-O-Fe_2O_3, where M is a divalent metal such as Zn, Ni, Co, Mn, etc., or a mixture of these. Ferrites are transparent to electromagnetic waves. An electromagnetic ray propagating through the ferrite encounters strong interaction with spinning electrons and gives rise to desirable magnetic properties in ferrites. The paired electrons in certain materials cancel their magnetisation effects due to electrons rotating in opposite directions. However, if unpaired electrons are present, they give rise to magnetic moments and hence magnetic properties. Thus a spinning electron may be taken as a small magnetic dipole. When a magnetic field is applied, it tries to align (in addition to its rotation) in the direction of the magnetic field forming a 'classical spinning gyroscope top'. (See Fig. 4.41 a and b). In ferrites the uncancelled electron spins are mutually parallel throughout domains of uniform magnetisation. Thus macroscopic magnetisation vector of a domain behave as one unit under the influence of field, as such in investigating the response of ferrites towards *r.f.* fields, classical mechanics may be applied to the system of electron spins.

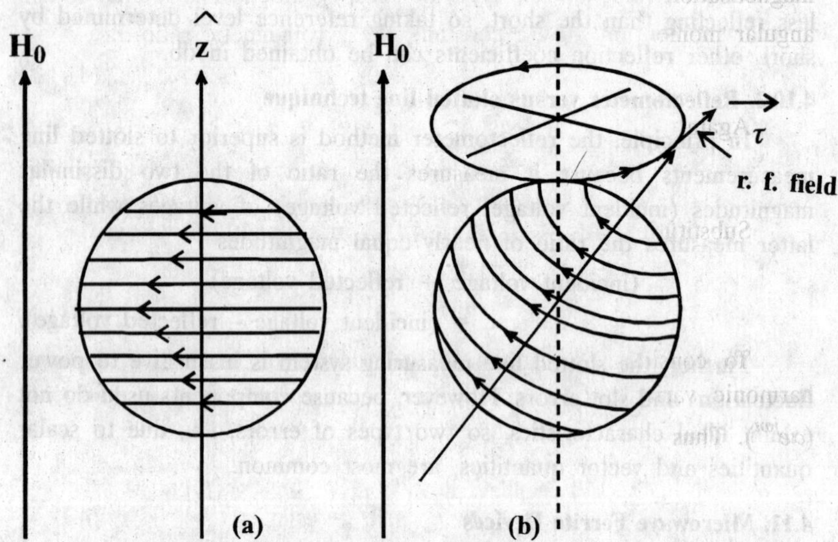

Fig. 4.41a & b. Illustration of spinning electron as gyroscope top.

4.11.2. Basic properties of ferrites

The use of ferrites in a number of microwave devices is based on the fact that propagation constants for different modes of polarisation (*i.e.*, the left- and right-handed circular polarisations) of an electromagnetic ray are different. This gives rise to nonreciprocal Faraday rotation. The desirable magnetic properties of ferrites can be obtained by considering the gyroscopic motion of the electron.

Permeability tensor

If τ be the torque exerted by the steady magnetic field H_0 when an electron is placed in it, then

$$\tau = \frac{d\mathbf{J}}{dt} \quad ....(4.11.1)$$

where J is spin angular momentum vector. This torque acts on the magnetic dipole (electron) having magnetic dipole moment M tending to rotate it into the alignment of the field. Due to angular momentum, spin does not change its angle with respect to the applied magnetic field but processes gyrescopically around H_0. It is this tendency towards precession in the presence of magnetising field that endows the properties to magnetic materials. The magnetic moment or magnetisation (magnetic moment per unit volume) M is related to the angular momentum J by a constant, the gyromagnetic ratio, *i.e.*,

$$\mathrm{M} = \gamma \mathbf{J} \quad ....(4.11.2)$$

Again

$$\tau = \mu_0(\mathbf{M} \times \mathbf{H}) \quad ....(4.11.3)$$

Substituting Eqs. 4.11.2 and 4.11.3 in Equ. 4.11.1, we find

$$\frac{1}{\gamma}\frac{d\mathrm{M}}{dt} = \mu_0(\mathrm{M} \times \mathrm{H}) \quad ....(4.11.4)$$

To consider propagation of microwave in ferrites, we assume harmonic variation of M with time because r.f. field is harmonic ($\alpha e^{j\omega t}$). Thus

$$\mathrm{M} = \frac{\tau\mu_0}{j\omega}(\mathrm{M} \times \mathrm{H}) \quad ....(4.11.5)$$

Equation (4.11.5) connects M and H, and by solving it, magnetic susceptibility constants $\left(\chi = \frac{M}{H}\right)$ may be obtained for our model which is an assembly of spins. To do so, we assume the magnetising field H as consisting of a small high frequency (*r.f.*) magnetic field H_1, superimposed on a constant polarising field H_0 in z-direction. The response of the medium (ferrite) to this H_0 is assumed to be a large constant magnetisation M_0 in the z-direction and time varying components of magnetization $\hat{x}\mathrm{M}_x$ and $\hat{y}\mathrm{M}_y$ in the x- and y-direction respectively. Thus we have

$$\mathrm{H} = (\hat{x}\mathrm{H}_x + \hat{y}\mathrm{H}_y)\, e^{j\omega t} + \hat{z}\mathrm{H}_0 \quad ....(4.11.6)$$

and

$$M = (\hat{x} M_x + \hat{y} M_y) e^{j\omega t} + \hat{z} M_0 \quad ....(4.11.7)$$

We have omitted time-varying components in z-direction because these are small as compared to high steady field H_0 in this direction. Substitution of Eqs. 4.11.6 and 4.11.7 in Eq. 4.11.5 gives components of magnetisation in terms of the r.f. field components, as

$$M_x = \frac{\omega_0 \omega_m}{\omega_0^2 - \omega^2} H_x + j \frac{\omega \omega_m}{\omega_0^2 - \omega^2} H_y \quad ....(4.11.8)$$

$$M_y = -j \frac{\omega_0 \omega_m}{\omega_0^2 - \omega^2} H_x + \frac{\omega \omega_m}{\omega_0^2 - \omega^2} H_y \quad ....(4.11.9)$$

$$M_z = 0 \quad ....(4.11.10)$$

where $\omega_0 = -\mu_0 \gamma H_0$ ....(4.11.11)

and $\omega_m = -\mu_0 \gamma M_0$ ....(4.11.12)

Equation 4.11.8 through 4.11.12 establishes relations between components of magnetization and the magnetic field. In the scalar case the ratio M/H expresses magnetic susceptibility χ of the medium. However, in our present case magnetization is not the same in all the directions so χ can be said to be a tensor. The components of χ can be obtained by transforming the above equations in the following matrix form :

$$\begin{bmatrix} M_x \\ M_y \\ M_z \end{bmatrix} = \begin{bmatrix} \chi_{xy} & \chi_{xy} & 0 \\ \chi_{yz} & \chi_{yy} & 0 \\ 0 & 0 & 0 \end{bmatrix} \begin{bmatrix} H_x \\ H_y \\ H_z \end{bmatrix} \quad ....(4.11.13)$$

where

$$\chi_{xx} = \chi_{yy} = \frac{\omega_0 \omega_m}{\omega_0^2 - \omega^2}$$

$$\chi_{xy} = -\chi_{yx} = \frac{j\,\omega \omega_m}{\omega_0^2 - \omega^2}$$

Again magnetic induction **B** is related to the magnetization **M** as

$$\mathbf{B} = \mu \mathbf{H} = \mu_0((\mathbf{H} + \mathbf{M}) \quad ....(4.11.14)$$

$$\begin{bmatrix} B_x \\ B_y \\ B_z \end{bmatrix} = \mu_0 \begin{bmatrix} 1 + \chi_{xx} & \chi_{yy} & 0 \\ -\chi_{yx} & 1 + \chi_{yy} & 0 \\ 0 & 0 & 1 \end{bmatrix} \begin{bmatrix} H_x \\ H_y \\ H_z \end{bmatrix} \quad ....(4.11.15)$$

or in matrix notaion

$$[B] = [\mu]\,[H] \qquad \text{....(4.11.16)}$$

where μ is the **Permeability Tensor** for the ferrite and can be written as

$$[\mu] = \begin{bmatrix} \mu & -jk & 0 \\ jk & \mu & 0 \\ 0 & 0 & \mu_0 \end{bmatrix} \qquad \text{....(4.11.17)}$$

where $$\mu = \mu_0\,(1 + \chi_{xx}) = \mu_0 \left(1 + \frac{\omega_0 \omega_m}{\omega_0^2 - \omega^2}\right)$$

$$k = \mu_0 \chi_{yx} = -\mu_0 \left(\frac{\omega \omega_m}{\omega_0^2 - \omega^2}\right)$$

where ω_0 is generally known as the **Gyromagnetic resonance frequency** because at $\omega = \omega_0$, $\mu = \mu_0$, and permeability is no more a tensor but comes a scalar. ω_m is a constant of a material and depends upon the strength of the saturation magnetization M_0 (see Eq. 4.11.12) in the ferrimagnetic domains and has values of the order of $2\pi \times 400$ to $2\pi \times 1000$ MHz.

If losses are present in ferrites, then a new term of damping is to be introduced in Eq. 4.11.3, which tends to reduce the precession angle ϕ Eq. 4.11.3 may be solved in a similar way to give permeability and susceptibility constants. For details reader may refer literature*.

4.11.3 Plane wave propagation in an infinite ferrite medium in the direction of bias (Faraday rotation)

We consider an infinite ferrite-filled region with a d.c. bias field given by $H_0 = \hat{z}H_0$, and a tensor permittivity $[\mu]$ given by (4.11.17). Maxwell's equation are :

$$\nabla \times E = -\,j\omega\,[\mu]\,H \qquad \text{....(4.11.18a)}$$

$$\nabla \times H = -\,j\omega\varepsilon\,H \qquad \text{....(4.11.18b)}$$

$$\nabla \cdot D = 0 \qquad \text{....(4.11.18c)}$$

$$\nabla \cdot B = 0 \qquad \text{....(4.11.18d)}$$

---

* Soohoo, R.F., **Microwave Magnetics Harper** and Row, N.Y., 1985.

Suppose plane wave propagation in the z-direction, with $\frac{\partial}{\partial x} = \frac{\partial}{\partial y} = 0$. Then the electric and magnetic fields are given in the form.

$$E = E_0 e^{-j\beta z} \quad \text{....(4.11.19a)}$$

$$H = H_0 e^{-j\beta z} \quad \text{....(4.11.19b)}$$

Using Eq. 4.11.17, the two curl equations 4.11.18 a, b then reduce to the following :

$$j\beta E_y = -j\omega\,(\mu H_x + jkH_y) \quad \text{....(4.11.20a)}$$

$$-j\beta E_x = -j\omega\,(-jkH_x + \mu H_y) \quad \text{....(4.11.20b)}$$

$$0 = -j\omega\,\mu_0 H_z \quad \text{....(4.11.20c)}$$

$$j\beta H_y = j\omega\varepsilon\, E_x \quad \text{....(4.11.20d)}$$

$$-j\beta H_y = -j\omega\varepsilon\, E_y \quad \text{....(4.11.20e)}$$

$$0 = j\omega\varepsilon\, E_z \quad \text{....(4.11.20f)}$$

From Equations 4.11.20c and 4.11.20f $E_z = H_z = 0$, as expected for **TEM** planes. We also have

$$\nabla \cdot D = \nabla \cdot B = 0, \text{ since } \partial/\partial x = \partial/\partial y = 0$$

The transverse field components are given by the Eqs. 4.11.20d,e as

$$Y = \frac{H_y}{E_x} = \frac{-H_x}{E_y} = \frac{\omega\varepsilon}{\beta} \quad \text{....(4.11.21)}$$

where Y is the wave admittance.

Eliminating H_x and H_y in Eqs. 4.11.20a and 4.11.20b using Eq. 4.11.21 gives

$$j\omega^2\varepsilon k E_x + (\beta^2 - \omega^2\mu\varepsilon)\, E_y = 0 \quad \text{....(4.11.22a)}$$

$$(\beta^2 - \omega^2\mu\varepsilon)\, E_x - j\,\omega^2\varepsilon k E_y = 0 \quad \text{....(4.11.22b)}$$

The determinant of set of equations 4.11.22a, b must vanish for a nontrivial solution,

$$\omega^4\varepsilon^2 k^2 - (\beta^2 - \omega^2\mu\varepsilon)^2 = 0$$

$$\beta_\pm = \omega\sqrt{\varepsilon\,(\mu \pm k)} \quad \text{....(4.11.23)}$$

Thus there are two possible propagation constants β_+ and β_-.

Fields associated with β_+ and β_-

Substituting β_+ in the Eq. 4.11.22 a or b, we get

$$j\omega^2 \varepsilon k E_x + \omega^2 \varepsilon k E_y = 0$$

or $$E_y = -jE_x$$

Then the electric field of Eq. 4.11.19a will have the following form :

$$E_+ = E_0 (\hat{x} - j\hat{y}) e^{-j\beta_+ z} \quad \text{....(4.11.24a)}$$

It is a right hand circularly polarised plane wave (RHCP).

The associated magnetic field is obtained by using Eq. 4.11.21 as

$$H_+ = E_0 Y_+ (j\hat{x} + \hat{y}) e^{-j\beta_+ z} \quad \text{....(4.11.24b)}$$

where Y_+ is the wave admittance for this wave.

$$Y_+ = \frac{\omega\varepsilon}{\beta_+} = \sqrt{\frac{\varepsilon}{\mu + k}} \quad \text{....(4.11.24c)}$$

Similarly, the fields associated with β_- are left-hand circularly polarized (LHCP).

$$E_- = E_0 (\hat{x} - j\hat{y}) e^{-j\beta_- z} \quad \text{....(4.11.25.a)}$$

$$H_- = E_0 Y_- (-j\hat{x} + \hat{y}) e^{-j\beta_- z} \quad \text{....(4.11.25.b)}$$

where $$Y_- = \frac{\omega\varepsilon}{\beta_-} = \sqrt{\frac{\varepsilon}{\mu - k}} \quad \text{....(4.11.25.c)}$$

We note that for an RHCP wave, the ferrite material can be represented with an effective permeability of $(\mu + k)$ and for LHCP it is euqal to $(\mu - k)$.

Faraday rotation—

The sum of electric field of an RHCP and an LHCP represent a linearly polarised electric field at $z = 0$

$$E|_{z=0} = \hat{x} E_0 = \frac{E_0}{2}(\hat{x} - j\hat{y}) + \frac{E_0}{2}(\hat{x} + j\hat{y}) \quad \text{....(4.11.26)}$$

From Eqs. (4.11.25a, b) the total field of Eq. 4.11.26 will propagate as

$$E = \frac{E_0}{2}(\hat{x} - j\hat{y})e^{-j\beta_+ z} + \frac{E_0}{2}(\hat{x} - j\hat{y})e^{-j\beta_- z}$$

$$= \frac{E_0}{2}\hat{x}\,(e^{-j\beta_+ z} + e^{-j\beta_- z}) - j\frac{E_0}{2}\hat{y}(e^{-j\beta_+ z} - e^{-j\beta_- z})$$

$$= E_0\left[\hat{x}\cos\left(\frac{\beta_+ - \beta_-}{2}\right)z - \hat{y}\sin\left(\frac{\beta_+ - \beta_-}{2}\right)z\right]e^{-j(\beta_+ + \beta_-)z/2} \quad ....(4.11.27)$$

This resultant wave is linearly polarised wave that has undergone a phase delay of $(\beta_- + \beta_+)z/2$. The new plane of polarisation makes an angle θ with the old (*i.e.*, $\hat{x}$)

$$\theta = \tan^{-1}(E_y/E_x) = \tan^{-1}\{-\tan(\beta_+ - \beta_-)z/2\}$$
$$= -(\beta_+ - \beta)\,z/2 \quad ....(4.11.28)$$

Thus plane of polarisation is rotated at the rate of $(\beta_+ - \beta_-)/2$ rad/metre.

If the direction of propagation is reversed, the plane of polarisation continues to be rotated by an angle θ in the same direction because β_+ and β_- are functions of magnetic field and not of the direction of motion. This property is known as **non-reciprocity** and used in designing non-reciprocal devices such as isolators and circulators.

The preceding discussion is valid so far as $\omega < \omega_0$ (ω's are functions of applied magnetic field). At $\omega = \omega_0$, the rotating magnetic field (r.f. circularly polarised waves) assumes the direction of precession and have the same frequency. Thus resonance occurs and travelling r.f. field aids electron precession thereby setting it to violent oscillations and absorbing the energy from the r.f. field. This is called **resonant absorption.**

Further, in this discussion we have assumed lossless ferrites. As a matter of fact when wave passes through ferrites, it will be attenuated in addition to phase delay. The attenuation is maximum at resonance.

4.11.4. Microwave ferrite devices

(A) Isolator

This microwave device permits unattenuated transmission in one direction (forward direction) but provides very high attenuation in the reverse direction (backward direction). This is generally used between the source and rest of the set-up to avoid overloading of the source due to reflected power. Two types of ferrite isolators are possible :

(i) Faraday-rotation isolator – As shown in Fig. 4.42, it consists of a 45° waveguide twist connected with a circular guide, which in turn is connected to another rectangular guide at the other end. The circular part has a known tapered length of ferrite placed under the biasing of the magnetic field in the forward direction. Two resistive cards are placed perpendicular to the electric field at the two ends.

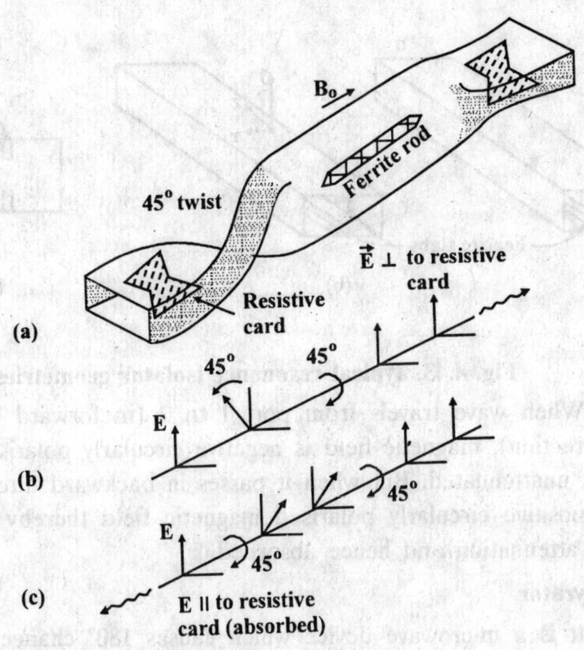

Fig. 4.42. Faraday rotation isolator.

When TE_{10} mode wave passes through 45° twist in forward direction (port 1 to 2) as shown in Fig. 4.42b the plane of its polarisation rotates through 45°. The ferrite rod causes an additional 45° rotation in the opposite direction. As a result outgoing wave has its electric field perpendicular to the resistive pads and so passes unattenuated. When it propagates in the reverse direction, the phase rotations due to ferrite and twist are additive (ferrite rotation is still in the same direction) and electric vector is rotated by 90° making it parallel to the resistive pad and hence absorbed.

(ii) Resonance isolator. In the vicinity of frequency $\omega_0 \approx \omega$, the attenuation constant for negative (left-handed) circular polarisation is much smaller as compared to positive (right-handed) polarisation. This property is put to use in a resonance isolator. Resonance isolator is designed by placing ferrite slab (or two slabs at a distance) such that r.f. magnetic field of TE_{10} mode is circularly polarised. The ferrite is magnetised by a static field applied in *y*-direction as shown in Fig. 4.43a, b and c.

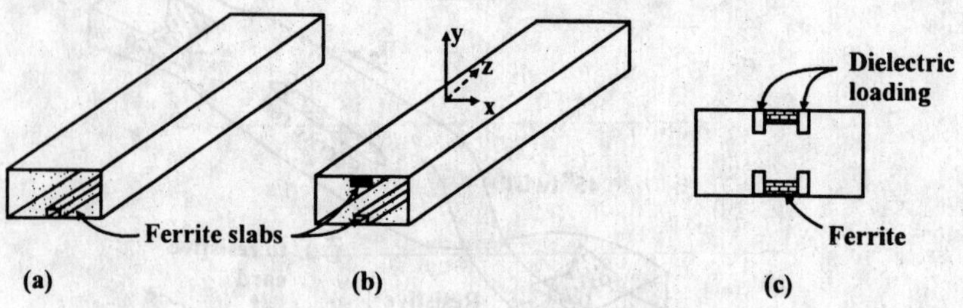

Fig. 4.43. Typical resonance isolator geometries.

When wave travels from port 1 to 2 (in forward direction, *i.e.* + z-direction), magnetic field is negative circularly polarised and wave passes unattenuated. But when it passes in backward direction it shall have positive circularly polarised magnetic field thereby experiencing heavy attenuation and hence absorbed.

(B) Gyrator

It is a microwave device which causes 180° change in phase of the waves propagating in the forward direction as compared to the waves travelling in backward direction. A ferrite gyrator, shown in Fig. 4.44a, consists of a 90° twist followed by a 90° negative ferrite rotator (rotation being in the same direction as that of the twist) placed in a cylindrical central section.

Consider a wave propagating from left to right. In passing through the twist, its plane of polarisation is rotated by 90° in counter-clockwise direction. Next, the ferrite produces an additional 90° rotation in the same direction. Thus, total rotation amounts to 180°. For the waves travelling from right to left, however, the two rotations cancel each other owing to Faraday rotation being non-reciprocal. A gyrator without 90° twist may also be designed as shown in Fig. 4.44b. In that case the second transition from cylindrical to rectangular is such that polarisation of the wave is rotated by 90°.

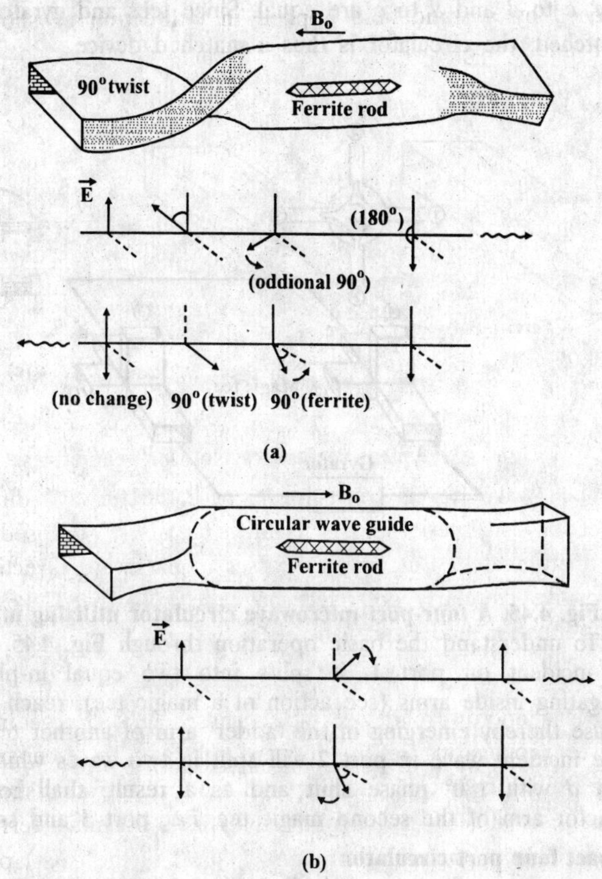

Fig. 4.44. Gyrators : (a) with 90° twise, (b) without 90° twist.

(C) Circulator

Circulator is a multiport device such that wave incident on n^{th} port is coupled to $(n + 1)^{th}$ port only, *i.e.*, if power is incident in port 1, port 2 is coupled but not ports 3 and 4. Microwave circulators with four ports (Fig. 4.45) are most common. A four-port circulator may be constructed from two magic tees or hybrid junctions and a gyrator which produces an additional phase shift of 180° for propagation in the direction from a to b. The electric lengths of propagation from b to a, c to d and d to c are equal. Since tees and gyrator ports are all matched, the circulator is thus a matched device.

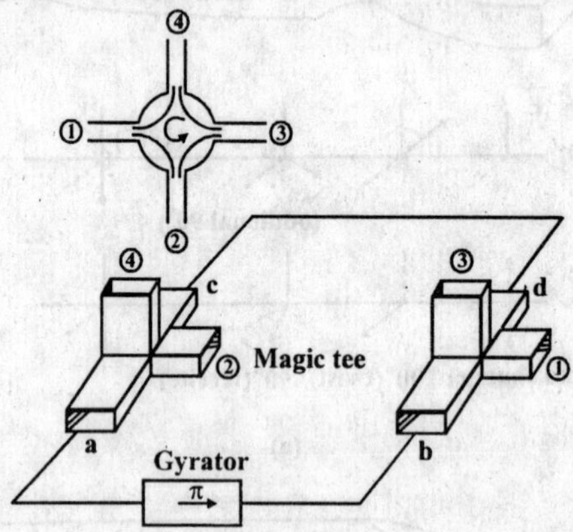

Fig. 4.45. A four-port microwave circulator utilizing magic tee.

To understand the basic operation through Fig. 4.45, consider a wave incident on port 1, it splits into two equal in-phase waves propagating inside arms (see action of a magic tee), reach at a and c in phase thereby emerging in the 'adder' arm of another tee, *i.e.*, port 2. The incident wave in port 2 will split in two waves which arrive at b and d with 180° phase shift and as a result, shall be added in subtractor arm of the second magic tee, *i.e.*, port 3 and so on.

Compact four port circulator

A compact four-port circulator may be constructed using 3 db side-hole directional couplers and two non-reciprocal 90° ferrite phase shifters. The latter consists of thin ferrite rod of length l placed in a rectangular wave guide where the magnetic field of TE_{10} mode is circularly polarised. A biasing magnetic field B_0 is applied in y-direction. Since two circular polarisations have different propagation constants β_+ and β_-; so a differential phase shift of $\pi/2$ between two polarisations may be obtained if the length of the rod is chosen as $(\beta_+ - \beta_-)l = \pi/2$.

A compact four-port circulator is shown in Fig. 4.46. Two phase shifters are biased in opposite directions. One guide is loaded with the ferrite non-reciprocal phase shifter while the other by a reciprocal dielectric phase shifter.

Consider a wave incident on port 1. This wave is split into two waves by first 3 db coupler. The upper wave undergoes a 90° phase change because of coupling character of the hole. This wave (in upper guide) shall reach port 2 with a relative phase 180° and the wave in lower waveguide at port 4, with a phase 90°. The second coupler again splits the waves such that resultant waves go out of phase and hence cancel out in port 4, while they go in phase and hence add in port 2. A similar analysis may be carried out to show that ports are coupled as 1 → 2 → 3 → 4 → 1 and not in the reverse direction.

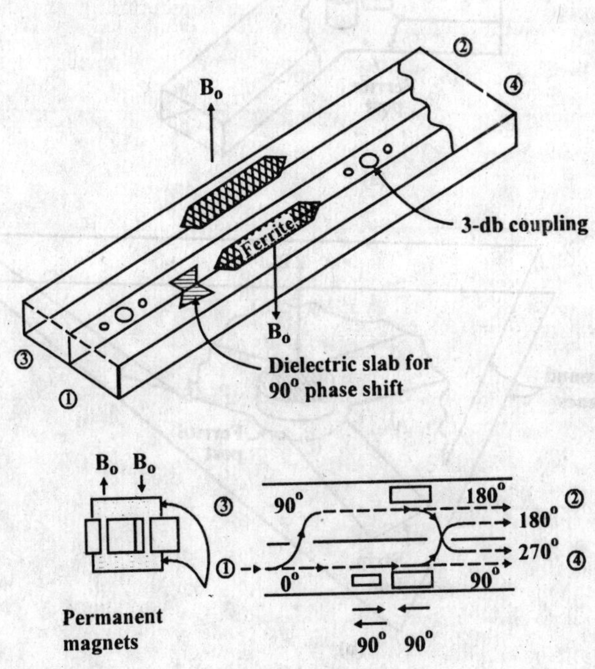

Fig. 4.46. Compact four-port circulator.

Three port circulator

A perfectly matched three-port circulator may also be designed. It consists of symmetric *y*-junction (Fig. 4.47) of three identical waveguides (or strip lines), with an axially magnetised ferrite rod placed at the centre. Microwave power incident in port 1 divides in the other two ports equally but ferrite causes phase variation in waves in such a way that the two are added in port 2 while subtracted in port 3, and so on. The basic properties of ferrite devices and various quantities are defined as follows.

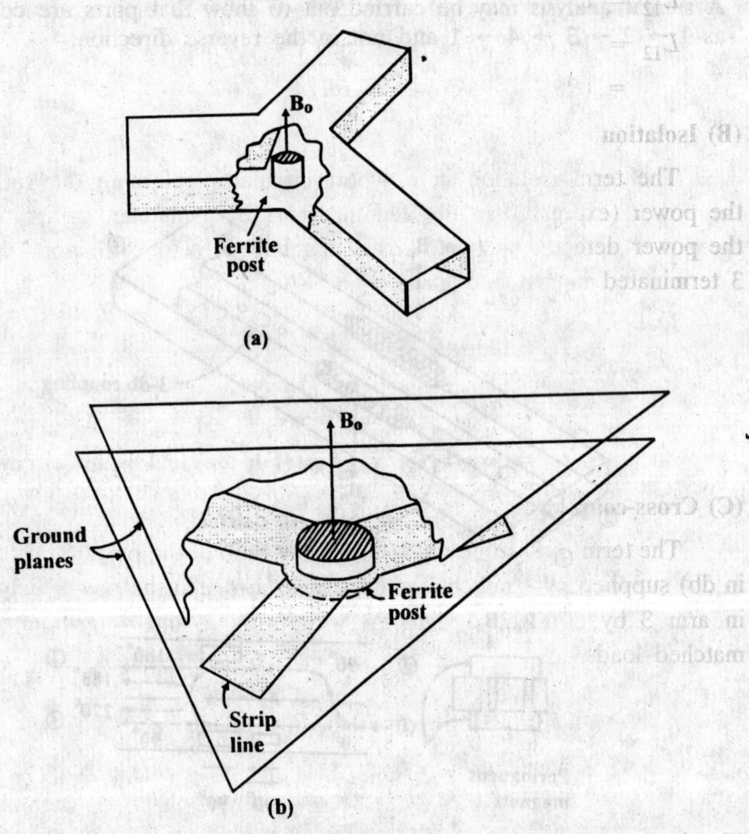

Fig. 4.47. Three port circulator.

4.11.5. Basic parameters of ferrite devices

(A) Insertion Loss

The ratio of the power (expressed in decibels) supplied by a matched source to the input arm (say 1), to the power detected by a matched detector in the coupling arm 2 with all other ports matched terminated, is defined as **insertion loss** or forward loss L_{12} of a circulator (or of any coupling devices). Clearly there may be many insertion loss parameters depeding upon the number of ports in a circulator, but since all the ports are identical so these parameters may be taken to be the same.

$$L_{12} = L_{23} = L_{34} = L_{41} \text{ (4-port circulator)}$$

$$L_{12} = 10 \log P_1/P_2 = 10 \log P_1 - 10 \log P_2$$

$$= (P_1 - P_2) \text{ (Power in dB)}$$

(B) Isolation

The term isolation in a 4-port circulator refers to the ratio of the power (expressed in db) fed in arm 1 by a matched generator to the power detected in port 4 by a matched detector with ports 2 and 3 terminated in matched loads.

$$I_{14} = 10 \log \frac{P_1}{P_4}$$

$$= (P_1 - P_4) \text{ expressed in dB}$$

$$= I_{21} = I_{32} = I_{43} \quad \text{(For an ideal 4-port circulator)}$$

(C) Cross-coupling

The term cross-coupling refers to the ratio of the power (expressed in db) supplied by a matched generator in arm 1 to the power detected in arm 3 by a matched detector with ports 2 and 4 terminated in matched loads.

$$C_{13} = 10 \log \frac{P_1}{P_3} = 10 \log P_1 - 10 \log P_3$$

$$= (P_1 - P_3) \text{ in dB}$$

Clearly $C_{13} = C_{24} = C_{31} = C_{42}$ for an ideal 4-port circulator.

(D) Input VSWR

Input VSWR of a 4-port circulator is the ratio of the maximum voltage to the minimum voltage of the standing waves existing on the line (slotted) when one port of the calculator (all ports being identical) terminates the line and all others have matched terminations.

4.12. Computer-Aided Design (CAD) for Microwave Circuits :

CAD programs for microwave circuit analysis and optimization are fast, powerful and accurate. These have the capability of analysing microwave circuits consisting of several lumped, passive and active components. There are several commercially available microwave CAD software packages such as SUPER COMPACT* and TOUCHSTONE* which are very useful tools for microwave enginner. With the use of CAD the microwave enginner could optimize the design by adjusting some of the circuit parameters to achieve the best performance. A paper model is developed which meets the specification. Then as engineering product can be built and tested. Thus, it saves the time and reduces cost of a design, while enhancing the quality.

Review Questions and Problems*

1. What are scattering coefficients of a microwave device ? Discuss the scattering properties of multiport junction and hence obtain the scattering matrix of a magic T. What are its uses ? Explain the use of magic T (1) as duplexer; (ii) as a mixer for a super-heterodyne receiver.
2. Explain the construction and working of two choke type movable short circuit used in microwave measurements.
3. Distinguish between *E*-plane and *H*-plane tees and hence discuss the construction and working of a magic-tee.
4. With the help of a diagram explain the working of 'Reflectometer'. Why is it an important part of a good microwave measurement laboratory ?
5. Explain the construction and working of wave guide phase shifter.
6. Explain the construction and working of precision variable attenuator. Discuss it frequency response and reflection losses.
7. Describe Bathe-hole coupler and explain its working. Obtain scattering matrix of a directional coupler.

---

* Registered trade mark of Compact Software Corp. and EEsof. Inc., Respectively.

* Selected from Universities examination papers.

8. Discuss various parameters of a directional coupler. Mention any two uses of disectional colepler.

9. Explain the use of magic-tee for a four port circulator.

10. Explain the operation of a circulator.

11. Write short nutes on any two of the following–
    (i) Rotary attenuator.
    (ii) Rotary phase shifter.
    (iii) Multi-hole directional coupler.
    (iv) Isolator.

12. What is meant by Faraday rotation ? Explain with the help of appropriate diagram the working of an isolator.

13. What are Ferrites ? What properties do they have ? Describe in detail a circulator and give its applications.

14. Explain the operation of Faraday Rotation Isolator and give its applications.

15. What are Ferrites ? Derive the permeability matrix for ferrites. Using the matrix explain the phenomenon of Faraday rotation. Explain the working of gyrator.

16. Discuss propagation of microwave energy in ferrites. Obtain an expression for Faraday rotation. What is a reciprocal effect ?

17. What do you understand by Faraday rotation? Obtain an expression for it. Is it a reciprocal effect ? Show that a lossless, matched, non-reciprocal, three-port microwave junction is a three-port circulator. Hence describe the essential features of a practical three port circulator.

18. What is Faraday rotation ? Show that it is a non-reciprocal effect. Hence explain the construction and working of a rotation isolator. State few desired properties of ferrites.

19. What are Ferrites ? Prove that for a ferrite, the permeability matrix is given by,

$$[\mu] = \begin{bmatrix} \mu & -jk & 0 \\ jk & \mu & 0 \\ 0 & 0 & \mu_0 \end{bmatrix}$$

where symbols have their usual meanings. Using this matrix, explain the rotation of plane of polarization of a plane electromagnetic wave propagation through the ferrite.

20. Show that scattering matrix for entirely symmetrical (120°) series. T-junction is given by

$$[S] = \frac{1}{3}\begin{bmatrix} 1 & 2 & 2 \\ 2 & 1 & -2 \\ 2 & -2 & 1 \end{bmatrix}$$

21. Show that scattering matrix for series T-junction matched at arm 3 is given by

$$[S] = \frac{1}{2}\begin{bmatrix} 1 & 1 & \sqrt{2} \\ 2 & 1 & -\sqrt{2} \\ \sqrt{2} & -\sqrt{2} & 0 \end{bmatrix}$$

22. Show that scattering matrix for shunt T-junction matched at arm 3 is given by

$$[S] = \frac{1}{2}\begin{bmatrix} -1 & 1 & \sqrt{2} \\ 1 & -1 & \sqrt{2} \\ \sqrt{2} & \sqrt{2} & 0 \end{bmatrix}$$

23. Show that scattering matrix for hybrid ring junction (rate-race, refer to Fig. 4.25) is given by

$$[S] = -\frac{1}{\sqrt{2}}\begin{bmatrix} 0 & 0 & 1 & 1 \\ 0 & 0 & 1 & -1 \\ 1 & 1 & 0 & 0 \\ 1 & -1 & 0 & 0 \end{bmatrix}$$

24. Show that the scattering matrix for an ideal unidirectional attenuator (isolator) without loss in the direction from arm 1 into arm 2 is given by

$$[S] = \begin{bmatrix} 0 & 0 \\ 1 & 0 \end{bmatrix}$$

25. Show that the scattering matrix for an ideal Y circulator (refer to Fig.4.47) is given by

$$[S] = \begin{bmatrix} 0 & 0 & 1 \\ 1 & 0 & 0 \\ 0 & 1 & 0 \end{bmatrix}$$

26. Show that the scattering matrix for a section of uniform lossless guide with an electric length $\theta = 2\pi L/\lambda_g$ or matched reciprocal phase shifter providing a θ phase shift is given by

$$[S] = \exp^{-j\theta} \begin{bmatrix} 0 & 1 \\ 1 & 0 \end{bmatrix}$$

27. Prove that the input impedance of a wave guide section terminated in a matched load has a real normalized value of unity.

5

Periodic Structures and Microwave Filters

5.1. Introduction

Waveguide and transmission lines loaded at regular intervals with reactive elements are referred to as periodic structures. Such structures have two basic properties, namely (1) passband-stopband characteristics, and (2) these structures support waves with phase velocities much less than the velocity of light. Passband stopband property is of interest for its frequency filtering aspect, while the ability of periodic structures having phase velocity much less than that of light is of basic importance for travelling-wave tube circuits. In a travelling wave tube, efficient interaction between electron beam and electromagnetic wave is obtained only if the phase velocity is equal to the beam velocity. Beam velocity is only 10 to 20 per cent of the velocity of light, hence considerable slowing down of the electromagnetic wave is required.

This chapter deals with the basic theory of periodic structures and microwave filters. These structures are usually analysed from both, a circuit and the field point of view. These concepts are described briefly in the following section.

5.2. Circuit Analysis and Structures

5.2.1. Capacitively loaded transmission line—

Consider a capacitive loaded transmission line as shown in Fig. 5.1. For a physically smooth transmission line, such as a co-axial line, the phase velocity is given by

$$\nu_p = (LC)^{-1/2} = (\mu_0\, \varepsilon_r\, \varepsilon_0)^{-1/2} \qquad ....(5.1)$$

where ε_r is the dielectric constant of the medium surrounding the central conductor. To reduce phase velocity, value of dielectric constant ε_r can be increased, but than the cross-sectional dimension of the line must be reduced to avoid the propagation of higher order modes.

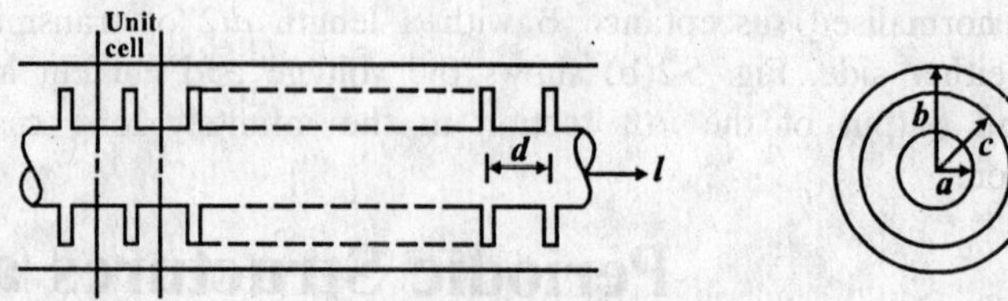

Fig. 5.1. Shunt capacitive loading of a coaxial line by means of thin circular diaphragms.

The phase velocity cannot be decreased by increasing the capacitance C per unit length because any change in the line configuration to increase C automatically decreases the series inductance L per unit length, since $LC = \mu_0 \varepsilon$. An effective increase in the shunt capacitance per unit length is possible, without the corresponding decrease in the series inductance L, if restriction on smoothness of the line can be removed. Hence by adding lumped shunt capacitance per unit length, value of L will not be affected and the phase velocity will be given by

$$\nu_p = \left[\left(C + \frac{C_0}{d}\right) L\right]^{-1/2} \quad \text{....(5.2)}$$

where C_0/d describes the capacitance C_0 added at intervals *d*. One method of adding shunt capacitive loading is by introducing thin circular diaphragms at regular intervals, as in Fig. 5.1. The fringing electric field in the vicinity of the diaphragm increases the local storage of electric energy and hence increase in shunt capacitance is achieved.

An approximate expression for the shunt susceptance of the diaphragm is

$$\overline{B} = \frac{B}{Y_c} = \frac{8(b-c)^2}{\lambda_0 c} \frac{\ln(b/a)}{[\ln (b/c)]^2} \ln \csc\left(\frac{\pi}{2} \cdot \frac{b-c}{b-a}\right) \quad \text{....(5.3)}$$

where $Y_c = [60 \ln (b/a)]^{-1}$ is the characteristic admittance of an air filled coaxial line. The circuit analysis of a periodic structure involves constructing an equivalent network for a single basic section first. Then it is followed by an analysis, for determining the voltage and current waves that may propagate along the network consisting of the cascade connection of an infinite number of the basic networks. Fig. 5.2(a) shows a basic unit for a loaded line of Fig. 5.1. It consists of a shunt normalised susceptance $\overline{B}$ with a length $d/2$ of transmission line on either side. Fig. 5.2(b) shows the voltage and current at the input and output of the nth section in the infinitely long cascade connection.

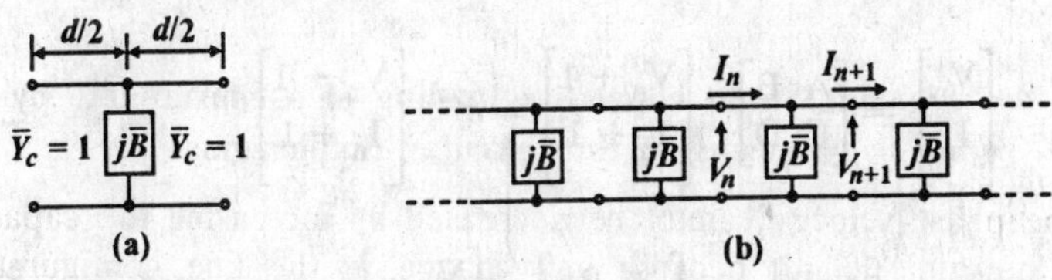

(a) Unit-cell of a coaxial line **(b) Cascade network of unit-cell**

Fig. 5.2.

The relationship between input and output variables V_n, I_n and V_{n+1}, I_{n+1} can be formed by using the ABCD transmission matrix for the unit cell. The unit cell may be broken down into three circuits in cascade i.e. a section of transmission line of length d/2 (electrical length $\theta/2 = k_0 d/2$), followed by a shunt susceptance $\overline{B}$, which in turn is followed by another length of transmission line.

Assuming lossless line sections the ABCD of the individual unit cell is–

$$\begin{bmatrix} A & B \\ C & D \end{bmatrix} = \begin{bmatrix} \cos\frac{\theta}{2} & j\sin\frac{\theta}{2} \\ j\sin\frac{\theta}{2} & \cos\frac{\theta}{2} \end{bmatrix} \begin{bmatrix} 1 & 0 \\ j\overline{B} & 1 \end{bmatrix} \begin{bmatrix} \cos\frac{\theta}{2} & j\sin\frac{\theta}{2} \\ j\sin\frac{\theta}{2} & \cos\frac{\theta}{2} \end{bmatrix} \quad \text{....(5.3a)}$$

The transmission matrix is the product of the above three matrices

$$\begin{bmatrix} V_n \\ I_n \end{bmatrix} = \begin{bmatrix} \cos\theta - \frac{\overline{B}}{2}\sin\theta & j\left(\frac{\overline{B}}{2}\cos\theta + \sin\theta - \frac{\overline{B}}{2}\right) \\ j\left(\frac{\overline{B}}{2}\cos\theta + \sin\theta + \frac{\overline{B}}{2}\right) & \cos\theta - \frac{\overline{B}}{2}\sin\theta \end{bmatrix} \begin{bmatrix} V_n + 1 \\ I_n + 1 \end{bmatrix} \quad \text{....(5.3b)}$$

If the periodic structure is capable of supporting propagating wave, the voltage and current at the $(n+1)^{\text{th}}$ terminal should be equal to voltage and current at the *n*th terminal, apart from a phase delay due to a finite propagation time. Thus we assume that

$$V_{n+1} = e^{-\gamma d}\, V_n \qquad .....(5.4a)$$

$$V_{n+1} = e^{-\gamma d}\, I_n \qquad .....(5.4b)$$

where $\gamma = j\beta + \alpha$ is the propagation constant from the periodic structure.

In terms of the transmission matrix for a unit cell

$$\begin{bmatrix} V_n \\ I_n \end{bmatrix} = \begin{bmatrix} A & B \\ C & D \end{bmatrix} \begin{bmatrix} V_n + 1 \\ I_n + 1 \end{bmatrix} = e^{\gamma d} \begin{bmatrix} V_n + 1 \\ I_n + 1 \end{bmatrix} \qquad ....(5.5a)$$

or
$$\left(\begin{bmatrix} A & B \\ C & D \end{bmatrix} - \begin{bmatrix} e^{\gamma d} & 0 \\ 0 & e^{\gamma d} \end{bmatrix} \right) \begin{bmatrix} V_{n+1} \\ I_{n+1} \end{bmatrix} = 0 \qquad ....(5.5b)$$

This is a matrix eigen value equation for γ. A nontrivial solution will only be obtained if the determinant vanishes. Hence The matrix eigen value equation for capacitively loaded coaxial line gives the relation for γ as

$$\cosh \gamma d = \cos\theta - \frac{\overline{B}}{2} \sin\theta \qquad ....(5.6)$$

where electric length $\theta = k_0 d$

When right hand side of Eq. 5.6 is less than 1

i.e. $\left| \cos\theta - \left(\frac{\overline{B}}{2}\right) \sin\theta \right| < 1$, then $\gamma = j\beta$ and $\alpha = 0$

$$\cos\beta d = \cos\theta - \frac{\overline{B}}{2} \sin\theta \qquad ....(5.7a)$$

When right hand side is >1, $\gamma = \alpha$ and $\beta = 0$, so that

$$\cosh \alpha d = \cos\theta - \frac{\overline{B}}{2} \sin\theta > 1 \qquad ....(5.7b)$$

Finely when the right hand side of Eq. 5.4 is less than -1, we must have $\gamma d = j\pi + \alpha$, so that

$$\cosh \gamma d = \cosh(j\pi + \alpha d) = -\cosh \alpha d = \cos\theta - \frac{\overline{B}}{2} \sin\theta < 1 \qquad ....(5.7c)$$

It is clear from Eq. 5.5 that there will be frequency bands for which propagation is unattenuated and there will be separate band of frequencies in which the wave is attenuated. Note that propagation in both the directions is possible since $-\gamma$ is also a solution. Another important parameter for the periodic loaded line is the periodic characteristic impedance of the line $\overline{Z}_B$.

$$\overline{Z}_B' = \frac{\overline{Z}_B + j\tan k_0 l}{1 + j\,\overline{Z}_B \tan k_0 l} \qquad \text{....(5.8)}$$

where l is the distance of the terminal plane in the $-$ z direction,

and $$\overline{Z}_B = \sqrt{\frac{C}{C + C_0/d}} \qquad \text{....(5.9)}$$

Note that the waves that may propagate along a periodic structure are known as Bloch waves by analogy with the quantum mechanical electron waves that may propagate through a periodic crystal lattice in a solid. This is why. the characteristic impedance is denoted by Z_B for the Bloach Wave. Periodic structures can also be analysed using wave analysis, *i.e.* in terms of the forward and backward propagating waves that can exist in a unit cell.

Other types of periodic structure can be composed of unsymmetrical two-port networks. Also the periodic structures are sometimes terminated in a load Z_L at the Nth terminal plane.

The total voltage and current at the nth terminal plane will be a superposition of an incident and reflected Bloch wave.

5.2.2. k_0–β diagram

The information contained in the eigenvalue equation for the propagation constant β in a periodic structure is usually plotted on a $k_0 - \beta$ (or $\omega - \beta$) plane. The β versus k_0 curves show the frequency bands for propagation and also the stopbands in which no propagation takes place. The resultant plot is called the Brillouin diagram.

For the capacitively loaded coaxial line,

$$\cos\beta d = \cos k_0 d - \frac{\overline{B}}{2}\sin k_0 d = \cos k_0 d - K k_0 d \sin k_0 d \qquad \text{....(5.8)}$$

where $\frac{\overline{B}}{2} = \frac{\omega C_0}{2 Y_c}$ has been expressed as K k_0d.. Curves of k_0d versus βd sketched in Fig. 5.3. For K = 1 *i.e.* for $\overline{B} = 2k_0d$.

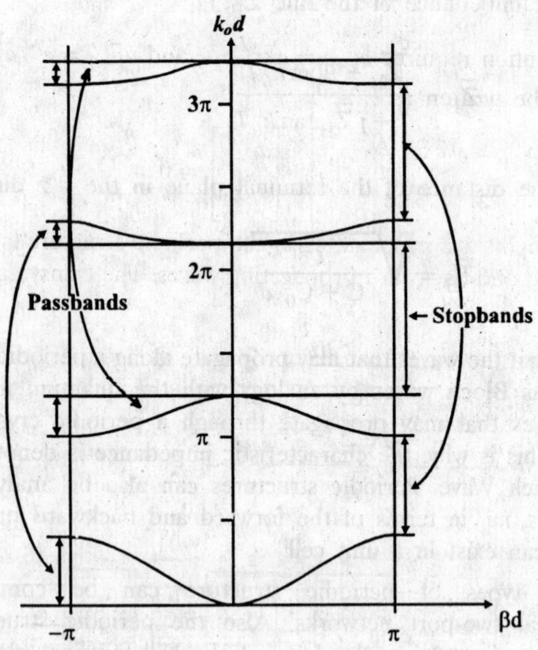

Fig. 5.3 Curves of k_0d versus βd

A low frequency passband exists for $0 < k_0d < 0.416\,\pi$. This passband is followed by a stopband and further alternating passbands and stopbands. As k_0d becomes large, the loading is increased, since B increased with k_0. This decreases the width of the passbands in terms of frequency.

5.2.3. Wave analysis of periodic structures

Periodic structures can also be analyzed in terms of the forward and backward propagating waves in the unit cell. In the wave approach the wave amplitude transmission matrix is used. Fig. 5.4.a,b, show the amplitudes in a unit cell and the cascaded structure. In Fig. 5.4b, the magnitude of the forward and backward wave at the kth and $(k+1)^{st}$

terminal plane are designated as a_k^+, a_k^- and a_{k+1}^+ and a_{k+1}^-, the two are related by the following relation

$$\begin{bmatrix} a_k^+ \\ a_k^- \end{bmatrix} = \begin{bmatrix} A_{11} & A_{12} \\ A_{21} & A_{22} \end{bmatrix} \begin{bmatrix} a_{k+1}^+ \\ a_{k+1}^- \end{bmatrix} \qquad \text{....(5.9)}$$

The solution requires $a_{k+1}^+ = e^{-\gamma d}\, a_k^+$, and $a_{k-1}^- = e^{\gamma d}\, a_k^-$. Hence Eq. 5.9 can be written as

$$\begin{bmatrix} A_{11} - e^{\gamma d} & A_{12} \\ A_{21} & A_{22} - e^{\gamma d} \end{bmatrix} \begin{bmatrix} a_{k+1}^+ \\ a_{k+1}^- \end{bmatrix} = 0 \qquad \text{....(5.10)}$$

The Bloch wave propagating in the periodic structure is made-up of the forward and backward propagating waves. The transverse electric

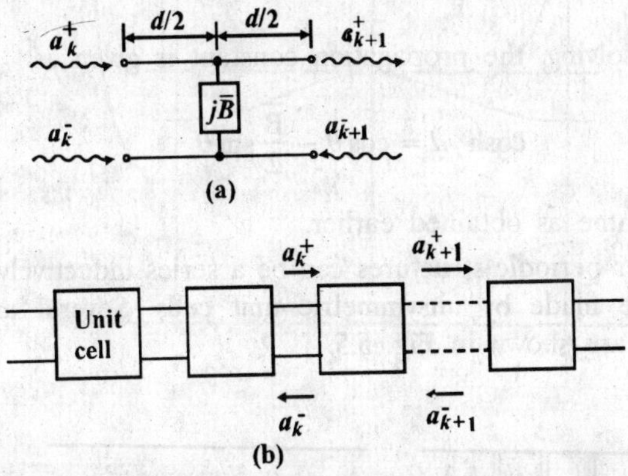

Fig. 5.4(a) Wave amplitude in a unit cell (b) Cascaded structure

field amplitude of the Bloch wave at the zeroth and K-th terminal plane is given as

$$V_{B0} = a_0^+ + a_0^- = a_0^+\,(1 + \Gamma_B) \qquad \text{....(5.11)}$$

$$V_{Bk} = a_k^+ + a_k^- = a_0^+\,(1 + \Gamma_B)e^{-\gamma kd} \qquad \text{....(5.12)}$$

The transverse magnetic field of the Block wave has the amplitude I_{Bk} as

$$I_{Bk} = a_0^+\,(1 - \Gamma_B)\, e^{-\gamma kd} \qquad \text{....(5.13)}$$

where Γ_B is the characteristic reflection coefficient. We also know from transmission line theory that characteristic impedance for the Block wave is

$$Z_B = \frac{1+\Gamma_B}{1-\Gamma_B} \qquad ....(5.14)$$

Now these wave-formulation can be applied to the capacitively loaded transmission discussed earlier. The [A] matrix for the unit cell is obtained by multiplying the three wave amplitude matrices for the unit cell of Fig. 5.4a as

$$[A] = \begin{bmatrix} e^{j\frac{\theta}{2}} & 0 \\ 0 & e^{-j\frac{\theta}{2}} \end{bmatrix} \begin{bmatrix} \frac{2+j\overline{B}}{2} & j\frac{\overline{B}}{2} \\ -j\frac{\overline{B}}{2} & \frac{4+\overline{B}^2}{2(2+j\overline{B})} \end{bmatrix} \begin{bmatrix} e^{j\frac{\theta}{2}} & 0 \\ 0 & e^{-j\frac{\theta}{2}} \end{bmatrix} \qquad ....(5.15)$$

On solving, the propagation constant is given as

$$\cosh \gamma d = \cos\theta - \frac{\overline{B}}{2}\sin\theta$$

which is same as obtained earlier.

Other periodic structures can be a series inductively loaded line, a structure made by unsymmetric unit cells. Several unsymmetrical structures are shown in Fig. 5.5.

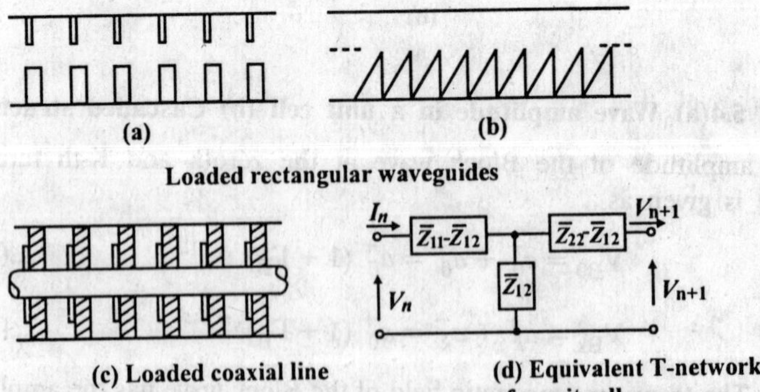

Fig. 5.5.

5.2.4. Floquet's theorem and spatial harmonics

We have noted that in an infinite periodic structure the field of a Bloch wave repeats at every terminal plane except for a propagation factor $e^{-\gamma d}$, (d is the length of the unit cell). Location of a terminal plane in a unit cell is arbitrary. If field in a unit cell is considered at a specific point then field at the same location in any other cell will have same value except for a propagation factor $e^{-\gamma d}$. Thus, if the field in the unit cell between $0 \leq z \leq d$ is $E(x, y, z)$, $H(x, y, z)$, the field in the unit cell located in the region $d \leq z \leq 2d$ will be

$$e^{-\gamma d}\, \mathrm{E}\,(x, y, z - d),\; e^{-\gamma d}\, \mathrm{H}\,(x, y, z - d)$$

Hence, fields in periodic structures are described by solutions of the form,

$$\mathrm{E}(x, y, z) = e^{-\gamma z}\, \mathrm{E_p}\,(x, y, z) \qquad \text{....(5.16a)}$$

$$\mathrm{H}(x, y, z) = e^{-\gamma z}\, \mathrm{H_p}\,(x, y, z) \qquad \text{....(5.16b)}$$

where E_p, H_p are periodic function of z with period d, for example,

$$\mathrm{E_p}\,(x, y, z + kd) = \mathrm{E_p}\,(x, y, z) \qquad \text{....(5.16c)}$$

Expressing the fields in a periodic structure in the form given by Eq. 5.16 is generally referred as Floquet's theorem.

Any periodic function such as $E_p(x, y, z)$ may be expanded into an infinite series

$$\mathrm{E_p}\,(x, y, z) = \sum_{k=-\infty}^{\infty} \mathrm{E_{pk}}\,(x, y)\, e^{-j2k\pi z/d} \qquad \text{....(5.17)}$$

Multiplying both sides by $e^{j2\pi l z/d}$ and integrating over a unit cell will result into

$$\mathrm{E}_{pl}\,(x, y) = \frac{1}{d}\int_0^d \mathrm{E_p}\,(x, y, z)\, e^{j2l\pi z/d} \qquad \text{....(5.18)}$$

The exponential function forms a complete orthogonal set, *i.e.*

$$\int_0^d e^{-j2\pi k z/d}\, e^{j2\pi l z/d}\, dz = \begin{cases} 0 & k \neq l \\ d & k = l \end{cases}$$

Hence, the field in a periodic structure may be expressed as

$$E(x,y,z) = \sum_{k=-\infty}^{\infty} E_{pk}(x,y)\, e^{-j\beta z - j2k\pi z/d}$$

$$= \sum_{k=\infty}^{\infty} E_{pk}(x,y)\, e^{-j\beta_k z} \quad ....(5.19)$$

where $\gamma = j\beta$ and $\beta_k = \beta + 2k\pi/d$. Each term in this expansion is called a spatial harmonic (or a Hartree harmonic) and has a propagation phase constant β_k. β_k will be negative whenever the integer k is sufficient negative. The corresponding phase velocity of the kth spatial harmonic is

$$v_{pk} = \frac{\omega}{\beta_k} = \frac{\omega}{\beta + 2k\pi/d} \quad ....(5.20)$$

v_p will be negative whenever β is negative. The group velocity of the kth harmonic is

$$v_{gk} = \frac{d\omega}{d\beta_k} = \left(\frac{d\beta}{d\omega}\right)^{-1} = v_g \quad ....(5.21)$$

which is same for all harmonics. From the above discussion, it is seen that approximately half of the spatial harmonics have phase and group velocities that are directed in the opposite directions.

All the spatial harmonics of the Bloch wave should be simultaneously present, so that the total field may satisfy all the boundary conditions.

5.2.5. Periodic structures for travelling wave tube

A common type slow wave structure used in travelling wave tubes is the helix (Fig 5.6a). These structures support an electromagnetic wave with a phase velocity equal to the velocity of electron beam. In the case of magnetron, the slow wave structure used is a vane and other type structures (see Chapter 6). The field analysis in such periodic structures are available in reference [1] in detail. Only the steps used in analysing a typical periodic structure are listed below :

1. Solve Helmholtz equation and use Floquet's theorem to obtain field expansions in each region of the periodic structure.

2. Apply boundary conditions on the fields at all common boundaries separating the different boundaries.

3. By Fourier analysis, convert the boundary conditions into algebraic equations for the amplitude constants.

4. Determine the eigenvalue equations for β from the set of homogeneous equations obtained from the algebraic equations.

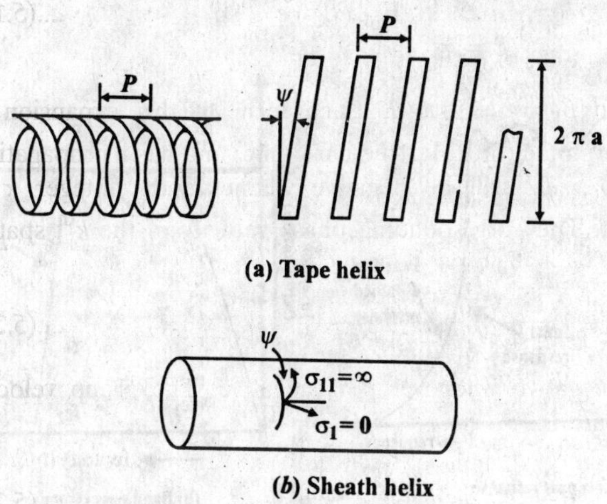

Fig. 5.6 Helical structures

5.3. Microwave Filters

5.3.1 Introduction

The ideal filter is a network that provides perfect transmission for all frequencies in certain passband region and infinite attenuation in stopband regions. Such ideal filters do not exist in practice, so the aim of filter design is to approximate the ideal requirements to within an acceptable tolerance. There are four general types of filters : (i) low pass, (ii) high pass, (iii) bandpass and (iv) bandstop characterized according to the range of frequencies passed or rejected. The response curves of these filters are shown in Fig. 5.7. The electric filters have numerous applications; for example,

1. Used in eliminating signal contamination such as noise in communication systems.
2. Used to separate relevant from irrelevant frequency components.
3. To detect signals in radio and TV's.
4. To band limit signals before sampling.
5. To convert sampled signals into continuous time signals.

6. To improve quality of audio equipment, *e.g.*, loudspeakers.
7. In time division to frequency division multiplex systems.
8. In speech synthesis.
9. In the equalization of transmission lines and cables.
10. In the design of artificial cochleas.

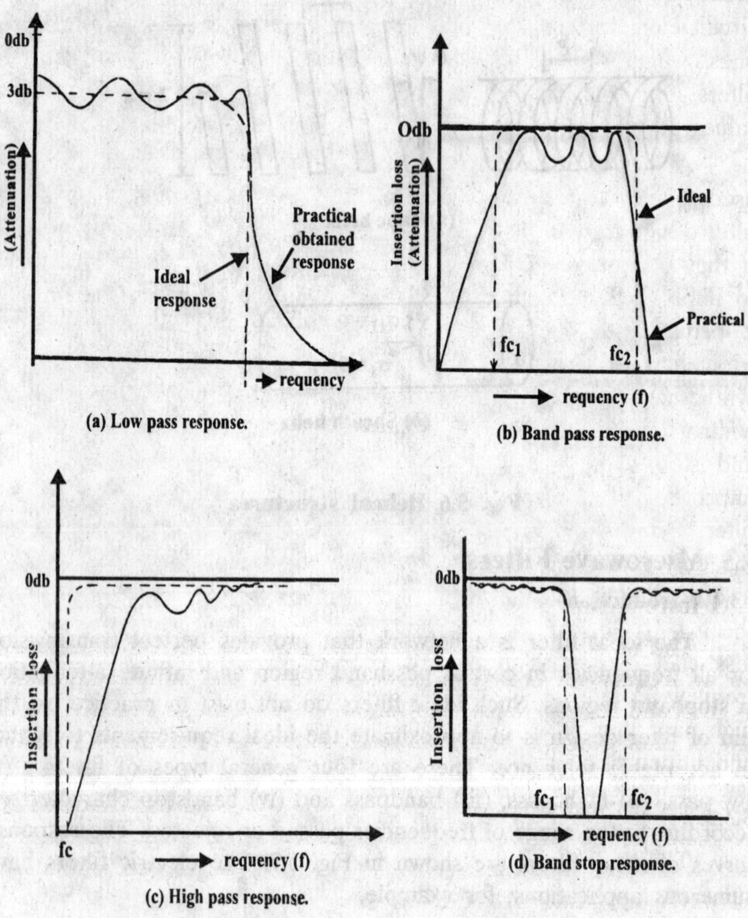

Fig. 5.7.

At low frequencies "building blocks" for filters design are ideal inductors and capacitors. These elements have very simple frequency characteristic and a complete synthesis technique has been developed to design the filter using these elements. The filter design problem at microwave frequencies where distributed parameter elements are used is much more complicated and no complete theory or synthesis procedure exists. The microwave filter is realized by using microwave circuit elements such as suitable lengths of waveguide or transmission lines, which replace all inductors and capacitors of low frequency filters. Once the lumped component values have been established these values are then transformed to the desired distributed components.

At low frequency two teachniques of filter design are commonly used. First is the image parameter method. This method provides a filter design having the required passband and stopband characteristics. If they do not meet the desired characteristic there is no simple way to improve the design. Second method is the insertion loss method, it begins with a clear cut specification of a physically realizable frequency characteristic, and from this a suitable filter network is synthesized. Hence the insertion loss method allows a high degree of control over the amplitude and phase characteristics in the passband and stop band. Also this method allows filter performance to be improved in a systematic manner, at the expense of a higher order filter. For this region the insertion loss method is preferable and is the only method considered in detail in the following sections. The insertion loss method, mainly comprises of following steps : (i) determine the low pass "prototype" network for the desired, specified insertion loss characteristics, normalized to 1 ohm termination and a cutoff frequency of 1 rad/sec.; (ii) transform the prototype structure into high pass, band pass or band stop structures using suitable frequency and impedance transformations.

5.3.2. Filter design by insertion loss method

The modern filter theory was developed by Darlington and subsequently improved by Mathaei. The highlights of their work are as follows :

(i) Assume a low pass "prototype" lumped circuit as shown in Fig. 5.8(a).The load impedance is chosen equal to 1Ω, and the generator impedance as R. The circuit in Fig. 5.8b is the dual of the circuit in Fig. 5.8a. Both circuits can be designed to give same power loss ratio. Here *g* represents the roots of the governing filter transfer function for *n*th order filter. These g values can be scaled to represent actual electric circuit elements in order to synthesize a desired filter response.

(ii) The elements are expressed in known parameters like VSWR, characteristic impedance.

(iii) Find out how many elements exist in a prototype circuit for a given insertion loss.

(iv) Find out frequency and impedance transformations that transform a low pass prototype network into a high pass, band pass or band stop network.

(v) Find out techniques that transform a lumped circuit into a distributed parameter circuit.

(vi) Change the network so developed into its microwave equivalent using either a microwave equivalent or the distributed one.

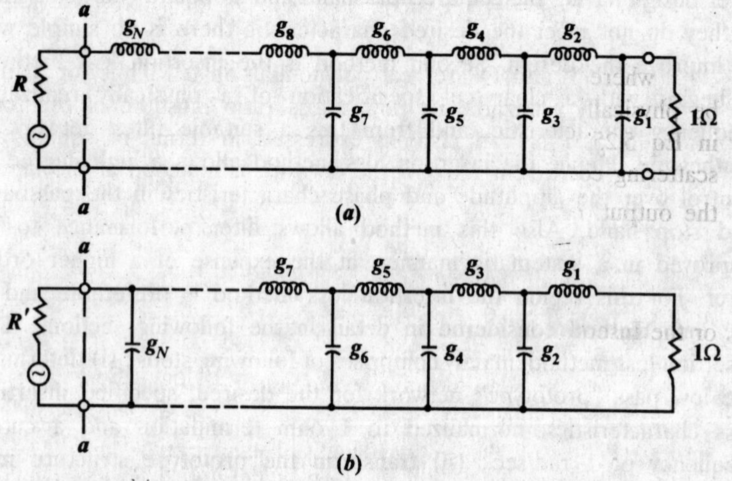

Fig. 5.8. Low pass ladder prototype filter networks

Basically the theory relies on the development of a lowpass prototype network for a given insertion loss (or scattering parameter) characteristic.

5.3.3. Characterization by power loss ratio

In the insertion loss method a filter response is defined by its insertion loss ratio P_{LR}.

$$P_{LR} = \frac{\text{Power available from source}}{\text{power delivered to load}} = \frac{P_{in}}{P_{load}}$$

$$= \frac{1}{1 - |\Gamma(\omega)|^2} \qquad \text{....(5.22)}$$

The insertion loss (I_L) in dB is

$$I_L = 10 \log P_{LR} \qquad \text{....(5.23)}$$

$|\Gamma(\omega)|^2$ is an even function of ω and can therefore be expressed as a polynomial in ω^2. Thus we can write

$$|\Gamma(\omega)|^2 = \frac{P(\omega^2)}{P(\omega^2) + Q(\omega^2)} \qquad \text{....(5.24)}$$

substituting this form in Eq. 5.22. gives

$$P_{LR} = = 1 + \frac{P(\omega^2)}{Q(\omega^2)} \qquad \text{....(5.25)}$$

where P and Q are real polynomials in ω^2. Thus for a filter to be physically realizable its power loss ratio must be of the form as in Eq 5.25. P_{LR} can also be expressed in terms of square of the scattering coefficient $|S_{21}|$ if the network is matched at the input and the output. *i.e.*

$$|S_{21}(j\omega)|^2 = \frac{1}{P_{LR}} \qquad \text{....(5.26)}$$

or the Insertion loss ratio I_L.

$$I_L = 10 \log_{10} P_{LR} = 10 \log_{10} |S_{21}|^{-2}$$

$$= 10 \log_{10} \left[1 + \frac{P(\omega^2)}{Q(\omega^2)}\right] \qquad \text{....(5.27)}$$

For a lossless junction [S] is unitary, hence for a two port network, we have

$$|S_{21}|^2 + |S_{11}|^2 = 1 \qquad \text{....(5.27)}$$

For a given insertion loss, $|S_{21}|^2$ is known from Eq. 5.26, $|S_{11}|^2$ can be calculated from Eq. 5.27. $|S_{11}|^2$ is connected to the input impedance of the network by the relation

$$Z_{in} = \frac{1}{Y_{in}} = \frac{1 + S_{11}(j\omega)}{1 - S_{11}(j\omega)} \qquad \text{....(5.28)}$$

We now discuss some practical filter responses.

5.3.4. Maximally flat

This characteristic is also called the binomial or Butterworth response and it provides the flattest possible passband response for a given filter. For a low-pass filter, choosing Q equal to unity and $P(\omega^2)$ equal to $k^2(\omega/\omega_c)^{2n}$ we obtain

$$P_{LR} = \frac{1}{|S_{12}|^2} = 1 + k^2 \left(\frac{\omega}{\omega_c}\right)^{2n} \quad ....(5.29)$$

where n is the order of the filter, and ω_c is the cutoff frequency. The pass band extends from $\omega = 0$ to $\omega = \omega_c$ at the band edge power loss ratio is $1+k^2$. If we choose it as -3 dB point, which is very common then $k = 1$. For $\omega > \omega_c$, the attenuation increases monotonically with frequency as shown in Fig 5.9a. For $\omega >> \omega_c$, $P_{LR} \approx k^2\left(\frac{\omega}{\omega_c}\right)^{2n}$, which shows that the insertion loss increases at the rate of 20 dB/decade.

5.3.5. Chebyshev filter

If a Chebyshev polynomial is used to specify the insertion loss of an n-order. For the low pass filter insertion loss is expressed as

$$P_{LR} = 1 + k^2 T_n^2 \left(\frac{\omega}{\omega_c}\right) \quad ....(5.30)$$

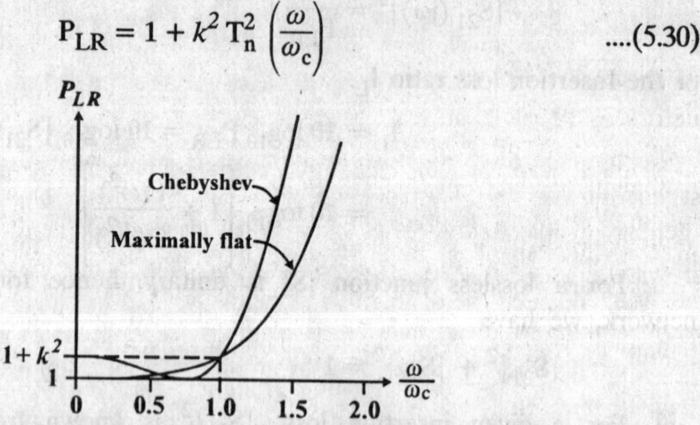

Fig. 5.9a. Maximally flat and equal ripple low pass filter response.

This will result in a sharp cutoff. The passband will have ripples of amplitude $1+k^2$, as shown in Fig 5.9, since $T_n(x)$ oscillates between ± 1 for $|x| \le 1$. For large x, $T_n(x) \approx \frac{1}{2}(2x)^n$, so that for $\omega >> \omega_c$ the insertion loss becomes

$$P_{LR} \approx \frac{k^2}{4}\left(\frac{2\omega}{\omega_c}\right)^{2n} \quad \text{....(5.31)}$$

which increases at the rate of $20n$ dB/decade. The insertion loss for the Chebyshev case is $(2^{2n})/4$ greater than the binomial response, at any given frequency where $\omega >> \omega_L$. Comparison of Butterworth and Chebyshev low pass filter show that Chebyshev filters have superior performance in the stop band and have a greater insertion loss rate than Butterworth filters with the same number of reactive components.

We will now consider the design of a low pass filter prototype which is normalized in terms of frequency and impedance. This normalization simplifies the design of filters for arbitrary frequency, impedance and type of the filter. The low pass prototypes are then scaled to the desired frequency and impedance.

If we let Z_{in} be the input impedance at the plane *aa* in Fig 5.8a the reflection coefficient will be

$$\Gamma = \frac{Z_{in} - R}{Z_{in} + R} \quad \text{....(5.32)}$$

The power loss ratio P_{LR} in terms of Z_{in} and R is

$$P_{LR} = 1 + \frac{|Z_{in} - R|^2}{2R\,(Z_{in} + Z_{in}^*)} \quad \text{....(5.33)}$$

At $\omega = 0$, all capacitors appear as infinite impedances and all inductors as zero impedances; hence $Z_{in} = 1$.

For a maximally flat filter or a Chebyshev filter with n odd, we must have unity power ratio at $\omega = 0$. This requires that we choose the generator impedance equal to unity. However, in case of Chebyshev filter with n even $P_{LR} = 1 + k^2$ at $\omega = 0$,

so that

$$1 + k^2 = 1 + \frac{(1 - R)^2}{4R}$$

or $$R = 2k^2 + 1 - \sqrt{4k^2\,(1 - k^2)} = \frac{1}{R'} \quad \text{....(5.34)}$$

Where R′ is the generator impedance in the dual network shown in Fig 5.8b. The required values of the element g_k in the ladder network can be obtained very readily by solving for Z_{in} and equating the power loss ratio as given by Eq. 5.33 to the desired power for n up to 3 or 4. As an example consider the case for $n = 2$ for the part in Fig. 5.8a, we find that

$$Z_{in} = j\omega L + \frac{1}{1 + j\omega C}$$

where $\in$ g_1, and $L = g_2$

Using (5.33), we get

$$P_{LR} = 1 + \frac{(1 - R)^2 + \omega^2 (L^2 + C^2R^2 - 2LC) + \omega^4 L^2C^2}{4R}$$

To make P_{LR} equal to unity at $\omega = 0$ and to obtain maximally flat response, we must choose $R = 1$ and equate coefficients of $\omega^2 = 0$ and ω^4 to be equal to 1.

$$1 = \frac{L^2C^2}{4}$$

or $LC = 2$, Hence $L = C = \sqrt{2}$

For Chebyshev response, we equate P_{LR} to

$$P_{LR} = 1 + k^2 T_2^2 (\omega/\omega_c) \qquad \text{....(5.35)}$$

We know that for Chebyshev polynomial,

$$T_1(x) = x,\ T_2(x) = 2x^2 - 1,\ T_3(x) = 4x^3 - 3x \text{ for } x = 1$$

$$T_n{}'(x) = 2x\, T_{n-1}(x) - T_{n-2}(x) = \cos(n \cos_x^{-1}) \text{ for } x \leq 1$$

$$= \cosh(n \cosh^{-1} x)$$

Substituting for T_2 in (5.35), we get

$$P_{LR} = 1 + k^2 T_2^2 (\omega/\omega_c) = 1 + k^2 [2(\omega/\omega_c)^2 - 1]^2 \qquad \text{....(5.36)}$$

to obtain the values of L and C.

This procedure can be extended to find the element values for filters with an arbitrary number of elements n, but for large n this scheme becomes very laborious to carry out. However the element values of ladder network have been prepared by number of people and are tabulated as listed in Table 5.1–5.2.

Table 5.1 gives such element values for maximally flat low pass filter prototypes for $n = 1$ to 7 and Table 5.2 gives for Chebyshev filter.

For the maximally flat network with a power loss ratio

$$P_{LR} = 1 + \omega^{2n}$$

The element values are given by

$$g_0 = 1$$

$$g_k = 2 \sin [(2k-1)\pi/2n] \qquad k = 1, 2 \ldots n \qquad \ldots(5.37)$$

where g_k is the value of either of inductance in henries or of capacitance in farads. Each end of the filter is terminated in a 1Ω resistance.

For a Chebyshev low pass filter with $\omega_c = 1$, the element values are given as

$$g_{n+1} = \begin{cases} 1 & n \text{ odd} \\ 2k^2 + 1 - 2k\sqrt{1-k^2} & n \text{ even} \end{cases}$$

When element g_n is a capacitor, $g_{n+1} = R$, but when g_n is an inductor, $g_{n+1} = 1/R$

$$g_k = \frac{4a_{k-1}\, a_k}{b_{k-1}\, g_{k-1}} \qquad k = 2, 3, 4, \ldots\ldots n$$

where $$a_k = \sin \frac{2k-1}{2n}\pi \qquad k = 1, 2, 3, \ldots\ldots n$$

$$b_k = \sinh^2 \frac{\beta}{2n} + \sin^2 \frac{k\pi}{n} \qquad k = 1, 2, 3, \ldots\ldots n$$

$$\beta = \ln \frac{\sqrt{1+k^2}+1}{\sqrt{1+k^2}-1}$$

$$g_1 = \frac{2a_1}{\sinh \beta/2n}$$

Table 5.1. Values of gk for Butterworth filter (IL = 3 dB at ω′ = 1)

k	n						
	1	2	3	4	5	6	7
1	2.0	1.414	1.0	0.7654	0.618	0.5176	0.445
2	1.0	1.414	2.0	1.8480	1.618	1.4140	1.247
3		1.000	1.0	1.8480	2.000	1.9320	1.802
4			1.0	0.7654	1.618	1.9320	2.000
5				1.0000	0.618	1.4140	1.802
6					1.000	0.5176	1.247
7						1.0000	0.445

Table 5.2. Values of g_k for chebyshev filter 0.1 dB ripple

k	n						
	1	2	3	4	5	6	7
1	0.3052	0.8430	1.0315	1.1088	1.1468	1.1681	1.1811
2	1.0000	0.6220	1.1474	1.3061	1.3712	1.4039	1.4228
3		1.3554	1.03315	1.7703	1.9750	2.0562	2.0966
4			1.0000	0.8180	1.3712	1.5170	1.5733
5				1.3554	1.1468	1.9029	2.0966
6					1.0000	0.8618	1.4228
7						1.3554	1.1811

More extensive tables are given in reference [6].

5.4 Frequency Transformations

The lowpass prototype filter with cutoff frequency at $\omega_c = 1$ and terminating impedance equal to 1Ω can be used as basis for the design of high pass and bandpass filters with arbitrary terminated load resistance. For the lowpass prototype filter, the frequency variable is denoted by ω'. The power loss ratio for the maximally flat and Chebyshev response can be expressed as

$$\omega' = f(\omega)$$

$$P_{LR} = 1 + P(\omega')^2 \qquad \text{....(5.39)}$$

If we wish to have load other than unity, *i.e.* R_L as the terminating load then the required filter reactances will be multiplied by R_L. Then the prototype filter reactances can be viewed as normalized with respect to R_L.

The new values of the inductance, capacitance and the generator resistance are given by

$$L_k' = R_L L_k$$

$$C_k' = C_k / R_L \qquad \text{....(5.40)}$$

$$R' = R_L R$$

which is nothing but impedance transformation. We see from this relation that the response characteristics of the new filter will be different from those of the original prototype filter depending upon the selection of the transformation function f(ω). The following transformation are commonly used.

5.4.1. Frequency Expansion

If we wish to change the cutoff from unity to some other value ω_c, then we choose

$$f(\omega) = \omega/\omega_c$$

Then $$P_{LR} = 1 + P\left(\frac{\omega^2}{\omega_c^2}\right) \quad \text{....(5.41)}$$

It is clear that cut off will occur when $(\omega/\omega_c) = 1$, *i.e.* at $\omega = \omega_c$ as shown in Fig 5.10a. The series reactances and shunt susceptance in the prototype filter will be replaced by new value of reactances and susceptances

$$j\,X'_k = j(\omega/\omega_c)\,L_k \quad \text{....(5.42)}$$

$$j\,B'_k = j\,(\omega/\omega_c)\,C_k$$

where $L_k' = L_k/\omega_c$ and $C_k' = C_k/\omega_c$

The power loss ratio in ferms of ω' and ω are compared in Fig. 5.10a and b.

If we replace the frequency variable ω' as

$$\omega' = f(\omega)$$

the power loss ratio because

$$P_{Lk} = 1 + P[f^2(\omega)]$$

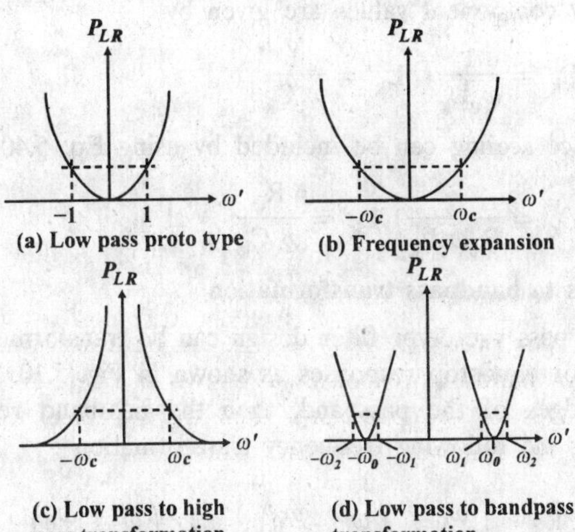

Fig. 5.10. Filter response

5.4.2 Low pass to high-pass transformation

Low pass to high pass filter is obtained by choosing f(ω) equal to $-(\omega_c/\omega)$. This power loss ratio P_{LR} is expressed as

$$P_{LR} = 1 + P\left(\frac{\omega_c}{\omega}\right)^2 \quad ....(5.43)$$

This transforms $\omega = 0$ to $\omega = \pm\infty$ and vice versa is shown in Fig. 5.10c. It interchanges the passband to stopband.

To realize the high pass response, replace each inductive element in the low pass network by a capacitive element, and the low pass capacitive element to inductive element. Thus an inductance in low pass case becomes a capacitance, *i.e.* $C_{HP} = \frac{1}{(\omega_c/\omega)L_{LP}}$ and a capacitance becomes an inductance according to $L_{HP} = \frac{1}{(\omega_c/\omega)\,C_{LP}}$ or more generally the series and the shunt susceptances in the new filter are chosen as follows :

$$j\,X_k' = -j\frac{\omega_c}{\omega}L_k = \frac{1}{j\omega C_k'} \quad ....(5.44a)$$

$$j\,B_k' = -j\frac{\omega_c}{\omega}C_k = \frac{1}{j\omega L_k'} \quad ....(5.44b)$$

The new component values are given by

$$C_k' = \frac{1}{\omega_c L_k},\; L_k' = \frac{1}{\omega_c C_k} \quad ....(5.45)$$

Impedance scaling can be included by using Eq. 5.40 to give

$$C_k' = \frac{1}{R_0\omega_c L_k},\; L_k' = \frac{R_0}{\omega_c C_k} \quad ....(5.46)$$

5.4.3. Low pass to bandpass transformation

The low pass prototype filter design can be transformed to have the bandpass or bandstop responses as shown in Fig. 5.10. If ω_1 and ω_2 are the edges of the passband, then the passband response is obtained using the following frequency transformation :

$$\omega' = f(\omega) = \frac{\omega_0}{\omega_2 - \omega_1}\left(\frac{\omega}{\omega_0} - \frac{\omega_0}{\omega}\right) = \frac{1}{\Delta\omega}\left(\frac{\omega}{\omega_0} - \frac{\omega_0}{\omega}\right) \quad ....(5.47)$$

where ω_0 is the geometric mean of ω_1 and ω_2.

$\omega_0 = \sqrt{\omega_1\omega_2}$ and $\Delta = \dfrac{\omega_2 - \omega_1}{\omega_0}$ is the fractional band width of the passband.

Equation 5.47 can be solved for ω to give

$$\omega = \omega' \frac{\omega_2 - \omega_1}{2} \pm \frac{1}{2}\sqrt{\omega'^2(\omega_2 - \omega_1)^2 + 4\omega_1\omega_2} \quad \text{....(5.48)}$$

The point $\omega' = 0$ has mapped into the points $\omega = \pm\,\omega_0$ and $\omega' = \pm\,1$ maps into the four points $\pm\,(\omega_2 - \omega_1)/2 \pm (\omega_2 + \omega_1)/2 = \pm\,\omega_2$ and $\pm\,\omega_1$. Thus the prototype filter passband between $\pm\,1$ maps into passband extending from ω_1 to ω_2 and $-\omega_1$ to $-\,\omega_2$, which represents bandpass filters with band centre at $\pm\,\omega_0$.

The filter elements are obtained by considering the frequency behaviour of series and parallel connection of L and C as shown in Fig. (5.11a). For the series circuit, we have

$$jX' = j\omega L + \frac{1}{j\omega C} = j\sqrt{\frac{L}{C}}\left(\omega\sqrt{LC} - \frac{1}{\omega\sqrt{LC}}\right)$$

Substitute $\sqrt{LC} = \dfrac{1}{\omega_0}$

$$jX' = j\sqrt{\frac{L}{C}}\left(\frac{\omega}{\omega_0} - \frac{\omega_0}{\omega}\right) \quad \text{....(5.49)}$$

Similarly for the parallel circuit

$$jB' = j\omega C + \frac{1}{j\omega L} = j\sqrt{\frac{C}{L}}\left(\frac{\omega}{\omega_0} - \frac{\omega_0}{\omega}\right) \quad \text{....(5.50)}$$

The desired frequency transformation is obtained, if we replace the reactance and susceptance $jX_k = j\omega L_k$ and $jB_k = j\omega C_k$ in the prototype filter by series and parallel tuned circuits, such that

$$jX_k' = j\sqrt{\frac{L_k'}{C_k'}}\left(\frac{\omega}{\omega_0} - \frac{\omega_0}{\omega}\right) = j\,L_k\frac{1}{\Delta}\left(\frac{\omega}{\omega_0} - \frac{\omega_0}{\omega}\right)$$

i.e. choose $L_k'\,C_k' = \dfrac{1}{\omega_0^2}$ for the series circuit

or $\sqrt{\dfrac{L_k'}{C_k'}} = \omega_0 L_k' = \dfrac{L_k\,\omega_0}{\omega_2 - \omega_1}$

or $$L_k{}' = \frac{L_k}{\omega_2 - \omega_1} \qquad \text{....(5.51)}$$

For the parallel circuit choose

$$\sqrt{\frac{C_k{}'}{L_k{}'}} = \omega_0 C_k{}' = \frac{\omega_0 C_k}{\omega_2 - \omega_1}$$

or $$C_k{}' = \frac{C_k}{\omega_2 - \omega_1} \qquad \text{....(5.52)}$$

The resultant filter network is represented in Fig. (5.11b).

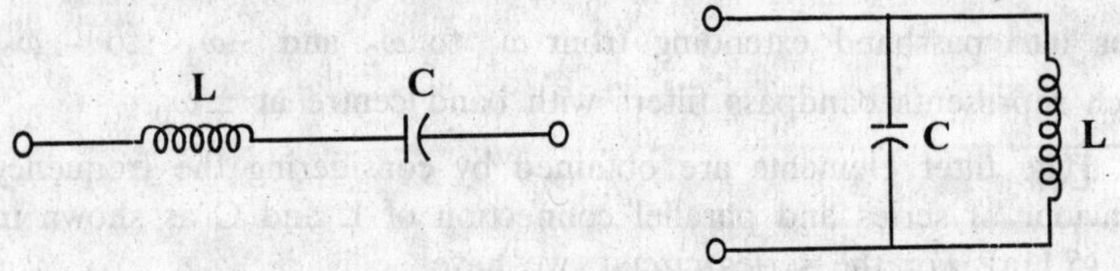

Fig. 5.11 a Series and parallel connection of L and C

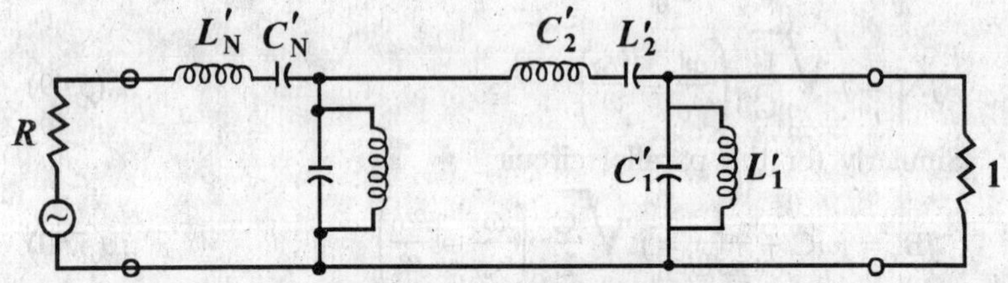

Fig. 5.11 b Bandpass filter configuration.

Lowpass to bandstop transformation is obtained by using the frequency transformation as given below :

$$\omega' = f(\omega) = \Delta\omega \left(\frac{\omega}{\omega_0} - \frac{\omega_0}{\omega} \right)^{-1}$$

Then series inductor of the lowpass prototype is converted to parallel LC circuits having elemental values given by

$$L_k{}' = \frac{(\omega_2 - \omega_1) L_k}{\omega_0^2}$$

$$C_k{}' = \frac{1}{(\omega_2 - \omega_1)\, L_k}$$

The shunt capacitor of the lowpass prototype is converted to series LC circuit having element value given by

$$L_k{}' = \frac{1}{(\omega_2 - \omega_1) C_k}$$

$$C_k{}' = \frac{(\omega_2 - \omega_1) C_k}{\omega_0^2}$$

The different element transformations from a lowpass prototype are summarized in Table 5.3.

Table 5.3. Summary of Prototype Filter Transformations

Low-pass	High-pass	Bandpass	Bandstop
Series inductor L	Series capacitor $\frac{1}{\omega_c L}$	Series inductor $\frac{L}{\omega_0 \Delta}$ in series with capacitor $\frac{1}{\omega_0 L}$	Parallel inductor $\frac{L\Delta}{\omega_0}$ and capacitor $\frac{1}{\omega_0 L \Delta}$
Shunt capacitor C	Shunt inductor $\frac{1}{\omega_c L}$	Parallel inductor $\frac{\Delta}{\omega_0 C}$ and capacitor $\frac{C}{\omega_0 \Delta}$	Series inductor $\frac{1}{\omega_0 L \Delta}$ in series with capacitor $\frac{C\Delta}{\omega_0}$

$$\Delta = \frac{\omega_2 - \omega_1}{\omega_0}$$

5.5. Richard Transformation and Kuroda's Identity for Microwave Filter implementation

At low frequencies the filter design can easily be implemented using the lump element filter design discussed in previous sections. But at microwave frequencies these lumped elements are realized by using distributed components of transmission lines, strip lines or microstrip lines. Richard transformation is used to convert lumped elements to transmission line sections. Along with this transformation

Kuroda's identities can be used to separate filter elements by using transmission line sections. These additional transmission line lengths do not affect the filter response.

5.5.1 Richard transformation

The transformation was introduced by P. Richard [6] to synthesize an LC network using open and short circuited transmission lines. We consider that L_k is replaced by the short circuited transmission line stub of length l and characteristic impedance and the capacitance C_k is replaced by open circuited stub of length l and characteristic admittance Y_k. The new reactance and susceptance functions become

$$jX_k' = j\,Z_k \tan \beta l = jZ_k \tan\left(\frac{\omega l}{c}\right)$$

$$= jZ_k \tan\theta = jg_k \tan\theta \qquad \text{....(5.53)}$$

$$jB_k' = jY_k \tan\theta = jg_k \tan\theta \qquad \text{....(5.54)}$$

and the power loss ratio for the filter is given by

$$P_{LR} = 1 + P(\tan^2\theta) \qquad \text{....(5.55)}$$

The frequency transformation $\omega' = \tan\theta$ maps the whole ω' axis periodically into intervals of length π in the θ domain. Hence the inductors and capacitors of a lumped element filter can be replaced with short-circuited and open-circuited stubs as illustrated in Fig. 5.12.

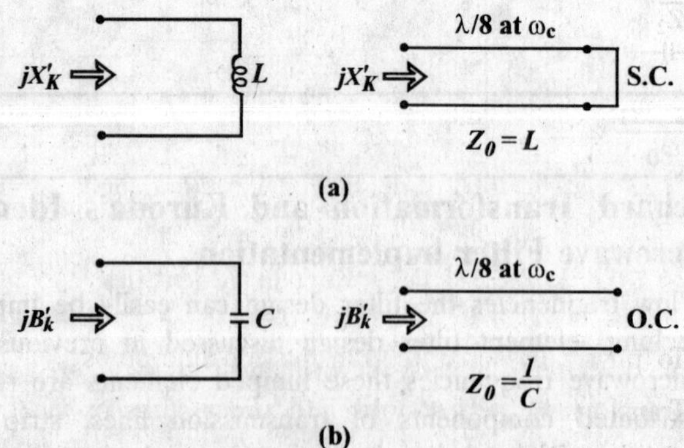

Fig. 5.12. Richard's transformation.

5.5.2. Kuroda's identities

Fig. 5.13 shows four network equivalences known as Kuroda's identities of the first and second kind. The equivalence are only valid in S plane defined as

$$S = j\Omega = j\tan\beta l = j\tan\theta \qquad ....(5.56)$$

These identities are used to achieve a more practical microwave filter implementation by performing any of the following operations :

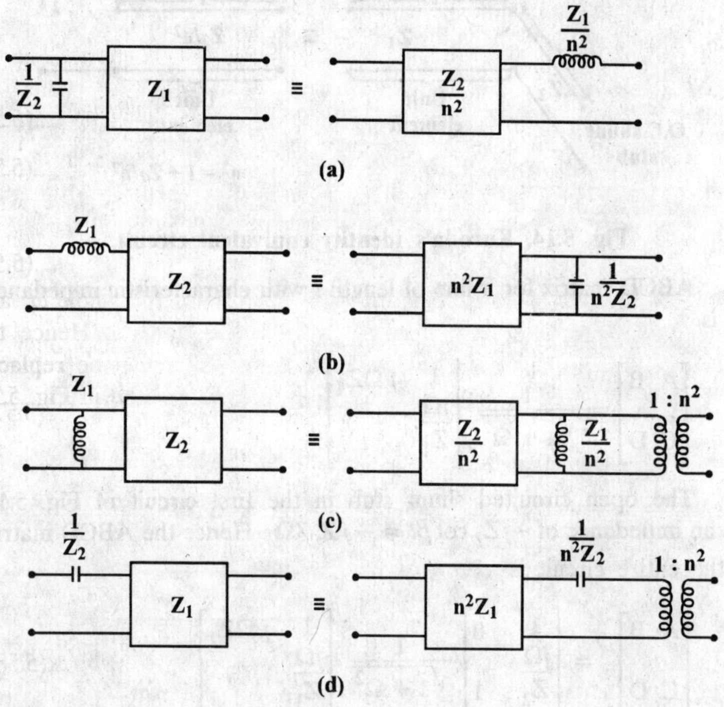

Fig. 5.13. Four Kuroda's Identities

1. To physically separate transmission line stubs
2. Transforming series stubs into shunt stubs or vice versa.
3. Change impractical characteristic impedances into more realizable ones.

Each box in the Fig. 5.13 represents a unit element or a transmission line of length $\lambda/8$ at $\omega = \omega_c$. The two circuits of identity (*a*) in Fig. 5.13 can be redrawn as in Fig. 5.14. We are going to show that these two networks are equivalent by showing that their ABCD matrices are identical.

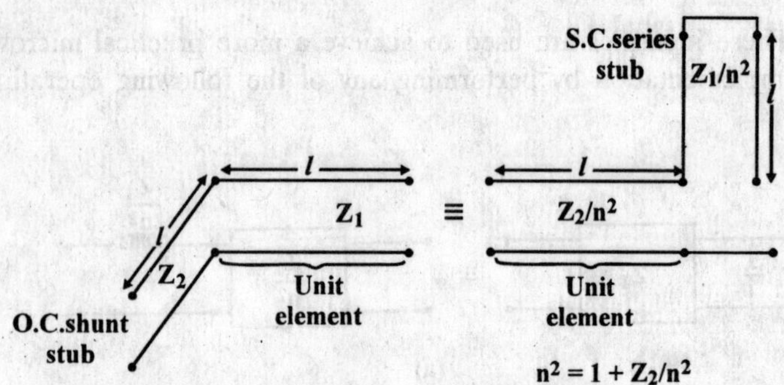

Fig. 5.14. Kuroda's identity equivalent circuit.

ABCD matrix for a line of length l with characteristic impedance Z_1 is

$$\begin{bmatrix} A & B \\ C & D \end{bmatrix} = \frac{1}{\sqrt{1+\Omega^2}} \begin{bmatrix} 1 & j\Omega Z_1 \\ \frac{j\Omega}{Z_1} & 1 \end{bmatrix} \qquad \text{....(5.57)}$$

The open circuited shunt stub in the first circuit of Fig. 5.14 has an impedance of $-jZ_2 \cot \beta l = -j\, Z_2/\Omega$. Hence the ABCD matrix of the entire circuit is

$$\begin{bmatrix} A & B \\ C & D \end{bmatrix}_L = \begin{bmatrix} 1 & 0 \\ \frac{j\Omega}{Z_2} & 1 \end{bmatrix} \frac{1}{\sqrt{1+\Omega^2}} \begin{bmatrix} 1 & j\Omega Z_1 \\ \frac{j\Omega}{Z_1} & 1 \end{bmatrix} \qquad \text{....(5.58)}$$

$$\begin{bmatrix} A & B \\ C & D \end{bmatrix} = \frac{1}{\sqrt{1+\Omega^2}} \begin{bmatrix} 1 & j\Omega Z_1 \\ j\Omega\left(\frac{1}{Z_1}+\frac{1}{Z_2}\right) & 1-\Omega^2\frac{Z_1}{Z_2} \end{bmatrix} \qquad \text{....(5.59)}$$

Now the short circuited series stub in the second circuit of Fig. 5.14 has an impedance of $j(Z_1/n^2)\tan\beta l = j\,(\Omega\, Z_1/n^2)$ so that the ABCD matrix of the entire circuit is

$$\begin{bmatrix} A & B \\ C & D \end{bmatrix} = \frac{1}{\sqrt{1+\Omega^2}} \begin{bmatrix} 1 & \dfrac{j\,\Omega}{n^2}(Z_1+Z_2) \\ \dfrac{j\Omega n^2}{Z_2} & 1-\Omega^2\dfrac{Z_1}{Z_2} \end{bmatrix} \quad \text{....(5.60)}$$

The results of Eq. 5.56b and Eq. 5.57 are identical if we choose $n^2 = 1 + Z_2/Z_1$. Other identities can also be proved similarly.

5.5.3. Impedance and admittance inverters

In microwave frequencies alternate presence of series and parallel tuned circuits in filters derived from lowpass prototype is not a desirable feature. It is possible to use only series or only shunt elements when implementing the filter with any particular transmission line. The Kuroda's identities or the method which uses impedances (K) or admittance (J) inverters can be used for this type of conversion. These are especially useful for narrow bandwidth (BW < 10%) bandstop or bandpass filters.

An impedance inverter is an ideal quarter wave transformer. A load impedance connected at one end is seen as an impedance that has been inverted with respect to the characteristic impedance squared at the input. Impedance inverter may be used to convert a bandpass filter network shown in Fig 5.15 in to a network containing only series tuned circuits. Similarly by using admittance inverters the band pass filter can be converted into a network using only parallel tuned circuits. Moreover, by choosing correctly the inverters all the inductors and capacitors can be chosen to have same values. Hence the J and K inverter make it possible to use identical series or paralled tuned resonators throughout the network.

In Fig 5.15a, consider the parallel admittance element connected on both sides by an ideal impedance inverter of characteristic impedance K^2. The input impedance is given by

$$Z_{in} = \frac{K^2}{Z_p} = K^2 Y_p = Y_p = Z_s \quad \text{....(5.61)}$$

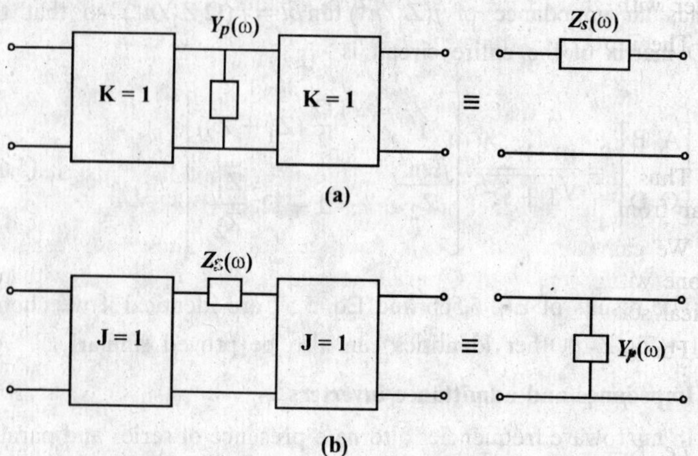

Fig. 5.15 (a) Impedance inverters. (b) admittance inverters.

Thus the shunt element with two impedance inverters converts the shunt admittance into an equivalent series impedance $Z_s(\omega) = Y_p(\omega)$. If Y_p is a parallel tuned resonator with $Y_p = j\omega C - \dfrac{j}{\omega L} = j\omega C\left(1 - \dfrac{\omega_0^2}{\omega^2}\right)$ will be converted into a series tuned circuit with $Z_s = j\omega L\,(1 - \omega_0^2/\omega^2)$.

The inductance L in henries will have the same numerical value as the capacitance C in farads. If we want to convert an admittance $Y_1 = j\omega C_1\left(1 - \dfrac{\omega_0^2}{\omega^2}\right)$ into a particular series tuned with arbitrary value of inductance L, then K should be chosen as

$$K^2\, j\omega C_1\left(1 - \frac{\omega_0^2}{\omega^2}\right) = j\omega L\left(1 - \frac{\omega_0^2}{\omega^2}\right) \qquad \text{....(5.62)}$$

or
$$K = \sqrt{\frac{L}{C_1}}$$

thus we can transform a shunt element into a series element having the same dependence on frequency but an arbitrary impedance level.

Fig. 5.15b shows a series element $Z_s(\omega)$ with an admittance inverter with characteristic admittance J connected on both sides.

The input admittance will be

$$Y_{in} = \frac{J^2}{Y_s} = J^2 Z_s = Y_p \quad \text{....(5.63)}$$

Thus the series element with the two admittance inverters will appear from the terminals to be an equivalent shunt admittance.

We can use inverters to convert the circuit shown in Fig. 5.16a into one with two identical parallel tuned resonators or one with two identical series tuned resonators.

For case (b), we choose K so that

$$K^2 j\omega C_1 (1 - \omega_0^2/\omega^2) = j\omega L_2 (1 - \omega_0^2/\omega^2) \quad \text{....(5.64)}$$

i.e. $K = \sqrt{L_2/C_1}$

for the case (c) J is chosen so that

$$J^2 j\omega L_2 \left(1 - \frac{\omega_0^2}{\omega^2}\right) = j\omega C_1 (1 - \omega_0^2/\omega^2) \quad \text{....(5.65)}$$

i.e. $J = \sqrt{C_1/L_2}$

For more detailed discussion on inverters, see [1].

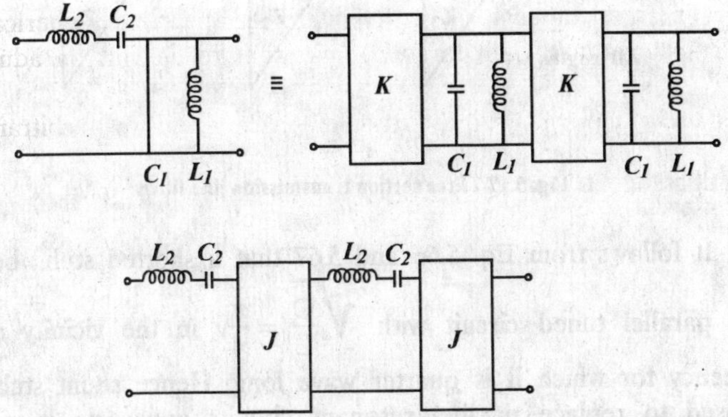

Fig. 5.16. Inverters used to convert a section of a filter into a network using only identical parallel or series tuned resonators.

5.5.4 Transmission line filters

Consider a typical three-section filter transformed to a three shunt stub structure shown in Fig. 5.17. The shorted stubs are quarter wave long at ω_0, the normalized input admittance in vicinity of frequency ω_0 is given as

$$Y_{in} = jy\,(\omega - \omega_0)\frac{l}{c} = jy\frac{\omega - \omega_0}{\omega_0}\pi/2 \qquad ....(5.66)$$

where l is the stub length and $\omega_0 l/c = \pi/2$. The input admittance of a parallel tuned circuit is given by

$$y_{in} = j\omega C + \frac{1}{j\omega L} = j\sqrt{\frac{C}{L}}\left(\frac{\omega}{\omega_0} - \frac{\omega_0}{\omega}\right)$$

$$\approx 2j\sqrt{\frac{C}{L}}\frac{\omega - \omega_0}{\omega} = 2j\,C\,(\omega - \omega_0) \qquad ....(5.67)$$

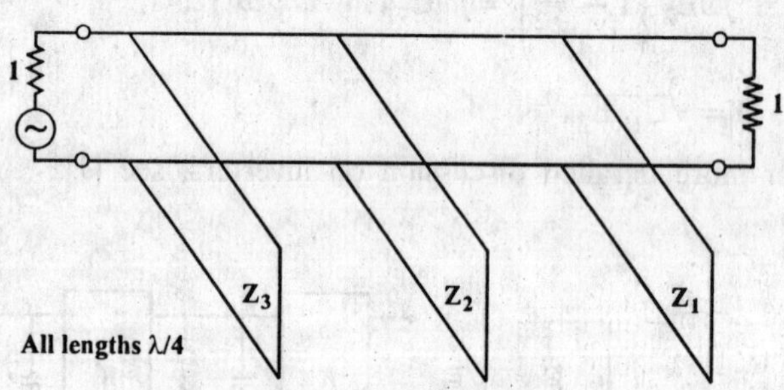

Fig. 5.17 Three section transmission line filter.

It follows from Eq. 5.66 and 5.67 that a shorted stub behaves as a parallel tuned circuit with $\sqrt{\frac{C}{L}} = \frac{\pi}{4}y$ in the vicinity of the frequency for which it is quarter wave long. Hence shunt stubs can be used to replace parallel resonant circuits appearing in a filter circuit. The stub length can be calculated from Eq. 5.62. Typical available coaxial line filters and their lumped equivalent are shown in Fig. 5.18. A low pass filter Fig. 5.18a consists of two re-entrant line sections separated by a concentric condenser. The structure behaves like low pass filter as long as re-entrant line sections are shorter than a quarter wavelength. At higher frequencies reactances of these sections can have poles and zeros, hence spurious passband can exist.

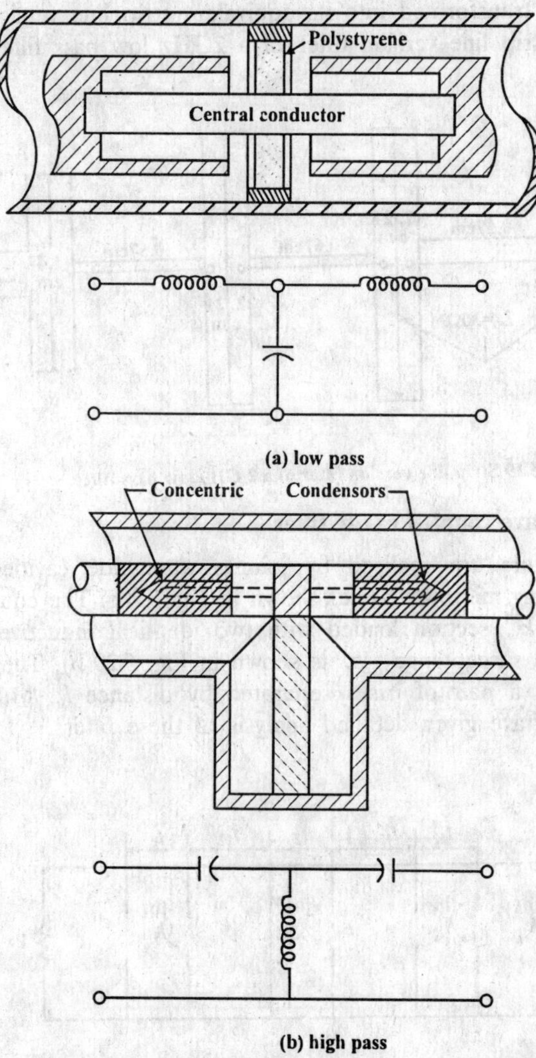

Fig. 5.18 A Mircowave coaxial line filter (a) low pass (b) high pass

The high pass coaxial filter Fig. 5.18b is differentiated from a low pass filter through the suitable frequency transformation discussed in section 5.4.2. Bandpass and bandstop filters may be similarly designed.

5.5.5 Strip line filters

Strip line filter is an import class of microwave filters. There are standard techniques [4] available by which a lumped or a distributed circuit may be transformed into its equivalent strip line version. Fig. 5.19 shows a strip line version filter of a 2GHz low pass filter.

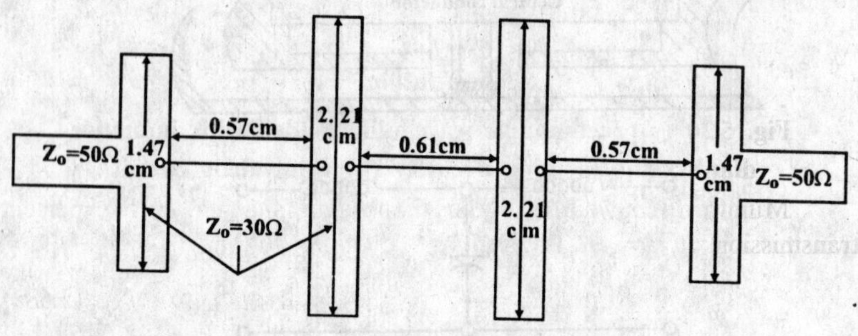

Fig. 5.19 Strip line version filter of a 2 GH_Z low pass filter.

5.5.6 Quarter wave coupled cavity filter

These filters are realised by joining waveguide cavities with quarter wave long microwave lines shown in Fig. 5.20a. The equivalent circuit for the kth section loaded with two identical inductive irises with normalised susceptance $-jb_k$ is shown in Fig. 5.20(b). The cavity k is formed by a pair of irises separated by distance l_k. **Mumford and Collin** [8] have given detailed analysis of these filters.

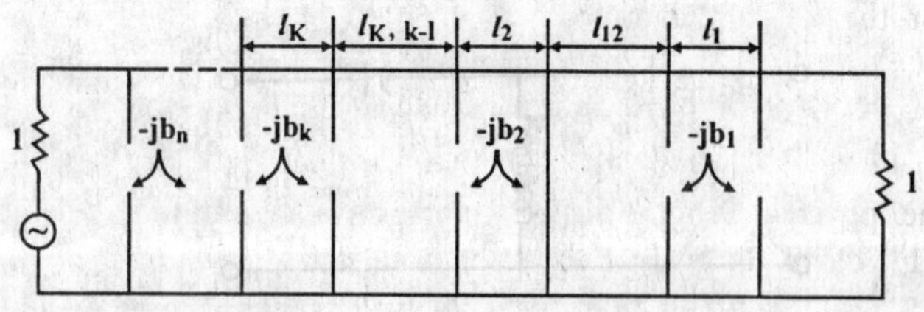

Fig. 5.20a

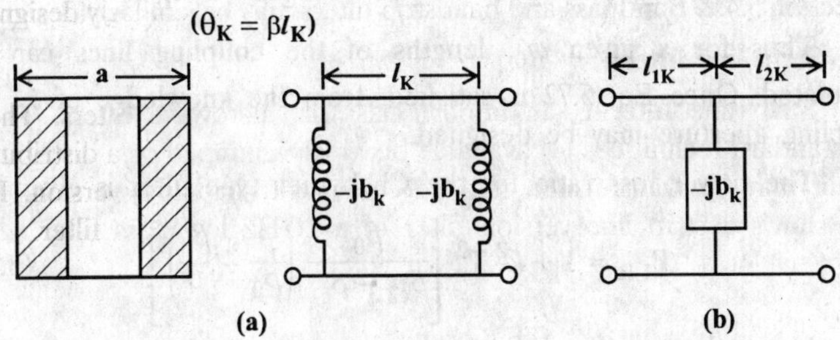

Fig. 5.20b.

Fig. 5.20 (a) rectangular waveguide loaded with inductive diaphragms forming a cavity (b) Equivalent circuit.

Mumford showed that the diaphragm spacing l_k for perfect transmission at $\omega = \omega_0$ is given by

$$\tan \beta_0 l_k = -2/b_k \qquad \text{....(5.68a)}$$

or

$$l_k = \frac{1}{\beta_0}\left[\tan^{-1}\left(\frac{-2}{b_k}\right)\right] \qquad \text{....(5.68b)}$$

where b_k is the normalized shunt susceptance of the kth cavity aperture. b_k is related to Q_k of the cavity as

$$Q_k = \frac{\tan^{-1}(2/b_k)}{2\sin^{-1} 2/(b_k^4 + 4b_k^2)^{1/2}} \approx \frac{\sqrt{b_k^4 + 4b_k^2}}{4}\tan^{-1}\left(\frac{2}{b_k}\right) \qquad \text{....(5.69)}$$

For high Q narrow band filter $B_k >> 1$ and can be approximated as

$$b_k = 2(Q_k^2 - 1)^{1/2} \qquad \text{....(5.70)}$$

For the kth resonator

$$Q_k \approx \frac{g_k}{2}\frac{\beta_0}{\beta_2 - \beta_1} \qquad \text{....(5.71)}$$

The physical length of the quarter wave coupling between k^{th} and $k+1^{th}$ cavity is given by

$$l_{k,k+1} = \frac{1}{\beta_0}\left(\frac{\pi}{2} - \theta_k - \theta_{k+1}\right)$$

$$= \frac{\lambda_{g_0}}{2\pi}\left(\frac{\theta_k + \theta_{k+1}}{2} - \frac{\pi}{2}\right) = \frac{l_k + l_{k+1}}{2} - \frac{\lambda_{g_0}}{4} \qquad \text{....(5.72)}$$

Thus for a given ω_0, lengths of the coupling lines can be calculated. Once Eq. 5.72 is satisfied, from the knowledge of b_k the coupling aperture may be designed.

The power loss ratio for the Chebyshev type filter is given by

$$P_{LR} = 1 + k^2 T_n^2 \left[\frac{\beta_0}{\beta_{c2} - \beta_{c1}}\left(\frac{\beta}{\beta_0} - \frac{\beta_0}{\beta}\right)\right] \qquad \text{....(5.73)}$$

Using the transformation

$$f(\omega/\omega_c) = \left[\frac{\beta_0}{\beta_{c2} - \beta_{c1}}\left(\frac{\beta}{\beta_0} - \frac{\beta_0}{\beta}\right)\right]$$

we can calcute all the required parameters.

Note that the reason for expressing P_{LR} in β's instead of ω'_s is that a waveguide is a dispersive device and hence β is a more reliable parameter than ω.

5.5.7 Direct coupled cavity filters

Cohn [9] has developed a design procedure for direct coupled cavity filters up to a band of 20 per cent. Figure 5.21a shows a directly coupled cavity filter consisting of a number of cavity resonators directly coupled by inductive irises. The separation between the cavities of this filter is zero so it is more compact than the corresponding quarter wave coupled filter. The normalized shunt susceptance required to decide cavity coupling are

$$b_1 = \frac{1 - \omega/g_1}{\sqrt{(\omega/g_1)}} \qquad \text{....(5.74a)}$$

$$b_2 = \frac{\sqrt{g_2 g_1}}{\omega}\left[1 - \frac{\omega^2}{g_1 g_2}\right] \qquad \text{....(5.74b)}$$

$$b_k = \frac{1}{\omega}\left[1 - \frac{\omega^2}{g_k g_{k-1}}\right]\sqrt{g_k g_{k-1}} \qquad \text{....(5.75)}$$

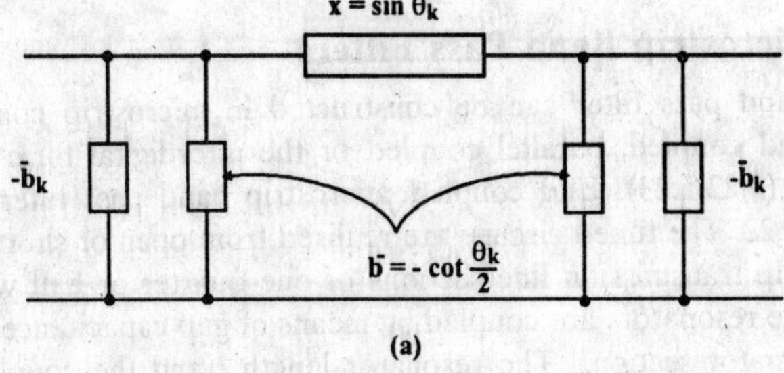

(a)

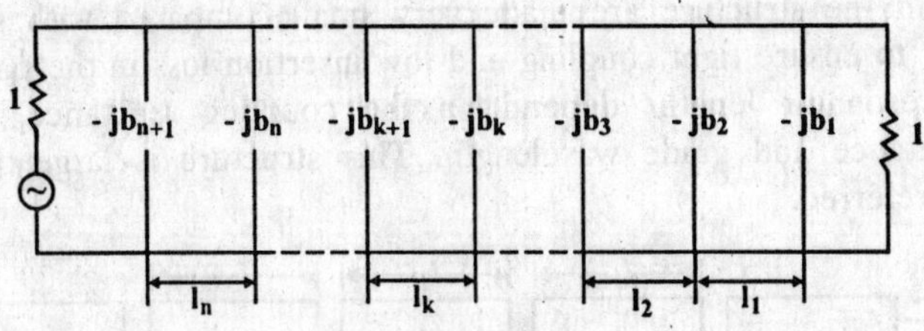

(b)

Fig. 5.21. Quarter wave coupled waveguide cavity filter

$$b_n = \frac{1 - \omega R/g_n}{\sqrt{(\omega R/g_n)}} \quad \text{....(5.76)}$$

where $\omega = \frac{\pi}{2} \frac{\beta_{c2} - \beta_{c1}}{\beta_0}$

and R = 1 for *n* odd in Chebyshev filter and for all integer values of *n* for Butterworth filter. If *n* is even in Chebyshev filter, then R is

$$R = 2a_m^2 + 1 - 2a_m \sqrt{(1 + a_m^2)} \quad \text{....(5.78)}$$

Also g_k are the elements of the prototype filter.

The length of the kth cavity at the centre frequency is

$$l_k = \frac{\lambda_{g_o}}{2} - \frac{\lambda g_o}{2\pi} (Q_k + Q_{k+1})$$

$$= \frac{\lambda g_0}{2} - \frac{\lambda g_0}{4\pi} \left[\tan^{-1} \frac{2}{b_{k+1}} + \tan^{-1} \frac{2}{b_k} \right] \quad \text{....(5.79)}$$

Thus, a direct coupled resonator may be designed

5.6. Microstrip Band Pass Filters

Band pass filter can be constructed in microstrip configuration using end coupled, parallel coupled or the interdigital form as shown in Figs. (5.22-5.23). End coupled microstrip band pass filter is shown in Fig. 5.22. The tuned circuits are realised from open or short circuited microstrip transmission line sections of one quarter or half wavelength long. The resonators are coupled by means of gap capacitances between the resonator sections. The resonator length l and the coupling space S can be calculated from the relations available in literature [1]. The gaps in the structure are made very small compared with substrate height to ensure tight coupling and low insertion loss in the pass band. The resonator lengths depend on the coupling reactance, the gap capacitance and guide wavelength. This structure is large, hence is not preferred.

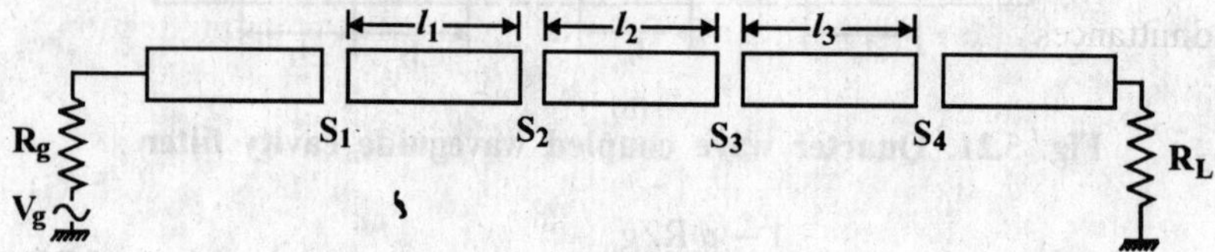

Fig. 5.22 End coupled microstrip band-pass filter

5.6.1 Microstrip parallel coupled filter

The parallel coupled filter shown in Fig. 5.24 is more compact than the end coupled filter described earlier. The coupling between resonators occur over a quarter-wave-long side of each resonator, hence the slot width is larger and the tolerance on the slot width is not very critical. The ends of each resonator section may be open-circuited or short-circuited. Detailed derivation of the coupling and impedance of parallel coupled filter is given in reference [6] using even and odd mode excitations. The expressions for design of a Chebyshev response n section band pass filter terminated in input and output lines of characteristic impedance Z_0 are summarised below. The maximum effective length of each resonator is calculated, the capacitive end loading effect is corrected for

$$l_e = \frac{\lambda_g}{4} - l_{eo} \qquad ....(5.80)$$

where l_{e0} is extension of the line length due to fringing field at the ends, is given by

$$l_{eo} = 4.12 \ln \left(\frac{\varepsilon_{eff} + 0.3}{\varepsilon_{eff} - 0.258}\right)\left(\frac{W/h + 0.262}{W/h + 0.813}\right) \quad ....(5.81)$$

$$\left(\frac{l_{co}}{h}\right)_{max} = \frac{2}{\pi} \ln 2 \approx 0.441 \text{ [reference (10)]} \quad ....(5.82)$$

The band pass circuit shown in Fig. 5.16 consists of series resonant circuit in the series arm and parallel resonant circuit in the shunt arm and they can be converted to either cascade of all parallel resonator networks together with impedance inverters K or to cascade of all series resonator networks together with admittance inverters J explained in section 5.5.3.

For all series network configurations with admittance inverters J, the admittances of the inverters are as follows. For the first coupling section,

$$\frac{J_{10}}{Y_0} = \left(\frac{\pi\Delta}{2g_0g_1}\right)^{1/2} \quad ....(5.83)$$

for the final coupling

$$\frac{J_{n+1,n}}{Y_0} = \left(\frac{\pi\Delta}{2g_ng_{n+1}}\right)^{1/2} \quad ....(5.84)$$

For the intermediate coupling section

$$\frac{J_{k+1,k}}{Y_0} = \left(\frac{\pi\Delta}{2\sqrt{g_kg_{k+1}}}\right) \qquad k = 1 \text{ to } n - 1 \quad ....(5.85)$$

where $\Delta = \dfrac{\omega_2 - \omega_1}{\omega_0}$ is the fractional bandwidth.

For the parallel coupled microstrip filter the line dimension are determined from the even and odd mode coupled line impedances which are given as

$$(Z_{oe})_{k+1,k} = Z_0\,(1 + J_{k+1,k}\, Z_0 + J_{k+1,k}^2\, Z_0^2) \quad ....(5.86)$$

and

$$(Z_{oo})_{k+1,k} = Z_0\,(1 - J_{k+1,k}\, Z_0 + J_{k+1,k}^2\, Z_0^2) \quad ....(5.87)$$

where Z_0 is the characteristic impedance of the input-output lines of the filter.

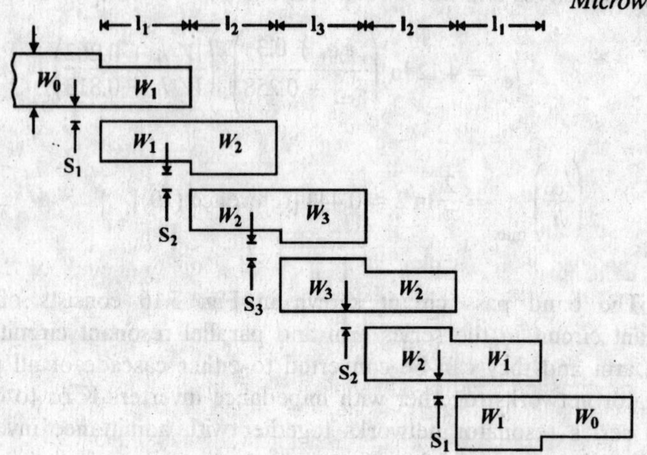

Fig. 5.23 Parallel coupled band-pass filter.

Example 5.1. Design a band pass filter having a 0.1 dB Chebyshev response, with N =3. The centre frequency is 2 GHz, the bandwidth is 200 MHz, and the impedance is 50 Ω.

The element values for the low pass prototype circuit are given as

$$g_1 = 1.0315 = L_1$$

$$g_2 = 1.1474 = C_2$$

$$g_3 = 1.0315 = L_3$$

$$g_4 = 1.000 = k_1$$

Also $\Delta = BW/\omega_0 = 0.1$

Then the impedance scaled and frequency transformed element values for the circuit of Fig. 5.15 is given as

$$L_1' = \frac{L_1 Z_0}{\omega_0 \Delta} = \frac{1.0315 \times 50}{2\pi \times 2 \times 10^9 \times 0.1} = 41 \text{ nH}$$

$$C_1' = \frac{\Delta}{\omega_0 L_1 Z_0} = \frac{0.1}{2\pi\, 2 \times 10^9 \times 50 \times 1.0315} = 0.154 \text{ pF}$$

$$L_2' = \frac{\Delta Z_0}{\omega_0 C_2} = \frac{0.1 \times 50}{2\pi \times 2 \times 10^9 \times 1.1474} = 0.3467 \text{ nH}$$

$$C_2' = \frac{C_2}{\omega_0 \Delta Z_0} = \frac{1.1474}{2\pi \times 2 \times 10^9 \times 0.1 \times 50} = 23.46 \text{ pF}$$

$$L_3' = \frac{L_3 Z_0}{\omega_0 \Delta} = 41 \text{ nH}$$

$$C_3' = \frac{\Delta}{\omega_0 L_3 Z_0} = 0.154 \text{ pF.}$$

Example 5.2. How many filter elements are required in designing a maximally flat low pass filter with a cutoff frequency of 4 GHz and a minimum attenuation of 15dB at 6 GHz, the line inapedance is 100 ohms.

Solution :

The number of reactive elements required are clculated from the relation

$$n = \frac{\log_{10}(10^{L(\omega)/10} - 1)}{2 \log_{10} (\omega/\omega_c)} = 4.219$$

where $L(\omega) = 15\text{dB}$

and $(\omega/\omega_c) = (6/4) = 1.5$

Hence the number of elements used are 5, from Table 5.1 the value of Low pass filter prototypes are

$$g_1 = g_5 = 0.6180$$

$$g_2 = g_4 = 1.6180$$

$$g_3 = 2.000$$

Using Eq. 5.40 and 5.41, scaled impedance and frequency element values can be obtained. Hence,

$$C_{K'} = C_k/(R_L \omega_C)$$

$$L_{K'} = R_L \, L_R/\omega_C$$

The capacitance and inductance values are

$$C_1 = C_5 = \frac{0.6180}{100 \times 2 \times 4 \times 10^9} = 2.46 \text{ pF}$$

$$L_2 = L_4 = \frac{1.6180 \times 100}{2 \times 4 \times 10^9} = 6.43\text{nH}$$

$$C_2 = \frac{2}{100 \times 2\pi \times 4 \times 10^9} = 7.95 \text{ pF}$$

References

1. Collins, R.E., **Foundation for Microwave Engineering,** McGraw-Hill Inc., International Edition, 1992.
2. Malherbe, J.A.G. **Microwave Transmission Line Filters,** Artech House Books, Dedham, Mass. 1979.
3. Ghose, R.N., **Microwave Circuit : Theory and Analysis,** McGraw-Hill Book Company, Inc., 1963.
4. H. Howe, **Strip Line Circuit Design,** Artech House Dedham, Mass. 1974.
5. Helszajn J. **Microwave planar passive circuits and filters,** John Wiley and Sons.
6. Mathaei, G.L., Young, L. and Johns, **EMT Microwave filters, impedance matching networks and coupling structures,** McGraw-Hill, New York, 1964.
7. Cohn S.B. **"Parallel coupled transmission line resonator filter",** IRE Trans on MTT.MTT-19, May 1971.
8. W.W. Mumford **"Maximally flat filters in Waveguides"** Bell System J., Vol. 27 (Oct. 1948).
9. S.B. Cohn **"Direct Coupled Cavity Filters".** Proc. IRE, vol., 45, Feb. (1957).
10. Cohn, S.B., **"Problems in strip transmission lines",** IRE Trans, PG MTT 3, No. 2, March 1955, pp. 119-126.
11. Temes, G.C. and Mitra, S.H. **"Modern Filter Theory and Design".** Wiley, New York (1973).
12. Wai-Kai-Chen **"The Circuits and Filters Handbook"** IEEE Press, 1995.
13. Rhodes, J.D., **Theory of Electric Filter,** John Wiley and Sons, Inc., New York, 1976.
14. Edward T., **"Foundations for Microstrip Circuit Design,** John Wiley and Sons 1981.

Problems and Review Questions

1. Compare the slow waves propagating in a coaxial line with that in a waveguide.
2. Find the eigen value equation for the propagation constant of a Bloch wave on a transonission line loaded at intervals & with series reactance X.

3. Design a lowpass 50 ohms chebyshev coaxial line filter with 0.2 dB passband ripple and the number of sections used is 3. The band edge frequency is 2 GHz
4. A 100 Ω transmission line is used to design a two-section half wave filter with a 7 percent bandwidth and a pass band tolerance k^2 = 0.1. The operating frequency is 4 GHz. A 100 Ω transmission line is used.
5. Design a band pass filter that will pass all frequencies from 1 to 4 GHz. The load impedance is 50 kΩ. specify all circuit components and draw the circuit. Draw equivalent series and shunt stub microwave filter.
6. Design a lowpass maximally flat filter having a pase band of 0 to 4 GHz and an attenuatiion of 20 dB at 6GHz. The characteristic impedance is 100 ohms.
7. Design a lowpass third order maximally flat filter using only series stubs, shunt stubs. The cutoff frequency is 6GHz and the impedence is 50 ohms.
8. Design a three cavity direct coupled microwave filter of chebyshev response. The passband is from 9GHz to 10 GHz with 0.1 dB ripple.

6
Microwave Tubes

In this chapter we shall discuss the high frequency limitations of conventional vacuum tubes, principles and ways to overcome these limitations and describe the devices that have enjoyed greatest technological success in microwave generation and amplification, namely, the magnetron, the klystron and the various travelling wave tubes (TWT).

6.1. High Frequency Limitations of Conventional Vacuum Tubes

With increasing frequency ($>$1GHz) the conventional vacuum tubes (triodes, tetrodes and pentodes) are less useful in amplification and generation because of two important limitations (i) parasitic circuit elements such as interelectrode- capacitances and lead inductances and (ii) effects due to transit time of electrons between elecrodes. These two effects have been analyzed in sections 6.1.1. and 6.1.2 respectively.

Other Limitations

In addition to these two effects there is

(1) Increase of Power Losses resulting from

(a) Skin effect : As the frequency is increased, the current flows more and more on the surface of the conductor because of the skin-effect. This results in ohmic losses in lead wires. This can be minimised by the use of conductors having low resistivity and large surface areas : planer electrodes.

(b) Electro magnetic radiation from the circuit : Lead wires become small antennas with a resulting radiation power loss. Radiation losses can be minimised by the use of electrode lead spacing of the order of 1/100 of a wave length or less.

(c) Dielectric losses : As variety of insulating materials are used inside the tube.

and (d) Charging current losses : I^2R losses caused by capacitance charging currents. These losses could be reduced by reducing interelectrode capacitance and by increasing the number of shunt paths along with the charging currents flow.

(2) Gain Bandwidth Product Limitation

Another limitation is caused by gain bandwidth product of the circuit which is given by

$$A_m\,(BW) = \frac{g_m}{C}$$

where A_m the maximum voltage gain at resonance, g_m = trans conductance and C = the capactance of the tank circuit. We note that gain band width product is indepedent of frequency. For a given tube a higher gain can be achieved only at the expense of bandwidth or higher bandwidth can be achieved only at the expense of gain. This restriction is applicable to a resonant circuit only.

6.1.1. Effect of Parasitic Circuit Elements

(Circuit-reactance limitation effect)

With increasing frequency of operation of an amplifier or an oscillator that uses conventional vacuum tubes it is found that the lead inductance* and interelectrode capacitances** of the tube become comparable to the external inductance and capacitance of resonator circuit and represent impedance that load the tube so as to affect the operation adversely. These effects are known as circuit-reactance limitation effects. To gain better understanding of these effects, we analyse the triode circuit shown in Fig. 6.1a. Its equivalent circuit in shown in Fig. 6.1b under the assumption that the interelectrode capacitances (C_{gk} and C_{gp}) and cathode lead inductance L_k are the only parasitic elements.

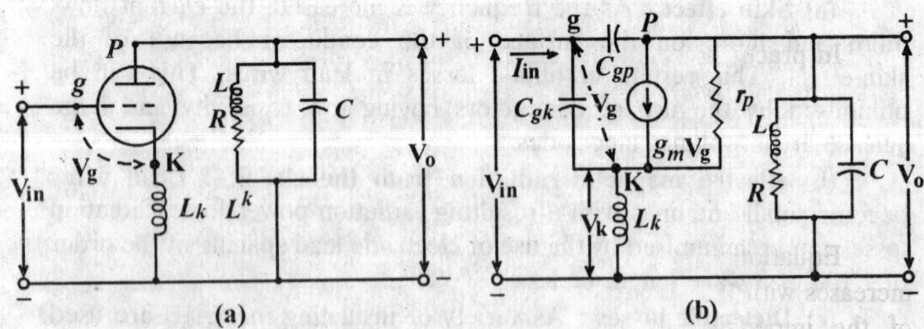

Fig. 6.1a. Triode circuit **Fig. 6.1b. Equivalent circuit**

* a lead of 2.5 inc. in length and 100 mils in diameter is equivalent to an inductance = 0.5 μH.

** Interelectrode capacitance C_{gk} is of the order of 0.5$\mu\mu$F.

Input Impedance :

Since $C_{gp} << C_{gk}$

and $\omega L_k << \dfrac{1}{\omega C_{gk}}$,

where C_{gk} is the interelectrode capactance between cathode and grid and C_{gp} is the interelectrode capacitance between grid and plate.

Input voltage V_{in} can be written as

$$V_{in} = V_g + V_k, \quad ....(6.1)$$

where V_k in the cathode voltage given by

$$V_k = j\omega L_k g_m V_g \quad ....(6.2)$$

The input current is given by

$$I_{in} = j\omega C_{gk} V_g \quad ....(6.3)$$

From Eqs. (6.1) and (6.2),

$$V_{in} = I_{in} \frac{(1+j\omega L_k g_m)}{j\omega C_{gk}} \quad ....(6.4)$$

∴ The input admittance is given by

$$Y_{in} = \frac{I_{in}}{V_{in}} = \frac{j\omega C_{gk}}{(1 + j\omega L_k g_m)} \quad ....(6.5)$$

In practical circuit $\omega L_k g_m << 1$ hence

$$Y_{in} \approx j\omega C_{gk} (1 - j\omega L_k g_m)$$

$$\approx j\omega C_{gk} + \omega^2 C_{gk} L_k g_m \quad ...(6.6)$$

Equation 6.6 shows that the input conductance $\omega^2 L_K C_{gk} g_m$ increases with the square of the frequency. It also means that real part of the impedance in inversely proportional to the square of the frequency. As the frequency increases it loads the tube and when the frequencies are above 1GHz the real part of the impedance becomes small enough to nearly short the signal. Consequently the output power decreases rapidly.

Load Impedance

Considering the resonant circuit of Fig. 6.1a in output circuit, it can be shown that real part of the load impedance is equal to $\frac{1}{R\omega_0^2C^2}$ *i.e.* the real part of the load impedance is inveresely proportional to the square of the frequency. Consequently, the output power is decreased rapidly.

Thus it is clear that parasitic elements limit the operation of conventional tubes at high frequencies. These effects could be minimized and high frequency limit of operation can be extended by incorporating the grid-cathode and grid-plate capacitances in to resonant cavities and or by planer construction of electrodes and reduced lead and tube dimensions.

6.1.2. Transit-time effect

Transit-time of electron between electrodes limits the operation of conventional tube at microwave frequencies. The electron transit time in defined as

$$T_g = \frac{d}{v_o} = \frac{d}{\sqrt{2\eta V_0}}$$

where $\eta = e/m$ Ratio of charge to mass of an electron

V_o = dc voltage

d = separation between cathode and grid

v_0 = electron velocity

At lower frequencies transit time (or angle) is a small fraction of the period of oscillations and is therefore insignificant. At microwave frequencies the transit time T_g is larger compared to the time period of the microwave signal. At lower frequncies an electron leaves the cathode and travels to the plate during the positive part of the grid voltage. At higher frequencies, the electron would leave the cathode when the grid is positive but before the electron passes the grid, the grid voltage might be negative or might even go through several cycles. Thus electron stream will be velocity modulated. This reduces the magnitude of mutual conductance and causes to have an imaginary component. The output voltage and current are no longer in phase because of a phase lag in the current produced by the finite transit time. This situation indicates that the output power is decreased.

From above discussion it is clear that the transit time effect can be minimized by (i) decreasing the interelectrode spacing and (ii) by increasing the operating voltage. The latter results into increase in power dissipation at the anode while the decrease of interelectrode spacing increases the interelectrode capacitance.

6.1.3. Lighthouse and Disk-seal Tubes

The high frequency limitations due to parasitic circuit elements and transit time were minimized by radical changes in spatial configuration, as in the light house tube in which the tube elements were made parts of the external circuit i.e. incorporating interelectrode capacitances into resonant cavities and reducing interelectrode spacing. Figure 6.2 shows the lighthouse tube.

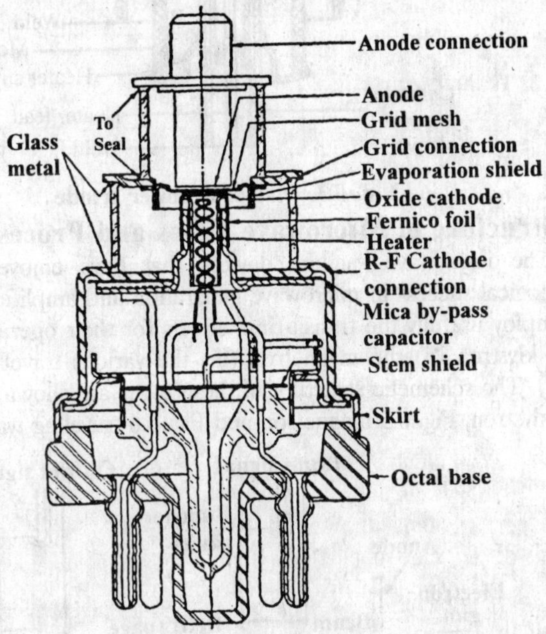

Fig. 6.2 Lighthouse tube structure

The problem of lead inductance and interelectrode capacitance has been solved in disk-seal tubes (Fig 6.3) by making the electrodes in the form of metal disks which are sealed to the glass envelope. Several devices were constructed that could overcome the frequency limitations. For details the reader is referred to chapter 9 of the Book-Microwave Principles by Reich et al

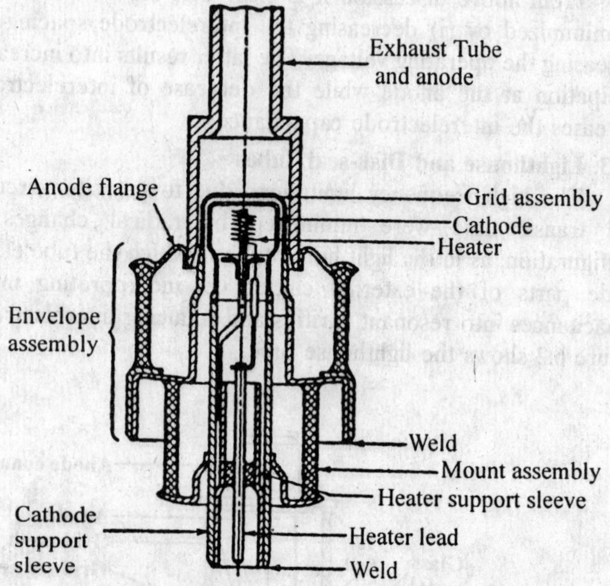

Fig. 6.3. Disk-seal power triode

6.2. Structure of Microwave Tubes and Processes

The microwave vacuum devices that have enjoyed the greatest technological success in microwave generation and amplification are those that employ usefully the transit-time effects for their operation. These are (i) the klystron (ii) the magnetron (iii) the various travelling wave tubes (TWTs). The schemetic structure of these tubes are shown in Fig. 6.4, two cavity klystron, Fig. 6.5 magnetron and Fig. 6.6 traveling wave Tube.

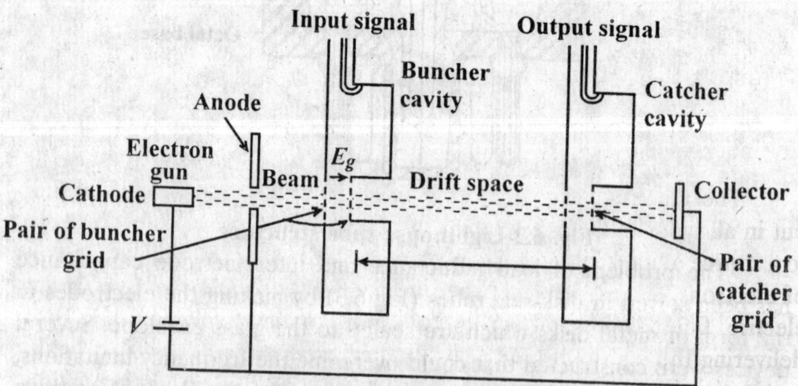

Fig. 6.4. Two-cavity Klystron

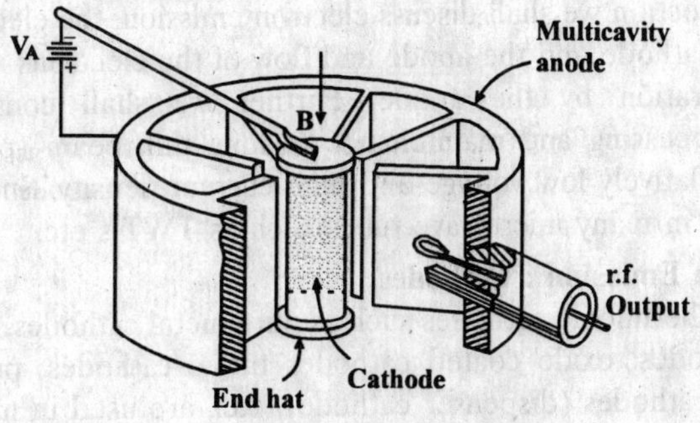

Fig. 6.5. Magnetron

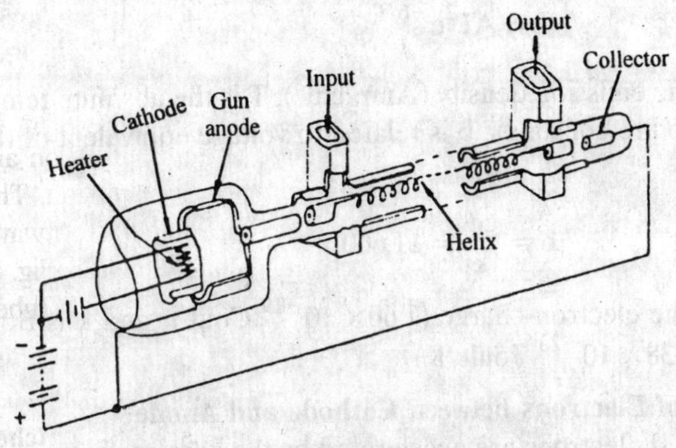

Fig. 6.6. Travelling wave tube

The mechanism of operation of these tubes may differ in detail but in all types it involves transfer of power from a source of dc voltage to a source of alternating voltage by means of a density modulated stream of electrons. This is accomplished by accelerating electrons in a direct electric field and retarding them in alternating electric field thus delivering the energy to ac field. The **processess** involved are (i) beam production (ii) velocity modulation (iii) conversion to density modulation (iv) transfer of energy and (v) collection of electrons. In any electron device these processes must take place, either sepearately (as in case of two-cavity klystron) or simultaneously (as in case of travelling wave tube).

6.3. Electron Beams

In this section we shall discuss electron emission, the electron flow between the cathode and the anode and flow of the electrons after their initial acceleration by the anode. Further we shall consider the production, focussing and maintenance of long thin beam (pencil like beam) at a relatively low voltage and high current density. Such beams are employed in many microwave tubes such as TWT's etc.

6.3.1. Electron Emission : Cathodes

Mostly thermionic cathodes such as pure metal cathodes, thoriated tungsten cathodes, oxide coated cathodes the L-cathodes, pressed or impregnated cathodes (dispenser cathode), etc., are used in microwave tubes. We are looking for cathodes which yield greater emission (low work function) and have longer life. The reader in referred to a Book-**Vacuum Electron Devices** by R Chatterjee and the **Special issue on Cathodes** IEEE Trans. Electron Devices, **36** (1989). The emission current density in given by equation (Richardson's equation)

$$J = AT^2 e^{-b/T} \qquad \text{.... (6.7)}$$

where J is the emission density (Amp/cm^2), T is the absolute temperature and A and b are constants, b is related to voltage equivalent of the work-function ϕ.

$$b = \frac{e\phi}{k} = 11{,}600\,\phi$$

where e is the electron charge (1.60×10^{-19} Coul.) and k is Boltzman's constant (1.38×10^{-23} Joule/K)

6.3.2. Flow of Electrons between Cathode and Anode

Emitted electrons are accelerated by the accelerating voltage V on the anode. Under the assumption that (i) initial velocity of the electrons is zero (ii) the electric field at the cathode is zero and (iii) normal emission from the surface of the cathode, the relation between anode voltage and current in any cathode anode configuration, i.e., electron gun, for space charge limited operation, is given by (Child's law)

$$I \propto V^{3/2} \qquad \text{....(6.8)}$$

Therefore, a figure of merit describing the performance of an electron gun may be defined as

$$K = \frac{I}{V^{3/2}}$$, where K is expressed in $A/V^{3/2}$ and is known as **perveance** which is independent of the size of the configuration and depends only on electrode shapes. Thus an electron beam of 3 ma at 100 volts has a perveance.

$$K = 3 \times 10^{-6} \text{ Amp./volt}^{3/2}$$
$$= 3 \text{ micro perveance}$$

We shall discuss the production of such beams, *i.e.* the design of electron gun in Section 6.3.5.

6.3.3. Electron Flow in Cylindrical Beams – Space Charge Spreading

Electron beam tends to spread due to mutual repulsion between electrons. In order to reduce the space-charge spreading (without any focussing mechanisms) the converging beam is launched aimed at the center of the tube which will be able to travel some distance before it spreads back to the original radius. In this situation the current is maximum at the centre where beam acquires a minimum radius r_m ($\dot{r} = 0$ at $r = r_m$) and then spreads. The beam envelope of such a beam is shown is Fig. 6.7.

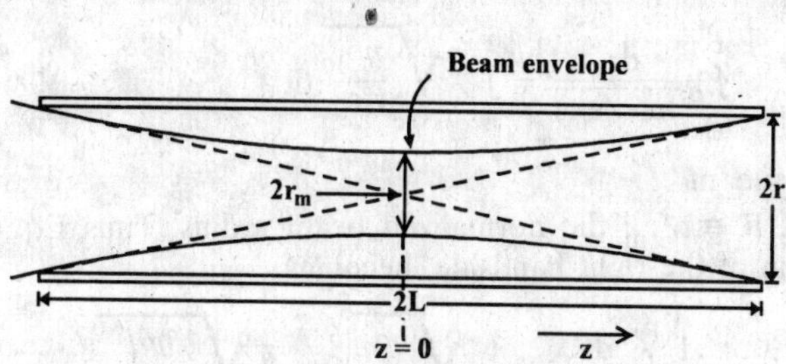

Fig. 6.7. Beam envelope. Launching a converging beam of radius r aimed at the center of the cylinder of length 2L and radius r.

The flow of each electron is influenced by all other electrons and in exact analysis one must calculate all the trajectories simultaneously including the space-charge effects due to all other electrons. This is not an easy task, however, an approximate close form solution could be obtained for a special case of considerable practical interest, namely, laminar beam having (i) the uniform charge density per unit length over the cross section and (ii) the axial velocity is also uniform over the cross section and is given by

$$v_0 = \sqrt{2\eta V_0}$$

i.e., the radial velocity of any electron is initially directly proportional to the distance from the axis. It also means that all trajectories are similar and the analysis of the outermost electron's trajectory will apply to any electron within the beam as well.

The radial equation of motion is given by

$$m\ddot{r} = eE_r = e\frac{\rho_1}{2\pi\varepsilon_0 r} \qquad \text{....(6.9)}$$

where $E_r = \dfrac{\rho_1}{2\pi\varepsilon_0 r}$ the radial electric field that of an infinite cylinder of charge density ρ_1 per unit length. This is nearly true for beam that is not converging too rapidly. $\rho_1 = I_0/v_0$ is the magnitude of the charge density per unit length. Multiplying both sides of equation 6.9 by r and on integration we obtain

$$\frac{m\dot{r}^2}{2} = \frac{e\rho_1}{2\pi\varepsilon_0} \ln r/r_m \qquad \text{.... (6.10)}$$

with the boundary condition that $\dot{r} = 0$ at the minimum radius $r = r_m$. Taking the origin at the point of minimum radius, Equation 6.10 may be rewritten as

$$\int_{r_m}^{r} \frac{dr}{\sqrt{\ln(r/r_m)}} = \int_{o}^{t} \sqrt{\frac{\eta\rho_1}{\pi\varepsilon_0}}\, dt \qquad \text{....(6.11)}$$

where $\eta = e/m$

Let $R \equiv r/r_m$ the normalized beam radius. Thus Eq. 6.11, after integration of the right handside, becomes

$$\frac{1}{R}\int_{1}^{R} \frac{dR}{\sqrt{\ln R}} = \frac{t}{r}\sqrt{\frac{\eta\rho_1}{\pi\varepsilon_0}} = \frac{z}{r}\sqrt{\frac{\eta\rho_1}{\pi\varepsilon_0 v_0^2}} \qquad \text{....(6.12)}$$

where $t = z/v_0$, z is the distance and v_0 is the velocity.

Equation 6.12 can be rewritten as

$$\frac{1}{R}\int_{1}^{R} \frac{dR}{\sqrt{\ln R}} = \frac{z}{r}\sqrt{\frac{I_0}{V_0^{3/2}} \frac{1}{2\pi\varepsilon_0\sqrt{2\eta}}} = \frac{z}{r}\sqrt{3 \times 10^4\, K} \qquad \text{...(6.13)}$$

where $K = I_0/V_0^{3/2}$ is perveance of the beam and factor $\dfrac{1}{2\pi\varepsilon_0\sqrt{2\eta}}$ is nearly equal to 3×10^4.

Equation 6.13 may be used in plotting the beam spreading curve using the values of the integral $\dfrac{1}{R}\int_{1}^{R} \dfrac{dR}{\sqrt{\ln R}}$ given in the Table 6.1.

TABLE 6.1*

R	$\int_I^R \frac{R}{\sqrt{\ln R}}$	$\frac{1}{R}\int_I^R \frac{R}{\sqrt{\ln R}}$
1.0	0.000	0.000
1.1	0.637	0.580
1.5	1.469	0.979
2.0	2.145	1.073
2.35	2.543	1.082
3.0	3.200	1.067
3.5	3.658	1.044
4.0	4.102	1.025
4.5	4.508	1.001
5.0	4.920	0.984

The curve is symmetrical, the converging portion of the beam has the same shape as the diverging portion (Fig. 6.7). Since the function on the left hand side of Eq. 6.13 has a maximum value of 1.082 at R = 2.35, the equation

$$\frac{z}{r}\sqrt{3 \times 10^4 K} = 1.082 \qquad \text{.... (6.14)}$$

determines the limiting conditions for various combination of z, r and K. The Eq. 6.14 *i.e.*, K perveance could be used to find the maximum value of the current that can be transmitted through a cylindrical tube of length 2L and radius r with beam just grazing the openings. Thus

$$\frac{L}{r}\sqrt{3 \times 10^4 K_{max.}} = 1.082$$

$$K_{max.} = \frac{I_0}{{V_0}^{3/2}} = 38.6 \times 10^{-6}\left(\frac{r}{L}\right)^2$$

$$K_{max.} = 39 \times 10^{-6}\left(\frac{r}{L}\right)^2 \qquad \text{.... (6.15)}$$

* Source : E. Jahnke and F. Emde, Tables of Functions, Fourth Edition, Dover Publication, Inc., New York, 1945.

The beam must enter at a specified angle. The optimal slope i.e. $\frac{dr}{dz} = \frac{r}{L}$ at $R = r/r_m = 2.35$. Equation 6.15 shows that with increasing beam perveance tunnel length becomes very small.

From equation 6.13 we can write

$$\int_1^R \frac{dR}{\sqrt{\ln R}} = \frac{R.z}{r}\sqrt{3 \times 10^4 K}$$

$$= \frac{z}{r_m}\sqrt{3 \times 10^4 K} = Z, \qquad \text{....(6.16)}$$

Where Z is reduced axial distance. A curve between reduced axial distance Z and normalized beam radius R is plotted in Fig. 6.8 which could be used for practical design of a tube in which a given beam (K) can be transmitted with beam just grazing the openings.

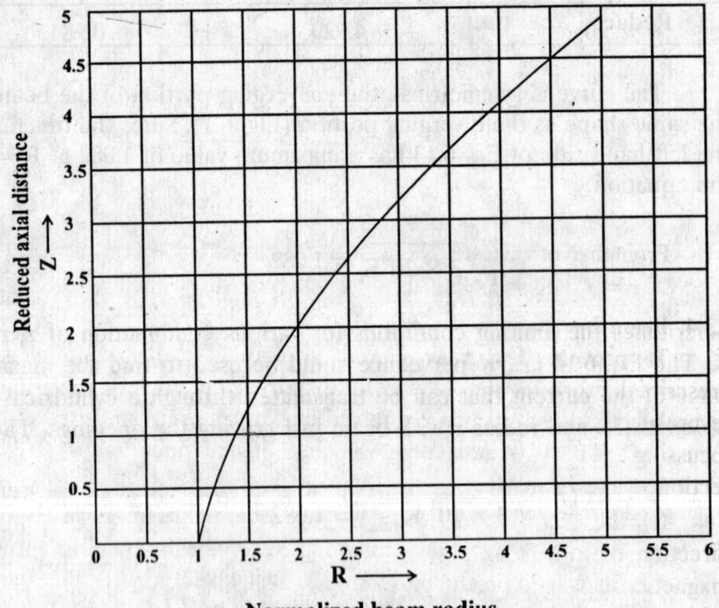

Fig. 6.8 A curve between reduced axial distance Z and normalized beam Radius R

From the graph it is clear that the beam expand in radius to twice the minimum (*i.e.* normalized ratio $R = 2$) value at the reduced axial distance $Z = 2.145$.

$$L = \frac{2.145}{\sqrt{3 \times 10^4 K}} \cdot r_m$$

$$= \frac{2.145}{174}\left[\frac{V_0^{3/2}}{I_0}\right]^{1/2} r_m$$

$$\approx 1.21 \times 10^{-2}\left[\frac{V_0^{3/2}}{I_0}\right]^{1/2} r_m \qquad \text{.... (6.17)}$$

Example 6.1. Find the distance in which 1 amp. beam at 10 kV with initial radius r_m = 1mm. will become in radius twice the minimum radius?

$$L = 1.21 \times 10^{-2} [10 \times 10^3]^{3/4} \times 0.1$$
$$= 1.21 \times 10^{-2} \times 10^3 \times 0.1$$
$$= 1.21 \text{ cm.}$$

Example 6.2. 3×10^{-6} amp/volt$^{3/2}$ perveance beam moves a distance of 0.5 cm from its minimum radius r_m = 0.1 cm. Find the new radius due to space charge spreading.

Reduced axial distance

$$Z = \frac{L}{r_m}\sqrt{3 \times 10^4 K}$$

$$= \frac{0.5}{0.1}\sqrt{3 \times 10^4 \times 3 \times 10^{-6}}$$

$$= 1.5$$

From the curve (Fig. 6.8.) normalized radius R = 1.6 for which Z = 1.5.

$\therefore r = 1.6\, r_m = 1.6 \times 0.1 = 0.16$ cm

6.3.4. Beam Focussing

To prevent the space charge spreading i.e. to maintain some prescribed cross-section of the long thin beam of very high density, several methods have been employed and are loosely spoken as "beam focussing". The two most common methods of maintaining the cross section of the beam are

(i) the beam is subjected to a magnetic field parallel to the direction of motion *i.e.* focussing of electron beam by a longitudinal magnetic field. It is produced by means of a solenoid. (ii) The beam is subjected to alternating magnetic field parallel to the direction of motion *i.e.* focussing of electron beam with periodic magnetic field. It is produced by periodic permanent magnets. It is prefered because of the lower total weight of the systems. The periodic focussing structure is shown in Fig. 6.9. The another method which has been used is ion trapping i.e. space charge neutralization by positive ions.

We shall discuss the first method because of its simplicity. The reader is referred to text books* by Pierce, Beck, Gewartowski, R. Chatterjee, Liao and Sisodia.

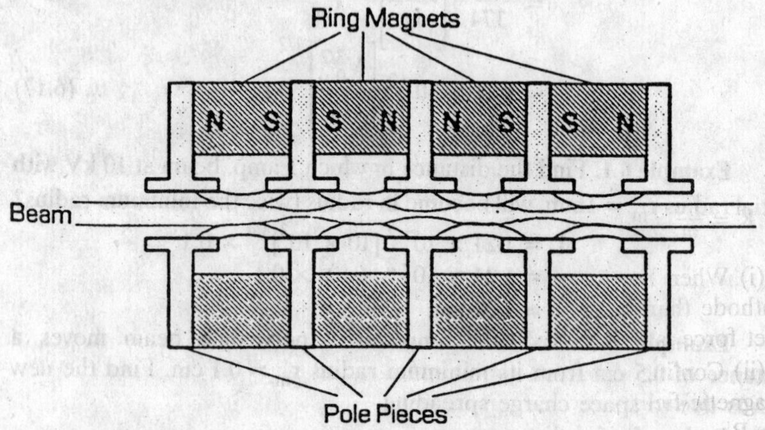

Fig. 6.9. Periodic permanent magnetic focussing structure.

6.3.4.1. Focusing Electron Beam by a Longitudinal Mangetic field

In this method, which is simple and commonly used, the electron beam is subjected to a magnetic field parallel to the direction of motion. In present discussion laminar beam (sec section 6.3.3) is assumed. In maintaining the cross-section of the beam a balance has to be achieved between space charge forces, centrifugal forces caused by angular electron motion and magnetic forces caused by the interaction between the axial field and the angular motion. The radial equation of motion for the general space charge balanced flow is

$$m\ddot{r} = mr\dot{\theta}^2 + er\dot{\theta}B + \frac{e\rho_1}{2\pi\varepsilon_0 r} \quad \text{.... (6.18)}$$

where $mr\dot{\theta}^2$ is the centrifugal force (outward), $-er\dot{\theta}B$ is the focussing force arising from the crossed product of angular velocity and axial magnetic field (inward), $\frac{e\rho_1}{2\pi\varepsilon_0 r}$ is the space charge spreading force (outward).

Dividing Eq. 6.18 by m we get

$$\ddot{r} = r\dot{\theta}^2 + \eta r\dot{\theta}B + \frac{\eta\rho_1}{2\pi\varepsilon_0 r} \quad \text{.... (6.19)}$$

With, utilization of

$$\dot{\theta} = \frac{\eta}{2\pi r^2}(\psi - \psi_c), \quad \text{(Busch's theorem)}^{**}$$

* Sec chapter 1.

** Sec Annexure 6.1.

and $\omega_L = \frac{\eta\psi}{2\pi r^2}$ Larmor precession frequency

and $\psi = \pi r^2 B$ the magnetic flux, the equation of motion 6.19 becomes

$$\ddot{r} = -r\omega_L^2 \left[1 - \left(\frac{\psi_c}{\psi}\right)^2\right] + \frac{\eta\rho_1}{2\pi\varepsilon_0 r} \quad \text{.... (6.20)}$$

$$\ddot{r} = -r\omega_L^2[1 - K^2] + \frac{\eta\rho_1}{2\pi\varepsilon_0 r} \quad \text{.... (6.21)}$$

where $K = \frac{\psi_c}{\psi}$, ψ_c is the magnetic flux at the cathode.

(i) When $K > 1$ *i.e.* $\psi_c > \psi$, that is the magnetic flux is greater at the cathode than in the interaction region, we find that $\ddot{r} > 1$; it means that net force is outward and no focussing can result.

(ii) Confined flow – When an electron gun is entirely immersed in the magnetic field, the flow is known as confined flow. It means $K = 1$ i.e. $B = B_c$

$$\psi = \pi r^2 B_c$$

$$\psi_c = \pi r_c^2 B_c$$

where r_c refers to the initial (cathode) value of the trajectory radius, the equation 6.20 becomes

$$\ddot{r} = -r\omega_L^2 \left(1 - \frac{r_c^4}{r^4}\right) + \frac{\eta\rho_1}{2\pi\varepsilon_0 r} \quad \text{....(6.22)}$$

$$= -4r\omega_L^2 (r - r_c) + \frac{\eta\rho_1}{2\pi\varepsilon_0 r} \quad \text{....(6.23)}$$

Where we have made the approximation $r + r_c \approx 2r$

when $r > r_c$, it gives net inward force

$r < r_c$, net outward force

It should also be noted that the focussing force increases with ω_L, *i.e.*, with the magnetic field. It is shown that $\dot{\theta} \propto \frac{1}{B}$ *i.e.* for $B \to \infty$. $\dot{\theta} \to 0$. It means that for maintaining the radius of the beam, very large axial magnetic field in needed. This flow is also known as **immersed flow.**

(iii) Balanced Flow – In general $\psi_c < \psi$, a perfect balance is obtained by definition that

$$\ddot{r} = 0 \text{ at } r = r_0$$

From equation 6.21 we get

$$\omega_L^2 (1 - K^2) = \frac{\eta\rho_1}{2\pi\varepsilon_0 r_0^2} \quad \text{....(6.24)}$$

ρ_1 is connected to the charge density ρ_0 per unit volume and the radius r_0 by

$$\rho_1 = \pi r_0^2 \rho_0$$

Substituting the value of ρ_1 in equation 6.24, we get

$$\omega_L^2 (1 - K^2) = \frac{1}{2}\frac{\eta\rho_0}{\varepsilon_0} = \frac{1}{2}\omega_\rho^2 \quad \text{....(6.25)}$$

It is equilibrium condition.

Where $\omega_\rho = \left(\dfrac{\eta\rho_0}{\varepsilon_0}\right)^{1/2}$ is the plasma frequency.

(iv) Brillouin Flow – It is a balanced flow in which $\psi_c = 0$, *i.e.* K=0

That is the electrons emitted from a magnetically shielded cathode are made to enter a constant magnetic field. Equation 6.25 becomes

$$\omega_L^2 = \frac{1}{2}\omega_\rho^2$$

$$\left(\frac{\eta B_{Br}}{2}\right)^2 = \frac{1}{2}\frac{\eta\rho_o}{\varepsilon_0}$$

$$= \frac{\eta\rho_1}{2\pi r_0^2 \varepsilon_0} = \frac{(\eta/2)^{1/2}}{2\pi r_0^2 \varepsilon_0}\frac{I_0}{V_0^{1/2}}, \quad \left[\rho_1 = \frac{I_0}{V_0} = \frac{I}{\sqrt{2\eta V_0}}\right]$$

$$\therefore \quad B_{Br} = \frac{8.30 \times 10^{-4}}{r_0}\left[\frac{I_0}{\sqrt{V_0}}\right]^{1/2} \text{Weber/m}^2 \quad \text{.... (6.26)}$$

That is B_{Br} is the magnetic field required for Brillouin flow for the beam with uniform charge distribution. This flow requires minimum magnetic field for maintanining the diameter of the electron beam in interaction region. It is difficult to achieve in actual practice. However one can use magnetic field 3-4 times the B_{Br} and let the cathode to be completely immersed in this field. The beam in this case is completely confined and maintain the original radius throughout the length of the tube.

Equation 6.26 can be written in terms of perveance of the beam K as

$$B_{Br} = \frac{8.30 \times 10^{-4}}{r_0}\left[KV_0\right]^{1/2} \text{Weber/m}^2 \quad \text{....(6.27)}$$

$$= \frac{830}{r_0}[KV_0]^{1/2} \text{gauss, where } r_0 \text{ is in cm.} \quad \text{....(6.28)}$$

For example (i) If beam current = 10ma and beam voltage V_0 = 1000 volts, and beam radius 0.5 mm. then the Brillouin magnetic field is 2.95×10^{-2} W/m^2 or 295 gauss

(ii) If beam perveance K= 1.36×10^{-6}, beam voltage = 3140V and beam radius = 0.157 cm. then the Brillouin magnetic field is nearly 350 gauss.

6.4. Electron Guns

An electron gun is a cathode-anode configuration in obtaining a stream of electrons and making it follow trajectories of the kind that is desired. Initially electron guns were usually designed using emperical methods until Pierce in 1940 suggested a more systematic method. The reader is referred to the Book – Theory and Design of Electron Beames, 2nd end., by J.R. Pierce. In Pierce gun (current is space charge limited) the cathode, the facussing electrode and accelerating electrode are so shaped that the field distribution along the beam edge is the same as that inside a beam of a complete configuration. It means that a potential is established which satisfies Laplace's equation $\nabla^2 V = 0$ in the charge free region outside the beam and inside the beam poisson's equation $\nabla^2 V = -\frac{\rho}{\varepsilon_0}$ is satisfied. Figure 6.10a show the electron gun for producing strip electron beam

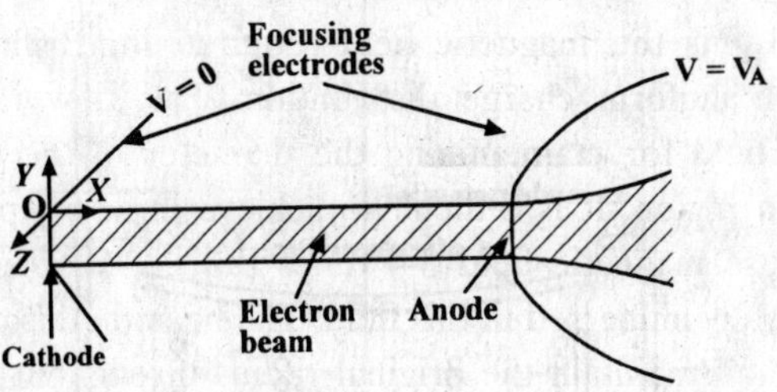

Fig. 6.10a. Electron gun for producing strip electron gun (Pierce)

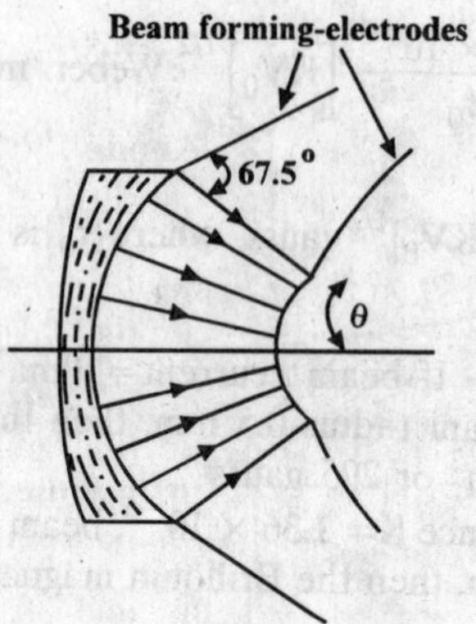

Fig. 6.10b. Spherical cathode electron gun (Pierce)

and 6.10b shows the schematic diagram of a spherical cathode electron gun. Fig. 6.11 shows the actual configuration of an electron gun used in a high power klystron/TWT with a spherical-cap cathode. Schematic diagrams of three electron guns those are commonly used in beam type microwave tubes are shown in Fig. 6.12. Electron beams of current density for greater than the cathode emission density are obtained in electron guns shown in Fig. 6.12a and 6.12b.

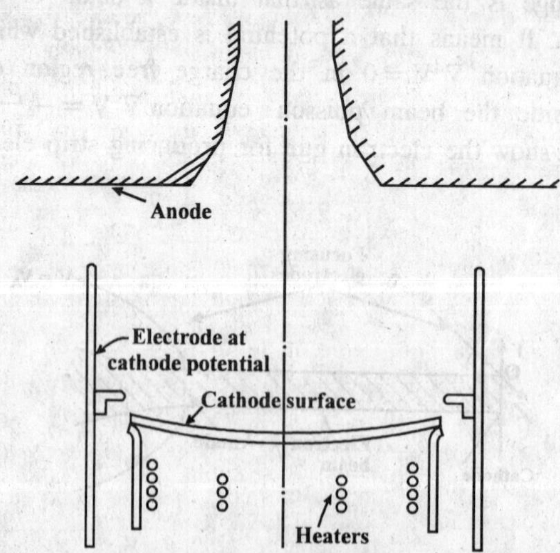

Fig. 6.11. Electron gun : actual configuration used in a high power klystron/TWT

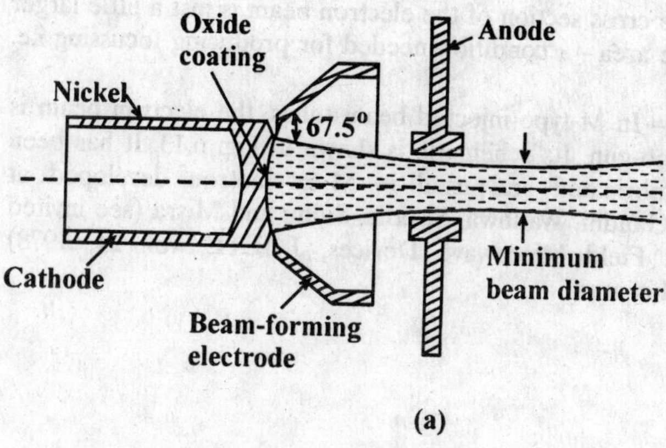

(a)

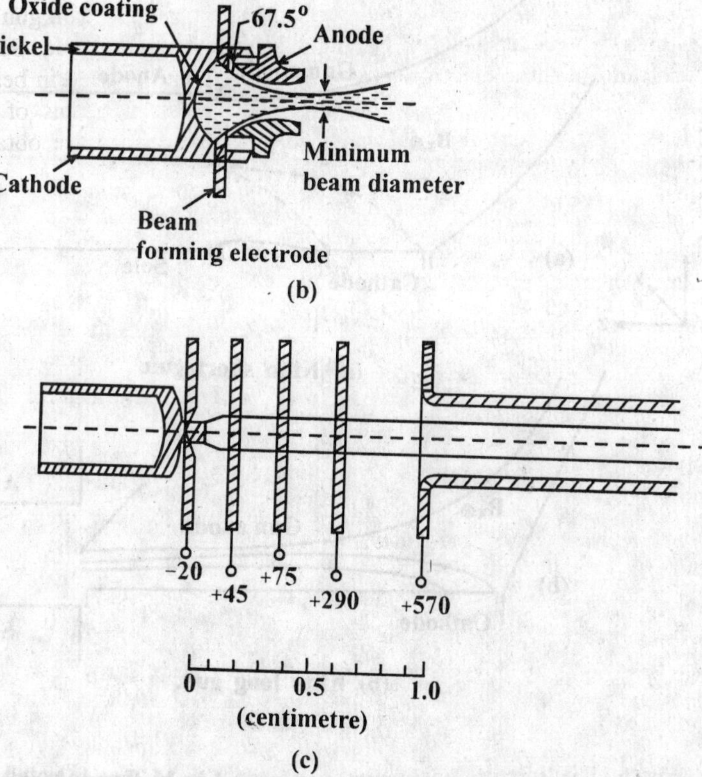

(c)

Fig. 6.12. Schemetic structure of electron guns used in O-type microwave tubes

The electron gun shown in Fig. 6.12c. is used to obtain confined flow in which the cross section of the electron beam is just a little larger than the cathode area – a condition needed for producing focussing i.e. inward force.

Kino Gun – In M-type injected beam tubes, the electron beam is produced by Kino-gun. Its schematic is shown in Fig. 6.13. It has been designed and fabricated and used in M-carcinotron developed at CEERI, Pilani. Gandhi, Wadhwa, Sisodia, Sidhu and Misra (see invited paper- Crossed Field Microwave Devices, J IETE, vol. 24, 1978) contributed in this area.

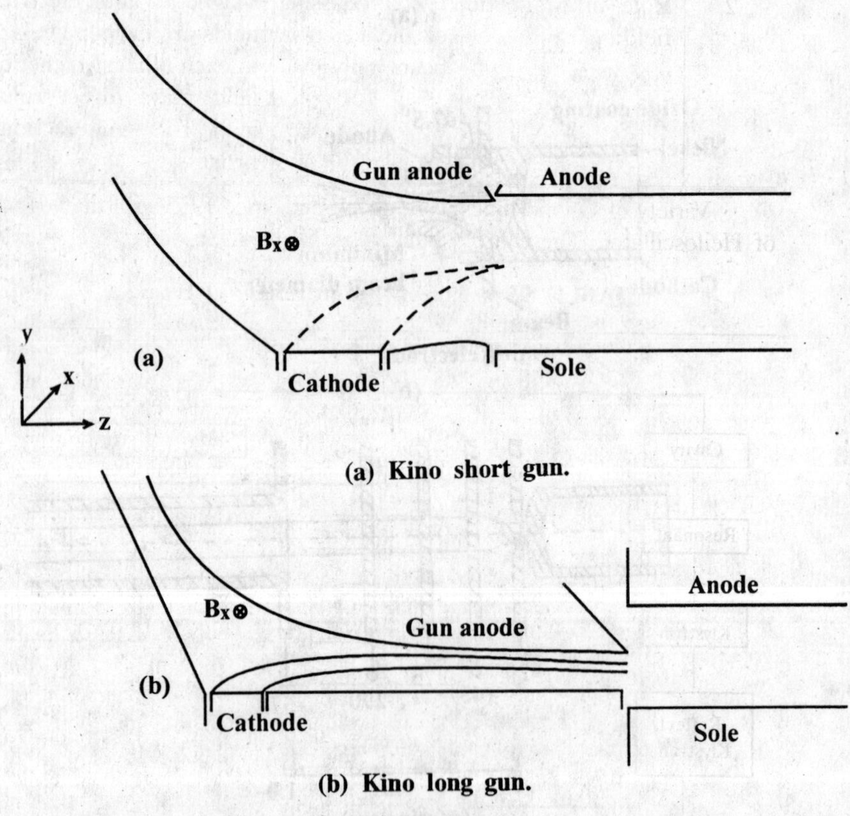

(a) Kino short gun.

(b) Kino long gun.

Fig. 6.13. Schematic of Kino-gun used in M-Type injected Beam Devices

6.5. Classification of Microwave Tubes

Microwave tubes can be broadly classified into two categories, namely, O-Type linear tubes (TWT, Klystrons) and M-Type tubes (magnetrons, crossed-field devices). The mechanism of operation in both the cases is essentially the same as mentioned in Section 6.2. The two main differences in the two types of tubes are listed in Table 6.5.1.

TABLE 6.5.1.

S. No.		O-Type tubes	M-Type tubes
1.	Energy conversion	Kinetic energy to r.f. energy	Potential energy to r.f. energy
2.	Role of Magnetic field	For focussing of the electron beam only	Magnetic and electric fields are perpendicular to each other. Magnetic field plays direct role in r-f interaction process.

Variety of O-type tubes were developed since 1935 with the advent of Heiloscillator. These are tabulated in Table 6.5.2. Since 1921, when

TABLE 6.5.2. Linear Beam Tubes (O-Type)

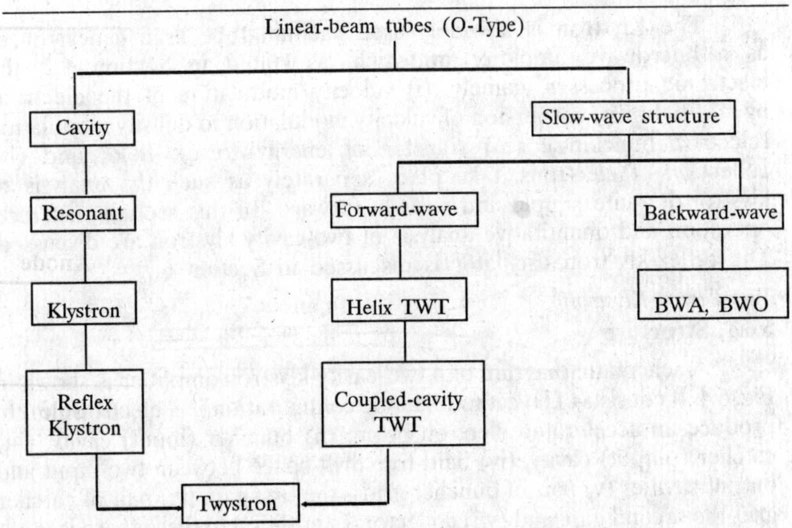

[Sources – Wadhwa, R.P., Crossed-Field Microwave Decives-JIETE Vol. 24, 1978, (II).

Hull invented the magnetron, variety of M-type tubes were developed. These are listed in Table 6.5.3 given on next page.

TABLE 6.5.3. M-Type Tubes.

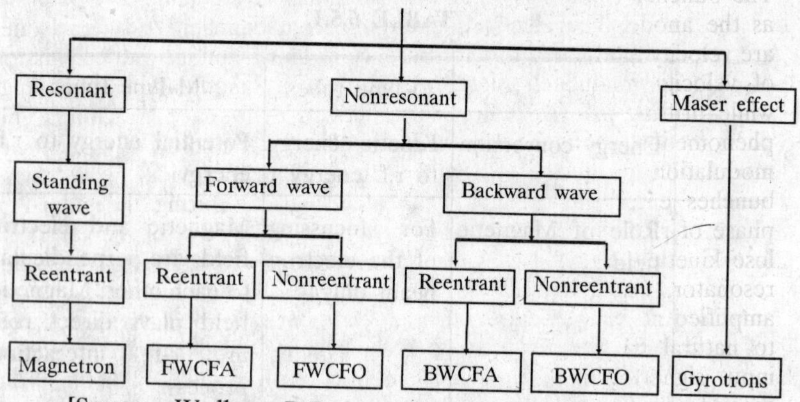

[Source – Wadhwa, R.P. op. cit.]

The scope of the book limits us to the discussion of klystrons, travelling wave tubes and magnetrons only. The reader is referred to text books listed in Chapter 1.

6.6. Klystrons

The Klystron is a widely used vacuum tube as a generator or as a microwave amplifier in which, as stated in Section 6.2, the electronic processes, namely, (i) velocity modulation of the electrons by r – f field; (ii) conversion of velocity modulation to density modulation (electron bunching); (iii) transfer of energy to r.f. field; and (iv) collection of electrons, take place separately as such the analysis of klystron is quite simple and straight-forward. In this section structure, operation and quantitative analysis of two-cavity klystron are discussed. The reflex-klystron oscillator is discussed in Section 6.7.

Two-Cavity Klystron

6.6.1. Structure

A schematic diagram of a two-cavity klystron amplifier is shown in Fig. 6.4. It consists of (i) cathode-anode configuration (*i.e.* electron gun) to produce an accelerated electron beam; (ii) buncher (input) cavity, (iii) catcher (output) cavity, (iv) field-free drift space between two input and output cavities (v) pair of buncher grid – the first gap, (vi) pair of catcher grid-the second gap, and (vii) collector. In addition to these there is input coupling loop in buncher (input) cavity and output coupling loop in catcher (output) cavity. Whole assembly is in vacuum envelope with vacuum sealed coaxial fittings for external connections.

6.6.2. Operation

The accelerated electron beam passes through a gap in the anode into a region between a pair of closely spaced buncher grids (first gap), across which an r.f. voltage exists, into a drift space, and then through another pair of catcher grids (second gap) to the collector. The buncher (input) cavity is kept generally at the same d.c. potential as the anode. The electrons emerging from buncher grids (gap one) are velocity modulated due to presence of an r.f. voltage and conversion of velocity modulated electrons into density modulation (bunching) while drifting in drift region and is called **drift-space bunching**. This phenomenon, commonly knowr as bunching, is the result of the velocity modulation produced at the first gap (buncher grids) when these bunches enter the second gap (catcher grids) during the retarding phase of r.f. field of the catcher resonator, then most of the electrons lose kinetic energy in crossing the second gap to r.f. field of catcher resonator, *i.e.*, r.f. input to the first resonator (buncher cavity) is amplified at catcher cavity. (Both cavities are identical and are tuned to natural frequency of the cavities which is also the frequency of input signal) Finally emerging electrons with reduced velocity from second gap (catcher grids) are collected by the collector.

Two-cavity klystron is capable of operation to frequencies in excess of 100 GHz. As an amplifier it offers pulse and CW power with medium bandwidth (2-15 per cent) and high gain (15-70 db). When sufficient energy is fed back from the catcher to the buncher in proper phase and if the loop gain has a magnitude of unity with a phase shift of multiple of 2π, it is double resonator klystron oscillator (Fig. 6.21).

6.6.3. Quantitative Analysis

(a) Velocity Modulation

Electrons in the electron beam produced in a cathode anode region and accelerated by a d.c. anode voltage V_0, passing through a pair of buncher grids (gap one), across which an r.f. voltage $V_1 \sin \omega t$ exist (ω is the frequency of the input signal and it is also the resonant frequency of the first cavity) are either accelerated or decelerated depending on the part of the cycle during which they cross the gap. The electrons which accelerated emerge with higher velocity than the entering velocity v_0 and those are decelerated emerge with velocities lower than the entering velocity v_0. Some electrons pass through at zero field and hence suffer no change in velocity. This variation of velocities of the electrons in the electron beam is known as **velocity modulation.**

The analysis is carried out with the following assumptions :

1. Electrons leave the cathode with zero velocity and the electron beam have uniform density in the cross-section of the beam.
2. Space charge effects are ignored.

3. The magnitude (V_1) of input microwave signal is much smaller than the de accelerating voltage (V_0), *i.e.*, $V_1 < V_0$.
4. r-f field is perfectly longitudinal.

Transit time across the first gap is negligible

It is assumed that the gap spacing and frequency is such that the transit time through gap (buncher grids) is small fraction of a cycle and is negligible.

The velocity of the electrons before entering the buncher grid is given by

$$v_0 = \sqrt{2\eta V_0} = 5.93 \times 10^5 \sqrt{V_0} \text{ m/s} \quad \text{....(6.6.1)}$$

where $\eta = e/m$ is the magnitude of the electron charge to mass ratio 1.76×10^{11} Coul/kg and V_0 is the anode-cathode potential difference in volts.

> (i) Let $V_0 = 1600$ V
> $v_0 = 5.93 \times 10^5 \times 40 = 2.37 \times 10^7$ m/s.
> (ii) if $V_0 = 900$ V
> $v_0 = 5.93 \times 10^5 \times 30$
> $= 1.779 \times 10^7$ m/s

The energy of an electron emerging from the gap at time t_1, is

$$eV = e(V_0 + V_1 \sin \omega t_1)$$

$$= eV_0 \left(1 + \frac{V_1}{V_0} \sin \omega t_1\right) \quad \text{....(6.6.2)}$$

where $V = V_0 + V_1 \sin \omega t_1$ is the instantaneous voltage at time t_1 (buncher cavity is at V_0 dc voltage).

This energy is equal to kinetic energy $\frac{1}{2}mv^2$, where v is the velocity of electron at time t_1.

$$\therefore \quad \frac{1}{2}mv^2 = eV_0 \left(1 + \frac{V_1}{V_0} \sin \omega t_1\right)$$

$$v = \sqrt{2\eta V_0 \left(1 + \frac{V_1}{V_0} \sin \omega t_1\right)}$$

$$v = v_0 \sqrt{\left(1 + \frac{V_1}{V_0} \sin \omega t_1\right)} = v_0 \sqrt{1 + \alpha \sin \omega t_1} \quad \text{....(6.6.3)}$$

where $v_0 = \sqrt{2\eta V_0}$ is the injected velocity and $\alpha = \frac{V_1}{V_0}$ and is known as **depth of modulation.**

As $V_1 << V_0$ *i.e.* $\alpha << 1$, then Eq. 6.6.3 may be written as

$$v = v_0 (1 + \frac{1}{2} \alpha \sin \omega t_1) \qquad ....(6.6.4)$$

It is noted from Eq. 6.6.4. that successive electrons are not travelling with the same velocity when they leave the first gap. The electron, which leave the gap at a time corresponding to

$$\omega t_1 = 2\pi n, \quad n = 0, 1, 2, 3$$

will suffer no change in velocity from the entering velocity v_0.

The electrons which leave at a time corresponding to

$$\omega t_1 = + \pi/2,$$

the maximum accelerating phase of buncher voltage will be moving with the maximum velocity

$$v_{max} = v_0(1 + \alpha/2)$$

The electrons which leave at a time corresponding to

$$\omega t_1 = - \pi/2,$$

the minimum accelerating phase of buncher voltage will be moving with the minimum velocity

$$v_{min} = v_0(1 - \alpha/2)$$

Thus the electrons which leave during the time

$$\pi/2\omega < t_1 < 0$$

will slow down (fall back) and those which leave during

$$0 < t_1 < \pi/2\omega$$

will move fast (catch up).

The equation 6.6.4 is the **equation of velocity modulation** at cavity frequency ω.

Finite transit time across the first gap (see Annexure 6.2)

When the transit time or transit angle across the gap is not zero the velocity modulation equation 6.6.4 is modified to

$$v = v_0 [1 + \frac{1}{2} \alpha \beta \sin \omega t_1] \qquad ....(6.6.5)$$

In above equation

$$\beta = \frac{\sin \omega\tau_g/2}{\omega\tau_g/2} = \frac{\sin \theta_{g/2}}{\theta_{g/2}}$$

is called the beam coupling coefficient; where $\tau_g = d/v_0$ is the electron transit time and $\theta_g = \omega\tau_g$ is the transit angle through the gap *d*. The equation 6.6.5 is obtained by calculating the work done by an electron while travelling through the gap (Annexure 6.2).

$$d = 1\text{mm}, \quad v_0 = 1.88 \times 10^7 \text{ m/s}, \quad f = 3\text{GHz}$$

$$\tau_g = \frac{1 \times 10^{-3}}{1.88 \times 10^7} = \frac{1}{1.88} \times 10^{-10} \text{ s (transit time)}$$

$$\omega\tau_g = \theta_g = \text{transit angle} = \frac{2\pi(3 \times 10^9) \times 10^{-3}}{1.88 \times 10^7} = 1 \text{ rad.}$$

$$\beta = \frac{\sin \theta_g/2}{\theta_g/2} = \frac{\sin\frac{1}{2}}{\frac{1}{2}} = 0.952 \approx 1$$

We see that when magnitude of transit time and transit angle is neligibly small, β is approaching 1, it implies a perfect beam coupling.

It is clear that finite transit time or transit angle is equivalent to a reduction in the magnitude of depth of modulation. In other terms it is reduction in the modulating voltage V_1.

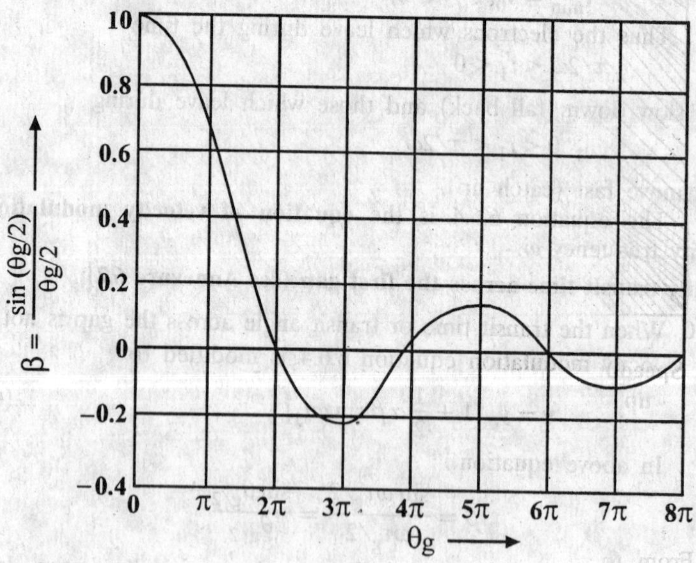

Fig. 6.14. Beam coupling coefficient β versus gap transit angle

The value of the beam coupling coefficient β depends on gap transit angle. Fig. 6.14 shows the plot of the beam-coupling coefficient β as a function of θ_g, the gap transit angle. It is observed that increasing the gap transit angle θ_g, decreases the coupling between the electron beam and the bunching cavity *i.e.* the velocity modulation of the beam for a given microwave signal is decreased [in the region of practical interest where $\theta_g \to 0$].

The velocity modulated electron beam while drifting in field free drift space between two cavities is converted into density modulation. This is discussed in the following section.

(b) Bunching of the electron beam

The electrons passing through the first gap at different instants t_1 travel at different velocities (Eq. 6.6.4) in the drift region. Those electrons that leave the first gap with higher velocities ($v > v_0$) catch up with those that left earlier with slower velocities ($v < v_0$). This is depicted in Fig. 6.15 in which the location of electron is plotted as function of time. This distance-time diagram is called as **Applegate diagram.**

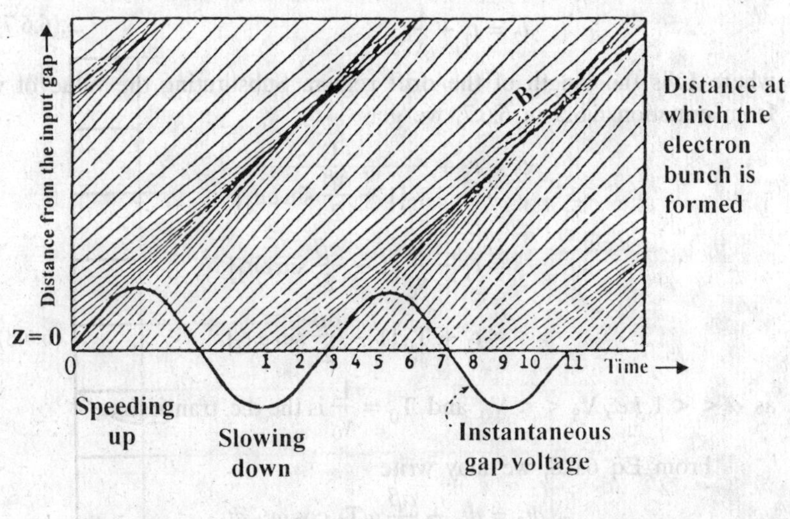

Fig. 6.15. Applegate diagram

From the Fig. 6.15 it is observed that electrons 1 through 3 leave the buncher cavity gap (first gap) during the deccelerating phase of r-f. voltage across the gap, with velocity less than velocity v_0, Electrons 3 to 5 leave the buncher cavity gap, during the accelerating phase of r-f. voltage across the gap, with higher velocity than v_0 and catch up with those electrons from 1 through 3 which left earlier with less velocity than v_0, forming an electron bunch depicted in the Fig 6.15 by intersecting bundle of lines marked B. The bunching process repeats once every cycle and electrons 1 through 5 over one-half of the cycle come together in a form of bunch at a definite drift distance from the first gap (buncher grids). Obviously at this distance the catcher cavity grids (second gap) should be located in order for the electron bunch to induce microwave fields in the catcher cavity.

(c) Quantitative analysis of electron bunching—r.f. current

The analysis is formulated on the basis of **law of conservation of charge.** It means that the net charge $I_0 dt_1$, leaving the buncher gap over an infinitesimal interval of time dt_1, arrives at catcher cavity gap as $I_2 dt_2$, where I_2 is the current at the catcher gap, dt_2 is arrival interval of time and I_0 is the dc current.

$$\therefore \quad I_2 dt_2 = I_0\, dt_1$$

or
$$I_2 = I_0 \frac{dt_1}{dt_2} \qquad \text{....(6.6.6)}$$

It is clear that t_2 is the arrival time for an electron for which departure time is t_1.

$$\therefore \quad t_2 = t_1 + \frac{L}{v} \qquad \text{....(6.6.7)}$$

where L is the length of the drift region. Substituting the value of v from equation 6.6.5 in 6.6.7, we get

$$t_2 = t_1 + \frac{L}{v_0[1 + \frac{\alpha\beta}{2} \sin \omega t_1]}$$

$$\approx t_1 + \frac{L}{v_0}[1 - \frac{\alpha\beta}{2} \sin \omega t_1]$$

$$\approx t_1 + T_0 [1 - \frac{\alpha\beta}{2} \sin \omega t_1] \qquad \text{....(6.6.8)}$$

as $\alpha << 1$, *i.e.*, $V_1 << V_0$ and $T_0 = \frac{L}{v_0}$ is the d.c. transit time.

From Eq 6.6.8, we may write

$$dt_2 = dt_1 - \frac{\alpha\beta}{2} \omega T_0 \cos \omega t_1\, dt_1$$

$$= dt_1 [1 - \frac{\alpha\beta}{2} \theta_0 \cos \omega t_1]$$

or
$$\frac{dt_1}{dt_2} = \frac{1}{[1 - \frac{\alpha\, \theta_0 \beta}{2} \cos \omega t_1]} \qquad \text{....(6.6.9)}$$

where $\theta_0 = \omega T_0$ the d.c. transit angle between the cavities.

For $L = 4$ cm, $v_0 = 1.88 \times 10^7$ m/s, $f = 3$ GHz

$$\theta_0 = \omega T_0 = \frac{\omega L}{v_0} = \frac{2\pi\,(3\times10^9) \times 4\times10^{-2}}{1.88 \times 10^7} = 40 \text{ rad.}$$

Substituting the value of $\frac{dt_1}{dt_2}$ from Eq. 6.6.9 in Eq. 6.6.6, we get

$$I_2 = \frac{I_0}{[1 - \frac{\alpha}{2}\theta_0 \beta \cos \omega t_1]}$$

$$= \frac{I_0}{[1 - X \cos \omega t_1]} \qquad \text{....(6.6.10)}$$

$$\approx I_0\,[1 + X \cos \omega t_1]$$

where $X = \frac{\alpha \theta_0 \beta}{2}$ is a dimensionless quantity called the **bunching parameter.** It is seen from Eq. 6.6.10 that bunching parameter depends on α, the drift angle $\theta_0 = \frac{\omega L}{v_0}$ and beam coupling coefficent β. The plot of $I_2(t_1)$ [equation 6.6.10] for various values of X is shown in Fig. 6.16.

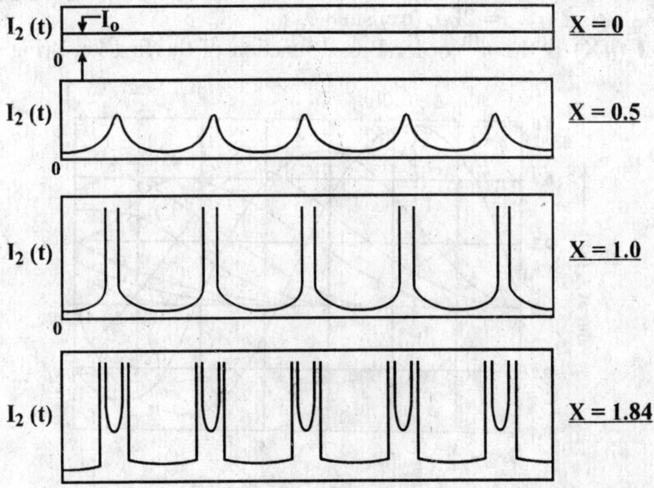

Fig. 6.16. Beam current $I_2(t_1)$ as function of time for various values of X the bunching parameter (which would correspond to different length L provided β and α are fixed).

It gives one pulse per cycle centred about the electron that crosses the input gap at $\omega t_1 = 2n\pi,\ n = 0, 1, 2, 3, \ldots\ldots$ It is seen from the Fig. 6.16 that for values $X > 1.0$ the catcher current is rich in the harmonics of the input frequency which is the resonance frequency of buncher cavity. This property is exploited in operating a klystron as an **harmonic generator.**

Fundamental component of $I_2(t_2)$

Since the output is usually tuned to the input frequency a Fourier analysis of the current I_2 at the catcher gap as function of the arrival time t_2 at second gap to find the amplitude of the fundamental component is in order. Expanding $I_2(t_2)$ in a Fourier series

we have $$I_2 = \sum_{n=0}^{\infty} [a_n \cos(n\,\omega t_2) + b_n \sin(n\omega t_2)] \quad \ldots(6.6.11)$$

where the coefficients

$$a_n = \frac{1}{\pi}\int_{-\pi}^{\pi} I_2 \cos n\omega t_2\, d(\omega t_2)$$

$$= 2I_0 J_n(nX)\cos n\,\theta_0$$

and $$b_n = \frac{1}{\pi}\int_{-\pi}^{\pi} I_2 \sin n\omega t_2\, d(\omega t_2)$$

$$= 2I_0 J_n(nx)\sin n\,\theta_0$$

where $J_n(nX)$ is the nth order Bessel function of the first kind (Fig. 6.17)

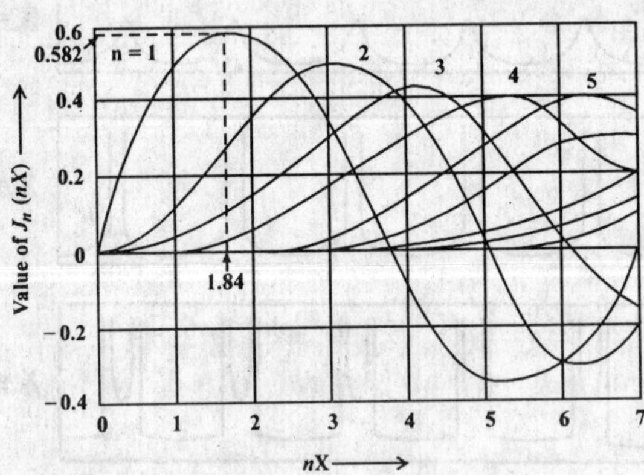

Fig. 6.17. Bessel function $J_n(nX)$ versus nX

* For evaluating coefficients reader is referred to texts by (i) Chodorow et al., and (ii) Gewartowski et al., op. cit. in chapter 1.

The current I_2 can therefore be written as

$$I_2 = I_0 + \sum_{n=1}^{\infty} 2I_0 J_n (nX) \cos n(\omega t_2 - \theta_0) \quad ....(6.6.12)$$

From Eq. 6.6.8 $\omega t_2 = \omega t_1 + \omega T_0 [1 - \frac{\alpha\beta}{2} \sin \omega t_1]$

$$= \omega t_1 + \theta_0 - \frac{\alpha\beta\theta_0}{2} \sin \omega t_1$$

$\therefore$ $\omega t_1 \approx \omega t_2 - \theta_0$ as $\frac{\alpha\beta\theta_0}{2} \sin \omega t_1$ is negligible

The fundamental component of the beam current at the frequency of the input gap ($n = 1$) is

$$I_f = 2I_0 J_1 (X) \cos (\omega t_2 - \theta_0) \quad ....(6.6.13)$$

$$= 2I_0 J_1 (X) \sin (\omega t_2 + \pi/2 - \theta_0)$$

The magnitude of $|I_f|$ is $2I_0J_1(X)$. This fundamental component I_f has its maximum amplitude at $X = 1.841$ (Fig. 6.17).

(d) Optimal length of drift region

The optimum distance L at which the maximum fundamental component occurs is computed.

$$X = 1.841 = \frac{\theta_0 \alpha\beta}{2}$$

$$= \frac{\omega \text{ Lopt}}{v_0} \frac{V_1}{2V_0}$$

$$\therefore \quad L_{opt} = 3.682 \times \frac{v_0 V_0}{\omega\beta V_1} \quad ....(6.6.14)$$

$$\propto \frac{1}{V_1}$$

The value of L_{opt} thus specifies the point at which the output cavity (catcher cavity) must be located. It is noted from Eq. 6.6.14 that (i) since $L_{opt} \propto \frac{1}{V_1}$ any variation in the input signal level would require a change in the drift length to maintain maximum gain. (ii) it would also appear that a very long drift space enables enormous gain to be obtained. However, debunching force combined with finite mass of electrons results in the amount of debunching increasing with the time the electron spent in the drift region.

$L_{opt} = 4cm$, $V_0 = 1000$ V, $\therefore$ $v_0 = 1.88\times10^7$ m/s, $\beta = 0.952, f = 3$GHz

From Eq. 6.6.14,

$$\therefore V_{1max} = \frac{3.682\times v_0 V_0}{\omega\beta L_{opt}} = \frac{3.68\times1.88\times10^7 \times 10^3}{2\pi\,(3\times10^9)\times0.952\times4\times10^{-2}} \approx 0.952$$

It is input gap voltage to give maximum voltage V_2.

(e) Transfer of energy – output power, efliciency

When the bunched electron beam passes through the retarding phase of catcher gap voltage, its kinetic energy is transfered to the field of the catcher cavity. These electrons emerge with reduced velocity are finally collected by the collector. For a two-cavity Klystron amplifier both cavities (buncher and catcher) are tuned to the signal frequency and the beam current at the catcher cavity is given by $2I_0\, J_1(X)\cos(\omega t_2 - \theta_0)$. Due to finite transit time of the beam through the catcher cavity gap, the effective beam current is reduced by the beam coupling coefficient β (Assumed identical buncher and catcher cavities i.e., β is same far both cavities) to $2\beta I_0\, J_1\,(X)\cos\,(\omega t_2 - \theta_0)$. The magnitude of the fundamental component of the beam current is

$$|I_f| = \beta 2I_0 J_1(X) \quad ....(6.6.15)$$

and V_2 is fundamental component of catcher gap voltage. The output power delivered to the catcher and the load is given by

$$P_{out} = \beta 2I_0 \frac{J_1(X)}{\sqrt{2}} \times \frac{V_2}{\sqrt{2}}$$

$$= V_2\beta I_0 J_1(X) \quad ....(6.6.16)$$

$$\therefore \text{ Efficiency of klystron } \eta = \frac{\text{Output power}}{\text{Input power}} = \frac{P_{out}}{P_{in}}$$

$$= \frac{V_2\beta I_0 J_1(X)}{2I_0 V_0} \quad ....(6.6.17)$$

$$= \frac{V_2}{V_0}\beta J_1\,(X) \quad ....(6.6.18)$$

If the coupling is perfect, $\beta = 1$, then

$$\eta = \frac{V_2}{V_0} J_1(X) \quad ....(6.6.19)$$

We know from Fig. 6.17 that when $X = 1.841$, $J_1(X) = 0.582$ the maximum value.

$$\therefore \quad \eta = \frac{V_2}{V_0} 0.582 \quad ....(6.6.20)$$

when $V_2 \rightarrow V_0$, *i.e.* $\frac{V_2}{V_0} \rightarrow 1$ then the maximum electronic efficiency is about 58%. Fig. 6.18 shows the variation of electronic efficiency of a klystron as function of catcher cavity transit angle θ_g since the efficiency is a function of β (β depends upon catcher gap transit angle).

In most of the klystron, the electronic efficiency ranges between 15% to 30%.

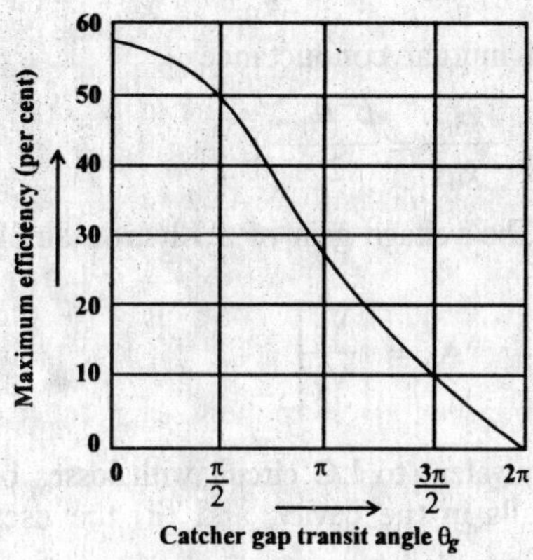

Fig. 6.18. Maximum efficiency of klystron versus transit angle.

(f) Mutual conductance of a klystron amplifier

It is defined as a ratio of induced (output) current to input voltage (r-f.)

$$|g_m| = \frac{|I_f|}{V_1} = \frac{2\beta I_0 J_1(X)}{V_1} \qquad \text{....(6.6.21)}$$

V_1 in terms of bunching parameter X is

$$V_1 = \frac{2V_0}{\beta\theta_0} X, \qquad \left[X = \frac{\alpha\theta_0\beta}{2} = \frac{V_1\theta_0\beta}{2V_0}\right]$$

Substituting the value of V_1 in Eq. 6.6.21, we get

$$|g_m| = \frac{2\beta I_0 J_1(X)}{2V_0 X}\beta\,\theta_0$$

$$= \beta^2\,\theta_0 \frac{I_0}{V_0}\frac{J_1(X)}{X}$$

The normalized mutual conductance

$$\frac{|g_m|}{g_0} = \beta^2 \theta_0 \frac{J_1(X)}{X} \qquad ....(6.6.22)$$

where $g_0 = \frac{I_0}{V_0}$ is the d.c. beam conductance.

For small signal parameter

$$J_1(X) \approx X/2$$

$$\therefore \qquad g_m \approx \beta^2 \theta_0 \frac{I_0}{2V_0}$$

or normalized mutual conductance

$$\frac{|g_m|}{g_0} = \frac{\beta^2 \theta_0}{2}$$

(g) Voltage Gain – The voltage gain of a Klystron amplifier is defined as

$$A_v = \left| \frac{V_2}{V_1} \right| \qquad ....(6.6.23)$$

A cavity is equivalent to LC circuit with losses because of (i) the resistance in the walls in the cavity; and (ii) the useful load coupled to cavity.

Figure 6.19 shows output equivalent circuit.

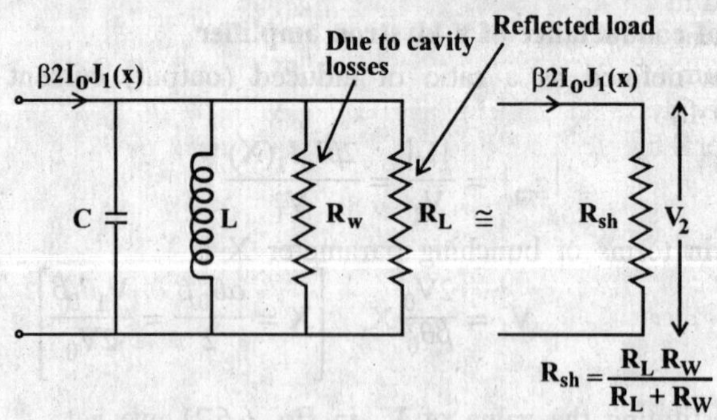

Fig. 6.19. Output equivalent circuit.

The fundamental component of current induced in the catcher cavity has a magnitude $= \beta 2 I_0 J_1(x)$

$$\therefore \qquad |V_2| = \beta 2 I_0 J_1(X)\, R_{sh}$$

$$\therefore \quad A_v = \frac{\beta^2\theta_0 2I_0 J_1(X)}{2V_0 X} R_{sh} \left(\text{since } |V_1| = \frac{2V_0}{\beta\theta_0} X \right)$$

$$= \beta^2 \theta_0 \frac{J_1(X)}{R_0 X} R_{sh} \quad \text{....(6.624)}$$

where $R_0 = V_0/I_0$ is the d.c. beam resistance

$$A_v = g_m R_{sh} \left(\text{Since } g_m = \beta^2\theta_0 \frac{I_0}{V_0} \frac{J_1(x)}{X} \right)$$

When $\beta = 1, \theta_0 = 40\text{rad}, R_{sh} = 30\ \text{K}\Omega, \frac{J_1(X)}{X} = \frac{0.582}{1.841}$

and $R_0 = 40\ \text{K}\Omega$

calculate voltage gain. From Eq. 6.6.24, we get

$A_v = \beta^2 \theta_0 \frac{J_1(X)}{R_0 X} . R_{sh}$; Substituting the values

$$= \frac{40 \times 0.582 \times 30 \times 10^3}{40 \times 10^3 \times 1.841} \approx 9.5$$

6.6.4. Multicavity Klystron

For achieving high overall gain, several two-cavity tubes are connected in cascade, feeding the output of each of the tubes to input of the following one. Instead of two cavities one can use number of cavities in one-vacuum envelope tube as shown in Fig. 6.20. There are varieties of multicavity klystron amplifier units capable of delivering tens of milliwalts up to several hunderd kilowatts of amplified output power.

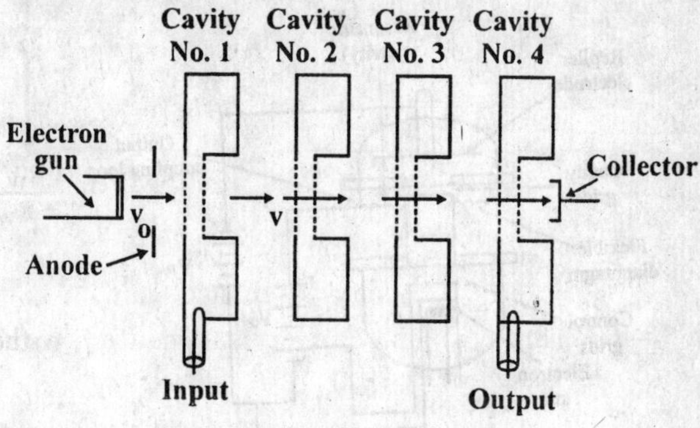

Fig. 6.20. Schematic diagram of a multicavity klystron.

6.7. Reflex Klystron

As mentioned in section 6.6.2 that two-cavity klystron can be made to oscillate by a positive feedback of power from output cavity to the input cavity as shown in Fig. 6.21. It is usually not constructed

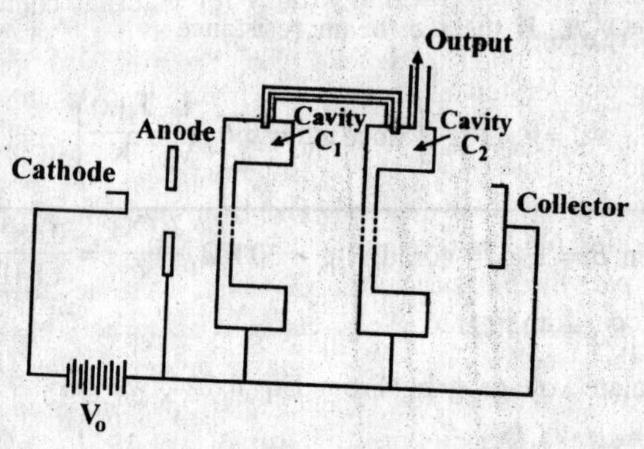

Fig. 6.21. Two-cavity klystron showing positive feedback use as an oscillator.

due to operational difficulties. As the frequency of oscillations is varied, the resonant frequency of each cavity and the feedback path phase shift is to be readjusted for a positive feedback which is cumbersome and is seldom used. These disadvantages were overcome in a single cavity low power klystron oscillator (reflex klystron). This type is widely used as a local oscillator in superheterodyne operations and in the laboratory for microwave measurements.

6.7.1. Structure

Figure 6.22 shows the schematic diagram of a reflex klystron. It consists of :

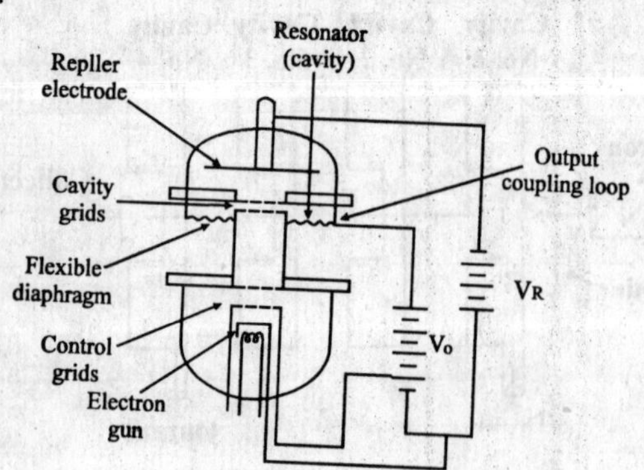

Fig. 6.22. Reflex klystron

(i) Cathode-anode configuration (electron gun) to produce an accelerated electron beam, (ii) Resonator (cavity); (iii) Flexible diaphragm; (iv) Control grid; (v) Pair of cavity grids (gap); (vi) Repeller electrode which is at a negative potential with respect to the cathode; and (vii) Output coupling loop. The whole assembly is sealed in vacuum envelope and vacuum fittings for external connections.

6.7.2. Operation

The accelerated electron beam from electron gun while passing through cavity gap is velocity modulated due to presence of microwave noise field (r.f. field) at cavity resonant frequency, generated due to d.c. voltage in the cavity circuit. Electron emerging from the gap are either accelerated or decelerated or no change in velocity depending upon the part of the rf cycle during which it crosses the gap. However these velocity modulated electrons will be turned back towards the cavity by the repeller due to its negative potential. The faster electrons ($v > v_0$) travel further in the repeller space as compared to slower one ($v < v_0$) and take longer time to return (Fig. 6.23).

The repeller space and repeller voltages can be adjusted in such a way that the electrons spread over a half cycle of oscillations leaving the modulating gap with different velocities return back to the gap in the form of bunch at a time which corresponds to the positive peak of the r.f. cycle of the cavity resonator (see Fig 6.23). On this return journey the bunched electrons pass through the gap during the retarding phase of r.f. field, lose their kinetic energy and give up to r-f. field in the cavity. When the energy delivered by the bunched electrons to the

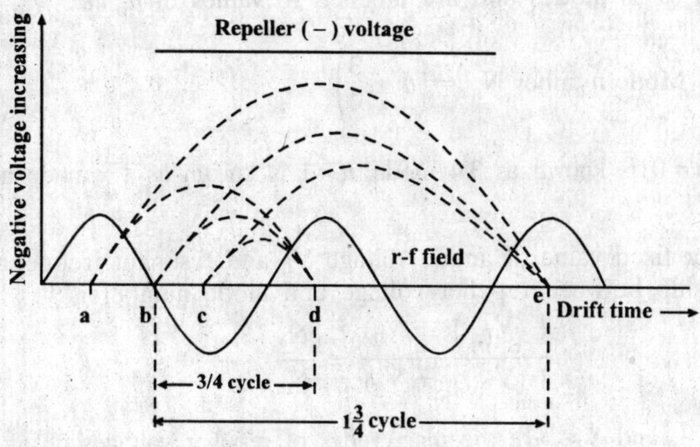

Fig. 6.23. Reflex klystron electron bunching and modes.

cavity is greater than the energy loss in the cavity, cavity could sustain the oscillations at the resonant frequency of the cavity. Oscillator output energy is taken from the cavity through coupling loop. The electrons are finally collected by the walls of the cavity or other grounded metal parts of the tube.

6.7.3. Transit Time and Mode Number

From above discussion, it is obvious that electron bunch should reach the resonator cavity at a time when the r-f. field retard the bunch and give up energy to reinforce the oscillations with in the cavity, *i.e.*, it should have proper transit time. From Fig. 6.23, it is clear that optimum transit time for the bunch to arrive at the cavity is $\left(n + \frac{3}{4}\right)$ cycles after the beam initially left the cavity.

∴ Transit time is related to the frequency by the relation :

$$T_0' = \frac{n + 3/4}{f} = \left(n + \frac{3}{4}\right) T \quad \text{....(6.7.1)}$$

where $T = \frac{1}{f}$ time period of r-f. voltage across the gap. In terms of transit angle,

$$\theta_0' = \omega T_o' = 2\pi f\left(n + \frac{3}{4}\right) T = \left(2\pi n + \frac{3}{2}\pi\right) \quad \text{....(6.7.2)}$$

where $n = 0, 1, 2, 3,.....$

From Eq. 6.7.1 and 6.7.2, it is clear that reflex klystron can be operated at different drift times (round trip transit time) which corresponds to different values of n. These different transit times are referred to as modes and are labelled to values of n, *i.e.*,

$$\text{Mode number } N_n = \left(n + \frac{3}{4}\right) \quad \text{....(6.7.3)}$$

where $n = 0$ is known as 3/4 mode, $n = 1$ is known as $|\frac{3}{4}$ mode and so on.

For fixed value of anode voltage V_0 and resonant frequency the relationship between repeller voltage and mode number is

$$\frac{(|V_{R_1}| + V_0)}{(|V_{R_2}| + V_0)} = \frac{N_2}{N_1} \quad \text{....(6.7.4)}$$

where V_{R_1} and V_{R_2} are the magnitudes of repeller voltages required to operate the klystron in mode number N_1 and N_2 respectively.

Substitution of mode number equation into repeller voltage relationship (Eq. 6.7.4) yields

$$\frac{(|V_{R_1}| + V_0)}{(|V_{R_2}| + V_0)} = \frac{n + 1 + \frac{3}{4}}{n + \frac{3}{4}} = \frac{n + 1.75}{n + 0.75} \quad \text{....(6.7.5)}$$

for to adjacent modes of operation. Figure 6.24 shows the variation of power output and frequency versus repeller voltage. These are known as mode curves. For $n = 0$ (*i.e.* $T_o' = \frac{3}{4}T$), the gain mechanism is usually not strong enough to over come system losses. Higher order modes ($n > 1$) are present at lower voltages.

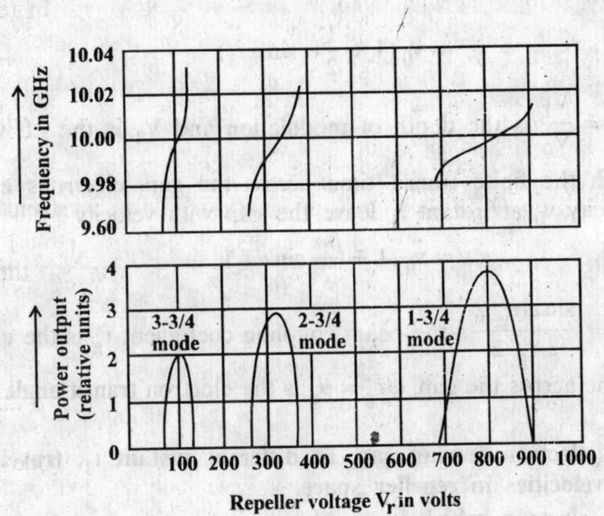

Fig. 6.24. Variation of power output and frequency versus repeller voltage (mode curves)

---

* SISODIA, M.L., and G.S. Raghuvanshi, Basic Microwave Γechniques and Laboratory Manual, New Age International (P) Ltd, reprint 2000. (Chapter 4)

Tuning* – Reflex Klystron oscillator can be electronically tuned (1 percent see, Fig. 6.24) as well as mechanically tuned (up to 30 per cent) by suitable tuning mechanism (changing the space between the grids of the resonator). Reflex klystrons are commercially available which are capable of delivering 10-2000 mW output power at frequency range 7 to 35 GHz. The efficiency is about 20 to 30 percent.

6.7.4. Quantitative Analysis

(a) Velocity Modulation

The analysis of a reflex klystron is similar to that of a two-cavity klystron. The accelerated electron beam with velocity,

$$v_0 = 0.593 \times 10^6 \sqrt{V_0} \qquad ....(6.7.6)$$

where V_0 is the accelerating voltage, enters the gap and leaves with a velocity v at instant t_1 (neglecting the transit time across the gap)

$$v = v_0 \left(1 + \frac{V_1}{V_0} \sin \omega t_1\right)$$

$$= v_0 \left(1 + \frac{1}{2} \alpha \sin \omega t_1\right) \qquad ....(6.7.7)$$

where, $\alpha = \frac{V_1}{V_0}$ is the depth of modulation and V_1 is the r.f. voltage.

With the finite transit time across the gap, electrons entering with velocity v_0 at instant t_1 leave the gap with velocity

$$v = v_0 \left(1 + \frac{\beta\alpha}{2} \sin \omega t_1\right) \qquad ....(6.7.8)$$

where $\beta = \frac{\sin \omega\tau_g/2}{\omega\tau_g/2}$, the beam coupling coefficient τ_g is the electron transit time across the gap, $\omega\tau_g = \theta_g$ is the electron transit angle across the gap.

The electron leaving gap, at different instant t_1, travels with different velocities in repeller space.

The electron, which leaves the gap at a time t_1 corresponding to

$$\omega t_1 = 2\pi n, \qquad n = 0, 1, 2, 3,.......$$

will suffer no change in velocity.

(b) Bunching, arrival time and modes

Suppose the voltage difference between the resonator and repeller is $(V_R - V_0)$ and the distance between the two is L. It is measured from the exit plane of the gap, *i.e.* $x=0$ (Fig. 6.25).

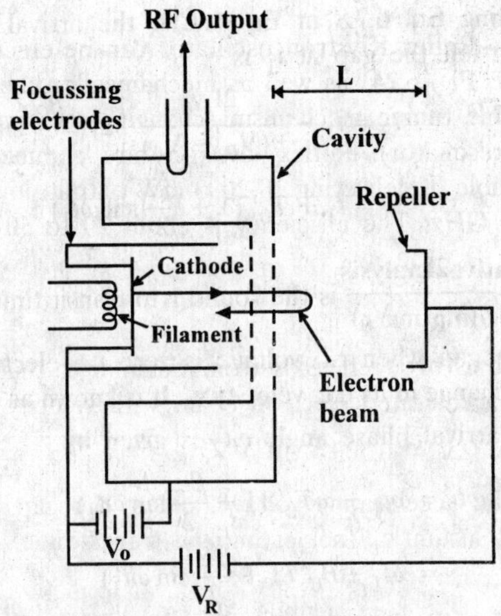

Fig. 6.25. Schematic diagram of Reflex klystron oscillator.

The force on the electron in the repeller space is given by

$$m\frac{d^2x}{dt^2} = \frac{e(V_R - V_0)}{L}$$

$$\therefore \quad \frac{d^2x}{dt^2} = \frac{\eta(V_R - V_0)}{L} \qquad ....(6.7.9)$$

where $\eta = e/m$ is the magnitude of the electronic charge to mass ratio $= 1.76 \times 10^{11}$ Coul/kg.

Integrating Eq. (6.7.9) twice, we obtain

$$x = \frac{\eta}{2}\frac{(V_R - V_0)}{L}(t - t_1)^2 + v(t - t_1) \qquad ....(6.7.10)$$

where $t = t_1$ is the instant when the electron leaves with a velocity v. The electron retarded as it approaches the negative repeller electrode, reverses its direction of travel, and travels towards the resonator gap and arrives at the gap x = 0 at the instant $t = t_2$ *i.e.,* **electron leaving $x = 0$ at t_1 arrives $x = 0$ at t_2.**

Thus the total transit time of the electron in the repeller space (round trip transit time) is

$$t_2 - t_1 = \frac{-2Lv}{\eta(V_R - V_0)} \qquad ....(6.7.11)$$

Substituting Eq. 6.7.8 in Eq. 6.7.11, the arrival time t_2 for the electron which left the gap at t_1 is

$$t_2 = t_1 - \frac{2Lv_0}{\eta(V_R - V_0)}\left(1 + \frac{\beta\alpha}{2}\sin\omega t_1\right)$$

$$= t_1 + T_0'\,(1 + \frac{\beta\alpha}{2}\sin\omega t_1) \quad \text{....(6.7.12)}$$

where $T_0' = -\frac{2Lv_o}{\eta(V_R - V_0)}$ is the round trip transit time of an electron that leaves the gap when r.f. voltage is zero *i.e.* electron which does not suffer any change in its d.c. velocity v_0. It is known as centre-of-bunch electron. The arrival phase angle ωt_2 is given by

$$\omega t_2 = \omega t_1 + \omega T_0'\,(1 + \frac{\beta\alpha}{2}\sin\omega t_1)$$

$$= \omega t_1 + \theta_0'\,(1 + \frac{\beta\alpha}{2}\sin\omega t_1) \quad \text{....(6.7.13)}$$

where $\theta_o' = \omega T_o'$ is the round trip transit angle of centre-of-bunch electron. It is clear (Fig. 6.23) that electrons between *a* and *c* centre around *b* arrive at the gap after reflecting from repeller at a retarding phase delivering energy to the cavity and sustaining oscillations. As discussed in Section 6.7.3 the optimum transit time T_0' for the bunch to arrive at the cavity is $\left(n + \frac{3}{4}\right)$T after the beam initially left the cavity, *i.e.*,

$$T_0' = \left(n + \frac{3}{4}\right)T$$

The optimum transit angle $\theta_0' = 2\pi\left(n + \frac{3}{4}\right) = (2\pi n + \frac{3\pi}{2})$.

Thus there are several values of T_0' or θ_0' satisfying the oscillation condition. These values correspond to various modes of a reflex klystron.

(c) Relation between accelerating voltage (V_0), repeller voltage (V_R) and repeller space (L)

The optimum value of T_0' is

$$T_0' = \frac{-2Lv_0}{\eta(V_R - V_0)} = \left(n + \frac{3}{4}\right)T \quad \text{....(6.7.14)}$$

for oscillation condition.

Substituting the value of $v_0 = \sqrt{2\eta V_0}$ in Eq. 6.7.14 and arranging

$$\frac{V_0}{(V_R - V_0)^2} = \frac{\eta}{8L^2}\left(n + \frac{3}{4}\right)^2 . T^2, \quad \left(T = \frac{1}{f}\right)$$

$$\frac{V_0}{(|V_R| + V_0)^2} = \frac{\eta}{8L^2 f^2}\left(n + \frac{3}{4}\right)^2 \qquad \text{....(6.7.14a)}$$

$$|V_R| = \frac{6.744 \times 10^{-6} fL\sqrt{V_0}}{\left(n + \frac{3}{4}\right)} - V_0 \qquad \text{....(6.7.14b)}$$

The smaller value of n correspond to higher value of V_R. Thus a particular mode of operation can be selected by the choice of repeller voltage (Eq. 6.7.14b).

For a selected gap-repeller spacing L, the various values of the repeller voltage V_R for oscillations can be obtained using Eq. (6.7.14,b), for a given value of V_0. Alternatively if the repeller voltage is fixed, the gap repeller spacing L can be determined.

(d) Power Output and Efficiency

The power output and efficiency of a reflex klystron can be determined in the same manner as that of a two-cavity klystron in Section 6.6. From the charge conservation law the net charge $I_0\, dt_1$ leaving the resonator cavity gap over an interval of time dt_1 arrives back to cavity gap over an interval of time dt_2 inducing current I_2. Thus

$$I_2 dt_2 = I_0 dt_1 \quad \text{(Charge conservation)}$$

$$\therefore \quad I_2 = I_0 \frac{dt_1}{dt_2} \qquad \text{....(6.7.15)}$$

From Eq. 6.7.12, we get

$$I_2 = \frac{I_0}{\left[1 + \frac{\beta\alpha\theta_0'}{2}\cos\omega t_1\right]}$$

$$\approx I_0\left[1 - \frac{\beta\alpha\theta_0'}{2}\cos\omega t_1\right]$$

$$\approx I_0[1 - X'\cos\omega t_1] \qquad \text{....(6.7.16)}$$

where $X' = -\frac{\theta_0' \alpha \beta}{2} = -\theta_0' \frac{\beta V_1}{2V_0}$ is bunching parameter and β is beam coupling coefficient and for small cavity gap $\beta \approx 1$, *i.e.* transit time across the gap is negligible.

X′ the bunching parameter has a negative sign with respect to the bunching parameter X of a two-cavity klystron amplifier. The beam current injected into the cavity gap from the repeller space flows in the negative direction. The fundamental component of the current induced in the cavity by the density modulated return electron beam is given by similar way as in case of two-cavity klystron.

$$I_f = 2I_0 J_1(X') \qquad \text{....(6.7.18)}$$

where $J_1(X')$ is the Bessel function of the first kind (see Fig. 6.26).

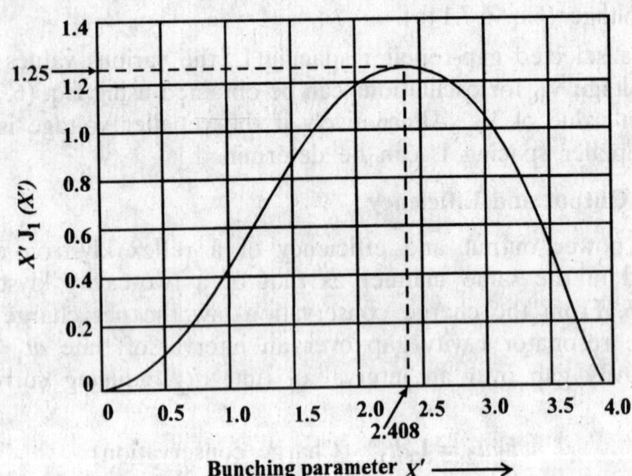

Fig. 6.26. X′ J1(X′) versus X′

The dc power supplied by the beam voltage V_0 is

$$P_{dc} = V_0 I_0$$

and the r.f. power delivered to the load is given by

$$P_{r.f.} = \frac{V_1 I_f}{2} = V_1 I_0 J_1(X') \qquad \text{....(6.7.19)}$$

The ratio of V_1 over V_0 is given by

$$\frac{V_1}{V_0} = \frac{2(X')}{(2\pi n + 3\pi/2)}$$

$$\therefore \qquad V_1 = \frac{2(X')V_0}{(2\pi n + 3\pi/2)} \qquad \text{....(6.7.20)}$$

Substituting the value of V_1 from Eq. 6.7.20 in Eq. 6.7.19, we get

$$P_{r.f.} = \frac{2I_0V_0(X')\,J_1(X')}{2\pi(n + 3/4)} \qquad \text{....(6.7.21)}$$

$$P_{r.f.} = \frac{I_0V_0(X')\,J_1(X')}{\pi(n + 3/4)} \qquad \text{....(6.7.22)}$$

From Fig. 6.26, it is clear that the factor $(X')J_1(X')$ reaches the naximum value of 1.25 at $X' = 2.408$ and $J_1(X') = 0.52$. Thus optimum naximum r.f. power would be

$$P_{r.f.(max.)} = \frac{0.3986 I_0 V_0}{(n + 3/4)} \qquad \text{....(6.7.23)}$$

$$\approx \frac{0.3986\, I_0 V_0}{N}$$

where $N = (n + 3/4)$, $n = 0, 1, 2, 3,.....$

Electronic efficiency from Eq. 6.7.22 is given below :

$$\text{Efficiency} = \eta = \frac{P_{r.f.}}{P_{dc}} = \frac{(X')\,J_1(X')}{\pi\,(n + 3/4)} \qquad \text{....(6.7.24)}$$

Maximum or optimum efficiency

$$\eta_{max} = \frac{0.3986}{(n + 3/4)} \qquad \text{....(6.7.25)}$$

The mode $n = 1$ *i.e.* $1\frac{3}{4}$ mode leads maximum r.f. power output (Eq. 6.7.23) and efficiency (Eq. 6.7.25).

$$P_{r.f.max} = 0.227\, V_0 I_0$$

$$\eta_{max} = 22.7\%$$

Example 6.7.1 *A reflex klystron is to be operated at frequency of 10 GHz, with dc beam voltage 400*V, *repeller space 0.1 cm for* $1\frac{3}{4}$ *mode. Determine optiman (maximum) value of power and corresponding repeller voltage for beam current of 30 mA.*

Solution :

From Eq. 6.7.14b, we can write

From Eq. 6.7.23

Given :
$I_0 = 30 \times 10^{-3}$ A
$V_0 = 400$ V
$n + \frac{3}{4} = 1\frac{3}{4} = 1.75$
$f = 10 \times 10^9$ Hz
$L_{opt} = 0.1 \times 10^{-2} = 10^{-3}$ m

$$P_{r.f.\,(max.)} = \frac{0.3986 \times I_0 V_0}{(n + 3/4)}$$

$$= \frac{0.398 \times 400 \times 30 \times 10^{-3}}{1.75}$$

$$= 2.73 \text{ watts}$$

$$|V_R| = \frac{6.744 \times 10^{-6} f L \sqrt{V_0}}{\left(n + \frac{3}{4}\right)} - V_0$$

$$= \frac{6.744 \times 10^{-6} \times 10 \times 10^9 \times 10^{-3} \times \sqrt{400}}{1.75} - 400$$

$$= \frac{6.744 \times 2 \times 10 \times 10}{1.75} - 400$$

$$V_R \approx -370.44 \text{ V}$$

Example 6.7.2. *Find the optimum length for* $1\frac{3}{4}$ *mode of a repeller space of reflex klystron which operates with centre frequency 9 GHz* with *dc beam voltage 600V and repeller voltage* $V_R = -250$ *V and* $\eta = 1.76 \times 10^{11}$ Coul/kg.

Solution : From Eq. (6.7.14a)

Given :
$V_0 = 600$ V
$\lvert V_R \rvert = 250$ V
$f_c = 9 \times 10^9$ Hz
$N = 1\frac{3}{4} = 1.75$

$$\frac{V_0}{(V_R + V_0)^2} = \frac{\eta}{8L^2} \frac{\left(n + \frac{3}{4}\right)^2}{f^2}$$

$$\therefore L^2 = \frac{\eta}{8} \frac{\left(n + \frac{3}{4}\right)^2}{f^2} \cdot \frac{(\lvert V_R \rvert + V_0)^2}{V_0}$$

$$\text{or} \qquad L = \sqrt{\frac{\eta}{8}} \, \frac{\left(n + \frac{3}{4}\right)}{f} \cdot \frac{(\lvert V_R \rvert + V_0)^2}{\sqrt{V_0}}$$

$$\text{or} \quad L = \frac{\sqrt{1.76 \times 10^{11}}}{\sqrt{8}} \times \frac{1.75}{9 \times 10^9} \times \frac{850}{\sqrt{600}}$$

$$= 10^{-3} \text{ m} = 0.1 \text{ cm}$$

(e) Admittance

Fig. 6.27 shows the equivalent circuit for the reflex klystron, where C, L, R represent equivalent lumped circuit components of the resonator cavity and $Y_e = G_e + jB_e$ is electronic admittance presented by bunches as the bunched electrons return to the cavity gap a little before the optimum transit time $T_0' = \left(n + \frac{3}{4}\right)T$, the r.f. beam current lags behind the field and an inductive reactance is presented to the external circuit and if the bunched electrons return slightly after T_0', a capacitive reactance appears in the circuit. The condition for ocillations is satisfied when G_e becomes negative.

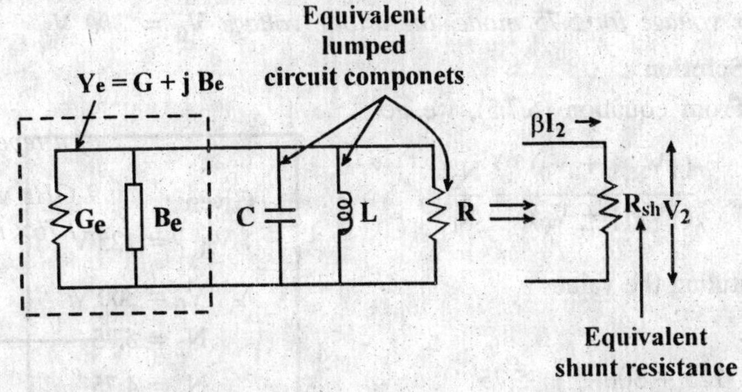

Fig. 6.27 Equivalent circuit of a reflex klystron

In Fig. 6.28, electronic admittance $Y_e = G_e + jB_e$ is plotted in the complex admittance plane. It shows the variation of G_e and B_e qualitatively. The origin in this plane corresponds to infinite repeller voltage. A decrease in repeller voltage moves outwards along the spiral. Oscillations can take place whenever $|G|$ is greater than G_{ext}, the conductance of the external circuit. When jB_e is negative, oscillations take place at a frequency higher than the resonance frequency of the cavity, whereas positive values of jB_e correspond to a lower frequency than the resonator resonance frequency. This leads to the frequency variation with the repeller voltage as shown in Fig. 6.28.

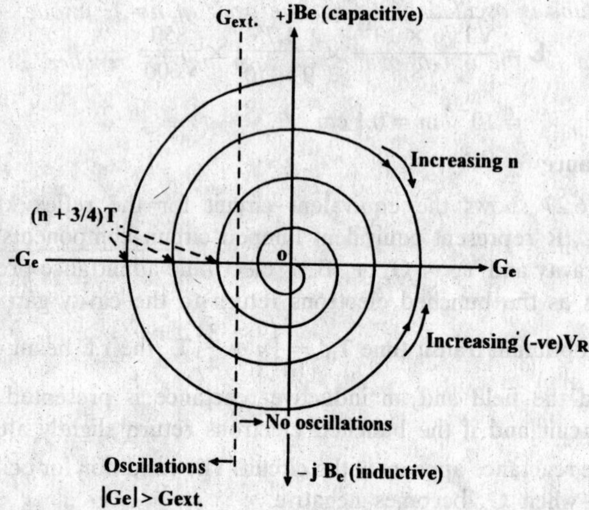

Fig. 6.28. Electronic admittance of reflex klystron.

Example 6.7.3. *4.75 mode the repeller voltage is-125*V *find the repeller voltage for 5.75 mode, the anode voltage* $V_0 = 300$ V

Solution :

From equation (6.7.5), we get

$$\frac{(|V_{R_1}| + V_0)}{(|V_{R_2}| + V_0)} = \frac{N_2}{N_1}$$

Given :
$|V_{R_1}| = 125$ V
$V_0 = 300$ V
$N_2 = 5.75$
$N_1 = 4.75$
$V_{R_2} = ?$

Substituling the values

$$\frac{125 + 300}{|V_{R_2}| + 300} = \frac{5.75}{4.75}$$

$$|V_{R_2}| = 51 \text{ V}$$

$$V_{R_2} = -51 \text{ V}$$

Example 6.7.4. *A reflex klystron operates under the following conditions :*

$V_0 = 600\text{V}$, $I_0 = 11.45\, mA$, $L = 1\, mm$.

$R_{sh} = 15\, K\Omega$, $f_r = 9\, GHz$

The tube is oscillating at f_r at the peak of $n = 1\frac{3}{4}$ mode. Assume $\beta = 1$ Find (a) the microwave gap voltage and (b) repeller voltage for the mode $\left(1\frac{3}{4}\right)$

Solution :

$I_0 = 11.45$ mA
$V_0 = 600$ V
$J_1(X') = 0.582$
for $X' = 2.408$
$R_{sh} = 15 \times 10^3\ \Omega$
$L = 10^{-3}$ m
$f = 9 \times 10^9$

(a) $V_2 = I_2 R_{sh} = 2I_0 J_1(X') R_{sh}$

$= 2 \times 11.45 \times 10^{-3} \times 0.582 \times 15 \times 10^3$

≈ 200V

(b) V_R for mode $1\frac{3}{4}$

$$|V_R| = \frac{6.744 \times 10^{-6} f_r L \sqrt{V_0}}{n + \frac{3}{4}} - V_0$$

$$= \frac{6.744 \times 10^{-6} \times 9 \times 10^9 \times 10^{-3} \times \sqrt{600}}{1.75} - 600$$

$\therefore V_R = -250$ V.

6.8. Travelling-Wave Tubes (TWTs)

Travelling-Wave Tubes (TWTs) are another class of O-type tubes which are widely used as broadband low and medium power microwave devices. A large variety of travelling wave tubes are available, that differ from one another in the type of structure (circuit) used in supporting a slow electromagnetic wave.

Helix travelling wave amplifiers are almost exclusively used for broadband application – such as wideband ground and satellite communication systems and antijaming and countermeasure radar systems etc. Octave bandwidths are possible with TWTs. Travelling wave tube oscillators, a more commonly known as backward wave oscillators (BOWs), have been devised which allow electronic tuning range of the order of 2 : 1. In this section structure, operation, and small signal analysis of helix travelling wave tube are presented.

6.8.1. Structure

A schematic diagram of a typical helix-type travelling wave tube in shown in Fig. 6.29a. (*Pierce depicted TWT as in Fig. 6.6.*) It consists of (i) a cathode anode configuration (eletron gun Fig. 6.10b.) to produce an electron beam with velocity close to the velocity of propagation of microwaves on the slow-wave structure; (ii) a long helix slow-wave structure (nonresonant) capable of propogating microwaves and at the same time enclosing an electron beam; (iii) a collector which is generally kept at a dc potential lower than that of the helix; (iv) input and output couplers; and (v) an external to vacuum envelope magnetic focussing structure usually long solenoid (see Section 6.3.4.). There is an attenuator at the céntre of the circuit which absorbs the reflecting wave from mismatch at the output.

6.8.2. Operation

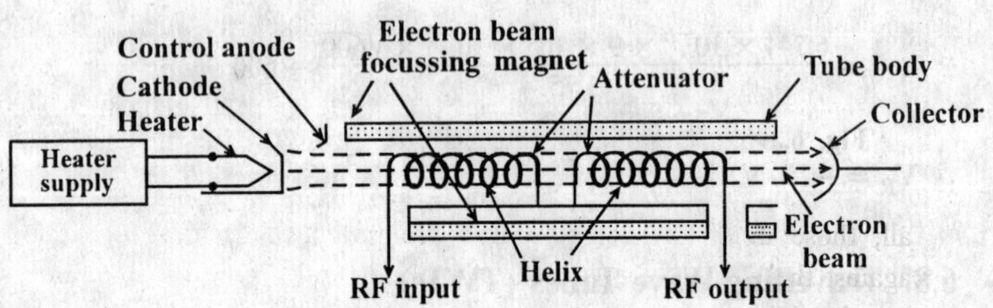

Fig. 6.29a. Schematic diagram of TWT (see figure 6.6 also).

We have seen that various electronic processes *i.e.*, velocity modulation, conversion to density modulation, transfer of energy etc., take place in two-cavity klystron in separate regions of the tube. On the other hand in travelling wave tube these processes take place continuously over the entire length of the slow-wave structure.* The

* Variety of slow-wave structures have been discussed in chapter 5 of the book.

applied signal propagates around the turns of helix, and produces an electric field along the axis of the helix which progresses along the axial direction with phase velocity which is small compared with the velocity of light. This axial time varying electric field produces velocity modulation in an otherwise uniform velocity which is approximately equal to the phase velocity (actually slightly greater) of electrons in the electron beam moving through the helix axis. The velocity modulation tends to bunch the electrons (Fig. 6.29b). As can be seen in the Fig. 6.29b, electrons near the zero amplitude value are not accelerated at

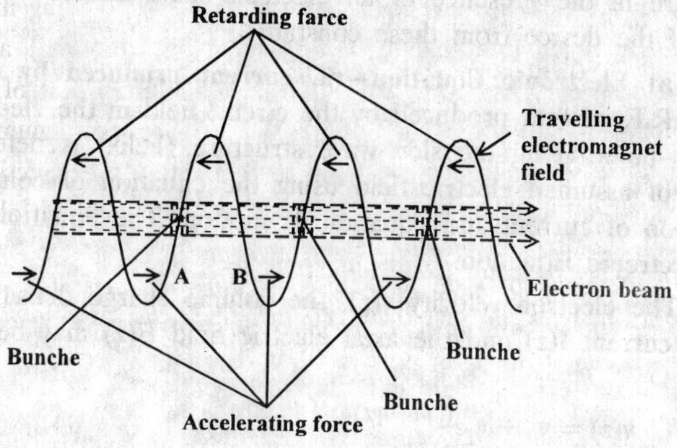

Fig. 6.29b. Bunching in a TWT due to interaction of electron beam with travelling electromagnetic field.

all; those in one- half cycle are accelerated (electric field directed against the electron flow accelerates); and those in the other half cycle are decelerated (electric field directed along the electron flow). The field obviously passess through zero at two points in each cycle. Consider the point A, electrons ahead of it are moving more slowly than the average and those behind it are moving faster than the average, than electrons tend to bunch themselves around point A. The zero-field point B (180° away) has a corresponding decrease in density associated with it. The action of the field is thus to produce bunching, similar to that of klystron, except electron travels with the field, so the field continually acts to increase the bunching i.e. velocity and density modulation occurs simultaneously in the same region. Since the dc electron velocity is slightly greater than the wave velocity, it results into a situation in which more electrons face the retarding field than the accelerating field, energy is thus lost by the electron beam and gained by the travelling-wave, resulting in an amplified amplitude signal. This cumulative interaction between the electrons and travelling waves along the axis can be discussed in terms of space charge waves on the beam.

6.8.3. Small signal analysis of travelling wave tube

The purpose of the following analysis is to determine the propagation constants of the space-charge waves that can exist on the structure in the presence of an electron beam and to calculate the gain of the device from these constants.

(a) Electronic Equation – r.f. current produced by the circuit field – R.F. current produced by the circuit field in the electron beam at any point along the slow-wave structure (helix) is determined in terms of assumed electric field using the equation of continuity, the defintion of current and equation of motion. The equation is known as Electronic Equation.

The electron velocity v(z), the volume charge density $\rho(z)$, the beam current I(z) and the axial electric field E(z) may be expressed as

$$v(z) = v_0 + v_1 e^{(j\omega t - \gamma z)} \qquad \text{....(6.8.1)}$$

$$\rho(z) = \rho_0 + \rho_1 e^{(j\omega t - \gamma z)} \qquad \text{....(6.8.2)}$$

$$I(z) = I_0 + i_1 e^{(j\omega t - \gamma z)} \qquad \text{....(6.8.3)}$$

and
$$E(z) = E_{z1} e^{(j\omega t - \gamma z)} \qquad \text{....(6.8.4)}$$

[$E_0 = 0$, since dc potential V_0 is constant along z-direction

$\therefore \dfrac{\partial V_0}{\partial z} = E_0 = 0$]

where $\gamma = \alpha_e + i\beta_e$ is the propagation constant of the axial waves. v_1, ρ_1 and i_1 are r.f. velocity, charge density and beam current respectively and are much smaller than corresponding dc quantities v_0, ρ_0 and I_0.

The beam current is the product of volume charge density $\rho(z)$ the velocity v(z) and beam area A. Thus I(z) could be written as

$$I(z) = I_0 + i_1 e^{(j\omega t - \gamma z)}$$
$$= \rho(z)\, v(z) \times \text{beam area A} \qquad \text{....(6.8.5)}$$

Substituting for $\rho(z)$ and $v(z)$ from Eq. 6.8.2 and 6.8.1 respectively in Eq. 6.8.5 and arranging, we get

$$I(z) \approx [\rho_0 v_0 + (\rho_0 v_1 + \rho_1 v_0)e^{(j\omega t - \gamma z)} + \rho_1 v_1 e^{2(j\omega t - \gamma z)}]A \quad ...(6.8.6)$$

The last term in the Eq. 6.8.6 is second order term involving the product of two small quantities ρ_1 and v_1 and is neglected. This yields ac component of the beam current (since $I_0 = \rho_0 v_0 A$).

$$i_1 = (\rho_0 v_1 + \rho_1 v_0)A \quad ....(6.8.7)$$

From the **current continuity equation**

$$\nabla . J = -\partial\rho/\partial t, \text{ we obtain}$$

$$\nabla . \frac{i_1}{A} = -\frac{\gamma i_1}{A} = -j\omega\rho_1 \quad ....(6.8.8)$$

$$\therefore \quad \rho_1 = -\frac{j\gamma i_1}{\omega A} \quad ....(6.8.9.)$$

Since

$$i_1 = (\rho_0 v_1 + \rho_1 v_0)A$$

$$= \left(\rho_0 v_1 - \frac{j\gamma i_1}{\omega A} v_0\right) A$$

$$\therefore \quad i_1\left[1 + \frac{j\gamma v_0}{\omega}\right] = \rho_0 v_1 A$$

Thus the expression for i_1, therefore, is derived as

$$i_1 = \frac{\omega \rho_0 v_1 A}{(\omega + j\gamma v_0)} \quad ....(6.8.9)$$

$$= \frac{j\beta_e \rho_0 A}{(j\beta_e - \gamma)} v_1 \quad ....(6.8.10)$$

where $\beta_e = \omega/v_0$ is defined as the phase constant of the velocity modulated electron beam and v_0 is the dc velocity of the electron beam.

From the equation of motion,

$$\frac{dv(z)}{dt} = \eta E(z) = \eta\frac{\partial V}{\partial z} = \eta\frac{\partial V_1}{\partial z} \quad ....(6.8.11)$$

Since the dc potential V_0 is constant along the flow of the electron beam so that $\frac{\partial V_0}{\partial z} \equiv 0$.

The left hand side of Eq. 6.8.11 can be written as :

$$\frac{dv(z)}{dt} = \frac{dv_1}{dt} = \frac{\partial v_1}{\partial t} + \frac{\partial v_1}{\partial z} \cdot \frac{\partial z}{\partial t}$$

$$= j\omega v_1 - \gamma v_1 (v_0 + v_1)$$

$$\approx j\omega v_1 - \gamma v_1 v_0$$

$$\approx (j\omega - \gamma v_0) v_1$$

∴ The equation (6.8.11) can be written as

$$(j\omega - \gamma v_0)\, v_1 = -\eta\gamma V_1$$

$$\therefore \quad v_1 = \frac{-\gamma\eta V_1}{v_0(j\beta_e - \gamma)} \qquad \text{....(6.8.12)}$$

Using Eq. 6.8.12 in Eq. 6.8.10. we have

$$i_1 = \frac{j\beta_e \rho_0 A}{(j\beta_e - \gamma)} \, \frac{-\gamma\eta V_1}{v_0(j\beta_e - \gamma)}$$

$$= \frac{jI_0\beta_e\gamma V_1}{2V_0(j\beta_e - \gamma)^2} \qquad \text{....(6.8.13)}$$

where $I_0 = -\rho_0 v_0 A$ and $v_0^2 = 2\eta V_0$ has been used. Equation 6.8.13 is called the **electronic equation.** It relates the r.f. beam current (convection current induce by the axial electric field) to the r.f. voltage on the slow-wave structure.

(b) Circuit equation : Electric field produced in the circuit by the r.f. current in the beam – The analysis is based on transmission line theory approach. Figure 6.30 depicts the equivalent circuit of the helix (helix is represented by lossless transmission line with series impedance Z per unit length and shunt admittance Y per unit length) in the vicinity of an electron beam which induces a current in the transmission line.

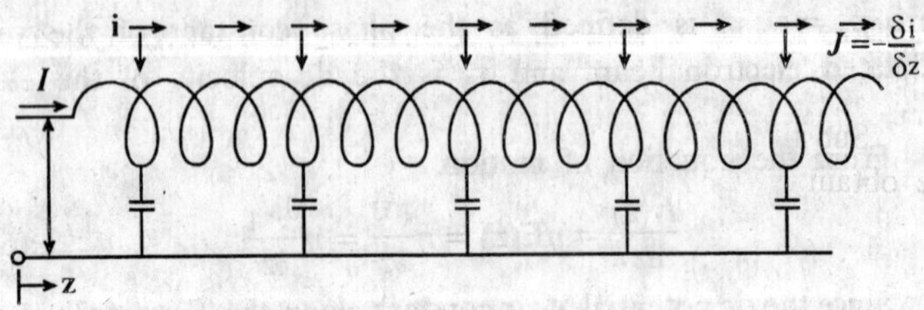

Fig. 6.30. Distributed circuit excited by electron beam.

From the transmission line relation,

$$\gamma_0 = j\sqrt{ZY} \qquad \text{....(6.8.14)}$$

and $Z_0 = \sqrt{Z/Y}$

where γ_0 is the propagation constant of the uncoupled helix and Z_0 is the characteristic impedance of the line (it is slow-wave structure (helix) to beam coupling impedance).

From Eq. 6.8.14

$$Z = -j\gamma_0 Z_0\,;\; Y = -j\gamma_0/Z_0 \qquad \text{....(6.8.15)}$$

The expressions for voltage and current per unit length for the network shown in Fig. 6.30 are, respectively

$$\frac{\partial V_1}{\partial z} = -jZI_1 \qquad \text{....(6.8.16)}$$

$$\frac{\partial I_1}{\partial z} = -jYV_1 + J \qquad \text{....(6.8.17)}$$

where J is the impressed current per unit length, due to coupling between electron beam and circuit, and is given by

$$J = -\frac{\partial i_1}{dz} \qquad \text{....(6.8.18)}$$

where i_1 = (beam area A) × ($\rho_0 v + \rho_1 v_0$) (See Eq. 6.8.7)

Assuming the various ac quantities as

$e^{j(\omega t - \gamma z)}$, from Eqs. 6.8.16 and 6.8.17, we get

$$-\gamma I_1 = -jYV_1 + \gamma i_1 \qquad \text{....(6.8.19)}$$

$$-\gamma V_1 = -jZI_1 \qquad \text{....(6.8.20)}$$

Substituting I_1 from Eq. 6.9.20 in Eq. 6.8.19, and rearranging we obtain

$$\therefore\; (\gamma^2 + ZY)V_1 = (\gamma^2 - \gamma_0^{\,2})V_1 = -j\gamma Z i_1 \qquad \text{....(6.8.21)}$$

$$\therefore \qquad V_1 = \frac{-\gamma\gamma_0 Z_0}{(\gamma^2 - \gamma_0^{\,2})} i_1 \qquad \text{....(6.8.22)}$$

This is the **circuit equation** relating the r.f. circuit voltage with the r.f. beam current i_1.

(c) The gain parameter C and gain – Substituting Eq. 6.8.22 into electronic Eq. 6.8.13. We obtain, the dispersion equation describing the TWT interaction of an electron beam with helix–the SWS as

$$\frac{jI_0\beta_0\gamma}{2V_0(j\beta_e-\gamma)^2}\,\frac{-\gamma\gamma_0Z_0}{(\gamma^2-\gamma_0^2)}=1$$

$$-\frac{j(Z_0I_0/2V_0)\,\gamma_0\beta_e\gamma^2}{(j\beta_e-\gamma)^2\,(\gamma^2-\gamma_0^2)}=1 \qquad ....(6.8.23)$$

In this equations

Z_0 = the helix to beam coupling impedance (characteristic impedance of the line)

I_0 = the beam current

V_0 = d.c. voltage equivalent to the beam velocity v_0.

$\gamma_0 = j\sqrt{ZY}$ propagation constant of circuit in absence of beam

$\beta_e = \omega/v_0$ where v_0 is the dc beam velocity $(= \sqrt{2\eta V_0})$

γ_0 = the complex propagation constant in the presence of the beam.

Rearranging 6.8.23, we can write

$$\frac{jI_0Z_0\gamma_0\gamma^2\beta_e}{2V_0(j\beta_e-\gamma)^2\,(\gamma_0^2-\gamma^2)}=1 \qquad ....(6.8.24)$$

or $$(\gamma_0^2-\gamma^2)\,(j\beta_e-\gamma)^2=\frac{j\gamma^2\gamma_0\beta_eZ_0I_0}{2V_0} \qquad ....(6.8.25)$$

Equation 6.8.25 is fourth order in γ and thus has four roots. That is four waves are set up on the circuit in the presence of the beam. The exact solutions of Eq. 6.8.25 can be obtained by numerical methods and a digital computer. However, the approximate solutions are given below :

For the travelling wave tube, we are particularly interested in a wave that propagates in the direction of electron flow of nearly the electron speed and which will account for the observed gain. Making a reasonable assumption that the electron speed is equal to that of circuit wave in the absence of beam interaction, we have

$$-\gamma_0 = -j\beta_e$$

If we further assume that γ differs from β_e by a small quantity ξ, we have

$$-\gamma = -j\beta_e + \xi \qquad ....(6.8.26)$$

Substitution of Eq. 6.8.26 in Eq. 6.8.24, results in

$$\frac{-Z_0 I_0 \beta_e^{\,2}(-\beta_e^{\,2}-2j\beta_e\xi+\xi^2)}{2V_0(2j\beta_e\xi-\xi^2)\xi^2}=1 \quad \text{....(6.8.27)}$$

In accordance with the assumption $\xi < \beta_e$ we may neglect the terms $2j\,\beta_e\xi$ and ξ^2 in numerator and ξ^4 in denominator, we obtain

$$\xi^3 = -\frac{jZ_0\,I_0\beta_e^{\,3}}{4V_0}$$

$$= -jC^3\beta_e^{\,3} \quad \text{....(6.8.28)}$$

where $C = \left(\frac{I_0 Z_0}{4V_0}\right)^{1/3}$ is the travelling wave gain parameter first suggested by Pierce.*

$$\therefore \quad \xi = [-j]^{1/3}\beta_e C$$

$$= \delta_n \beta_e C$$

Where $\delta_n = (-j)^{1/3}$ [n = 0, 1, and 2) and its. three roots are

$$\delta_1 = \frac{\sqrt{3}}{2} - j/2 \quad \text{(correspond to n = 0)}$$

$$\delta_2 = -\frac{\sqrt{3}}{2} - j/2 \quad \text{(correspond to n = 1)}$$

$$\delta_3 = j \quad \text{(correspond to n = 2)}$$

$$\therefore \quad -\gamma = -j\beta_e + \xi$$

$$= -j\beta_e + \delta_n\beta_e C$$

or

$$\gamma_n = j\beta_e - \delta_n\beta_e C$$

Thus the values of three propagation constants are–

$$\gamma_1 = -\beta_e C\frac{\sqrt{3}}{2} + j\beta_e\left(1+\frac{C}{2}\right) \quad \text{....(6.8.29a)}$$

---

* Pierce J.R. : **Theory of the Beam-type Travelling Wave Tube, Proc. I.R.E. 35, 111 – 123 (1947).**

$$\gamma_2 = \beta_e C\frac{\sqrt{3}}{2} + j\beta_e\left(1 + \frac{C}{2}\right) \qquad ....(6.8.29b)$$

$$\gamma_3 = j\beta_e(1 - C) \qquad ....(6.8.29c)$$

Thus, it is obvious that three waves are set up on the circuit in the presence of the electron beam. The waves corresponding to γ_1 and γ_2 propagate more slowly than the circuit wave when the beam is absent. From modified phase constant we can write–

$$\beta_e(1 + C/2) = \frac{\omega}{v_0/\left(1+\frac{C}{2}\right)} = \frac{\omega}{v_p}$$

i.e., $v_{p_1} < v_0$. Similarly $v_{p_2} < v_0$

Thus the first two waves have phase velocities slightly less than the beam velocity.

Amplitude of each of the wave varies as $e^{j\omega t - \gamma_n z}$. Substituting the values of γ_1 and γ_2 and arranging, we get the amplitudes of the waves with propagation constant γ_1 and γ_2 respectively varying as

$$e^{\sqrt{3}/2\,\beta_e Cz} \,.\, e^{j[\omega t - \beta_e(1+\frac{C}{2})z]} \qquad ....(6.8.30a)$$

$$\text{and } e^{-\sqrt{3}/2\beta_e Cz} \,.\, e^{j[\omega t - \beta_e(1+\frac{C}{2})z]} \qquad ....(6.8.30b)$$

we note from Eq. 6.8.30a that the wave corresponding to γ_1 is a growing wave with distance and energy flows from the electron beam to wave whereas the wave corresponding to γ_2 (Eq. 6.8.30b) is a decaying wave with distance and energy flows from the wave to electron beam.

Similarly, we find that the wave corresponding to γ_3 is unattenuated, but is faster than the first two waves. Its phase constant is

$$\beta_e(1 - C) = \frac{\omega}{v_0/(1-C)}$$

$$= \frac{\omega}{v_{p_3}} \quad \text{where} \quad v_{p_3} = \frac{v_0}{(1-C)}, \text{ i.e. } v_{p_3} > v_0$$

The amplitude of the wave with propogation constant γ_3 varies as $e^{j[\omega t - \beta_e(1-C)]}$, thus the wave is unattenuated and no energy exchange occurs between the wave and the electron beam.

Fourth root wave–As Eq. 6.8.24 or 6.8.25 is quadratic as such the propagation constant γ has four roots. The fourth root δ_4 corresponding to the backward travelling wave and can obtained

$$\xi_4 = -jC^2/4$$

$$\text{and} \quad \gamma_4 = -j\beta_e - \beta_e C\delta_4$$

$$\therefore \qquad \gamma_4 = -j\beta_e\left(1 - \frac{C^3}{4}\right) \qquad \text{....(6.2.29)}$$

This is a backward wave set up at output and travels towards input end with a velocity slightly higher than the velocity of the electron beam. Usually the structure is perfectly matched so that there is no backward wave. Attenuator is usually put at the centre of the tube which absorbs the reflected backward wave if any due to some mismatch.

The above analysis although based on the transmission line equations which are strictly valid only at low frequencies, are actually good approximation for periodic structure like helix at high frequencies if the phase velocities of interest are small compared to the velocity of light and gives a surprisingly good quantitative accuracy.

Gain relation :

From the above discussion it is clear that total circuit voltage is the sum of the three forward voltages corresponding to the three forward travelling waves. The input signal voltage at the input end z=0) naturally splits into three, that is

$$V(0) = V_1 + V_2 + V_3$$

With the proper boundary conditions*, it can be shown that

$$V_1 = V_2 = V_3 = \frac{V(0)}{3} \qquad \text{....(6.8.31)}$$

and looks logical, as at the input end, there is no reason why at the start any wave may have more or less voltage than the other. Therefore, the amplitude of the growing wave

$$V(z) = \frac{V(0)}{3} e^{\frac{\sqrt{3}}{2}\beta_e C z}$$

When $z = L$, the circuit length then

$$V(L) = \frac{V(0)}{3} e^{\frac{\sqrt{3}}{2}\beta_e C L}$$

$$= \frac{V(0)}{3} e^{\sqrt{3}\pi NC} \qquad \text{....(6.8.32)}$$

where $\beta_e L = 2\pi N$, N is the circuit length in electronic wave length, that is

$$N = \frac{L}{\lambda_e} \quad \text{and} \quad \beta_e = \frac{2\pi}{\lambda_e}$$

The output power gain in decible is

$$A_p = 10 \log \left|\frac{V(L)}{V(0)}\right|^2 = 10 \log \left[\frac{1}{3} e^{\sqrt{3}\pi NC}\right]^2$$

---

* Pierce J.R., **Travelling Wave Tubes**, D. Van Nostrand, New Jersey, 1950.

$$= -9.54 + 47.3\,NC \quad \text{db.} \qquad \text{....(6.8.33)}$$

where NC is a numerical number. From Eq. 6.8.33 it can be noted that power gain is proportional to the circuit length in electronic wave length and the gain parameter C of the circuit. For larger C, larger gain for the same physical length of the tube.

There is initial loss at the circuit input of 9.54 db due to splitting of signal into three waves of equal magnitude and growing wave voltage is only one-third of the total input voltage.

It is observed that with the increase of r.f. input power, r-f. output power attains a maximum and finally starts decreasing (Fig. 6.31a).

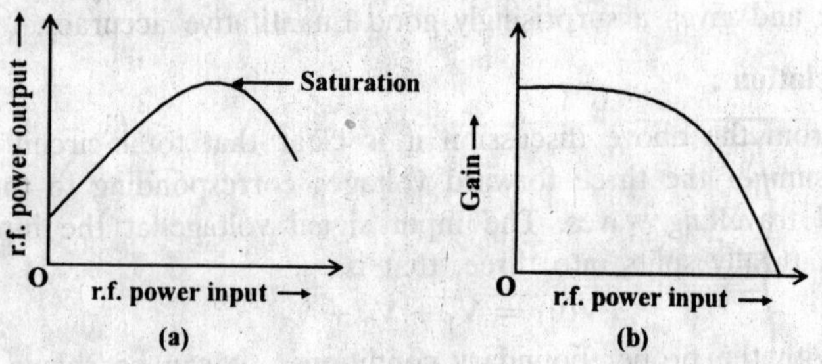

Fig. 6.31. r-f. power output and gain characteristics

The point at which r.f. output power attains maximum is termed as saturation point and the gain at that point is known as saturation gain (Fig. 6.31a). For low r.f. inputs, the small signal gain is almost constant (Fig. 6.31b). These tubes are known for their low noise and wide bandwidth characteristics. As such, as mentioned earlier, they have been extensively used in microwave communication systems. CEERI, Pilani has developed TWTs in our country and are being used in number of microwave systems.

Example 6.8.1. A helix travelling wave tube operates at 4 GHz under a beam voltage $V_0 = 4$ kV, and a beam current 20 mA. If the helix impedance (Z_0) is 100 ohm and circuit length N=30, find the out put power gain.

Solution : From Eq. 6.8.33 the gain in decible is given by

$$A_p = -9.54 + 47.3\,NC$$

and Gain parameter $C = \left(\frac{I_0 Z_0}{4V_0}\right)^{1/3}$

Substituting the value of I_0, Z_0, V_0, we find

$$C = \left[\frac{20 \times 10^{-3} \times 100}{4 \times 4 \times 10^3}\right]^{1/3}$$

$$= 0.5 \times 10^{-1}$$

$$\therefore \text{ Gain } A_p = -9.54 + 47.3 \times 0.5 \times 10^{-1} \times 30$$

$$= 61.41 \text{ db}$$

Given :
$Z_0 = 100\ \Omega$
$I_0 = 20$ mA
$V_0 = 4$ kV
$N = 30$

For high power operation coupled cavity travelling wave tubes are available. In these, instead of helix, coupled cavity shown in Fig. 6.32: is used. It overcomes the thermal limitation of helix type TWT.

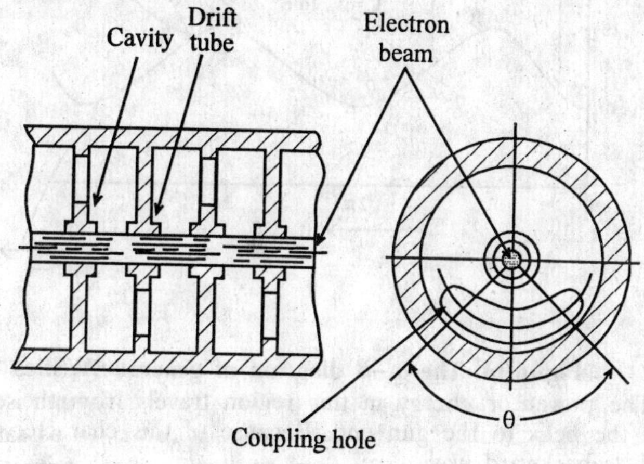

Fig. 6.32. Coupled cavity

6.9. Backward Wave Oscillators :

The schematic diagram of Backward wave Oscillator (BWO) is shown in Fig. 6.33 and as seen it is very similar to that of a travelling wave amplifier. In this growing wave travels in a direction opposite to

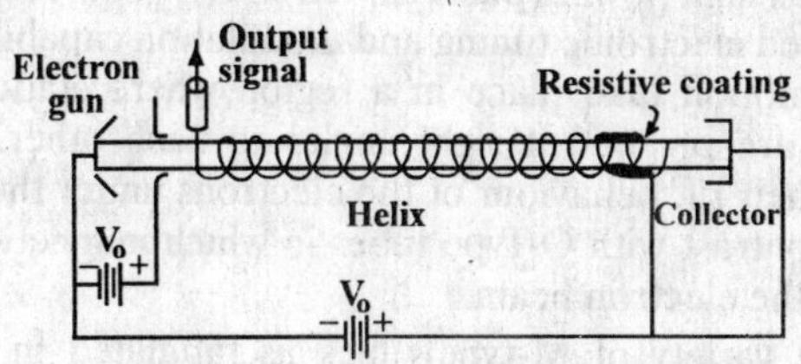

Fig. 6.33. Schematic diagram of BWO.

that of the electron beam. From the dispersion curve, *i.e.*, $\omega - \beta$ diagram for any periodic SWS there is a region in which the phase velocity is positive (ω/β) but the group velocity $v_g = d\omega/d\beta$ is negative (see portion BC in diagram, Fig. 6.34).

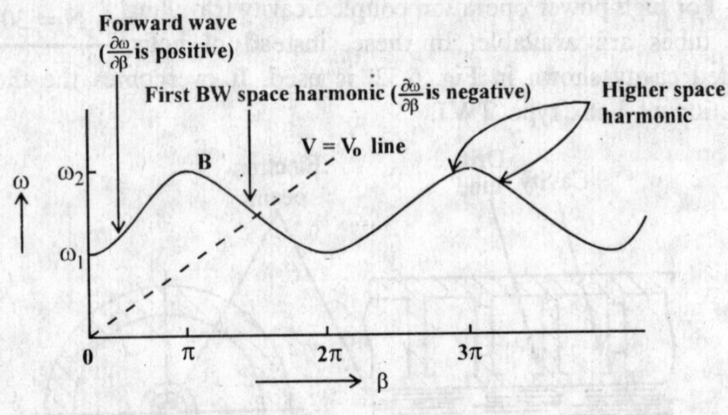

Fig. 6.34. The ω–β diagram of general SWS.

The power or energy in this region travels from the collector end of the helix to the gun end. Because of this characteristic it is termed as backward wave.

The electron beam velocity can be varied by changing the helix (SWS) voltage V_0 so that the beam is synchronous with the phase velocity of the backward wave at different frequencies $\omega_1 < \omega < \omega_2$ (Fig. 6.34). This property makes BWO a voltage tunable oscillator.

6.10. M–Type Tubes (Crossed–Field Tubes) – Magnetrons

M-Type tubes are another class of microwave vacuum tubes which are widely used as high power (pulse as well as CW) sources of microwave power with limited electronic tuning and modulation capabilities. In these tubes electron motion take place in a region where static electric and magnetic fields are present at right angles to each other. These fields strongly affect their r.f. behaviour of the electrons under the action of r.f. fields. It is in contrast with O-Type tubes in which magnetic field is used merely to focus the electron beam.

There are variety of M-type tubes as tabulated in Table 6.4. In this section magnetrons are studied. Magnetrons are grouped into three types, *viz.* (i) the negative resistance magnetron (split-anode magnetron); (ii) the cyclotron–frequency magnetron; and (iii) the multicavity travelling wave magnetron. The first two were developed in the early days of the magnetron development. The reader is referred to literature*. The multicavity travelling wave magnetrons are superior in performance and technically highly developed devices. These are discussed in some detail below.

6.11. Multicavity Travelling Wave Magnetrons :

Variety of multicavity travelling wave magnetrons such as the cylindrical magnetron, a coaxial magnetron, voltage tunable magnetron, inverted coaxial magnetron, and the frequency-agile magnetron etc. were developed and commercially available. We will limit our discusson to cylindrical multicavity magnetron oscillator which is best known of these devices and its planar version are described.

6.11.1. Cylindrical multicavity magnetron – Structure/Building blocks

Figure 6.35(a) shows the schematic diagram of a cylindrical multicavity magnetron oscillator. It consists of (1) a coaxial cathode. (2) a multicavity cylindrical anode block, *i.e.*, several reentrant cavities are connected to the gap and is kept at high dc potential. It is a slow-wave structure. (3) cathode anode space where electron moves and interaction takes place. (4) coaxial line output coupling generated microwave power to the outside. (5) a permanent magnet (not shown in Fig. 6.35a) to provide magnetic field along the axial length of the cathode and perpendicular to radial dc electric field.

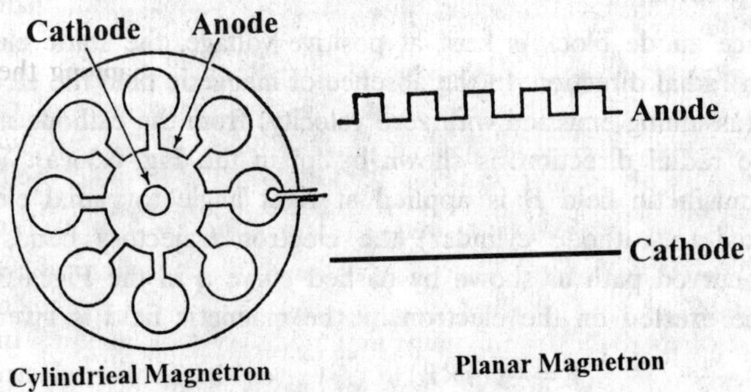

Fig. 6.35(a). A multicavity magnetron

*. Brownwell, A. B. and Beam, R.E., **Theory and Application of Microwaves,** McGraw-Hill, Inc. New York (1947).

2. **Collins, G.B., Microwave Magnetrons;** MIT Radiation Laboratory Series, Vol. 6, McGraw-Hill, Inc., New York (1948).

Figure 6.35(b) shows the various types of magnetron anode blocks, viz. (1) hole and slot, (2) vane; (3) slot, (4) rising sun, and (5) strap.

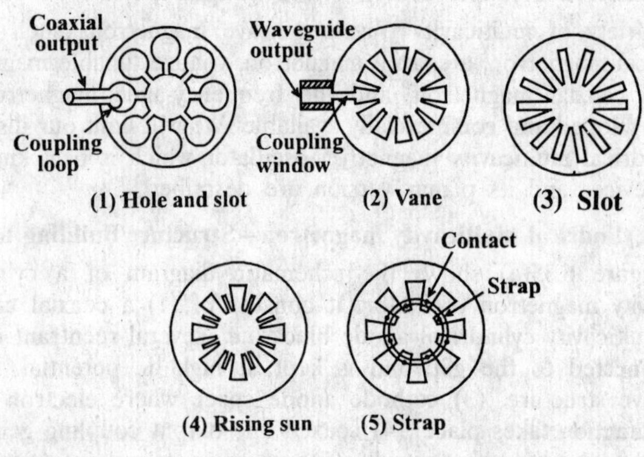

Fig. 6.35 (b). Various types of magnetron anodes.

6.11.2. Operation

Since anode block is kept at positive voltage, the static electric field is in radial direction. In the absence of magnetic field the electron emitted (assuming emission with zero velocity) from the cathode moves along the radial direction as shown by 'p' in the Fig. 6.36(a). When a small magnetic field B is applied at right angle to radial electric field (axial to cathode cylinder) the electron trajectory bends and follow a curved path as shown by dashed curve q in the Fig. 6.36(a). The force exerted on the electron by the magnetic field is given by

$$\mathbf{F} = -e(\mathbf{v} \times \mathbf{B})$$

As, the magnetic field is increased the magnetic force exerted on electron increases and the radius of curvature of electron paths (shown by dashed curves) decreases. Above a certain value of the B_c called the cut-off field electrons are returned to the cathode (electron paths as shown by dashed curves *r* and *s*) and the anode current is cut-off. In general, when $B > B_c$ and under the influence of radial electric field

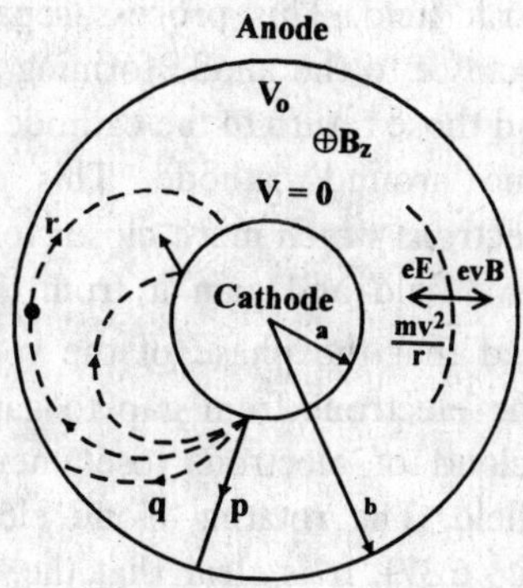

Fig. 6.36(a) Electron trajectories at various magnetic fields.

E_r the electron take curved path such as *r* and *s*. When these rotating electrons pass through the fringing r.f. field of the gap (Fig. 6.36 b) due to excitation of anode cavities by r.f. noise voltage, they are either accelerated or decelerated by the action of this r.f. field. The electrons, which are accelerated by r.f. fringing field, are pushed back towards the cathode because accelerated electrons experience increased magnetic force $[-e(\mathbf{v}\times\mathbf{B})]$ due to its increased velocity.

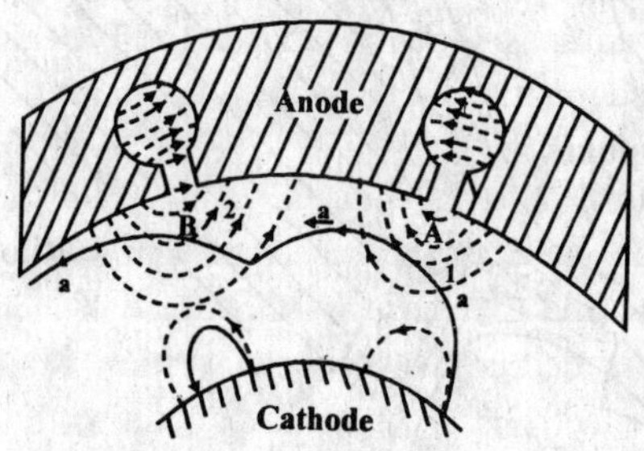

Fig. 6.36(b) Electron trajectories in the presence of r.f. field.

Those electrons which are deccelerated by the r.f. fringing field are pushed closer to the anode as retarded electrons experience reduced magnetic force $[-e(\mathbf{v}\times\mathbf{B})]$ due to its reduced velocity and loss of energy to the r.f. field. This process separates the electrons into those which move closer to the anode forming a cloud of electrons (density modulation) and those return to the cathode. Returned electrons form an electron cloud around cathode. This cloud is known as **Brillouin cloud**. The electrons which move closer to the anode continue to lose energy to the r.f. field and gain it from the dc field.

Thus it is required that the phase of the voltage at the various gaps and velocity of the electrons from gap to gap must be properly synchronised so that cloud of electrons lose energy to the r.f. field and gain it from dc. field. The rotating cloud electrons is similar to spokes of electrons (Fig. 6.37). It is clear that the electronic processes in magnetron are really the same as of travelling wave tube. The sorting of electron takes place due to static crossed electric and magnetic fields and transverse r.f. field play an important role. The magnetron could also be operated as an amplifier in which r.f. field grows similar to travelling wave tube.

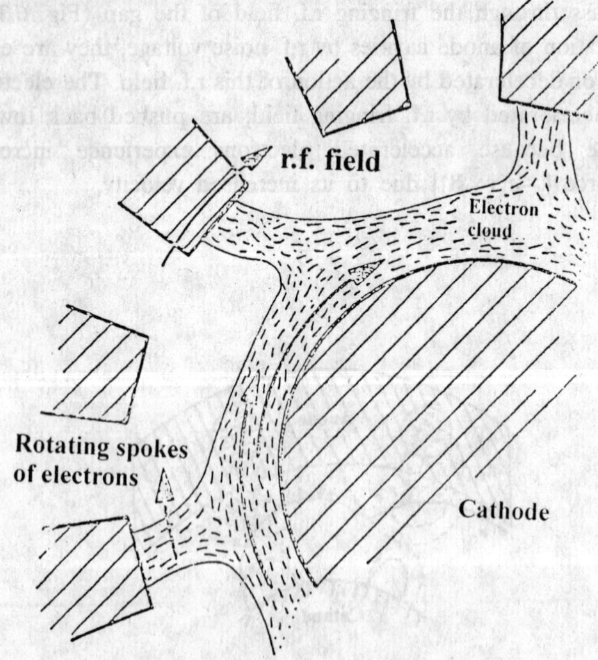

Fig. 6.37. Spoke pattern in magnetron.

6.11.3 Quantitative analysis

(a) Hull cut-off magnetic field and cut-off voltage in cylindrical magnetron – From the discussion in Section 6.11.2, it could be concluded that for a specific applied voltage on anode there is corresponding level of magnetic field B necessary for electrons emitted from the cathode to just graze the anode block and travel in interaction space between the cathode and anode. The anode current will be zero. This magnetic field is known as **Hull cut-off magnetic field** and conversely for a specific magnetic field there is a corresponding anode voltage for which anode current will be zero.

This voltage is known as Hull cut-off voltage. The relations for Hull cut-off magnetic field and voltage are derived below.

Let b and a are anode and cathode radii, respectively (Fig. 6.36). V_0 is the voltage applied between the anode and cathode and a magnetic field B is into the page as shown in Fig. 6.36. It is in positive z-direction.

There are three forces acting on an electron moving in curved path of radius of curvature r and velocity **v** in the interaction space of the cylindrical magnetron, *viz.*, (i) force due to electric field $(-eE_r)$, force due to magnetic field $[-e(\mathbf{v}\times\mathbf{B})]$ and the centrifugal force $\left(\frac{mv^2}{r}\right)$. These three forces are radial as shown in Fig. 6.36a. In equilibrium, for the electron to move in a circular orbit of radius r, the equation of motion is given by

$$\frac{mv^2}{r} + eE_r = evB \qquad \text{....(6.11.1)}$$

where $E_r = \frac{V_0}{r} \ln \frac{b}{a};$ here, b and a are anode and cathode radii respectively and V_0 is applied voltage on anode.

Cyclotron frequency

When $E_r = 0$, the electron moves in a circular path and returns to the cathode.

From Eq. 6.11.1.

$$\frac{mv^2}{r} = evB \qquad \text{....(6.11.2)}$$

or

$$\frac{v}{r} = \omega_c = \frac{e}{m} B = \eta B \qquad \text{....(6.11.3)}$$

is called **cyclotron angular frequency.**

The equation of motion for an electron in crossed electric (E_r) and magnetic field (B). is given by

$$\mathbf{F} = m\frac{d\mathbf{v}}{dt} = -e\left[\mathbf{E_r} + \mathbf{v} \times \mathbf{B}\right] \quad \text{....(6.11.4)}$$

where **v** is the electron velocity.

As we are discussing the motion of an electron in cylindrical multicavity magnetron, the equation of motion (Eq. 6.11.4) in cylindrical coordinates are

$$\frac{d^2r}{dt^2} - r\left(\frac{d\theta}{dt}\right)^2 = \eta E_r - \eta r\frac{d\theta}{dt}B_z \quad \text{....(6.11.5a)}$$

and
$$\frac{1}{r}\frac{d}{dt}\left(r^2\frac{d\theta}{dt}\right) = \eta B_z\frac{dr}{dt} \quad \text{....(6.11.5b)}$$

Where $B = B_z$ is assumed in the +z-direction

Equation 6.11.5 (b) can be written as

$$\frac{d}{dt}\left(r^2\frac{d\theta}{dt}\right) = \frac{1}{2}\omega_c\frac{d(r^2)}{dt} \quad \text{....(6.11.6)}$$

where $\omega_c = \eta B_z$ is the cyclotron frequency. Integration of Eq. 6.11.6, gives

$$r^2\frac{d\theta}{dt} = \frac{1}{2}\omega_c r^2 + K \quad \text{....(6.11.7)}$$

where K is an integration constant. Applying boundary condition $r = a, \frac{d\theta}{dt} = 0$ in Eq. 6.11.7, we get

$$K = -\frac{1}{2}\omega_c a^2$$

∴ Eq. 6.11.7 becomes

$$r^2\frac{d\theta}{dt} = \frac{1}{2}\omega_c r^2 - \frac{1}{2}\omega_c a^2$$

∴ The angular velocity is expressed by

$$\frac{d\theta}{dt} = \frac{1}{2}\omega_c\left(1 - \frac{a^2}{r^2}\right) \quad \text{....(6.11.8)}$$

The kinetic energy of the electrons is given by

$$eV = \frac{1}{2}m\left[\left(\frac{dr}{dt}\right)^2 + \left(r\frac{d\theta}{dt}\right)^2\right] \quad \text{....(6.11.9)}$$

as electron has a tangential as well as a radial velocity.

For grazing the anode $r = b$, $V = V_0$, and $\frac{dr}{dt} = 0$; Eq. 6.11.9 becomes

$$b^2 \left(\frac{d\theta}{dt}\right)^2 = \frac{2e}{m} V_0 = 2\eta V_0 \qquad \text{....(6.11.10)}$$

Substitution of Eq. 6.11.8 into Eq. 6.11.10 results in

$$b^2 \left[\frac{1}{2}\omega_c \left(1 - \frac{a^2}{b^2}\right)\right]^2 = 2\eta V_0 \qquad \text{....(6.11.11)}$$

Substituting $\omega_c = \eta B_c$ at grazing and solving Eq. 6.11.11 for B_c, we obtain :

$$B_c = \frac{(8V_0/\eta)^{1/2}}{b\left(1 - \frac{a^2}{b^2}\right)} \qquad \text{....(6.11.12a)}$$

The relation 6.11.12 is known as **Hull cut-off** magnetic field. Substituting the value of

$\eta = 1.759 \times 10^{11}$ C/kg the Eq. 6.11.12a becomes

$$B_c = \frac{6.75 \times 10^{-6}\, b}{(b^2 - a^2)} \sqrt{V_0}\ \text{Wb/m}^2 \qquad \text{....(6.11.12b)}$$

When $b >> a$

$$B_c = \frac{6.75 \times 10^{-6}}{b} \sqrt{V_0}\ \text{Wb/m}^2 \qquad \text{....(6.11.12c)}$$

Here V_0 is in volts and b is in metre. The relation 6.11.12 is known as **Hull cut-off magnetic field**. This means that if $B_z > B_c$ for a given V_0 the electron will not reach the anode, *i.e.* anode current is zero. Conversely the cut-off voltage for a given B_z is given by

$$V_c = \frac{\eta}{8} B_z^{\,2} b^2 \left(1 - \frac{a^2}{b^2}\right)^2 \qquad \text{....(6.11.13)}$$

It is also called the **Hull cut-off voltage** equation. It means that when $V_0 < V_c$ for a given B_z, the electron will not reach the anode.

Figure 6.38 shows the typical trajectories of electron at various magnetic fields. Equation 6.11.12. predicts that anode current should fall abruptly to zero above cut-off magnetic field B_c for a given anode voltage. But it is not observed in actual measurement. The anode current decreases gradually as shown in Fig. 6.39.

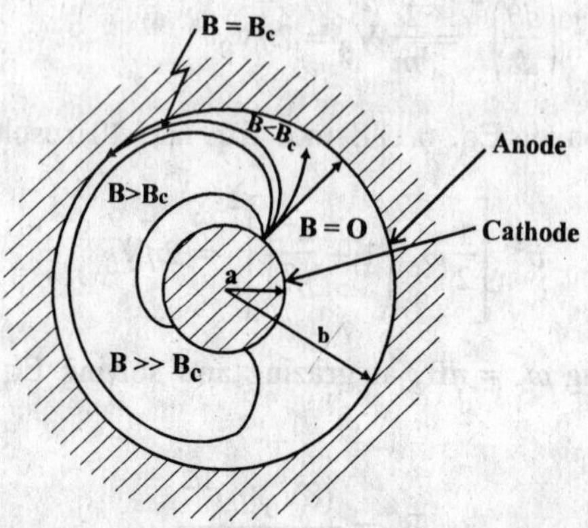

Fig 6.38. Typical trajectories of electron at various magnetic fields.

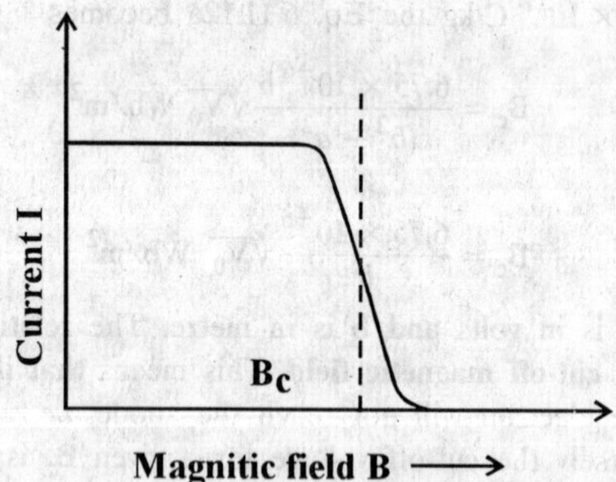

Fig. 6.39. Variation of anode current with magnetic field in magnetron.

The gradual decrease of anode current is attributed to the space charge effects and in actual the electrons are emitted from cathode with the Maxwellian distribution of velocities (electron emitted with velocity $\neq 0$). In a practical magnetron a magnetic field $B >> B_c$ is used which reduces the outer radius of Brillouin cloud around the cathode.

(b) Linear Magnetron – If the cylindrical geometry of Fig. 6.35 is opened out into a planar form as shown Fig. 6.40 it is a Linear Magnetron. Its analysis is simpler and Hull cut-off voltage is given by

$$V_c = \frac{1}{2}\frac{e}{m} B_z^{\,2} d^2 = \frac{1}{2} \eta \, B_z^{\,2} d^2 \qquad ....(6.11.14)$$

where d is the distance between cathode and anode.

The Hull cut-off magnetic field is expressed as

$$B_c = \frac{1}{d}\sqrt{\frac{2m}{e} V_0} = \frac{1}{d}\sqrt{\frac{2V_0}{\eta}} \qquad ....(6.11.15)$$

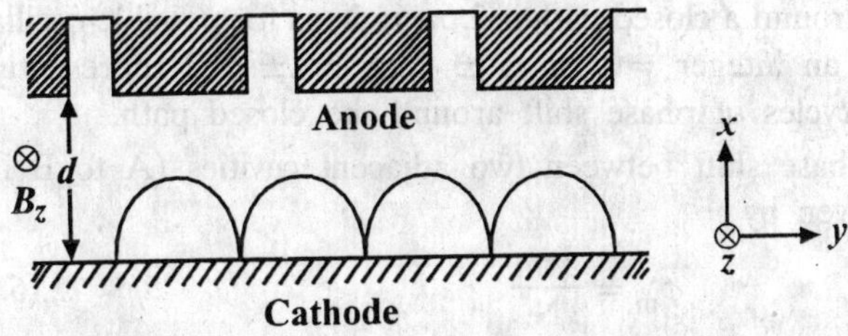

Fig. 6.40. Electron path in a linear mangetron

(c) Hartree condition/Voltage – Substituting the value of $E_r = \frac{V_0}{r} \ln \frac{b}{a}$ in Eq. 6.11.1 the anode potential V_0 is given by

$$V_0 = \left(\omega_e r^2 \ln \frac{b}{a}\right) \left(B - \frac{\omega_e}{\eta}\right) \qquad ....(6.11.16)$$

where ω_e = v/r is electron angular velocity which is moving in circular path of radius r.

Taking, $\quad ln \frac{b}{a} \approx \frac{2(b-a)}{(b+a)}$ and $r = \frac{b+a}{2}$, Eq. 6.11.16 becomes :

$$V_0 = \omega_e \frac{(b^2 - a^2)}{2} \left[B - \frac{\omega_e}{\eta}\right] \qquad ....(6.11.17)$$

It will be necessary to synchronise electron angular velocity to the velocity of travelling waves on the multicavity structure magnetron.

(d) Modes (Relationship between the frequency of oscillation ω_m and the angular velocity of electron ω_e)

The angular velocity of the electron $\omega_e = d\theta/dt$

and it travels around the interaction space in a time

$$T = \frac{2\pi}{\omega_e} \quad \text{....(6.11.18)}$$

The time taken by the electron to move from the centre A of one anode gap to B (See Fig. 6.36 b) for next adjacent anode gap is given by

$$T_1 = \frac{2\pi}{N\omega_e} \quad \text{....(6.11.19)}$$

where N = number of resonant coupled cavities in the anode block (slow wave structure)

Due to N resonant coupled cavities, there exists N resonate frequencies or modes (see equivalent resonant circuit in Fig. 6.42a).

As the slow-wave structure is closed on itself, therefore, the total phase shift around a closed path is $2\pi m$ radians for possible oscillations, where m is an integer $= 0, \pm 1, \pm 2, \pm 3 .... \pm N/2$ representing the number of cycles of phase shift around the closed path.

The phase shift between two adjacent cavities (A to B in Fig. 6.36,b) is given by

$$\phi_m = \frac{2\pi m}{N} \quad \text{....(6.11.20)}$$

If we assume that the electron has the same direction of rotation as the a.c. field, the travelling electron sees a phase difference of $(\omega_m T_1 - \phi_m)$ radians between corresponding points A and B of two adjacent cavities (Fig 6.36,b). Mechanism of oscillations as explained earlier requires that the electron has to experience a maximum retarding force in both positions and lose energy to the resonator (cavity), this phase shift seen by the electron must be an integral multiple of 2π radian *i.e.*,

$$\omega_m T_1 - \theta_m = 2\pi n \quad \text{....(6.11.21)}$$

where $n = 0, \pm 1, \pm 2, \pm 3$ ....Substituting Eq. 6.11.19 and 6.11.20 into Eq. 6.11.21 and on arranging for ω_e, obtain

$$\omega_e = \frac{\omega_m}{(m + nN)} \quad \text{....(6.11.22)}$$

or in terms of $\omega_m = (m + nN)\, \omega_e = K\omega_e$
where $K = (m + nN)$ may be negative or positive. Equation 6.11.22 expresses a relation between angular velocity of electron in terms of frequency of oscillation. Also different values of K represent different modes of oscillations.

The phase velocity in the azimuthal direction for the nth spatial harmonic for the mth resonant mode is

$$v_{pmn} = \frac{\omega_m r}{(m + nN)}$$

Substituting Eq. 6.11.22 into Eq. 6.11.17, we obtain

$$V_0 = V_H = \frac{\omega_m}{(m + nN)} \frac{(b^2 - a^2)}{2} \left(B - \frac{\omega_m}{\eta(m + nN)} \right) \quad \text{....(6.11.23)}$$

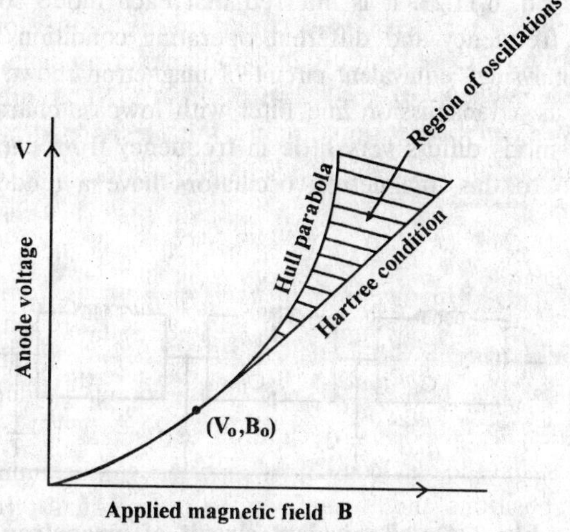

Fig. 6.41. Shaded area indicates region of oscillation.

This relation is known as **Hartree condition for oscillations**. When $m = N/2$, it means $\phi_m = \pi$ that is opposite phase shift in successive cavities and excitation is maximum in cavities. This mode is known as **π-mode** and is commonly used for magnetron oscillators. Substituting $m = N/2$ in Eq. 6.11.23, we obtion Hartree voltage for π-mode

$$V_{H_\pi} = \frac{\omega_{N/2}(b^2 - a^2)}{N(1+2n)} \left[B - \frac{2\omega_{N/2}}{\eta N(1+2n)} \right] \quad \text{....(6.11.24)}$$

A plot of Hull cut-off voltage and Hartree voltage V_H with magnetic field B is shown in Fig. 6.41; where the region of oscillation is shown by shaded area.

From the above discussion and analysis, it is necessary to adjust the magnetic field B and d.c anode voltage V_0 to obtain the proper value of ω_e so that Eq. 6.11.21 for the desired mode is satisfied. From Eq. 6.11.22 there can be a large number of modes possible in a magnetron. However only few of these modes have practical significance, as most of them yield low power output and low efficiency.

6.11.4. Mode jumping and mode separation

From Eq. 6.11.23. it is inferred that each mode corresponds to a different frequency and different operating conditions. It has been shown by analysing* equivalent circuit of magnetron shown in Fig. 6.42a. which acts as a tansmission line filter with lowpass characteristic that the various mods differs very little in frequency from each other (Fig. 6.42b). Due to this, magnetron oscillators have a tendency to jump

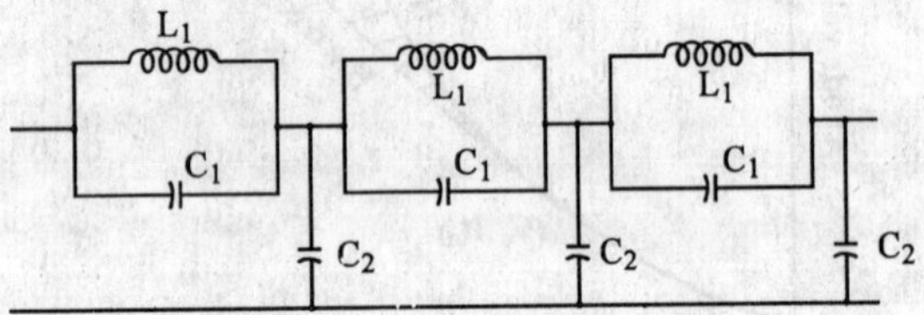

Fig. 6.42a. Equivalent circuit of magnetron

---

* From the low pass equivalent circuit shown in Fig. 6.42a, (where each of the identical cavities is replaced by its L_1C_1 equivalent circuit. C_2 is the coupling capacitance between the cavity vane and the cathode due to which mutual coupling between various cavities take place. It can be shown that $\left(\frac{\omega_m}{\omega}\right)^2 \approx \frac{1}{1+\frac{C_2}{C_1\left(1-\cos\frac{2\pi m}{N}\right)}}$ where ω_m is mode frequency, and ω is the fundamental resonant frequency of the cavities given by $\omega = \frac{1}{\sqrt{L_1C_1}}$ In obtaining the above relation we used the relation $\cos\phi_m = 1 + \frac{Z_1}{2Z_2}$, where $\phi_m = \frac{2\pi m}{N}$ the phase shift (Eq. .6.11.20); Z_1 = total series impedance and Z_2 total shunt impedance per section.

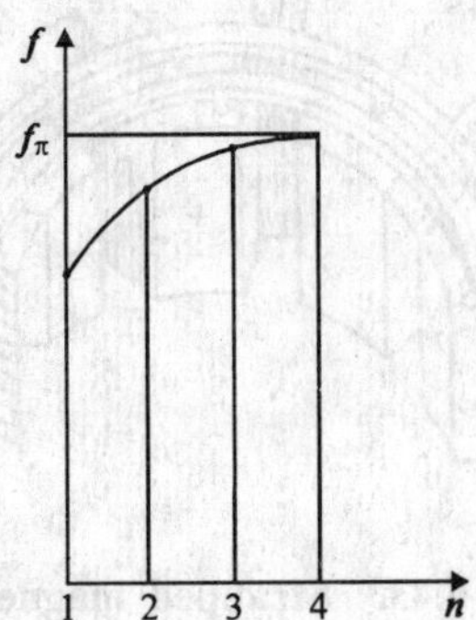

Fig. 6.42b. Variation of mode frequency versus mode numbers.

from one mode to another mode under slight variation in operating conditions. This results in an abrupt change in frequency of oscillations and power output This is known as **mode jumping.** It is observed from Fig. 6.42b that it would be difficult to separate the π-mode from the next immediate mode for maximum power output. Mode separation is achieved or in other words mode jumping is prevented by connecting two metallic straps to anode segments as shown in Fig. 6.43.

In this arrangement one strap is connected to the even numbered anode segments and the other strap to the odd numbered anode segments. It means that for the π-mode each strap is at same potential and no π-mode current flows in strap. The straps add in parallel to the capacitor (Fig. 6.42a) of each slot, thus causing a shift in mode frequency distribution. In other words the added capacitance depresses the π-mode resonance frequency greatly.

6.11.5. Pulling and Pushing of frequency

The variation in frequency with variation in load impedance of a magnetron is called **Frequency Pulling**, the variation in frequency with variation in operating voltages and currents is called **Frequency Pushing.**

6.11.6. Tuning of magnetron

It is achieved by varying the effective inductance or the effective capacitance of the resonators. The arrangement is shown in Fig. 6.44. In case of arrangement 6.44(a) an inductance is varied by sliding a

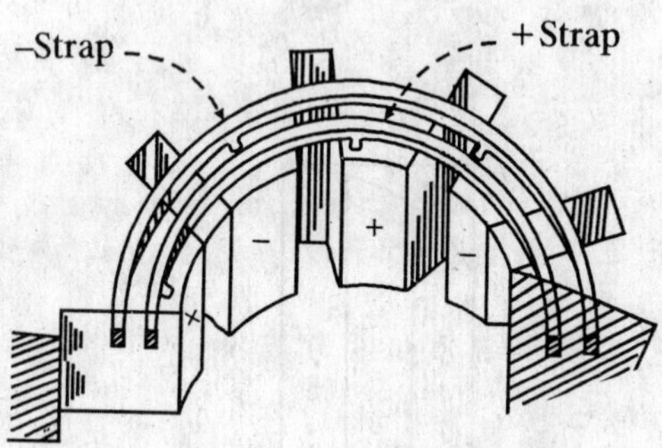

Fig. 6.43. Strapped magnetron

conducting plunger into or out of the resonator. In case of arrangement 6.44(b) the capacitance is varied by moving annular strap into or out of groves in the anode.

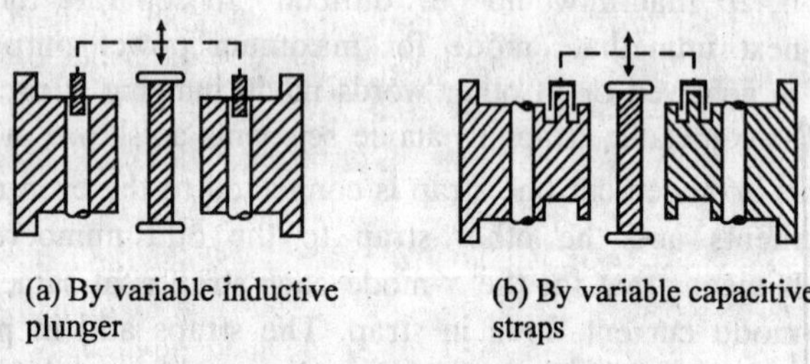

Fig. 6.44. Tuning of magnetron.

6.11.7. Power and efficiency of magnetron

We have seen that noise voltage grows because of the energy supplied by the electrons moving towards the anode. Thus potential energy of electron is transferred to the r.f. field while kinetic energy remains more or less constant. The average drift velocity in the θ direction,

$$v_\theta = \frac{E}{B_z}$$

is constant for a given applied dc voltage V_0 and axial mangetic field B. It results into high electronic efficiency (η)of conversion of d.c. power into microwave power.

$$\eta = \frac{eV_0 - \frac{1}{2} m_e v_0^2}{eV_0} \approx 1 - 2.84\,(E/B_z)^2/V_0$$

where V_0 is applied voltage in volts and B in gauss.

There are commercially available magnetrons capable of producing pulsed power of the order of megawatts and CW power of several kilowatts with efficiencies ranging between 50 to 80 per cent.

6.11.8. Operating characteristics

Commercially available magnetrons are supplied with performance charts. One typical chart is shown in Fig. 6.45. It gives contours of constant power output, constant efficiency and constant magnetic field strength as function of the dc anode voltage and current. From this one could select the optimum operating point. Another method of graphical representation is Riecke diagram. One such diagram is shown in Fig. 6.46. It shows the contours of constant power output and

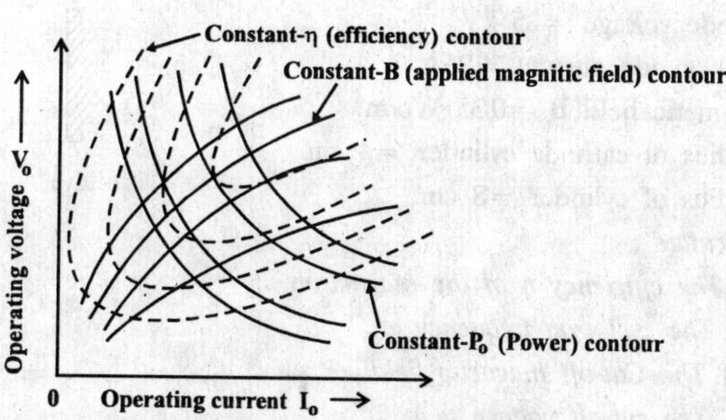

Fig. 6.45. Performance chart of magnetron

constant frequency plotted on a Smith chart. It's data are experimentally obtained by varying the load impedance and observing the power output and frequency. From such performance chart one could select the optimum load impedance.

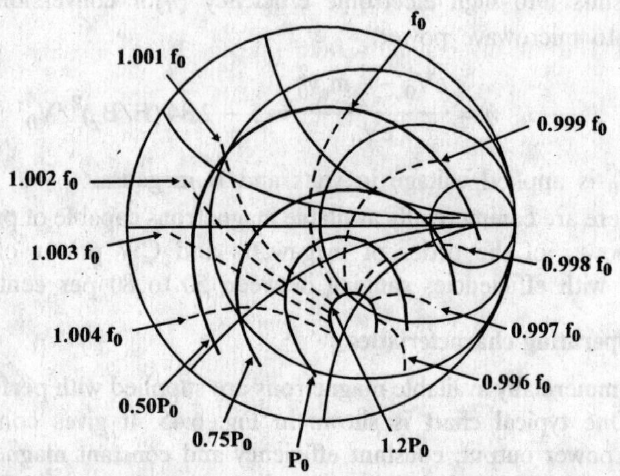

Fig. 6.46. Riecke diagrams showing contours of constant power output and constant frequency, plotted on a Smith chart. (–, contours of constant power output, ---, contours of constant frequency)

Example 6.11.1. *A 250* kW *pulsed cylindrical magnetron is operated with the following parameters –*

Anode voltage = 25 kV

Peak anode current = 25A

Magnetic field B = 0.35 Wb/m^2

Radius of cathode cylinder = 4 cm.

Radius of cylinder = 8 cm.

Calculate :

(i) The efficiency η of the magnetron

(ii) The cyclotron frequency ω_c.

(iii) The Cut-off magnetic field.

(iv) The cut-off voltage.

Solution :

(i) Efficiency $\eta = \dfrac{P_{out}}{P_{in}} = \dfrac{250 \times 10^3 \times 10^2}{25 \times 10^3 \times 25} = 40$ percent

(ii) The cyclotron frequency $\omega_c = \dfrac{e}{m} B$

$$= 1.76 \times 10^{11} \times 0.35$$

$$= 0.616 \times 10^{11} \text{ radians.}$$

(iii) The cut-off magnetic field [Eq. 6.11.13b]

$$B_c = \frac{6.75 \times 10^{-6} \times 8 \times 10^{-2}}{(64 - 16) \times 10^{-4}} \sqrt{25 \times 10^3}$$

$$= 0.018 \text{ Wb/m}^2 = 18 \text{ mWb/m}^2$$

(iv) The cut-off voltage

$$= \frac{1}{8} \eta B^2 b^2 \left(1 - \frac{a^2}{b^2}\right)^2$$

$$= \frac{1}{8} \times 1.76 \times 10^{11} (0.35)^2 \times (8 \times 10^{-2})^2 \left(1 - \frac{4^2}{8^2}\right)^2$$

$$= 151.58 \text{ kV}$$

6.12. Characteristics of tubes at Glance :

Figures 6.47 and 6.48 summarize the frequency versus power performance of magnetsons, reflex klystrons, klystrons and helix travelling wave tubes. From the Fig. 6.47 we find that magnetrons are capable of very high CW power outputs in the range of several kilowatts. On the other hand reflex klystrons are capable of very low power outputs in the range of few miliwatts. From the graph of Fig. 6.48 we see that klystrons are capable of peak powers in the megawatt

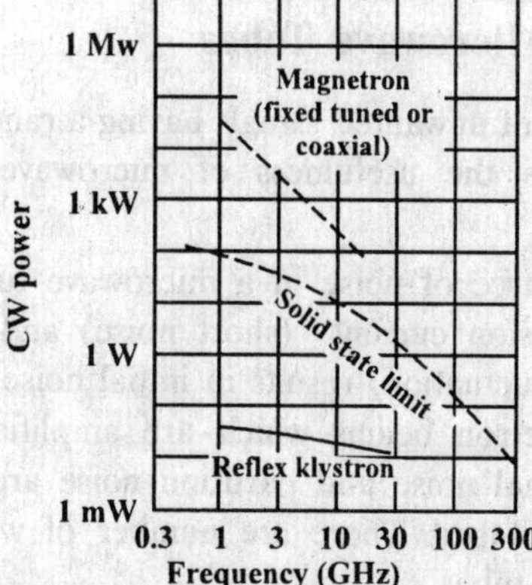

Fig. 6.47. Frequency versus power performance of reflex klystrons and magnetrons (oscillators)

range and helix TWTs are capable of power in the range of several hundred watts.

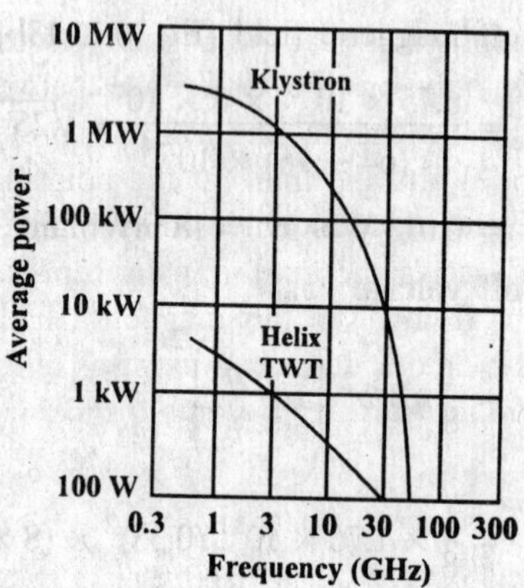

Fig. 4.48. Frequency versus powers performance of klystrons and helix TWTs (amplifiers)

Travelling wave tubes are characterised by very wide band width ranging from 30 to 120% and efficiency in the range of 20 to 40%. Two cavity klystrons are narrow bandwidth amplifiers, can produce gain about 20 db and power elficiency inrange of 30-50%. Klystrons have very low AM and FM noise. Magnetrons are very noisy, however thy have AM efficiency of 80% or more.

6.13. Noise* in Microwave Tubes

Noise consists of unwanted signals having a random or incoherent nature, which limits the usefulness of microwave tubes and their associated circuits.

The major source of noise in a microwave tube is the cathode where random emission current (short noise) and random emission velocities (velocity fluctuation) results in initial noise current and noise velocity on the electron beams which are amplified and appear as output noise. Thermal noise and partition noise are other sources of noise in microwave tubes. There are number of ways to reduce the noise in microwave tubes.

O-Type devices are superior to M-Type devices with regard to noise behaviour.

* Noise Power, Noise Temperature, Noise Figure etc., are discussed in Annexure 6.3

Annexure 6.1

Busch's Theorem*

Busch's theorem states that the angular velocity of any electron at any point depends only on the difference between the total fluxes (magnetic) linked by the charge ring at the two electron positions, the initial (at the cathode) and the final (at the point under consideration). The angular velocity is independent of the detailed trajectory between these two points. [Busch's theorem actually represents conservation of angular momentum. It involves the magnetic field when the electron motion in a magnetic field is described in terms of the Hamiltonian form of dynamics.] Equation, which represents the Busch's theorem is.

$$\dot{\theta} = \frac{\eta}{2\pi r^2}(\psi - \psi_c) \qquad \text{....(6.1.1)}$$

where $\eta = e/m$, the ratio of electron charge to electron mass; ψ is the magnetic flux linked at the point under consideration, ψ_c is the magnetic flux linked at the initial position (at the cathode) and r is the radius of the electron beam. This relation is established below :

In this we shall assume that the magnetic field is axially symmetric, *i.e.*, independent of θ. For the establishment of above mentioned equation we consider the transition region of the micrwave tube, *i.e.*, the region between electron gun and interaction region (Fig. A6.1).

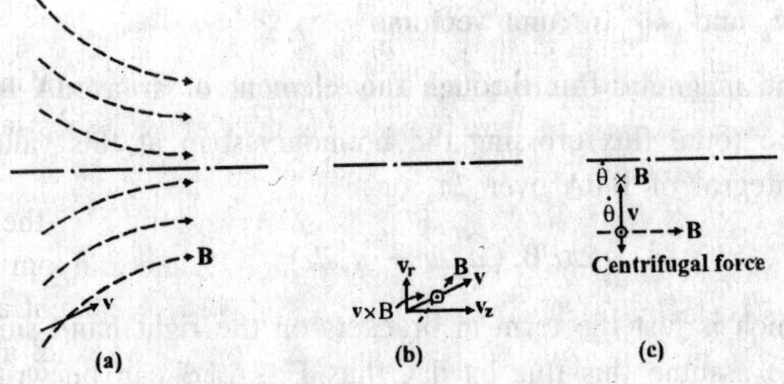

Fig. A6.1. (a) and (b) refer to transition region, (c) refers to uniform-flow region.

---

1. Chodorow, M. and Charles, S., **Fundamentals of Microwave Electronics,** McGraw-Hill Book company New York, 1964.
2. Pierce, J.R., **Theory and Design of Electron Beams,** 2nd edn., Van Nostrand Reinhold, New York, 1954

An electron moving with a velocity **v** interact with **B** to produce a **F** = c (**v** × **B**) is directed out of the paper. The angular velocity $\dot{\theta}$ resulting from this force causes the electron to interact with the axial magnetic field in the interaction region to produce an inward (focussing) force. The angular velocity also produces an outward centrifugal force, which actually reduces the focussing force. In this region, **B** is parallel to the axial component of velocity and no interaction with that velocity results.

To compute θ, we recall that the rate of change of angular momentum equals the moment rF_θ of the angular force,

$$\frac{d}{dt}(mr^2\dot{\theta}) = re(-\dot{r}B_z + \dot{z}B_r) \qquad ....(6.1.2)$$

Equation (6.12) is multiplied by $2\pi dt$ yields

$$2\pi d(mr^2\dot{\theta}) = -e[2\pi r(B_z dr - B_r d_z)] \qquad .....(6.1.3.)$$

where dr and dz are the components of the electron trajectory during the time dt. A vector area $d\mathbf{A}$ generated by rotating this trajectory element through an infinitesimal angle $d\theta$ would be

$$\text{dA} = r\,d\,\theta(\hat{a}_z\,dr - \hat{a}_r\,dz)$$

where $\hat{a}_z$ and $\hat{a}_n$ are unit vectors.

The magnetic flux through this element of area **dA** is **B.dA**.

The totlal flux crossing the boundary strip at this value of r; z is the integral of **B·dA** over 2π, or

$$2\pi r\,\mathbf{B}.\,(\hat{a}_z\,dr - \hat{a}_r\,dz)$$

which is just the term in brackets on the right hand side of Eq. 6.1.3. We assume this flux by dψ, thus Eq. 6.1.3 can be written as

$$2\pi d(mr^2\dot{\theta}) = -\,ed\psi \qquad ....(6.1.4.)$$

Integrating 6.1.4 we write

$$\int d(mr^2\dot{\theta}) = -\frac{e}{2\pi}\int d\psi$$

$$(mr^2\dot{\theta}) - (mr^2\dot{\theta})_c = -\frac{e}{2\pi}(\psi - \psi_c)$$

where the subscript *c* refers to the value in the electron gun region (at the cathode). In most application, $\dot{\theta} = 0$ there, which dtermines the lower limit of the integral and yields.

$$\dot{\theta} = \frac{\eta}{2\pi r^2}(\psi - \psi_c) \qquad \text{....(6.1.5)}$$

This equation is mathematical representation of Busch's theorem.

Annexure 6.2

Beam Coupling Parameter – Effect of Finite Transit Time Across the Cavity Gap

While discussing velocity modulation in klystron, it is mentioned that due to finite transit time across the cavity gap the amplitude (V_1) of a.c. voltage is modified by a factor

$$\beta = \frac{\sin \beta_0 \, d/2}{\beta_0 \, d/2} \qquad \text{....(A.6.1.1)}$$

which is known as **Beam coupling parameter or factor;** where $\beta_0 = \dfrac{\omega}{V_0}$ is the dc propagation constant and *d* is the width of the gap (Fig. A.6.2.1). To study the effect of transit time, we calculate the change of energy of an electron as it passes through the cavity gap under the electric force $F = eE$, where $E = E_g e^{j\omega t}$ in which $E_g = V_1 d$. Here V_1 = amplitude of the a.c. voltage and *d* is the gap distance (Fig. A.6.2.1).

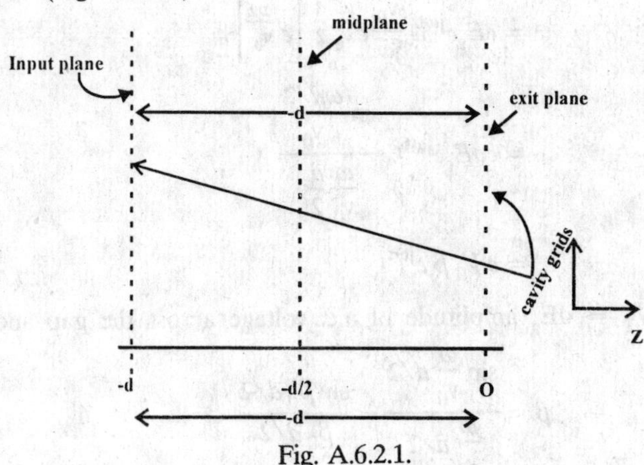

Fig. A.6.2.1.

If the time at which a particular electron passes the midplane $z = \frac{-d}{2}$ is t_1, then the position of such electron after certain interval of time t, is given by

$$z = -\frac{d}{2} + v_0 (t - t_1) \quad \text{....(A.6.1.2)}$$

where v_0 is the velocity of electron beam. From Eq. A.6.1.2, we can write

$$t = \frac{1}{v_0}\left(z + \frac{d}{2} + v_0 t_1\right) \quad \text{....(A6.1.3)}$$

Thus, the electric field at time t, wouid be

$$E = E_g e^{\frac{j\omega}{v_0}\left(z + \frac{d}{2} + v_0 t_1\right)} \quad \text{....(A.6.1.4)}$$

Work done in moving an electron through cavity gap is given

$$W = \int_{-d}^{0} eE_g\, e^{\frac{j\omega}{v_0}\left(z + \frac{d}{2} + v_0 t_1\right)} dz$$

$$= eE_g e^{j\omega t_1} e^{\frac{j\omega}{v_0}\frac{d}{2}} \int_{-d}^{0} e^{\frac{j\omega z}{v_0}} dz$$

$$= eE_g e^{j\omega t_1} \frac{v_0}{j\omega} e^{\frac{j\omega}{v_0}\frac{d}{2}} \left[e^{\frac{j\omega z}{v_0}}\right]_{-d}^{0}$$

$$= edE_g e^{j\omega t_1} \frac{\sin\frac{\omega d/2}{v_0}}{\frac{\omega}{v_0}\frac{d}{2}}$$

$$= e\,V_1 \beta\, e^{j\omega t_1} \quad \text{....(A.6.1.5)}$$

where $V_1 = dE_g$ amplitude of a.c. voltage across the gap and

$$\beta = \frac{\sin\frac{\omega}{v_0} d/2}{\frac{\omega}{v_0} d/2} = \frac{\sin \beta_0\, d/2}{\beta_0\, d/2} \quad \text{....(A.6.1.6)}$$

It is known as beam coupling factor or parameter. It is clear that the amplitude is reduced by a factor β. This is the effict of the finite transit time across the gap.

When we have a small grid spacing and very small transit angle $\beta_0 d = \frac{\omega d}{v_0}$, β approaches close to unity.

Annexure 6.3

Noise Power, Equivalent Noise Temperature and Noise Figure

Noise Power

At microwave frequencies it has been shown that due to random motion of electrons in a resistor R rms value of voltage fluctuations produced across the resistor terminals is given by

$$v_n = \sqrt{4kTBR} \quad \text{......(A6.3.1)}$$

Where k = 1.380 × 10^{-23} J/K is Boltzmann's constant.

T is the temperature, in degrees kelvin (K) B is the band width of the system, in Hz

R is the resistance, in Ω.

Equation A6.3.1 is known as Rayleigh-Jeans equation and it is mostly used in microwave work. Using the Th-evenin equivalent circuit of the noisy resistor, the maximum available noise power from the noisy resistor at temperature T K is given by

$$P_n = kTB \quad \text{......(A6.3.2)}$$

Equivalent Noise Temperature

An arbitrary source of noise could be replaced by a noisy resitor of R at temperature T_e so that from it same noise power available as given by noise source, then

$$T_e = \frac{P_n}{kB} = \frac{P_s}{kB} \quad \text{.....(A6.3.3)}$$

T_e is known as **equivalent noise temperature**. Thus, equivalent noise temperature of an arbitrary noise source is equal to that temperature of noisy resistor R at which maximum available noise power is equal to noise power available from the noise source. Therefore any arbitrary noise source can be characterised with an equivalent noise temperature T_e, Thus, a noisy microwave component can be characterized by an **equivalent noise temperature.**

Noise Figure

Noise figure is an another parameter of a microwave component (passive and active) which is defined as

$$F = \frac{\text{Signal–to–noise ratio at input}}{\text{Signal–to–noise ratio at output}}$$

$$= \frac{S_i/N_i}{S_0/N_0} \geq 1$$

$$= \frac{S_i}{S_o}\frac{N_0}{N_i} \geq 1 \qquad \text{.....(A6.12.3)}$$

Where S_i is the input signal

S_0 is the output signal

N_i is the input noise power

N_0 is the output noise power

If the component is noisy, the output noise power will be increased more than the output signal power (input signal and input noise power will be amplified by the same factor but there will be an additional noise power due to noisy component) so that the output signal to noise ratio will be reduced. Noise figure is the measure of this reduction in signal-to-noise ratio. Let microwave component is characterized by a gain G, a band width B and an equivalent noise temperature T_e, the input noise power $N_i = k\ T_0\ B$ and the output noise power N_0 is a sum of the amplified input noise power (GkT_0B) and the internally generated noise is given by

$$N_0 = kGB\,(T_0 + T_e) \qquad \text{....(A6.3.4)}$$

The output signal S_0 is

$$S_0 = GS_i$$

Substituting these values in the expression

$$F = \frac{S_i}{S_0}\frac{N_0}{N_i}$$

$$= \frac{S_i}{GS_0} \cdot \frac{kGB(T_0 + T_e)}{k\,T_0\,B}$$

$$= 1 + \frac{T_e}{T_0} \geq 1 \qquad \text{....(A6.12.5)}$$

$$\text{In dB, } F = 10 \log \left(1 + \frac{T_e}{T_0}\right) \text{ dB} \geq 0$$

If the microwave component were noiseless, T_e would be zero, giving F = 1 or 0 dB.

Here we have assumed that the input power is equivalent to the noise power resulting from a noisy resistance at T_0 = 298 K. Rearranging Eq. A6.3.5, we can write

$$T_e = (F - 1)\, T_0 \qquad \text{....(A6.3.7)}$$

Thus, noise property of microwave component is characterized by equivalent noise temperature or by noise figure as such they are inter-chanaeable.

PROBLEMS AND REVIEW QUESTIONS*

1. An electron beam has the following parameters :
   (a) accelerating voltage V_0 = 1000 V
   (b) beam current I_0 = 0.03 A
   (c) radius r = 0.2 cm
   Determine : (1) the beam perveance, (2) space charge density ρ_0 (3) the velocity v_0, (4) the radial displacement of an electron located at the beam boundary during the time it takes the beam to move a distance $z = 5$ cm (use Eq. 6.13, find normalized R from the graph, Fig. 6.8)
2. How far does the beam of 110 mA beam at 1.7 kV, travel before its radius becomes twice the initial value 0.2 cm.
3. Calculate the Brillouin magnetic field for the beam of problem 2.
4. A two-cavity klystron amplifier has the following parameters :
   $V_0 = 1000$ V, $f = 5$ GHz, Cavity gap = 1 mm.
   Find : (i) the gap transit angle; and (ii) the optimum length of the drift region.

* Selected from various universities examination papers.

5. A two-cavity klystron amplifier has the following parameters :
V_0 = 1200 V, I_0 = 25 mA, R_0=30 KΩ, f = 10 GHz, d = 1 mm, L = 4 cm, R_{sh} = 30 kΩ
Calculate : (i) the input voltage for maximum output voltage; (ii) the voltage gain in decibles ; (iii) efficiency.

6. A reflex-klystron has the following parameters :
V_0 = 2500 V, L = 6 mm, f = 3 GHz
Calculate the repeller voltage for which tube can oscillate in $1\frac{3}{4}$ mode and $3\frac{3}{4}$ mode.

7. A. reflex-klystron has the following parameters :
V_0 = 800 V, L=1.5mm R_{sh}=15 kΩ, f = 9GHz
calculate : (i) the repeller voltage for which the tube can oscillate in $1\frac{3}{4}$ mode; (ii) the direct current necessary to give a microwave gap voltage of 200 V; and (iii) electron efficiency.

8. A TWT has the following parameters :
V_0 = 3 kV, I_0 = 4 mA, f = 10 GHz, Z_0 = 30 ohm and N = 50.
Calculate : (i) the gain parameter; and (ii) power gain in db.

9. An X-band pulsed cylindrical magnetron has the following parameters :
V_0 = 30 kV, I_0 = 90A, B_0=0.01 Wb/m^2,
a = 4 cm and b = 8 cm.
Calculate : (i) the cyclotron angular frequency; (ii) the cut-off magnetic field; and (iii) the cut-off voltage.

10. A travelling wave tube (TWT) operates under the following parameters :
Beam voltage V_0=3 kV, Beam Current I_0=30 mA, characteristic impedance of helix Z_0 = 10 Ω, Circuit length =50 and Frequency f=10 GHz.
Determine (a) the gain parameter; and (b) the output power gain in decibles.

11. A reflex klystron having an accelerated field of 300 volts oscillates at a frequency of 10 GHz with a retarding field of 500 volt. If its cavity is returned to 9 GHz, what must be the new value of retarding field for oscillations in the same mode to take place ?

12. Explain space charge spreading of electron beam. Derive an expression for maximum perveance K that can be transmitted with the beam just grazing two ends of a cylinder of length 2L and diameter $2a$. Calculate the value of maximum K when $2L = 6$ cm and $2a = 2$cm.

13. Mention different types of electron flow. Explain Brillouin flow and derive an expression for Brillouin magnetic field B_M.

14. What is velocity modulation ? How is it achieved in a two cavity klystron ? Describe the construction and working of a reflex klystron.

15. What are limitations of conventional tubes at microwave frequencies? Describe construction and working of a two cavity Klystron amplifier. Explain in detail bunching process and obtain expression for bunching parameter. Compare two cavity klystrons with TWT as microwave amplifier.

16. Name different methods of generating microwave power. Describe with necessary theory, the working of a reflex klystron. Explain how frequency stabilization is achieved in this tube?

17. (a) Give construction of a magnetron. Derive Hull cut-off voltage equation and explain the process of generation of microwaves by a cavity magnetron operated in π-mode. Describe in brief applications of magnetrons.

    (b) How does the reflex klystron work ? Discuss its operating characteristics and applications.

18. Describe the phenomenon of velocity modulation in two-cavity klystron and explain how microwave power is amplified by the interaction of velocity modulated beam with electromagnetic field in the two-cavity klystron.

19. Describe the mechanism of velocity modulation in a two cavity klystron and hence obtain an expression for the bunched beam current. Also find out condition for maximum power output.

20. Explain physically the following in connection with a reflex klystron.

    (a) Velocity modulation and electron bunching,

    (b) Condition for obtaining power output,

(c) Mounting of klystron on a rectangular wave guide for exciting TE_{10} mode in it.

21. (a) Draw the electronic admittance diagram of a reflex klystron and explain the phenomenon of electronic tuning.

    (b) Describe the experimental method for studying the charactertstics of a reflex klystron.

22. Draw a labelled schematic diagram of Helix TWT and show that output power gain of TWT is

$$G = -\ 9.54 + 47.3\ \text{CN db}$$

23. Describe with necessary theory the amplification of microwaves by O-type travelling wave tube.

    In what respect is it superior to klystron two cavity amplifier?

24. Giving necessary theory explain the mechanism of oscillations in a multicavity magnetron.

    Discuss the various modes of oscillations and their separation by means of straps. Obtain an expression for the efficiency of this oscillator. How would you represent its operating characteristics graphically ?

25. What do you understand by thermal noise in a microwave tube ? Define equivalent noise temperature and noise figure.

26. Describe the construction and working of a magnetron as oscillator. Show that in a magnetron the angular velocity of electron is related with the frequency of oscillation by the relation:

$$\omega_e = \frac{2\pi f}{(m+nN)}$$

    Where N is the number of resonators in magnetron and m and n are integers.

27. (a) Write the causes of Noise in microwave tubes. Explain Noise Figure and Noise Temperature.

    (b) Explain what do you mean by space-charge spreading. Mention different types of electron flow.

28. Show the variation of cut-off voltage and Hartree voltage with magnetic field. Indicate the operating range.

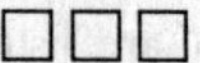

7

Solid State Microwave Devices

7.1. Introduction

Microwave tubes as signal generator were available for quite some time. It was possible to obtain microwave power at complete range of microwave frequencies and at various power levels. Proper functioning of the tubes require high anode voltages, high magnetic fields for focussing the beam and special type of guns. These requirements tend to increase weight and cost of the tubes. Recent developments in semiconductor technology has made it possible to design solid state generators at microwave frequencies, which may be used in large number of applications.

Solid state oscillators generally require low voltages for operation and do not require an electron gun or focussing magnetic fields, hence are generally very compact and light weight. For space application these characteristics are particularly useful. The power capability of these devices can be improved by proper power combining techniques and can be improved considerably over the single device. However, the level remains significantly below that which can be achieved by tubes. FET MESFET, BARITT, Tunnel diodes, Gun diodes and IMPATT devices are the most commonly used semiconductor devices for generation of microwave power. These devices show good cw and pulsed power, efficiency and reliability. Bipolar transistor, high electron mobility transistors are also used successfully for microwave power generation.

The primarily used semiconductors for different devices are gallium arsenide (GaAs) and Silicon. Recently indium phosphide devices are also gaining popularity due to their low noise characteristics. The characteristics of the commonly used semiconductors are listed in Table 7.1.

Table 7.1. Properties of semiconductors used in microwave devices at 290 K

Semiconductor	Energy band gap W_g(eV)	Electron effective mass m_e/m_0	Hole effective mass m_h/m_0	Mobility cm^2/sec μ_e	Mobility cm^2/sec μ_h	Intrinsic number density n_i (cm^{-3})	Dielec-tric constant
Silicon (Si)	1.15	0.31	0.59	1450	500	1.4×10^{10}	11.8
Gallium Arsenide (GaAs)	1.43	0.07	0.50	9000	400	1.4×10^{6}	12.5
Indium Phosphide (InP)	1.34	0.08	0.40	4500	150	1.97×10^{9}	14.0
Germanium	0.7	0.17	0.37	3800	1800	2.2×10^{13}	16.0

In the table intrinsic number density is obtained from the equation

$$n_i^2 = n_e n_h = \frac{32\pi^3 K^3 T^3 (m_e m_h)^{3/2}}{h^6} e^{-Wg/kT} \quad \text{....(7.1)}$$

where n_e and n_h represent the number of density of free electrons and holes per cubic centimeter, having effective mass m_e and m_h respectively,

K is Boltzmann constant (1.38×10^{-23} Joule/K)

h is Planck's constant (6.625×10^{-34} Joule-sec)

T is absolute temperature of the material in Kelvin

W_g is the band gap of the semiconductor.

n_e and n_h indicate the number of electrons and holes in the undoped material and are equal to each other. The addition of a donor impurity such that the number of free electrons become much larger than the number of holes, results in an *n*-type material. The donor impurities are usually P, As and Sb for silicon and Sn and Se for gallium arsenide. Similarly, addition of acceptor impurities such as B, Al, Ga and In for silicon, Zn and Cd for GaAs results in free holes which are greater than electrons and will make a *p*-type material. Depending upon donor concentration, the materials can be classified as n^- or ν, n^+ and n^{++}, the first represent weakly n type, and the n^+ and n^{++} material corresponding to n type materials with high and very high electron densities respectively. Similarly the corresponding *p*-type materials are denoted as p^- or π, p^+ and p^{++}.

In this chapter some of the most widely used semiconductor devices are described. Semiconductor diodes are two terminal devices while transistors are three terminal devices. There are two types of microwave transistors *(i)* the bipolar transistors (BPTs) and *(ii)* the field effect transistors (FETs). First we will describe the various types of solid state diodes, then the transistors.

Microwave Semiconductor Diodes

7.2. PIN Diodes

The structure of a PIN diode consists of a heavily doped *p*-region and a heavily doped *n*-region separated by a layer of high resistivity material that is nearly intrinsic and is shown in Fig. 7.1. In actual practice, the *i*-region is either a high resistivity *p*-layer (called π) or a high resistivity *n*-layer (called ν). The doping profile, space charge density and electric field are shown in Fig. 7.2

The resistance of the intrinsic region is very high, hence most of the applied voltage falls across this region. The device can be used as a switch with switching speed $= \dfrac{W}{2v_s}$, where v_s = saturation velocity in *i*-region.

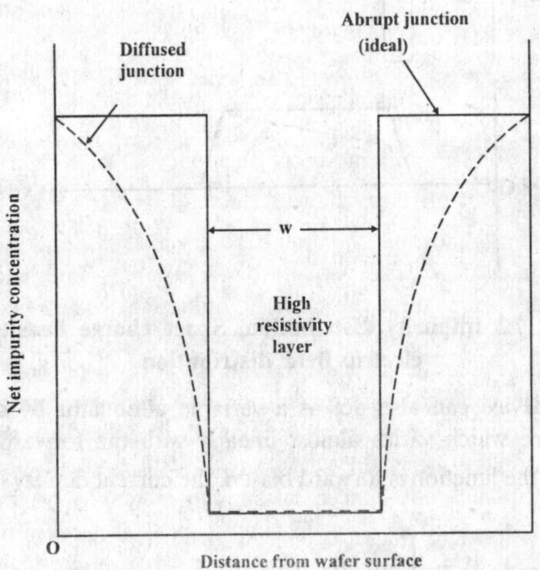

Fig. 7.1 Impurity concentration in PIN Junction

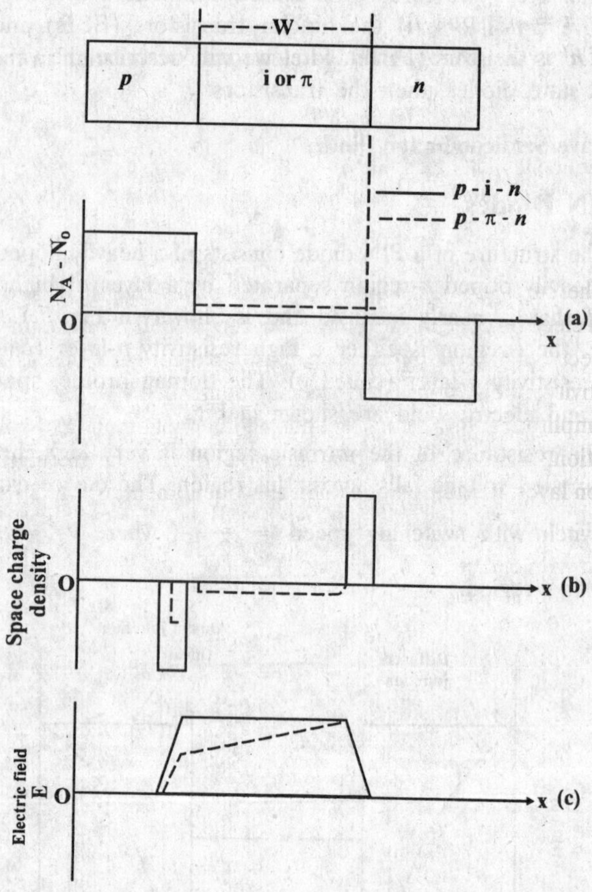

Fig. 7.2 Impurity distribution, Space charge density, electric field distribution

This device can also act as a variable attenuator by controlling the resistance which varies almost linearly with the forward current.

When the junction is forward biased, the current density is given by

$$J = \int_0^W qU dx \qquad ...(7.2)$$

where $U = \frac{n(x)}{\tau}$ the recombination rate

$n(x)$ = injected carrier concentration

τ = life time

If n' is the average injected electron concentration in the i-region

$$J = \int_0^W \frac{qn'}{\tau_a}\, dx \qquad \text{....(7.3)}$$

or

$$J = \frac{qn'W}{\tau_a} \qquad \text{....(7.4)}$$

The current in the i-layer depends on its length W and n' is the injected electron concentration which in turn depends on the forward bias. The effect of controlling current density on forward bias is known as conductivity modulation. Electronically controlled PIN diodes and their use in amplitude modulation depends on the phenomenon of conductivity modulation. The ordinary *p-n* junction diodes have relatively thin depletion layer, hence do not exhibit this phenomenon.

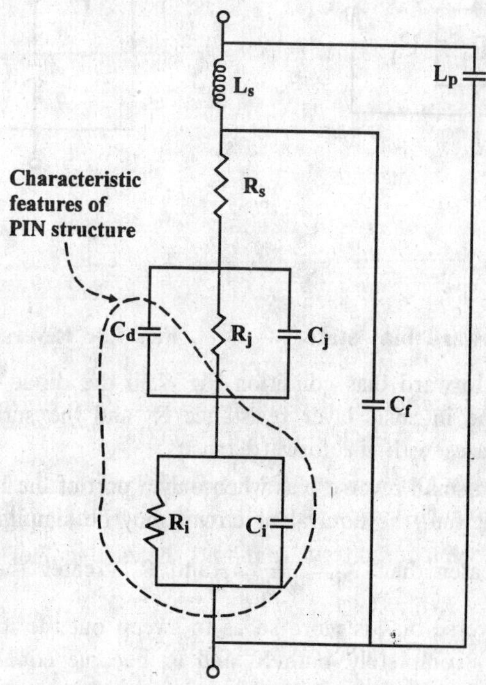

Fig. 7.3a Equivalent circuit of a PIN diode

An equivalent circuit of PIN diode is shown in Fig. 7.3a where L_s is the lead inductance, C_p is package capacitance, C_f is fringing capacitance, C_d represents diffusion capacitance due to charge storage caused by current flow through the intrinsic region, R_i and C_i represent the resistance and capacitance of high resistance I region, R_j and C_j are junction resistance and capacitance respectively. Equivalent circuit of PIN diodes under forward and reverse bias are shown in Fig. 7.3 b,c.

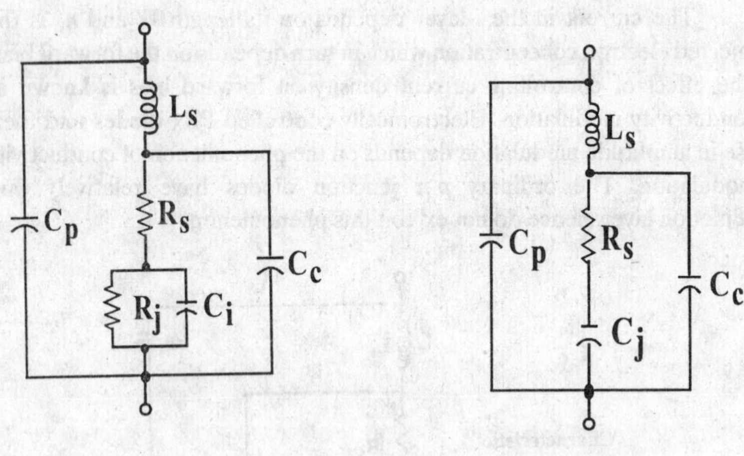

Fig. 7.3b Forward bias state **Fig. 7.3c Reverse bias state**

Under forward bias condition Fig. 7.3b the diode resistance R_f consists of the intrinsic layer resistance R_i and the series resistance R_s. R_i decreases with the forward bias.

Under a small reverse bias when only a part of the high resistivity layer is swept out, the equivalent circuit may be simplified by taking R_j much greater than $X_j = \frac{1}{\omega C_j}$, and R_i greater than $X_i = \frac{1}{\omega C_i}$. When the reverse bias is more so as to sweep out the high resistance layer (I-layer) completely, both X_i and R_i become equal to zero and is shown in Fig. 7.3c.

7.2.1. PIN diode parameters

The diode equivalent circuit employed for the analysis are shown in Fig. 7.3b,c for forward and reverse bias conditions respectively. Using reverse bias equivalent circuit (Fig. 7.3c) following expressions for the reverse bias admittance are obtained

$$Y_r = \frac{(1/R_s)\,(f/f_{co})^2}{\left(\frac{f}{f_{co}}\right)^2 + \left[1 - \left(\frac{f}{f_r}\right)^2\right]^2} + j\omega\left\{\frac{C_j\left[1 - \left(\frac{f}{f_r}\right)^2\right]}{\left(\frac{f}{f_{co}}\right)^2 + \left[1 - \left(\frac{f}{f_r}\right)^2\right]^2} + C_p\right\} \quad ....(7.4)$$

where $\omega = 2\pi f$ rad/sec

$f_{co} = \frac{1}{2\pi R_s C_j}$ = diode cut off frequency

$f_r = \frac{1}{2\pi\sqrt{L_s C_j}}$ = reverse bias series resonance frequency.

Usually f/f_{co} is small hence equation (7.4) can be approximated as

$$Y_r = \frac{\left(\frac{1}{R_s}\right)\left(\frac{f}{f_{co}}\right)^2}{\left[1 - \left(\frac{f}{f_r}\right)^2\right]^2} + j\omega\left\{\frac{C_j}{\left(1 - \frac{f}{fr}\right)^2} + C_p\right\} \quad ....(7.5)$$

Diodes are selected so that $\left(\frac{f}{f_r}\right)^2 << 1$, then Eq. 7.5 can be written as

$$Y_r = G + jB = \left(\frac{1}{R_s}\right)\left(\frac{f}{f_{co}}\right)^2 + j\omega\,[C_j + C_p] \quad ....(7.6)$$

Expression for impedance under forward bias can be written in a simple form when $(\omega C_p) << (\omega L_s)^{-1}$ as

$$Z_f = R + jX = R_f + j\omega L_s$$

7.2.2. PIN diode switches

PIN diode is used as microwave switch. The performance of a switch depends on two parameters, insertion loss and isolation. Insertion loss is the ratio in dBs of the power incident at the input to the power transmitted by the switch when in on condition. Isolation is a measure of the power transmitted when the switch is in the off condition. The PIN diodes have very high resistance when reverse biased and very low resistance when in the forward bias condition. Typical values are several kilo ohms in reverse bias, and less than one ohm under forward bias condition. These values are much higher or lower than waveguide impedance, hence when mounted in a waveguide the diode behaves as open circuited or short circuited element under the two bias conditions.

For switching applications the PIN diodes may be mounted across the transmission lines as series mounted or in the shunt mounted configuration.

(i) Shunt mounted configuration

The diode is connected across a transmission line in shunt mounted configuration as shown in Fig. 7.4 a, its equivalent circuit is also shown in the Fig. 7.4b. A shunt mounted switch is 'on' when the diode is reverse biased (high impedance) and 'off' when the diode is forward biased (low inpedance). Fig. 7.4(b) illustrates it.

For calculation of insertion loss consider Fig. 7.4c

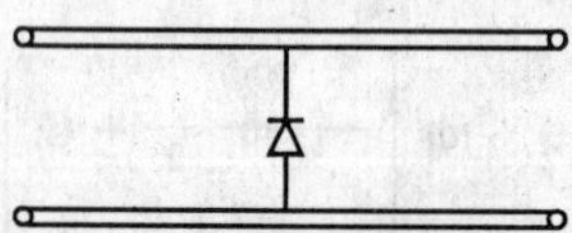

Fig. 7.4a Shunt Mounted PIN Switch.

For an ideal switch, power delivered to the load is

$$P_0 = \frac{I^2}{Y_0} \qquad \text{....(7.7)}$$

The power delivered to the load when the diode admittance (G + jB) is also taken into account is

$$P_d = (2IY_0)^2/\{Y_0\,[(2Y_0 + G)^2 + B^2]\} \qquad \text{....(7.8)}$$

From Eq. 7.7 and 7.8, the insertion loss may be written as

$$I_L = I_0 \log_{10} (P_0/P_d)$$

$$I_L = 10 \log_{10} \{(1 + G/2Y_0)^2 + (B/2Y_0)^2\} \quad \text{....(7.9)}$$

This relation indicates that the insertion loss I_L can be reduced by increasing Y_0 or by reducing the characteristic impedance of the guide. The insertion loss can also be reduced by decreasing B. The susceptance B can be made zero by adding an inductive susceptance in parallel such that it forms a resonant circuit at operating frequency. Eq. 7.9 gives the value of isolation when G and B correspond to the forward bias equivalent circuits of Fig. 7.3b.

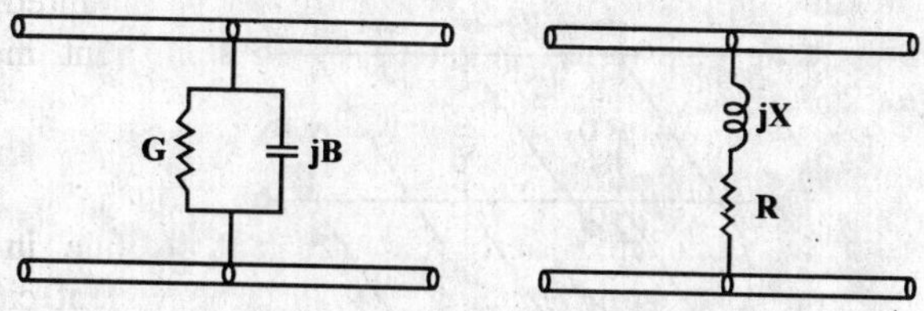

Fig. 7.4b. Equivalent circuit

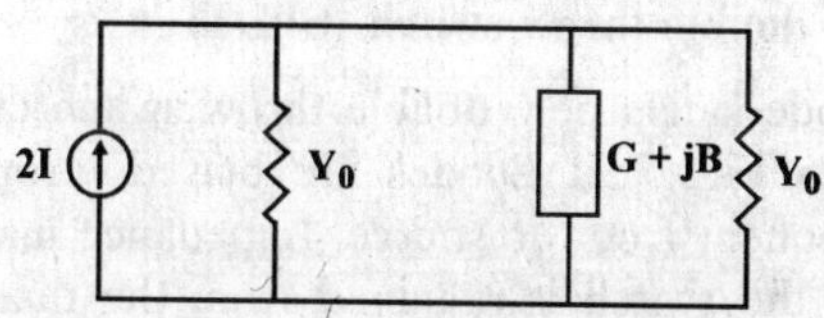

Fig. 7.4c.

(ii) Series mounted configuration

Similarly the insertion loss for the series mounted diode shown in Fig. 7.5 a can be analysed from the equivalent circuit of Fig. 7.5b and can be written as

$$I_L = 10 \log_{10} \{(1 + R/2Z_0)^2 + (X/2Z_0)^2\} \quad \text{....(7.9a)}$$

In this case the insertion loss can be reduced by increasing Z_0 the characteristic impedance of the transmission line. PIN diode switches are used in real-time-delay phase shifters used in phased array radar systems (Fig. 7.7a, b, c).

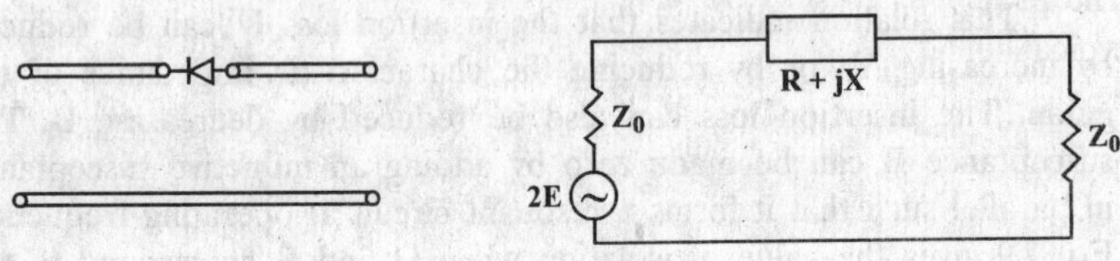

Fig. 7.5a Series mounted configuration

Fig. 7.5b Equivalent Circuit

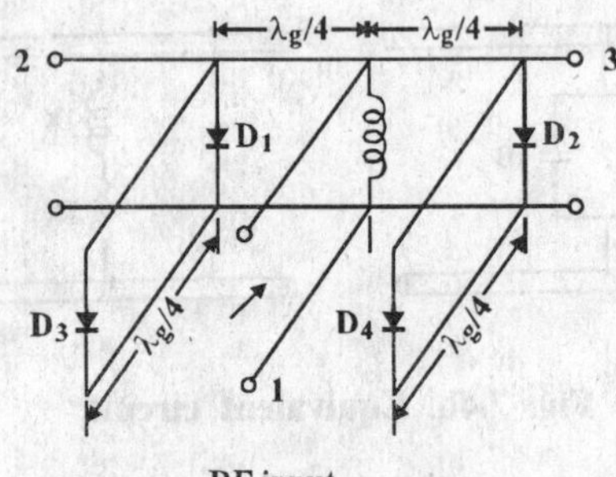

Fig. 7.5c SPDT double switch

7.2.2a. Single pole double throw switch (SPDT)

The PIN diode single pole double throw switch circuit using two diodes is shown in Fig. 7.5c. Diodes are biased through RF chokes to isolate ac component from dc source. Impedance matching between RF feed line and the switch is obtained from the quarter wave lines which provide zero impedance when the switch is OFF (open circuit) and infinite impedance when the switch is ON (short circuit). Thus when D_1 is forward biased Z_{iz} is infinite, when D_2 is reverse biased Z_{iz} is equal to 0. In this situation the input RF power is directed to port (3), and the port (2) remains isolated. Input power can be switched to port (2) keeping port (3) isolated by changing bias of D_1 and D_2, *i.e.* D_1 is reverse biased and D_2 forward biased.

7.2.3. PIN diode as limiters

PIN diodes are also used as microwave limiters, as such a passive protective device. The P-I-N diodes are needed in radars to prevent high transmitting power from damaging the receiver. They act as short circuit during the transmit period, due to an applied forward bias which results in very low resistance (approximately a short circuit), this reduces the power that reaches the receiver drastically. Limiters use shunt mounted diodes. The presence of excess power, switches off the power (hence bias). A typical limiter circuit is shown in Fig. 7.6a.

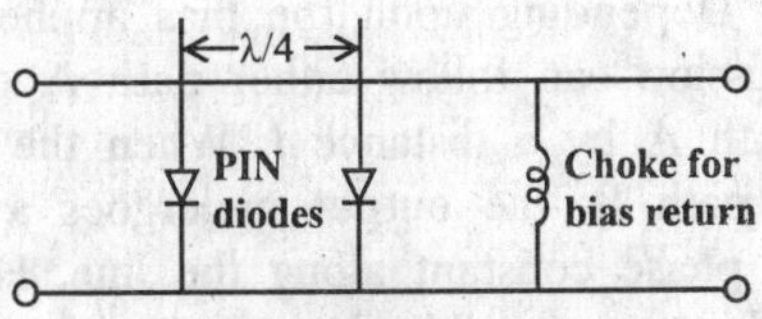

Fig. 7.6a PIN diode limiter

Two PIN diodes are connected in shunt across a transmission line. The diodes are spaced $\lambda/4$ apart so that the individual reflection cancels and a low VSWR is obtained. The choke in the circuit provides a return path for the self bias current. During limiting operation, the threshold voltage across the diode is equal to the junction potential V_j. At high voltage levels, the voltage across the diode exceeds the junction potential V_j making the diode resistance very low. The circuit behaves as closed switch and the incident power is reflected back. The input-output characteristic of a practical limiter deviates from the ideal curve because the transition from high reverse to low forward resistance is not abrupt, Fig. 7.6b.

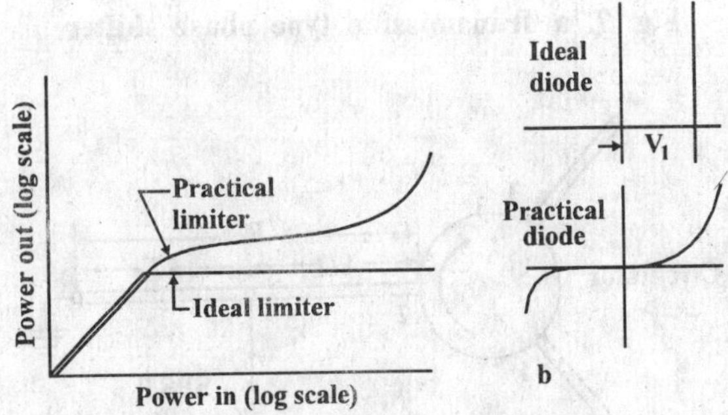

Fig. 7.6b. Practical and ideal limiter

7.2.4. PIN Diode as phase shifters

Electrically controlled phase shifters at microwave frequencies may be obtained by using PIN diode. When the phase shift changes continuously from one value to another, this device is called continuously variable (or analog) phase shifter. Microwave bridges and equipments require continuously varying phase shifters. In other application like phased array antennas, phase shifters having discrete value of the phase shift are used. These are also called digital phase shifters.

Two possible configurations (1) a transmission type, and (2) the reflection type, digital phase shifters can be designed by using diodes and transmission line section as shown in Fig. 7.7a, b & c. The transmission type phase shifter uses two single pole double throw (SPDT) switches. Depending upon the bias applied to two switches the signal transmission can follow either path A or path B. Path B is longer than path A by a distance l. When the signal is switched from path A to path B, the output undergoes a phase shift of βl radians, β is the phase constant along the line. Hence two discrete values of phase shift are possible.

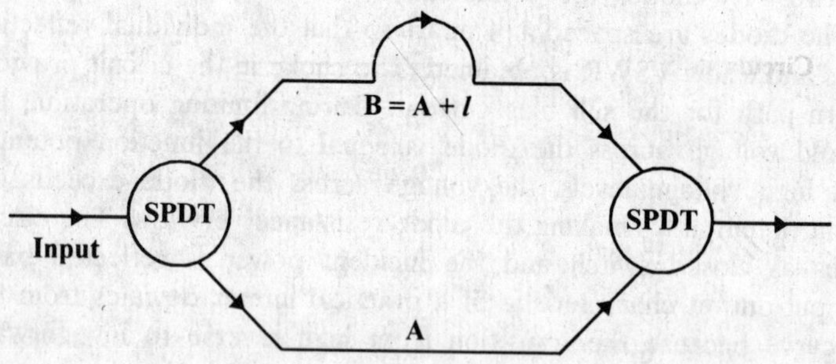

Fig. 7.7a Transmission type phase shifter

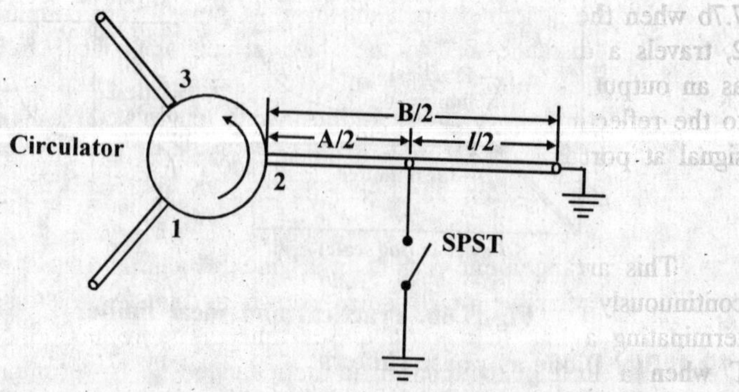

Fig. 7.7b Reflection type phase shifter

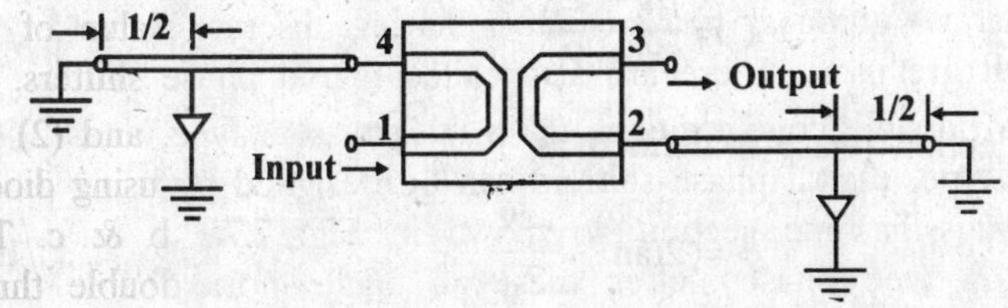

Fig. 7.7c Reflection type phase shifter using directional coupler

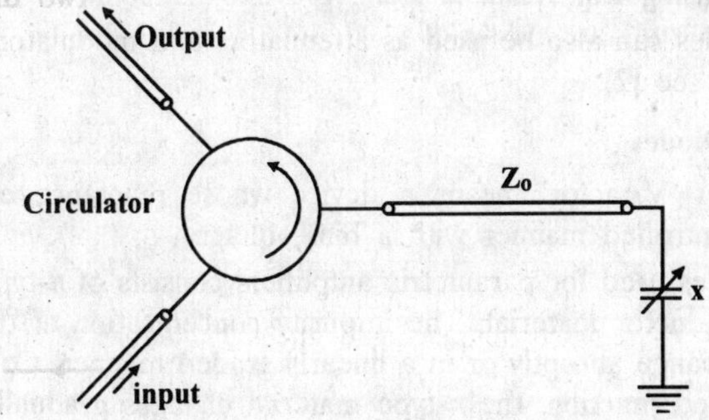

Fig. 7.7d

Reflection type phase shifter shown in Fig. 7.7b uses one SPST switch and a circulator. Alternatively a 3 dB direction coupler and two SPST switches may be employed as shown in Fig. 7.7c. In Fig. 7.7b when the switch is open an input at port 1 gets coupled to port 2, travels a distance B/2 to the short circuit and back, and appears as an output at port 3. When the SPST switch is closed, the distance to the reflecting short circuit reduces to a length A/2 and the output signal at port 3 goes through a phase shift given by

$$\phi = \beta\,(B - A) = \beta\, l \qquad ....(7.10a)$$

This arrangement results in a one bit digital phase shifter. A continuously variable phase sifter shown in Fig. 7.7a is designed by terminating a line in a variable reactance. The reflection coefficient Γ when a line of characteristic impedance Z_0 is terminated in a reactance X is given as

$$\Gamma = \frac{jX - Z_0}{jX + Z_0}$$

Reflection phase is defined as

$$\phi = 2\tan^{-1}\frac{-X}{Z_0} \qquad \text{....(7.10b)}$$

If a varactor diode is used, the value of X can be varied from X_1 to X_2 by varying the reverse bias applied to the diode. This will change the phase shift continuously from ϕ_1 to ϕ_2. Their values can be calculated using Eq. 7.10b.

PIN diodes can also be used as attenuators and modulators. For further details see [2].

7.3. Varactor Diodes

The term 'Varactor' means a device whose reactance can be varied in a controlled manner with a bias voltage.

The diodes used for parametric amplifiers consists of *n*-type and *p*-type semiconductor material. The impurity concentration at the *p-n* junction can change abruptly or in a linearly graded manner. Consider a linearly graded junction, the *n*-type material changes gradually and in a linear fashion over to the p-type material in a distance d as shown in Fig. 7.8a. This variation can be obtained by gradually reducing the doping or concentration of donor atoms to zero in the region $x = d/2$ to $x = 0$, and then increasing the concentration of acceptor atoms in the region $x = 0$ to $x = -d/2$ Fig. 7.8b. The difference between the acceptor atom density N_a and the donor atom density N_d will vary linearly with x across the junction and can be expressed as

$$N_a - N_d = Kx$$

where K is a constant.

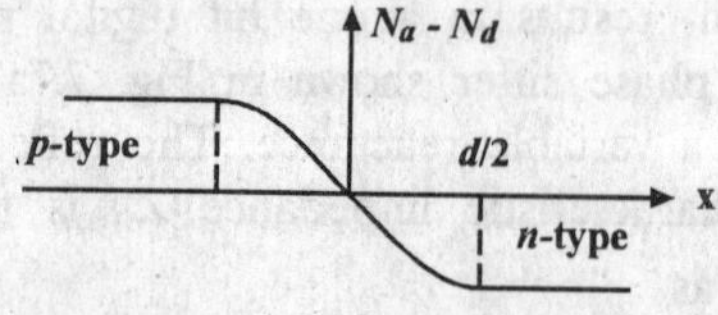

Fig. 7.8a The linearly graded junction.

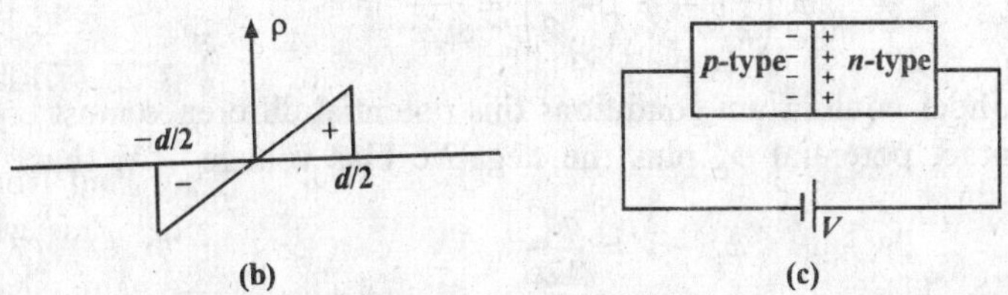

Fig. 7.8b, c The linearly graded junction.

7.3.1. Analysis of graded junction

When there is a gradient in the impurity concentration densities, charge carriers (electrons/holes) will diffuse from a region of high concentration to one of low concentra tion. Thus the electrons will diffuse to the *p*-type side and holes to the *n*-type side of the junction. This diffusion continues until a space charge distribution of sufficient strength is set up to produce a force that is equal and opposite to the effective force created by the concentration gradients. When equilibrium reaches, a small region which is free of charge carriers is produced and is called the depletion region. The space charge and the resultant electric field built up on either side of the junction constitutes an equivalent capacitor. On applying a reverse bias the electrons and holes will be forced further apart. The junction capacitance will reduce due to this widening of the depletion layer. If an ac voltage is superimposed on the bias voltage, it is possible to vary the junction capacitance with time. The linearly varying space charge density (per unit cross section area) is represented by $\rho = qx$ where q is a suitable constant.

Poisson's equation for the potential ϕ is written as

$$\frac{d^2\phi}{dx^2} = -\frac{\rho}{\varepsilon} = -\frac{q}{\varepsilon}x \qquad \text{....(7.11)}$$

Integrating and using the boundary conditions that the electric field $\left(\frac{d\phi}{dx}\right)$ is zero for $|x| > \frac{d}{2}$ and $\phi = 0$ at $x = 0$, we get

$$\phi = -\frac{qx}{2\varepsilon}\left(\frac{x^2}{3} - \frac{d^2}{4}\right) \qquad \text{....(7.12a)}$$

The potential difference across the junction is

$$\phi\left(\frac{d}{2}\right) - \phi\left(-\frac{d}{2}\right) = \frac{qd^3}{12\varepsilon} \qquad \text{....(7.12b)}$$

Under equilibrium conditions this potential difference must equal the contact potential ϕ_c plus the negative bias voltage $-$ V, thus

$$\phi_c - V = \frac{qd^3}{12\varepsilon} \qquad \text{....(7.13)}$$

The total stored charge per unit area is given by

$$Q = \int_0^{d/2} qx\, dx = \frac{qd^2}{8} \qquad \text{....(7.14)}$$

Eliminating d using Eq. 7.13, Q is expressed as

$$Q = \frac{q}{8}\left[\frac{12\varepsilon(\phi_c - V)}{q}\right]^{2/3} \qquad \text{....(7.15)}$$

The capacitance is a function of voltage, it is defined as the ratio of an incremental change in $\phi_c - V$. Thus the capacitance per unit cross-sectional area is

$$C = \frac{dQ}{d(\phi_c - V)} = \varepsilon\left[\frac{q}{12\varepsilon(\phi_c - V)}\right]^{1/3} \qquad \text{....(7.16)}$$

From this equation it can be seen that the junction capacitance C is nonlinear, since it depends on the voltage V. For an abrupt junction diode, C is proportional to $(\phi_c - V)^{-1/2}$. If C is a linear element, Q = CV.

Denote $\phi_c - V = V_0$ and in addition a pumping voltage $v_p = V_p \cos \omega_p t$ is applied, then the capacitance becomes a function of time.

$$C(t) = \varepsilon\left(\frac{q}{12\varepsilon V_0}\right)^{1/3}\left(1 + \frac{V_p}{V_0}\cos\omega_p t\right)^{-1/3} \qquad \text{....(7.17)}$$

In this case the nonlinear capacitance is also a function of time, and can be represented by a Fourier series expansion of the form

$$C(t) = \sum_{n=0}^{\infty} C_n \cos n\omega_p t \qquad \text{....(7.18)}$$

The coefficients C_0 and C_n are given by

$$C_0 = \frac{\varepsilon}{2\pi}\left(\frac{q}{12\varepsilon V_0}\right)^{1/3}\int_{-\pi}^{\pi}\left(1+\frac{V_p}{V_0}\cos\theta\right)^{-1/3} d\theta \qquad \text{....(7.19a)}$$

$$C_n = \left(\frac{q}{12\varepsilon V_0}\right)^{1/3}\int_{-\pi}^{\pi}\left(1+\frac{V_p}{V_0}\cos\theta\right)^{-1/3} \cos n\theta \, d\theta \qquad \text{....(7.19b)}$$

where $\theta = \omega_p t$.

The coefficients can be evaluated using numerical techniques. The important conclusion drawn from these derivations is that *C(t)* is a function of time which can be represented by a Fourier series containing all harmonics of pumping frequency f_p.

It is important to note that these coefficients are not, in general, linear functions of the ac voltage V_p or the voltage V_0. As the junction capacitance *C(t)* is a nonlinear capacitance, the principle of superposition cannot be used for arbitrary ac signal amplitudes. However to use the superposition principle, under small-signal conditions a Taylor series expansion of *C(t)* about an operating point may be used and only the linear term in the signal amplitude is retained.

In addition to the capacitance associated with the diode junction, there is a shunt conductance due to the bulk resistance of the material in depletion layer. This shunt conductance is proportional to the area, and *C* is also proportional to area, the ratio is independent of the cross-sectional area of the diode. Shunt conductance of the depletion layer is small and often neglected. The series resistance of *p* and *n* type semiconductor material outside the depletion layer is more important. When the diode is encapsulated and leads are put on, an additional shunt capacitance C_p due to the cartridge and a series inductance arising from the leads are also present. The equivalent circuit is thus of the from shown in Fig. 7.9a.

C_j is the junction capacitance, R_s is the series resistance and R_p is the parallel equivalent resistance of generation recombination current, diffusion current and surface leakage current. Both C_j and R_s decrease with the reverse bias voltage while R_p generally increase with voltage. The efficiency of a varactor is expressed as a quality factor *Q*, which is the ratio of energy stored to energy dissipated.

$$Q \approx \frac{\omega C_j R_p}{1+\omega^2 C_j^2 R_p R_s} \qquad \text{....(7.20)}$$

The maximum value of Q can be obtained at a frequency $\omega = \omega_0$,

where $$\omega_0 = \frac{1}{C_j\,(R_p R_s)^2} \qquad ....(7.21)$$

and $$\theta_{max} = \left(\frac{R_p}{4R_s}\right)^{1/2} \qquad ....(7.22)$$

For a given bias, Q varies as $(\omega C_j R_p)$ at low frequencies and as $\left(\frac{1}{\omega C_j R_s}\right)$ at high frequencies. Fig 7.9b shows a qualitative graph of the relationship between Q versus frequency and bias voltage.

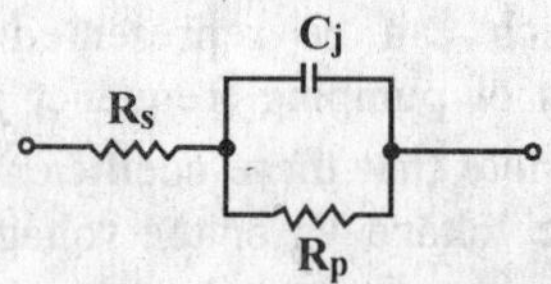

Fig. 7.9a Simplified equivalent circuit of a varactor

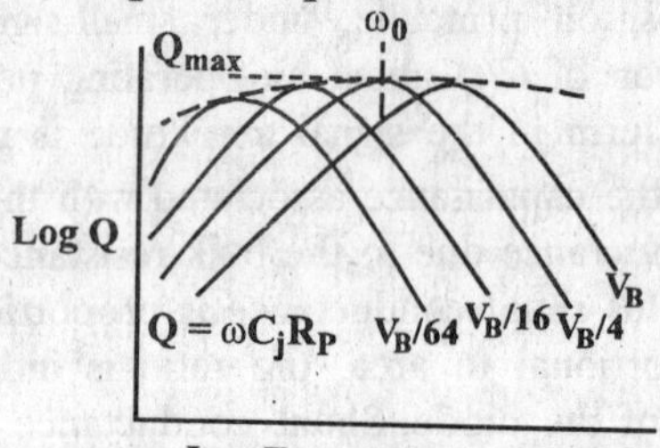

Fig. 7.9b Q versus frequency.

Varactor diodes can be used for many applications [13].

(1) It is used in low noise parametric amplifiers and up converters.

(2) The variable capacitance of this device can be used as a timer for changing the oscillation of a resonant circuit. For such application the varactor should at least have a capacitance range of 5 : 1 to 10 : 1.

(3) The varactor diode produces harmonics due to the nonlinear reactance. Hence they can be used in the construction of solid state microwave sources which are harmonic generators using lower frequency sources.

(4) They are also used in mixing and detection of signals.

A typical microwave varactor diode is shown in Fig. 7.10a and the doping density profile in Fig 7.10b. The doping density at the edges where metal contacts are made should be large enough to reduce the unwanted resistance R_s due to undepleted regions in series with the junction capacitance C_j in the equivalent circuit Fig. 7.10c the series inductance L_s and the overall shunt capacitance are due to connecting lead and the cartridge capacitance respectively. The main function of the varactor is to act as a capacitance, hence the reactance $\frac{1}{\omega C_j}$ should be much larger than R_s at the highest frequency at which the varactor is to be used. In this condition R_s is negligible and the equivalent circuit of the varactor is primarily the voltage variable capacitance.

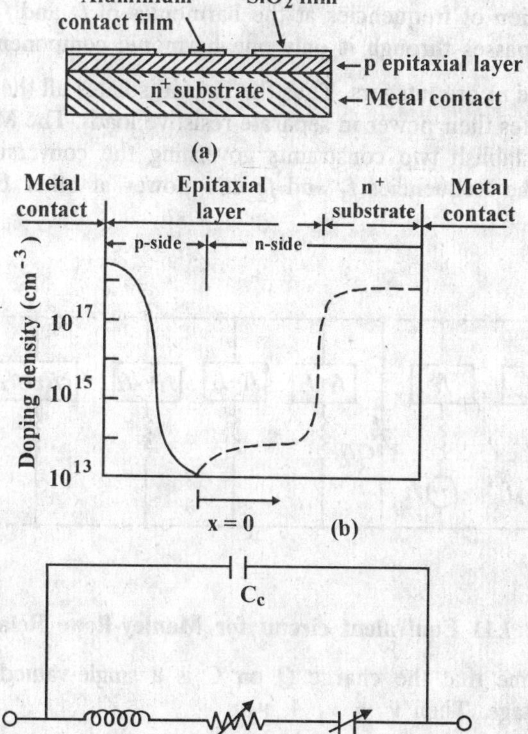

Fig. 7.10 (a) Typical layout of a varactor diode; (b) a typical doping density profile of a microwave varactor diode; (c) varactor equivalent circuit.

7.3.2 Manley-Rowe relation [14]

Two useful relations connecting the power at different frequencies flown into and out of a nonlinear reactance have been derived by Manley and Rowe and are known as the Manley-Rowe relations. Using these relations it is possible to determine whether or not power gain is possible in a reactive frequency conversion when the frequency of the signal is raised or lowered.

The circuit used by Manley and Rowe is shown in Fig. 7.11. The sources have sinusoidal frequencies f_1 and f_2, and infinite number of loads in series with ideal band pass filters connected in shunt with a nonlinear capacitance. The nonlinear capacitance $C(t) = C$ causes the generation of frequencies at the harmonics of f_1 and f_2. The band pass filter passes through it only one harmonic component $(n_{f_1} + m_{f_2})$ where n and m are integers. Thus the circuit isolates all the frequencies and dissipates their power in separate resistive loads. The Manley-Rowe relations establish two constraints governing the conversion of input power at the frequencies f_1 and f_2 into power at other frequencies.

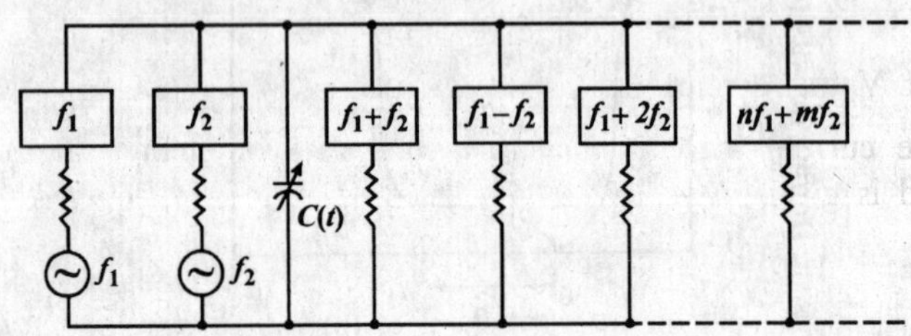

Fig. 7.11 Equivalent circuit for Manley-Rowe Relations

Assume that the charge Q on C is a single-valued function of the ac voltage. Then $v = v_1 + v_2$

or $v = V_1 \cos \omega_1 t + V_2 \cos \omega_2 t$ applied across it and

$Q = Q(v)$. Expanding Q by a Taylor series in v, we obtain

$$Q = Q(0) + \frac{\partial Q}{\partial v} v + \frac{1}{2} \frac{\partial^2 Q}{\partial v^2} v^2 \qquad \text{....(7.23)}$$

All the derivatives are evaluated at $v = 0$.

Eq. 7.23 shows that all powers of ν occur. ν can be written in exponential form as

$$\nu = \frac{V_1}{2}(e^{j\omega_1 t} + e^{-j\omega_1 t}) + \frac{V_2}{2}(e^{j\omega_2 t} + e^{-j\omega_2 t})$$

The charge Q will have frequencies at all harmonics of f_1 and f_2, if currents at all frequencies are permitted to pass through.

The voltage developed across C will also contain all possible harmonics. Hence it is clear that in this case Q is a function of all voltages present. The general expansion of Q will have the form

$$Q = \sum_{n=-\infty}^{\infty} \sum_{m=-\infty}^{\infty} Q_{nm}\, e^{j(n\omega_1 + m\omega_2)t} \qquad ....(7.24)$$

As charge is a real function of time, we must have $Q_{-n-m} = Q_{nm}^*$ so that n, m and $-n$, $-m$ when combined form a real function of time with frequency $n\omega_1 + m\omega_2$

The total voltage V can be expressed as a function V(Q) of the charge. Hence V can also be expressed in similar form as Eq. 7.24, thus

$$V = \sum_{n=-\infty}^{\infty} \sum_{m=-\infty}^{\infty} V_{nm}\, e^{j(n\omega_1 + m\omega_2)t} \qquad ....(7.25)$$

For V to be real $V_{-n-m} = V_{nm}^*$

The current through C is the total rate of change of Q with time, and is given by

$$I = \frac{dQ}{dt} \sum_{n=-\infty}^{\infty} \sum_{m=-\infty}^{\infty} j(n\omega_1 + m\omega_2)\, Q_{nm} e^{j(n\omega_1 + m\omega_2)t}$$

$$= \sum_{n=-\infty}^{\infty} \sum_{m=-\infty}^{\infty} I_{nm}\, e^{j(n\omega_1 + m\omega_2)t} \qquad ....(7.26)$$

where $I_{nm} = j(n\omega_1 + m\omega_2)\, Q_{nm}$

As C is a purely reactive element, there can be no net power into or out of C. If we assume ω_1 and ω_2 are not comparable (either in amplitude, phase or time period), there will be no time average power due to interacting harmonics. The average power at the frequencies $\pm|n\omega_1 + m\omega_2|$ is

$$P_{nm} = (V_{nm} I_{nm}^* + V_{nm}^* I_{nm})$$

$$= (V_{nm} I_{nm}^* + V_{-n-m} I_{-n-m}^*) = P_{-n-m} \qquad ....(7.27)$$

Since the time average of

$$(I_{nm}e^{j(n\omega_1 + m\omega_2)t} + I_{-n-m}e^{-j(n\omega_1 + m\omega_2)t})\,(V_{nm}e^{j(n\omega_1 + m\omega_2)t} + V_{-n-m}e^{-j(n\omega_1 + m\omega_2)t})$$

is $V_{nm}I_{-n-m} + V_{-n-m}I_{nm} = V_{nm}I^*_{nm} + V^*_{nm}I_{nm} = V_{nm}I^*_{nm} + V_{-n-m}I^*_{-n-m}$

conservation of power can therefore be expressed as

$$\sum_{n=-\infty}^{\infty}\sum_{m=-\infty}^{\infty} P_{nm} = 0 \quad ....(7.28)$$

Since $P_{nm} = P_{-n-m}$ from 7.27. We multiply each term by $(n\omega_1 + m\omega_2)/(n\omega_1 + m\omega_2)$ and split the sum in to two parts. So that the relation (7.28) can be expressed in the form

$$\omega_1 \sum_{n=-\infty}^{\infty}\sum_{m=-\infty}^{\infty} \frac{nP_{nm}}{n\omega_1 + m\omega_2} + \omega_2 \sum_{n=-\infty}^{\infty}\sum_{m=-\infty}^{\infty} \frac{mP_{nm}}{n\omega_1 + m\omega_2} = 0 \quad ....(7.29)$$

We now show that each double sum must vanish separately.

1. Replace each $I_{nm}/(n\omega_1 + m\omega_2)$ by jQ_{nm}

2. Then $P_{nm}/(n\omega_1 + m\omega_2)$ become $-j\,V_{nm}\,Q^*_{nm} - jV_{-n-m}\,Q^*_{-n-m}$ and does not depend directly on ω_1 or ω_2

3. For any choice of ω_1 and ω_2, it is possible to adjust the network external to C so that the currents which result in the network keep the amplitude of the V_{nm} unchanged.

As Q_{nm} depend on V_{nm}, hence they also remain unchanged.

4. On these consideration from Eq. 7.29, it is possible now to change ω_1 and ω_2 arbitrarily but keep the two double sums unchanged. Hence Eq. 7.29 will hold for arbitrary ω_1 and ω_2 only if

$$\sum_{n=-\infty}^{\infty}\sum_{m=-\infty}^{\infty} \frac{nP_{nm}}{n\omega_1 + m\omega_2} = 0 \quad ....(7.30)$$

$$\sum_{n=-\infty}^{\infty}\sum_{m=-\infty}^{\infty} \frac{mP_{nm}}{n\omega_1 + m\omega_2} = 0 \quad ....(7.31)$$

that is, the coefficients of ω_1 and ω_2 must vanish separately. These relations can also be written in somewhat different form. The first sum in Eq. 7.30 is written as

$$\sum_{n=0}^{\infty}\sum_{m=-\infty}^{\infty} \frac{nP_{nm}}{n\omega_1 + m\omega_2} + \sum_{n=0}^{\infty}\sum_{m=-\infty}^{\infty} \frac{-nP_{-n-m}}{-n\omega_1 - m\omega_2} \quad ....(7.32)$$

where n and m have been replaced by $-n$, $-m$ in the second term. Since $P_{-n-m} = P_{nm}$, the two parts are equal, hence Eq. 7.30 – 7.31 can be written as

$$\sum_{n=0}^{\infty} \sum_{m=-\infty}^{\infty} \frac{nP_{nm}}{n\omega_1 + m\omega_2} = 0 \qquad \text{....(7.33)}$$

$$\sum_{m=0}^{\infty} \sum_{n=-\infty}^{\infty} \frac{mP_{nm}}{n\omega_1 + m\omega_2} = 0 \qquad \text{....(7.34)}$$

where P_{nm} is the power flowing into the nonlinear reactance at frequency $(n\omega_1 + m\omega_2)$. Eqs. 7.33 – 7.34 are the standard Manley-Rowe relations. These are the general power-conservation relations and do not depend on any specific circuit since we have not made any reference to the external circuit in the derivation of these relations.

To demonstrate the usefulness of the Manley-Rowe relations, consider load only at frequency $(\omega_1 + \omega_2)$ and let load at all other harmonics be open circuited. Hence currents can exist only at f_1, f_2 and $(f_1 + f_2)$ frequencies.

Hence the only terms present in the two equations 7.33 and 7.34 are $n = \pm 1, m = 0$ and $n = 0, m = \pm 1$ and $n = m = \pm 1$. If we write $\omega_1 + \omega_2 = \omega_3$ we get

$$\frac{P_{10}}{\omega_1} + \frac{P_{11}}{\omega_3} = 0 \qquad \text{....(7.35a)}$$

$$\frac{P_{01}}{\omega_2} + \frac{P_{11}}{\omega_3} = 0 \qquad \text{....(7.35b)}$$

As power is applied at ω_1 and ω_2, then P_{10} and P_{01} have to be positive, Therefore P_{11} is negative and power is delivered from the nonlinear capacitance C at the frequency ω_3. If it is considered that ω_1 is the input frequency, ω_2 is the pump frequency than ω_3 is the output frequency. The signal gain is given by

$$-\frac{P_{11}}{P_{10}} = \frac{\omega_3}{\omega_1} = 1 + \frac{\omega_2}{\omega_1} \qquad \text{....(7.35c)}$$

A parametric amplifier of this type is called an up-converter. In any practical amplifier, losses will always be present, hence gain will be less than ω_3/ω_1. Eq. 7.35c sets the criterion for maximum gain from which a practical up-converter can be judged.

7.3.3. Applications of varactor diodes

(1) Parametric up convertor

In the up-converter signal frequency is at ω_s, the pump frequency is applied at ω_p and the output is obtained at higher frequency $(\omega_s+\omega_p)$. There will be three voltages at these frequencies and can be represented as

$$v_s = \text{Re}\,(V_s e^{j\omega_s t}) = \frac{1}{2}(V_s e^{j\omega_s t} + V_s^* e^{-j\omega_s t})$$

$$v_p = \text{Re}\,(V_p e^{j\omega_p t}) = \frac{1}{2}(V_p e^{j\omega_p t} + V_p^* e^{-j\omega_p t}) \quad \text{....(7.36 a,b,c)}$$

$$v_o = \text{Re}\,(V_o e^{j\omega_p t}) = \frac{1}{2}(V_o e^{j\omega_0 t} + V_o^* e^{-j\omega_0 t})$$

We can write current in terms of v_p and v_s assuming v_s very small.

$$i = \frac{dQ(v_p)}{dt} + \frac{d}{dt}\left(\frac{dQ}{dv} \quad \begin{matrix} v_s \\ r_s = 0 \end{matrix}\right) \quad \text{....(7.37a)}$$

If the pumping voltage is very small the junction capacitance of the varactor can be written as

$$C(t) = C_0(1 + 2M\cos\omega_p t) \quad \text{....(7.37b)}$$

In terms of the voltages v_s, v_p and v_o the expression 7.37 can be expressed as

$$i = \frac{dQ(v_p)}{dt} + \frac{1}{2}\frac{d}{dt}\, C_0\,(1 + 2M\cos\omega_p t)\times$$
$$(V_s e^{j\omega_s t} + V_s^* e^{-j\omega_s t} + V_0 e^{j\omega_0 t} + V_0^* e^{-j\omega_0 t}) \quad \text{....(7.38)}$$

Let the current at ω_s and ω_0 are expressed as

$$i_s = \frac{1}{2}\,(I_s e^{j\omega_s t} + I_s^* e^{-j\omega_s t}) \quad \text{....(7.39)}$$

$$i_0 = \frac{1}{2}\,(I_0 e^{j\omega_0 t} + I_0^* e^{-j\omega_0 t}) \quad \text{....(7.40)}$$

The current I_s and I_0, in terms of signal current i_s and output i_0 can be expressed as

$$I_s = j\omega_s C_0 V_s + j\omega_s C_0 M V_0 \quad (7.41a)$$

$$I_0 = j\omega_0 C_0 V_0 + j\omega_0 C_0 M \omega_0 V_s \quad (7.41b)$$

The junction capacitance may be expressed by an admittance matrix

$$\begin{vmatrix} I_s \\ I_0 \end{vmatrix} = \begin{bmatrix} j\omega_s C_0 & j\omega_s C_0 M \\ j\omega_0 C_0 M & j\omega_0 C_0 \end{bmatrix} \begin{vmatrix} V_s \\ V_0 \end{vmatrix} \qquad \text{....(7.41c)}$$

The parameter M is proportional to the pump voltage and gives the coupling between the voltages at the two frequencies ω_s and ω_0.

Fig 7.12a illustrates an equivalent circuit model of an up-convertor. The scries tuned circuits are chosen so that the three circuit loops have resonant frequencies of ω_s, ω_0 and ω_p and current due to these frequencies can exist. The three circuit loops are coupled together through the time varying part C of C_s only. Therefore for the two frequencies ω_s and ω_0 the equivalent circuit can be reduced to that of Fig. 7.12b. The box labled *C(t)* in this circuit is an equivalent impedance network that maintains the relationship given in Eq. 7.32 between the terminal currents and voltages. Circuit in Fig. 7.12b can be analysed like any other conventional network. Going through extensive circuit analysis we can obtain current I_0 and from this the power gain G_0. In Fig. 7.12a it was assumed that there were no losses present, the presence of circuit losses were small compared with losses presented by diode resistance R_s and the external loading due to R_g and R_L. Eq. (7.41c) can be solved for V_s and V_0 in terms of I_s and I_0 to obtain I_0 and G_0.

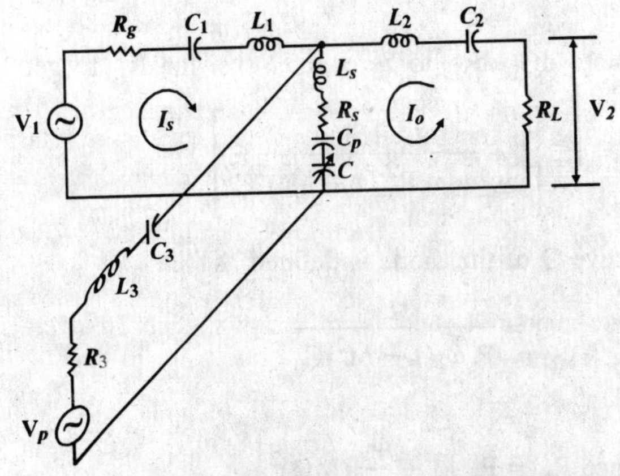

Fig. 7.12a Equivalent circuit model of an up-converter

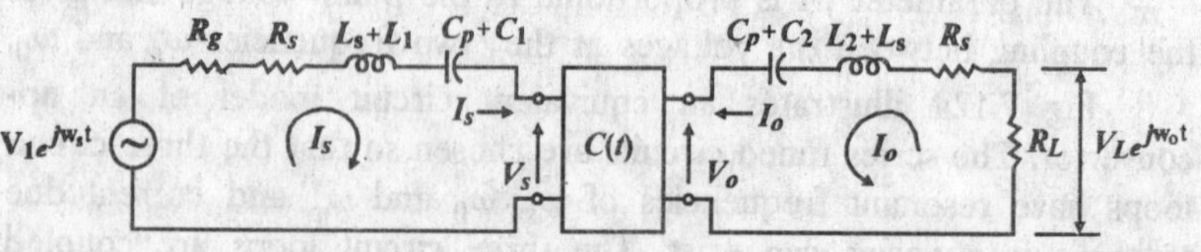

Fig. 7.12b Reduced equivalent circuit for an up-converter

$$I_0 = \frac{-jV_1M\omega_0C_0(1-M^2)}{M^2 + (R_g+R_s)(R_L+R_s)\,\omega_0\omega_s(1-M^2)^2C_0^2} \quad \text{....(7.42)}$$

$$\text{and } G_0 = \frac{4|I_0|^2 R_L R_g}{V_1^2} \quad \text{....(7.42a)}$$

To obtain maximum gain R_g and R_L are adjusted so that the value of R_g and R_L are equal, hence to maximize the Eq. 7.42a

$$G_0 = \frac{4R_L^2M^2}{\omega_s^2(1-M^2)^2C_0^2\left[(R_L+R_S)^2 + \dfrac{M^2}{\omega_0\omega_s(1-M^2)^2C_0^2}\right]^2}$$

Equate dG_0/dR_L to zero and solve for R_L to get

$$R_L = R_s\left[1 + \frac{M^2}{\omega_0\omega_sR_s^2(1-M^2)^2C_0^2}\right]^{1/2} \quad \text{....(7.43b)}$$

The effective Q of the diode is defined as

$$Q = \frac{1}{R_s\omega_s(1-M^2)C_0} \quad \text{....(7.44a)}$$

$$\text{Hence } R_L = R_s\left[1 + \frac{\omega_s}{\omega_0}(MQ)^2\right]^{1/2} \quad \text{(7.44b)}$$

and the maximum gain is

$$G_0 = \frac{\omega_0}{\omega_s}\frac{\delta}{(1+\sqrt{1+\delta})^2} \quad \text{(7.44c)}$$

where $\delta = (\omega_s/\omega_0)\,(MQ)^2$. According to the Manley-Rowe relation, the maximum gain of the up convertor is $\frac{\omega_0}{\omega_s}$. The factor $\delta/(1+\sqrt{1+\delta})^2$ may therefore be regarded as a gain-degradation factor. As the diode Q approaches infinity, that is as R_s goes to zero, and S approaches infinity the gain degradation factor becomes unity. Hence for a loss less diode, gain becomes equal to ω_0/ω_s.

High gain can be achieved with an up-convertor, provided the ratio of ω_0/ω_s (output frequency to input frequency) is large. At higher microwave frequency maintaining this ratio high is not very practical, and for this reason up-convertors are usually used below 1 GHz frequency. Higher gain can be obtained from the negative-resistance parametric amplifier, which is discussed in the next section.

(ii) Negative-Resistance parametric amplifier :

The most important use of the varactor diode is for low noise parametric amplifiers which are used as front ends of the microwave receivers in long range radars, satellite, ground stations, microwave communication links etc. In the negative-resistance parametric amplifiers currents are permitted to exist at the signal frequency ω_s, pump frequency ω_p, and the idler frequency $\omega_i = \omega_p - \omega_s$. The equivalent circuit model for parametric amplifier can be depicted in Fig. 7.13

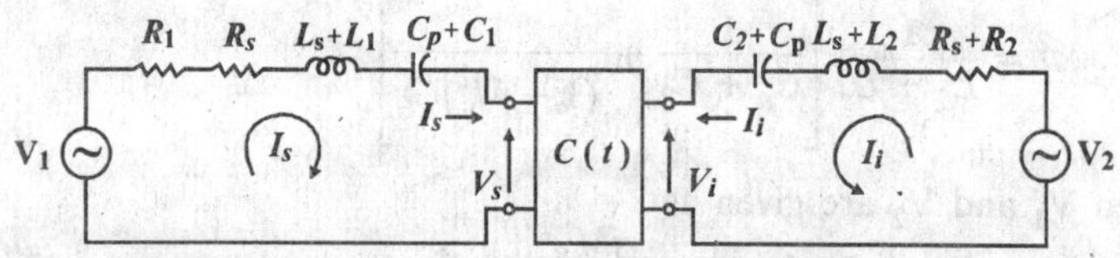

Fig. 7.13. Equivalent circuit for a negative resistance parametric amplifier

The voltage V_0 in Eq. 7.38 is replaced by $v_i = \frac{1}{2}(V_i\, e^{j\omega_i} + V_i^*\, e^{-j\omega_i})$ and introduce the idler current $i_i = \frac{1}{2}(I_i e^{j\omega_i t} + I_i^*\, e^{-j\omega_i t})$.

We may solve for I_s and I_i in terms of V_s and V_i in the way it was solved for the up-converter. For $\omega_i = \omega_p - \omega_s$,

$$\begin{bmatrix} I_i \\ I_s^* \end{bmatrix} = \begin{bmatrix} j\omega_i C_0 & j\omega_i C_0 M \\ -j\omega_s C_0 M & -j\omega_s C_0 \end{bmatrix} \begin{bmatrix} V_i \\ V_s^* \end{bmatrix} \qquad \text{....(7.45a)}$$

$$\begin{bmatrix} V_i \\ V_s^* \end{bmatrix} = \frac{1}{1-M^2} \begin{bmatrix} \dfrac{1}{j\omega_i C_0} & \dfrac{M}{j\omega_i C_0} \\ \dfrac{-M}{j\omega_s C_0} & \dfrac{-1}{j\omega_s C_0} \end{bmatrix} \begin{bmatrix} I_i \\ I_s^* \end{bmatrix} \quad \text{....(7.45b)}$$

For the circuit of Fig. 7.13, the following equations are written

$$V_1 = I_s \left[R_1 + R_s + j\omega_s(L_1 + L_s) + \frac{1}{j\omega_s(C_p + C_1)} + \frac{1}{j\omega_s(1-M^2)C_0} \right] + \frac{M}{(1-M^2)j\omega_i C_0} I_i^* \quad \text{....(7.46a)}$$

$$V_2 = I_i \left[R_2 + R_s + j\omega_i(L_2 + L_s) + \frac{1}{j\omega_i(C_s + C_2)} + \frac{1}{j\omega_i(1-M^2)C_0} \right] + \frac{M}{(1-M^2)j\omega_s C_s} I_s^* \quad \text{....(7.46b)}$$

If we impose the timing conditions

$$\omega_s^2 = \frac{1}{L_1 + L_s} \left[\frac{1}{C_p + C_1} + \frac{1}{(1-M^2)C_0} \right]$$

$$\omega_i^2 = \frac{1}{L_2 + L_s} \left[\frac{1}{C_p + C_2} + \frac{1}{(1-M^2)C_0} \right]$$

Then V_1 and V_2 are given as

$$V_1 = (R_1 + R_s)\, I_s - \frac{jM}{\omega_i(1-M^2)C_0} I_i^* \quad \text{....(7.47a)}$$

$$V_2 = (R_2 + R_s)\, I_i - \frac{jM}{\omega_s(1-M^2)C_0} I_s^* \quad \text{....(4.47b)}$$

If we assume $V_2 = 0$, I_i can be determined from Eq. 7.47 and the gain G_0 evaluated from

$$G_0 = \frac{4R_1R_2|I_i|^2}{V_1^2} \quad \text{....(7.48a)}$$

On substituting for I_i and V_1, G_0 can be written as

$$G_0 = \frac{4R_1R_2M^2}{\left[R_1 + R_s - \dfrac{M^2}{(R_2 + R_s)\omega_i\omega_s(1 - M^2)^2C_0^2}\right]^2 (R_2 + R_s)^2\,\omega_s^2\,C_0^2\,(1 - M^2)^2} \quad \text{....(7.48b)}$$

The third term in square brackets of the denominator can be equated to the negative resistance-R, hence G_0 can be expressed as

$$G_0 = \frac{4R_1R_2[\omega_i(1 - M^2)C_0R]^2}{M^2(R_1 + R_s - R)^2} \quad \text{....(7.49)}$$

The parametric amplifier discussed above is called a negative resistance converter, since it is possible to take the output at the same frequency as the input, *i.e.* at ω_s. It R_1 is split into a generator resistance R_g plus a load resistance R_L, the power delivered to R_2 is $\frac{1}{2}R_L|I_s|^2$. In this case the power gain will be

$$G_0 = \frac{4R_gR_L|I_s|^2}{V_1^2} \quad \text{....(7.50)}$$

Is can be calculated from Eq. (7.47) to give G_0 as

$$G_0 = \frac{4R_gR_L}{(R_g + R_L + R_s - R)^2} \quad \text{....(7.51)}$$

where R as assumed earlier equals to

$$R = \frac{M^2}{(R_2 + R_s)\,\omega_i\omega_s(1 - M^2)^2C_0^2} \quad \text{....(7.52)}$$

It can be seen that if R is made equal to $R_1 + R_s$ very high gain can be obtained. Too high gain may cause oscillations, which forbids making $R_1 + R_s$ very close to R.

The negative resistance –R arises in the following manner :

(1) The signal pump power when applied to the non-linear capacitance, frequency mixing occurs.

(2) As current at idler frequency (ω_p–ω_s) is allowed to exist, further frequency mixing of power at the ω_s, (ω_p–ω_s) and ω_p occurs.

(3) This later mixing causes harmonics of ω_p and $\omega_p - \omega_s$ to be generated, power at ω_s is also generated. When the power generated through frequency mixing exceeds that being supplied at the signal frequency ω_s, the diode appears to have negative resistances.

(4) If idler current is not permitted to exist, the negative resistance vanishes. From Eq. 7.52 if R_2 is made equal to infinity (open circuit for the idler current) then idler current vanishes.

The negative resistance parametric amplifier with input and output at the same frequency are not very stable. The reason for this is that in a microwave system R_g and R_L are the impedances seen looking into the input and output transmission line ports. If the loads connected to these ports are not matched, reflected waves occur. Reflected waves in the output return to the amplifier, get amplified and then fed both to the input and output lines. This makes the gain function of the external generator and load impedances.

To improve the stability of the amplifier, a circulator at input of the parametric amplifier is used as shown in Fig. (7.14).

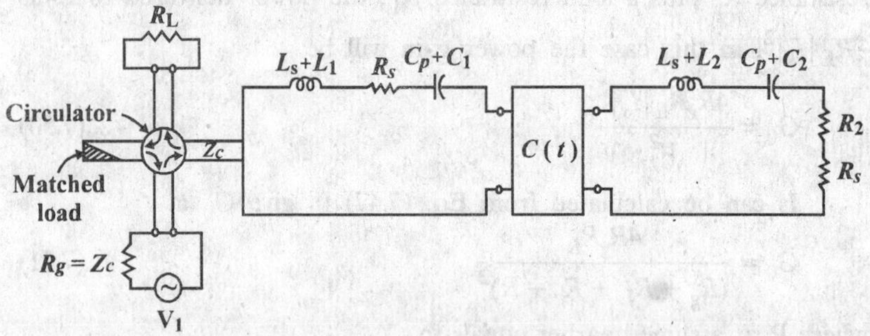

Fig. 7.14 Circulator used in a negative resistance parametric amplifier

The use of a circulator makes the load termination R_L for the amplifier equal to the characteristic impedance of the transmission line independent of the generator or load impedances Z_g and Z_L, when $R_L = R$.

$$G_0 = \frac{4R^2}{(R_L + R_s - R)^2} \quad \text{....(7.53)}$$

When a circulator is used, the optimum value of R_L is twice than it is without a circulator. Hence using circulator improves the gain by 6 dB. For further details see [1].

7.3.4. Noise properties of parametric amplifiers

The noise produced by parametric amplifiers is the thermal noise in the resistances in the equivalent circuit. Let us analyse it for the up-converter shown in Fig. 7.12a. The input thermal noise at frequency ω_s is that arising from the generator resistance R_g. The mean square voltage across R_g is $e_1^2 = 4kTR_g\Delta f$. The diode circuit losses can be neglected in comparison to resistance R_s. Other source of noise in the signal circuit generated across R_s has a mean square noise voltage $e_2^2 = 4kT_sR_s\Delta f$ at frequency ω_s. The equivalent noise temperature of the diode at frequency ω_s is denoted by T_s. The noise at frequency ω_s is amplified and converted at the output frequency ω_0.

Replace the voltage V_1 by $\sqrt{e_1^2 + e_2^2}$ in Fig. 7.11a, the amplified output noise at mid-band is given by

$$P_1 = |I_1^2| R_L = \frac{R_L\,(e_1^2 + e_2^2)\, M^2 \omega_0^2\, C_0^2\, (1 - M^2)^2}{[M^2 + (R_g + R_s)(R_L + R_s)\, \omega_0 \omega_s\, (1 - M^2)^2 C_0^2]^2} \quad ....(7.54)$$

Introduce the midband gain G_0 in the definition of P_1 from equation 7.43, we get

$$\rho_1 = \frac{e_1^2 + e_2^2}{4R_g} G_0 = \frac{k\Delta f(R_g T + R_s T_s)}{R_g} G_0 \quad ....(7.55)$$

Noise is also generated in the output circuit at frequency ω_0 across the resistance R_s. If the diode temperature at the frequency ω_0 is T_0, an equivalent noise voltage $e_3^2 = 4k\, T_0\, R_s\, \Delta f$ appears across R_s in the output circuit. Solve for the noise current I_2. Also calculate $P_2 = |I_2|^2 R_L$, we obtain for P_2

$$P_2 = \frac{\omega_s^2\, (1 - M^2)^2\, C_0^2\, (R_s + R_g)^2\, G_0 e_3^2}{4\, R_g M^2}$$

$$= \frac{\omega_s^2\, (1 - M^2) C_0^2 (R_s + R_g)^2\, kT_0 R_s\, \Delta f\, G_0}{R_g M^2} \quad ....(7.56)$$

The total output noise power at frequency ω_0 is $P_n = P_1 + P_2$. The input noise power available from R_g is $kT\Delta f$. Hence the noise figure is given by

$$F = \frac{P_1 + P_2}{G_0 kT\Delta f} = 1 + \frac{R_s T_s}{R_g T} + \frac{\omega_s^2 (1 - M^2)^2 C_0^2\, (R_s + R_g)^2\, R_s T_0}{R_g M^2 T} \quad ....(7.57)$$

Gain G_0 was defined as output power divided by the available power from the input signal source, so that F as evaluated above conforms to the accepted definition of noise figure. Take the diode noise temperature at the two frequencies ω_s and ω_0 equal to T_d, we obtain

$$F = 1 + \frac{R_s}{R_g}\frac{T_d}{T}\left[1 + \frac{(R_s + R_g)^2}{M^2Q^2R_s^2}\right] \quad ....(7.58)$$

R_g for maximum gain is obtained after introducing the diode Q from Eq. 7.44a.

$$R_g = R_L = R_s\left(1 + \frac{\omega_s}{\omega_0}M^2Q^2\right)^{1/2} \quad ....(7.59)$$

Thus the noise figure under maximum gain condition is given by

$$F = 1 + \frac{T_d}{T}\left(1 + \frac{\omega_s}{\omega_0}M^2Q^2\right)^{-1/2}\left(1 + \frac{\{1 + [1 + (\frac{\omega_s}{\omega_0})\, M^2Q^2]^{1/2}\}^2}{M^2Q^2}\right)$$

$$= 1 + \frac{T_d}{T}\left(1 + \frac{\omega_s}{\omega_0}M^2Q^2\right)^{-1/2} \quad ....(7.60)$$

F for typical parametric amplifier is of the order of 1.3 dB which shows low noise property of these amplifiers.

The noise properties of negative resistance parametric amplifiers have been analyzed and measured by Ueonahara etc. The noise theory for a negative resistance parametric amplifiers employing a circulator in which the output signal is taken at the same frequency as the input *i.e.* at ω_s can also be worked out on similar pattern.

7.4. Tunnel Diodes

7.4.1. Introduction

A tunnel diode comprises of a *p-n* junction in which both p and n sides are heavily doped with impurities of the order of $10^{19}/cm^3$, the depletion layer width is very small (typically few Å). Hence there exists a high probability that carriers tunnel through the potential barriers even if they do not possess sufficient kinetic energy (K.E.) to pass over it. Esaki published the classical paper on Tunnel diode in 1958 and established its potential for microwave applications. The tunnel phenomenon is a majority carrier effect. The tunneling time of carriers through the potential energy barrier is not governed by the classical time concept (that is the transit time is equal to the barrier width divided by the carrier velocity) but by the quantum transition probability per unit time. Tunnel diodes are used for microwave oscillation, amplification and in binary memory devices. Tunnel diodes are low cost, light weight, low noise, high speed devices and need low power for operation, while they have high peak current to valley-current ratio.

Tunnel diodes are formed from Ge, GaAs and other materials like GaSb. Fig 7.15 shows typical I-V characteristics of Ge and GaAs diodes. These diodes show negative differential resistance (NDR) over a part of their I-V characteristic. The negative differential resistance is a result of majority carrier tunneling across the extremely narrow barrier of the diode. This is a majority carrier effect and hence is very fast.

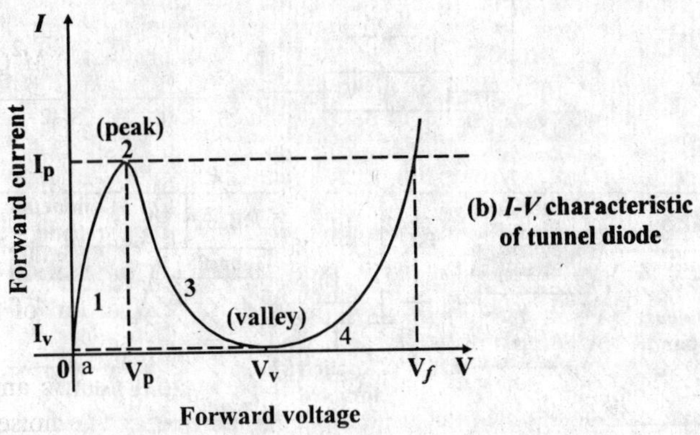

Fig. 7.15. I-V Characteristics of a Tunnel diode

7.4.2. Principles of operation :

There are two conditions that should be satisfied so that quantum mechanical tunneling can take place. These are (1) If the barrier is less than 3Å, there is finite possibility that the particles will tunnel through the potential barrier, even though they do not have enough energy to pass over the same barrier.

(1) Under open circuit or at zero bias condition, the upper levels of electron energy of both *p*-type and *n*-type are at the same Fermi level as shown in Fig. 7.16(a) There are no empty states on one side of the junction and filled states on the other side, hence no charge flow in either direction across the junction and the current is zero as shown at point a of the I-V characteristic curve of the tunnel diode Fig. 7.15.

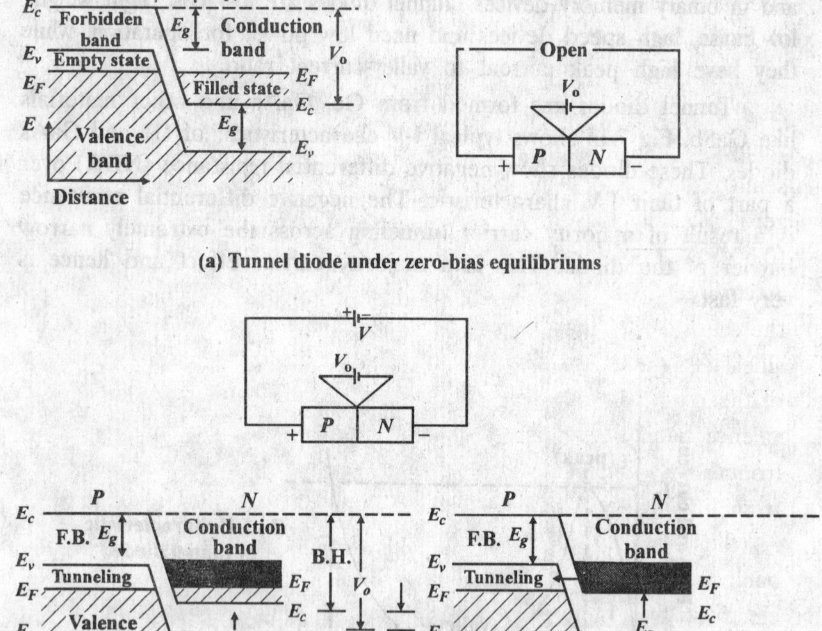

(a) Tunnel diode under zero-bias equilibriums

(1) $0 < V < V_p$ **(2)** $V = V_p$

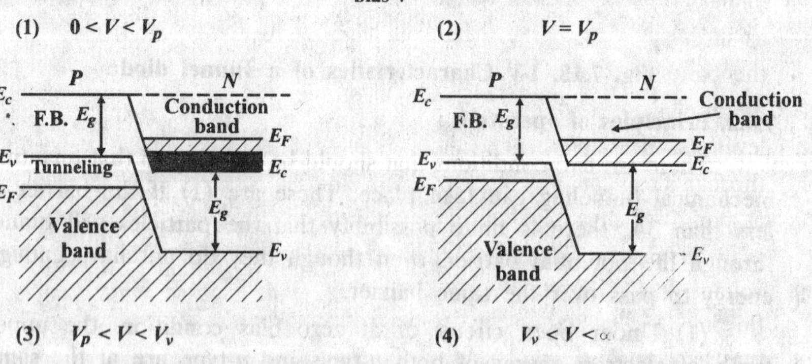

(3) $V_p < V < V_v$ **(4)** $V_v < V < \infty$

(b) Tunnel diode with applied foward bias

Fig. 7.16. Energy band diagram of a Tunnel diode

(2) Besides, the thin barrier, there must be filled energy states on one side of the barrier from which the particles will tunnel and allowed empty states on the other side into which particles penetrate through at the same energy level. In order to understand the tunnel effect we analyze the energy band diagram of the tunnel diode shown in Fig. 7.16.

In ordinary diodes the Fermi level exist in the forbidden band. As the tunnel diodes are very heavily doped, Fermi level exists in the valence band for *p*-type and in the conduction band in *n*-type semiconductors. When the tunnel diode is forward biased between zero and the value that would produce peak tunneling current I_p $(0 < V < V_p)$, the energy diagram is shown in part (1) of Fig. 7.16b. Accordingly, the potential barrier is decreased by the magnitude of the applied forward bias voltage. A difference in Fermi levels in both sides is created. Since there are filled states in the conduction band of the n-type at the same energy level as allowed empty states in the valence band of the *p* type, the electrons tunnel through the barrier from the *n*-type to the *p*-type, giving rise to a forward tunneling current from the *p*-type to the *n*-type as shown in sector (1) of Fig. 7.16b. As the forward bias is increased to V_p, the picture of the energy band is as shown in part (2) of Fig. 7.16b. Maximum number of electrons can tunnel through the barrier from the filled states in the *n*-type to the empty states in the *p*-type, giving rise to the peak current I_p in Fig. 7.15. If the bias is further increased, the condition shown in part (3) of Fig 7.16b is reached. The tunnelling current decreases as shown in sector (3) of Fig. 7.15. Finally, at a very large bias voltage, the band structure of part (4) of Fig. 7.16b is obtained. Since there are now no allowed empty states in the *p*-type at the same energy level as filled states in the *n*-type, hence no electrons can tunnel through the barrier and the tunneling current drops to zero as shown at point (4) of Fig. 7.15.

When the forward bias voltage V is increased above the valley voltage V_v, the ordinary injection current I at the *p-n* junction starts flowing. This injection current increases exponentially with the forward bias as indicated by the dashed curve of Fig. 7.15. The total current, given by the sum of the tunneling current and the injection current, results into the volt-ampere charecteristic of the tunnel diode as shown in Fig. 7.15.

7.4.3. Tunnel Diode Amplifiers

The negative-resistance characteristic of tunnel diode is utilized for fabricating microwave ascillators and amplifiers. The I-V characteristic of a tunnel diode with three load lines is shown in Fig. 7.17.

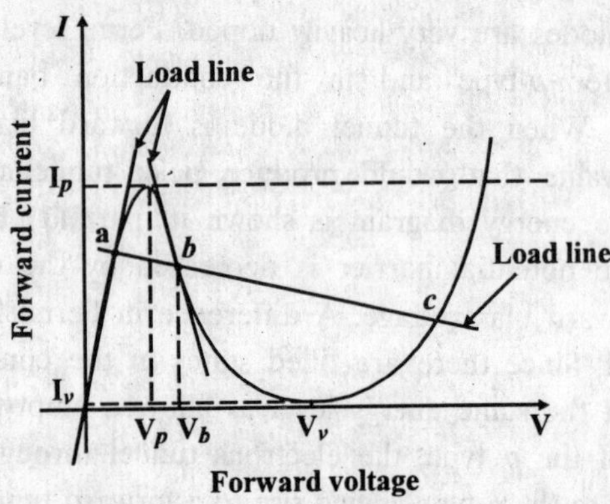

Fig. 7.17. I-V Characteristic of Tunnel diode with load line.

The abc load line intersects the characteristic curve in three points, points a and c are stable points, and point b is astable point. If the voltage and current vary about b. The final values of I and V would be given either by point a or c, but not by b. Since the tunnel diode has two stable states for this load line. The circuit is called bistable, and it can be utilized as a binary device in switching circuits.

The second load line intersects the I-V curve at point b only, this point is stable and shows negative conductance that enables the tunnel diode to function as a microwave amplifier or oscillator. The circuit with a load line crossing at point b in the negative resistance region is called astable. Another load line crossing point a in the positive-resistance region indicates a monostable circuit. The negative conductance in Fig. 7.18 is given by

$$-g = \frac{\partial i}{\partial v} \quad v_b = -\frac{1}{R_n} \qquad ....(7.61)$$

where R_n is the magnitude of negative resistance. For a small variation of the forward voltage V_b, the negative resistance is constant and the diode circuit behaviour is stable. A small signal equivalent circuit for the tunnel diode operated in the negative resistance region as shown is Fig. 7.18 and Here R_s and L_s are the resistance and inductance of packaging circuit, C is the junction capacitance usually measured at valley point.

– R is the negative resistance

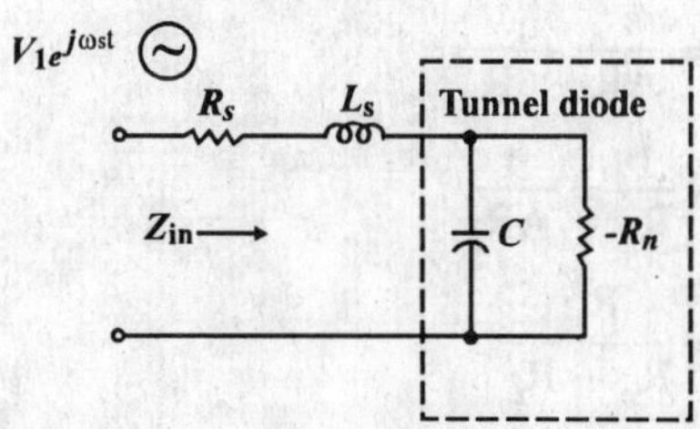

Fig. 7.18. Equivalent circuit of tunnel diode.

Typical values for a tunnel diode are

$R_s = 1\ \Omega$, $L_s = 5$ nH, C = 20 pF and $-R_n = 30\ \Omega$

The input impedance is

$$Z_{in} = R_s + j\omega L_s + \frac{(R_n)\left(\dfrac{j}{\omega C}\right)}{-R_n - \dfrac{j}{\omega C}} \qquad \text{....(7.62)}$$

$$Z_{in} = R_s - \frac{R_n}{1 + (\omega R_n C)^2} + j\left[\omega L_s - \frac{\omega R_n^2 C}{1 + (\omega R_n C)^2}\right] \qquad \text{....(7.63)}$$

For resistive cut off frequency, the real part of Z_{in} should be zero, we get from equation (7.63).

$$f_c = \frac{1}{2\pi R_n C}\sqrt{\frac{R_n}{R_s} - 1} \qquad \text{....(7.63)}$$

For the self resonance frequency, the imaginary part of the input impedance must be zero. Thus

$$f_r = \frac{1}{2\pi R_n C}\sqrt{\frac{R_n^2 C}{L_s} - 1} \qquad \text{....(7.64)}$$

The tunnel diode can be connected either in series or in parallel with a resistive load as an amplifier.

The equivalent circuits are shown in Fig. 7.19a

(1) For parallel loading the gain is equal to

$$\frac{V^2}{R_l} = \frac{V^2}{AR_l} + \frac{V^2}{R_n}$$

where $\frac{1}{R_l} - \frac{1}{R_n} = \frac{1}{AR_l}$

$$A = \frac{R_n}{R_n - R_l} \qquad \text{....(7.65)}$$

When the negative resistance R_n of the tunnel diode approaches the load resistance. A approaches infinity and the system goes into oscillation.

(2) For series loading as shown in Fig. 7.19b the power gain is found as follows :

$$A = \frac{R_l}{R_l - R_n}$$

$$= \frac{1}{1 - R_n/R_l} \qquad \text{....(7.66)}$$

The device remains stable in the negative resistance region without switching if $R_l < R_n$.

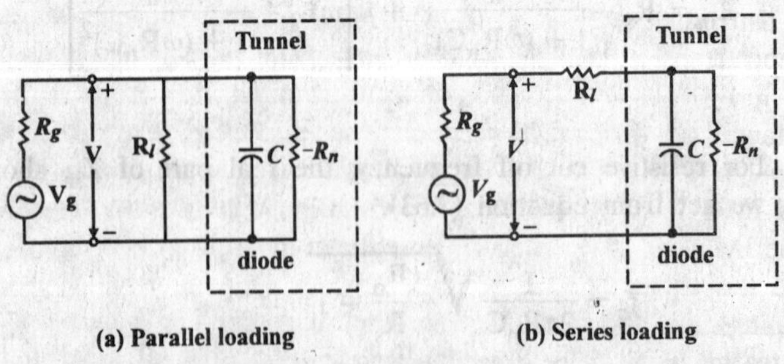

Fig. 7.19 (a) parallel loading (b) Series loading

A tunnel diode connected to a circulator can act as a negative resistance amplifier as shown in Fig. 7.20. A microwave circulator is a multiport junction in which the power may flow only from part 1 to part 2 to part 3, in the direction shown in figure. Microwave circulators with four ports are most commonly used. If the circulator is lossless and has a positive characteristic impedance R_0, an amplifier with infinite gain can be built by selecting a negative-resistance tunnel diode whose input impedance has a real part equal to $-R_0$ and an imaginary part equal to zero. The reflection coefficient is infinite and is given as

$$\Gamma = \frac{-R_n - R_0}{-R_n + R_0} \quad \text{....(7.67)}$$

By setting $R_n = R_0$, an amplifier with infinite gain can be built.

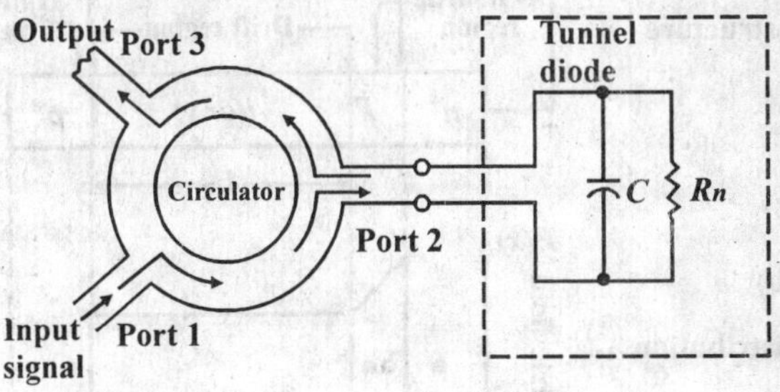

Fig. 7.20. Tunnel diode connected to circulator.

7.5. IMPATT and Related Avalanch Transit Time Devices

Introduction : The word IMPATT is acronym for impact ionization avalanch transit time. These diodes employ impact-ionization and transit time properties of semiconductor structures to produce negative resistance at microwave frequencies. In 1958, Read proposed an n^+–p–i–p^+ structure showing negative resistance properties [7]. Using Read IMPATT diodes Lee et al [8] in 1965, first reported oscillations. In the IMPATT device negative resistance arise from two delays, which cause the current to lag behind voltage. (1) Avalanche delay caused by finite build up time of avalanche current. (2) The transit time delay due to the finite time taken by the carriers to cross the drift region. When these two delays add up to 180°, the diode electronic resistance becomes negative corresponding to that frequency.

The IMPATT diode is one of the most powerful solid state sources of microwave power. For this device typical dc to rf conversion efficiency is 5 to 10%, and frequencies are as high as 100 GHz with silicon diodes. The other mode in this class of devices is the TRAPATT mode, which represents trapped plasma avalanche triggered transit operation. Its typical conversion efficiency is from 20 to 60%.

Allied devices like the BARITT [9] is also an important device at microwave frequencies.

7.5.1. The Physics of IMPATT diodes

The basic operating principle of IMPATT diode can be understood clearly by studying the structure proposed by READ in 1959 known as READ diode. A READ diode structure, doping profile and dc electric field distribution is shown below in Fig. 7.21.

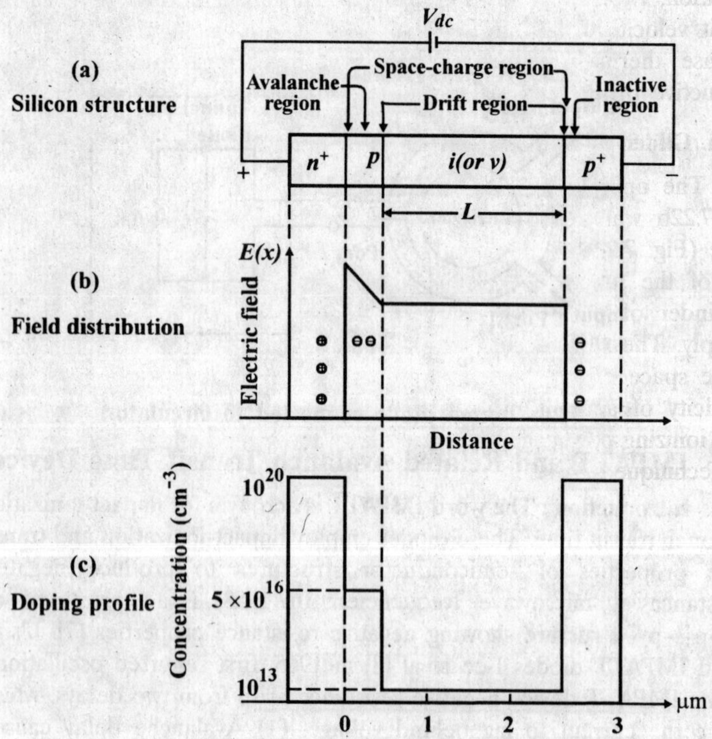

Fig. 7.21. Read diode, Structure, Field distribution and doping profile

When a large reverse bias voltage is applied, some electrons and holes in the region of peak field gain enough energy, and this makes them impact and knock electrons off, or ionize atoms in the crystal lattice. Thus, an impact ionization mechanism creates an electron-holes pair. The electron and holes thus created are accelerated by the field in opposite direction, and can cause additional impact ionization events which result in large multiplication of current or avalanche break down occurs. The multiplied hole current exit to the left of the avalanche zone or in the *p* region, and the multiplied electron current exist to the right or in the *n* region. By proper selection of the doping levels and the thickness of the *p* and *n* region, the transit time delay associated with the hole and electrons moving across their drift regions will generate r-f frequencies in a desired frequency band.

From the above discussion we conclude that for IMPATT operation, two effects are important : (1) Impact ionization, (2) slow transit velocities. Fast transit velocities require thick substrate, which increase thermal resistance, this excessive temperature will cause destructive processes like alloying etc. to occur.

7.5.2a. Gilden and Hines analysis of $p^+ - n$ Read diode

The operation of an avalanche diode can be understood from Fig. 7.22b which shows the field distribution in an avalance p^+–n diode (Fig. 7.22a) A thin part of space charge region exists on the *n* side of the junction, where avalanche multiplication occurs. In the remainder of the space charge region the carrier drift but do not multiply. The drift occurs with the limiting drift velocity v_d for most of the space charge region, as the field involved are very high. For simplicity of analysis, we assume that electrons and holes have the same ionizing power and they move with the same limiting drift velocity V_d. Technique of Gilden and Hines [30] are used to analyse this diode.

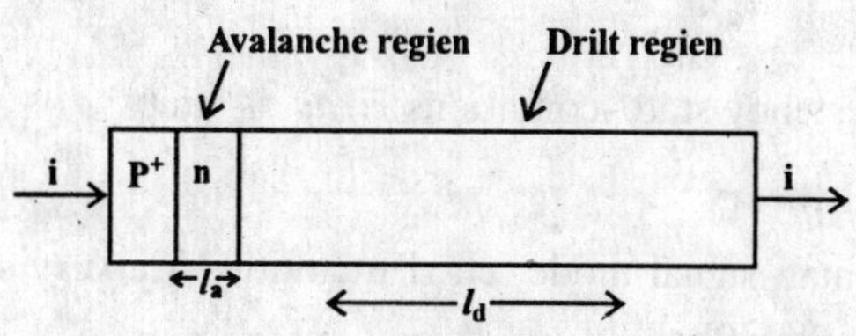

Fig. 7.22a. IMPATT diode (p^+–n dio de)

If p and n are the hole and electron densities, the current densities J_p and J_n are given as below :

$J_p = -ev_d p$ and $J_n = -ev_d n$. The electron-hole pairs are being generated at the rate $\alpha v_d(n+p)$, thermal generation is assumed to be negligible.

The equations of continuity are

$$\frac{\partial P}{\partial t} = -\frac{1}{e}\frac{\partial J_p}{\partial x} + \alpha v_d(n+p) \quad \text{....(7.68)}$$

$$\frac{\partial n}{\partial t} = \frac{1}{e}\frac{\partial J_n}{\partial x} + \alpha v_d(n+p) \quad \text{....(7.69)}$$

where α is the ionization rate.

Add these two equations and put $J_p + J_n = J_a(t)$. Eliminate p and n with the help of the definitions for J_p and J_n, and integrate with respect to x over the avalanche region. If we define the transit time as $\tau_a = l_a/v_d$. Then

$$\tau_a\frac{dI_a}{dt} = (I_p - I_n)\Big|_0^{la} + 2I_a\int_0^{l_a}\alpha dx \quad \text{....(7.70)}$$

In this equation current densities are replaced by currents. If we assume that we are within the avelanche regions so that the junction saturation currents can be neglected, At $x = 0$, $I_p = I_a$, and $I_n = 0$. Also at $x = l_a$, $I_p = 0$ but $I_n = I_a$. Hence Eq. 7.70 can be written as

$$\frac{dI_a}{dt} = \frac{2I_a}{\tau_a}(\overline{\alpha}\, l_a - 1) \quad \text{....(7.71)}$$

where $\overline{\alpha} = \frac{1}{l_a}\int_0^{l_a}\alpha\, dx$ is the average value of α over the avalanche region. For steady-state conditions $\overline{\alpha}\, da$ is unity.

Small signal theory :

In a small signal mode, all rf quantities are very small compared with the dc bias quantities.

Now introduce small-signal deviations. That is, put

$$F = F_0 + F_a, \qquad I_a = I_0 + i_a \quad \text{....(7.72a)}$$

$$\overline{\alpha} = \overline{\alpha}_a + \overline{\alpha}'_a F_a, \qquad \overline{\alpha} l_a = 1 + l_a + \alpha_a^{-1} F_a \quad \text{....(7.72b)}$$

where $\bar{\alpha}'_a$ is the derivative of $\bar{\alpha}$ with respect to F.

Taking into account that F_a and i_a are small-signal perturbations in electric field and current. Substitute these in Eq. 7.71 and neglect second order terms. As the signals are sinusoidal *i.e.* vary as exp ($j\omega t$), $d/dt = j\omega$. current has two components these are the conduction current and the displacement current. Total current i is the sum of these currents. The avalanche conduction current can be written as

$$i_a = \frac{2\bar{\alpha}'_a l_a I_0 F_a}{j\omega\tau_a} = \frac{2\bar{\alpha}'_a I_0}{j\omega\tau_a} v_a \quad ....(7.73)$$

The displacement current in the avalanche zone is

$$i_{da} = j\omega\varepsilon\varepsilon_0 A F_a = j\omega\frac{\varepsilon\,\varepsilon_0 A}{l_a} v_a \quad ....(7.74)$$

where $v_a = F_a l_a$ is the ac voltage across the avalanche region and A is the junction area, see Fig. 7.22b. Hence the total current i is

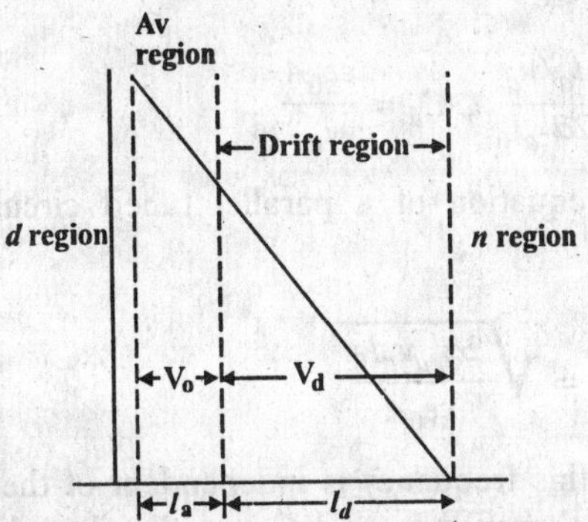

Fig. 7.22b. Field distribution in a avalanching $p^+ - n$ diode.

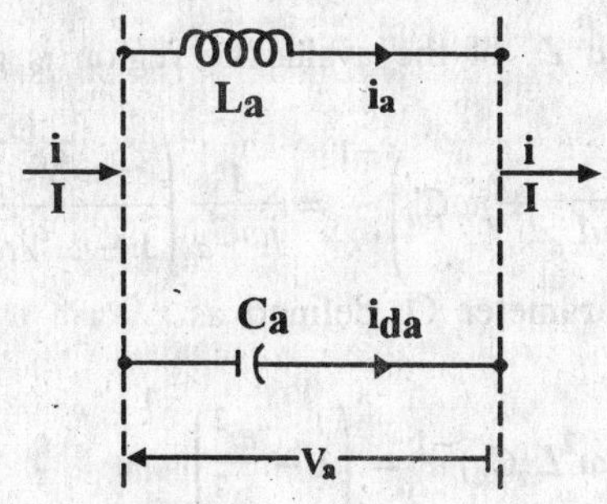

Fig. 7.22c. Current flow in the avalanche region

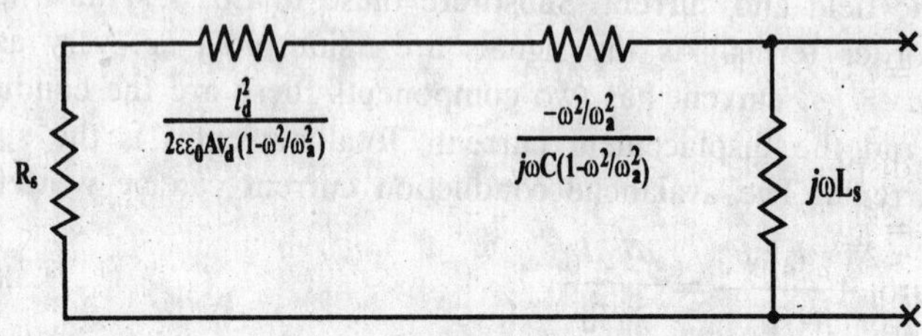

Fig. 7.22d. Equivalent circuit for the small θ.

$$i = i_a + i_{da} = \left(\frac{1}{j\omega L_a} + j\omega C_a\right) v_a \quad \text{....(7.75)}$$

$$\text{where } L_a = \frac{l_a/v_d}{2\bar{\alpha}'_a I_0}, \; C_a = \frac{\varepsilon\varepsilon_0 A}{l_a} \quad \text{....(7.76)}$$

This is the equation of a parallel tuned circuit, tuned at the angular frequency ω_a

$$\omega_a = \frac{1}{\sqrt{L_a C_a}} = \sqrt{\frac{2\bar{\alpha}'_a v_d I_0}{\varepsilon\varepsilon_0 A}} \quad \text{....(7.77)}$$

We see that this frequency is independent of the avelanche zone thickness length la, because L_a and C_a are distributed parameters and the resonant frequency is a parameter of each small section of the avalanche region.

The impedance Z_a of the avalanche region is given as

$$Z_a = \frac{v_a}{i} = \left(\frac{1}{j\omega L_a} + j\omega C_a\right)^{-1} = \frac{1}{j\omega C_a}\left(\frac{-\omega^2/\omega_a^2}{1-\omega^2/\omega_a^2}\right) \quad \text{....(7.78)}$$

Introduce a parameter Q, defined as

$$Q = \frac{i_a}{i} = (1-\omega^2 L_a C_a)^{-1} = \left(1-\frac{\omega^2}{\omega_a^2}\right)^{-1} \quad \text{....(7.79)}$$

The convection current i_c, drifts in the drift region unattenuated with the drift velocity v_d. The convection current i_c is continuous at the boundary of the drift region, hence can be written as

$$i_c(x) = i_a \exp\left(-\frac{j\omega x}{v_d}\right) = iQ \exp\left(-\frac{j\omega x}{v_d}\right) \qquad ....(7.80)$$

The displacement current is given as

$$i_d(x) = j\omega\varepsilon\varepsilon_0 \, AF_a(x) \qquad ....(7.81)$$

The total current $i = i_c(x) + i_d(x)$ is independent of x, the ac field strength in the drift-region

$$F_a(x) = i\frac{1 - Q\exp(-i\omega x/v_d)}{j\omega\varepsilon\varepsilon_0 A} \qquad ....(7.82)$$

Integrate this expression over the drift length *la* to obtain the ac voltage v_d, across the drift region.

$$v_d = \frac{l_a i}{j\omega\varepsilon\varepsilon_0 A}\left\{1 - \frac{1}{1 - \dfrac{\omega^2}{\omega_a^2}}\left[\frac{1 - \exp(-j\theta)}{j\theta}\right]\right\} \qquad ....(7.83)$$

where $\theta = \dfrac{\omega l_a}{v_a} = \omega\tau_d$ is the transit angle, τ_d is the transit time through the drift region.

If $C_d = \varepsilon\varepsilon_0 A/l_d$ is the capacitance of the drift region, the impedance of the drift region is

$$Z_d = \frac{v_{dv}}{i} = \frac{1}{j\omega C_d}\left(1 - \frac{(\sin\theta)/\theta}{1 - \omega^2/\omega_a^2}\right) + \frac{1}{\omega C_d}\left[\frac{(1-\cos\theta)/\theta}{1 - \omega^2/\omega_a^2}\right] \qquad ....(7.84)$$

$$= \frac{1}{j\omega C_d}\left(1 - \frac{(\sin\theta)/\theta}{1 - \omega^2/\omega_a^2}\right) + \frac{l_d^2}{2\varepsilon\varepsilon_0 A v_d}\left[\frac{2(1-\cos\theta)/\theta^2}{1 - \omega^2/\omega_a^2}\right]$$

Beyond the drift region, the remaining part of the diode has a series resistance R_s, the total impedance of the device is

$$Z_{to} = R_s + Z_d + Z_a$$

$$= R_s + \frac{l_d^2}{2\varepsilon\varepsilon_0 A v_d}\left[\frac{2(1-\cos\theta)/\theta^2}{1 - \omega^2/\omega_a^2}\right] + \frac{1}{j\omega C_d}$$

$$\left[\frac{1 - \frac{\sin\theta}{\theta} - \left(\omega^2/\omega_a^2\right)\left(\frac{1 + la/l_d}{1 - \omega^2/\omega_a^2}\right)}{1 - \frac{\omega^2}{\omega_a^2}}\right] \quad \text{....(7.85)}$$

θ is relatively small, so $(\sin\theta)/\theta \approx 1$ and $2(1 - \cos\theta)/\theta^2 \approx 1$ Eq. 7.85 may then be written as

$$Z = R_s + \frac{l_d^2}{2\varepsilon\varepsilon_0 A v_d}\left(\frac{1}{1 - \omega^2/\omega_a^2}\right) + \frac{1}{j\omega C}\left(\frac{-\omega^2/\omega_a^2}{1 - \omega^2/\omega_a^2}\right) \quad \text{....(7.86)}$$

where $C = \varepsilon\varepsilon_0 A/(l_a + l_d)$ is the net capacitance of the space charge region, when the diode is biased just below avalanche breakdown. The second term in Eq. (7.86) is negative for $\omega > \omega_a$. The third term has similarity with a parallel resonant circuit which includes the diode capacitance C and a shunt inductor. Hence, to make the diode oscillate, a parallel inductance L has to be added to the equivalent circuit.

It is clear from the second term that strong negative-resistance effects occur for relatively small transit angles. This negative resistance effect shows, why the diode will oscillate for frequencies $\omega > \omega_a$. Thus we understand that avalanche diodes will oscillate at microwave frequencies.

Avalanche multiplication

The velocity of electron and holes drift in the space charge region at a constant velocity v_d and is about 10^7 cm/s for silicon. The field throughout the space charge region is above 5 kV/cm. The transit time of a hole across the drift length L is

$$\tau = \frac{L}{v_d} \quad \text{....(7.87a)}$$

and the avalanche multiplication factor is

$$M = \frac{1}{1 - (V/V_b)^n} \quad \text{....(7.87b)}$$

where

V = applied voltage

V_b = avalanche break down voltage

n = 3 to 6 for silicon is a numerical factor depending on the doping of p^+-n or n^+-p junction.

The break down voltage for a silicon P^+-n junction can be expressed as

$$|V_b| \approx \frac{\rho_n \mu_n \varepsilon_s |E_{max}|_b^2}{2} \quad \text{....(7.87c)}$$

where

ρ_n = resistivity

μ_n = electron mobility.

ε_s = semiconductor permittivity

E_{max} = maximum break down of the electric field

Fig. 7.23 shows the avalanche break down voltage as a function of impurity at a p^+–n junction for several semiconductors.

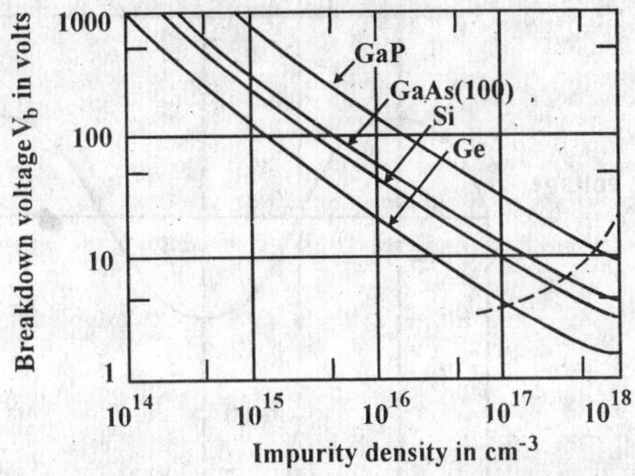

Fig. 7.23. Breakdown voltage versus impurity doping

To understand the working of a Read diode, consider that the Read diode is mounted in a microwave resonant circuit, the a c voltage in the microwave cavity is maintained at a given frequency. Let us assume that the field is just below the critical field for avalanche break down. If an RF voltage is superimposed over this bias, the total field will go above the requirement for avalanche breakdown during the positive half cycle. Throughout this interval an exponential increase of the avalanche charge continues. During the negative half cycle the total field is below this critical value and the avalanche process decays. The growth rate of the carriers is exponential and peak charge is obtained at the end of the positive half cycle of the AC. This build up of the avalanche charge is shown in Fig. 7.24.

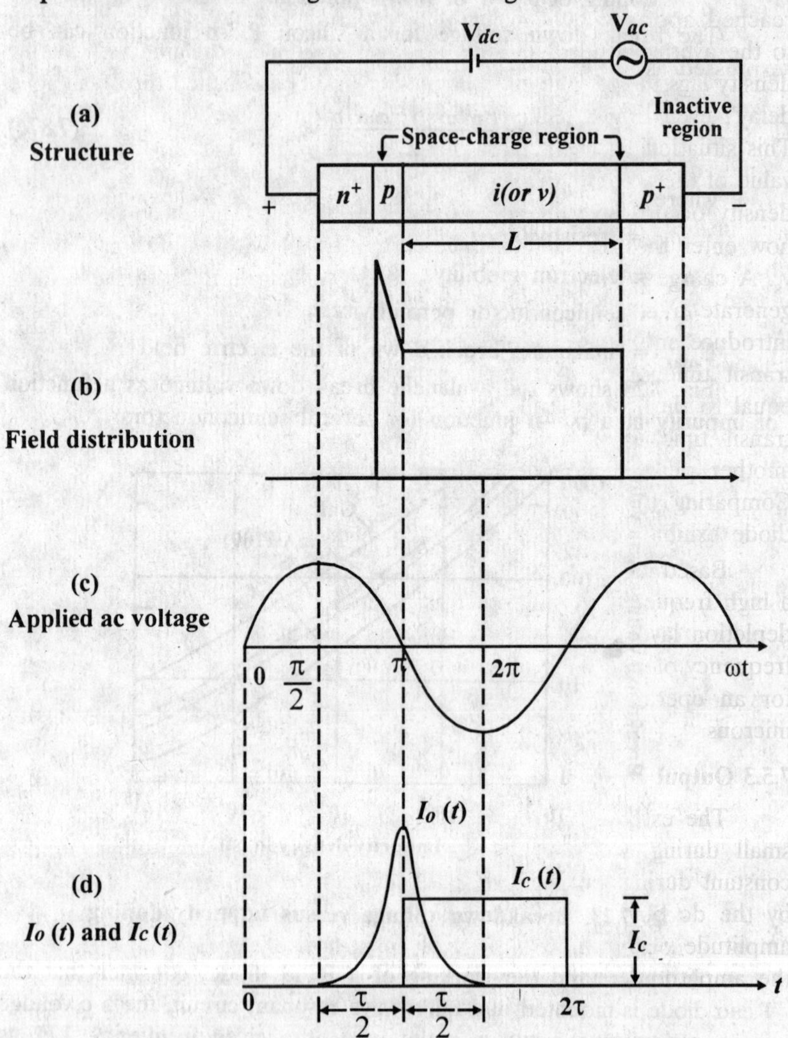

Fig. 7.24. Field Voltage and Current in Read diode

As the electric field changes periodically with time the impact ionization rate per carrier follows the field charge nearly instantaneously. However, the carrier density does not follow the field charge exactly, because the carrier generation also depends on the number of carriers already present. As such, even the field has crossed its maximum value, the carrier density keeps increasing, because the carrier generation rate is still above the average value. The maximum carrier density is reached approximately, when the field has decreased from the peak to the average value E_0. Thus the ac variation of the injected carrier density lags the ac voltage by about 90° and this is called the 'avalanche delay', even though the ionization rate is in phase with the ac field. This situation is shown as the injected current in Fig. 7.24a. The peak value of the ac field occurs at $\pi/2$ but the peak of the injected carrier density occurs at a delay of $(\pi/2 - \pi)$ or 90°. The injected carriers now enter the drift region, where they travel with saturation velocity v_s. A charge moving at constant velocity within an electric field would generate a constant velocity in the external circuit. This will again introduce another delay of 90° known as transit time delay. The finite transit time of the carriers results in a current pulse of a duration equal to the transit time. If the width of the *i*-layer is such that the transit time through it is half AC cycle, the external current has another phase delay of 90°. Hence the total delay will be of 180°. Comparing the ac voltage and the external current shows that the diode exhibits a negative resistance at its terminals.

Based on these arguments, Read pointed out that one can design a high frequency negative resistance diode. As pointed out earlier the depletion layer width should be equal to half the time period of the frequency of operation. The saturation velocity for Si is $\approx 10^7$ cm/sec, for an operation at 5 GHz the width of the *i*-layer should be 10 microns.

7.5.3 Output Power and Quality Factor

The external current $I_e(t)$ approaches a square wave, it is very small during the positive half cycle of the ac voltage and almost constant during the negative half cycle. The direct current I_d supplied by the dc bias is the average external current. It is noted that the amplitude of variation of $I_e(t)$ is approximately equal to I_d. If Va is the amplitude of the ac voltage, the ac power delivered is given by

$$P = 0.707\ V_a I_d \text{ W/unit area} \qquad ....(7.45)$$

The quality factor Q is defined as

$$Q = \omega \frac{\text{maximum energy stored}}{\text{average dissipated power}}$$

The Read diode supplies ac energy, hence it has negative Q while Q of the cavity is positive. At the stable operating point, the negative Q of the diode is equal to the positive Q of the cavity circuit. If the amplitude of the ac voltage increases, the stored energy or energy of oscillation increases faster than the energy delivered per cycle. For stable oscillations this is the necessary condition.

7.5.3. Equivalent circuit of IMPATT diode :

An equivalent circuit for the IMPATT diode package is shown in Fig 7.25.

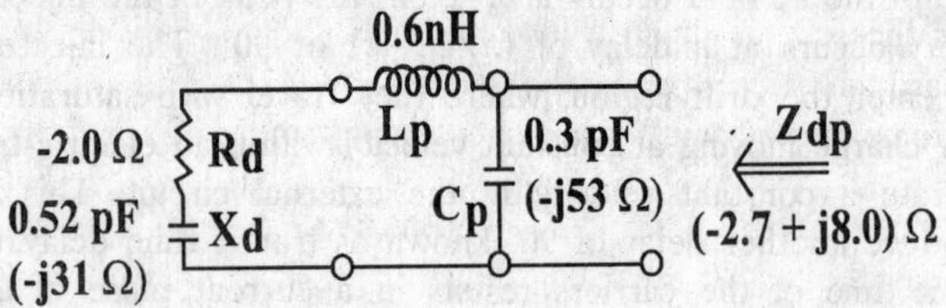

Fig. 7.25. Equivalent Circuit for the IMPATT diode package

The negative resistance R_D is in series with a reactance X_D. The package is described by a series inductance L_p and a shunt capacitance C_p. The value of L_p is changed by the microwave circuit surrounding the diode. Typical values for a commercially available diode is also shown in the Fig. 7.25. Some important properties of chip equivalent circuit 7.25. are (1) The magnitude of negative resistance. R_D is generally much smaller than that of the reactance X_D resulting in the chip impedance mainly comprising of X_D. (2) X_D in most cases of interest can be approximated with the reactance of chip junction capacitance at the break down voltage. (3) Values of net negative resistance are generally small compared to the usual transmission line impedance. Typical value vary between – 0.7 ohms to – 2.0 ohms.

Various types of circuits have been reported for IMPATT diode oscillators and amplifiers. These can be classified in three groups : broadly tunable circuits, low Q circuits and high Q.

7.5.5. IMPATT diode oscillators and amplifiers

(i) Broadly tunable circuit

These are very flexible circuits that can be used for the study of IMPATT diode properties in laboratory. One of them is the multiple slug tuned cavity in a coaxial cavity as shown in Fig. 7.26(a) and (b). In the figure there are two low characteristic impledance regions equal to 10 and 20 ohms. Location of these slugs can be changed by sliding them over the central conductor. Normally the distance between slugs is $\lambda/4$ at central frequency. By adjusting the position of slugs, its is possible to match diodes of different impedances. When the distance between the first slug B and the shorted end of the coaxial line S is approximately half wave length, this region behaves as a resonator and the two slugs control the coupling between the cavity and the output line. A tunable waveguide oscillator circuit, Fig. 7.26b shows the schematic illustration of a tunable wave guide oscillator. A standard short can be used for tuning. For smaller tuning range requirements, a fixed short and a tuning screw can be used.

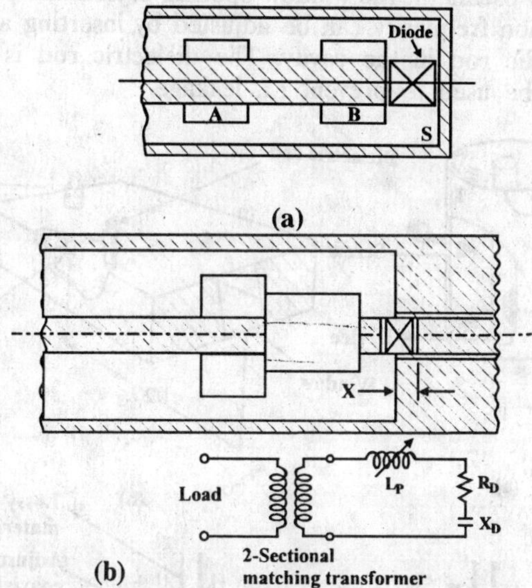

Fig. 7.26. Broadly tunable circuit.

(ii) Low Q oscillator and amplifier circuit

These are the simplest possible IMPATT diode circuits. They do not possess frequency tunability. These low Q circuits are primarily used in applications where the frequency stability and noise capability of the diode can be controlled by injection phase locking techniques. They are typically used as FM transmitters, CW Doppler radar transmitters and as up-convertor pump. Circuit configuration for these oscillators include coaxial circuits with suitable transformation from the diode to transmission line impedance and waveguide circuit with the diode mounted on a post at a fixed distance from the shorted end.

(iii) High Q Low Noise Oscillators

The noise performance and frequency stability achieved with these circuits is comparable with local oscillator requirements in radar, telemetery and telecommunication receivers. Sufficient power is available from these oscillators to make them suitable for low power transmitters and for parametric amplifier pumps, as well as for police radars. A coupled coaxial waveguide oscillator is most commonly used for this class of oscillators. The design consists of a coaxial resonator which is strongly coupled to a high Q waveguide resonator as shown in Fig. 7.27. Fig. 7.27a and 7.27b shows a coaxial cavity oscillator and waveguide cavity oscillator. The oscillation frequency in the coaxial cavity oscillator is adjusted by inserting a screw through the sidewall and the loading can be adjusted by rotating the coupling loop to the load. In the waveguide cavity oscillator, the window opening determines the loading, and the oscillation frequency can be adjusted by inserting a dielectric rod or a metallic rod in the cavity. The dielectric rod is preferred because it can be used to prevent r.f. leakage.

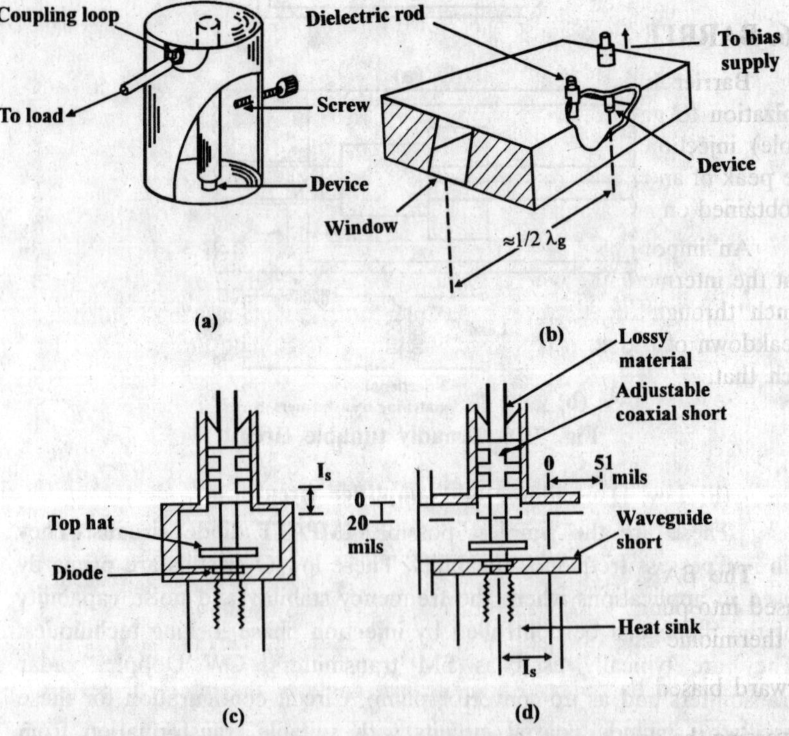

Fig. 7.27 (a) Coaxial cavity oscillator (b) waveguide cavity oscillator (c), (d) Resonate cap (top hat) circuit.

At millimeter wave frequencies the cavity dimensions become very small and losses are substantial. Circuit loss is crucial for low impedance IMPATT diodes. To overcome this problem, resonant cap circuits as shown in Fig. 7.27c and 7.27d are used. The impedance presented to the diode is controlled by the diameter of the disk, or the movable waveguide short circuit.

7.5.6. IMPATT diode power combiners

Efficient power combiners have been considered. A combiner with modest number of these diodes could fill important radar transmitter's applications.

Power combiners can be designed in two configurations – (1) A cluster of these devices can be combined at the device level in a region which remains small compared with a wavelength, (2) the devices can be combined at the circuit level to achieve desired output power.

7.6. BARRIT Diodes

Barrier Injection Transit Time (BARRIT) devices avoid impact ionization to get rid of high noise [9]. In these devices, the minority (hole) injection is provided by punch through of the drift region at the peak of an rf cycle in say, a *p-n-p* structure. The negative resistance is obtained on account of the drift of the injected holes to the collector.

An important essential requirement for the BARRIT device is that the intermediate drift region must be completely depleted to cause punch through the emitter base junction without causing avalanche breakdown of the base collector junction. The doping density must be such that.

$$\int_0^{W_d} N_d(x)dx = E_{max} < E_{BD} \quad \text{....(7.89)}$$

The BARITT diode is basically a back-to-back pair of diodes biased into punch through condition. Microwave oscillations occur due to thermionic injection and diffusion of minority carriers across the forward biased barrier and a $\frac{3\pi}{2}$ transit angle of the injected carriers traversing the drift region. BARITT diodes are low in power efficiency, but have good signal to noise performance, and are useful as local oscillators in microwave receivers. Fig. 7.28a show a BARITT diode.

It consists of a M–n–M structure. The energy band diagram at thermal equilibrium is shown in Fig. 7.28b. Where Q_{n1} and Q_{n2} are the barrier heights for the metal-semiconductor contacts respectively.

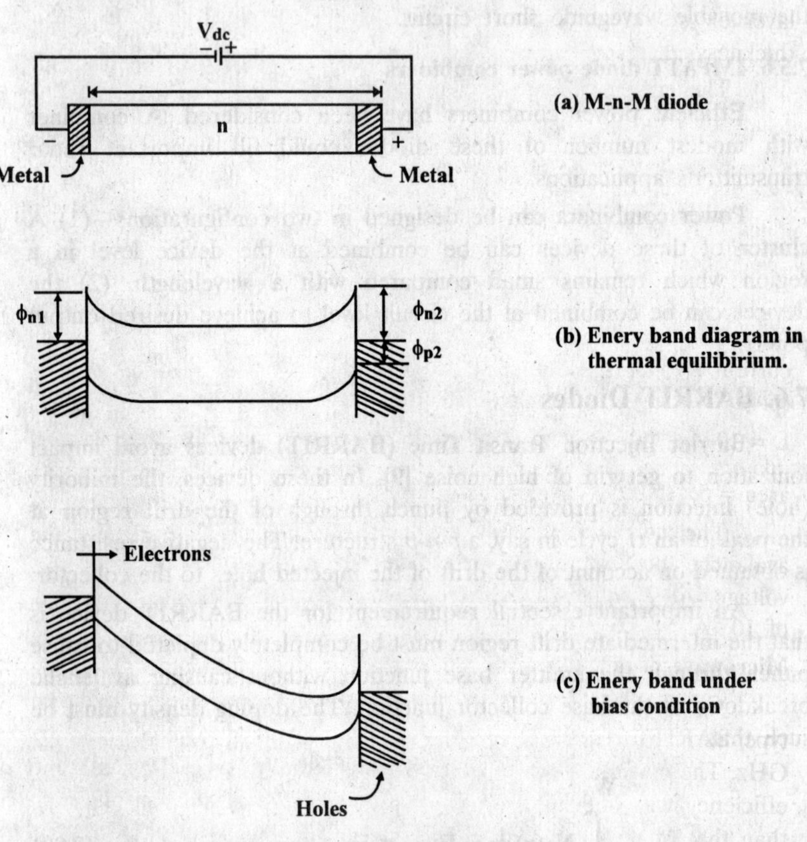

Fig. 7.28 M-n-M diode.

A n-type crystal wafer of about 10 micron thickness is sandwitched between two Pi-Si shottkey barrier contacts of about 10.0 micron thickness to obtain this structure of Fig. 7.28. For this Pt-Si-Si-PtSi structure, $\phi_{n_1} = \phi_{n_2} = 0.85$ eV. The hole barrier height for the forward-biased contact is about 0.15 eV. The mechanisms responsible for the microwave oscillations are (1) the rapid increase of the carrier injection process caused by the decreasing potential barrier of the forward-biased metal semiconductor contact. (2) An apparent $\frac{3\pi}{2}$ transit angle of the injected carrier traversing the semiconductor depletion region. The rapid increase in terminal current with applied voltage (above 30V) as shown in Fig. 7.28c is caused by thermionic hole injection into the semiconductor as the depletion layer of the reverse biased contact reaches through the entire device thickness.

The critical voltage is approximately given by

$$v_c = \frac{qNL^2}{2\varepsilon_s}$$

where N = doping concentration

L = semiconductor thickness

ε_s = semiconductor dielectric permittivity.

The breakdown voltage is double of the critical voltage. The current voltage characteristic of the silicon MSM structure ($pt - Si - Si - Pt\,Si$) were measured for a device with dimensions as $L = 10\,\mu m$, $N = 4\times10^{14}\,cm^3, \phi_{n_1} = \phi_{n_2} = 0.85$ eV and area = $5\times10^{-4} cm^2$ at 77K and 300K.

The current increases as shown in Fig. 7.28d is not due to avalanche multiplication, as is clear from the magnitude of the critical voltage. At 77K the rapid increase in current is stopped at a current of 10^{-5}A.

Microwave performance

Continuous-wave (CW) microwave performance of the M-n-M type BARITT diode observed was over the entire C band of 4 to 8 GHz. The maximum power observed was 50 mW at 4.9 GHz, maximum efficiency was about 1.8%. The noise measure is substantially lower than that of a silicon IMPATT diode and is comparable to that of a GaAs transfer oscillator [9].

7.7. TRAPATT Diodes

TRAPATT stands for trapped plasma avalanche triggered transit mode. It was first reported by Prager et.al. [10]. It is a high efficiency microwave oscillator capable of operating from several hundred megahertz to several gigahertz. The operating principle of the diode is that a high field avalanche zone propagates through the diode and fills the depletion layer with a dense plasma of electrons and holes that become trapped in the low field region behind the zone [11, 12].

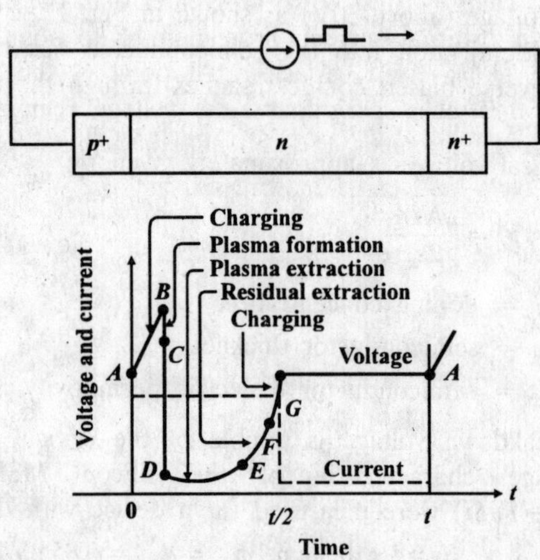

Fig. 7.29. Voltage and Current Waveforms for TRAPATT diode

A typical voltage waveform for the TRAPATT mode of avalanche P^+-n-n^+ diode operating with an assumed square wave current is shown in Fig. 7.29. At point A the electric field is uniform throughout the sample and its magnitude is large but less than the value required for avalanche breakdown. At point A the current is turned on, at this instant only charge present are due to thermal generation, the diode initially charges like a capacitor and the magnitude of the electric field reaches above the breakdown voltage. When the particle current exceeds the external current and the electric field is depressed throughout the depletion region, causes the voltage to decrease. This is shown in the figure from point B to C. during this time interval electric field is sufficiently large for the avalanche to continue, and a dense plasma of electrons and holes is created. Some of the electrons and holes drift out of the ends of the depletion layer, and the field is further depressed, hence 'traps' the remaining plasma. The voltage then decreases to point D. A long time is required to remove the plasma because the total plasma charge is large compared to the charge per unit time in the external circuit. At point E the plasma is removed, but a residual charge of electrons remains in one end of the depletion layer and a residual charge of holes in the other end.

As the residual charge is removed, the voltage increases from point E to point F. At F all the charge generated internally has been removed. This charge is just equal or greater than the external charge supplied by the external current. From point F to point G, the diode charges again like a fixed capacitor. At point G the diode current goes to zero for half a period and the voltage remains constant at V_A until the current comes back on and the cycle repeats.

The electric field can be expressed as

$$E(x,t) = E_m - \frac{qN_A}{\varepsilon_s}x + \frac{Jt}{\varepsilon_s} \quad \text{....(7.90)}$$

where

N_A = Doping concentration of *n* region

ε_s = Semiconductor permittivity

E_m = The value of electric field at a given distance *x* into the depletion region and is obtained by setting

$E(x, t)$ = E_m. We get from Eq 7.90

$$t = \frac{qN_A}{J}x \quad \text{....(7.91)}$$

Differentiating Eq. 7.91 with respect to t, we get v_z the avalanche-zone velocity

$$v_z = \frac{dx}{dt} = \frac{J}{qN_A}$$

Thus the avalanche zone will quickly sweep across almost entire diode, and the diode will be filled by highly conducting electron hole plasma whose space charge depresses the voltage to low values. The drift velocity depends on particles mobilities, hence the transit time of the carrier becomes much longer than the transit time τ_s

$$\tau_s = \frac{L}{v_s} \quad \text{....(7.92)}$$

where v_s is the saturated carrier drift velocity.

Because of the large extraction time of the electron hole plasma, TRAPATT diodes operate at comparatively low frequencies below 10 GHz. The noise behaviour of TRAPATT diodes is even worse than that of the IMPATT diodes, because extremely large fluctuations occur in the start up of the current by avalanche multiplication.

TRAPATT oscillators have high output power and high efficiency. Voltage during plasma extraction period is very low, hence very high efficiency. These oscillators are mostly used for pulse operation. The maximum efficiency achievable in this mode is about 80%. A typical silicon TRAPATT diode when used for the pulsed operation in 1-2 GHz range gave output power of 1 KW and efficiency about 60 per cent.

7.8. Gunn Diode

Introduction

Transferred electron devices (TEDs) or Gunn diodes are one of the most important microwave devices used as local oscillators and as power amplifiers unlike transistors the Gunn diodes are bulk effect devices. The Gunn diode is fabricated from compound semiconductors such as gallium-Arsenide (GaAs), Indium Phosphide (InP) or Cadmium-Telluride (CdTe). TEDs operate with 'hot' electrons whose energy is very much greater than the thermal energy. Gunn diodes have been operated up to 100 GHz with CW power levels reaching 2 watts, efficiencies of up to 15 per cent, and pulse power levels of about 500W at about 20 per cent efficiency. These devices are tunable over a wide frequency range, have low noise characteristics, and are simple to fabricate and inexpensive.

7.8.1. Device physics

In 1963, Gunn discovered that coherent microwave output was generated when a dc electric field was applied across a short *n*-type sample of GaAs, or InP. The dc electric field was of the order of threshold value of 3-5 kV/cm. The efficiency of oscillations was approximately equal to reciprocal of the carrier transit time across the length of the sample. In 1963 Ridley, Watkinson and Hilsum [15] proposed a theory of negative differential resistance (NDR) according to which there is a decrease in carrier velocity (mobility) with an increase in the electric field. Some materials like GaAs, InP etc. show negative diferential mobility, the mechanism responsible for this (NDM) is a field induced transfer of conduction band electrons from a low energy, high mobility valley to higher energy, low mobility satellite valley.

Some materials like GaAs show two valleys in the conduction band as shown in Fig. 7.30 with the characteristics given in table 7.2.

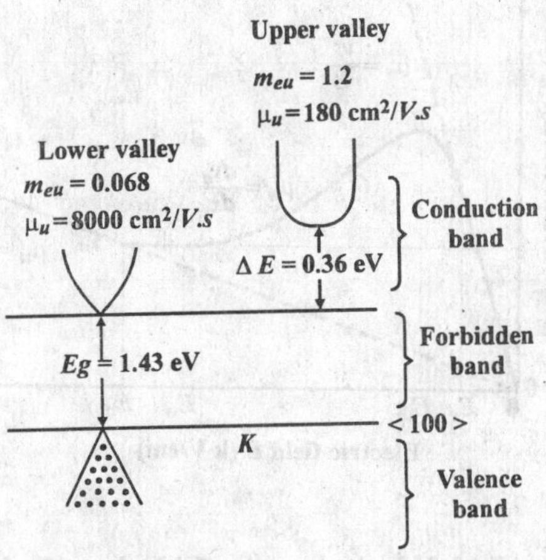

Fig. 7.30. Two valley model of n-type GaAs

At zero voltage, the average energy of the electrons is the thermal energy KT (0.025 eV at room temperature). This energy is less than the energy gap ΔE between two valleys in the conduction band, hence most of the electrons are in the lower valley Γ. As the voltage is increased, the electrons are accelerated by the electric field. Electrons in the lower vallelly (Γ) get transferred to the X valley. When the energy gained by the electrons from the applied electric field is comparable to ΔE, the rate of transfer of electrons from lower to upper valley increases. This transfer of electrons from Γ to X valley gives rise to a velocity versus field characteristic as shown in Fig. 7.31. The negative differential mobility characteristic of GaAs may be used for amplification or generation of microwaves. On the basis of Redley - Watkins - Helsum Theory the conditions necessary for the transferred electron effect to occur can be summarised as follows :

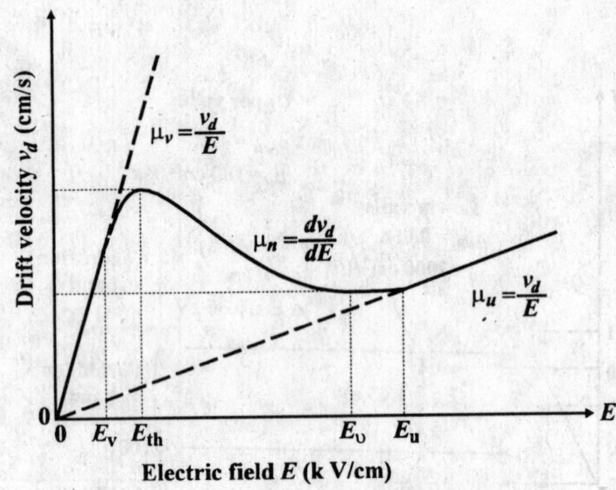

Fig. 7.31 Velocity versus field characteristic

(1) The separation between the lower Γ and upper X valley must be much larger than thermal energy (≈ 0.026 eV) at room temperature, *i.e.* $\Delta E = (E_X - E_\Gamma) > KT$

(2) The separation energy ΔE between the valleys must be smaller than the gap energy so that the electric field required for electron transfer is much smaller than the breakdown field.

(3) Electrons in the lower valley must have high mobility small effective mass and a low density of states (so that electron transfer from upper valley is not allowed) whereas those in the upper valley must have low mobility, large effective mass and high density of state. In other words, electron velocities (dE / dK) must be much larger in the lower valley than in the upper valley.

The two most popular elemental semi-conductors Si and Ge do not meet all these criteria, while some compound semi-conductors like GaAs, InP and CdTe do satisfy these criteria.

The negative differential resistivity can be of two types in a bulk solid state III-IV compound when either a voltage or a current is applied to the terminals of a sample the voltage controlled and current controlled modes are shown in Fig. 7.32. In the voltage controlled mode, the current density can be multivalued whereas in the current controlled mode the voltage can be multivalued.

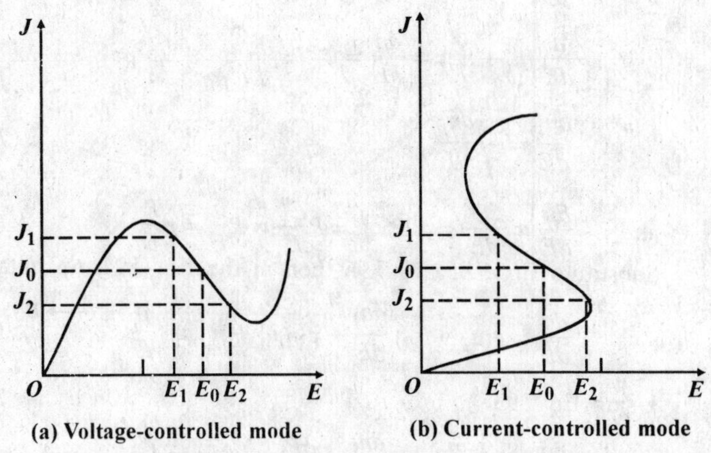

(a) Voltage-controlled mode

(b) Current-controlled mode

Fig. 7.32. Multiple values of current density for negative resistance.

Table 7.2.

Valley	Effective mess m_e	Mobility μ	Seperation ΔE
Lower	$M_{el} = 0.068$	$\mu_l = 8000$ cm^3/V Sec	$\Delta E = 0.36$ eV
Upper	$M_{eu} = 1.2$	$\mu_u = 180$ cm^2/V Sec	$\Delta E = 0.35$ eV

7.8.2. Negative differential resistance :

Let us understand the mechanism of negative differential resistance in a semiconductor. Consider *n*-type GaAs sample with upper and lower valleys. Let the electron densities in the upper and lower valleys to be n_u and n_l, μ_u and μ_l the electron mobilities in the upper and lower valleys respectively. Then the conductivity σ of the *n*-type GaAs is given by Eq. 7.93.

$$\sigma = J/E = e(n_l\mu_l + n_u\mu_u) \qquad \text{....(7.93)}$$

On applying high electric field to the GaAs sample, the electrons are accelerated and their effective temperature rises above the lattice temperature. The electron densities n_l, n_u and the mobilities (μ_l, μ_u) both are functions of the electric field, Differentiating equation (7.93) with respect to E, We obtain

$$\frac{d\sigma}{dE} = e\left(\mu_l \frac{dn_l}{dE} + \mu_u \frac{dn_u}{dE}\right) + e\left(n_l \frac{d\mu_l}{dE} + n_u \frac{d\mu_u}{dE}\right) \qquad \text{....(7.94)}$$

If $(n_l + n_u) = n$, the total current density, and it is also assumed that μ_l, and μ_u are proportional to E^{P}, where P is constant, then

$$\frac{d}{dE}(n_l + n_u) = \frac{dn}{dE} = 0 \qquad \text{....(7.95a)}$$

$$\text{or} \quad \frac{dn_l}{dE} = -\frac{dn_u}{dE} \qquad \text{....(7.95b)}$$

$$\text{and} \quad \frac{d\mu}{dE} \propto \frac{dE^p}{dE} = PE^{p-1} = P\frac{E^p}{E} \propto P\frac{\mu}{E} = \mu\frac{P}{E} \qquad \text{....(7.96)}$$

Substitute Eq. 7.95a to 7.96 then in the Eq. 7.94, we obtain

$$\frac{d\sigma}{dE} = e(\mu_l - \mu_u)\frac{dn_l}{dE} + e(n_l\mu_l + n_u\mu_u)\frac{P}{E} \qquad \text{....(7.97)}$$

Using Eq 7.93

$$\frac{d\sigma}{dE} = e(\mu_l - \mu_u)\frac{dn_l}{dE} + \frac{\sigma P}{E} \qquad \text{....(7.97b)}$$

When Ohm's law, (J = σE) is differentiated with respect to E. It results into

$$\frac{dJ}{dE} = \sigma + \frac{d\sigma}{dE}E \qquad \text{....(7.98)}$$

This can be rearranged into

$$\frac{1}{\sigma}\frac{dJ}{dE} = 1 + \frac{d\sigma/dE}{\sigma/E} \qquad \text{....(7.99)}$$

We see, from Eq. 7.99, for negative resistance current density J must decrease with increasing field E, or the ratio dJ/dE must be negative. This is only possible, when right hand side term of equation 7.99 is less than zero, or the condition,

$$-\frac{d\sigma/dE}{\sigma/E} > 1 \qquad \text{....(7.100a)}$$

is satisfied. Using Eq. 7.97b

$$-\frac{E}{\sigma}\left[e(\mu_l - \mu_u)\frac{dn_l}{dE} + \frac{\sigma p}{E}\right] > 1 \qquad \text{....(7.100b)}$$

$$\text{or } -\frac{Ee(\mu_l - \mu_u)}{\sigma}\frac{dn_l}{dE} - P > 1$$

Substitute for σ from Eq. 7.93

$$-\frac{Ee(\mu_l - \mu_u)}{e(\mu_l n_l + \mu_u n_u)}\frac{dn_l}{dE} - P > 1 \quad \text{....(7.100c)}$$

Replace $n_u/n_l = f$, we obtain

$$\left[\left(\frac{\mu_l - \mu_u}{\mu_l + \mu_{uf}}\right)\left(-\frac{E}{n_l}\frac{dn_l}{dE}\right) - P\right] > 1 \quad \text{....(7.101)}$$

Eq. 7.101 gives the condition for negative resistance.

Field exponent P is a function of lattice scattering mechanism and is a large negative quantity. This factor makes impurity scattering undesirable because if it is dominant, the mobility will rise with increase in field, and *P* becomes positive. But when lattice scattering is dominant, *P* is negative and will depend upon the lattice and carrier temperature. In Equation 7.101, the term in first bracket must be positive in order to satisfy unequality. This will be possible, if $\mu_l > \mu_u$, that is, the electrons should be transferred from the low mass valley to high mass valley when the electric field is applied (heated). When $\mu_l >> \mu_u$, the 1st term $\left(\frac{\mu_l - \mu_u}{\mu_l + f\mu_u}\right)$ tends to be one, and this is the maximum value this factor can attain. The factor (dn_l/dE) in the second bracket must be negative. This factor represents the rate at which electrons transfer to upper valley with respect to the electric field, which in turn depends on the differences between the electron densities, electron temperature and energy gap between the two valleys. Hence we conclude.

(1) *P* must be negative and large.

(2) $\frac{\mu_l - \mu_u}{\mu_l + f\mu_u}$ should be positive; *i.e.*, $\mu_l > \mu_u$.

(3) dn_l/dE should be negative.

(4) Electrons must be transferred from lower valley to upper valley when they are excited by electric field.

7.8.3. Criterion for classifying the modes of operation

Gunn diodes are basically made from an *n*-type GaAs. The concentration of free electrons ranging from 10^{14} to 10^{17} per cubic centimeter at room temperature. Typical dimensions of the device are 150 × 150 μm in cross section and 30 μm long. The various modes depend on the parameters of the material and on the operating conditions. During the early stage charge accumulation, the time rate of growth of space charge layer is given by

$$Q(X, t) = Q(X - vt, 0) \exp\left(\frac{t}{T_d}\right) \quad \text{....(7.102)}$$

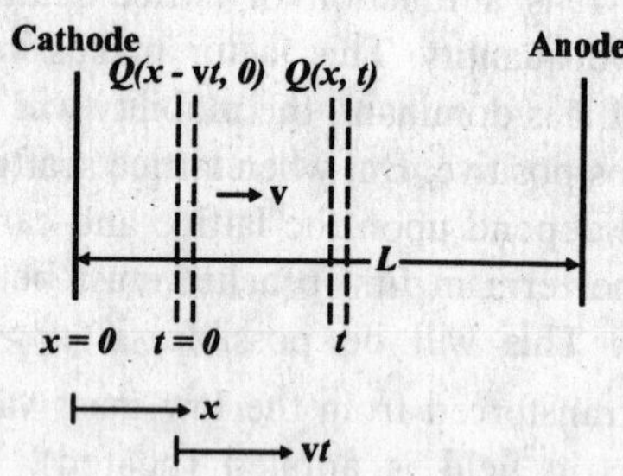

Fig. 7.33 Space charge accumulation travelling with a velocity v.

A pictorial representation of Eq. 7.102 is shown in Fig. 7.33. If Eq. 7.102 is valid throughout the entire transit time of the space charge layer, the growth factor, which gives the factor of maximum growth is given by

$$\text{Growth factor} = \frac{Q(L, L/v_v)}{Q(0, 0)} = \exp(L/v\,\tau_d) = \exp(Ln_0\, e/\mu_n/\varepsilon v) \quad \text{....(7.103)}$$

The space charge layer is assumed to start at the cathode ($x=0$) at t = 0 and arrive at the anode (x = L) at t = L/v. For a large space charge growth, the factor $\left(\frac{Ln_0 e|\mu_n|}{\varepsilon v}\right)$ must be larger than unity. Therefore

$$n_0 L > \frac{\varepsilon v}{e|\mu_n|} \quad \text{....(7.104)}$$

This equation gives the criterion for classifying the modes of operations for the Gunn effect diode. For n-type GaAs, the value of $\varepsilon v/(e\,|\mu_n|)$ is about $10^{12}/\text{cm}^2$, where $|\mu_n|$ is assumed to be 150 $\text{cm}^2/\text{V.s.}$

7.8.4. Domain formation

We have learnt that negative differential resistance occurs by applying electric field of certain range to a multivalley semiconductor compound such as *n*-type GaAs. We can also demonstrate that a decrease in drift velocity by increasing electric field leads into the formation of a high field domain for microwave generation and amplification.

In the *n*-type GaAs diode the majority carriers are electron. At low voltage, the GaAs is ohmic, since the drift velocity of the electrons is proportional to the electric field the conduction current density in the diode is given by

$$J = \sigma E_x = \frac{\sigma V}{L}\hat{x} = \rho\, v_x \hat{x} \quad \text{....(7.104)}$$

where J = Conduction current density

σ = Conductivity

E_x = Electric field in the x direction

L = Length of the diode

V = Applied voltage

ρ = Charge density

v = Drift velocity

$\hat{x}$ = Unit vector

The current is carried by free electrons that are drifting through a background of fixed positive charge. The domain formation can be explained by the JE plot shown in Fig. 7.34.

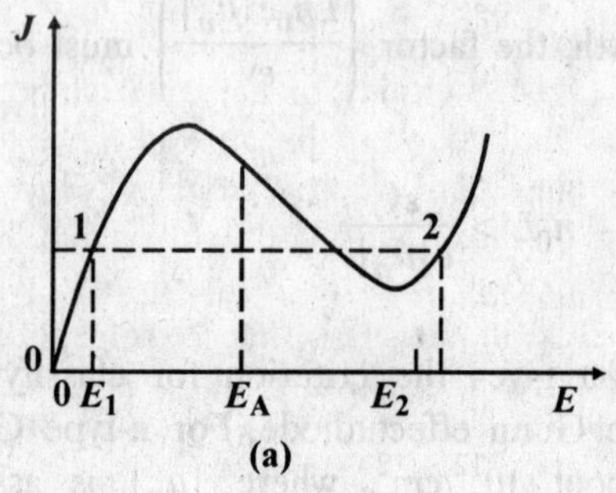

(a)

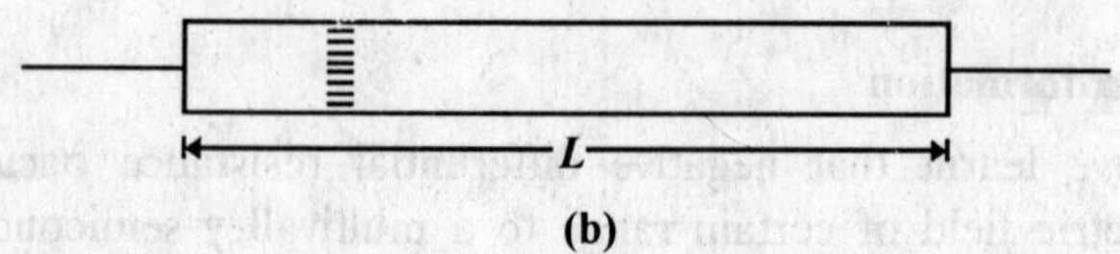

(b)

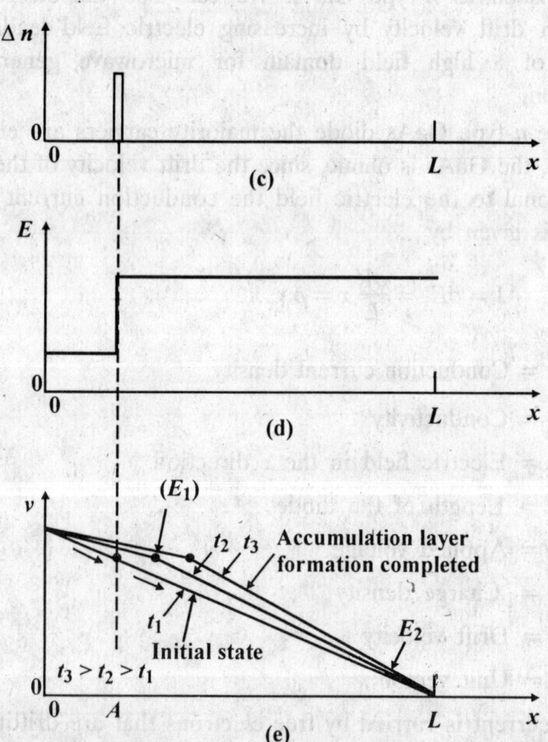

(e)

Fig. 7.34. Formation of Electron accumulation layer in GaAs.

It is assumed that at point A in the JE plot of Fig. 7.34b, there exists an excess (accumulation) of negative charge that could be due to a random noise fluctuation or because of a non-uniformity in doping in the GaAs sample. An electric field is created by these excess charges as shown in Fig. 7.34d. The field on the left side of the point A is lower than at point A if the diode is biased at point E_A on the JE curve. This situation implies that charges (current) flowing into point A is greater than that flowing out of point A, thereby increasing the space charge accumulation. This process continues until the low and high fields reach values outside the differential negative resistance region and settle at points 1 and 2 in Fig 7.34a. This pure accumulation layer is the simplest form of space charge instability. When positive and negative charges are separated by a small distance then a dipole domain is formed as shown in Fig. 7.35.

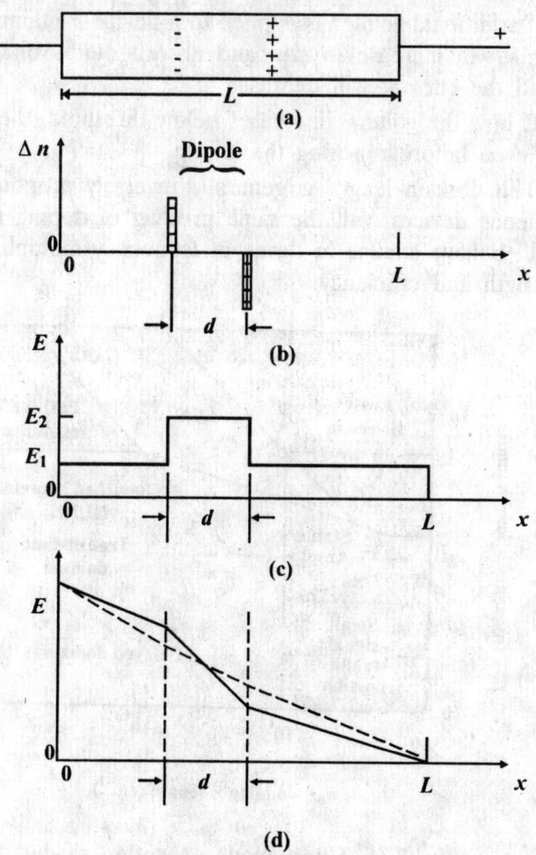

Fig. 7.35. Formation of an electron dipole layer in GaAs.

The electric field inside the domain will be greater than the field on either side of the dipole shown in Fig. 7.35c. Because of the negative differential resistance the current in the region of low field side will be greater than that in the high field side as shown in Fig. 7.35 (c). The two field values tend towards equilibrium condition outside the negative differential resistance region, where the low and high field current become equal. When the high field domain disappears at the anode a new dipole field will start forming at the cathode, and the process is repeated.

In general, the high field domain has the following properties :

1. A domain will start to form whenever the electric field in a region of sample increases above the threshold electric field and will drift through the device. When the electric field increases, the electron drift velocity decreases and the diode exhibits negative resistance.

2. If additional voltage is applied to a device containing a domain, the domain will increase in size and absorb more voltage than was added and the current will decrease.

3. If now the voltage decreases below threshold, the domain will disapper even before reaching the anode.

4. The domain length is generally inversely proportional to the doping, hence devices with the same product of doping multiplied by length will behave similar in terms of frequency multiplied by length voltage/length and efficiency.

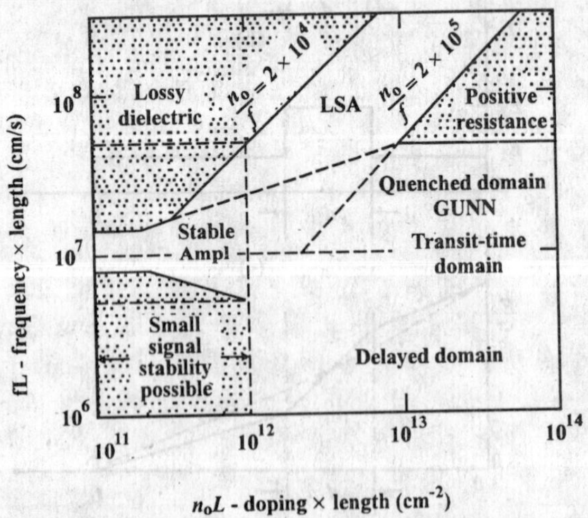

Fig. 7.36. Gunn diode operation modes

Modes of operation :

The formation of a strong space charge instability depends on the condition that enough charge is available in the crystal and the device is long enough so that a space charge of required strength can be built up within the transit time of the electrons. Copeland [16] proposed four basic modes of operation for the uniformally doped bulk diodes with low resistance contacts as shown in Fig. 7.36. This figure gives a mode chart [17] for Gunn diodes with f_L versus n_0L. The four modes are given below in Fig. 7.36.

7.8.5. Gunn oscillation mode

In the Gunn oscillation modes, the range of n_0L is given by $10^{12}/cm^2 < (n_0L) < 10^{14}/cm^2$. When $n_0L > 10^{12}$ cm^2 in GaAs, the space charge perturbations in the specimen increases exponentially in space and time as given by Eq. 7.102. A high field domain is formed and moves from the cathode to anode. The frequency of the oscillations is given by

$$f = \frac{v_{dom}}{L_{eff}}$$

where v_{dom} is the velocity of the electron in the domain and L_{eff} is the effective length that the domain travels from the time it is formed till the time a new domain starts forming.

Gunn considered several circuit configurations for describing the behaviour of oscillation in GaAs devices. When the circuit is mainly resistive or the voltage across the diode is constant, the period of oscillation is the time required for the domain to drift from the cathode to the anode. This mode is not usually used in mocrowave oscillations. For this mode $fL = 10^7$ cm/sec and $n_0L = 10^{12}$ cm^2. Negative conductivity devices are usually operated in resonant circuits, such as high-Q resonant microwave cavities. When the diode is in a resonant circuit, the frequency can be tuned to a range of about an octave without loss of efficiency [18].

In the normal Gunn domain mode, the high field domain drifts along the diode from the cathode to the anode when the electric field is greater than the threshold value E_{th}. If the low field value drops below the sustaining field E_s as shown in Fig. 7.37 the drift of the high field domain ends. The sustaining drift velocity v_s for GaAs is about 10^7 cm/s. Since the electron drift velocity v varies with the electric field, there are five possible domain modes for the Gunn oscillation mode.

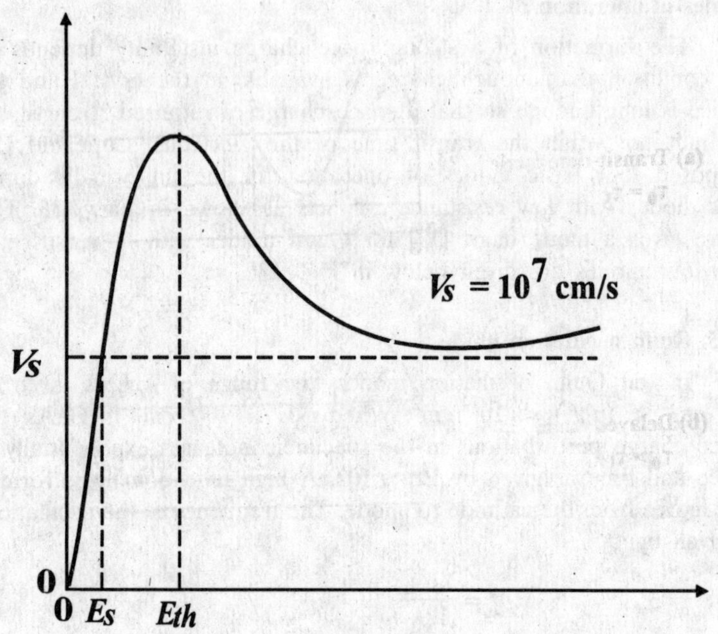

Fig. 7.37 Electron drift velocity versus electric field.

(i) Transit time gunn domain mode

In this mode fL $\approx 10^7$ cm/s. When the electron drift velocity v_d is equal to the sustaining velocity v_s, the high-field domain is stable. The electron drift velocity v_d is given by $v_d = v_s = fL = 10^7$ cm/s. In this case the period of oscillation τ_t is equal to the transit time τ_0 or $\tau_0 = \tau_t$. Fig. 7.38(a) illustrates this situation. In this case the efficiency is below 10% because the current is collected only when the domain arrives at the anode. The value of n_0L for this mode is 10^{12} cm^2. The resonant frequency of the resonant circuit is equal to the transit time frequency for this mode.

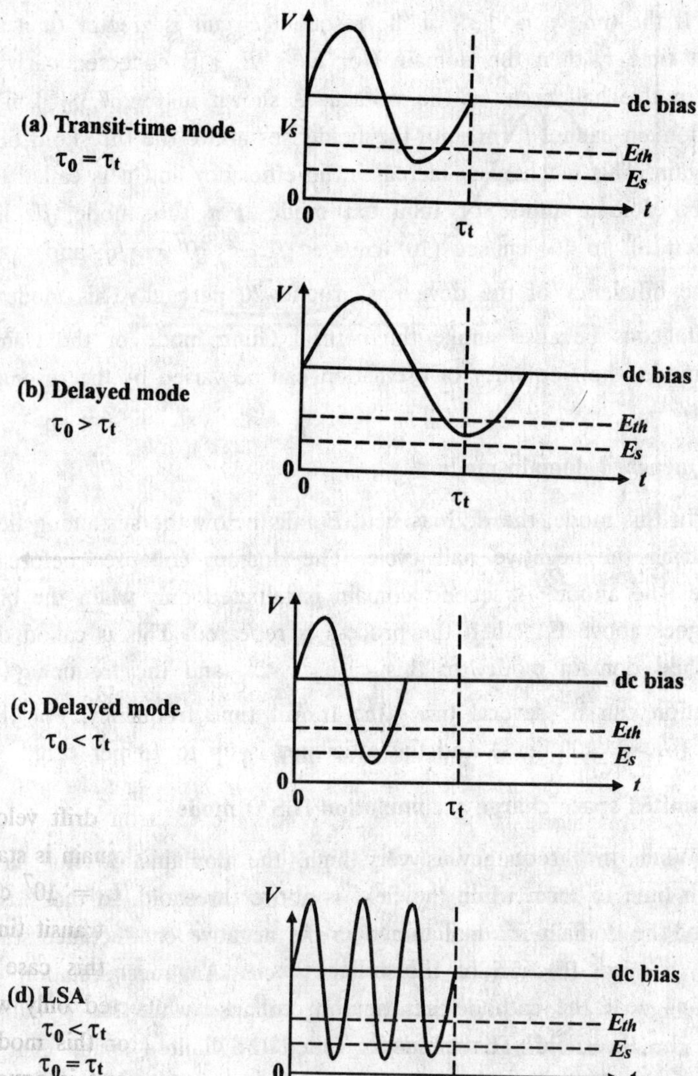

Fig. 7.38. Gunn domain modes

(ii) Delayed domain mode

If the time period τ_0 of the resonant circuit is greater than the transit time τ_t then the domain (for $E < E_{th}$) is collected early in the negative half cycle of the voltage as shown in Fig. 7.38(b). The new domain cannot form until the field rises above the threshold field E_{th} again. This mechanism increases the efficiency and it is called the delayed domain mode or inhibited mode. For this mode, fL lies between 10^6 to 10^7 cm/sec (10^6 cm/s $< fL <$ 10^7 cm/s), and $\tau_0 > \tau_t$. The efficiency of the device is around 20 percent. This mode is advantageous because unlike the natural Gunn mode or the transit time mode, the frequency of oscillation can be varied by the resonant circuit.

(iii) Quenched domain mode

In this mode, the dc bias field E falls below the sustaining field E_s during the negative half cycle. The domain collapses before it reaches the anode. A second domain is initiated only when the bias field goes above E_{th}, then the process is repeated. This is called the quenched domain mode. In this case $\tau_0 < \tau_t$ and the frequency of oscillation can be several times the transit time frequency. For this mode ($fL > 2\times10^7$ cm/s) and the efficiency is up to 13 per cent.

(iv) Limited space charge accumulation (LSA) mode

When the frequency is very high, the domains do not have enough time to form while the field is above threshold. In that case, most of the domain are maintained in the negative conductance state during a large fraction of the voltage cycle. Any accumulation of electrons near the cathode has time to collapse while the signal is below the threshold. This mode is called the limited space charge accumulation (LSA) mode and it is the simplest mode of operation. It consists of a uniformaly doped semi-conductor without any internal space charge. The internal electric field is uniform and proportional to the applied voltage. The current in the device is proportional to the drift velocity at this field level. The efficiency of the device reaches about 20%.

The requirements for the LSA mode are that the period τ_0 of the resonant circuit is not more than a few times amplitude of the dielectric relaxation time τ_d in the negative conductance region, but should be much large than τ_d for the low field conductance region so that any accumulation of electrons will collapse while the signal is below threshold. This mode is shown in Fig. 7.38 in which $\tau_0 = 3\tau_d$. For *n*-type GaAs, the product of doping and length (n_0L) is about 10^{12} per cm^2. At the low frequency limit, the drift velocity is taken to be

$$v_l = fL = 5 \times 10^6 \; cm/s \qquad ....(7.105)$$

The ratio of n_0L to fL yields

$$\frac{n_0}{f} = 2 \times 10^5 \qquad ....(7.106)$$

At the upper-frequency limit it is assumed that the drift velocity is

$$v_u = fL = 5 \times 10^7 \; cm/s$$

Now the ratio of n_0L to fL is

$$\frac{n_0}{f} = 2 \times 10^4 \qquad (7.107)$$

Both upper and lower boundaries of the LSA mode are indicated in Fig. 7.36.

(v) Stable amplification mode ($n_0L < 10^{12}/cm^2$)

When the N_0L product of the device is less than about $10^{12}/cm^2$. The device exhibits amplification at the transit time frequency rather than spontaneous oscillation. This is possible because the negative conductance is utilized without domain formation. Generally there are too few electrons for domain formation within the transit time. Therefore amplification of signals near the transit time frequency can be accomplished. This mode was first observed by Thim and Barber [19]. Uenohara [20] showed that there are several types of amplification depending on the *fL* product of the device as shown in Fig. 7.38.

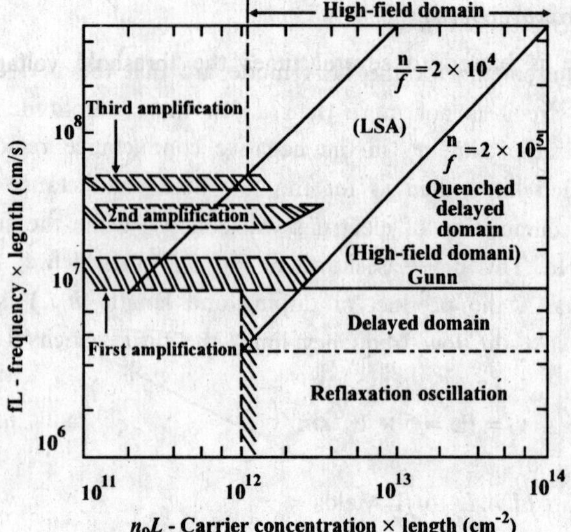

Fig. 7.38 (e) Gunn mode chart

The various modes of operation for Gunn diodes are generally classified on the basis of the times in which various processes occur. These times are the following :

τ_t = domain transit time

τ_d = dielectric relaxation time at low field

τ_g = domain growth time

τ_0 = natural period of oscillation of a high Q external electric circuit.

7.8.6. Limited space-charge accumlation mode (LSA diodes)

The working parameters for this mode are n_0L should be greater than $10^{12}/cm^2$ and n_0f should lie within 2×10^5 to 2×10^4 s/cm^3 so that the high field domains and the space charge layers do not have sufficient time to build up. The magnitude of RF voltage is kept sufficiently large to derive the diode below threshold during each cycle in order to dissipate space charge. Also, the portion of the time in each cycle when the *RF* voltage is above threshold must be short enough to prevent the domain formation and the space charge accumulation. Only initially the accumulation of charges starts near the cathode; rest of the sample remains fairly homogeneous. Thus with limited space-charge accumulation the remainder of the sample appears as a series negative resistance that increases the frequency of the oscillations in the resonant circuit. In the LSA mode the diode is placed in a resonator tuned to an oscillation frequency of $f_0 = 1/\tau_0$

and the device is biased to several times the threshold voltage as shown in Fig. 7.39.

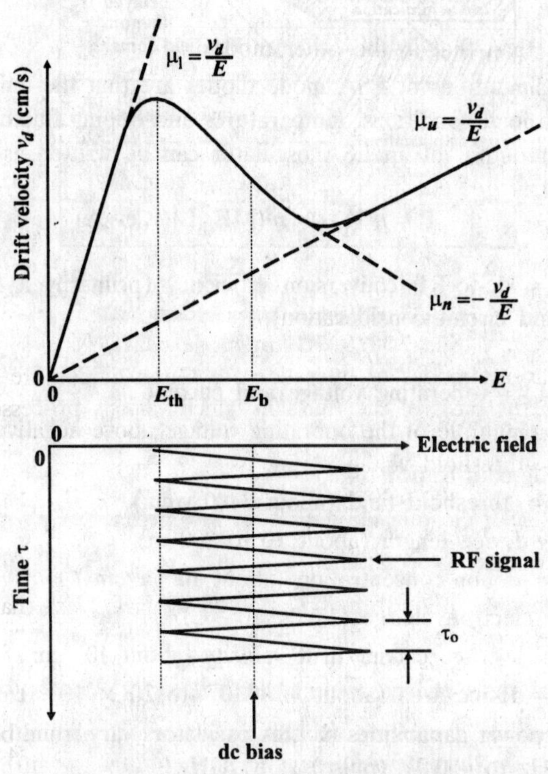

Fig. 7.39 LSA mode operation

As soon as the RF voltage swings beyond the threshold, the space charge starts building up at the cathode. The oscillation period τ_0 of the RF signal is less than the domain growth period (τ_g), the total voltage swings below the threshold before the domain can form. Further more, since τ_0 is much greater than the dielectric relaxation time τ_d, the accumulation space charge is drained in a very small fraction of the RF cycle. Hence, the device spends most of the RF cycle in the negative-resistance region, and the space charge is not allowed to build up. The frequency of oscillation in the LSA mode is independent of the transit time of the carriers and depends only on the circuits external to the device. The power impedance product does not fall off as $\frac{1}{f_o^2}$; hence the output power in the LSA mode can be greater than that in the other modes.

The limitations of LSA mode diodes are that the output is very sensitive to load conditions, temperatures and doping fluctuations [21]. The power output of an LSA oscillator can be written as

$$P = \eta V_0 I_0 = \eta (ME_{th}L)(n_0 e \nu_0 A) \qquad ....(7.108)$$

where η = dc-to-RF conversion efficiency (primarily a function of material and circuit consideration).

V_0, I_0 = operating voltage and current

M = multiple of the operating voltage above negative resistance threshold voltage.

E_{th} = threshold field (about 3400 v/cm)

L = device length (about 10 to 200 m)

n_0 = donor concentration (about 10^{15} e/cm^3)

e = electron charge (1.6×10^{-19}C)

ν_0 = average carrier drift velocity (about 10^7 cm/s)

A = device area (about 3×10^{-4} to 20×10^{-4} cm^2)

The power capabilities of LSA oscillators vary from 6 kW (pulse) at 1.75 GHz to 400 W (pulse) at 51 GHz.

Practical gun oscillators are mounted in coaxial, waveguide and YIG-tuned stripline configurations, we will describe most commonly used waveguide cavity Gunn oscillator. The Gunn diode is mounted on a cylindrical metal post centred in the broad wall of a rectangular waveguide as shown in Fig. 7.40a. This configuration consists of a waveguide section, separated from the output waveguide by an iris. This cavity operates in a TE_{11} mode. The admittance of the packaged device is resonated by the total admittance of the circuit. Fig. 7.40b shows the equivalent circuit of a post mounted packaged Gunn diode waveguide oscillator. The network on the right side of the Gunn diode is represented by the waveguide admittance Y_w of a short circuited waveguide transmission line of length L and characteristic admittance

Y_0 and propagation constant γ. An equivalent T network consisting of series susceptances C_b and a shunt susceptance consisting of the series combination of L_a and C_g represents the resonant post. La is the inductance associated with the magnetic energy stored in a simple full-height post, and C_g is associated with the capacitive energy stored in the gap between the end of the post and the waveguide. The load admittance transformed to the plane of the post is represented by Y_L. The equivalent circuit of the packaged Gunn diode is given in Fig. 7.40c; where $R = \frac{-1}{G}$ is the negative resistance, C = equivalent capacitance, R_s = bulk semi-conductor and contact resistance, L_p = package inductance, and C_p is the package capacitance.

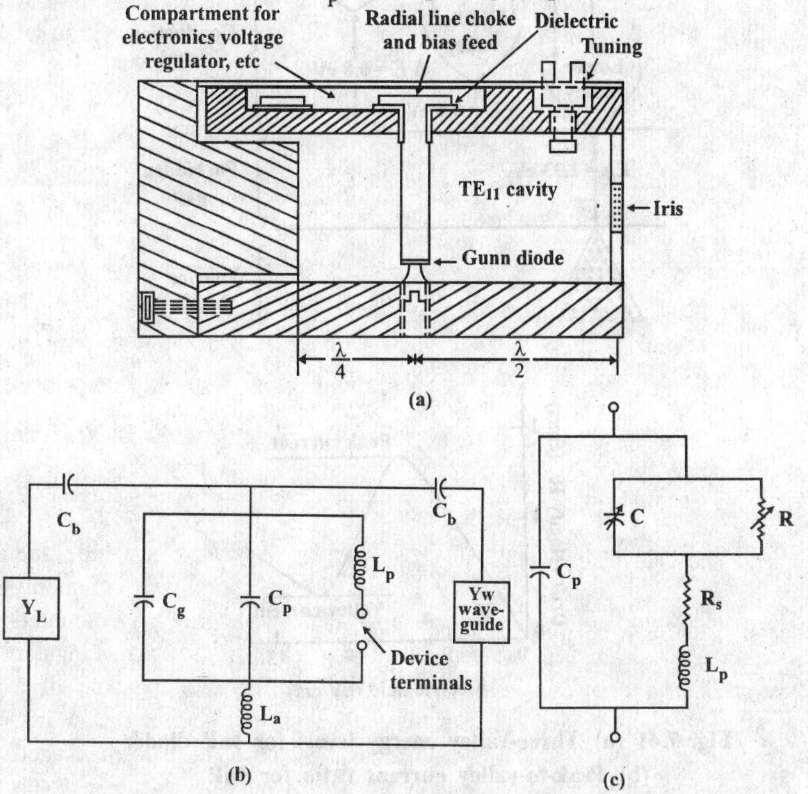

Fig. 7.40 Waveguide Gunn diode oscillator and equivalent circuit (a) Waveguide Gunn diode oscillator; (b) equivalent circuit of waveguide Gunn diode oscillator; (c) equivalent circuit of a packaged Gunn diode.

7.9. InP Diodes

Gunn observed the Gunn effect in GaAs and also in InP. Both the GaAs diode and the InP diode operate basically the same way in a circuit with dc voltage applied at the electrodes. In this section the n-type InP diode is discussed. Indium phosphide diode works as a three level device [22]. Fig. 7.41a shows the three valley model for Indium phosphide.

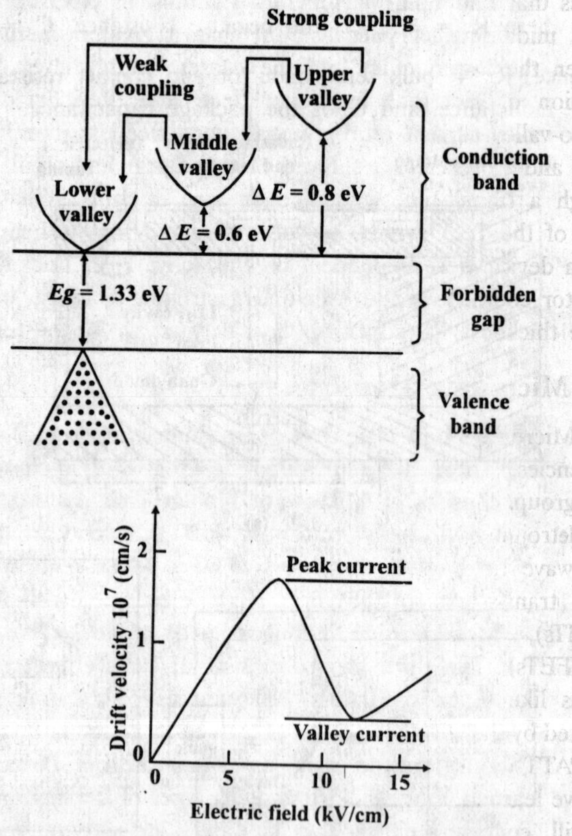

Fig. 7.41 (a) Three-Valley energy levels for InP diode. (b) Peak-to-valley current ratio for InP.

The InP has a lower-valley energy level, one middle valley and an upper valley energy level. The InP diode has a large peak-to-valley current ratio because the electron transfer starts rapidly as the field increases as shown in Fig. 7.41b. This situation occurs because the coupling between the lower valley and upper valley in InP is comparatively weaker than in GaAs. The middle valley energy level provides the additional energy loss mechanism required to avoid breakdown caused by the high energies acquired by the lower-valley electrons from the weak coupling. It can be seen from Fig. 7.41a that the lower valley is weakly coupled to the middle valley but strongly coupled to the upper valley to prevent breakdown. This situation ensures that under normal operating conditions electrons concentrate in the middle valley. Because InP has a greater energy separation between the lower valley and the nearest energy levels, the thermal excitation of electrons has less effect, and the degradation of its peak-to-valley current ratio is about four times less than in GaAs [23]. Taylor and Colliner [24] showed that epitaxial InP oscillators operate through a transit-time phenomenon and do not oscillate in a bulk mode of the LSA type. They also observed that frequency obtained from a device were dependent on the active layer thickness. The InP oscillator could be tuned over a large frequency range, bounded only by the thickness, by adjusting the cavity size.

7.10. Microwave Transistors

Microwave solid state devices are gaining importance at microwave frequencies. There are four different groups of microwave devices. First group consists of Microwave bipolar junction transistor (BJT), and Hetrojunction bipolar transistor (HBT), Second group consists of Microwave field effect transistors (FETs), Metal-semiconductor field effect transistors (MESFETs), High electron mobility transistors (HEMTs), Metal oxide semiconductor field effect transistors (MOSFETs). The third group consists of Bulk effect semiconductor devices like Gunn oscillators. The devices of the fourth group are operated by the avalanche effect of the semiconductors IMPATT diodes, TRAPATT diodes are the examples of this category. In earlier sections we have learned about the 3rd and 4th types of devices. In this section we will concentrate on the 1st and 2nd group three terminal semiconductor devices. These semiconductor transistors have replaced bulky, low power microwave tubes. The microwave transistors give very good performance, high reliability, less maintenance and are cost effective. The bipolar transistor is usually fabricated in Silicon (Si) for frequency range from UHF to about S-band (3 GHz). Microwave power technology has advanced significantly during past four decades, as the technology is advancing, the upper frequency limit for these transistors is being continuously extended, and at the present time the devices are capable of producing useful power up to 30 GHz. The microwave transistor is a nonlinear device, its principle of operation is similar to that of the low frequency device, but requirements for dimensions, process control, heat sinking and packaging are much more stringent. Bipolar transistors can also be fabricated using GaAs compound. GaAs devices offer high performance. But the Si transistors are durable, integrable, cheap and have much higher gain. For these reasons, Si transistors dominate in amplifier applications at lower microwave frequencies and are also used for local oscillator applications.

7.10.1. Bipolar transistor general consideration

Basic operation of microwave bipolar transistor is identical to that for transistors at low frequencies. General input, output power and power gain are defined as below :

The input power is given by

$$P_{in} = i_{in}^2 R_{in} \quad \text{....(7.109)}$$

and the output power may be written as

$$P_{out} = i_{out}^2 R_{out} \quad \text{....(7.110)}$$

Power gain is obtained

$$P_0/P_{in} = [i_{out}/i_{in}]^2 [R_{out}/R_{in}] \quad \text{....(7.111)}$$

Ratio i_{out} / i_{in} is the AC current gain factor denoted by h_{fe}.

It is also expressed as f_t/f, where f_t is the cutoff frequency corresponding to a current gain value of unity, where f is the operating frequency. Eq. 7.111 can be written as

$$\text{Power gain} = (f_t/f)^2 (R_{out}/R_{in}) \quad \text{....(7.112)}$$

The transistor parameters that influence power gain are (i) f_t (it should be large); (ii) R_{out} (should be large); and (iii) R_{in} (should be small).

Figure 7.42 shows a microwave transistor in planar configuration. A microwave transistor is fabricated by a 'planar technology'. The fabrication processes are identical to those used for low frequency transistors. A wafer of n^+ silicon is used as the substrate. A thin layer of n-type silicon is grown over this substrate by 'epitaxial growth'. This makes the n-region of the collector. An insulating layer of SiO_2 is thermally grown over the n-region. The base layer diffusion pattern is then cut into the silicon dioxide layer by employing the photoresist method. The base layer is formed by diffusion of *p*-type impurities. After the *p*-type base diffusion, the emitter junction is formed either by diffusion (in which case the device is called a double diffusion transistor) or by alloying (in which case the device is known as diffused-base-alloyed-emitter transistor). Finally by metallization process ohmic contacts are made to the emitter and the base. The collector contact is made from the bottom surface of the n^+ substrate.

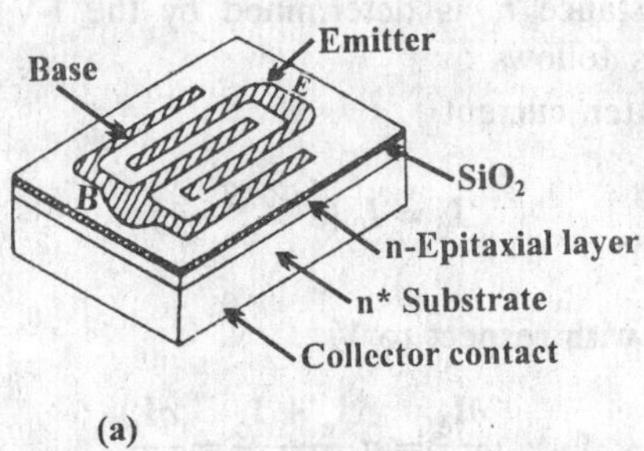

(a)

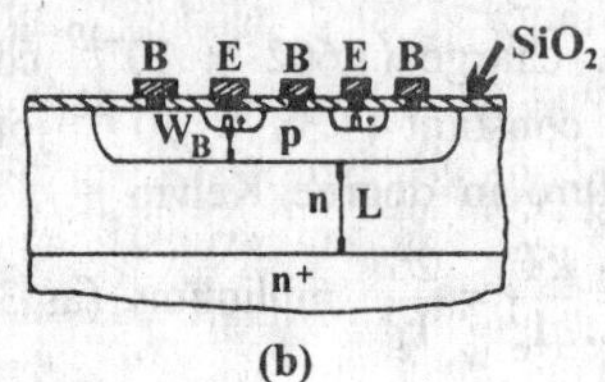

(b)

Fig. 7.42 Planar geometry of a n-p-n transistor.

7.10.2. Dependence of device design on various parameters :

(1) Cut off frequency (f_t)

In the case of transistors, their high frequency operation is limited by the transit time, this is the time taken by the charge carriers (electrons for *n-p-n* and holes for *p-n-p* transistors) to move from the emitter to the collector. Based on the transit time of the charge carriers, a cut-off frequency called transit time cut off frequency (f_t) may be defined as

$$f_t = \frac{1}{2\pi\tau} \quad ..(7.113)$$

τ is the transit time; this time is composed of four parts : (i) emitter charging time τ_e, (ii) base transit time τ_b, (iii) collector space charge transit time τ_{sc}, and (iv) collector charging time τ_c. These parameters are discusseed in detail in [26].

(a) Emitter charging time—It is the product of the resistance and transition capacitance of forward biased emitter base junction

$$\tau_e = r_e C_e$$

The resistance r_e is determined by the I-V characteristic of a *p-n* junction as follows :

The emitter current

$$I_e = I_0 (e^{qV/kT} - 1) \quad \text{....(7.114)}$$

differentiate it with respect to V,

$$\frac{\partial I_e}{\partial V} = q \frac{I_e + I_o}{kT} \approx \frac{qI_e}{kT} \quad \text{....(7.115)}$$

where

q = electronic charge (1.602×10^{-19} coulombs)
k = Boltzman constant (1.38×10^{-23} joules/deg) and
T = Temperature in degree Kelvin

thus $\quad r_e = \dfrac{kT}{qI_e} = \dfrac{26}{I_e}$ milliohms (at 300K)

The capacitance C_e is the junction capacitance given by

$$C_e = C_o \Big/ \left(1 - \frac{V}{V_i}\right)^{1/n} \quad \text{....(7.116)}$$

where V_i is the contact potential, n is a constant whose value is 2 for an abrupt junction and 3 for a linearly graded junction, C_o is the junction capacitance at zero bias. In addition to C_e given by Eq. 7.116, capacitance caused by packaging (stray capacitance) and miller capacitance defined as C_c $(1 + g_m R_L)$ adds to C_e.

Emitter charging time forms a considerable fraction of the total transit time. τ_e can be reduced by decreasing the emitter area and increasing the operating current I_e. A value of τ_e near 10 picosecond is typical for an f_t of 6 GHz.

(b) Base transit time : When the base is uniformly doped, the transit of carriers through the base is solely by diffusion. If D is the diffusion constant and W the base width, the base transit time may be written as

$$\tau_b = \frac{W^2}{2D} \qquad \text{....(7.117)}$$

This expression can be derived from the definition of the diffusion constant D. Diffusion current is related to the diffusion constant as

$$J = -Dq\frac{\partial n}{\partial x} \qquad \text{....(7.118)}$$

If the doping in the base region is not uniform, there is a built-in electric field. This electric field arises because of non-uniform distribution of acceptors (in *p*-type) or donors (in *n*-type) and may be evaluated using Gauss's law. In this case, the base transit time τ_b may be written as

$$\tau_b = W^2/\eta D \qquad \text{....(7.119)}$$

where η is a function of the buit-in field. For a diffused base alloyed emitter structure typical value of η is 4. Typical value of τ_b for a 6 GH_z cut off transistor is 2 picosecond.

(c) Collector space charge transit time (τ_{sc}) : At the operating bias, the depletion layer in the collector region has a finite width which is determined by the impurity concentration in the collector body and the reverse voltage applied to the collector base junction. Because high fields in the depletion layer, the velocity of carriers traversing the region saturates at a value determined by ionized inpurity scattering. If the depletion width is X and the saturation velocity of carriers is v_s, the transit time is given by X/v_s.

Here, it is assumed that electrons get accelerated to the velocity v_s over a distance much smaller as compared to X. One more factor which has to be taken into account is that the ac voltage across the depletion region excites a displacement current in this region. This causes a phase shift in the total current flowing across the depletion region. Consequently, effective transit time is reduced.

Typical value of τ_{sc} for a cut off frequency of 6 GHz is 12 picosecond.

(d) Collector charging time τ_c : Collector charging time is the product of r_c the collector resistance, and C_c which is the collector depletion layer capacitance, hence $\tau_c = r_c C_c$ ....(7.120)

In a conventional diffused transistor, the collector has resistivity determined by the doping level necessary to achieve the desired breakdown voltage, the resistance r_c is determined by the spreading resistance and is usually so high that r_c C_c product is one of the major limiting factors in frequency response.

The value of r_c can be minimized by the use of an epitaxial structure as shown in Fig. 7.42. In this configuration the collector depletion layer extends completely across the high resistivity epitaxial layer. The collector region resistance $r_c = \rho_c L_c/A$; where ρ_c is the resistivity of the substrate and is kept very low. L_c is its thickness and A is the area. Typical value of τ_c for a 6 GHz cut-off frequency is 1 picosecond.

So we conclude that the transit time decreased by (a) decreasing the emitter area and thus reducing the emitter charging time, (b) having non-uniform doping in base region so that the built in field reduces the base transit time, and (c) by using an epitaxial collector for reducing the collector series resistance.

Output resistance (R_{out}) and input resistance (R_{in})

R_{out} and R_{in} are two import resistances, for obtaining the output power gain. Output resistance R_{out} is given by the load line slope. The load line is a function of the output power, configuration of operation, and the operating voltage, as such, is independent of the transistor, however, it is shunted by the collector capacitance. Condition for large output impedance is achievable by minimizing the collector capacitance or by making the base area smaller.

The input resistance R_{in} is governed by the emitter geometry and the spacing between emitter and base contacts. At microwave frequencies skin effect causes most of the emitter current to flow near its edges, and therefore, R_{in} is inversely proportional to the distance between the emitter and the base contact.

Thus, in order to obtain an optimum performance from a microwave transistor, emitter periphery should be maximized and the base area should be minimised. The ratio of emitter to base area is known as aspect ratio and is an important parameter for transistor performance.

7.10.3. Physical structure

All microwave transistors are now planar in the form and almost all are in Si, *n-p-n* type. The geometry can be (a) interdigitated, (b) overlay, and (c) matrix type as shown in Fig. 7.45. The interdigitated type is for a small signal and power but the overlay and matrix type are used for power transistors only. Several of these transistors can be used in parallel to give high output of 2 to 10 W up to 4 GHz [25].

For high frequency applications, the *n-p-n* structure is preferred because the electron mobility (μ_n = 1500 cm^2/ v.s.) is much higher than the hole mobility ($\mu_p = 450\, cm^2$/v.s.). The limitations of the bipolar transistor are because it is difficult to get physical base width less than 0.1-0.15 μm and emitter strap widths less than 1 μm. Fig 7.42b gives a schematic diagram of a microwave bipolar transistor (interdigitated) and its cross-section.

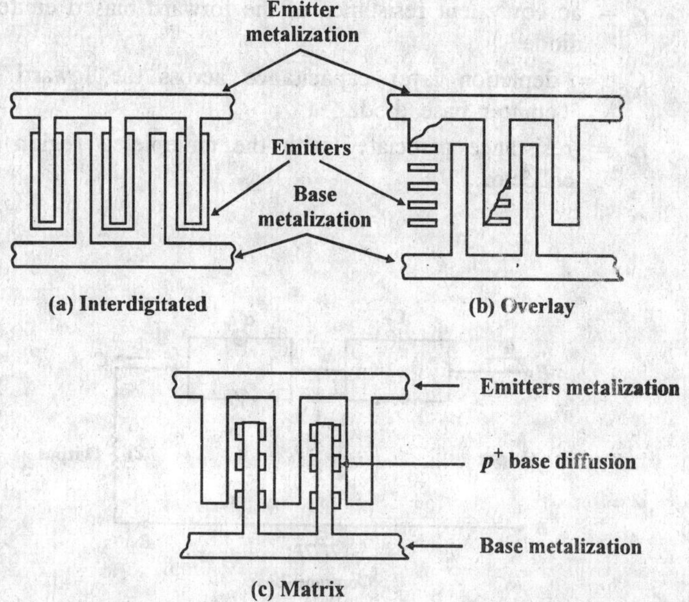

Fig. 7.43. Geometries of microwave power transistor.

Internal tuning for microwave transistors

At the input and output terminals of a transistor, matching transformers are required for impedance matching at the two terminals for maximum power transfer. In recent years the use of internal tuning has also come into prominance. This technique uses MOS chip capacitor and discrete band wire lengths placed inside the transistor package to raise one or both of the input and the output impedance of the device to the level of commonly used transmission lines at input and output (say 50 ohms). The capacitance and inductance values used are determined from the impedance characteristics of the transistor chip. Devices of this type provide broader bandwidth and greatly simplify the circuit designers problem with respect to matching to very low impedances.

7.10.4 Equivalent circuit of a bipolar transistor

The equivalent circuits of common base (CB) and common emitter (CE) configurations of microwave bipolar transistor are shown in Fig. 7.44a. The various circuit parameters are

r_b = base spresding resistance.

C_c = collector-base depletion layer capacitance.

r_e = ac equivalent resistance of the forward biased emiter-base diode.

C_e = depletion layer capacitance across the foward biased emitter base diode.

r_c = resistance associated with the undepleted region of the collector.

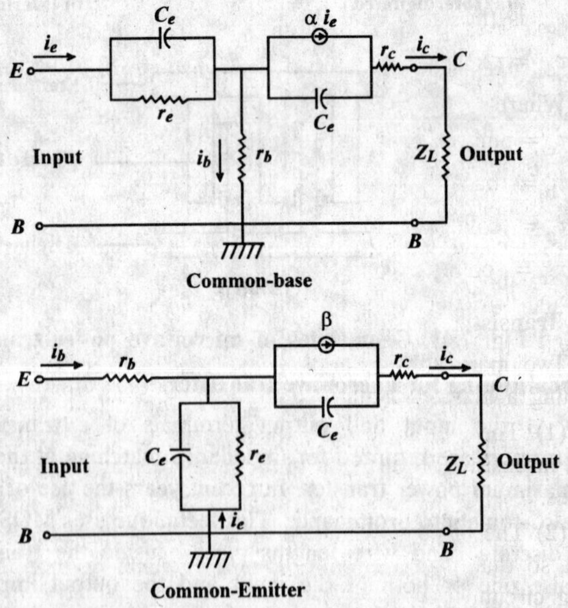

Fig. 7.44a. Microwave bipolar transistor equivalent circuits.

At microwave frequencies common emitter configuration is frequently used, because it reduces the negative feedback on account of the base to collector capacitance.

The common base current gain is given by

$$\alpha(f) = \frac{\alpha_0}{1 + jf/f_\alpha} \qquad \text{....(7.120)}$$

For common emitter case the current gain is expressed as

$$\beta(f) = \frac{\alpha(f)}{1 - \alpha(f)} \qquad \text{....(7.121a)}$$

$$= \frac{\beta_0}{1 + j(f/f_p)} \qquad \text{....(7.121b)}$$

where $\beta_0 = \alpha_0/(1 - \alpha_0)$ and $f_\beta = (1 - \alpha_0)f_\alpha$

The frequency at which $|\beta| = 1$ (collector shorted) is called the common emitter unity gain frequency (f_t) when $f_t = \dfrac{1}{2\pi\tau_{ec}}$ as defined in Equation 7.113.

τ_{ec} is the emitter to collector delay time and is given by

$\tau_{ec} = \tau_e + \tau_b + \tau_c + \tau_{sc}$

Where

τ_e = emitter charging time

τ_b = base transit time

τ_c = collector charging time

τ_{sc} = collector base depletion layer transit time.

7.10.5 Transistor biasing

Two main considerations have to be taken into account, while designing a biasing circuit

(1) The biasing circuit must provide a stable operating point that is insensitive to variation in the device parameters and temperature changes.

(2) The biasing circuit must be isolated from the high frequency circuit so that high frequency signal currents do not flow in the dc biasing circuit.

To meet the first requirement a dc feedback path is provided in the biasing circuit. To meet the second requirement a high impedance high frequency circuit element is inserted in series with the dc components; and by using low impedance capacitive bypass circuit to shunt high frequency currents around the dc circuit elements.

The bias circuit shown in Fig. 7.44b provides a stable operating point. The bias circuit is isolated from the transistor by using series inductors between the device terminals and the bias circuit resistors. In a microwave amplifier the RF chokes (inductors) are often replaced by a quarter wave high impedance transmission line or a combination of transmission line sections.

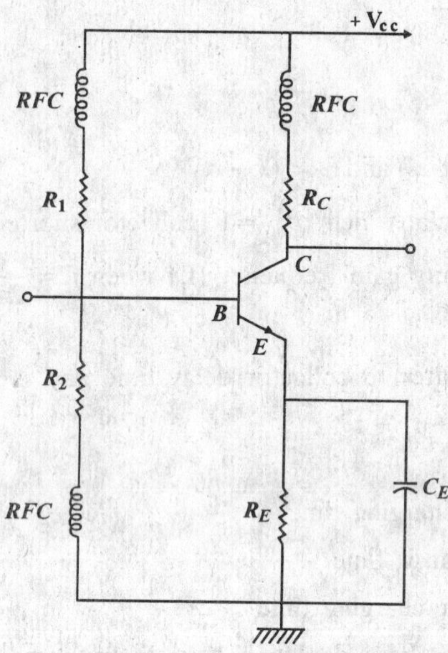

Fig. 7.44b. Biasing Circuits

7.10.6. Oscillator circuit design

Basic circuit design for microwave applications are similar to that of oscillators at lower frequencies. The common configuration of oscillators at low frequency are the Colpitts, Hartley and Clapp type, these are also used at microwave frequencies. The inductance and capacitors used in feed back loop, of these oscillators are realized in the form of transmission line sections. Fig. 7.45a shows a low frequency colpitt oscillator at microwave frequencies. For its realisation stripline technique is used. The base of the transistor is directly grounded to the ground plane of the stripline board Fig. 7.45b. The capacitance

C_1 is provided by the base to emitter capacitance of the device. Feed back is provided by the phase resonant loop with L_2 and C_2. In the input circuit L provides the necessary reactance to tune the output capacitance and T is a quarter wave transformer which transforms the real part of the collector impedance to about 50 ohms. C_m provides adjustment to the matching network. C_F represents feed through capacitor for the DC bias.

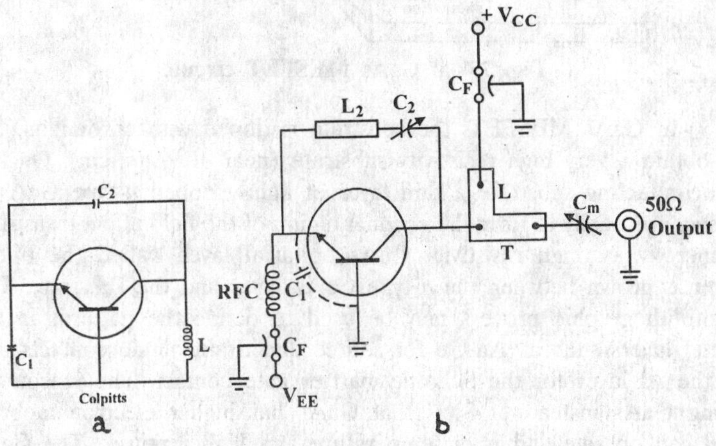

Fig. 7.45. Colpitt's Oscillator

7.11. Field Effect Transistors

Field effect transistors offer certain advantages over bipolar transistor, when used in microwave amplifier design. These are the lower noise characteristics and the high frequency operation. The high operating frequency is due to the higher electron mobility in gallium arsenide, which is the material used in field effect transistor compared to silicon material used for bipolar transistors. The higher electron mobility and the absence of shot noise are important features for low noise characteristic. The first microwave field effect transistors were metal semiconductor field effect transistors (MESFETS).

7.11.1. MESFET configuration

The metal-semiconductor field-effect transistor (MESFET) is a part of a family of field-effect transistor (FET). FETs at microwave frequencies are mostly fabricated in GaAs and use a metal-semiconductor (MES) Schottky junction for the gate contact. Fig. 7.46a shows the schematic diagram of a GaAs MESFET.

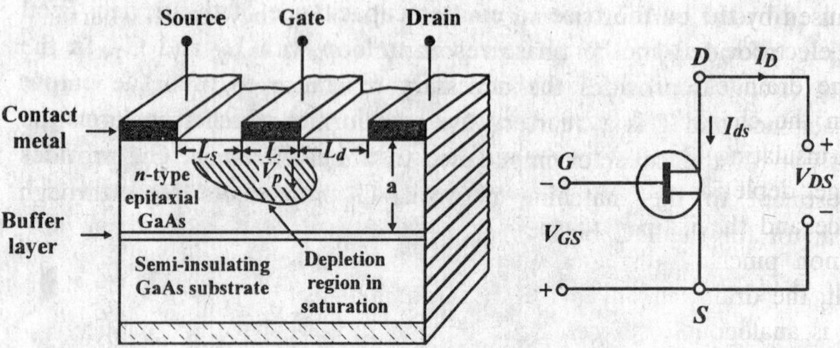

Fig. 7.46a. GaAs MESFET circuit

In GaAs MESFETs the substrate is doped with chromium (Cr) to obtain a very high resistivity substrate (near 10^8 ohm-cm). On this nonconducting substrate a thin layer of lightly doped *n*-type GaAs is grown epitaxially to form the channel region of the field effect transistor. Generally a high resistivity GaAs epitaxial layer, called the buffer layer is grown between the *n*-type GaAs layer and the substrate. The photolithographic process may be used to define the patterns in the metal layers such as Au-Ge for source and drain ohmic contacts and in the Al layer for the Schottky barrier gate contact. The reason for using GaAs instead of Si is that GaAs has higher electron mobility and can operate at higher temperature and higher power. The GaAs MESFET can also be grown using ion implantation.

The MESFET device is an interdigitated structure, fabricated by using an *n*-type GaAs epitaxial film about 0.15 to 0.35 μm, on a semi insulating substrate about 100 μm. The *n*-channel layer is dopped with either sulphur or tin in a doping concentration N between $8 \times 10^{16}/\text{cm}^3$ and $2 \times 10^{17}/\text{cm}^3$. The electron mobility in the layer is in the range of 3000 to 4500 cm^2/Vs. The source and drain contacts are Au-Ge, Au-Te, or Au-Te-Ge Alloys. A contact metallization pattern of gold is used to bring the source, drain and gate contacts out to bonding pads over the semi-insulating substrate. A buffer layer of about 3 μm with a doping concentration of 10^{15} to 10^{16} cm^{-3} is often fabricated between the active *n*-type epitaxial layer and the semi-insulating substrate.

In the MESFET of Fig. 7.46a voltage is applied in the direction to reverse bias the junction between the source and the gate, while the source and the drain electrodes are forward biased, under these conditions. The majority carriers (electrons) flow in the *n*-type epitaxial layer from the source electrode, through the channel beneath the gate, to the drain electrode. A voltage drop along the length of the channel is caused by the current flowing through it so that the Schottky-barrier gate electrode becomes progressively more reverse biased with respect to the drain electrode. As a result of this, a charge depletion is set up in the channel and gradually pinches off the channel against the semi-insulating substrate towards the drain end. The height of the charge depletion region increases as the reverse bias between the source and the gate increases. The decrease of the channel height in the non pinchet off region increases the channel resistance . As a result, the drain current I_s will be modulated by the gate voltage V_{gs}. This is analogous to the collector current I_c varying with the collector voltage V_{ce} with the base current I_b as a parameter in a bipolar transistor. Hence, a family of curves of the drain current I_d versus the V_{ds} between the source and the drain with the gate voltage V_{gs} as parameter can be drawn for a unipolar Schottky-barrier gate GaAs FET, as shown in Fig. 7.46b.

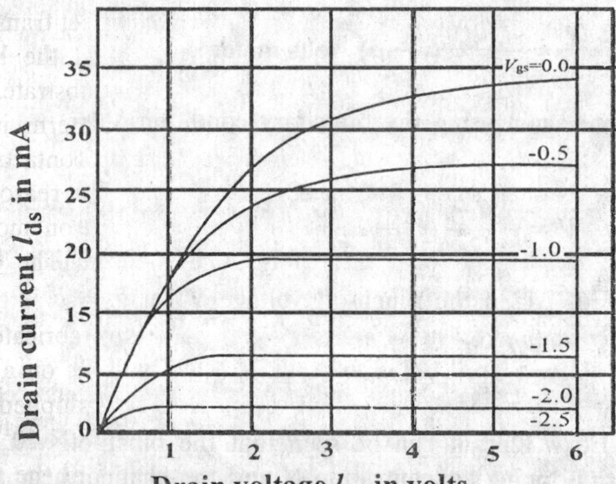

Fig. 7.46b. Voltage-Current characteristics.

The transconductance of a FET is defined as

$$g_m = \frac{dI_d}{dV_g} \quad V_d = \text{constant} \qquad \text{....(7.121)}$$

It is seen from Eq. 7.121 that for a fixed drain to source voltage V_{ds}, the drain current I_d is a function of the gate voltage V_{gs}. The drain current I_d is controlled by the field effect of the gate voltage V_{gs}, hence this device is called the field effect transistor (FET). When the drain current is increasing continuously, the ohmic voltage drop between the source and channel, reverse biases the junction further as a result, the channel is eventually pinched off. When the channel is pinched off, the drain current I_d remains almost constant even if the drain-to-source voltage V_{ds} is continuously increased.

The pinch off voltage is the gate reverse voltage that removes all the free charge from the channel. Poisson's equation in the *n*-channel, in terms of volume charge density is

$$\frac{d^2V}{dy^2} = -\frac{\rho}{\varepsilon} = \frac{-q_e N}{\varepsilon} = -\frac{q_e N}{\varepsilon_r \varepsilon_0} \quad \text{....(7.122)}$$

where ρ = volume charge density, q_e is charge of the electron, N = electron concentration, ε and ε_0 are the permittivity of the material and of free space respectively. Using the boundary conditions, that

$$E = -\frac{dV}{dy} = 0 \text{ at } y = a$$

$$\frac{dV}{dy} = -\frac{q_e N}{\varepsilon}(y - a) \text{ volts/meter} \quad \text{....(7.123a)}$$

Integrate again using the boundary condition V = 0 at y = 0, results as

$$V = -\frac{q_e N}{2\varepsilon}(y^2 - 2ay) \quad \text{....(7.123b)}$$

From Eq. 7.123b the pinch-off voltage V_p at $y = a$ is given by

$$V_p = \frac{q_e N a^2}{2\varepsilon_s} \text{ Volts} \quad \text{....(7.123c)}$$

From Eq. 7.123c, it can be seen that the pinch-off voltage is a function of the doping concentration N and the channel height *a*. The highest value of N that is possible is limited by the gate breakdown voltage. Therefore, the pinch-off voltage may be made large enough so that drift saturation effects just become dominant.

7.11.1. Small-Signal equivalent circuit :

At microwave frequencies, the metal-semiconductor field effect transistor (MESFET) has a very short channel length, and its velocity saturation should occurs in the channel before reaching the pinched path. The cross section and equivalent circuit of the MESFET is shown in Fig. (7.47). In this figure the intrinsic and extrinsic elements for 1 μm gate length and 500 μm gate width MESFET are listed below in bracket :

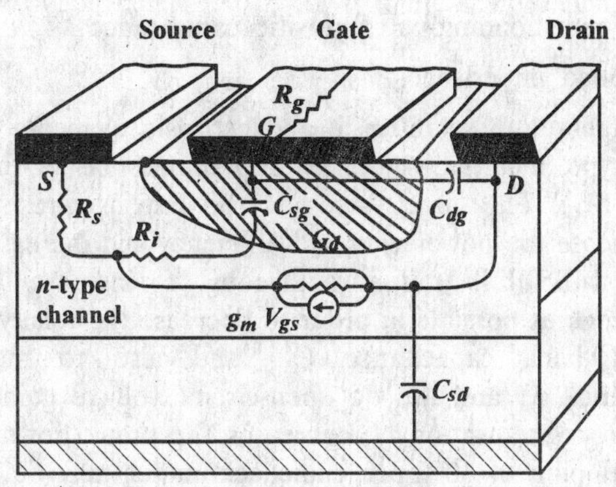

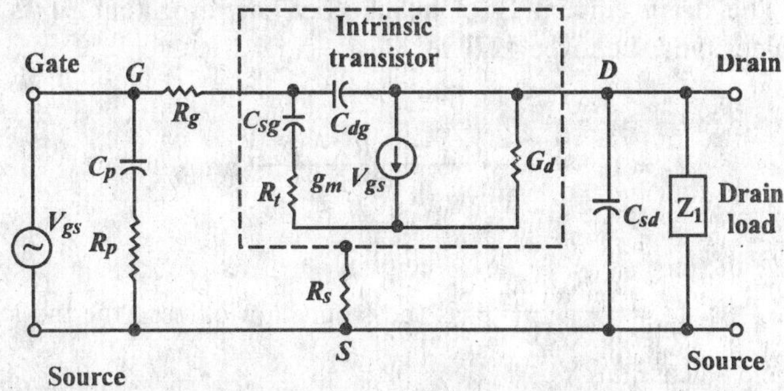

Fig. 7.47. Cross section and equivalent circuit of MESFET

g_m = transconductance of the MESFET (53 m mhos)
G_d = drain conductance
R_i = input resistance (2.6 Ω)
C_{gs} = gates-source capacitance (0.62 pF)
C_{gd} = gate drain (feed back) capacitance (0.02 pF)

Extrinsic elements :

R_g = gate metallization resistance (2.9 Ω)
R_s = Source gate resistance (2.1 Ω)

C_{ds} = drain-source capacitance (0.12 pF)

R_p = gate bonding-pad parasitic resistance

C_p = gate bonding-pad parasitic capacitance

Z_l = load impedance.

The values of these intrinsic and extrinsic elements depend on the channel type, material, structure, and dimensions of the Schottky barrier gate FET. The large values of the Extrinsic resistances will seriously decrease the power gain and efficiency and increase the noise figure of the MESFET. It is advantageous to increase the channel doping N as high as possible in order to decrease the relative influence of the feed back capacitance C_{gd} and also to increase the transconductance g_m and the dc open-circuit voltage gain. However, an increase in concentration N, decreases the break down voltage of the gate. A doping of 10^{18} per cubic centimeter may be considered as an upper limit.

The drain current I_d of a Schottky barrier gate FET is derived by Zuleeg and Lehovec [27] as

$$I_d = I_p \frac{3[(\mu^2 - \rho^2) - 2(\mu^3 - \rho^3)]}{1 + \eta\,(\mu^2 - \rho^2)} \text{ amp.} \qquad \text{....(7.124)}$$

Where $I_p = \dfrac{q_e N_d \mu\, a Z V_p}{3L}$ is the saturation current for the schottkey case at $V_g = 0$

μ = low field mobility in square meters per volt second

q_e = 1.6×10^{-19} coulomb is the electron charge

N_d = doping concentration in electrons per cubic meter

a = channel height

Z = channel depth or width

L = gate length

V_p = pinch off voltage as defined in Eq. 7.123c

$u = \left(\dfrac{V_{ds} + |V_{gs}|}{V_p}\right)^{1/2}$ is the normalized sum of the drain and gate voltages with respect to the pinch-off voltage.

$\rho = \left(\dfrac{|V_g|}{V_p}\right)^{1/2}$ is the normalized gate voltage with respect to the pinch off voltage.

$\eta = \dfrac{\mu |V_p|}{v_s L} = \dfrac{v}{v_s}$ is the normalized drift velocity with respect to the saturation drift velocity.

$v_s =$ saturation drift velocity

$v = \dfrac{\mu E_x}{1 + \dfrac{E_x}{v_s}}$ is the drift velocity in the channel

E_x = absolute value of the electric field in the channel.

Fig. 7.46b shows a plot of the drain current I_d versus the drain voltage V_{ds} with the gate voltage V_{gs} as a parameter for a typical *n*-channel GaAs MESFET. The drain current has a maximum at $\mu = \mu_m$ given by

$$u_m^3 + 3u_m \left(\frac{1}{z} - \rho^2\right) + 2\rho^3 - \frac{3}{z} = 0 \qquad \text{....(7.125)}$$

where $z = \mu |V_p|/(v_x L)$ is the ratio between the small-field velocity extrapolated linearly to the field Vp/L and the saturation velocity.

Substitution of Eq. 7.125 into Eq. 7.124 yields the saturation drain current as

$$I_{d\,(sat)} = 3\, I_{dss}\, (1 - u_m)/z \qquad \text{....(7.126)}$$

The transconductance in the saturation region is given by

$$g_m = \left.\frac{\partial I_{d\,(sat)}}{\partial |V_g|}\right|_{V_d = \text{constant}} = \frac{g_{max}(u_m - \rho)}{1 + z(u_m^2 - \rho^2)} \qquad \text{....(7.127)}$$

In practice, the drain current and mutual conductance of a GaAs MESFET can be expressed by

$$I_{ds} = I_{dss} \left(1 + \frac{|V_g|}{V_p}\right)^2 \qquad \text{....(7.128)}$$

and $$g_m = \frac{2I_{dss}}{|V_p|}\left(1 + \frac{|V_g|}{V_p}\right) \quad ....(7.129)$$

The cut off frequency of a schottky barrier gate FET in a wide-band-lumped circuit is given by [28] as

$$f_{co} = \frac{g_m}{2\pi C_{gs}} = \frac{v_s}{4\pi L}\text{ Hz} \quad .....(7.130)$$

where C_{gs} = gate source capacitance, L, v_s have already been defined. The maximum of oscillation depends on the device transconductance and the drain resistance in a distributed circuit [27]. It is given as

$$f_{max} = \frac{f_{co}}{2}(g_m R_d)^{1/2} = \frac{f_{co}}{2}\left[\frac{\mu E_p(u_m - \rho)}{2(1 - u_{m)}}\right]^{1/2} \quad ....(7.131)$$

where R_d = drain resistance

g_m = device transconductance

E_p = electric field at the pinch-off region in the channel

u_m = saturation normalization of u

For ρ = 0 (*i.e.*, V_{gs} = 0), and $\eta >> 1$, f_{co} becomes

$$f_{co} = \frac{v_s}{4\pi L} \text{ and } u_m << 1$$

$$f_{max} = \gamma(v_s/L)(3/\eta)^{1/3}\text{ Hz} \quad ....(7.192)$$

where γ = 0.14 for $\mu E_p/v_s = 13$

and γ = 0.18 for $\mu E_p/v_s = 20$ for GaAs

The experimental value for the maximum frequency of oscillation for a gallium arsenide FET with gate length less than 10 μm is

$$f_{max} = \frac{33 \times 10^3}{L}\text{ Hz} \quad ....(7.193)$$

where L is the gate length in meters. L is of the order of 0.5 μm

The maximum values of f_{max} is obtained by the transit time τ as is used for finding the cutoff frequency f_{co}.

$$f_{co} = \frac{1}{2\pi\tau} = \frac{V_s}{2\pi L}\text{ Hz} \quad ....(7.194)$$

The highest frequency of oscillation for maximum power gain with the input and output networks matched is given by Dingler. et. al. as

$$f_{max} = \frac{f_{co}}{2}\left(\frac{R_d}{R_s + R_g + R_i}\right)^{1/2} \text{ Hz} \quad \text{....(7.195)}$$

where

R_d = drain resistance

R_s = source resistance

R_g = gate metalization resistance

R_i = input resistance.

Example 7.1. An IMPATT diode power amplifier has negative resistance R_d = – 20 ohms, Load resistance R_L = 40 ohms. find power gain.

$$\text{Gain} = \left[\frac{-|R_d| - R_L}{-|R_d| + R_L}\right]^2 = \frac{-2-4}{-2+4} = 9$$

Example. 7.2. In an up-convertor parametric amplifier, the figure of merit for a diode nonlinear capacitor is 8, and the ratio of the output frequency fo over the signal frequency is 8. The diode temperature is 300K.

Calculate the following :

(a) Power gain and noise figure in decibels.

(b) Bandwidth for γ = 0.2

$$\text{Power Gain} = \frac{f_0}{f_s}\frac{8}{(1+\sqrt{1+8})^2}$$

$$\frac{f_0}{f_s} = 8$$

$$\gamma = 0.2$$

Figure of merit = γQ = 8

$$8 = \frac{f_s}{f_o}(\gamma Q)^2 = \frac{1}{8}(8)^2 = 8$$

$$P = 8\frac{8}{(1+\sqrt{9})^2} = \frac{8 \times 8}{16} = 4$$

$P_{dB} = 10 \log_{10}(4) = 6.02$ dB

The noise figure $F = 1 + \frac{2T_d}{T_0}\left[\frac{1}{\gamma Q} + \frac{1}{(\gamma Q)^2}\right]$

$$= 1 + \frac{2 \times 300}{300}\left[\frac{1}{8} + \frac{1}{8^2}\right]$$

$$= 1 + 2 \times \left(\frac{9}{64}\right) = 2.28$$

Band width (BW) $= 2\gamma\sqrt{\frac{f_0}{f_s}}$

$$= 2 \times 0.2 \times 8 = 3.2$$

Example 7.3. A Gunn diode has a drift length of 2 μm. What minimum voltage is required to initiate the Gunn mode ?

Since a voltage gradient in excess of 3.3 kV/cm will start Gunn mode.

drift length = 2 μm

hence minimum voltage required is

$V_{min} = 3.3 \times 10^3 \times 2 \times 10^{-4} = 0.66V$

Example 7.4. In certain Gunn diode of active lengths 10 μm; the drift velocity of electrons is 2×10^7 cm/s. Calculate the natural frequency of the diode.

$$f = \frac{V_d}{L} = \frac{9 \times 10^7}{10 \times 10^{-4}}$$

$$= 20 \text{ GHz}$$

Example 7.5. A GaAs MESFET, has the following parameters :

Electron concentration : $N_d = 7 \times 10^{17}\ cm^{-3}$

Channel height : $a = 0.15\ \mu m$

Relative dielectric constant : $\varepsilon_r = 13.0$

Charge : $q = 1.6 \times 10^{-19}$

Calculate the pinch-off voltage.

The pinch-off voltage is given as

$$V_p = \frac{qN_d a^2}{2\varepsilon_s}$$

$$= \frac{1.6 \times 10^{-19} \times 7 \times 10^{23} \times (0.15 \times 10^{-6})^2}{2 \times 13.0 \times 8.854 \times 10^{-12}}$$

$$= \frac{1.6 \times 7 \times 10^4 \times 0.0225}{26 \times 8.854}$$

$$= 10.5 \text{ volts}$$

Example 7.6. A typical GaAs MESFET has the following parameters :

$R_g = 2.5\ \Omega$ $\quad R_i = 2.5\ \Omega$ $\quad g_m = 50$ mV

$R_d = 42\ \Omega$ $\quad R_s = 3.2\ \Omega$ $\quad C_{gs} = 0.66$ pF

(1) Determine the cut-off frequency.

(2) Find the maximum operating frequency.

The cutoff frequency is

$$f_{co} = \frac{g_m}{2\pi C_{gs}} = \frac{0.05}{2\pi \times 0.66 \times 10^{-12}}$$

$= 12.26$ GHz

The Maximum frequency is

$$f_{max} = \frac{f_{co}}{2}\left(\frac{R_d}{R_s + R_g + R_i}\right)^{1/2}$$

$$= \frac{12.26 \times 10^{19}}{2}\left(\frac{425}{3.2 + 2.5 + 2.5}\right)^{1/2}$$

$$= 44.13 \text{ GHz}$$

Example 7.7. A Certain *n*-channel GaAs MESFET has the following parameters :

Permittivity of free space $\varepsilon_0 = 8.854 \times 10^{-12}\ F/m$

Electron concentration : $N_d = 8 \times 10^{17}\ cm^{-3} = 8 \times 10^{23}\ m^{-3}$

Channel height : $a = 0.1\ \mu m$

Relative dielectric constant : $\varepsilon_r = 13.10$

Channel length : $L = 12\ \mu m$

Channel width : $Z = 40\ \mu m$

Electron mobility : $\mu = 8000\ cm^2V^{-1}S^{-1}$

Drain voltage : $V_d = 4.5$ Volts

Gate voltage : $V_g = -\ 1.5$ Volts.

Saturation drift velocity : $v_s = 2 \times 10^5\ m/s$

Charge of the electron : $q_e = 1.6 \times 10^{-19}$

Calculate the following parameters

a. The princh-off voltage V_p

b. The velocity ratio η

c. Saturation Current at $V_g = 0$

d. The drain current I_d.

Solution :

$\varepsilon_s = \varepsilon_0\, \varepsilon_r$

(a) From Eq. (7.123c)

$$V_p = \frac{q_e N_d a^2}{2\varepsilon_s}$$

$$V_p = \frac{1.6 \times 10^{-19} \times 8 \times 10^{23} \times (0.1 \times 10^{-6})^2}{2 \times 8.854 \times 10^{-12} \times 13.10}$$

$= 5.5178$

(b) From eq. (7.124)

$$\eta = \frac{\mu |V_l|}{v_s L}$$

$$= \frac{0.08 \times 5.5178}{2 \times 10^5 \times 12 \times 10^{-6}}$$

$= 0.182$

(c) From eq, (7.124)

$$I_p = \frac{q N_d\, \mu a\, Z\, V_p}{2L}$$

$$= \frac{1.6 \times 10^{-19} \times 8 \times 10^{23} \times 0.08\,(0.1 \times 10^{-6}) \times 40 \times 10^{-6} \times 5.5178}{2 \times 12 \times 10^{-6}}$$

$= 0.9417 \times 10^{-2} = 9.4\, mA$

(d) From Eq. (7.124) $u = \left(\dfrac{V_d + |V_g|}{V_p}\right)^{1/2}$

$$u = \left(\frac{4.5 + 1.5}{V_p}\right)^{1/2} \quad u = 1.043, u^2 = 1.088, u^3 = 1.135\,\rho = 0.2718,$$

$$\rho^2 = 0.0739, \rho^3 = .0206$$

$$\rho = \left(\frac{1.5}{V_p}\right)^{\frac{1}{2}}$$

Then the drain current is

$$I_d = I_p \frac{3(u^2 - \rho^2) - 2(u^3 - \rho^3)}{1 + \eta\,(u^2 - \rho^2)} \text{ amp.}$$

$$= 0.94 \times 10^{-2} \frac{[3(1.088 - 0.0739) - 2(1.135 - 0.0206)]}{1 + 0.182(1.088 - 0.0739)}$$

$$= 0.94 \times 10^{-2} \times 0.687 = 6.45 \text{ mA}$$

REFERENCE

1. S.Y. Liao, **Microwave Devices and Circuit**, Prentice-Hall of India Private Ltd., 1995 (Third Ed.).
2. S.M. Sze, **Physics of Semiconductor Devices,** Wiley Eastern Ltd., 1981.
3. R. Chatterjee, **Microwave and Millimeter-Wave Semiconductor Devices**, Affiliated East-West Press Pvt. Ltd. 1997
4. M.S. Tyagi **Semiconductor Materials and Devices,** John Wiley & Sons ed. 1991.
5. K.C. Gupta, **Microwaves,** Wiley Eastern Limited 1979.
6. H.A Watson, **Microwave Semiconductor Devices and their Circuit Application,** Mc-Graw Hill Inc., 1969.
7. READ, W.T., **A Proposed High-Frequency Negative-Resistance Diode**. Bell System Tech. J, **37** 401-446 (1958)
8. Lee, C.A. et.al., **The Read Diode and Avalanche, Transit Time, Negative-resistance Oscillator.** App. Phy. Letters, 6, 89 (1965)
9. COLEMAN, D.J. Jr, and S.M. SZE, **A Low Noise Metal Semiconductor-Metal (MSM) Microwave Oscillator;** Bell System. Tech. J.,50,1645-1699, May-June, 1971
10. RAGER, H.J. etal., **High Power High Efficiency Silicon Avalanche Diodes at Ultra High Frequencies,** Proc. IEEE (Letters), **55,** 586-587, April, 1967.

11. CLORFEIWE, A. S., et. al; **A Theory for the High Efficiency Mode of Oscillation in Avalanche Diodes.** RCA Rev. **30**, 397-421, September, 1969.
12. DELDACH, B. C. Jr., and D. L. SCHARFTTER, **Device Physics of TRAPATT Oscillators.** IEEE Trans. In Electron Devices, ED-17, 9-21 January, 1970.
13. VENDER ZIEL, A., **On the Mixing Properties of Nonlinear Capacitances**. J. Appl. Phys., 19, 999-1006, November 1948.
14. MANLEY, J. M., and H. E. ROWE, **Some General Properties of Non-linear Elements** - **Pt. I, General Energy Relations,** Proc. IRE, **44**, 904, July 1956.
15. Ridley, B.K., **Specific Negative Resistance in Solids.** Proc. Phy. Soc. (London), **82**, 954-966, Dec. 1963.
16. Copeland, J. A., **Stable space charge layers in two-valley semi conductors.** J. Appl. Phys. 37, Nov. 9, 3602, August 1966.
17. Copeland, J.A., **Characterization of bulk negative resistance diode behaviour**. IEEE Trans. In Electron Devices ED-14, No. 9, 436-441, September 1967.
18. Hobson, G.S., **Some Properties of Gunn-effect Oscillation in a Biconical cavity,** IEEE Trans, Electron Devices ED-14, 9, 526-531, 1967.
19. Thim, H. W., and M. R. Barber, **Observation of Multiple High Field Domains in** n-GaAs. Proc. IEEE, 56, 110 (1968).
20. Uenohara, M., **Bulk Gallium Arsenide Devices.** Chapter 16 in H. A. Watson (Ed), Microwave Semiconductor devices and their Circuit Applications. McGraw-Hill Book Company, New York, 1969.
21. Wilson, W.E., **Pulsed LSA and TRAPATT Sources for Microwave systems.** Microwave J. 14, No. **8**, August 1971, 87-90.
22. G.B.L, **Three-level Oscillator in Indium Phosphide**. Physics Today, **23,** 19-20, December 1970.
23. Colliver, D., and B. Prew, **Indium Phosphide : Is it Practical for Solid State Microwave sources ? Electronics 110-113, April 10, 1972.**
24. Taylor, B.C., and D. J. Colliver, **Indium Phosphide Microwave Oscillators**. IEEE Trans. on Electrons Devices, ED-18, No. 10, 835-840, October 1971.
25. SOBOL, H., and F. STERZER, **Solid State Microwave Power Sources. IEEE Spectrum,** 4, 32, April 1972.
26. JOHNSON, E.O., **Physical Limitations on Frequency and Power Parameters of Transistors**. RCA Rev., 26, No. **6**, 163-177, June 1965.

27. Zuleeg, R. and Lehovec, K., **High Frequency and Temperature Characteristics of GaAs Junction Field-effect Transistors in the Hot Electron Range,** in Proc. symp. GaAs, Institute of Physics confi., series, No. 9, pp. 240-245, 1970.

28. Lehovec, K. and Zuleeg, R., **Voltage Current Characteristics of GaAs J. FETs in the Hot Electron Range**, Solid State Electronics, **13**, 1415-1426, 1970.

Problems and Review Questions

1. Why is GaAs superior to silicon as a microwave semiconductor material ?
2. Explain the principle of operation of the Gunn diode.
3. What is the fundamental difference between bulk and junction, effect semiconductor devices ?
4. Why is the tunnel diode important in microwave work ?
5. Discuss the differences between transferred electron devices and avalanche transit time device.
6. Describe the modes of operation for Gunn diodes.
7. Describe the Ridley-Watkins-Hilsum theory.
8. For a transit-time domain mode, the domain velocity is about 1×10^7 cm/s. Determine the drift length of the diode at a frequency of 10 GHz. Can the device operate at 8.0 GHz and 12 HGz frequencies ? Justify the modes of operation involved at these two frequencies.
9. In a bipolar transistor, the emitter charging time constitutes 40 per cent of the total transit time. Calculate the percentage change in the cut-off frequency when the emitter current is increased from 100 mA to 200 mA.

   All other parameters are assumed to be constant.
10. Estimate the terminal values of voltage and current for a 300 mW Gunn oscillator at 14 GHz. The CW efficiency is 3% and the threshold electric field Eth for GaAs is 3000 V/cm. Assume the Gunn oscillater transit time equal to the period of oscillation, and the dc bias equal to three times the threshold voltage. Calculate the length of the active region, the threshold voltage and the d.c. bias. Calculate the input power P_{in} and the *d.c.* bias current I_{bias}.

11. Describe the advantage and disadvantage of the parametric devices.
12. For a MESFET, $g_m = 53$ mhos, Rg = 2.9 ohms L = 150 μm, $\nu_0 = 2\times10^7$ cm/s. Calculate f_{co} and f_{max}.
13. A PIN diode has a resistance of 1 ohm in forward bias and 10 kilo-ohm in reverse blas. All reactances associated with the diode may be neglected. The diode is shunt mounted across a 50 ohm line to obtain an SPST swtich. Calculate the insertion loss and the isotation.
14. A silicon P^+-n-p transistor has impurity concentrations of 5×10^{18}, 10^{16} and 10^{15} cm^{-3} in the emitter, base and collector respectively. The base width is 1.0 μm and the device cross-sectional area is $3mm^2$. The emitter-base junction is forward-biased to 0.5 V and the base-collector junction is reversed biased to 5V, calculate (a) the minority carrier concentration at the emitter-base junction and (b) the minority carrier charge in the base region.
15. An IMPATT diode has a drift length of 2μm. Determine (a) the drift time of the carriers and (b) the operating frequency of the IMPATT diode.

8

Strip Lines and Microwave Integrated Circuits

8.1. Introduction

Earlier to year 1965 nearly all microwave equipment utilized coaxial or wave guide lines. With the introduction of monolithic microwave integrated circuits (MMICs), planar transmission lines have become more suitable and are used extensively because they provide a free and accessible surface on which solid state devices can be attached. A planar geometry implies that the characteristics of the element can be determined from the dimensions in a single plane. Several configurations for planar transmission lines have been realized. Some of these lines support TEM modes, others hybrid or higher order modes. Figure 8.1 shows some of the transmission lines used in MMICs.

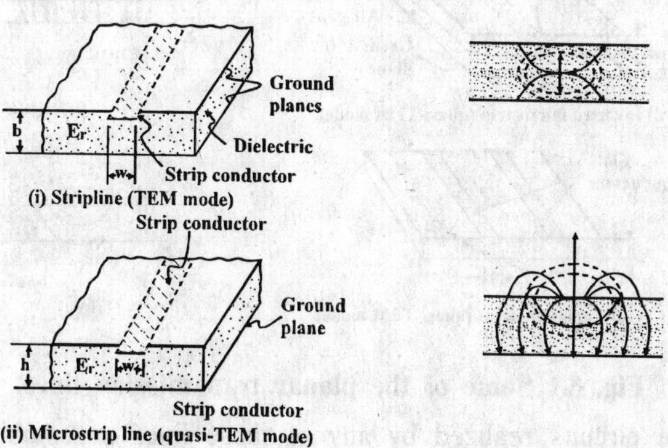

Fig. 8.1 Some of the planar transmission lines.

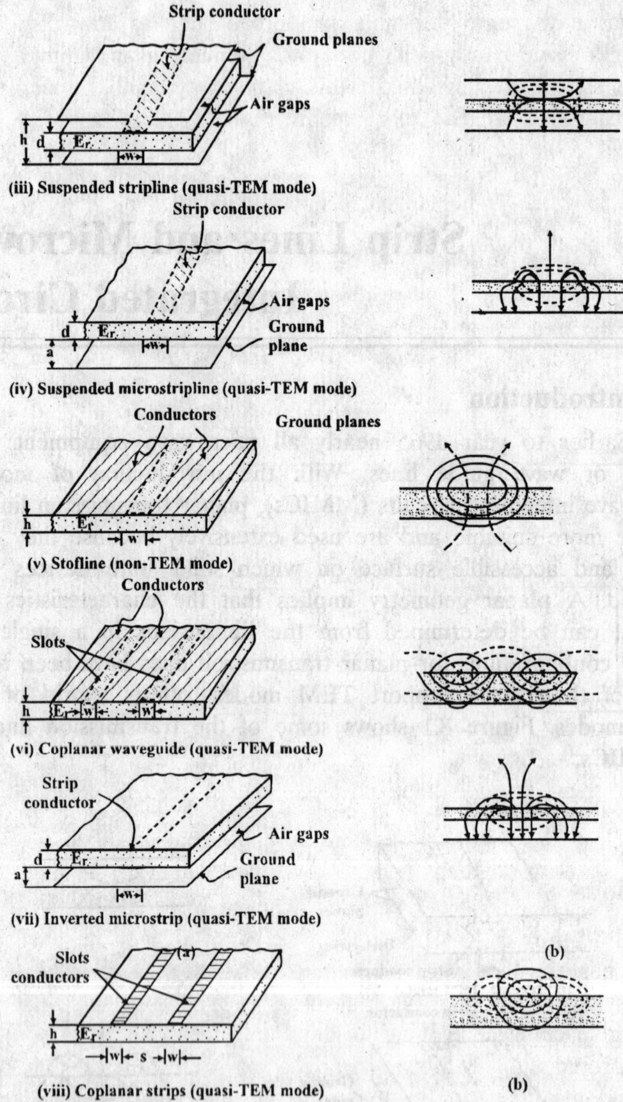

Fig. 8.1 Some of the planar transmission lines.

The circuits realized by any of these lines or combination of them have distinct advantages such as light weight, small size, improved performance, better reliability and reproducibility and low cost. Figure 8.2 shows various configurations of a special kind of line known as Fin-lines which are frequently used at microwave and millimeter wave frequencies. These lines have some desirable properties such as low dispersion, broad single mode bandwidth, moderate attenuation and compatibility with solid state chip devices. In this chapter we shall be describing these transmission lines in more detail.

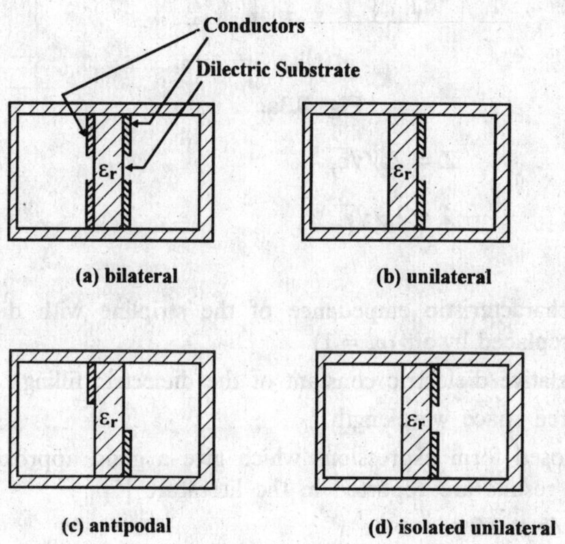

Fig. 8.2. Various fin line configurations.

8.2. Various Strip Lines

8.2.1. Strip lines

The basic structure of a strip line consists of a flat strip conductor situated symmetrically between two large ground planes with the intervening space homogeneously filled with a dielectric. The dominant mode of propagation in a strip line is a pure TEM mode that is the electric and magnetic field components lie entirely transverse to the direction of propagation. The strip lines can also support higher order TM and TE modes but these are generally avoided. The field in the stripline concentrate around the strip conductor and decay rapidly with distance away from the strip in the lateral direction shown in Fig. 8.3a. The characteristic impedance Z and the guide wavelength λ of the homogeneous stripline are given by

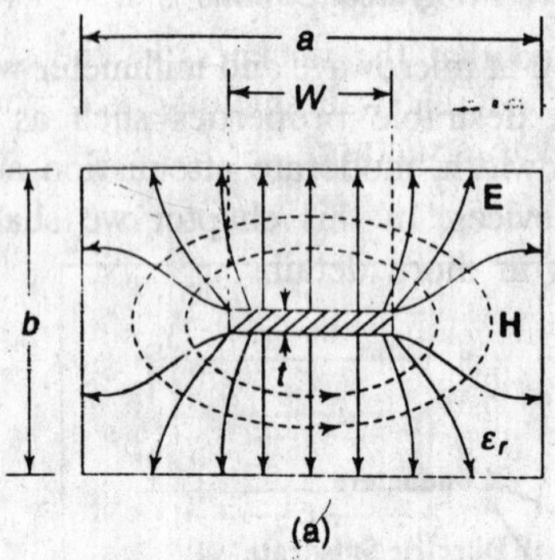

Fig. 8.3a.

$$Z = Z_0/\sqrt{\varepsilon_r} \qquad ....(8.1)$$

$$\lambda = \lambda_0/\sqrt{\varepsilon_r} \qquad ....(8.2)$$

where

Z_0 = characteristic empedance of the stripline with dielectric replaced by air ($\varepsilon_r = 1$)

ε_r = relative dielectric constant of the dielectric filling

λ_0 = free space wavelength

The closed form expressions which give a good approximation to the exact results are reported in the literature [5].

For $W/b \le 0.5$

$$Z\sqrt{\varepsilon_r} = 29.979 \ln\left[2\frac{(1+\sqrt{k})}{(1-\sqrt{k})}\right] \qquad ....(8.3)$$

For $W/b \ge 0.5$

$$Z\sqrt{\varepsilon_r} = \frac{29.979\,\pi^2}{\ln\left[2\frac{(1+\sqrt{k'})}{(1-\sqrt{k'})}\right]} \qquad ....(8.4)$$

Therefore

$$k = \text{Sech}\,(\pi W/2b) \qquad ....(8.5a)$$

$$k' = \text{Tanh}\,(\pi W/2b) \qquad ....(8.5b)$$

where

W = the strip width

b = ground plane spacing

Here it is assumed that the thickness of the strip conductor is negligible. A complete metallic wall shielding is generally provideded by enclosing the complete structure.

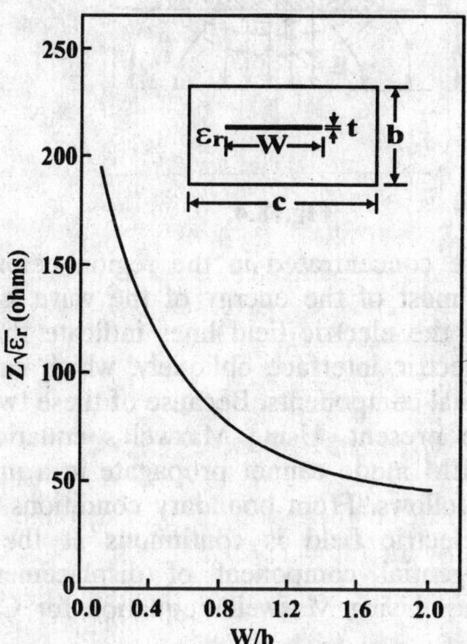

Fig. 8.3b. Variation of $Z\sqrt{\varepsilon_r}$ as a function of W/b of symmetric stripline.

The sidewall separation C is chosen large enough (C/W ≥ 10) so that the walls have negligible effect on the propagation characteristics. Figure 8.3b shows the variation in $Z\sqrt{\varepsilon_r}$ as a function of W/*b* for a stripline with C/W = 35. It can be seen that $Z\sqrt{\varepsilon_r}$ is independent of $\sqrt{\varepsilon_r}$.

For practical circuits, the dimensions of the stripline are chosen keeping in view that the operation is restricted in the TEM mode and the losses are kept minimum. The strip line is an excellent medium for realizing passive components. A microstrip directional coupler has excellent directivity and high isolation because of its operation in TEM mode.

8.2.2. Microstrip

Unlike the stripline, the microstrip as shown in Fig. 8.1b (ii) is an inhomogeneous line.

Microstrip line has a very simple geometry. These lines are used extensively to interconnect high speed logic circuits. Microstrip line consists of a metallic strip attached to a dielectric sheet. On the other side of the dielectric it has a ground plane. Approximate electric and magnetic fields in a microstrip are sketched in Fig. 8.4. Most of the

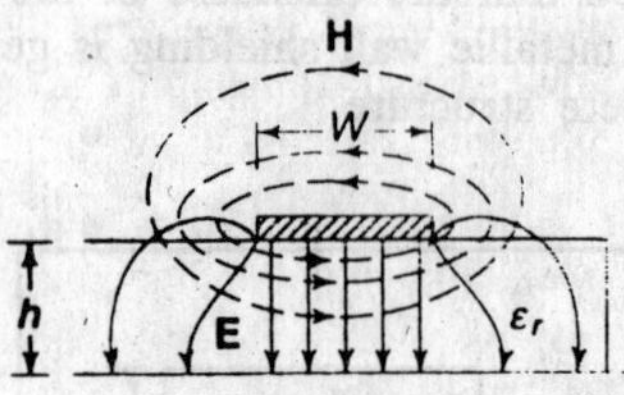

Fig. 8.4.

electric field lines are concentrated in the region below the strip in the dielectric, hence most of the energy of the wave is concentrated there. Distribution of the electric field lines indicate that the E lines approach the air-dielectric interface obliquely, which can be resolved in tangential and normal components. Because of these two components of electric fields are present. Using Maxwell's equations it can be shown that a pure TEM mode cannot propagate in a microstrip. This can be explained as follows. From boundary conditions the tangential component of the electric field is continuous at the air-dielectric interface, hence tangential component of displacement density D becomes discontinuous. Using Maxwell's equation for Curl H we can write

$$(\nabla \times H)_x \,|_{air} \neq (\nabla \times H)_x \,|_{diel} \qquad \text{....(8.6)}$$

If Hz is zero (*i.e.* if the mode is pure TEM), Eq. 8.6 gives $\partial H_y/\partial z \,|_{air} \neq \partial H_y/\partial z \,|_{diel}$

or $$H_y \,|_{air} \neq H_y \,|_{diel} \qquad \text{....(8.7)}$$

Inequality in Eq. 8.7 violates the field matching conditions for tangential component of magnetic field.

This implies that Hz should be a non-zero quantity for Eq. 8.6 to be satisfied. Hence it is concluded that a pure TEM mode cannot be supported by a microstrip line. However since the major portion of electric field lines is concentrated below the strip, the electric field crossing the air dielectric boundary is small. As such the deviation from the TEM mode is small and may be ignored for most of the circuit design applications [1,2,3,4].

Hence it is clear that the non TEM properties of microstrip are caused by the existance of two different dielectric constants in the line cross-section, not by the physical asymmetry of the line. If the relative dielectric constant of the dielectric layer is one, then the line shown in Fig. 8.1(ii) would be a TEM line.

Static parameters

For any TEM type transmission line the characteristic impedance at high frequency may be expressed as

$$Z_0 = \sqrt{L/C} \quad \text{or} \quad Z_0 = v_p L \quad \text{or} \quad Z_0 = 1/v_p C \qquad \text{....(8.8a,b,c)}$$

where v_p is the phase velocity of the wave travelling along the line.

The phase velocity is also given as

$$v_p = \frac{1}{\sqrt{LC}} \qquad \text{....(8.9)}$$

If we assume that the substrate of the microstrip line is removed (effectively) then we will have an air filled line along which the wave will travel with the velocity of light $c(c = 2.99793 \times 10^8$ m/s) in free space. The characteristic impedance of this air filled "microstrip" line is, say Z_{01} where L remains unaltered and C_1 is the capacitance per unit length for this structure.

Since $v_p = c$,

$$Z_{01} = \sqrt{\frac{L}{C_1}} \qquad \text{....(8.10a)}$$

or $$Z_{01} = cL \quad \text{or} \quad Z_{01} = \frac{1}{cC_1} \qquad \text{....(8.10b, c)}$$

Combining Eqs. 8.8a, 8.10 b and c yield a very significant result

$$Z_0 = \frac{1}{c\sqrt{CC_1}} \qquad \text{....(8.11)}$$

This means we can evaluate the characteristic impedance, if only we can evaluate the capacitance per unit length of the structure with and without the presence of the dielectric substrate.

The effective microstrip permittivity ε_{eff}

For the air-spaced microstrip line the propagation velocity is given by

$$c = \frac{1}{\sqrt{LC_1}} \qquad \text{....(8.12)}$$

Dividing Eq. 8.12 by Eq. 8.9 and squaring, we obtain

$$\frac{C}{C_1} = \left(\frac{c}{v_p}\right)^2 \qquad \text{....(8.13)}$$

The capacitance ratio C/C_1 is termed as the effective microstrip permittivity ε_{eff}, an important microstrip parameter. From Eq. 8.13 ε_{eff} is given as

$$\varepsilon_{eff} = \left(\frac{c}{v_p}\right)^2 \qquad \text{....(8.14)}$$

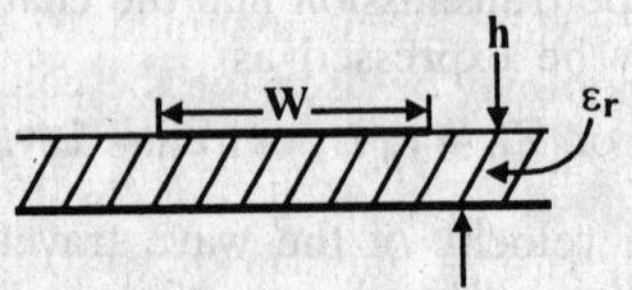

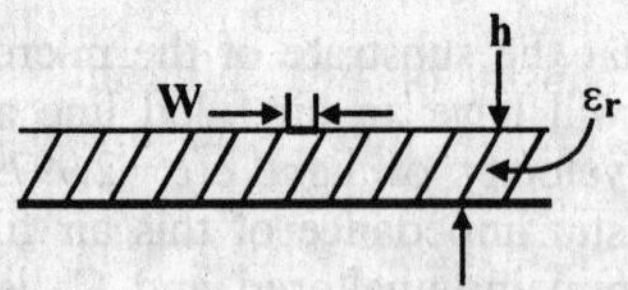

Fig. 8.5 Extremely wide (W >>h) and extremely narrow (W <<h) microstrip lines

A useful relationship between Z_0, Z_{01} and ε_{eff} can be obtained by combining Eq. 8.8c, 8.10c, 8.13 and 8.14. The result is

$$Z_0 = \frac{Z_{01}}{\sqrt{\varepsilon_{eff}}}$$

or $$Z_{01} = Z_0 \sqrt{\varepsilon_{eff}} \quad ....(8.15)$$

Effect of very wide and very narrow lines is indicated in Fig. 8.5. For the very wide lines nearly all the electric field is confined to the substrate dielectric and the structure resembles a parallel-plate capacitor. Therefore at this extreme

$$\varepsilon_{eff} \rightarrow \varepsilon_r$$

In the case of very narrow lines the field is almost equally shared by the air ($\varepsilon_r = 1$) and the substrate so that at this extreme,

$$\varepsilon_{eff} \approx \frac{1}{2}(\varepsilon_r + 1)$$

The range of ε_{eff} is

$$\frac{1}{2}(\varepsilon_r + 1) \le \varepsilon_{eff} \le \varepsilon_r \quad ....(8.16)$$

A convenient form of expressing effective microstrip permittivity is as follows

$$\varepsilon_{eff} = 1 + q\,(\varepsilon_r - 1) \quad ....(8.17)$$

where q is called the filling factor and has the limits

$$\frac{1}{2} \le q \le 1$$

Some useful published microstrip line formula

When a pure TEM mode is assumed to exist the method of conformal transformation may be used for the calculation of microstrip line parameters. For a practical microstrip line having a mixed dielectric configuration the analysis is carried out in two stages. First the capacitance is calculated for a uniform dielectric microstrip line. This result is then extended to cover the real microstrip case simply by replacing the 'uniform' dielectric constant ε_r by the effective dielectric constant ε_{eff}. Wheeler in 1965 [2] has given a conformal transformation useful for microstrip analysis and derived microstrip design formula based on it. These consist of two different relations for wide (a) ($W/h > 2$) and (b) narrow ($W/h < 2$) microstrip lines because of the different approximations used. In the 1977 paper, Wheeler [15] has reported an empirical relation that covers both the ranges. Owens carefully investigated the ranges of applicability of many of the expressions given by Wheeler [15], comparing the calculated results with very accurate numerical computations. The most accurate expressions for synthesis as well as analysis are given below.

Analysis formulae

For narrow lines with $W/h \le 2$

$$Z_0 = \frac{119.9}{\sqrt{2(\varepsilon_r + 1)}}\left\{H' - \frac{\varepsilon_r - 1}{2(\varepsilon_r + 1)}\left[0.4516 + \frac{0.2416}{\varepsilon_r}\right]\right\} \qquad \text{....(8.18)}$$

where $H' = \ln\left[\frac{4h}{W} + \left\{\left(\frac{4h}{W}\right)^2 + 2\right\}^{1/2}\right]$

For wide lines with $W/h \ge 2$

$$Z_0 = \frac{376.7}{\sqrt{\varepsilon_r}}\left\{\frac{W}{h} + 0.8825 + 0.1645\left[\frac{\varepsilon_r - 1}{\varepsilon_r^2}\right] + \frac{\varepsilon_r + 1}{\pi\varepsilon_r}\left\{1.4516 + \ln\left(\frac{W}{2h} + 0.94\right)\right\}\right\}^{-1} \qquad \text{....(8.19)}$$

Effective relative permittivity

For narrow lines with $W/h \le 1$

$$\varepsilon_{eff} = \frac{\varepsilon_r + 1}{2}\left\{1 - \frac{(\varepsilon_r - 1)}{2H'(\varepsilon_r + 1)}\left(0.4516 + \frac{0.2416}{\varepsilon_r}\right)\right\}^{-2}$$

For wide lines with $W/h \ge 1$

$$\varepsilon_{eff} = \frac{\varepsilon_r + 1}{2} + \frac{\varepsilon_r - 1}{2} \times F \qquad \text{....(8.20)}$$

where $F = \left[1 + 10\frac{h}{W}\right]^{-0.555}$ ....(8.21)

Synthesis (Line geometry)

For $8 \leq \varepsilon_r \leq 12$,

$$\frac{W}{h} = \frac{8}{\exp(A) - 2\exp(-A)} \quad \text{....(8.22)}$$

with $$A = \frac{Z_0\sqrt{2(\varepsilon_r + 1)}}{119.9} + \frac{1}{2}\frac{(\varepsilon_r - 1)}{(\varepsilon_r + 1)}\left[0.4516 + \frac{0.2416}{\varepsilon_r}\right] \quad \text{....(8.23)}$$

For wide strips

$$\frac{W}{h} = \frac{2}{\pi}\left[(B-1) - \ln(2B-1) + \frac{\varepsilon_r - 1}{2\varepsilon_r}\left\{\ln(B-1) + 0.293 - \frac{0.577}{\varepsilon_r}\right\}\right] \quad \text{....(8.24)}$$

with $$B = \frac{59.96\pi^2}{Z_0\sqrt{\varepsilon_r}} \quad \text{....(8.25)}$$

Variation of microstrip characteristic impedance Z with W/*h* is shown in Fig. 8.6 for the three different values of ε_r and Fig. 8.7 shows the corresponding variation in ε_{eff}.

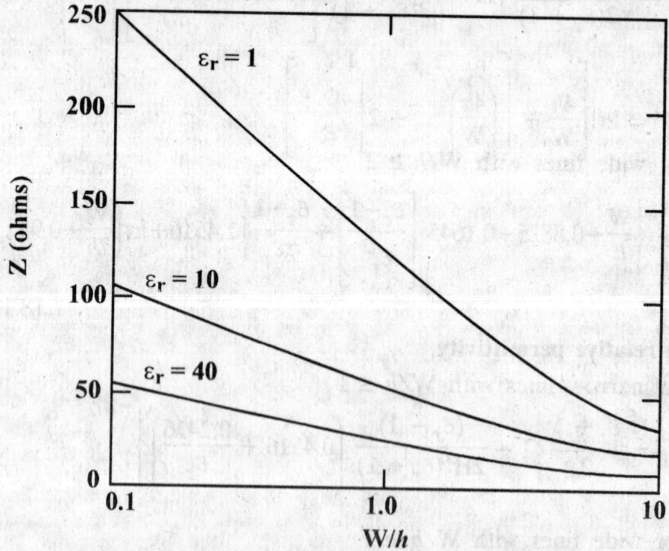

Fig. 8.6. Variation of Z_0 as a function of W/*h* for the quasi-static microstrip line.

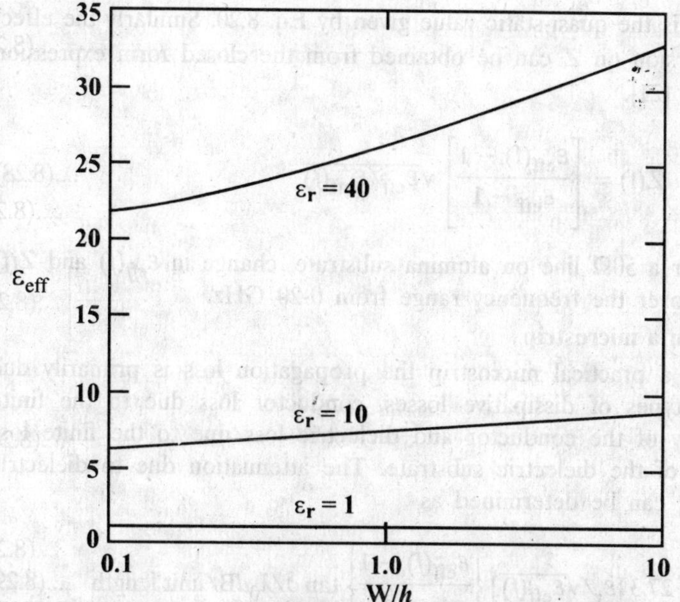

Fig. 8.7. Variation of ε_{eff} for the quasi-static microstrip as a function of W/*h* line.

Empirical formula for the maximum frequency up to which quasi-static formulae can be used is given by

$$f_{stat} = \frac{21.3}{(W + 2h)\sqrt{\varepsilon_r + 1}} \text{ GHz} \qquad \text{....(8.26)}$$

where W and *h* are in mm.

Effect of dispersion

At high frequencies, fields tend to concentrate more in the dielectric substrate. Therefore ε_{eff} increases with increase in frequency, and as the frequency becomes very high (tends to infinity) its value approaches the substrate permittivity ε_r. Approximate closed form dispersion formula to compute the frequency dependent ε_{eff} denoted as ε_{eff} (f) are listed below [17].

$$\varepsilon_{eff}(f) = \left[\frac{\sqrt{\varepsilon_r} - \sqrt{\varepsilon_{eff}}}{1 + 4F^{-1.5}} + \sqrt{\varepsilon_{eff}}\right]^2 \qquad \text{....(8.27a)}$$

where

$$F = \frac{4h\sqrt{\varepsilon_r - 1}}{\lambda_0}\{0.5 + [1 + 2\log(1 + \left(\frac{W}{h}\right))]^2\} \qquad \text{....(8.27b)}$$

and ε_{eff} is the quasi-static value given by Eq. 8.20. Similarly the effect of dispersion on Z can be obtained from the closed form expression given by [21].

$$Z(f) = \left[\frac{\varepsilon_{eff}(f) - 1}{\varepsilon_{eff} - 1}\right] \sqrt{\varepsilon_{eff}/\varepsilon_{eff}(f)} \quad \text{....(8.28)}$$

For a 50Ω line on alumina substrate, change in $\varepsilon_{eff}(f)$ and $Z(f)$ is 10% over the frequency range from 0-20 GHz.

Losses in a microstrip

In a practical microstrip the propagation loss is primarily due to two types of dissipative losses, conductor loss due to the finite resistivity of the conductor and dielectric loss due to the finite loss tangent of the dielectric substrate. The attenuation due to dielectric loss [25] can be determined as

$$\alpha_d = 27.3\,[\varepsilon_r/\sqrt{\varepsilon_{eff}(f)}]\left\{\frac{\varepsilon_{eff}(f) - 1}{\varepsilon_r - 1}\right\} \tan\delta/\lambda_0 \text{dB/unit length} \quad \text{....(8.29)}$$

where $\tan\delta$ is the loss tangent of the dielectric

δ = skin depth

$= (1/R_s\sigma)$ ....(8.30a)

σ = conductivity of the metal

R_s = Surface resistivity of the conductor. ....(8.30b)

is equal to

$R_s = \sqrt{\omega\mu_0/2\sigma}$

The attenuation due to conductor loss for wide lines is given approximately[3] by

$$\alpha_c = R_s/Z_0W \quad \text{Np}/m \quad \text{....(8.30c)}$$

For most microstrip substrates, conductor loss is more significant than dielectric loss. However exception may be with some semiconductor substrates.

The total attenuation constant α is given by

$$\alpha = (\alpha_c + \alpha_d) \quad \text{dB/unit length}$$

Fig. 8.8 shows the variation in α as a function of substrate height.

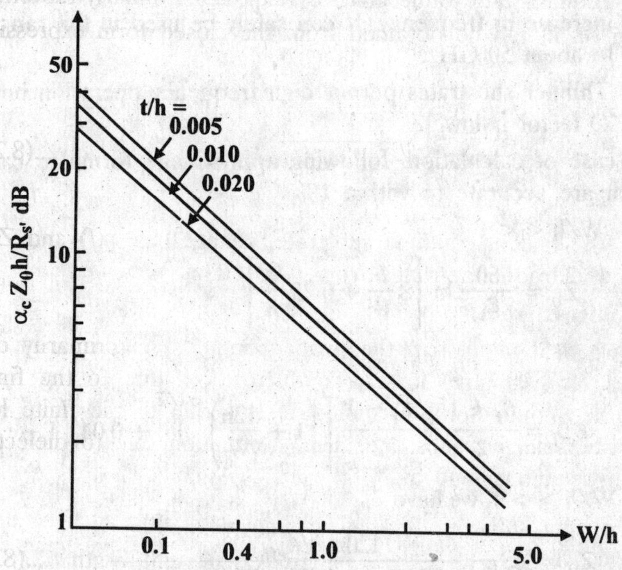

Fig. 8.8 Variation of attenuation constant with W/h

Higher order modes in microstrip

When the width of the microstrip line is large, a transverse resonance mode is exhibited which can couple strongly with the quasi-TEM mode. While narrow strip width TM surface wave mode starts propagating and significant coupling takes place between the quasi-TEM mode and the TM-surface wave mode.

The lower limit for Z in a microstrip is 20 Ω which is set by the onset of transverse resonance mode. The upper limit is 120 and is set by the smallest realizable value of W. One major advantage of microstrip is that its surface is accessible for mounting passive as well as active discrete devices. It is also used for realizing a variety of circuit forms and combining several circuit functions.

Limitations of microstrip

(i) Most of the field in a microstrip is concentrated in the dielectric substrate, a slight change in ε_r due to temperature variation or batch to batch variation changes the impedance and guide wavelength considerably.

(ii) Circuit dimensions at high frequencies are very small and results in fabrication problems.

(iii) The conductor loss in the microstrip increases with an increase in frequency. It can safely be used in the range up to about 50 GHz.

(iv) Thinner substrates permit high frequency operation but the Q factor is low.

For ease of calculation, following approximate formulae can be used which are accurate to within 1%

For $W/h << 1$

$$Z_0 \approx \frac{60}{\sqrt{\varepsilon_{eff}}} \ln \left[8\frac{h}{W} + 0.25\frac{W}{h} \right]$$

where

$$\varepsilon_{eff} = \frac{\varepsilon_r + 1}{2} + \frac{\varepsilon_r - 1}{2} \left[\left(1 + \frac{12h}{W}\right)^{-1/2} + 0.04\left(1 - \frac{W}{h}\right)^2 \right]$$

For $W/h >> 1$, we have

$$Z_0 \approx \frac{120\pi/\sqrt{\varepsilon_{eff}}}{W/h + 1.393 + 0.667 \ln (W/h + 1.444)}$$

For this condition ε_{eff} is

$$\varepsilon_{eff} \approx \frac{\varepsilon_r + 1}{2} + \frac{\varepsilon_r - 1}{2} \left(1 + \frac{12h}{W}\right)^{-1/2}$$

8.3. Inverted Microstrip

The inverted microstrip is shown in Fig. 8.1(iii). The line is etched on lower side of the substrate, there is no conductor on the opposite side of the substrate and ground plane is separated from the substrate by an air space. Thus the substrate mainly supports the microstrip lines and most of the field lines are within the air between the strip and the ground plane. This ensures that the wavelength is long relative to that in conventional microstrip operated at similar frequencies (it also indicates that inverted microstrip can be operated satisfactorily at higher frequencies also). For a required value of characteristic impedance comparatively wider line is obtained in the inverted microstrip line than in conventional microstrip. This reduces conductor dissipation and relaxes fabrication tolerances [5].

8.4. Suspended Stripline

The suspended stripline shown in Fig. 8.1 (iv) is the most useful variant of the stripline. It is essentially an inhomogeneous stripline in which the substrate carrying the strip conductor is placed symmetrically between the two ground planes thereby creating an air gap on either side of the substrate. The dominant mode of propagation is quasi-TEM. The introduction of air gap results in the reduction of the effective dielectric constant of the propagating medium. This structure therefore permits larger circuit dimensions leading to relaxed dimensional tolerences and increased accuracy of circuit fabrication as compared with the microstrip. By choosing a sufficiently thin substrate, the effective dielectric constant can be made close to air thereby extending the frequency range of operation in the dominant mode, which reduces to nearly TEM [22]. Because of these advantages the suspended line is ideally suited for operation in millimeter wave range.

Alternatively suspended stripline is viewed as, it results when the ground plane of inverted microstrip is made to totally enclose the structure, that is the air gap is at both the top and the bottom. The losses in this closed structure are low, hence it results in fairly high Q factor, but unwanted wave guide modes can easily be excited at higher frequencies. The excitation of waveguide modes can possibly be prevented either by bringing the top and bottom walls very close together and or by introducing various structures to act as mode suppressors. In the first case the separations become so small that there is insufficient space for the incorporation of semiconductor devices or other passive devices. In the second case introduction of mode suppressors represents a new design problem. In both the cases the basic structure is not compatible with shunt mounted semiconductor devices [7]. The suspended stripline was studied by Brenuer [17] who made use of finite difference method [18] to obtain computation expressions.

Propagation characteristics

As discussed above, an air gap on both sides of the strip reduces the effective dielectric constant and consequently the strip dimensions are nearly two to three times larger than in a microstrip, for the same microstrip characteristic impedance. A graph showing the comparison of impedance characteristics of microstrip with those of suspended microstrip and inverted microstrip are shown in Fig. 8.9. Another importance of the air gaps is the reduction in the conductor loss as shown in Fig. 8.10. The total dissipative loss in a 50 ohm microstrip at 5-10 GHz range is of the same order as that in a suspended or inverted microstrip around 60 GHz.

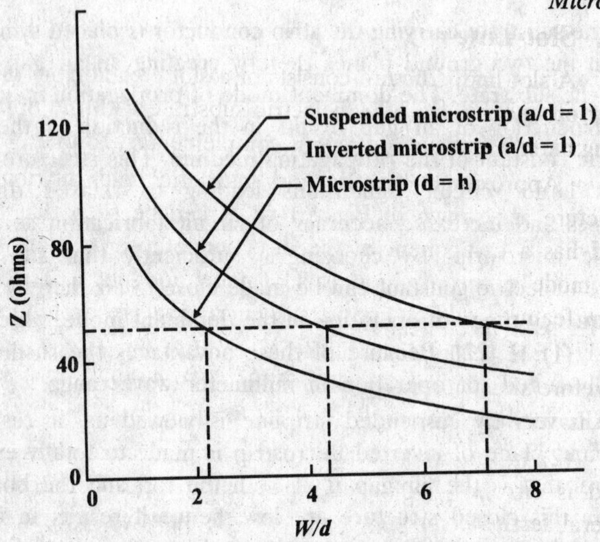

Fig. 8.9. Comparison of impedance characteristics of microstrips Fig. 8.1 (ii), suspended microstrop Fig. 8.1 (iv) and inverted microstrip Fig. 8.1 (iii). $\varepsilon_r = 3.78$.

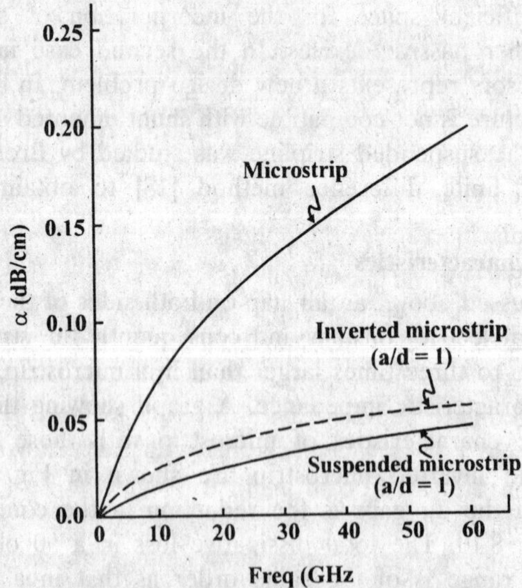

Fig. 8.10. Comparison of attenuation constant $\alpha(=\alpha_c + \alpha_d)$ versus frequency of 50 Ω line in microstrip Fig. 8.1 (ii), suspended microstrip Fig. 8.1(iv) and inverted microstrip Fig. 8.1 (iii).

8.5. Slot-Line

A slot line structure consists of a slot etched from the conducting layer on one surface of a dielectric substrate with the opposite surface being bare. The structure is thus complementary to that of a microstrip.

Approximate electric and magnetic field distributions in this structure are shown in Fig. 8.1(v). It can be seen that the magnetic field has a component in the direction of propagation as well. Thus the mode of propagation is TE mode and not a TEM mode. The main features of slot line versus microstrip are as follows [8]

(1) In a slot line, both the conductors are in one plane, and therefore shunt mounting of components (active or passive) across the line is very convenient.

(2) In the cross section of the line, at some region the magnetic field is circularly polarized. This feature can be used in design of several ferrite components such as resonance isolators.

(3) In a microstrip, a high value of characteristic impedance is produced by very narrow strip width. On the other hand in the slot line, large slot width will provide high impedance. As we know there is technological limitation on the fabrication of very narrow lines, higher impedances can be easily realized in a slot line.

(4) Slot line is more dispersive than microstrip, *i.e.* variations of Z_0 and λ/λ_g with frequency are larger.

(5) The slot line mode resembles the TE_{10} of a rectangular waveguide but it differs from it in that it has no cutoff frequency.

Propagation characteristics

As discussed earlier Fig. 8.11 shows the variation in the slot line impedance Z as a function of W/*h* along with that of microstrip. It is clear from the figure, that the characteristic impedance Z in a slot line increases with an increase in the slot width whereas in the case of microstrip Z decreases with an increase in the strip width.

Also due to non-TEM nature of the slot line it is quite dispersive, hence Z and ε_{eff} vary considerably with frequency (Fig. 8.12). In comparison the variation in microstrip over the same frequency range is negligible. One major disadvantage of slot line is that its Q factor is low around 100 as compared with other planar transmission line.

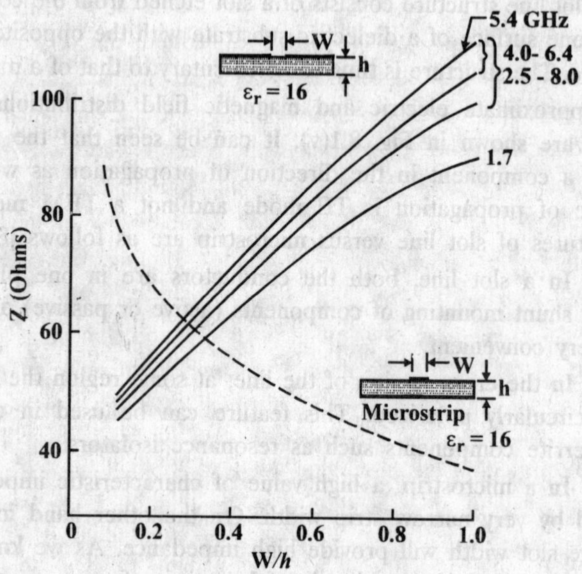

Fig. 8.11. Comparision of impednance characteristics of slot line with microstrip

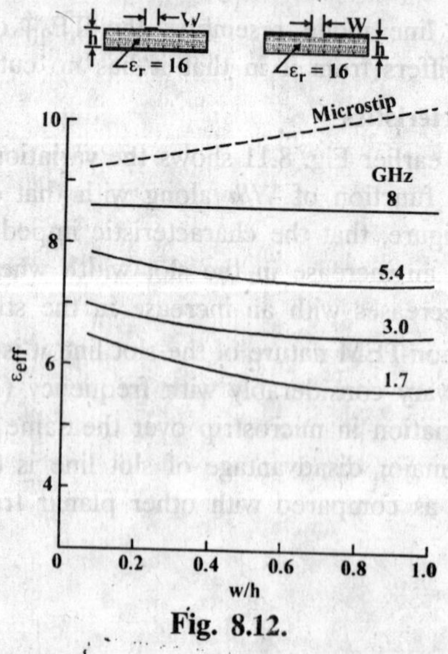

Fig. 8.12.

8.6. Coplanar Lines

A coplanar line consists of a strip of metallic film deposited on the surface of the dielectric slab with two ground planes running adjacent and parallel to the strip on the same side. This is shown in Fig. 8.1(vi). A coplanar waveguide is a coupled slot line in which the signal is applied to the centre conductor with repect to the two ground conductors on the two sides. The shape of this structure is distinctly different from any of the lines considered so far because the metallization is formed on one side of the substrate alone. Some interesting features of coplanar lines are listed below

(1) As we have learnt slot line geometries are well suited for shunt mounting of components across the slot and the microstrip is convenient for series mounting of components but in a coplanar line both series and shunt mounted components can be easily incorporated [9].

(2) Coaxial to coplanar line and microstrip-to-coplanar line transitions can be achieved easily.

(3) Dimensions of a coplanar line can be tapered for a uniform impedance to connect a wide dimensioned component (*e.g.* a SMA connector) to a small device chip or lumped element.

(4) Both balanced and unbalanced modes are possible in a coplanar line. Thus this transmission line finds extensive application in balanced mixers, balanced modulators, etc. where both the balanced and unbalanced signals are present.

(5) Elliptically polarized magnetic field region is located in this geometry. This characteristic is used in design of several ferrite components.

The open nature of this structure represents one limitation, that it results in considerable radiation at higher microwave frequencies. For more details consult the book by Gupta etal. [9]

Consider an infinitely thick substrate and conductors of zero thickness ($b = 0$). The characteristic impedance by using conformal mapping is given by

$$Z_c = \frac{Z_0}{\sqrt{8(\varepsilon_{r+1})}} \frac{k'(\mu)}{k(\mu)} \, \Omega$$

where $$\mu = (1 + 2g/W)^{-1}$$

and $k(\mu)$ is the complete first order elliptical integer.

8.7. Fin Line ('E-Plane' circuits)

Figure 8.2 show fin line structures. It is a totally shielded rectangular conducting box (like rectangular waveguide, but the modes are not waveguide modes) in which dielectric substrate is fixed, usually centrally located across two of its faces. A metal circuit is deposited on one side of the substrate and a slot pattern on this metal conductor forms the fin line circuit. Since the substrate of fin line lies in the E-plane of the rectangular waveguide, these lines are also called E-plane transmission lines. Fin lines are frequently used in millimeter wave integrated circuits (MWICs) because of their favourable properties such as low dispersion broad single mode band width, moderate attenuation, and compatibility with solid state chip devices. From Fig. 8.2 it is evident that fin-line structures are quasiplanar as compared to microstrip-like structures [10,11].

8.8. Image Line

At very high microwave frequencies of the order of hundreds of GHz, the wavelengths become comparable with practically realistic dielectric 'slab' cross sectional dimensions. The geometry of an image line as shown in Fig. 8.13 comprises a rectangular dielectric slab of relative permittivity ε_r backed by a perfectly conducting ground plane. The image line supports hybrid modes (E^y_{mn} & E^x_{mn}). The largest field components of the image line are in the transverse directions the modes are essentially of the TEM kind and can be grouped into two families designated by E^y_{mn} and E^x_{mn}. The superscripts denote the electric field component in the direction of propagation and the sub-scripts m and n designate the number of half cycle variations of the field components within the guide along the x and y directions respectively. $m = n = 1$ corresponds to the dominant modes for this line. The Q factors available at frequencies above 100 GHz is of the order of several thousands. Image lines have the limitations of poor compatibility with active devices, mutual coupling and of radiations from discontinuities and bends. The other problem with these lines is that the dielectric/metal adhesives are very lossy and this reduces the practical loaded Q factor. Other salient features of the image line are that it is suitable for passive as well as active integrated circuits. The ground plane supports the dielectric substrate and provides a heat sink and dc biasing for active devices. The use of high resistivity semiconductor as the dielectric material allows the fabrication of active devices such as oscillators, mixers, phase shifters, modulators etc. directly into the transmission line [11, 12].

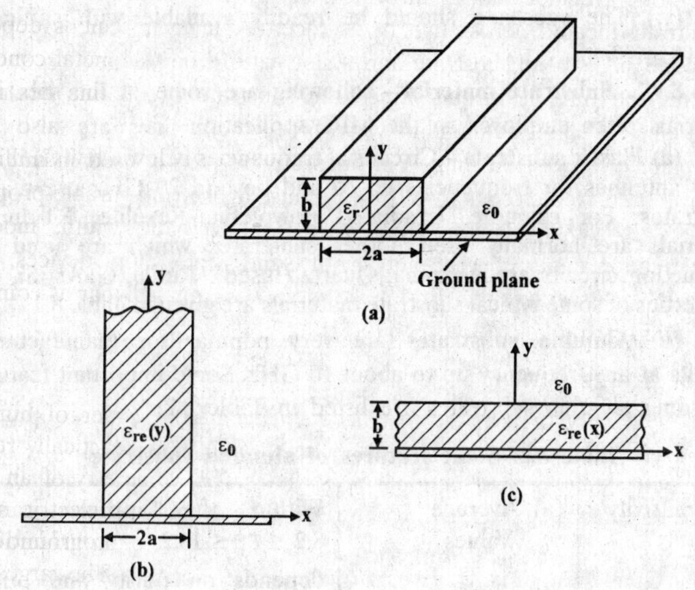

Fig. 8.13. Image-line geometry.

8.9. Choice of Substrate for MICs.

Several factors that need to be considered in selecting a particular substrate are its mechanical, thermal, electronic and economical aspects, which influence the decision process leading to the correct choice for a specific type of MIC and their applications.

The most important criterion which should be taken into account are as follows

(i) The cost of the substrate should be justified in the light of application of the overall system costs.

(ii) The technology chosen should be thin or thick film.

(iii) The frequency ranges involved must be taken into account because this will influence the thickness and permittivity of the dielectric substance selected.

(iv) The surface finish of the substrate should be sufficiently good so that conductor losses can be maintained at tolerably low levels.

(v) The mechanical strength and thermal conductivity should be sufficient for the desired application.

(vi) The substrate should be readily available with sufficient surface area.

8.9.1. Substrate material – Following are some of the substrate materials often employed in the MIC application

(a) Plastic substrate – Circuits at frequencies below a few GHz and array antennas for frequencies up to and beyond 20 GHz use plastic substrates. For example, Irradiated polyolefin, Rexolite, RT-duroid materials are normally used. Other substrates which are used for production circuits are Alumina, Quartz (fused), Rutile, GaAs, Si, etc. Properties of some typical substrate materials are given in Table 8.1.

(b) Alumina substrates are very popular for manufacturing circuits at any frequency up to about 10 GHz. Some important features regarding alumina substrates are listed in Table 8.2.

Table 8.2. Some features of alumina substrate

Permittivity	(a) Average Values	Within the approx. range $8.2 \le \varepsilon_r \le 10.2$, considerably depends on purity and other factors.
	(b) Variation from batch to batch	Hence it should be taken into account in design (worsens with deteriorating purity).
	(c) Material dispersion	Significant, $\frac{1}{\varepsilon_r}(\partial \varepsilon_r / \partial f)$ through microwave frequencies. Some dipolar behaviour, amount depends on impurities.
Dielectric loss ($\tan \delta$)		Present to varying extent.
Anisotropy		Depends on method of manufacture (caused by preferential orientation of crystallites).
Surface flatness		Improper flatness (bowing) can often occur to a significant extent with cheaper substrates.

Table 8.1. Properties of substrates used in MICs

Material	ε_r approx.	$\tan\delta \times 10^4$ at 10 GHz	Surface roughness (μm)	Thermal conductivity W/cm K	Special Features
Alumina (99.5%)	9.6–10.4	1	0.05 (polished)	0.37	Au coated substrates, widely used in microwave range.
Fused quartz (99.5%)	3.78	1	0.006–0.025	0.017	Reproducible substrates, minimum thickness 0.05 mm, smooth surface, useful in mm range, high cost.
Sapphire (single crystal)	$\varepsilon_{r1} = 9.6$ $\varepsilon_{r11} = 11.6$	1	0.005–0.025	0.42	Reproducible substrates, smooth surfaces, anisotropic, high cost.
Rutile (TiO_2)	85	40	0.25–2.5	0.05	Reduced size components, rough surface, ε_r temperature sensitive.
Beryllia BeO 98%	6.3	60	0.05–1.25	2.5	High conductivity, rough surface, compound substrate.
RT-duriod 5880	2.2–2.3	3–7	0.075–1 4.25–8.75	0.0026	Cu-coated, large sheet size minimum thickness 0.1mm, easily machinable, low cost.
RT-duroid 6010	10.2–10.7	10–15			Cu-coated, high ε_r, easily machinable, high loss.
Kapton	3–3.5				Flexible substrates, minimum thickness 0.025 mm, easily machinable, low cost.
Si	11.7–12	40–150	< 0.025	0.9	
GaAs	12–13	10–60	< 0.025	0.3	

(c) Other very useful substrate is sapphire, it is one of the most expensive substrates having the following unique features.

(i) It is optically transparent. Hence chip devices can be marked for attachment since the underside can be viewed.

(ii) It has high permittivity (≈11). This is almost compatible with high resistivity silicon. It results in small size of the microstrip components due to the reduced wavelength.

(iii) Sapphire substrates are highly reproducible, *i.e.* all pieces are essentially identical in dielectric properties.

(iv) Surface finish is of optical grade which results in low power loss from surface roughness.

(v) Thermal conductivity is quite high, being about 30 per cent higher than the best alumina.

8.9.2. Conductor materials – The ideal conductor materials used for monolithic microwave integrated circuits should have high conductivity, low temperature coefficient of resistance, good adhesion to the substrate, good etchability and solderability and shoud be easily deposited or electroplated. Generally used conductor materials are Gold (Au), Silver (Ag), Copper (Cu), Aluminium (Al), Chromium (Cr), etc.

8.10. Thin-Film Manufacture

Microwave grade hybrid circuits place some stringent demands on the accuracy and repeatability on the circuit technology. These demands can be met by carefully controlled thin film manufacturing process which is normally used for the great majority of MICs. "Clean room" areas are used for the manufacturing purposes. Gold and copper are the most commonly used conductors for the deposition on the substrates [13,14]. Copper is preferred because of its superior conductivity and lower price but a final gold film must be evaporated over the copper to provide an environmental protective layer. The necessary thickness of the metal film may be determined by considering the skin depth in the metal at the lowest frequency of interest. At about 4 GHz the skin depth in copper is approximately 1 μm. At least 4 to 5 skin depths should be deposited, hence, the required thickness will be 4 to 5 μm. Practical techniques used for the deposition are

(a) Evaporation or sputtering a very thin "seed" layer of a suitable metal onto the surface of the substrate.

(b) Evaporation or sputtering a very thin layer of conductor metal on to this 'seed' layer.

(c) Electroplating the bulk conductor metal on to layer (b). Steps *a* and *b* provide mechanical and electric foundation layers on which good quality bulk conductor metal is electroplated.

Circuit definitions for MICs are obtained by selective photo etching of metallised substrate. First of all a layout of the circuit is drawn and a photo mask is prepared. The size of this mask is equal to the actual size of the circuit. This mask has a negative transparency, *i.e.* transparent at the portions where metallisation is required.

The substrates are cleaned to a very high specification and a thin layer of photo resist emulsion spread evenly over it. This layer is exposed to the ultra-violet rays through the circuit mask. Exposed portions corresponding to the circuit pattern harden up. Unexposed photo resist is dissolved away and etching of the metal (copper or gold) is carried out. Required metallization pattern is protected by hardened photo resist and thus left unetched on the substrate. This photoresist layers on the final circuit pattern is removed chemically.

Once the required circuit pattern has been etched on the substrate, discrete (active or passive) devices are mounted. The mounting of series-connected devices can be accomplished by bonding the device across a gap in the microstrip. Other devices well suited for MICs are wire-bonded device chips, leadless inverted devices, ceramic carriers and beam lead devices. Shunt mounting on the microstrip circuits is carried out by drilling a hole through the substrate (usually by an ultrasonic grinder). The device is mounted between the ground plane and a strip placed over the microstrip to bridge the hole. Devices in "pill" or "micropill" packages are well suited for this application. Shunt mounting of devices in a slot line circuit is fairly easy. The device is mounted across the slot. Device packages that are suitable for series mounting in a microstrip are also equally suited for shunt mounting in slot line circuits. Bonding techniques for connecting devices depend on the circuit metallisation and type of the device package used. Normally soldering is used with the copper clad laminates and thermo-compression bonding is used for gold metallisation, low-temperature indium solders and conductive epoxies may also be used.

8.11. Thick-Film Manufacture

Thick film technology has become well established in the low-cost manufacture of hybrid microcircuits at lower-than-micro wave frequencies and for densely packaged digital subsystems [15]. Compared with thin film technology this is relatively low cost. Thick film materials and techniques have been developed for MICs operating at frequencies upto about 20 GHz [16]. The losses associated with the thick film conductors are more than that for thin-film conductors. The method commonly used for the manufacture of thick film MICs are

(a) Thick film patterns are printed and fired on to the ceramic substrate-usually alumina but occasionally quartz [17].

(b) A printed circuit technique is used to etch the desired pattern in the copper clading of the plastic substrate (usually polyolefin).

8.12. Advantages of MICs

MICs are preferred over the conventional microwave circuits for the following reasons – (a) small size and weight (b) reproducibility and reliability, (c) improved performance in some cases and (d) eventual cost reduction when produced in large quantities.

8.12.1. Reduction in size : There is large reduction in cross section for MIC transmission lines. An X-band wave guide is 1 inch by 0.5 inch size whereas cross-section required for a 50 ohm microstrip on alumina substrate is of the order of 0.25 inch by 0.25 inch. High dielectric constant substrates reduce the guide wave length by a factor equal to the square root of effective dielectric constant. For alumina circuits a reduction of 2.5 to 3.0 is obtained, hence the size of the distributed elements of the circuits reduces in the same ratio. A further reduction in the size is achieved by use of lumped elements in place of distributed elements. The lumped elements are an order of magnitude smaller than distributed elements. In MICs large complicated circuits can be produced by photo-etching on a single metallization, hence it eliminates inter-connection which saves considerable volume occupied by connectors. Also in this fabrication process the input output parts can be located at the desired location. In MICs it is possible to use encaplusated device chips. These device chips occupy much smaller space than packaged devices.

8.12.2. Reproducibility and reliability

Thin film deposition and photo-etching techniques used in MIC fabrication leads to a very uniform product. Increased reliability of MICs are achieved

(1) Microwave semi-conductor devices used in MICs have longer life as compared to that of tubes.

(2) Fewer number of connectors are required for achieving a given sub-system function.

(3) More durable connections between device and circuit are obtained because of improved bonding techniques. Relative motion among various parts of the circuit is less, therefore the circuit construction is more rigid.

8.12.3. Improvement in performance

In MICs transverse dimensions of the microwave structure are compatible with the size of the device chips while in the conventional microwave circuits, device mounting structures like posts, etc., introduce additional reactances which limit the circuit performance. Elimination of these reactances in MICs increases the circuit bandwidth and device impedance level. Combinations of different micro-strip lines in the same circuit introduces another degree of flexibility in circuit design. These factors improve the performance of MICs.

8.12.4. Reduction in cost

In conventional microwave circuits, time consuming and expensive operation of precision machining has been replaced in the case of MICs, with techniques like photo-etching which are much quicker and cheaper. The cost of fabrication of MICs is to a considerable extent independent of the circuit complexity. For example, etching out a micro-strip section or a filter circuit requires about the same effort. Once the mask is prepared large-scale production does not require any additional tools. Also the MICs can use semiconductor devices in chip form which are much cheaper than the packaged devices.

8.13. Limitations of MICs

There are some difficulties associated with the design and usage of MICs. Most of these are because of the fact that once an MIC has been fabricated there is hardly any provision for adjustment of circuit parameters. Screws and plungers etc. cannot be incorporated in MICs to improve the circuits performance like in conventional microwave circuits. Hence the circuits have to be designed fairly accurately taking all the parameters into account so that adjustments after fabrication are reduced to minimum. One application of MIC is a microstrip patch antenna and is discussed in detail in the following section.

To design circuits accurately precise characterization of semiconductor devices is needed.

8.14. Microstrip Patch Antenna

Microstrip patch antenna consist of metal patch that are large with respect to normal transmission line widths. A patch radiates from fringing fields around its edges. Impedance match occurs when a patch resonates as a resonator cavity. When matched the antenna achieves peak efficiency. Figure. 8.14 illustrates a rectangular patch antenna

The edges of a patch appear as slots whose excitations depend on the internal fields of the cavity. In the general analysis of an arbitrary shaped patch, the patch is considered to be a resonant cavity with metal (electric) walls of the patch and the ground plane, and magnetic walls around the edges. In the analysis the effect of fringing field is taken care of by increasing the effective size to account for the capacitive susceptance of fringing fields and the radiation admittance is ignored to find the resonant frequency. The far field is integrated to find the radiated power and the radiation conductance. The fields at the ends can be resolved into normal and tangential components with respect to the ground plane. The normal component are out of phase due to patch length being $\lambda/2$. Therefore the far fields produced by them cancel in the broad side direction. The tangential components (those parallel to the ground plane) are in phase, and the resulting fields combine to give the maximum radiated field normal to the surface of the structure; *i.e*, the boadside direction. Therefore the patch may be respresented by two slots $\lambda/2$ apart excited in phase and radiating in the half space above the ground plane.

Various types of feed configurations are used in microstrip antennas. Four generally used feeds are (1) microstrip line, (2) coaxial probe, (3) aperture coupling and proximity coupling. Microstrip feed line in a conducting strip is usually of much smaller width compared to the patch. It is easy to fabricate and easy to match by controlling the inset position and simple to model. However surface waves and spurious feed radiation increase with substrate thickness, limiting the band width. The coaxial feed is easy to fabricate and match, also has low spurious radiation. It has narrow bandwidth and is more difficult to model for thick substrates.

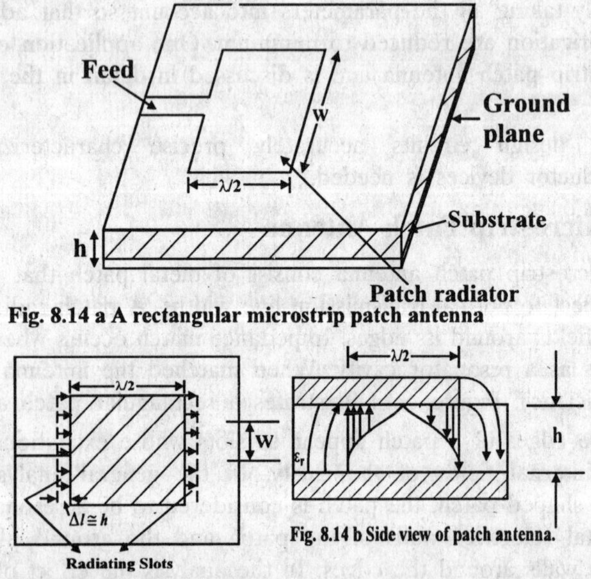

Fig. 8.14 a A rectangular microstrip patch antenna

Fig. 8.14 b Side view of patch antenna.

Fig. 8.14 c Top view of radiating element

Fig. 8.14 Illustrates a rectangular microstrip patch antenna.

Principal Patch Shapes

Various shapes of patch antennas are possible; some of these are shown in Fig. 8.15.

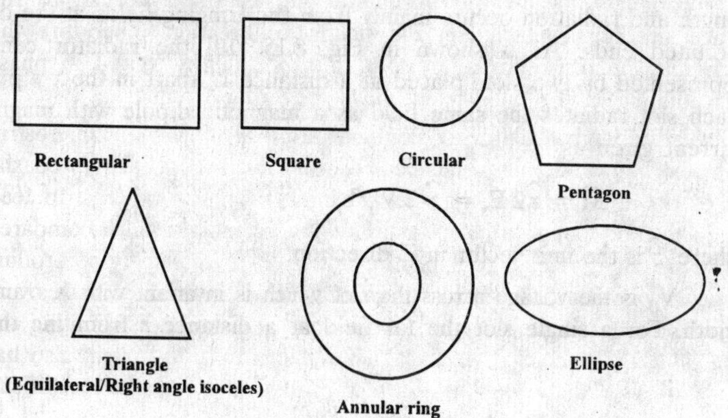

Fig. 8.15

8.14.1 Rectangular microstrip antenna

The simplest microstrip patch configuration is rectangular microstrip antenna with the basic antenna element being a strip conductor on a thin dielectric substrate backed by a ground plane.

Methods of analysis

Many methods of analysing microstrip antennas are available in literature.

The most popular models are the transmission line, cavity and full wave. The transmission line model is easiest of all, it gives good physical insight but is less accurate. The cavity model is more accurate compared to the transmission line model, but at the same time more complex.

(a) Transmission line model

Transmission line model is the simplest for analysis of the patch and the results obtained are adequate for most engineering purposes and require less computation. The limitation of this model are that it can only be applied to rectangular or square patch geometry and the accuracy is limited. However the analysis provides a reasonable interpretation of the radiation mechanism while simultaneously giving simple expressions for the characteristics. This method is suitable for moderate bandwidth antennas [19].

In this mode the microstrip radiator element is treated as a line resonator with no transverse field variations. The fields vary along the length and radiation occurs mainly from the fringing fields at the open circuited ends. As is shown in Fig. 8.15 [19] the radiator can be represented by two slots placed at a distance L apart in the *x-y* plane. Each slot radiates the same field as a magnetic dipole with magnetic current given as

$$\vec{M} = \hat{z}\, 2\, E_x = \hat{z}\, 2\, V_0/h \qquad \text{....(8.31)}$$

where $\hat{z}$ is the unit vector in Z direction.

V_0 is the voltage across the slot which is invariant with X over the width. For a single slot the far field at a distance r from the origin is

$$E_\phi = -j\, 2V_0 W k_0 \frac{\exp(-jk_0 r)}{4\pi r} F(\theta, \phi) \qquad \text{....(8.32)}$$

$$E_\theta = 0 \qquad \text{....(8.33)}$$

where

$$F(\theta,\phi) = \frac{\sin\left(\dfrac{k_0 h}{2} \sin\theta \cos\phi\right) \sin\left(\dfrac{k_0 W}{2} \cos\theta\right)}{\left(\dfrac{k_0 h}{2} \sin\theta \cos\phi\right)\left(\dfrac{k_0 W}{2} \cos\theta\right)} \sin\theta \qquad \text{....(8.34)}$$

For $\theta = \pi/2$, $F(\theta)$ will represent the E-plane pattern which can be determined from equation given below

$$F(\phi) = \frac{\sin\left(\dfrac{k_0 h}{2} \cos\phi\right)}{\left(\dfrac{k_0 h}{2} \cos\phi\right)} \sin\theta \qquad \text{....(8.35)}$$

Similarly, for $\phi = \pi/2$, $F(\theta)$ will represent the H-plane pattern and may be written as

$$F(\theta) = \frac{\sin\left[\frac{k_0 W}{2}\cos\theta\right]}{\left[\frac{k_0 W}{2}\cos\theta\right]}\sin\theta \qquad \text{....(8.36)}$$

Hence for two slots spaced a distance L apart, the E plane radiation pattern is

$$F(\phi) = \frac{\sin\left(\frac{k_0 h}{2}\cos\phi\right)}{\left(\frac{k_0 h}{2}\cos\phi\right)}\cos\left[\frac{k_0 L}{2}\cos\phi\right] \qquad \text{....(8.37)}$$

whereas the H-plane radiation pattern is independent of L and is given by $F(\theta)$.

The radiated power may be obtained by integrating the real part of the poyanting vector over the hemisphere and may be expressed for $h<\lambda_0$ as

$$P_r = \frac{V_0^2 I_1}{240\,\pi^2} \qquad \text{....(8.38)}$$

where

$$I_1 = \int_0^{\pi} \sin^2\left[\frac{ko W\cos\theta}{2}\right]\tan^2\theta\sin\theta\, d\theta \qquad \text{....(8.39)}$$

The radiation resistance R_r is then given by

$$R_r = \frac{V_0^2}{2P_r} = \frac{120\,\pi^2}{I_1^2} \qquad \text{....(8.40)}$$

For $\quad W < \lambda_0,\; R_r = 90\lambda_0^2/W^2 \qquad$ ....(8.14)

$\quad W > \lambda_0,\; R_r = 120\lambda_0/W \qquad$ ....(8.42)

Using the expression for the normalised line extension Δl, the slot susceptance represented by a capacitance is expressed as

$$C = \frac{\Delta l\sqrt{\varepsilon_{eff}}}{cZ_0} \qquad \text{....(8.43)}$$

where Z_0 is the characteristic impedance of the microstrip line and c is the velocity of light. Hence the input impedance of the radiating element can be expressed as

$$Y_{in} = G + jB + Y_0 \frac{G + j\,(B + Y_0 \tan \beta L)}{Y_0 + j(G + j\,B \tan \beta L)} \quad \text{....(8.44)}$$

where $G = 1/R_r$, $B = \frac{k_0 \Delta l \sqrt{\varepsilon_{eff}}}{Z_0}$, β is the propagation constant $= 2\pi \frac{\sqrt{\varepsilon_0}}{\lambda_0}$ and $Y_s = \frac{1}{Z_0}$

$$\tan \beta L = \frac{2Y_0 B}{B^2 + G^2 - {Y_0}^2} \quad \text{....(8.45)}$$

$$Y_{in}(z) = 2G \left[\cos^2 (\beta\, z) + \frac{G^2 + B^2}{Y_0^2} \sin^2 (\beta z) - \frac{B}{Y_0} \sin (2\beta z) \right]^{-1} \quad \text{....(8.46)}$$

where z is the distance of the feed point from the corner. This expression can be further simplified for the practical case of $G/Y_0 < 1$, and $B/Y_0 < 1$, to

$$Y_{in}\,[Z] = \frac{2G}{\cos^2 (\beta z)} \quad \text{....(8.46a)}$$

which is valid every where except for $\beta z = \pi/2$.

Further the mutual conductance for the interaction between the two radiating slots is

$$g_{12} = \frac{1}{120\pi^2} \int_0^{\pi} \frac{\sin^2 \left[\frac{\pi W}{\lambda_0} \cos \theta \right] \tan^2 \theta \sin \theta \, J_0 \left[\frac{2\pi L}{\lambda_0} \sin \theta \right]}{G} \, d\theta \quad \text{....(8.47)}$$

where $J_o(n)$ is the Bessel function of zeroeth order

$$Y_{in}\,(Z) = 2\,(G \pm g_{12}) / \cos^2 (\beta z) \quad \text{...(8.14.18)}$$

The input admittance at the feed point is

$$Y_1 = Y_0 \left[\frac{Z_0 \cos \beta L_1 + jZ_\omega \sin \beta L_1}{Z_\omega \cos \beta L_1 + jZ_0 \sin \beta L_1} + \frac{Z_0 \cos \beta L_2 + jZ_\omega \sin \beta L_2}{Z_\omega \cos \beta L_2 + jZ_0 \sin \beta L_2} \right] \quad .....(8.49)$$

where $Z_w = 1/Y_w$ and Z_0 is the characteristic impedance of the microstrip

$$X_L = \frac{377}{\sqrt{\varepsilon_r}} + \tan \left[\frac{2\pi h}{\lambda_0} \right] \quad ....(8.50)$$

hence the input impedance is

$$Z_{in} = Z_1 + jX_L \quad ....(8.51)$$

where $Z_1 = 1/Y_1$

$$G_\omega^d = \frac{f_d}{f_a} \sqrt{\varepsilon_{eff}}\, G_\omega^a \quad ....(8.52)$$

$$B_\omega^d = \frac{\Delta l_d\, f_d}{\Delta l_a\, f_a}\, \varepsilon_{ff}\, B_\omega^a \quad ....(8.53)$$

where the superscripts *a* and *d* respectively denote quantities for air and actual dielectric, in this way line extension Δl's are calculated.

Example 8.1. A stripline has the following constants W = 0.05 cm, **t** = 0.005 cm and b = 0.4 cm, ε_r = 2.4. Find the characteristic impedance of the line.

Sol. : $\frac{W}{b-t} = \frac{0.05}{0.4 - 0.005} = 0.01266$

and $\frac{t}{b} = \frac{0.005}{0.4} = 0.0125$

Since $\frac{W}{b-t} \leq 0.5$

Eq. 8.3 should be used to find Z_0

$$K = \text{sech}\,(\pi W/2b)$$

$$= \text{sech}\,[\pi \times 0.05/(2 \times 0.4)] = 0.98$$

$$Z = \frac{1}{\sqrt{\varepsilon_r}} \left\{ 29.979 \ln \left[2 \frac{(1+\sqrt{K})}{(1-\sqrt{K})} \right] \right\}$$

$$= \frac{1}{\sqrt{2.4}} \left\{ 29.979 \ln \left[2 \frac{(1+\sqrt{.98})}{(1-\sqrt{.98})} \right] \right\} = 115.7\ \Omega$$

Example 8.2. A microstrip line is built on a substrate with a dielectric constant of 10. The substrate thickness is 0.010 mm. Calculate the line width and guide wave length for a 50Ω line operating at 10GHz. What is the effective dielectric constant for this case ?

Given	Calculate
$\varepsilon_r = 10$	$W = ?$
$h = 0.010$	$\lambda_g = ?$
$f = 10$ GHz	$\varepsilon_{eff} = ?$
$Z = 50\ \Omega$	

Z and ε_r are known, hence the line can be synthesized using following steps

For Z = 50 Ω from graph 8.6, find $\frac{W}{h} \cdot \frac{W}{h} = 0.9$

h = 0.01; hence W = 0.009

$W/h \le 1$

Formula to be used for finding ε_{eff} is given below

$$\varepsilon_{eff} = \frac{\varepsilon_r + 1}{2} + \frac{\varepsilon_r - 1}{2}\left[\left(1 + \frac{12h}{W}\right)^{-1/2} + 0.04\left(1 - \frac{W}{h}\right)^2\right]$$

$$= 6.6890$$

$$\lambda_g = \frac{\lambda_0}{\sqrt{\varepsilon_{eff}}} = 1.15995 \text{ cm}$$

Example 8.3. A microstrip line is to be designed on alumina substrate having relative dielectric constant ε_r = 8.2. The W/h ratio is = 0.95. Compute the effective relative dielectric constant, the characteristic impedance Z_0, the phase velocity, and the guide wave length.

The effective dielectric constant is obtained from the relation given in Ex. 8.2.

$$\varepsilon_{eff} = \frac{8.2 + 1}{2} + \frac{8.2 - 1}{2}\left[\left(1 + \frac{12}{0.95}\right)^{-1/2} + 0.04\,(1 - 0.95)^2\right]$$

$$= 5.575$$

The characteristic impedance Z_0 is calculated from the relation

$$Z_0 = \frac{60}{\sqrt{\varepsilon_{eff}}} \ln\left(\frac{8}{W/h} + 0.25\frac{W}{h}\right)$$

$$= \frac{60}{\sqrt{5.575}} \ln\left[\frac{8}{0.95} + 0.25\,(0.95)\right] = 54.85\ \Omega$$

The phase velocity is

$$v_p = \frac{3 \times 10^8}{\sqrt{5.575}} = 1.27 \times 10^8 \text{ m/s}$$

The wavelength is

$$\lambda = \frac{\lambda_0}{\sqrt{\varepsilon_r}} \left[\frac{\varepsilon_r}{1 + 0.63\,(\varepsilon_r - 1)\,(W/h)^{0.1255}} \right]^{1/2}$$

For $W/h \geq 0.6$

$$\lambda = \frac{\lambda_0}{\sqrt{8.2}} \left[\frac{8.2}{1 + 0.63\,(8.2 - 1)\,(0.95)^{0.1255}} \right]^{1/2} = 0.426\,\lambda_0$$

References

1. Gupta, K.C, and Singh, A. **"Microwave Integrated Circuits"**, Wiley Eastern, New Delhi (1974). Apart from discussions on various aspects of MICs this book contains an extensive bibliography of papers on MICs published during 1967 to 1973.

2. Wheeler, H.A., **"Transmission-line Properties of a Strip on a Dielectric Sheet"**, IEEE Trans., MTT-13, pp. 172-185 (1965)

3. Gupta, K.C., Garg Ramesh and Bahl I.J., **"Microstrip line and slotlines,"** Artech House (Mass, U.S.A.), 1979

4. Schneider, M.V., **"Microstrip lines for microwave Integrated Circuits"**, The Bell System Technical Journal, May-June 1969, pp. 1421-1444.

5. Gunston, M.A.R., **"Microwave Transmission - line Impedance Data"**, Van Nostrand Reinhold Company, London, 1972.

6. Ganguly, A.K. and Spielman, B.E. **'Dispersion Characterstics for Arbitrarily Configured Transmission Media"**, IEEE Trans, MTT- **25**, No. 12. December 1977, pp. 1138-1141.

7. Villotte, J.P. Aubourg, M., Garault Y., **"Modified Suspended Striplines for Microwave Integrated Circuits'**, Electron-Lett. **14.** No. 18, 31 Aug. 1978, pp. 602-603.

8. Holder, P.A.R. **"X-band Microwave Integrated Circuits using slotline and Coplanar waveguide".** The Radio and Electronic Engineer, 48, No 1/2, January/Fabruary 1978, pp. 38-42.

9. Meier, P.J., **"Millimeter Integrated Circuits Suspended in the E-plane of Rectangular Waveguide".** IEEE Trans., MTT-26, No. 10, October 1978, 726-733.

10. Knox, R.M. **"Dielectric Waveguide Microwave Integrated Circuits - an overview"**, IEEE Trans., MTT-**24**, No. 11, November 1976, pp. 806-814.

11. Hinken, J.H., **"Waveguides for Microwave Integrated Circuits"**, Proceedings of Ninth European Microwave conference, 17-21 September 1976, Brighton, England, pp. 650-660.

12. Caulton, M., and Sobol, H., **"Microwave Integrated Circuit Technology a Survey"**, IEEE J. Solid-State Circuits, SC-5, December 1970, pp. 292-303.

13. Ladbrooke, P.H., England, E.H., and Potok, M. H. N., **"A specific thin-film technology for microwave integrated circuits"**, IEEE Trans on Manufacturing Technology, MFT-**2**, No. 2, December 1973, pp. 53-59.

14. Harper, C.A. (Ed.), **"Handbook of Thick Film Hybrid Micro-electronics"**, McGraw - Hill Book Co., New York, U.S.A., 1974.

15. Wheeler, H.A., **"Transmission - line properties of a strip on a dielectric sheet on a plane"**, IEEE, Tran. MTT-25 P. (C31-647, 1977)

16. Brenner, H.E., **"Numerical solution of TEM-Line Problems Involving Inhomogeneous Media"**, IEEE Trans. MTT, vol. MTT-**15**, August 1967, pp. 485-487

17. Wen, C.P. **"Coplanar Waveguide A surface strip transmission line suitable for non-reciprocal cryromagnetic device application".** IEEE Trans, Microwave theory Tech., Vol. MTT-**17**, December 1969, pp 1087-1090.

18. Bahl, I. J. and Bhartia, P., **"Microstrip Antenna"**, Artech House, Inc, Dedhem, 1982.

19. James, J.R. and Hall, P.S., **"Hand Book of Microstrip Antenna"**, Vol. I.

20. Munson, R.E., **"Conformal Microstrip Antennas and Microstrip Phased Arrays"**, IEEE. Trans. Antenna Propagation., vol. A P-22, January 1974, pp. 74-78.

21. Hammerstad, E.O., **"Equation for microstrip circuit design"**, Proc. 5th European Microstrip conf, Humburg, September, 1975, pp. 268-272.

22. Carver, K.R. James W. Mink, **"Microstrip Antenna Technology"**, IEEE Trans, Antennas Propagation, Vol. A P-29, Nol, pp. 2-24, January 1981.

23. Knorr, J.B. and Kuchler, K.D., **"Analysis of coupled slots and coplanar strips on dielectric substrate"**, IEEE Trans., MTT, Vol. MTT-23, pp. 541-548, July 1975.

24. Yamashita, E. Atsuki, K. and Ueda, T., **"An approximate dispersion formula of microstrip lines for computer aided design of microwave integrated circuits"**, IEEE Trans. Microwave Theory Tech., Vol. MTT-27, pp. 1036-1038, Dec. 1979.

25. E.J. Denlinger, **"Losses in microstrip lines"**, IEEE Trans. Microwave theorg Teeh., Vol. MTT-28, pp. 513-522, June 1980.

Problems and Review Questions

1. A quartz substrate of relative dielectric constant = 3.8 and tan δ = 0.0001 has a microstrip, the W/h ratio is 5. Find the (a) effective permittivity, (b) Z_0, (c) α_d at 10GHz.
2. A microstrip line is etched on a fibreglass epoxy material having ε_r = 5.23, h = 8 mil, t = 2.8 mils, the width of the line W = 10 mils. Write a FORTRAN program to compute the characteristic impedance Z_o of the line.
3. Design a 50 Ω stripline with fused quartz substrate of relative dielectric constant = 3.8 and h = 1.5 mm. Calculate the cutoff wavelengths for higher order TM_{11} and TE_{10} modes.
4. A microwave circuit is constructed on a 40 × 80 mm piece of 1.59 mm thick substrate having ε_r = 2.5. The circuit is completely shielded by a metallic base with the top plate at a height of 15 mm above the substrate. Calculate the expected frequency for the lowest order waveguide resonance.
5. Calculate the characteristic impedance of a stripline having constants W = 0.14 cm, t = 0.004 cm and b = 0.3 cm if the substrate relative permittivity is 2.3.

□□□

[illegible] et al., "Transition for [illegible]", [illegible] Microwave [illegible] Symposium, September [illegible].

Lange, J., "Interdigitated [illegible]", IEEE Trans. [illegible], [illegible].

1. [illegible] of relative dielectric constant = 6.5 and [illegible] for (a) [illegible] (b) Z_0 (c) [illegible] at 10 GHz.

9

Antenna Theory and Analysis

9.1. Introduction

This chapter is intended to provide simple treatment for understanding radio and microwave antennas. The emphasis is placed upon description of various types of antennas, their characteristics and necessary mathematical treatment to explain fully their radiating properties. An antenna is defined as a "means for radiating or receiving radio waves". In other words the antenna is a structure between free space and a guiding device. Antenna is required to concentrate the radiation energy in some directions and suppress it in others [1].

9.2. Types of Antennas

The various types of antennas encountered are listed below

9.2.1. Wire antennas

These antennas are the most familiar as these can be seen virtually everywhere-on automobiles, buildings, ships, aircrafts and spacecrafts, etc. There are various types of wire antennas such as a straight wire, loop and helix as shown in Fig. 9.1.

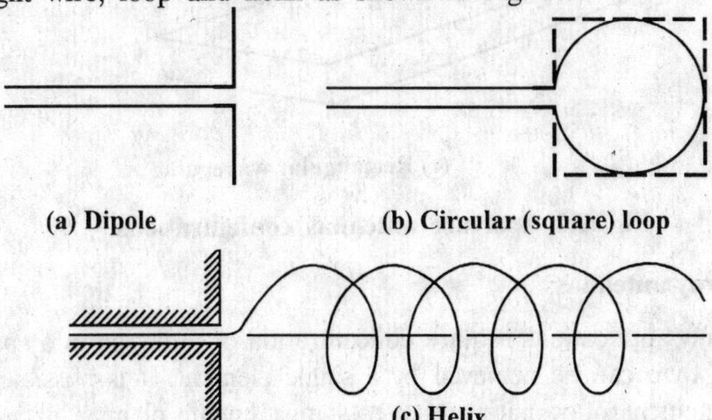

(a) Dipole (b) Circular (square) loop

(c) Helix

Fig. 9.1 Wire antenna configurations.

9.2.2. Aperture antennas

Antennas of this type are shown in Fig. 9.2 and are very useful for aircraft and spacecraft applications because they can be easily mounted on the body of these vehicles.

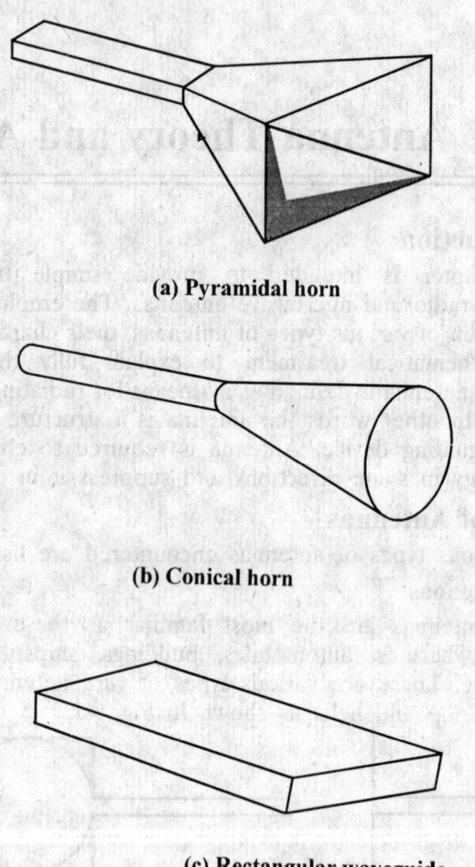

(a) Pyramidal horn

(b) Conical horn

(c) Rectangular waveguide

Fig. 9.2 Aperture antennas configurations.

9.2.3. Array antennas

Many applications require concentration of radiation in a specific direction than can be achieved by a single element. It is possible that an arrangement of radiating elements in a linear, plannar or in any other geometric configuration will result in the desired radiation characteristics. Typical examples of arrays are shown in Fig. 9.3.

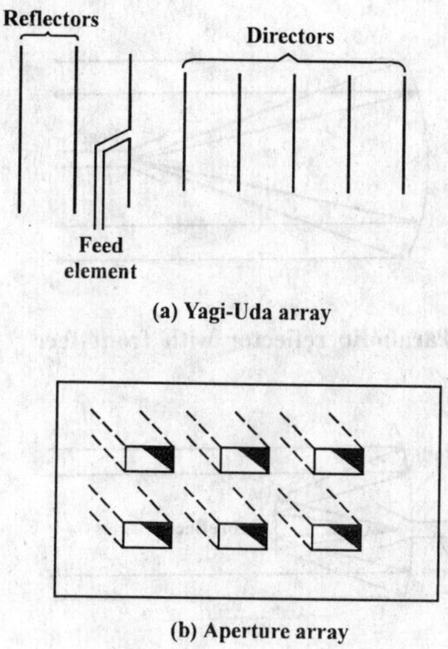

(a) Yagi-Uda array

(b) Aperture array

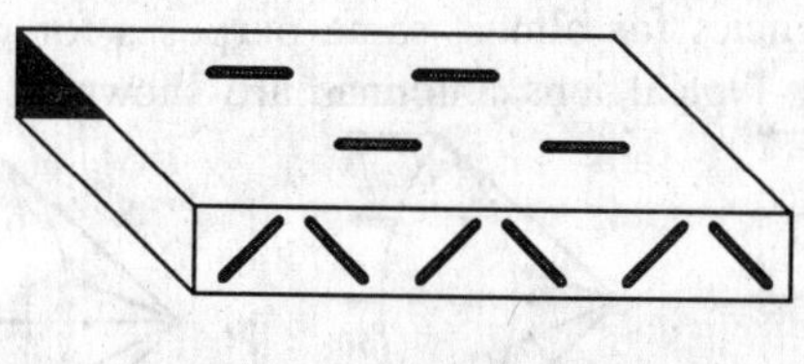

(c) Slotted-waveguide array

Fig. 9.3 Typical wire and aperture array configurations.

9.2.4. Reflector antennas

For long distance communication of signals parabolic and cassegrain reflector antennas are used as shown in Fig 9.4a & b. These antennas can be used to transmit signals to millions of miles.

9.2.5. Lens antennas

It is well known from the knowledge of geometric optics that lenses are used to collimate incident divergent energy and to prevent it from spreading in undesired directions. By choosing appropriate material and shape of the lenses, they can be used to transform various forms of divergent energy into plane waves. Lens antennas are mostly used

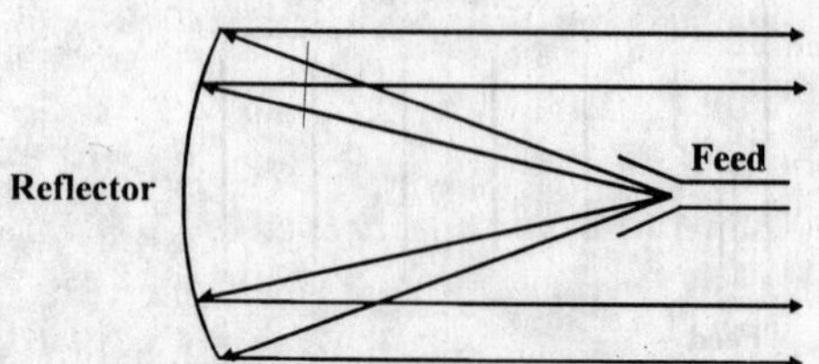

(a) Parabolic reflector with front feed

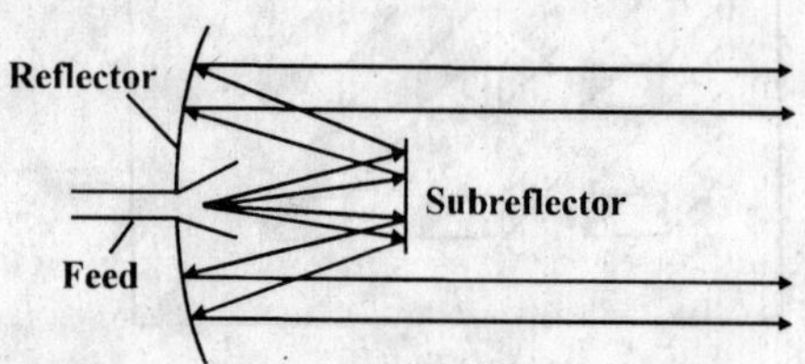

(b) Parabolic reflector with Cassegrain feed

Fig. 9.4 Typical reflector configurations

at very high frequencies for almost same purposes for which reflector antennas are used. Typical lens antennas are shown in Fig. 9.5.

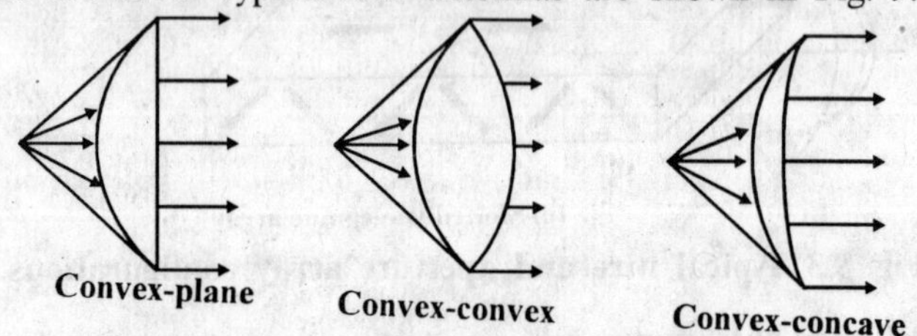

(a) Lens antennas with index of refraction $n < 1$

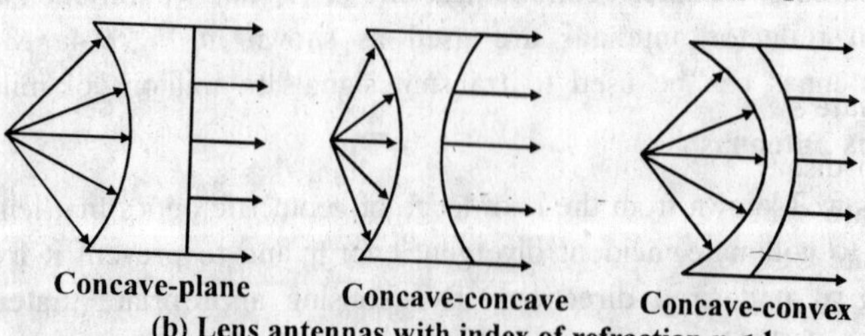

(b) Lens antennas with index of refraction $n < 1$

Fig. 9.5 Typical lens antenna configurations

9.3. Fundamental Parameters of Antennas

9.3.1. Radiation pattern

An antenna radiation pattern is defined as "a graphical representation of the radiation properties of the antenna as a function of space coordinates". Radiation properties include radiation intensity, field strength, phase or polarization. A three-dimensional radiation pattern of infinitesimal dipole is shown in Fig. 9.6a. Half wave dipole, short dipole and isotropic radiation patterns are compared in Fig. 9.6b.

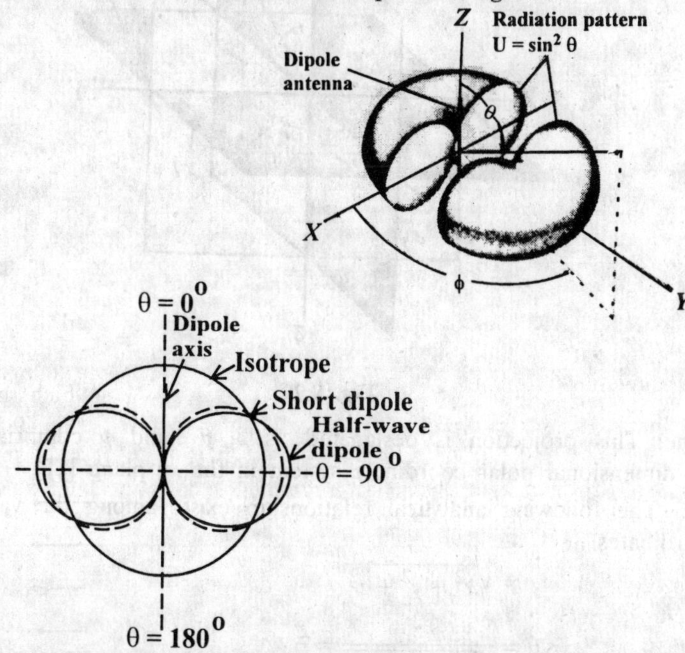

Fig. 9.6b Haff-wave-dipole, short-dipole, and isotrope patterns compared for equal power radiated (electric-intensity patterns), in plane containing dipole waves.

Coordinate system

To discuss the radiation pattern of an antenna, an appropriate coordinate system is needed. Fig. 9.7 shows a cartesian and spherical coordinate systems needed in most of antenna work. Fig. 9.7 shows a point P defined in cartesian coordinates, whereas the spherical coordinates are shown in terms of the line going directly from the origin to the point P and the projection of this line on to the *x-y*

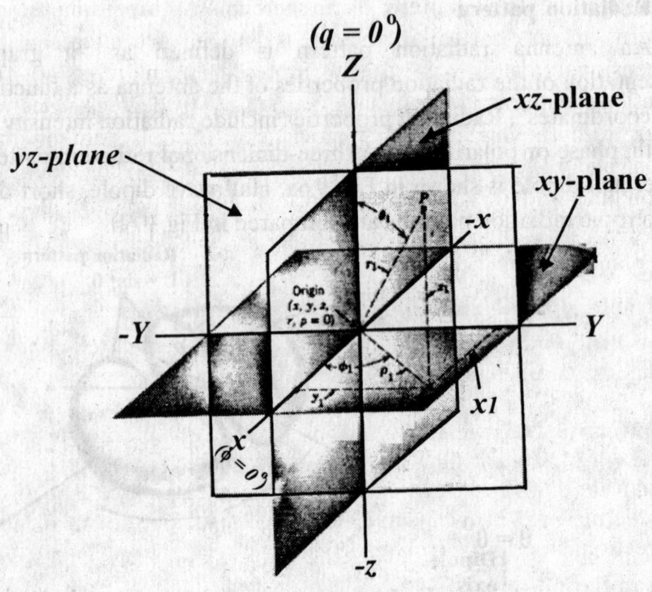

Fig. 9.7

plane. This projection is designated as ρ, θ and ϕ comprises a two-dimensional polar coordinate system in the *xy* plane [1].

The following analytical relationship exists among the various coordinates.

$$r = \sqrt{x^2 + y^2 + z^2} \quad \text{....(9.1a)}$$

$$\cos\theta = \frac{z}{\sqrt{x^2 + y^2 + z^2}} = \frac{z}{r} \quad \text{....(9.1b)}$$

$$\tan\theta = \frac{y}{x} \quad \text{....(9.1c)}$$

$$x = r \sin\theta \cos\phi \quad \text{....(9.2a)}$$

$$y = r \sin\theta \sin\phi \quad \text{....(9.2b)}$$

$$z = r \cos\theta \quad \text{....(9.2c)}$$

$$\rho = \sqrt{x^2 + y^2} = r \sin\theta \quad \text{....(9.3)}$$

$$x = \rho \cos\phi \quad \text{....(9.4)}$$

$$y = \rho \sin\phi \quad \text{....(9.5)}$$

Patterns in a plane

Although the total pattern of an antenna is three-dimensional, the pattern in a particular plane is often of interest. The three-dimensional pattern is usually represented in terms of the two-dimensional patterns in two planes that are at 90° degree angles with each other, with the origin of a spherical coordinate system on their intersection line. The $\phi = 0°$ direction is taken to lie along the intersection line and this plane is equivalent to *x-y* plane of Fig. 9.7 and the $\theta = 0°$ direction is equivalent to *x-z* plane. These are called principal planes of the coordinate system.

9.3.1. Isotropic, directional and omni-directional patterns

An isotropic radiator is defined as "a hypothetical antenna having equal radiation in all directions. An isotropic radiator is not physically realizable, but it is often taken as a reference for expressing the directive properties of practical antennas. A directional antenna is one "having the property of radiating or receiving electromagnetic waves more effectively in some direction than in others". An omni-directional pattern is defined as one "having a non-directional pattern in azimuth and a directional pattern in elevation.

9.3.2. The radiation intensity

Radiation intensity in a given direction is the power radiated from an antenna per unit solid angle in that direction. Mathematically, it is expressed as

$$U = r^2 W_{rad} \qquad \text{....(9.6)}$$

where U = radiation intensity (W/unit solid angle)

W_{rad} = radiation density (W/m^2)

9.3.3. Directive gain and directivity

Directive gain in a given direction is defined as "the ratio of the radiation intensity in that direction to the radiation intensity of a reference antenna". The reference antenna is taken to be an isotropic source.

Directivity generally is the value of directive gain in the direction of its maximum value.

Mathematically, this can be written as

$$D_g = \frac{U}{U_0} = \frac{4\pi U}{P_{rad}} \qquad \text{....(9.7)}$$

where, D_g = Directive gain (dimension less)

U_0 = Radiation intensity of isotropic source (W/unit solid angle)

P_{rad} = total radiated power (W)

$$D_0 = \frac{U_{max}}{U_0} = \frac{4\pi U_{max}}{P_{rad}} \qquad ....(9.8)$$

where,

D_0 = Directivity (dimensionless)

U_{max} = Maximum radiation intensity (W/unit solid angle)

9.3.4. Power gain

Power gain in a given direction is 4π times the ratio of the radiation intensity in that direction to the total power delivered to the antenna. Power gain is usually taken in the direction of maximum radiation. Mathematically it can be expressed as

$$\text{Power gain} = 4\pi \frac{\text{radiation intensity}}{\text{total input power}} = 4\pi \frac{U(\theta, \phi)}{P_{in}} \qquad ....(9.9)$$

9.3.5. Antenna efficiency

Total antenna efficiency takes into account losses at the input terminals and within the structure of the antenna.

$$e_t = e_r\, e_c\, e_d \qquad ....(9.10)$$

e_t = total overall efficiency

e_r = reflection mismatch efficiency = $(1 - |\Gamma|^2)$

e_c and e_d are the conduction and dielectric efficiency. e_c and e_d together contribute towards radiation efficiency, *i.e.*, $e_{cd} = e_c\, e_d$ = antenna radiation efficiency.

9.3.6. Bandwidth

It is defined as "the range of frequencies within which the performance of the antenna, with respect to some characteristic (say the gain, input impedance or efficiency) is satisfactory. The definition of the bandwidth of antenna is less precise than the definitions of any other parameters.

9.3.7. Input impedance

Input impedance of an antenna is the ratio of the voltage to current at a pair of terminals. Here we are interested in the input impedance at the input terminals of the antenna. In the Fig. 9.8a, the input terminals are the points *a-b*. The ratio of the voltage to current at these terminals with no load attached, defines the impedance of the antenna as

$$Z_A = R_A + j\,X_A \qquad ....(9.11)$$

where,

Z_A = Antenna impedance at terminals a–b (Ω)

R_A = Antenna resistance at terminals a–b (Ω)

X_A = Antenna reactance at terminals a–b (Ω)

Resistive part consists of two components

$$R_A = R_r + R_L \quad \text{....(9.12)}$$

where,

R_r = Radiation resistance of the antenna

R_L = Loss resistance of the antenna

The antenna is connected to a generator with internal impedance

$$Z_g = R_g + j\,X_g \quad \text{....(9.13)}$$

where,

R_g = Resistance of generator impedance (Ω)

X_g = Reactance of generator impedance (Ω)

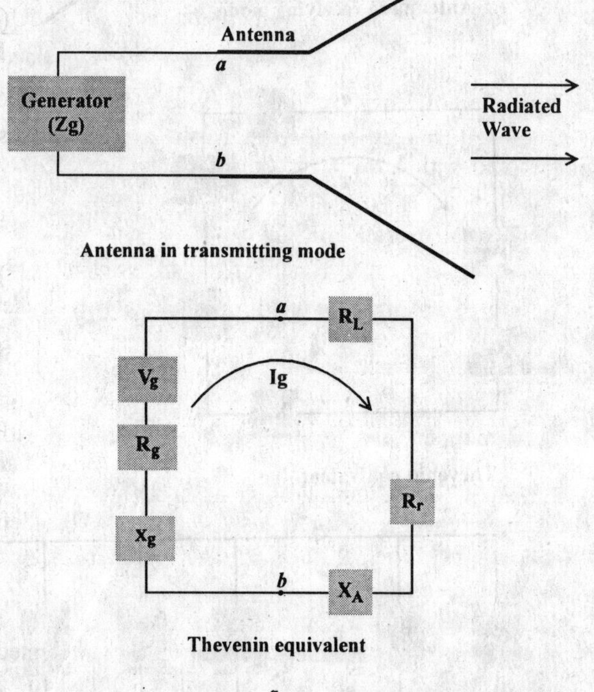

Fig. 9.8a Transmitting antenna and its equivalent circuits.

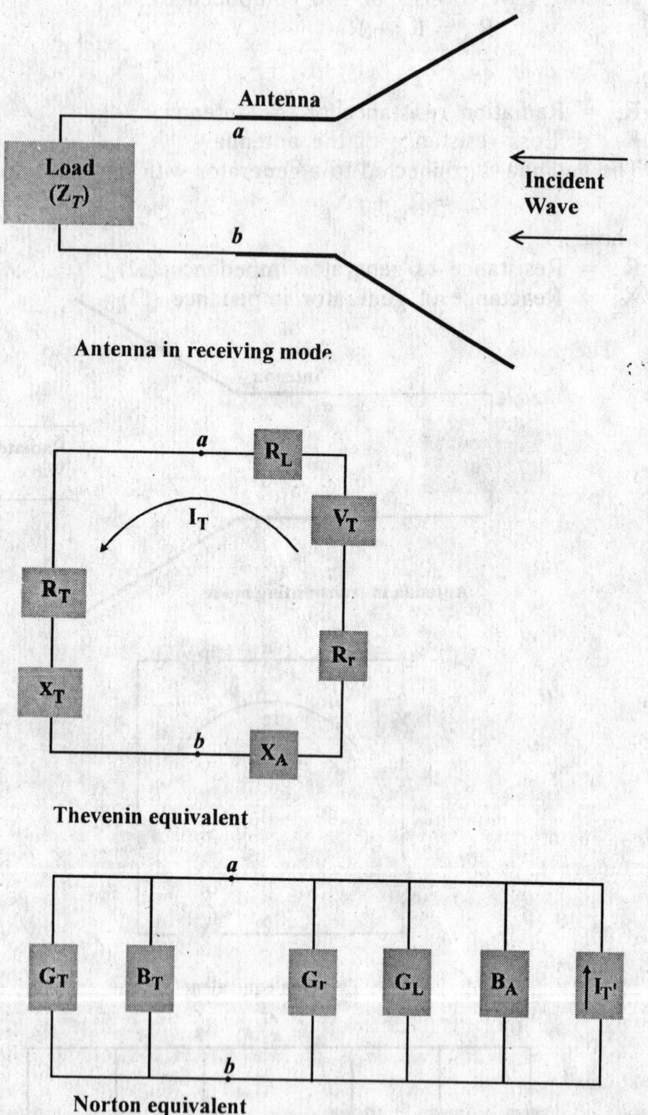

Fig. 9.8b Antenna and its equivalent circuits in the receiving mode.

If the antenna is in transmission mode, the antenna and generator can be represented by an equivalent circuit shown in Fig. 9.8a.

We are going to find power delivered to R_r for radiation and the amount of power lost as heat in R_L.

The current in the loop is given as

$$I_g = \frac{V_g}{Z_t} = \frac{V_g}{Z_A + Z_g} = \frac{V_g}{(R_r + R_L + R_g) + j(X_A + X_g)} \text{ (A)} \qquad ....(9.14)$$

and its magnitude is given by

$$|I_g| = \frac{|V_g|}{[(R_r + R_L + R_g)^2 + (X_a + X_g)^2]^{1/2}} = \frac{|V_g|}{[N_r]^{1/2}}$$

where $[N_r]$ is defined as $[(R_r + R_L + R_g)^2 + (X_A + X_g)^2]$
The power delivered to antenna for radiation is

$$P_r = \frac{1}{2}|I_g|^2 R_r = \frac{|V_g|^2}{2}\left[\frac{R_r}{[N_r]^{1/2}}\right] \text{ (W)} \qquad ....(9.15)$$

Power dissipated as heat is

$$P_L = \frac{1}{2}|I_g|^2 R_L = \frac{|V_g|^2}{2}\left[\frac{R_L}{[N_r]^{1/2}}\right] \text{ (W)} \qquad ....(9.16)$$

The remaining power is dissipated as heat on the internal resistance R_g of the generator, and is given by

$$P_g = \frac{|V_g|^2}{2}\left[\frac{R_g}{[N_r]^{1/2}}\right] \text{ W} \qquad ....(9.17)$$

Maximum power will be delivered to the antenna when the antenna resistance (R_A) is conjugate matched to the generator impedance, that is

when $\quad R_r + R_L = R_g$
and $\quad X_A = -X_g$
For this case

$$P_r = \frac{|V_g|^2}{2}\left[\frac{R_r}{4(R_r + R_L)^2}\right] = \frac{|V_g|^2}{8}\left[\frac{R_r}{(R_r + R_L)^2}\right] \qquad ....(9.18)$$

$$P_L = \frac{|V_g|^2}{8}\left[\frac{R_L}{(R_r + R_L)^2}\right] \qquad ....(9.19)$$

$$P_g = \frac{|V_g|^2}{8R_g} \qquad ....(9.20)$$

From Eq. 9.15 to 9.17, it is clear that

$$P_g = P_r + P_L$$

The power supplied by the generator during the conjugate matching is

$$P_s = \frac{1}{2} V_g I_g^* = \frac{1}{2} V_g \left[\frac{V_g^*}{2(R_r + R_L)}\right] = \frac{V_g^2}{4}\left[\frac{1}{R_r + R_L}\right] \quad \text{....(9.21)}$$

Half of the total power supplied by the generator is dissipated as heat in the internal resistance (R_g) of the generator and other half is delivered to the antenna. This happens in the conjugate match condition. A part of the power which is delivered to the antenna is radiated, rest is dissipated as heat. If the antenna is lossless (e_{cd} = 1), then half of the total power supplied by the generator is radiated by the antenna during conjugate matching [8].

The antenna in receiving mode can also be handled similarly, the equivalent circuit is shown in Fig. 9.8b. The discussion for the antenna and its load in receiving mode parallels that for the transmitting mode.

The input impedance of an antenna is generally a function of frequency and it also depends on other factors like geometry, method of excitation and its proximity to surrounding objects.

We discuss more on radiation resistance which is a concept applicable only to antennas in which radiation is associated with a definite current in a conductor.

The radiation resistance R_r from Eq. 9.15 is given as

$$R_r = \frac{2P_r}{I_g^2}$$

When P_r is in watts, I_g in amperes the radiation resistance R_r will be obtained in ohms. The radiation resistance of some type of antennas can be calculated. For other types the calculation cannot be made practically, and the value must be obtained by measurement. Typical values of radiation resistance range from a fraction of ohms to several hundred ohms. The very low values are undesirable because they imply large antenna current and thereby the possibility of considerable ohmic loss of power. That is, more power is dissipitated as heat loss than as radiation. An excessively high value of radiation resistance would also be undesirable because it would require very high voltage to be applied to the antenna. Very high values do not occur in practical antennas, whereas very low values sometimes do occur.

9.3.8. Antenna effective aperture

An antenna in the receiving mode captures the receiving electromagnetic waves and extracts power from them. This is true for all types of antenna-may be a wire, aperture, array etc. The effective aperture for any of these antennas is defined as the ratio of power delivered to the load to the incident power density. This can be expressed as :

$$A_e = \frac{P_T}{W_i} = \frac{|I_T|^2 R_T/2}{W_i} \qquad \text{....(9.22)}$$

where

A_e is the effective aperture (area) (m^2)

P_T is the total power delivered to the load (W)

W_i is the power density of incident wave (W/m^2)

We can write A_e as

$$A_e = \frac{|V_T|^2}{2W_i}\left[\frac{R_T}{(R_r + R_L + R_T)^2 + (X_A + X_T)^2}\right] \qquad \text{....(9.23)}$$

Under conditions of maximum power transfer

$$R_r + R_L = R_T \text{ and } X_A = -X_T$$

$$A_{em} = \frac{|V_T|^2}{8W_i}\left[\frac{1}{R_r + R_L}\right] \qquad \text{....(9.24)}$$

The effective aperture of an antenna is not necessarily same as the physical aperture. If the antenna has constant amplitude and phase distribution, the effective aperture is equal to physical aperture. The maximum effective aperture of wire antenna is greater than the physical area. Thus the wire antenna can capture much more power than is intercepted by its physical size [8].

9.4. The Mechanism of Antenna Radiation

A very simplistic approach is used to explain radiation mechanism. If the ends of a parallel wire transmission line are spread 180° apart as shown in Fig. 9.9 we would have a simple antenna. We note that an electric field exists between the two wires due to a sinusoidal supply voltage V_s. Only one electric line of force is shown in Fig 9.9 for simplicity. In reality, an infinite number of such lines would surround the antenna, and magnetic lines of force would encircle these electric lines at right angles. The polarity signs (+ and –) represent an arbitrary instantaneous polarization of the voltage on the antenna. In the Fig. 9.10a it is also assumed that the value of V_s is maximum. As V_s

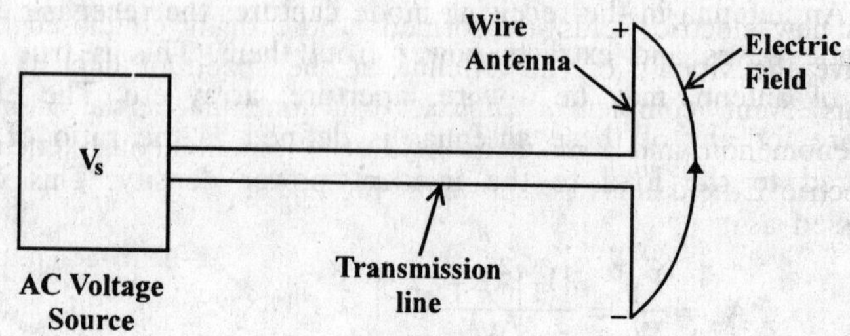

Fig. 9.9 A Simple Antenna

decreases, the electric lines of force will begin to collapse, as shown in Fig. 9.10a, b and c. Finally as shown in part d of the Fig. 9.10, V_s

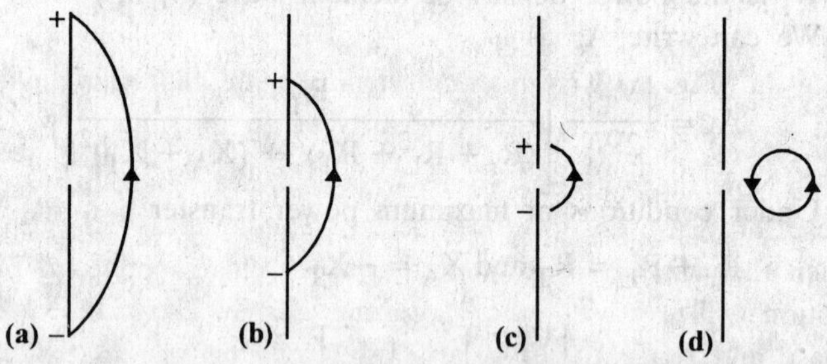

Fig. 9.10 Formation of the radiation elecric field.

drops to zero, and the electric lines of force collapse completely, forming a loop. This loop falls back onto the antenna, but the polarity of V_s reverses quickly and a new electric field is formed opposite to the one in Fig. 9.10 as shown in Fig. 9.11. The direction of this newly

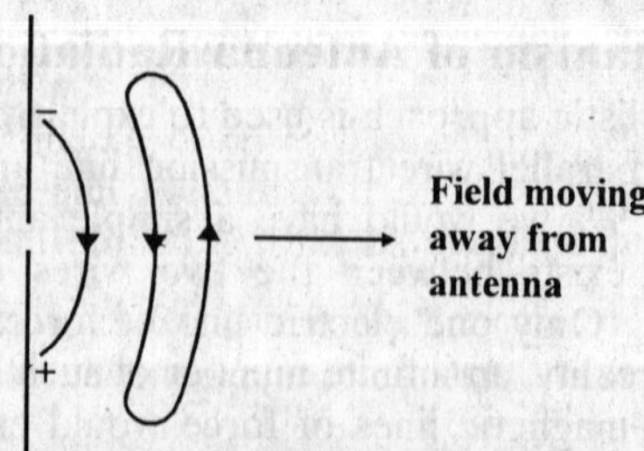

Fig. 9.11 Radiation field leaving the antenna

formed electric field repels the closed loop away from the antenna and distorts its shape into the elongated form as shown in Fig. 9.11. As new electric fields are formed these distorted closed loops will leave the vicinity of the antenna at the speed of light, 3×10^8 m/s. This event completely encircles the antenna as a 3-dimensional phenomenon, and a magnetic field exists simultaneously encircling the electric E-field lines as shown in Fig. 9.12.

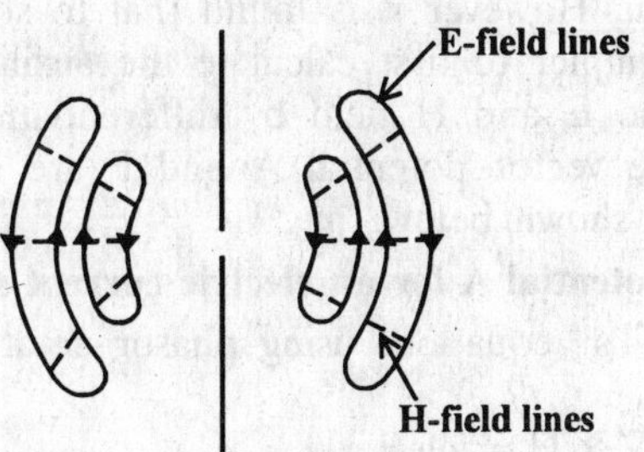

Fig. 9.12 complete electromagnetic radiation field leaving the vicinity of an antenna.

Now the question arises, what is the mechanism which sustains these TEM waves once they leave the antenna. The answer is that when the waves are radiated they form close loops and once set in motion, will always induce the other (E → H or H → E) in time phase and space quadrature. Thus it can be concluded that electric charges (currents) are required to excite the fields but are not needed to sustain them and may exist in absence of them.

All the fields in the vicinity of the antenna do not represent radiation fields. When the antenna polarity reverses, some of these field components "collapse" upon the conductor, causing induced voltage and current associated with the inductance and capacitance of the antenna conductor. These field components decrease rapidly with distance from the antenna. These fields are known as the near fields of the antenna. On the other hand the radiation field propagate to astronomical distances. [13]

9.5. Potential Functions and Electromagnetic Fields

In the electromagnetic propagation problems explained in earlier chapters, it is seen that electromagnetic fields were defined and we were required to find out the sources. But in the radiation problems it is required to find how these fields are related to their sources, *i.e.* to the charges and currents which produce them.

It is common practice in the analysis of radiation problems that we introduce auxiliary functions known as vector potentials, which will aid in the solution of the problems. The most common vector potential functions are the A (magnetic vector potential) and F (electric vector potential). The introduction of the vector potential often simplifies the solution. It is possible to calculate the E, H fields directly from the source current densities J and M (electric and magnetic current density) by integration. However it is found that to solve radiation problems, it is much simpler to first calculate the auxiliary potentials and then determine the E and H field by differentiation. For further reading see [12]. The vector potential A and F are derived from Maxwell's equations as shown below.

The vector potential A for an electric current source

Maxwell's equations using phasor notation (for constant scalar ε and μ) are

$$\nabla \times \mathrm{H} = j\omega\varepsilon \mathrm{E} + \mathrm{J} \quad \text{....(9.25)}$$

$$\nabla \times \mathrm{E} = -j\omega\mu \mathrm{H} \quad \text{....(9.26)}$$

$$\nabla . \mathrm{E} = \rho/\varepsilon \quad \text{....(9.27)}$$

and
$$\nabla . \mathrm{H} = 0 \quad \text{....(9.28)}$$

The vector potential A is generated by a given harmonic electric current J. The magnetic flux B is always sinusoidal (*i.e.* $\nabla.\mathrm{B} = 0$). Hence, it can be represented as curl of another vector A.

$$\nabla . \nabla \times \mathrm{A} = 0 \quad \text{....(9.29)}$$

Thus we define

$$\mathrm{B_A} = \mu \mathrm{H_A} = \nabla \times \mathrm{A} \quad \text{....(9.30)}$$

Or
$$\mathrm{H_A} = \frac{1}{\mu} \nabla \times \mathrm{A} \quad \text{....(9.31)}$$

Substituting Eq. 9.31 in Eq. 9.26, we get

$\nabla \times \mathrm{E_A} = -j\omega \nabla \times \mathrm{A}$ which can be written as

$$\nabla \times (\mathrm{E_A} + j\omega \mathrm{A}) = 0 \quad \text{....(9.32)}$$

Eq. 9.32 is satisfied if $(\mathrm{E_A} + j\omega\mathrm{A})$ is represented as the gradient of a scalar

$$\mathrm{E_A} + j\omega \mathrm{A} = -\nabla \mathrm{V} \quad \text{....(9.33)}$$

The scalar potential V is defined in such a way that for slowly varying fields ($j\omega\mathrm{A} \approx 0$) it is identical to the scalar potential used in electrostatic fields. In this case the electric field strength can be expressed as

$$\mathrm{E_A} = -\nabla \mathrm{V} - j\omega \mathrm{A} \quad \text{....(9.34)}$$

Eqs. 9.31 and 9.34 show how the field quantities H and E may be expressed in terms of a vector potential A and a scalar potential

V. Expressions 9.31 and 9.34 for H and E satisfy two of the Maxwell's equations 9.26 and 9.28. The remaining two of the Maxwell's equations may be used to derive differential equation for the potential functions. Substitution of Eqs. 9.31 and 9.34 in 9.25 gives,

$$\frac{1}{\mu}\nabla \times \nabla \times A = -j\omega\varepsilon \nabla V + \varepsilon\omega^2 A + J$$

Using the identity $\nabla \times \nabla \times A = \nabla \nabla . A - \nabla^2 A$ in the above relation can be written as

$$\nabla^2 A + \omega^2 \mu\varepsilon A = -\mu J + j\omega\mu\, \varepsilon \nabla V + \nabla \nabla . A \qquad ....(9.35)$$

This is one of the required differential equations.

The second one is obtained by substituting Eqn. 9.33 into 9.27, we obtain

$$\nabla^2 V + j\omega\nabla . A = -\frac{\rho}{\varepsilon} \qquad ....(9.36)$$

The equations 9.35 and 9.36 are complicated because of the fact that they are coupled, that is, the unknown V and A are appearing in both equations. Further the two equations do not yield unique solution. From Helmholtz theorem it is clear that any vector field due to a finite source is specified uniquely if both the curl and divergence of the field are specified. The curl of A is given in Eq. 9.31 but its divergence has not been defined. There is also some arbitrariness in defining the scalar potential as in equation 9.34. If the divergence of A in equation 9.35 and 9.36 is set equal to $-j\,\omega\mu\,\varepsilon V$, these equations become uncoupled and reduce to standard wave equations with source terms included *viz.*,

$$\nabla^2 A + \mu\varepsilon\omega^2 A = -\mu J \qquad ....(9.37)$$

$$\nabla^2 V + \mu\varepsilon\omega^2 V = -\frac{\rho}{\varepsilon} \qquad ....(9.38)$$

These are vector wave equations.

The condition chosen that

$$\nabla . A = -j\omega\mu\varepsilon V \qquad ....(9.39)$$

is known as **Lorentz Gauge condition.** The solution of the two Eqs. 9.37 and 9.38 is given by the following potential functions :

$$A(r, t) = \frac{\mu}{4\pi}\int \frac{J(r', t - R/c_v)}{R}\, dV' \qquad ....(9.40)$$

$$V(r, t) = \frac{1}{4\pi\varepsilon}\int \frac{\rho(r', t - R/c_v)}{R}\, dV' \qquad ....(9.41)$$

where $R = |r - r'|$ as shown in Fig. 9.13 (9.42)

Since a time delay R/c_v is involved these potentials are known as retarded potentials. c_v is the velocity of propagation in the medium.

Potential functions for sinusoidal oscillations

We should take into account the phase delay due to the distance R between a source point and the observation point. It is well known

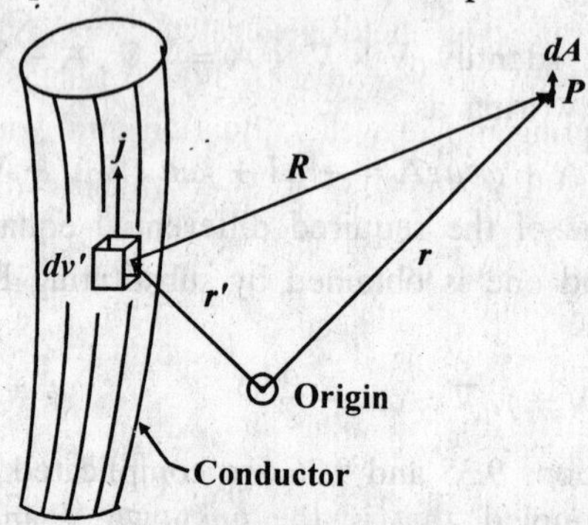

Fig 9.13 Geometry for calculating retarded potential due to current density J.

that a uniform plane wave travelling in the R direction would have a phase variation of the factor $e^{-j\beta R}$. Hence the potential integrals should be modified by the inclusion of an exponential phase factor as

$$A(r) = \frac{\mu}{4\pi} \int J(r') \frac{e^{-j\beta R}}{R} dV' \quad \text{....(9.43)}$$

$$V(r) = \frac{1}{4\pi\varepsilon} \int \rho(r') \frac{e^{-j\beta R}}{R} dV' \quad \text{....(9.44)}$$

Using phasor notation the expression for the magnetic and electric field strengths are

$$H_A = \frac{1}{\mu} \nabla \times A \quad \text{....(9.45)}$$

$$E_A = -\nabla V - j\omega A \quad \text{....(9.46)}$$

where vector and scalar potentials are related by the Lorentz gauge condition

$$\nabla . A = -j\omega\mu\varepsilon V \quad \text{....(9.47)}$$

The scalar potential V may be eliminated from Eq. 9.46 using Eq. 9.47 to give

$$E_A = \frac{\nabla\nabla.A}{j\omega\varepsilon\mu} - j\omega A \quad \text{....(9.48)}$$

Hence we see that the fields E and H can be expressed entirely in terms of A.

The vector potential F for a magnetic current source M

Magnetic currents are physically unrealizable, but equivalent magnetic currents arise when we use the volume or the surface equivalence theorem. The field generated by a harmonic magnetic current in a homogeneous region with J = 0 but M ≠ 0 must satisfy ∇.D = 0. Substituting in Maxwell's equation and working out detailed analysis as in section (c), we get a wave equation in F as

$$\nabla^2 F + k^2 F = -\varepsilon M \quad \text{....(9.49)}$$

where $k^2 = \omega^2 \mu \varepsilon$

from which E_F and H_F can be obtained.

F is obtained from the integral,

$$F = \frac{\varepsilon}{4\pi} \int\int\int_v \frac{Me^{-jkR}}{R} dv' \quad \text{....(9.50)}$$

Thus total field is $E = E_A + E_F$ (9.51)

$$H = H_A + H_F \quad (9.52)$$

9.6. Oscillating Electric Dipole (Infinitesimal Dipole)

A good example to use vector potential is in calculation of electromagnetic fields of an alternating current element (oscillating electric dipole) in free space. A current element I*dl* refers to a filamentary current I flowing along an elemental length dl. It is assumed that the length is very short and the current is constant through out the very short length *dl.* Any physical antenna will be actually consisting of a large number of such short elements joined end to end. Therefore, if the electromagnetic field of this building block is known, the fields of any actual antenna having a specified current distribution can be determined [8].

Fig. 9.14 shows one such current element I *dl* cos *ωt* located at the origin of a spherical coordinate system. We will find the E and H fields at any point P.

Find the vector potential A at point P. The general expression for A is given by

$$A(r) = \frac{\mu}{4\pi} \int \frac{J\left(t - \dfrac{r}{C_v}\right)}{R} dV' \quad \text{....(9.53)}$$

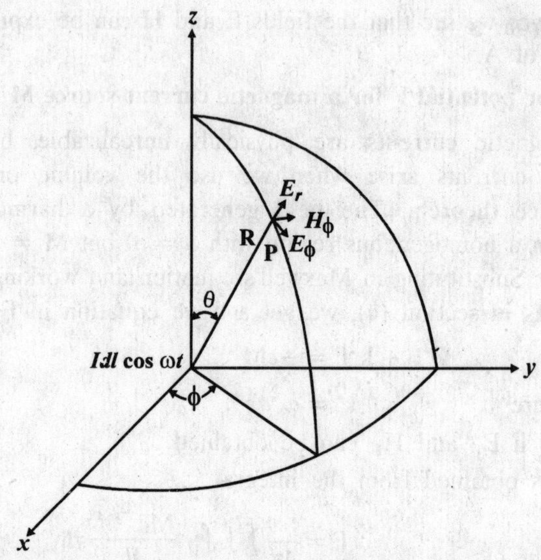

Fig 9.14 A current element at the origin of a spherical co-ordinate system

The integration over the volume in Eq. 9.53 consists of integration over the area of the wire and over its length. The current density J integrated over the cross-sectional area of the wire will result in just the current I, and this is assumed to be constant along the length dl and gives the total volume integral of J as I *dl.* Hence the vector potential A for this particular problem will be directed in *z* direction (the direction of the current element) only, and is written as

$$A_z = \frac{\mu}{4\pi}\left[\frac{Idl\cos\omega(t - r/c_v)}{r}\right] \quad \text{....(9.54)}$$

The magnetic field H can be determined throught the relation

$$\mu H = \nabla \times A$$

Write curl in spherical coordinates for obtaining three components of H (H_r, H_θ, H_ϕ)

From Fig. 9.14, it is seen that the spherical components of A in terms of A_z for this case are given by

$$A_r = A_z \cos\theta; \quad A_\theta = -A_z \sin\theta; \quad A_\phi = 0 \quad \text{....(9.55)}$$

Also we note that because of symmetry $\partial/\partial\phi = 0$

From the $\nabla \times A$ relation, we get

$$\mu H_r = (\nabla \times A)_r = 0$$

$$\mu H_\theta = (\nabla \times A)_\theta = 0$$

and
$$H_\phi = \frac{1}{\mu r}\left[\frac{\partial}{\partial r}(rA_\theta) - \frac{\partial A_r}{\partial \theta}\right]$$

$$H_\phi = \frac{I\,dl}{4\pi r}\left[\frac{\partial}{\partial r}\left\{-\sin\theta\cos\omega\left(t-\frac{r}{c_v}\right)\right\} - \frac{\partial}{\partial\theta}\left\{\frac{\cos\theta}{r}\cos\omega\left(t-\frac{r}{c_v}\right)\right\}\right]$$

$$= \frac{I\,dl\sin\theta}{4\pi}\left[\frac{-\omega\sin\omega\left(t-\dfrac{r}{c_v}\right)}{rc_v} + \frac{\cos\omega\left(t-\dfrac{r}{c_v}\right)}{r^2}\right] \quad ....(9.56)$$

The electric field strength E can be obtained from the Maxwell's curl equation :

$$\nabla \times H = \varepsilon\frac{\partial E}{\partial t}$$

or
$$E = \frac{1}{\varepsilon}\int \nabla \times H\,dt \quad ....(9.57)$$

Taking the curl of Eqn. 9.56 and then integrating with respect to time gives component of E as

$$E_\theta = \frac{I\,dl\sin\theta}{4\pi\varepsilon}\left(\frac{-\omega\sin\omega t'}{rc_v^2} + \frac{\cos\omega t'}{r^2 c_v} + \frac{\sin\omega t'}{\omega r^3}\right) \quad ....(9.58)$$

$$E_r = \frac{2I\,dl\cos\theta}{4\pi\varepsilon}\left(\frac{\cos\omega t'}{r^2 c_v} + \frac{\sin\omega t'}{\omega r^3}\right) \quad ....(9.59)$$

H_ϕ is rewritten as

$$H_\phi = \frac{I\,dl\sin\theta}{4\pi}\left(\frac{-\omega\sin\omega t'}{rc_v} + \frac{\cos\omega t'}{r^2}\right) \quad ....(9.60)$$

Where $t' = \left(t - \dfrac{r}{c_v}\right)$

Equations 9.58 to 9.60 give the E–H field components by the simple current element.

If we consider the rms values of a time varying field of the form $e^{-j\omega t}$ and use the cosine term as the reference phasor, then the sine term lags behind the cosine phasor and can be represented by a phasor of $-j$; similarly, the negative sine term can be represented by a phasor of $+j$. The phase constant β will be used to replace the ratio ω/c_v.

$$\text{i.e.} \qquad \cos \omega \left(t - \frac{r}{c_v}\right) \rightarrow \cos (\omega t - \beta r) \Rightarrow e^{-j\beta r}$$

$$\sin \omega \left(t - \frac{r}{c_v}\right) \rightarrow -j \sin (\omega t - \beta r) \Rightarrow -je^{-j\beta r}$$

Then the expressions 9.58 to 9.60 can be written as

$$H_\phi = \frac{j\beta^2 I\, dl}{4\pi}\left[\frac{1}{\beta r} - \frac{j}{(\beta r)^2}\right] \sin\theta \,.\, e^{-j\beta r} \qquad \text{....(9.61)}$$

$$E_\theta = 30 j\beta^2 I\, dl \left[\frac{1}{\beta r} - \frac{j}{(\beta r)^2} - \frac{1}{(\beta r)^3}\right] \sin\theta .\, e^{-j\beta r} \qquad \text{....(9.62)}$$

$$E_r = 60\beta^2 I\, dl \left[\frac{1}{(\beta r)^2} - \frac{j}{(\beta r)^3}\right] \cos\theta . e^{-j\beta r} \qquad \text{....(9.63)}$$

$e^{j\omega t}$ term is assumed to be present in all cases. This is another form of writing the field componants.

The component H_ϕ consists of two components, one of which varies inversely as r and the other inversely as r^2. The second term relates to the induction field and will predominate at points close to the current element.

Near the antenna, that is at distance $<0.01\lambda$, the $\frac{1}{r}$ and $\frac{1}{r^2}$ terms can be ignored in comparison to $\frac{1}{r^3}$. The H_ϕ component can be ignored since it does not have a $\frac{1}{r^3}$ term. The E_r and E_θ components are given by

$$E_r = -\frac{j\,60\,I\,dl}{r^3}\cos\theta .\, e^{-j\beta r} \qquad \text{....(9.64)}$$

$$E_\theta = -\frac{j\,30\,I\,dl}{r^3}\sin\theta .\, e^{-j\beta r} \qquad \text{....(9.65)}$$

It can be seen that the E_r vector is twice in magnitude of the E_θ vector, and have a phase difference of 90 degrees.

The ratio of E_r to E_θ in the near field is given by

$$\frac{E_r}{E_\theta} = 2\cot\theta \qquad \text{....(9.66)}$$

9.6.1. Fields at large distances from the dipole

The significance of these components will now be studied. At large distance the terms that are inversely proportional to the square and cube of the distance will be reduced to very small magnitude, and thus can be ignored. Hence radial component of the electric field can be ignored. The electric and magnetic fields at large distances from the dipole from Eqs. 9.58 and 9.60 can be written as

$$E_\theta = \frac{I\,dl\sin\theta}{4\pi\varepsilon}\left[\frac{\omega\sin\omega\left(t-\frac{r}{c_v}\right)}{rc_v^2}\right] \qquad \text{....(9.67)}$$

$$H_\phi = \frac{I\,dl\sin\theta}{4\pi}\left[\frac{\omega\sin\omega\left(t-\frac{r}{c_v}\right)}{rc_v}\right] \qquad \text{....(9.68)}$$

To calculate the total average power radiated in the far field, we take the vector product of H_ϕ and E_θ and integrate it over a sphere. In order to perform this integration we consider an elemental thin annular shell on a sphere as shown in Fig. 9.15.

Its width is $r\,d\theta$ and its circumference is $2\pi r\sin\theta$ thus its area is $2\pi r^2\sin\theta d\theta$. The total average power radiated is found by integrating this annular shell with respect to θ from 0 to π in order to get the area over the whole sphere.

Thus the total average power (P_{ave}) is given by

$$P_{ave} = \frac{1}{2}\int_0^\pi \left(\frac{\omega^2 I^2 dl^2 \sin^2\theta}{16\pi^2 r^2 c_v^3 \varepsilon}\right) 2\pi r^2 \sin\theta\, d\theta \qquad \text{....(9.69)}$$

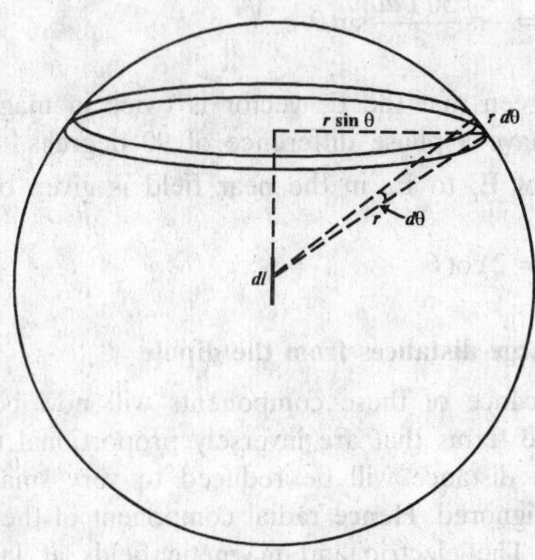

Fig. 9.15. Total power radiated over a sphere

$$= \frac{\omega^2 I^2 dl^2}{16\pi\, c_v^3 \varepsilon} \int_0^{\pi} (\sin^3\theta\, d\theta)$$

$\sin^3\theta$ can be written as $\sin\theta\,(1 - \cos^2\theta)$, P_{ave} will be

$$P_{ave} = \frac{\omega^2 I^2 dl^2}{16\pi\, c_v^3 \varepsilon} \left[-\cos\theta + \frac{\cos^3\theta}{3} \right]_0^{\pi}$$

$$= \frac{I^2 dl^2 \omega^2}{12\pi\, c_v^3 \varepsilon} \qquad \text{....(9.70)}$$

For free-space propagation the velocity c_v is equal to speed of the light and is equal to $\frac{1}{\sqrt{\mu_0 \varepsilon_0}}$. Thus the total average power is given by

$$P_{ave} = \frac{\pi I^2 dl^2}{3\lambda^2} \sqrt{\frac{\mu_0}{\varepsilon_0}} \qquad \text{....(9.71a)}$$

This is the total average power radiated by a current element carrying a uniform current along its length. This current element is called a Hertzian dipole. In practice a Hertzian dipole cannot be realized, but a very short dipole $< \lambda/10$ is fairly good approximation [14]. The current amplitude along the length of a radiating wire decreases uniformily from a maximum at the centre to zero at the ends and a triangular distribution is a good aproximation for a short dipole. Then the average current is taken as half of the maximum, and thus $I^2/4$ should be substituted for I^2 in Eq. 9.71a to give the total average power as

$$P_{ave} = \frac{\pi I^2 dl^2}{12\lambda^2}\eta_0 \quad \text{....(9.71b)}$$

where η_0 is the free space impedance $= 120\pi$.

9.6.1(a) Radiation resistance

Total average power given by Eq. 7.71a is equivalent to familier expression of $I^2R/2$, in this case since the element is radiating this is known as the radiation resistance. Thus the expression for the radiation resistance of the current element is given by

$$R = \frac{2\pi}{3}\eta_0 \left(\frac{dl}{\lambda}\right)^2 \quad \text{....(9.72a)}$$

η_0 is the free space impedance, its value is 120π. Hence

$$R = 80\pi^2 \left(\frac{dl}{\lambda}\right)^2 \quad \text{....(9.72b)}$$

is the radiation resistance of a current element of length dl through which a constant current I flows.

If we assume that the current distribution is triangular, which is more realistic situation, we get the radiation resistance given as

$$R = 20\pi^2 \left(\frac{dl}{\lambda}\right)^2 \quad \text{....(9.72c)}$$

Since for the same current I the short practical dipole of length l will radiate only one quarter as much power as the curent element of the same length which has the current I through its entire length (the field strength at every point reduces to one half, so the power density will be reduced to one quarter). Therefore the radiation resistance of a practical short dipole is one quarter that of the current element of the same length.

9.7. Radiation From a Quarter Wave Monopole or Half Wave Dipole

In order to calculate the electromagnetic fields of longer antennas, it is essential to know the current distribution along the antennas. If the antenna is centre fed open circuited transmission line it is assumed that a sinusoidal current distribution is justified for calculating approximate field distribution along the length of the line. For thin wire antennas sinusoidal current distribution is a fairly good assumption, for more accurate results it is necessary to use current distribution close to the actual one. Fig 9.16a shows a centre-fed dipole with a sinusoidal current distribution and Fig. 9.16b shows the corresponding

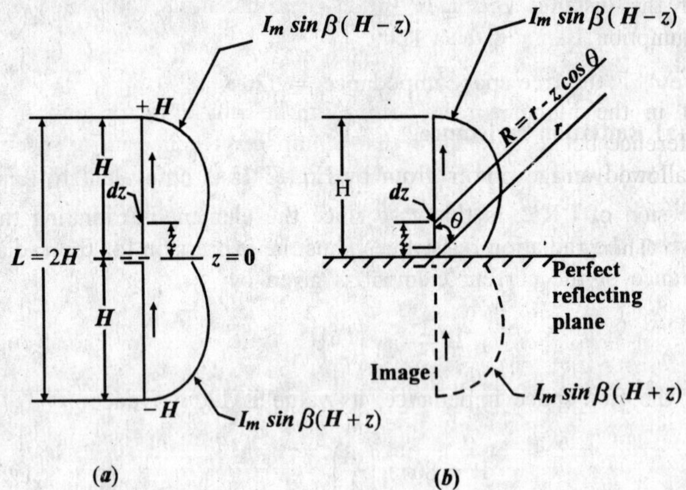

Fig. 9.16a Centre-fed dipole with assumed sinusoidal current distribution; (b) corresponding monopole.

monopole. In Fig. 9.16 b the vertical antenna is fed against an infinitely large perfectly conducting plane, has the same radiation characteristics above the plane as does the dipole antenna of length L in free space shown in Fig. 9.16a. Thus the dipole of length 2 H and the base fed antenna of Fig. 9.16b can be solved as one problem.

Now we are illustrating the method to calculate radiation from a $\lambda/4$ monopole or a $\lambda/2$ dipole. Fig. 9.16 shows that the current is sinusoidally distributed along the length of the antenna. Thus

$$I = I_0 \sin\beta(H-z) \qquad z > 0$$

$$I = I_0 \sin\beta(H+z) \qquad z < 0$$

where I_0 is the value of current maximum. The vector potential A at a point P due to the current element Idz will be

$$dA_z = \frac{\mu I \, e^{-j\beta R} \, dz}{4\pi R} \quad \text{....(9.73)}$$

R is the distance from the current element to the point P. The total vector potential at P due to all the current elements over the entire length of the antenna will be

$$A_z = \frac{\mu}{4\pi} \int_{-H}^{0} - \frac{I_0 \sin \beta (H + z) e^{-j\beta R} dz}{R} + \frac{\mu}{4\pi} \int_{0}^{H} \frac{I_0 \sin \beta (H - z) e^{-j\beta R} dz}{R} \quad \text{....(9.74)}$$

For the distance factor R in the denominator at the far field the assumption is made that

$$R \approx r$$

but in the numerator R occurs in the phase factor and it is the difference between R and r that is important hence no approximation is allowed and we write from the Fig. 9.16a

$$R = r - z \cos \theta$$

Then the expression for A_z becomes

$$A_z = \mu I_0 \frac{e^{-j\beta r}}{4\pi r} \left[\int_{-H}^{0} \sin \beta (H + z) \, e^{j\beta z \cos \theta} \, dz + \int_{0}^{H} \sin \beta \, (H - z) \, e^{j\beta z \cos \theta} dz \right]$$

When $H = \lambda/4$ (case of a monopole) :

$\sin \beta (H \pm z) = \cos \beta z$ and the integral becomes

$$A_z = \frac{\mu I_0 e^{-j\beta r}}{4\pi r} \int_{0}^{H} \cos \beta z \left(e^{j\beta z \cos \theta} + e^{-j\beta z \cos \theta} \right) dz \quad \text{....(9.76)}$$

Using appropriate trigonometric and Euler relation, on simplification we get

$$A_z = \frac{\mu I_0 e^{-j\beta r}}{2\pi \beta r} \left[\frac{\cos (\pi/2 \cos \theta)}{\sin^2 \theta} \right] \quad \text{....(9.77)}$$

Following the procedure outlined in section (9.6) when the current is entirely in z-direction only H_ϕ component is left and from the curl equation it is written as

$$\mu H_\phi = \frac{-\partial A_z}{\partial r} \sin\theta$$

On substituting for A_z

$$H_\phi = \frac{jI_0 e^{-j\beta r}}{2\pi r}\left[\frac{\cos(\pi/2\cos\theta)}{\sin\theta}\right] \qquad ....(9.78)$$

Electric field strength for the radiation field of the $\lambda/4$ monopole or $\lambda/2$ dipole is

$$E_\theta = \frac{j60\, I_0}{r}\left[\frac{\cos(\pi/2\cos\theta)}{\sin\theta}\right] \qquad ....(9.79)$$

Average value of poynting vector which is one-half the peak value of $[E_\theta H_\phi]$ is given as

$$P_{ave} = \frac{\eta I_0^2}{8\pi^2 r^2}\left[\frac{\cos^2(\pi/2\cos\theta)}{\sin^2\theta}\right]$$

The total power radiated through a hemispherical surface of radius *r* will be

$$\int P_{ave}\, da = \frac{\eta I_0^2}{4\pi}\int_0^{\pi/2} \frac{\cos^2(\pi/2\cos\theta)}{\sin\theta}\, d\theta \qquad ....(9.80)$$

Evaluation of the integral in equation 9.80 is not very straight forward. It can be solved by substitution method or numerically using Simpson's or trapezoidal rule.

The numerical value of the integral obtained is

$$\int_0^{\pi/2} \frac{\cos^2(\pi/2\cos\theta)}{\sin\theta}\, d\theta = 0.609$$

Hence, the power radiated through the hemispherical surface is

$$\text{Radiated power} = \frac{0.609\,\eta\, I_0^{\,2}}{4\pi}$$

In this expression I_0 is the peak current. In terms of effective current the radiated power would be

$$\text{Radiated power} = \frac{0.609\,\eta\, I_{eff}^2}{2\pi}$$

$$= 36.5\ I_{eff}^2$$

Therefore the radiation resistance of a quarter wave monopole antenna is 36.5 ohms.

For the half wave dipole antenna in free space, power would be radiated through a complete spherical surface, that is, the power radiated would be twice for that of a monopole and the radiation resistance of half wave dipole is

$$R_{rad} = 73 \text{ ohms.}$$

General expressions for the distant electric field of a dipole antenna of any length L = 2H is given by

$$E = \frac{j\,60\,I_0 e^{-j\beta r}}{r}\left[\frac{\cos(\beta H\cos\theta) - \cos\beta H}{\sin\theta}\right] \text{ V/m.}$$

As the length of a dipole is increased beyond the point where it can be considered as short in terms of a wave length the radiation pattern changes as indicated in Fig. 9.17. The radiation pattern for a Hertzian dipoles, half wave dipole and for antenna lengths of $1\frac{1}{2}$ and 2 wave length are shown in Fig. 9.17.

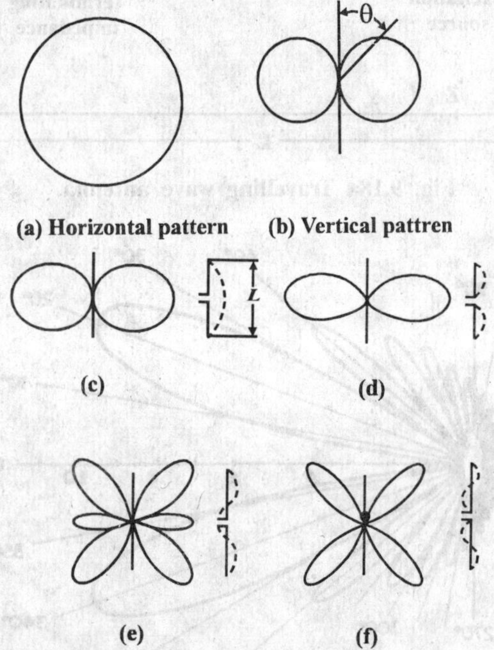

Fig. 9.17 Radiation patterns of center-fed vertical dipoles (a) horizontal pattern for all lengths, (b) vertical pattern for short dipole, Vertical pattern for dipole lengths (c) one-half wavelength (d) one wave-length (e) one-and-a-half wavelengths (f) two wave-lengths. The assumed current in each case is shown dashed.

9.8. Travelling Wave Antennas or Non-Resonant Antenna

In the last section it was shown that an open transmission line could form an efficient radiator. These antennas have standing wave distribution of current. Sometimes antennas are terminated to make them non-resonant or there are no reflected waves, hence no standing waves as shown in Fig 9.18a and they have a travelling wave distribution. Assuming negligible attenuation of the wave along the antenna and a

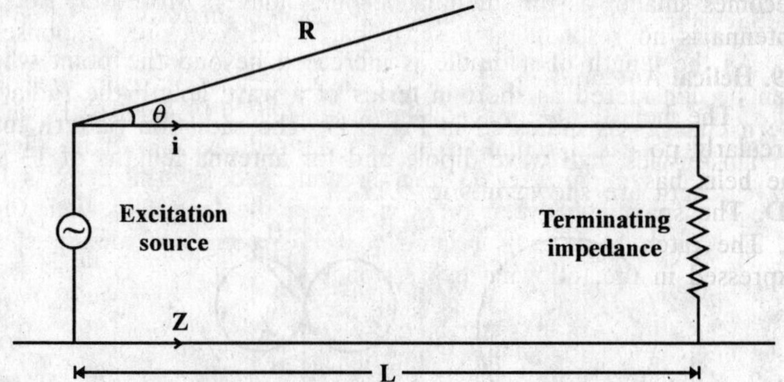

Fig. 9.18a Travelling wave antenna.

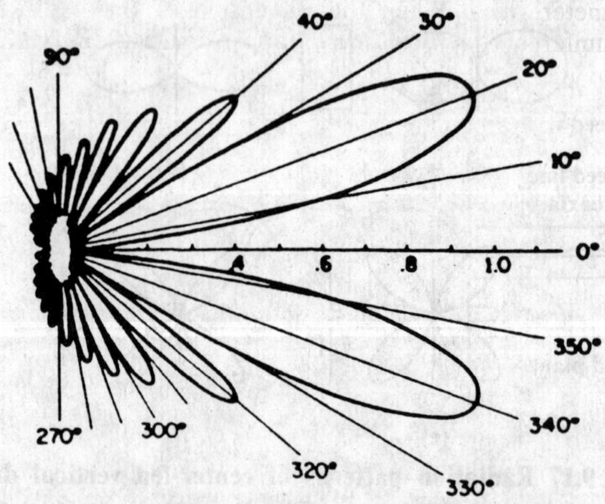

Fig. 9.18b Radiation pattern of a travelling wave antenna six wavelengths long.

wave velocity equal to c, the expression for E field of a travelling wave antenna can be written as

$$E = \frac{30I_0 \sin\theta}{r(1 - \cos\theta)} [2 - 2\cos\{\beta L(1 - \cos\theta)\}]^{1/2} \quad ....(9.83)$$

Fig 9.18b shows the radiation pattern of a travelling wave antenna having a length of six wave lengths

From the radiation pattern in Fig. 9.18b it is seen that the pattern is not symmetrical about the $\theta = 90$ degrees plane, the pattern shows a leaning in the direction of the current flow. The angle θ between the axis of the antenna and the direction of maximum radiation becomes smaller as the antenna becomes longer. Moreover, since the antenna is nonresonant, it has a broad band frequency response.

9.9. Helical Antenna

The helical antenna as shown in Fig. 9.19 is useful, when a circularly polarized radiation field is desired. As shown in Fig. 9.19 the helix has a diameter D, the circumference of the helix is C = πD. The spacing between turns is S, and the length of each turn is L. The pitch angle α is related to the spacing and diameter as is expressed in the following expression [14] :

$$\tan\alpha = \frac{S}{\pi D} \quad ....(9.84)$$

where pitch angle α is in degrees, the spacing is in metres, and D is the diameter of the helix in meters.

A helical antenna can radiate in several modes depending upon its parameter sizes. When the dimension of the helix are such that the circumference of one turn is approximately one wave length, the

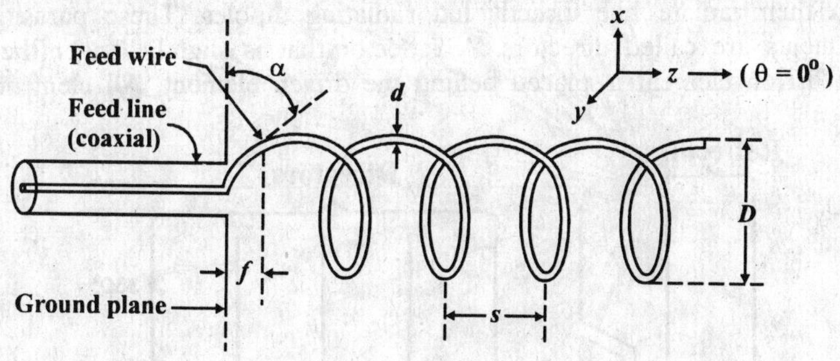

d - diameter of wire
D- diameter of helix
s- turn spacing
f- spacing of helix from ground plane
α- pitch angle

Fig. 9.19 Helical antenna.

antenna radiates in the axial mode. In this mode the radiation is circularly polarized and has a maximum value in the direction of the helix axis and the minor lobes are relatively small. In this mode of radiation the antenna has relatively large band-width and good efficiency. Most axial mode helices are of uniform diameter, but helices of non-uniform diameter are used to give wider bandwidth and improved radiation characteristics. If the circumference, pitch and length of the helix are small compared to a wavelength so that the current is approximately uniform in magnitude and phase in all parts of the helix, the normal mode of helix is excited, that is, the radiation is maximum in the plane normal to the helix axis. The radiation may be elliptical or circularly polarized, depending upon the helix dimensions. This mode of radiation is characterized by relatively narrow band width and poor efficiency. When we increase the number of turns we get a narrower beam, which is expected since it amounts to increasing the aperture of an antenna [14].

9.10. Yagi-UDA Antenna

This antenna named after the inventors in Japan consists of a single driven dipole and a number of slightly shorter parasitic dipoles in front of it, as shown in Fig. 9.20. The driven element is a resonant dipole or it could be a folded dipole. In the front of this dipole there are other dipoles which are called parasitic because they are not directly fed by electromagnetic signal but have currents induced in them in the same way as the current from the primary coil of a transformer induces current in the secondary. These parasitic dipoles can then radiate like directly fed radiating dipoles. These parasitic elements are called directors. A reflector that is slightly longer then the driven element is placed behind the driven element. All elements

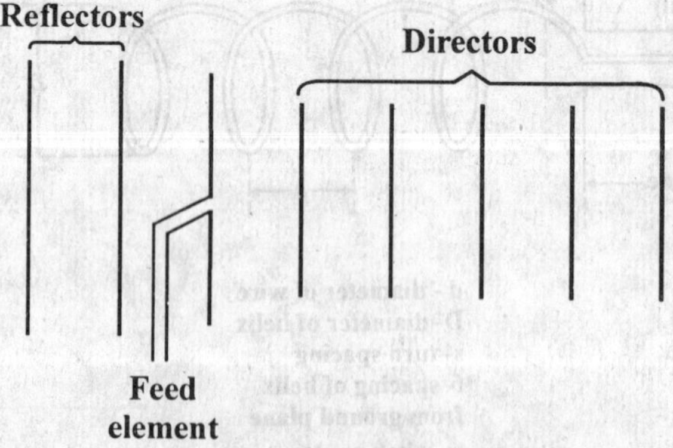

Fig. 9.20 Yagi-Uda antenna.

are parallel to each other and in the same plane. The antenna radiates in the end fire direction from the reflector towards the shorter directors. Increasing the number of directors increases the gain.

9.11. Antenna Arrays

Radio antennas have mainly two functions. The first is to "radiate" the electromagnetic energy generated by the radio-frequency source at the transmitter and guided by the transmission lines to the antenna. Antenna's role in this case is that of an impedance transforming device to match the impedance of transmission line to that of free space. The other function of the antenna is to direct energy in the desired direction and suppress the radiation in those direction in which it is not wanted.

A omni-directional radiator radiates uniformly in all directions and is known as an isotropic radiator. There is no radiator of electromagnetic energy which can be identified as isotropic radiator, since all antennas have some directivity. Omni-directional characteristics of a single antenna are very desirable for commercial broadcast purposes where receiving stations are located in all directions from the transmitter. For microwave communication, radar, remote sensing and other special applications, highly directive antennas are desirable than can be obtained by a single antenna, hence antenna arrays are used. An antenna array is an assembly of two or more antenna elements (generally half wave dipoles) situated very close to each other so that their induction fields interact. By an appropriate choice of (a) spacing

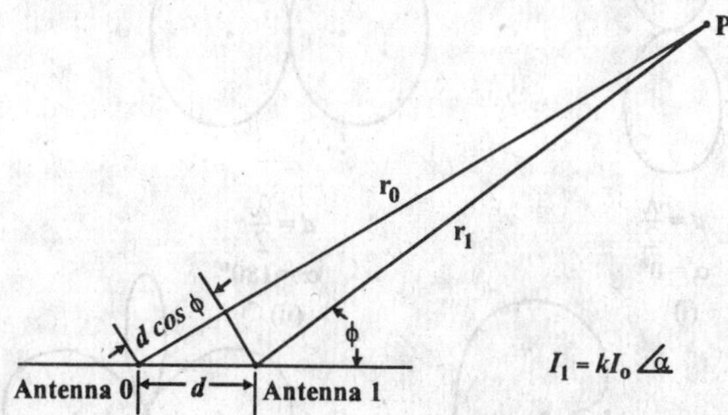

Fig. 9.21 A two-element array of nondirectional radiators.

between elements and (b) phase difference between the currents feeding the elements, various specialized patterns may be obtained.

One of the simplest arrays consists of two non-directional vertical radiators placed closely as shown in Fig. 9.21.

Consider a point P sufficiently remote from the antenna system, the radius vectors to the point P can be considered parallel and it is possible to write

$$r_1 = r_0 - d\cos\phi \qquad \text{....(9.85)}$$

in the phase factor of the fields, and

$\frac{1}{r_1} = \frac{1}{r_0}$ for the magnitude part of the fields. The phase difference between the radiations from the two antennas will be

$$\psi = \beta d \cos \phi + \alpha$$

where $\beta d = (2\pi/\lambda)d$ is the path difference in radians and α is the phase angle by which the current I_1 leads I_0. The sum of the fields of this system will be

$$E = E_0 (1 + K e^{j\psi}) \qquad \text{....(9.86)}$$

where E_0 is the field strength due to antenna (0) alone and K is the ratio of the magnitudes of I_1 and I_0. The magnitude of total field strength is given by

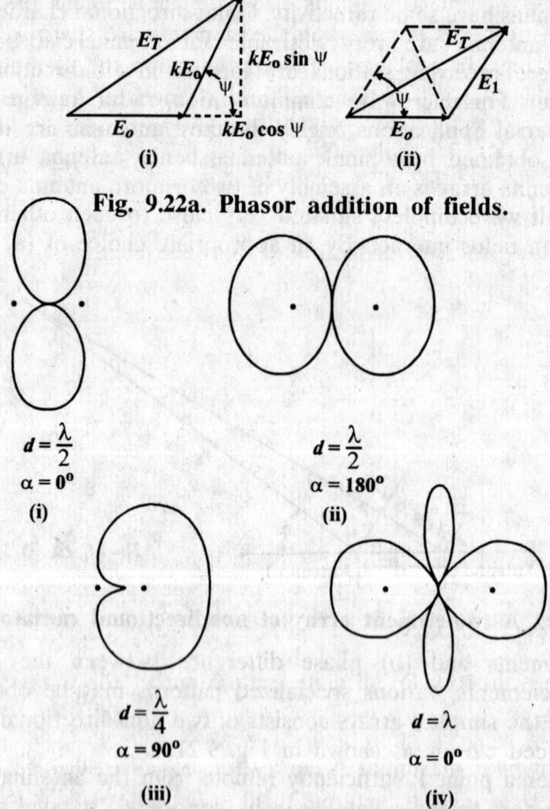

Fig. 9.22a. Phasor addition of fields.

Fig. 9.22b Radiation patterns of two nondirectional radiators fed with equal currents at various spacings and phasings.

$$E_T = |E_0 (1 + K e^{j\psi})|$$
$$= E_0 \sqrt{(1 + K\cos\psi)^2 + K^2 \sin^2\psi} \quad \text{....(9.87)}$$

In the particular case where the antenna currents have equal magnitude

Eqn. 9.87 becomes $E_T = 2E_0 \cos\frac{\psi}{2}$

$$= 2E_0 \cos\left(\frac{\pi d \cos\phi}{\lambda} + \frac{\alpha}{2}\right) \quad \text{....(9.88)}$$

Shown in Fig. 9.22a. The radiation patterns resulting from this expression for various spacings and phasing are shown in Fig. 9.22b.

9.11.1. Linear arrays

To obtain a very narrow beam a multi-element linear or planar array is used. An array is linear when the elements are spaced equally along a straight line. In a planar array configuration the elements are placed in a plane. We will obtain the field strength of an n element uniform linear array. The field strength for these elements is given as

$$E_T = E_0\, |1 + e^{j\psi} + e^{j2\psi} + e^{j3\psi} + \ldots\ldots\ldots\, e^{j(n-1)\psi}| \quad \text{....(9.89a)}$$

where $\psi = \beta d \cos\phi + \alpha$

and α is the progressive phase shift between elements. Equation 9.89a resembles a geometric progression and can be written as

$$\frac{E_T}{E_0} = \left|\frac{1 - e^{jn\psi}}{1 - e^{j\psi}}\right| \quad \text{....(9.89b)}$$

$$= \left|\frac{\sin\frac{n\psi}{2}}{\sin\frac{\psi}{2}}\right| \quad \text{....(9.90)}$$

The maximum value of this expression is n and occurs when $\psi = 0$.

This is the direction of principal maximum of the array [1].

When $\psi = 0$, $\beta d \cos\phi + \alpha = 0$.

Hence principal maximum occurs when $\cos\phi = -\frac{\alpha}{\beta d}$.

The expression 9.90 is zero, when

$$\frac{n\psi}{2} = \pm k\pi \qquad k = 1, 2, 3$$

These are the nulls of the array system, first null occurs when $\psi_1 = \frac{2\pi}{n}$.

For a broad side array the maximum radiation occurs when $\phi = \pi/2$ and this results in $\alpha = 0$

Hence $\cos\phi = \psi/\beta d$

The first null accurs at an angle $\cos(\pi/2 + \Delta\phi)$

where $\cos(\pi/2 + \Delta\phi) = \frac{\psi_1}{\beta d} = \frac{2\pi}{n\beta d} = \frac{\lambda}{nd}$

If $\Delta\phi$ is small it is given approximately by

$$\Delta\phi \approx \frac{\lambda}{nd} \quad \text{.....(9.91)}$$

The width of the principal lobe is approximately equal to the angle between the nulls on either side of the principal maxima or $2\Delta\phi$. Hence width of the main lobe $= \frac{2\lambda}{nd}$ which is twice the reciprocal of the array length in wavelengths. Fig. 9.23a shows a broad side array system. Note that each individual antenna receives the same amount of energy from the transmitter and each is excited in phase with the other elements. The proper phasing is achieved by placing the elements $\lambda/2$ apart and crossing the feed points as shown in Fig. 9.23a. Each four elements are shown in phase, + along the top, – along the bottom. Therefore each of the individual donut patterns combine, forming the resultant bidirectional radiation pattern having maximum directivity perpendicular to the plane of the array. Fig. 9.23b shows the three dimenstional radiation pattern of a broad side array.

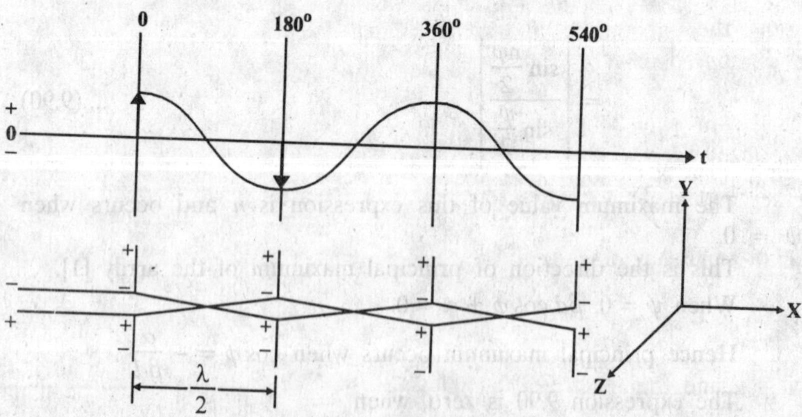

Fig. 9.23a Broadside array.

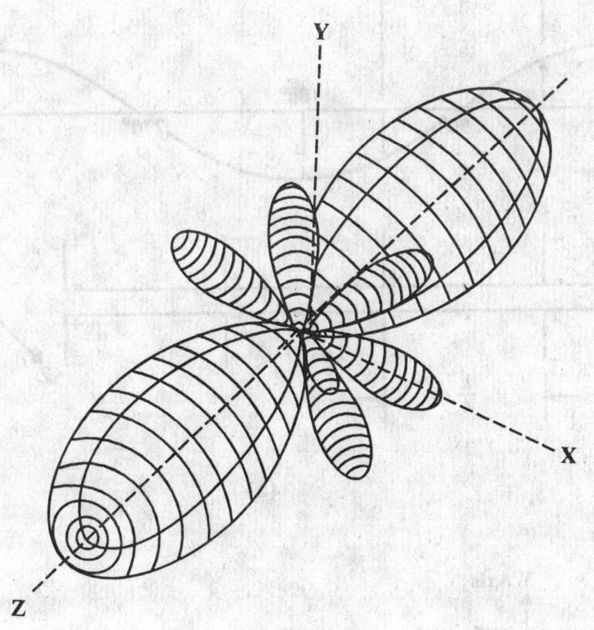

Fig. 9.23b. Solid radiation pattern of a broadside array.

(i) End fire array

For an end fire array the maximum radiation is along the line of the array i.e. at $\phi = 0$. Hence $\alpha = -\beta d$ and $\psi = \beta d(\cos\phi - 1)$. The first null is at $\phi_1 = \Delta\phi$

$$\text{or } \psi_1 = \beta d(\cos\phi_1 - 1) = -\frac{2\pi}{n}$$

$$\text{or } (\cos\Delta\phi) - 1 = -\frac{\lambda}{\text{nd}}$$

For small $\Delta\phi$ this is approximately equal to

$$\left(\frac{\Delta\phi}{2}\right)^2 = \frac{\lambda}{nd}$$

and the width of the principle lobe $= 2\Delta\phi$

$$\text{or} \qquad 2\Delta\phi = 2\sqrt{\frac{2\lambda}{nd}} \qquad \text{....(9.92)}$$

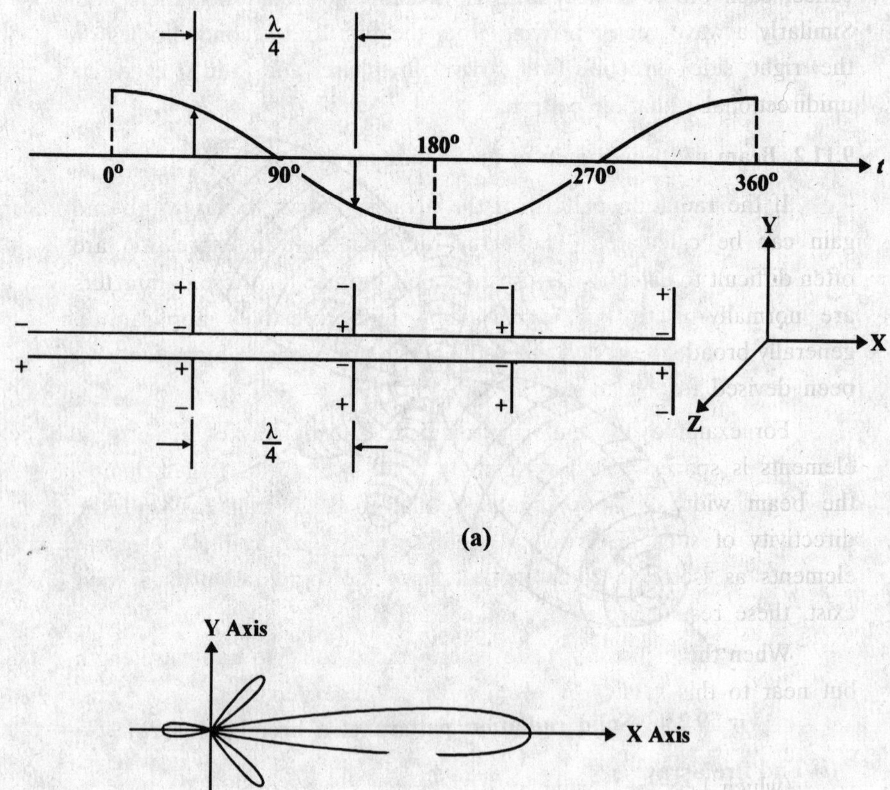

Fig. 9.24 Radiation pattern of an endfire array

Hence the width of principal lobe of an end fire array is greater than that of a uniform broad side array. In end fire array shown in Fig. 9.24(a) elements are spaced $\lambda/4$ apart and are fed 90 degrees out of phase. As is clear from the figure, the first and third (2nd and 4th) dipoles are out of phase, they cancel out each others radiation at right angles to the array. Because of this there is no radiation normal to the plane of the array. See Fig. 9.24b

A wave leaving the first dipole and moving to the left is $\lambda/4$ closer to some remote point than a wave leaving the second dipole also to the left side. So the waves arriving some time later at the remote point on left will be 180 degree out of phase, and will therefore cancel each other. Hence there is virtually no radiation on left side. Similarly a wave vector arriving from the first and second dipoles on the right side direction will arrive in phase and add to give a unidirectional radiation pattern.

9.11.2. Beam width and gain of broad-side arrays

If the radiation pattern of the array is known, beam width and gain can be calculated. The array radiation pattern expression are often difficult to calculate, approximation formulae for these parameters are normally used. For narrow-beam high directivity applications, generally broad side arrays are used, hence approximate formulae have been devised for broad-side arrays.

For example if a uniform broadside linear array of n isotropic elements is spaced a half wavelength apart, when n is larger than 3, the beam width is approximately equal to $102/n$ degrees and the directivity of such an array is equal to n. We always talk of array elements as isotropic radiators but since isotropic radiators do not exist, these results are somewhat academic.

When the element spacing is not exactly equal to half-wavelength but near to this value, the beam-width formula becomes

$$\text{B.W.} = 51\lambda/nd \text{ degree}$$

(which becomes equal to $102/n$ for $d = \lambda/2$).

Broad-side arrays are often made unidirectional by placing a reflecting screen behind the array. When such array is large the beam width and directivity are given by the formulae of the following type

$$\text{B.W.} = K_1 \left(\frac{\lambda}{nd}\right) \qquad \text{....(9.93)}$$

$$D = K_2 \left(\frac{4\pi A}{\lambda^2}\right) \qquad \text{....(9.94)}$$

where K_1 and K_2 are of the order of one or slightly less, if the beam width is expressed in radians. If the beamwidth is expressed in degrees K_1 is around 60, slightly less for a uniform array, and some-what more for tapered arrays. For a tapered array the constant K_2 in Eq. 9.94 is less than one.

9.11.3. Array tapering for side lobe reduction

We have learned from earlier discussions that directional antenna patterns are characterized by minor lobes in addition to the main lobe or lobes. Generally these minor lobes are undesired. It is desirable to minimize the strength of these secondary lobes in comparison to the main-lobe strength. The minor lobes immediately adjacent to the main lobe are of greatest importance. The term "side lobe ratio" refers to the ratio of the main-beam power density to the power density of the largest minor lobe. It is also the figure of merit of the antenna, since larger its value the better the antenna performance from the point of view of favouring main-lobe signals and discriminating against signals from other directions.

In the preceding discussions of broadside arrays it has been assumed that all the array elements are of equal strength and all are in phase. In this condition the side lobe level obtained is approximately 20 or 13 dB. But this side lobe level is high for many applications and is unacceptable. For example in Radar systems, general requirement of side-lobe level is 30 to 40 dB.

The technique that has been developed for reducing minor lobes is called "tapering". This term refers to nonuniform current strength of the elements of the array. It has been found that minor lobes are reduced in amplitude if the centre elements of the array radiate more strongly than the end elements, the strength is gradually tapered from centre to end according to some mathematical function.

9.11.4. Dolph-Tchebyscheff array

This array has many practical applications. The theory and procedure for this array was worked out by C.L. Dolph and is based on the use of mathematical function called Tchebyscheff polynonials [a]. It is primarily a compromise between uniform arrays and binomial arrays.

The Tchebyscheff polynomial is defined by

$$T_m(x) = \cos(m \cos^{-1} x) \qquad -1 < x < +1 \qquad \text{....(9.95)}$$

$$T_m(x) = \cosh(m \cosh^{-1} x) \qquad |x| > 1 \qquad \text{....(9.96)}$$

The general shape of $T_m(x)$ is shown in Fig. 9.25. for both m even and m odd.

By inspection, $T_0(x) = 1, \quad T_1(x) = x$

The higher order polynomials can be derived as follows

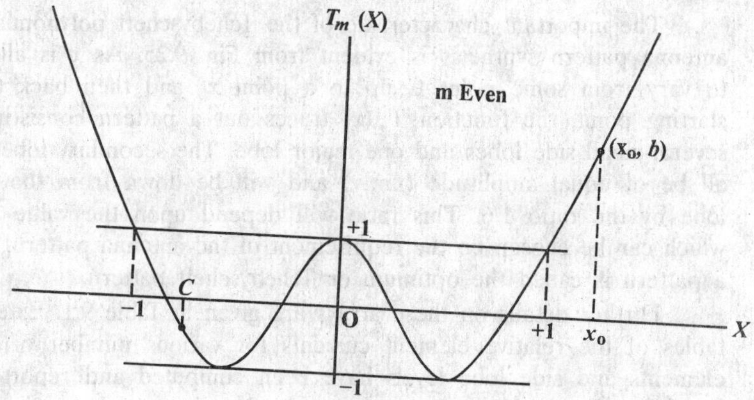

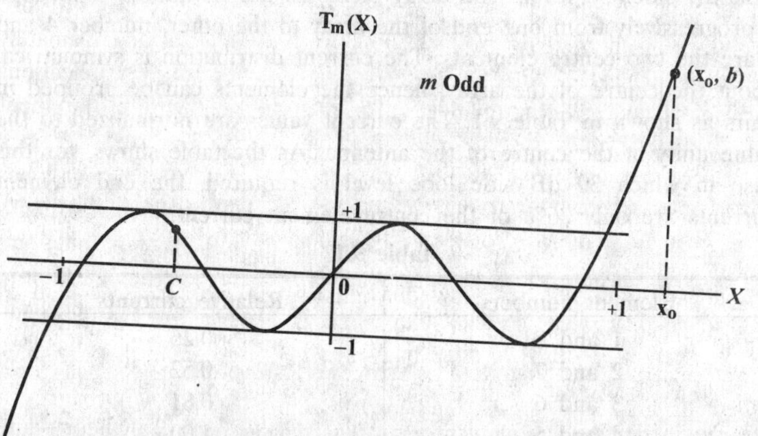

Fig. 9.25 Tchebyscheff polynomials, T_m (x) for m even and m odd.

$$T_2(x) = \cos(2 \cos^{-1} x) = \cos 2\delta$$

Where $\delta = \cos^{-1} x$ or $x = \cos \delta$

Now since $\cos 2\delta = 2\cos^2 \delta - 1$

$$T_2(x) = 2x^2 - 1$$

Also it can be shown that

$$T_{m+1}(x) = 2T_m(x)\, T_1(x) - T_{m-1}(x) \qquad \text{....(9.97)}$$

so that $T_3(x) = 4x^3 - 3x$

$$T_4(x) = 8x^4 - 8x^2 + 1$$

and so on.

The important characteristic of the Tchebyscheff polynomial for antenna pattern synthesis is evident from Fig. 9.25. As x is allowed to vary from some point C up to a point x_0 and then back to its starting point, the function $T_m(x)$ traces out a pattern consisting of several small side lobes and one major lobe. The secondary lobes will all be of equal amplitude (unity) and will be down from the main lobe by the ratio 1/6. This ratio will depend upon the value of x_0 which can be chosen on the requirement of the antenna pattern. Such a pattern is called the optimum or Tchebyscheff pattern.

Further details on these arrays are given in Table 9.1. Extensive tables of the relative element currents for various number of array elements and side lobe levels have been computed and reported in literature. A sample of these tabulated values is given below in Table 9.1. This table array is for an eight-element linear array designed for a 30-dB sidelobe level. The array elements are numbered 1 through 8 progressively from one end of the array to the other, number 4 and 5 are the two centre elements. The current distribution is symmetrical about the centre of the array, hence the elements can be grouped in pairs as shown in Table 9.1. The current values are normalized to the value unity at the centre of the antenna. As the table shows, for this case in which 30 dB side lobe level is required, the end element currents are only 26% of the centre element current.

Table 9.1

Element numbers	Relative currents
1 and 8	0.26
2 and 7	0.52
3 and 6	0.81
4 and 5	1.00

The Dolph-Tchebyscheff distribution of currents results in side lobes that are all of the same amplitude, in contrast with the uniform distribution for which the side lobes adjacent to the main beam are the largest, the remaining ones becoming progressively smaller with increasing angle from the main lobe. In the case of Tchebyscheff arrays, the number of side lobes in the complete radiation pattern increases as the size of the array (number of elements) increases. For this reason, although increasing the number of elements decrease the beam width, but the side lobes increase and hence the gain (directivity) decreases. This statement can be viewed in Fig. 9.26. The uppermost curve represents the gain that would be obtained with uniform distribution and show that the gain for this case is always greater than the tapered array gain. Other curves in the figure also show that

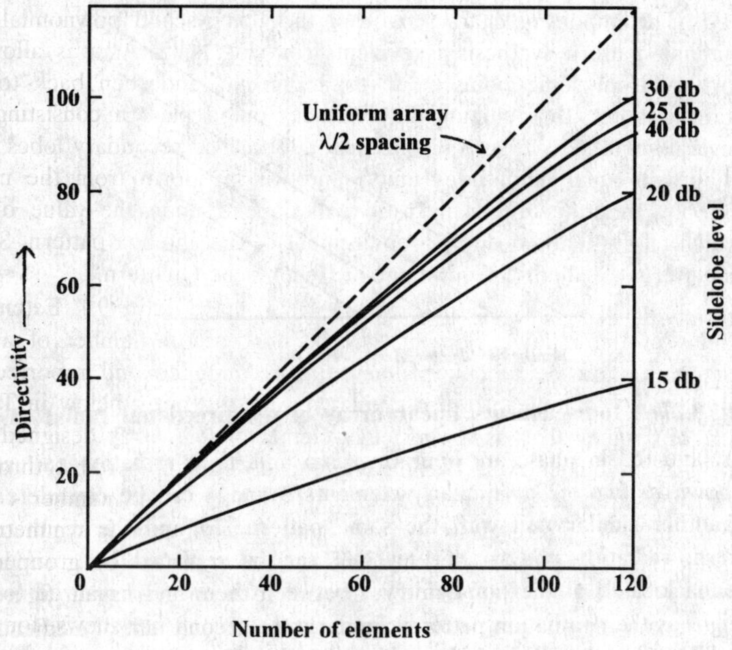

Fig. 9.26.

reducing the taper does not always increase the gain, in fact increasing the number of element increases the gain.

It is possible to eliminate the side lobes completely, in principle, by means of a binomial current distribution explained in the next sections.

9.12. Multiplication of Patterns

The principle of pattern multiplication provides a useful concept for the determination of field patterns for antenna arrays, and for synthesis of arrays to produce specific field patterns. By the use of this principle, the field pattern of a complicated array may often be obtained as the product of the field patterns of two simpler arrays whose patterns are known or are easily determined. Consider a four element array of antennas in Fig. 9.27 in which spacing between elements is $\lambda/2$ and the currents are in phase $\alpha = 0$. The pattern can be obtained by directly adding the phasor fields of the four elements as we have done in the case of two element array. However the same radiation pattern can be found from the following consideration. The pattern of antennas (1) and (2) spaced $\lambda/2$ distance

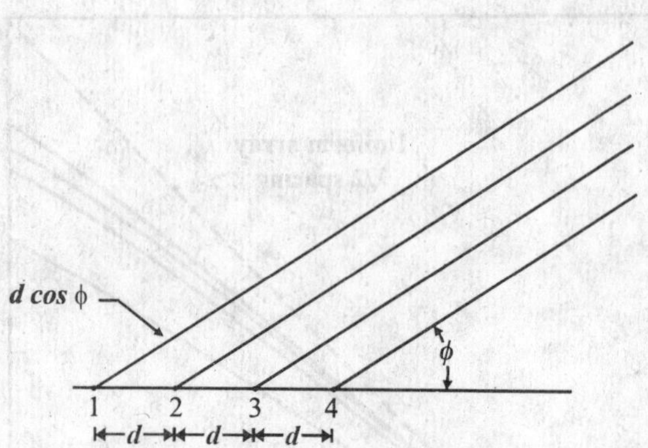

Fig. 9.27 A four-elements linear array of nondirectional radiators.

apart and fed in phase are operating as a unit, their radiation pattern is shown in Fig. 9.28a. Similarly elements 3 and 4 can be considered as another similar unit with the same pattern. To find the resultant pattern, radiation pattern of unit one can be replaced by a single antenna located at the point midway between them and having figure of eight as their radiation pattern. Similarly the second unit of elements 3 and 4 replaced at their midpoint by a single unit of another radiation pattern of figure of eight. Now problem left, is to determine the radiation pattern of two similar antennas which are having radiation pattern as figure of eight and are spaced by λ and fed in phase. Radiation pattern of such unit is given in Fig. 9.28b. The resultant pattern for the original four element array is obtained as the product of the pattern of Fig. 9.28b by the pattern of the unit as shown in Fig. 9.28c

The application of this principle can be applied to more complicated arrays. Using this procedure lengthy calculations to find the approximate radiation pattern of complicated arrays can be avoided [8].

9.12.1. Binomial array

For a uniform linear array it is found that as the length of array is increased in order to increase the directivity, secondary lobes appear in the pattern. Some applications require a single narrow lobe without minor lobes (secondary lobes).

John Stone suggested that the excitation coefficients of a binomial array is given by the binomial series expansion of the function $(1+x)^{m-1}$ given as :

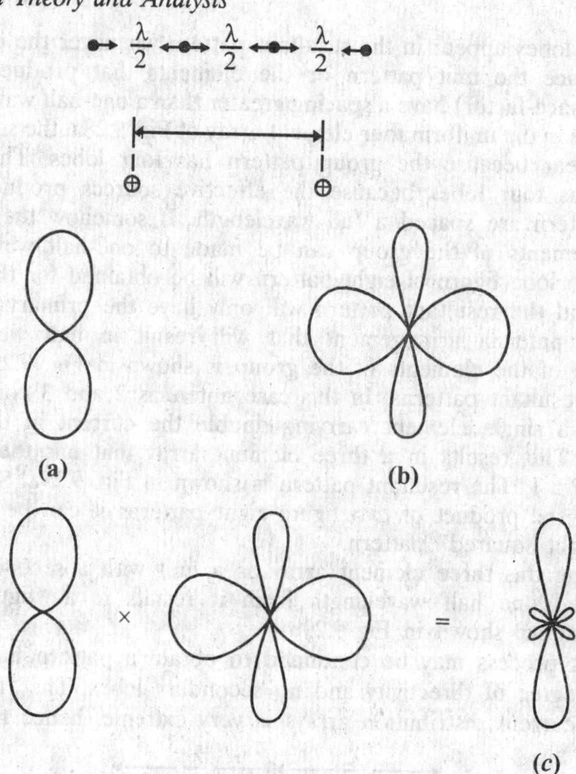

Fig. 9.28 Multiplication of patterns.

$$(1+x)^{m-1} = 1 + (m-1)x + \frac{(m-1)(m-2)}{2!}x^2 + \frac{(m-1)(m-2)(m-3)}{3!}x^3 + ... \quad ....(9.98)$$

Where m = 1, 2, 3, ...

For various values of m, the amplitude current coefficients are given as

For three element

1 : 2 : 1

For four elements

1 : 3 : 3 : 1

For five elements

1 : 4 : 6 : 4 : 1 and so on

The radiation pattern of a binomial array can be derived by the principle of multiplication of patterns. In the study of uniform array using the principle of pattern multiplication, it was shown that the secondary lobes appear in the resultant pattern whenever the elements that produce the unit pattern or the elements that produce group pattern (space-factor) have a spacing greater than a one-half wavelength.

Thus in the uniform four element array of Fig. 9.28a, the secondary lobes appear because the group pattern has four lobes. The group pattern has four lobes because the effective sources producing the group pattern are spaced a full wavelength. If somehow the spacing of the elements of the group can be made to one-half wavelength, then a two lobe figure of eight pattern will be obtained for the group pattern and the resultant pattern will only have the primary lobes.

The antenna arrangement that will result in half wavelength seperation of the elements of the group is shown in Fig. 9.29a along with the resultant patterns. In this case antennas 2 and 3 coincide to represent a single element carrying double the current in the other elements. This results in a three element array that has the current ratio 1 : 2 : 1. The resultant pattern is shown in Fig. 9.29a. Since this pattern is the product of two figure-eight patterns it can be called a "figure-eight squared" pattern.

Using this three element array as a unit with a second similar unit placed one half wavelength from it results in a "figure eight cubed" pattern shown in Fig 9.29b.

This process may be continued to obtain a pattern having any desired degree of directivity and no secondary lobes. The "taper" in binomial current distribution arrays is very extreme, hence this array

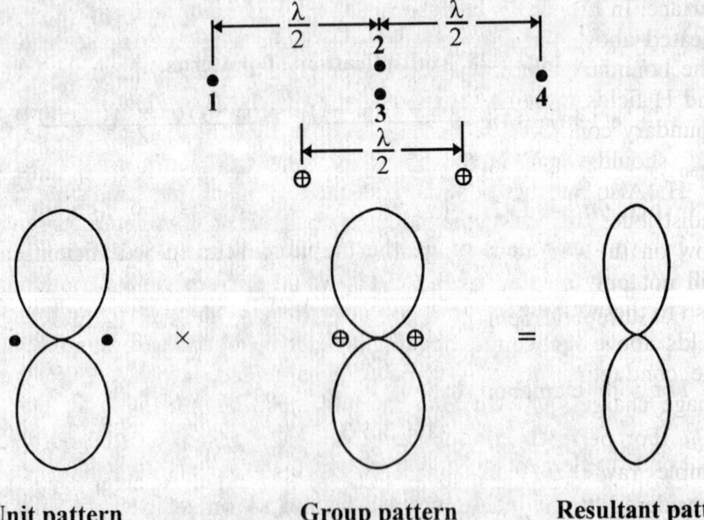

Fig. 9.29a An array that produces a pattern without secondary lobes.

is hardly ever used in practice. The beam width and gain are poorer for a given number of elements, than they would be with for a very low side lobe Dolph Tchebyscheff array.

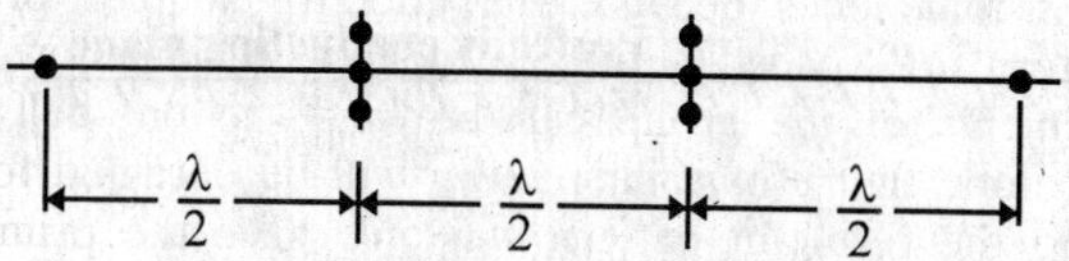

Fig. 29b A four-element array with a "figure-eight cubed" pattern.

9.13. Effect of the Earth on Vertical Patterns

The radiation pattern shown so far have been obtained on the assumption that the antenna was situated in free space far removed from any other conducting bodies or reflecting surfaces. In practice antennae are always erected right at, or within few wavelengths off, the surface of the earth, or some other reflecting surface. In such situation currents flow in the reflecting surface and the radiation pattern is modified. The magnitude and phases of these induced currents will depend upon the frequency, σ and E of the reflecting surface. In Fig. 9.30a below, are shown horizontal and vertical antennas located above the earth which we assume to be perfectly conducting. The boundary conditions for tangential and normal components for E and H fields must be satisfied at the dielectric conductor surface. The boundary conditions to be satisfied are that the tangential component E_{tan} should vanish at the boundary, so should the normal component of H. Also at the boundary surface E is normal and the charges redistribute themselves and due to tangential components currents will flow on the conducting surface. The total electric and magnetic field will not only be due to the charges and currents on the antenna but also to these "induced" charges and currents. The electric and magnetic fields above the conducting region can be obtained by assuming that the conducting plane is removed and replaced with suitably located image charges and currents as shown in Fig. 9.30a.

For perfectly conducting planes same results can be obtained by simple ray theory as shown in Fig. 9.30b. The resultant field is considered to be made up of direct and reflected waves from the actual and image antennae. The vertical component of the E field for the incident wave is reflected without phase reversal whereas the horizontal component has a 180 degree phase reversal.

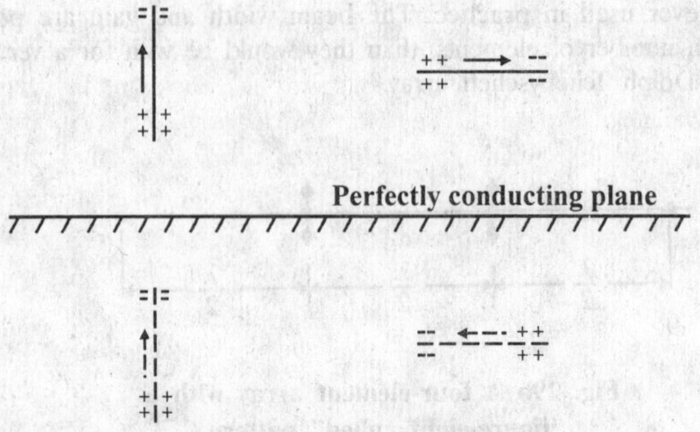

Fig. 9.30a Image charges and currents replace the charges and currents induced in the conducting plane.

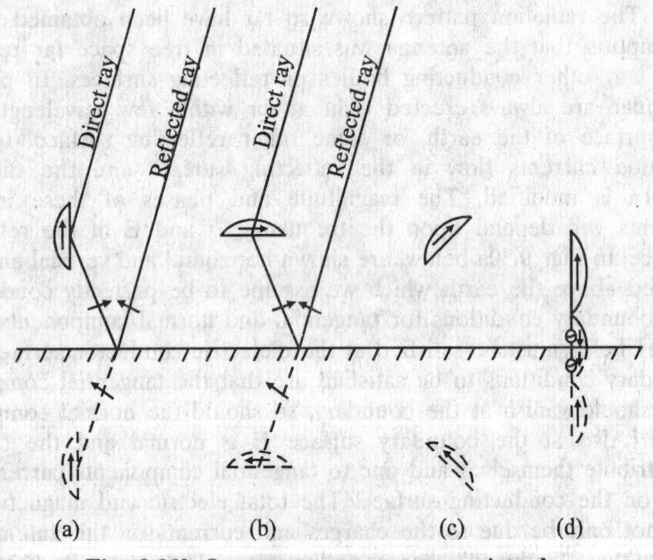

Fig. 9.30b Image antennas act as virtual souces for the reflected waves.

9.14. Aperture Antennas and Concept of Magnetic Currents

Aperture antennas are most common at microwave frequencies. The most popular aperture antenna (horn) configurations are shown in Fig. 9.31a. The wave guide horns as shown may be square, rectangular, circular or can take any other configuration. Aperture antennae are specially suitable for space application because they can be mounted on the surface of the spacecraft or aircraft. Sources of radiation for aperture antenna are both time varying electric field and time varying magnetic fields. Time varying electric field is equivalent to magnetic current. We will introduce the concept of magnetic currents and equivalence principle which are helpful in finding out the radiation pattern for apertures and horns.

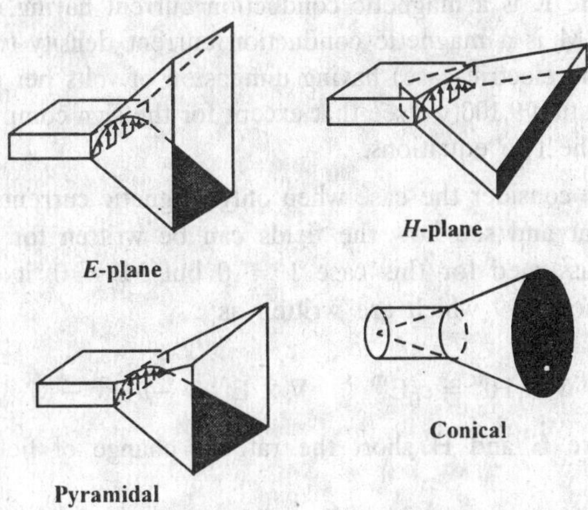

Fig. 9.31a Typical electromagnetic horn antenna configurations.

9.14.1. Magnetic currents

The two Maxwells curl equations are

$$\nabla \times H = \frac{\partial D}{\partial t} + J \text{ and } \nabla \times E = -\frac{\partial B}{\partial t}$$

D, J and B are the densities of electric displacement current, electric conduction current and magnetic displacement current respectively. There is no quantity corresponding to J i.e. a magnetic conduction current since no isolated magnetic charge exists. In many situations it is more convenient to obtain solutions of electromagnetic problems using fictitious magnetic currents and charges. Although in such problems fields are actually produced by a certain distribution of electric current and charge. For example the radiation field for an aperture is from page 9.52found using magnetic current and charges. Therefore expressions for the fields due to magnetic charges and currents will now be developed.

Maxwell's curl equation using magnetic current and charges can be modified as follows

$$\nabla \times H = \frac{\partial D}{\partial t} + J \ , \quad \nabla \times E = \frac{-\partial B}{\partial t} - M \qquad \text{....(9.99)}$$

or in the integral form

$$\oint H.ds = \dot{\psi} + I \quad \oint E.ds = -\dot{\Phi} - K \qquad \text{....(9.100)}$$

where K is a magnetic conduction current having dimensions of volts and M is a magnetic conduction current density (corresponding to J for the electric case) having dimension of volts per square meter. From equation 9.100 we see that except for the sign complete symmetry exists in the two equations.

Now consider the case when only magnetic currents and charges are present and see how the fields can be written for this case. As we have assumed for this case $J = 0$ but $M \neq 0$, it should satisfy the equation 9.99 which are written as

$$\nabla \times H^m = \varepsilon_0 \dot{E}^m \qquad \nabla \times E^m = -\mu \dot{H}^m - M \qquad \text{....(9.101)}$$

where $\dot{E}$ and $\dot{H}$ short the rate of change of fields with time $\left(\frac{\partial}{\partial t}\right)$.

These should be compared with the familiar relations written for electric current only *i.e.* $M = 0$ but $J \neq 0$ In this case the curl equations are

$$\nabla \times E^e = -\mu \dot{H}^e \qquad \nabla \times H^e = \varepsilon_0 \dot{E}^e + J \qquad \text{....(9.102)}$$

The superscripts e and m refer to fields due to electric and magnetic currents respectively. Comparison of equations 9.101 & 9.102 shows them to be identical sets (except for sign) if electrical and magnetic quantities are interchanged *i.e.* H^m, E^m, M, μ and ε replaced to E^e, H^e, J, ε and μ respectively. We can now adopt the procedure outlined in section 9.5a (for electric current) for finding the potentials due to magnetic currents.

In this case F is defined as electric vector potential and ϕ_m as an arbitrary magnetic scalar potential. Then Electric field E^m can be found from the curl equation.

$$E^m = -\frac{1}{e} \nabla \times F \qquad \text{....(9.103)}$$

$$\text{and } H^m = -\nabla \phi_m - j\omega F \qquad \text{....(9.104)}$$

and the vector wave equation in F can be written as

$$\nabla^2 F + k^2 F = -\varepsilon M \qquad ....(9.105)$$

F and ϕ_m have solutions of the form

$$F = \frac{\varepsilon}{4\pi}\int \frac{Me^{-j\beta R}}{R} dV \text{ and } \phi_m = \frac{1}{4\pi}\int \rho_m \frac{e^{-j\beta R}}{\mu R} dV \qquad ....(9.106)$$

In a problem where both electric and magnetic current and charge distribution are involved, the total magnetic and electric field strengths will be given as sum of the two

i.e. $E = E^e + E^m$ and $H = H^e + H^m$

Hence the fields have to be calculated by expressions

$$E = -\nabla V - j\omega A - \frac{1}{\varepsilon}\nabla \times F \qquad ....(9.107)$$

$$H = -\nabla \phi_\mu - j\,\omega F + \frac{1}{\mu}\nabla \times A \qquad ....(9.108)$$

9.14.2. Field equivalence principle

The field equivalence is a principle by which actual sources such as an antenna are replaced by equivalent sources. The equivalence principle is based on uniqueness theorem which states that "a field in a lossy region is uniquely specified by the sources within the region plus the tangential components of the electric field over the boundary, or the tangential components of the magnetic field over the boundary, or the former over part of the boundary and the later over the rest of the boundary" [12].

The equivalence principle is explained by considering an actual radiating source, which is electrically represented by current densities J_1 and M_1 as shown in Fig. 9.31b. The source radiates fields E_1 and

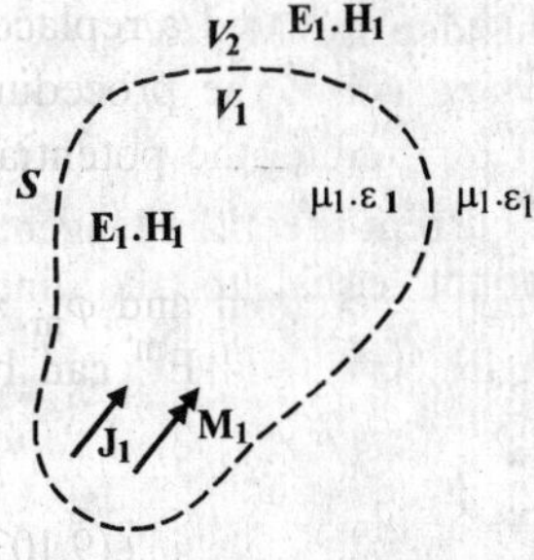

Fig. 9.31b Actual problem

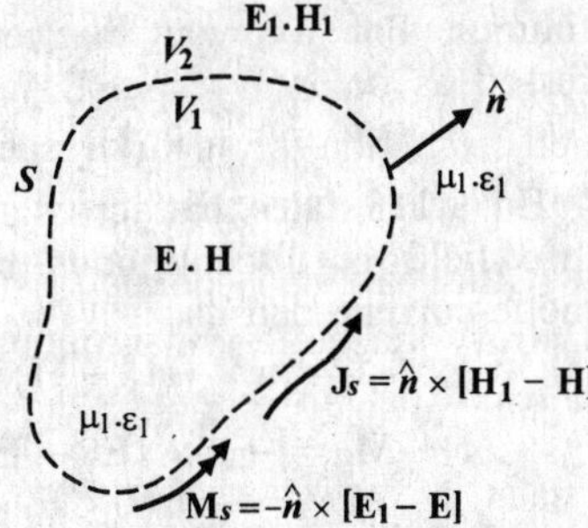

Fig. 9.31c Equivalent problem

H_1 every where. We are interested in devising a method to find fields outside a closed surface S which encloses both the current densities as shown in Fig. 9.31b. The volume inside S is denoted as V_1 and outside as V_2. To accomplish the task of finding fields at V_2 an equivalent problem as shown in Fig. 9.31c is formulated. The original sources J_1 and M_1 are removed and we assume that fields E and H exist inside S and fields E_1 and H_1 outside of S. These fields must satisfy the boundary conditions on the tangential electric and tangential magnetic field components. Thus on the imaginary surface S there must exist the equivalent sources. Eq. 9.107 and 9.108 can be written in terms of vector potentials only.

$$E = \frac{1}{j\omega\mu\varepsilon} \nabla \times \nabla \times A - \frac{1}{\varepsilon} \nabla \times F \qquad \text{....(9.109a)}$$

$$H = \frac{1}{j\omega\mu\varepsilon} \nabla \times \nabla \times F + \frac{1}{\mu} \nabla \times A \qquad \text{....(9.109b)}$$

One other salient aspect of magnetic current must be considered. It was found that tangential H was discontinuous across an electric current sheet (although tangential E remained continuous). The discontinuity in tangential H was equal to the linear current density Js as shown in the relation.

$$H_{1(tan)} - H_{2(tan)} = J_s \quad \text{(amp/m)}$$

The electric current density J_s and tangential H are mutually perpendicular, this can be indicated by the vector relation

$$J_s = \hat{n} \times (H_1 - H_2) \qquad \text{(amp/m)} \qquad \text{....(9.110)}$$

where $\hat{n}$ is the unit vector normal to the current sheet and is regarded positive when pointing to the side that contains H_1. In the same way it is found from Eq. 9.100 that tangential E is discontinuous across a magnetic current sheet, whereas tangential H remains continuous. For a linear magnetic current density M_s (V/m) it is expressed as below

$$M_s = -\hat{n} \times (E_1 - E_2) \qquad \text{....(9.111)}$$

Eq. 9.111 states that across a magnetic current sheet the tangential electric field is discontinuous by an amount equal to the linear magnetic-current density.

$$J_s = \hat{n} \times (H_1 - H)|_{H=0} \qquad \text{....(9.112)}$$

$$M_s = -\hat{n} \times (E_1 - E)|_{E=0} = -\hat{n} \times E_1 \qquad \text{....(9.113)}$$

and they radiate in an unbounded space. The current densities J_s and M_s are equivalent only within V_2 as they produce the original fields (E_1H_1) only outside S. Field (E, H) is a different field than the original field (E_1H_1) which has resulted inside the surface S. Since the fields in Eqs. 9.112 and 9.113 radiate in an unbounded medium V_2, fields from these surface current can be found from equations 9.107 and 9.108. We have used the tangential component of both E and H, because by using the tangential component of either E or H one can determine the radiation field completely. Hence an equivalent problem can be found which require only the magnetic currents (tangential E) or only electric currents (tangential H). This requires modifications to the equivalent problem of Fig. 9.31c.

The region within S is not of interest, hence the field within it can be any thing and it can even be equal to zero. In that case Fig. 9.31 can be modifical to Fig. 9.32 and Eq. 9.112 and 9.113 to

$$J_s = \hat{n} \times H_1 \quad \text{....(9.114)}$$

$$M_s = -\hat{n} \times E_1 \quad \text{....(9.115)}$$

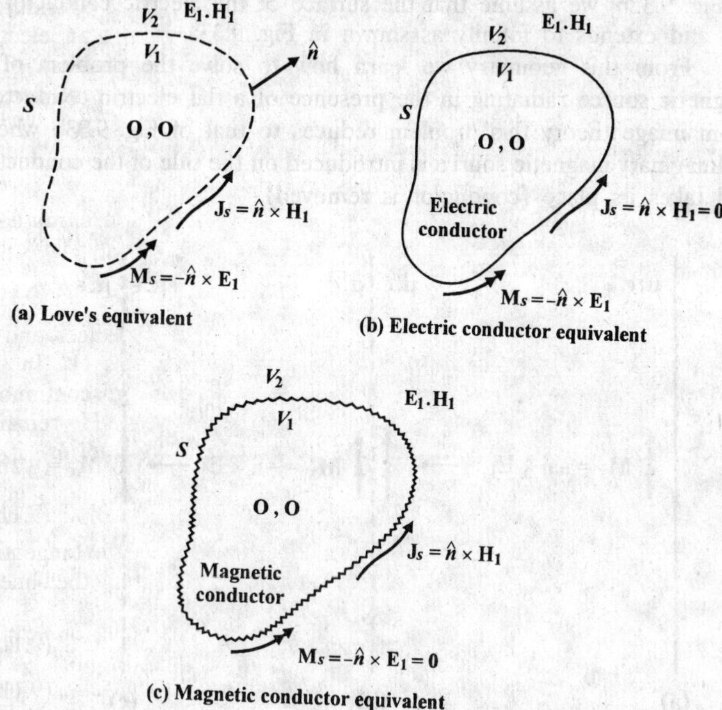

Fig. 9.32 Equivalence principle models.

This modification is known as Love's equivalence principle and is shown in Fig. 9.32a. It produces a null field within the imaginary surface S. Since the values are E = 0 and H = 0 within S, they will not change if the properties of the medium within it are changed. Let us assume that it is replaced by a perfect electric conductor ($\sigma = \infty$). As the electric conducter takes its place as in Fig. 9.32b, the electric current density J_s which is tangent to the surfaces, is short circuited by the electric conductor and the equivalent problem of Fig. 9.32a reduces to that of Fig. 9.32b. That is there exists only a magnetic current density M_s over S and it radiates the original fields E_1H_1 in the presence of electric conductor outside of S. The difficulty in trying to use equivalent problem in Fig. 9.32b is that equations (9.106 – 9.108) can not be used because the current densities do not radiate into an unbounded medium. The problem of a magnetic current radiating in the presence of an electric conducting surface must be solved.

We can also replace the perfect electric conductor inside S by perfect magnetic conductor as shown in Fig. 9.32c which will short the magnetic current. We again face similar problem as for Fig. 9.32b.

To begin to see the utility of the field equivalence principle as in Fig. 9.32b, we assume that the surface of the electric conductor is flat and extends to infinity as shown in Fig. 9.33a.

From this geometry we learn how to solve the problem of a magnetic source radiating in the presence of a flat electric conductor. From image theory this problem reduces to that of Fig. 9.33b where an imaginary magnetic source is introduced on the side of the conductor and takes its place (conductor is removed).

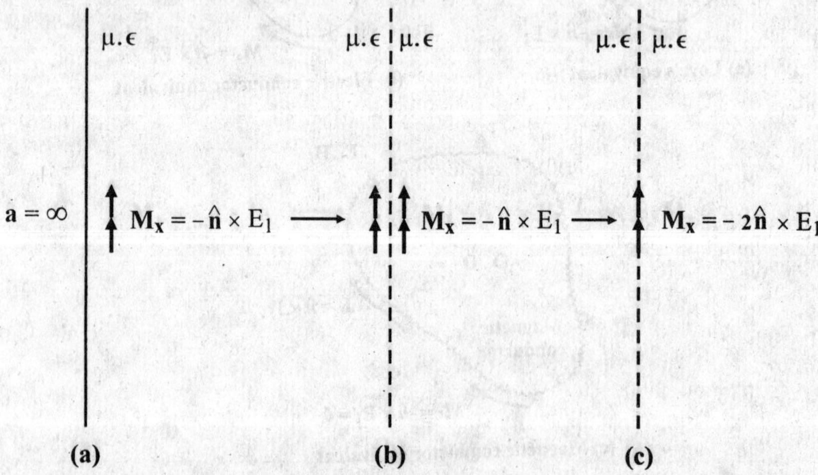

Fig. 9.33

Since the imaginary source is in the same direction as the equivalent source, the equivalent problem of Fig. 9.33b reduces to that of Fig. 9.33c. The magnetic current is doubled and it radiates in an unbounded medium. Equations 9.107 and 9.108 can be used to find the correct field on the right side of the interface.

9.15. Field of a Secondary or Huygens' Source

Huygens' Principle may be used in a qualitative manner to predict radiation pattern for any type of radiator. This principle states that the electromagnetic field at any point in space may be obtained by considering each point on the wave front as a source of spherical waves and superimposing the effect of all these sources at the far field point in question. Consider an element of area of an advancing wave front in free space as shown in Fig. 9.34. This element of area dx dy is on the wave front of a uniform plane (TEM) wave, which is advancing in the z direction. This element of wave front has electric field strength $E_x°$ and magnetic field strength $Hy° = E°_x/\eta_0$ and can be treated as a secondary source which can be replaced by electric and magnetic sheets. The directions and densities of these current sheets will be

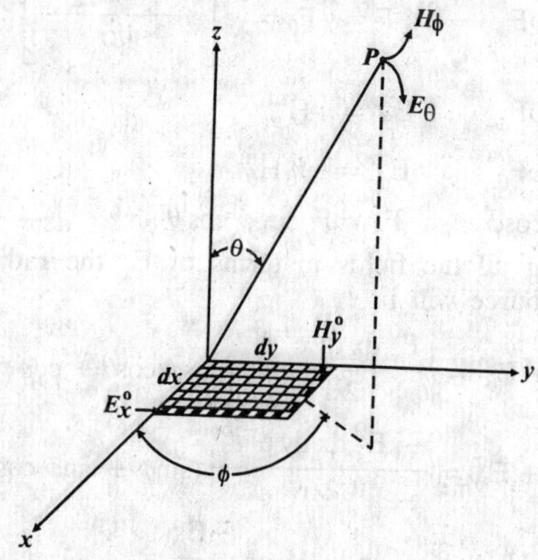

Fig. 9.34 Radiation from a Huygens' source.

$$J_x = -H_y^0 = \frac{E_x^0}{\eta} \text{ and } M_y = -E_x^0 \qquad ....(9.116)$$

The element of area dx dy of electric surface current density J_x constitutes an electric current element $(J_x dy)d_x$, and similarly the element of area of magnetic surface current density M_y constitutes a magnetic current element $(M_y dx)$ dy. We have to determine the radiation fields of these current elements. As we require the radiation fields, only the vector potentials will be considered.

At large distances the electric field of the electric current element will be

$$E^e = -j\omega A \text{ and } A = \hat{x} A_x = \hat{x} \mu \left[\frac{(J_x dy)\, dx\, e^{-j\beta r}}{4\pi r} \right] \quad ...(9.117)$$

The θ and ϕ components of the radiation field of the electric current element will be

$$E_\theta^e = -j\omega A_\theta \qquad H_\phi^e = \frac{E_\theta^e}{\eta} \quad ....(9.118a, b)$$

$$E_\phi^e = -j\omega A_\phi \qquad H_\theta^e = -\frac{E_\phi^e}{\eta} \quad ....(9.119a, b)$$

where

$$A_\theta = A_x \cos\phi \cos\theta \text{ and } A_\phi = -A_x \sin\phi \quad ....(9.119c)$$

Similarly radiation fields for the magnetic current element are

$$H^m = -j\omega F \qquad F = \hat{y} F_y = \hat{y} \varepsilon \left[\frac{(M_y dx) dy_e^{-i\beta r}}{4\pi r} \right] \quad ....(9.120a, b)$$

$$H_\phi^m = -j\omega F_\phi \qquad E_\theta^m = \eta H_\phi^m \quad ....(9.121a, b)$$

$$H_\theta^m = -j\omega F_\theta \qquad E_\phi^m = -\eta H_\theta^m \quad ....(9.122a, b)$$

$$F_\phi = F_y \cos\phi \qquad F_\theta = F_y \sin\phi \cos\theta \quad ....(9.123a, b)$$

Expressing all the fields in terms of E_x^0 the radiation field of the Huygen's source will be

$$E_\theta = E_\theta^e + E_\theta^m = \frac{j E_y^0\, dx\, dy\, e^{-j\beta r}}{2\lambda r} (\cos\phi \cos\theta + \cos\phi) \quad ....(9.124)$$

$$E_\phi = E_\phi^e + E_\phi^m = \frac{-j E_x^0\, dx\, dy\, e^{-j\beta r}}{2\lambda r} (\sin\phi + \sin\phi \cos\theta) \quad ....(9.125)$$

$$H_\phi = \frac{E_\theta}{\eta} \text{ and } H_\theta = \frac{-E_\phi}{\eta} \quad ....(9.126)$$

In the plane ϕ =0, the magnitude of the electric field strength is

$$|E_\theta| = \frac{E_y^0\, dx\, dy}{2\lambda r} [1 + \cos\theta] \qquad |E_\phi| = 0 \quad ....(9.127)$$

In the plane ϕ = 90 degree, the magnitude of the electric field is

$$|E_\theta| = 0, \quad |E_\phi| = \frac{E_x^0\, dx\, dy}{2\lambda r} [1 + \cos\theta] \quad ....(9.128)$$

The radiation is maximum in the forward direction ($\theta = 0$), it is zero in the backward direction ($\theta = 180$ degrees). This in a way explains why an electromagnetic wave once launched, continues to propagate in the forward direction. Actually an electric current sheet alone radiates equally on both sides, similarly a magnetic current sheet radiates on both sides, but crossed electric and magnetic current sheets of proper relative magnitude and phase can be made to radiate on one side only [1, 3].

9.15.1 Application of Huygens' principle

Radiation through an aperture

Consider a rectangular aperture ab in a perfectly absorbing screen of infinite extent which occupies the z = 0 plane, see Fig. 9.35. A uniform plane electromagnetic wave travelling in the z direction is incident from z

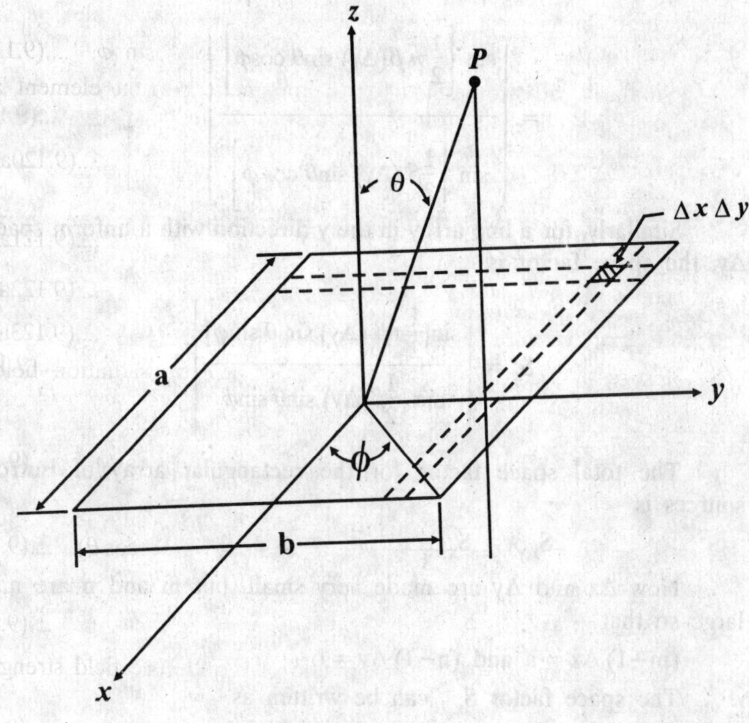

Fig. 9.35 An element of area on an advancing wave front.

(bottom) direction. We will find the radiation through the aperture in the positive z direction. We assume that the incident wave is completely absorbed at the bottom surface of the screen so that there is no reflection at the aperture. Hence the field strength at the aperture will be just of the incident wave. Aperture part is divided into a large number of Huygens' sources of area da = Δx Δy and the aperture may be treated as a rectangular array of such sources all fed in phase. For a uniform array of isotropic radiators arranged in x direction and having a uniform spacing dx. The radiation pattern or space factor is

$$S_x = \left|1 + e^{j\psi} + e^{2j\psi} + \ldots\ldots\ldots\ldots + e^{j(m-1)\psi}\right| \quad \ldots(9.129)$$

$$= \left|\sum_{0}^{m-1} e^{j\beta(\Delta x)\sin\theta\cos\phi}\right|$$

$$= \left|\frac{\sin\left[\frac{1}{2}m\,\beta(\Delta x)\sin\theta\cos\phi\right]}{\sin\left[\frac{1}{2}\beta(\Delta x)\sin\theta\cos\phi\right]}\right| \quad \ldots(9.130)$$

Similarly, for a line array in the y direction with a unform spacing Δy, the space factor is

$$S_y = \left|\frac{\sin[\frac{1}{2}n\beta(\Delta y)\sin\theta\sin\phi]}{\sin[\frac{1}{2}\beta(\Delta y)\sin\theta\sin\phi}\right| \quad \ldots(9.131)$$

The total space factor for the rectangular array of isotropic sources is

$$S_{x,y} = S_x S_y$$

Now Δx and Δy are made very small, but m and n are made large so that

$(m-1)\,\Delta x = a$ and $(n-1)\,\Delta y = b$

The space factor $S_{x,y}$ can be written as

$$S_{xy} = \frac{ab}{\Delta x\Delta y}\left|\frac{\sin(\frac{1}{2}\beta\,a\sin\theta\cos\phi)}{(\frac{1}{2}\beta\,a\sin\theta\cos\phi)}\cdot\frac{\sin(\frac{1}{2}\beta\,b\sin\theta\sin\phi)}{(\frac{1}{2}\beta\,b\sin\theta\sin\phi)}\right| \quad \ldots(9.132)$$

Multiplying this space factor by the radiation from the unit Huygens' source gives the total radiation from the aperture as in Eq. (9.124) and (9.125)

$$E_\theta = \frac{jE^\circ_x abe^{-j\beta r}}{2\lambda r}[(1+\cos\theta)\cos\phi]\left|\frac{\sin u_1}{u_1} - \frac{\sin v_1}{v_1}\right| \quad ....(9.133)$$

$$E_\phi = \frac{-jE^\circ_x abe^{-j\beta r}}{2\lambda r}[(1+\cos\theta)\cos\phi]\left|\frac{\sin u_1}{u_1} \cdot \frac{\sin v_1}{v_1}\right| \quad ....(9.134)$$

where $u_1 = \frac{1}{2}\beta\, a \sin\theta \cos\phi$ and $v_1 = \frac{1}{2}\beta\, b \sin\theta \sin\phi$

This is also known as diffracted field.

In the (x-z) plane, $\phi p = 0$, or π $E_\phi = 0$ and the E_θ field is given by

$$E_\theta = \frac{jE^\circ_x abe^{-j\beta r}}{2\lambda r}(1+\cos\theta)\left|\frac{\sin u}{u}\right| \quad ....(9.135)$$

where $$u = \left[\frac{1}{2}\beta\, a \sin\theta\right] = \frac{\pi a}{\lambda}\sin\theta$$

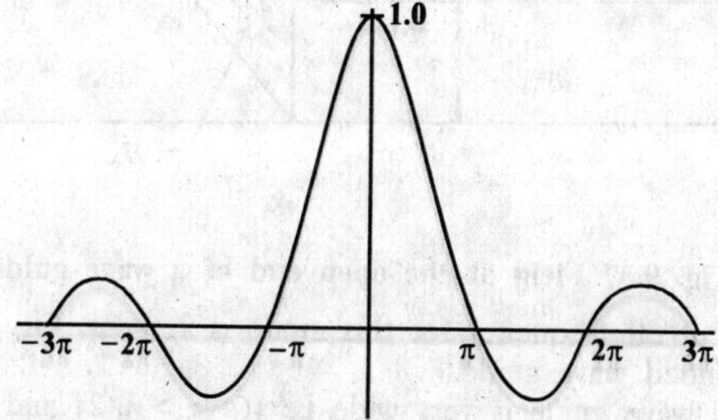

Fig. 9.36 Plot of (sin u)/u.

The expression $\frac{\sin u}{u}$ occurs in many radiation problems and is plotted in Fig. 9.36 as a function of u.

The first null of this pattern occurs when $u = \pi$. Thus for an aperture of width equal to one λ the first null occurs when θ = 90 degrees. For aperture widths smaller than one λ there is no null in the pattern which that is a very broad beam. For very large apertures the beam is quite narrow. When θ is very small $\sin\theta \approx \theta$ and

$$u \approx \frac{\pi a \theta}{\lambda}$$

For $a = 10\lambda$ the first null occurs at $\theta_0 = 0.1$ radian or 5.7 degrees.

9.15.2. Application to open ended wave guides

In this case we assume that the fields at the open end are approximately the same as they would be if the guide was not terminated but continued on to infinity. The waveguide is supporting dominant mode TE_{10}. The fields at the open end are given by

$$E_y^0 = E^0 \sin\frac{\pi x}{a}, \quad H_x^0 = \frac{1}{\eta}\sqrt{1 - \left(\frac{\lambda}{\lambda_c}\right)^2}\, E_y^0 \qquad \text{....(9.136)}$$

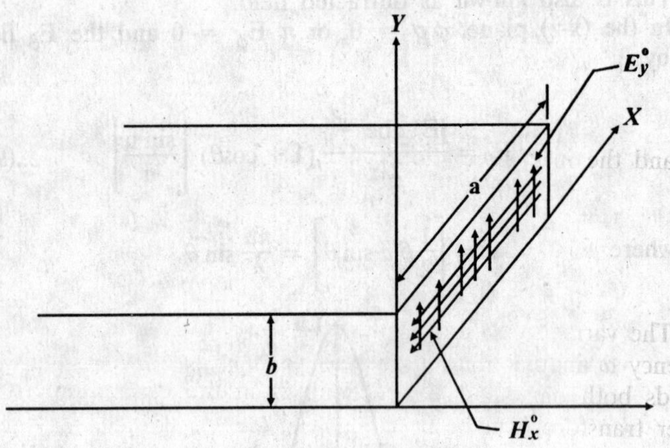

Fig. 9.37 Field at the open end of a wave guide.

The cut off frequency for this mode is $\lambda_c = 2a$. Fig. 9.37 shows the open ended wave guide.

If the wave guide is very wide i.e $((a >> \lambda/2)$ and is carrying the dominant mode, in this case ratio of electric field to magnetic field $E_y^0/H_x^0 \approx \eta$ and the problem reduces to that of a rectangular aperture, except for the variation of E and H fields in the x direction across the mouth of the guide. If the guide is operating near the cutoff i.e. at $\lambda \to 2a$ than H_x becomes very small and η becomes very large, hence there will be large mismatch between the impedance of the guide and the free space (at the open end of the guide). As such most of the energy is reflected back from the open end and very less energy is radiated. Also the radiation pattern approaches closely to that which would have resulted from a magnetic current sheet alone rather than from crossed electric and magnetic current sheets.

To find the radiation pattern of a waveguide or horn theoretically, a rigorous mathematical treatment is required. There are two basic methods described in the literature.

(1) In the first approach vector and scalar potential from the electric and magnetic currents are accurately formulated and far field radiation field obtained using proper coordinate transformations as is described in [12].

This approach gives good results for both geometrical and irregular shape radiators.

(2) In the second approach the electric and magnetic field are formed at the apertures, and then for calculating the far field radiation pattern Fourier transform of the aperture field is calculated. If the field is a function of x, its Fourier transform is

$$V(K_x) = \int_{-\infty}^{\infty} v(x)\, e^{jk_x x} dx \qquad \text{....(9.137)}$$

and the inverse relation is

$$\nu(x) = \frac{1}{2\lambda} \int_{-\infty}^{\infty} V(K_x)\, e^{-jk_x x}\, dK_x \qquad \text{....(9.138)}$$

The variables K_x and x play the same role as time t and radian frequency ω in the Fourier analysis of time signals. If the functions depends both on x and y direction (as in the case of aperture) its Fourier transform will be

$$U(k_x, k_y) = \int_{-\infty}^{\infty} \int_{-\infty}^{\infty} u(x,y)\, e^{jk_x x + jk_y y}\, d_x d_y \qquad \text{....(9.139)}$$

and the inverse relation is

$$u(x, y) = \frac{1}{4\pi^2} \int \int_{-\infty}^{\infty} U(k_x, k_y)\, e^{-jk_x x - jk_y y}\, dk_x dk_y \qquad \text{....(9.140)}$$

For the given problem if the electric field is known the wave equation in E is written and then take its Fourier transform with respect to x, y and z is the direction of propagation, the electromagnetic field radiated in z direction will have the solution of the form $e^{-jK_z z}$. Finally one arrives at the far field E (r) from which H can be found as

$$H = \frac{1}{Z_0}(a_r \times E) \qquad \text{....(9.141)}$$

Detailed calculations are derived by R.E. Collins (Antenna and radiowave propagation Ch 4). Fourier transform technique can be applied to geometrical shape radiators [10].

9.16. Radiation from Electromagnetic Horns

When greater directivity is desired a waveguide can be flared out to form an electromagnetic horn. The common rectangular horn shapes are possible as shown in Fig. 9.38a.

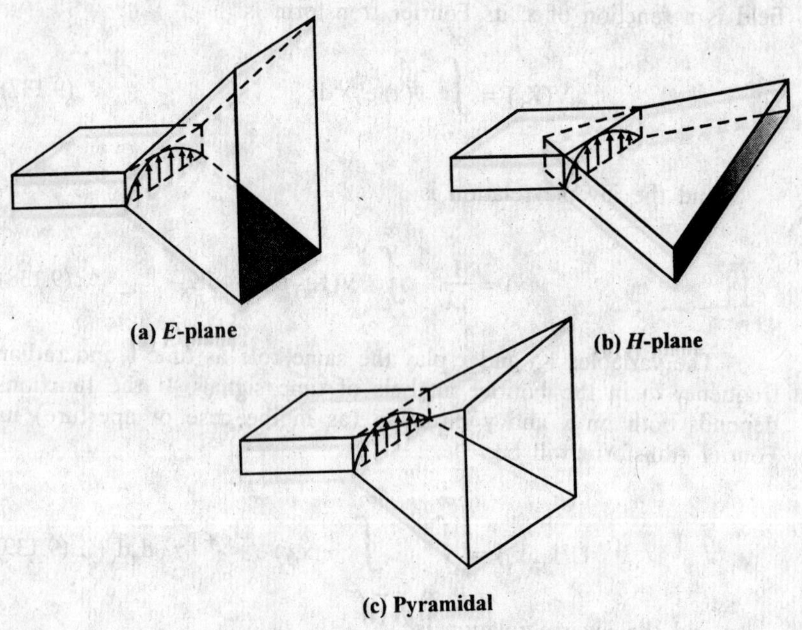

Fig. 9.38a Typical electromagnetic horn antenna configurations.

9.16.1. E-plane sectoral horn

In the E-plane sectoral horn as shown in Fig. 9.38b we can see that the broad walls of the wave guide are flared in the direction parallel to the electric field vector and the flare angle is $2\psi_e$. The narrow dimension of the guide is increased from b to b_1 at the open mouth of the horn, whereas the broad dimension remains at the same value. The flared walls have a virtual apex. The virtual length l_1 are longer than the virtual perpendicular distance ρ_e by δ. This difference causes the spherical waves emanating from the virtual apex to have a phase difference at the edges of the horn compared with the wave front at the center of the horn. The phase difference ϕ is given as

$$\phi = \frac{2\pi\delta}{\lambda} \quad \text{....(9.142)}$$

When the phase difference is π the waves from the edges are out of phase from those from the center, hence they distructively interfere. As a result there is a decrease in gain and an increase in the side lobe level.

Lets find a relationship between the phase deviation δ and the loss in gain due to this. δ is expressed in terms of λ.

Consider triangle from Fig. 9.38b, we can see that

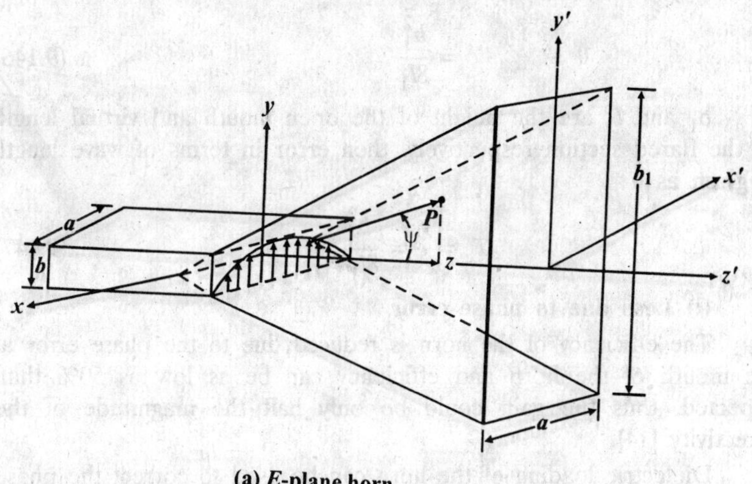

(a) *E*-plane horn

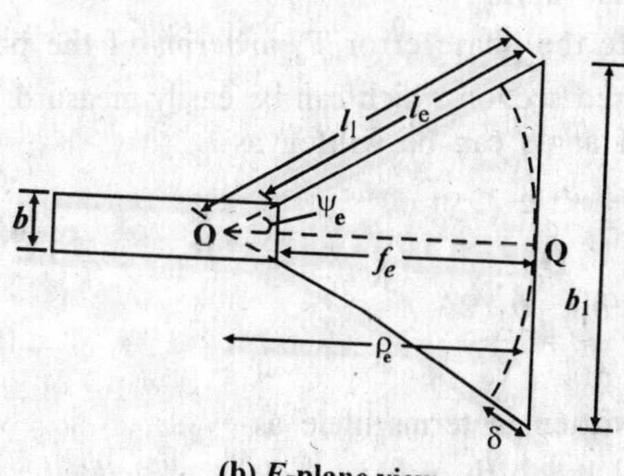

(b) *E*-plane view

Fig. 9.38b E-plane horn and coordinate system.

$$\rho_e^2 = l_1^2 - \left(\frac{b_1}{2}\right)^2 \qquad \text{....(9.143)}$$

Since $$\rho_e = l_1 - \delta \qquad \text{....(9.144)}$$

$$(l_1 - \delta)^2 = l_1^2 - \left(\frac{b_1}{2}\right)^2$$

or $$2l_1\,\delta - \delta^2 = \frac{b_1^2}{4} \qquad \text{....(9.145)}$$

As δ is small compared to l_1, δ^2 is neglected in comparison to $2l_1$. Now δ is written as

$$\delta = \frac{b_1^2}{8l_1} \qquad \text{....(9.146)}$$

b_1 and l_1 are the height of the open mouth and virtual length of the flared section respectively, then error in terms of wave length is given as

$$T_e = \frac{\delta}{\lambda} = \frac{b_1^2}{8l_1\lambda} \qquad \text{....(9.147)}$$

(i) Loss due to phase error

The efficiency of the horn is reduced due to the phase error at the mouth of the horn and efficiency can be as low as 50% than expected, thus the gain could be only half the magnitude of the directivity [14].

Dielectric loading of the horn can be used to correct the phase error. Efficiencies as high as 90% are achievable with zero phase taper at the mouth of the horn.

It is useful to write the phase error T_e in terms of the physical slant length l_e of the flared section which can be easily measurd. From Fig. 9.38b the flare half angle can be written as

$$\sin\psi_e = \frac{b_{1/2}}{l_1} \qquad \text{....(9.148)}$$

Also $$\frac{b_1}{l_1} = \frac{b_1/2}{l_e} \qquad \text{....(9.149)}$$

Thus Te can be written in terms of le as

$$T_e = \frac{b_1(b_1 - b)}{8\lambda l_e} \qquad \text{....(9.150)}$$

The maximum gain of a horn is directly proportional to the size of the aperture. The aperture size can be increased by having a large flare angle ($2\psi_e$) and/or having a long flare length. To limit the phase variation to quarter wave length (for the E-plane sectorial horn) at the highest frequency of operation, it is preferred to have long horn with small flare angle.

The flare semi angle in terms of length l_1 can be written as from the Fig. 9.38b

$$\cos \psi_e = \frac{\rho_e}{l_1} = \frac{\rho_e}{\rho_e + \delta} \quad ....(9.151)$$

or

$$\rho_e = \frac{\delta \cos \psi_e}{(1 - \cos\psi_e)} \quad ....(9.152)$$

Since the virtual length ρ_e is not easy to measure, it is more convenient to express ψ_e in terms of physical length l_e and the heights b and b_1. Referring to the same figure once more we can write

$$\tan \psi_e = \frac{b_1}{2\rho_e} = \frac{b_1 - b}{2f_e} \quad ....(9.153)$$

$$\rho_e = \left(\frac{b_1}{b_1 - b}\right) f_e$$

$$f_e^2 = l_e^2 - \left(\frac{b_1 - b}{2}\right)^2 \quad ....(9.154)$$

Also

$$\frac{\rho_e}{f_e} = \frac{b_1}{b_1 - b} \quad ....(9.155)$$

Hence

$$\rho_e = \left(\frac{b_1}{b_1 - b}\right) \sqrt{l_e^2 - \left(\frac{(b_1 - b)}{2}\right)^2} \quad ....(9.156)$$

The linear gain G_e of an E plane horn is given by the formula from Balanis (P. 546)

$$G_e = \frac{64\, a\, \rho_e}{\pi \lambda b_1} \left[C^2 \left(\frac{b_1}{\sqrt{2\lambda\rho_e}}\right) + S^2 \left(\frac{b_1}{\sqrt{2\lambda\rho_e}}\right) \right] \quad ....(9.157)$$

where a is the width of the wave guide feeding the horn, ρ_e is the virtual length of the horn, b_1 is the height of the open mouth of the horn, C and S are the Fresnel cosine and sine integrals defined as below–

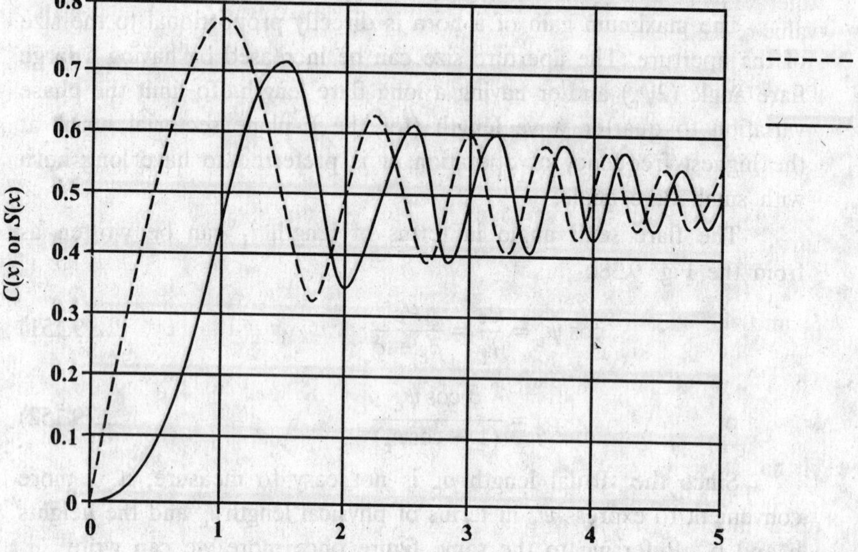

Fig. 9.39 Fresnel cosine and sine integrals.

$$C(x) = \int_0^x \cos\left(\frac{\pi}{2}x^2\right) dx \qquad \text{....(9.158)}$$

$$S(x) = \int_0^x \sin\left(\frac{\pi}{2}x^2\right) dx \qquad \text{....(9.159)}$$

The values of the Fresnel cosine and sine integrals are shown in Fig. 9.39.

9.16.2. H-Plane sectorial horn

In the H-plane horn, as shown in figure 9.40, the narrow walls of the wave guide are flared in the plane parallel to the magnetic field vector and the flare angle is $2\,\psi_h$. The broad dimension of the guide is increased from a to a_1 at the open mouth of the horn, whereas the narrow dimension remains same at the same value b. The flared walls have a virtual apex and the virtual length l_2 to the open end are longer than the length ρ_h (the virtual perpendicular distance) by δ. This difference causes the spherical waves emanating from the virtual apex to have a phase difference at the edges of the horn. This phase difference results in a reduction in gain as in the case of the E-plane horn described earlier. In this case a maximum phase difference of 135 degrees can be tolerated [E-plane case the tolerable phase difference was 90°] This phase difference **corresponds** to a value of d equal to $3\lambda/8$.

The phase deviation or error in terms of wavelengths T_h can be derived in the same way as for E-plane horn

$$T_h = \frac{\delta}{\lambda} = \frac{a_1^2}{8 l_2 \lambda} \quad \text{....(9.160a)}$$

$$l_h = \frac{\delta \cos \psi_h}{[1 - \cos \psi_h]} \quad \text{....(9.160b)}$$

The virtual flare length ρ_h is related to the physical flare length l_h and the widths a and a_1 of the waveguide horn by the expression

$$\rho_h = \left(\frac{a_1}{a_1 - a}\right) \sqrt{l_h^2 - \left(\frac{a_1 - a}{2}\right)^2} \quad \text{....(9.160c)}$$

where a_1 is the width of the aperture of the horn and l_h is the virtual slant length of the flared section.

The efficiency of the horn is reduced by the phase error at the open mouth, and the effective aperture is only about 50% of the physical aperture.

The numeric gain of the H-plane sectorial horn shown in Fig. 9.40 is given by.

$$G_h = \frac{4\pi\, b\, \rho_h}{a_1 \lambda} \{[C(u) - C(v)^2] + [S(u) - S(v)]^2\} \quad \text{....(9.161)}$$

where b is the height of the waveguide feeding the horn, ρ_h is the virtual length of the horn, a_1 is the width of the horn aperture. C(u) and C(v) are the Fresnel cosine integral of u and v respectively. S(u) and S(v) are the Fresnel sine integral of u and v.

Fresnel cosine and sine integral are defined in Eq. 9.158-159 and u and v are given by

$$u = \frac{1}{\sqrt{2}}\left(\frac{\sqrt{\lambda \rho_h}}{a_1} + \frac{a_1}{\sqrt{\lambda \rho_h}}\right) \quad \text{....(9.162)}$$

$$v = \frac{1}{\sqrt{2}}\left(\frac{\sqrt{\lambda \rho_h}}{a_1} - \frac{a_1}{\sqrt{\lambda \rho_h}}\right) \quad \text{....(9.163)}$$

The Fresnel cosine and sine integrals can be obtained from Fig. 9.39, which shows the gains divided by the width a in terms of the wavelength. Closer examination of these curves show that the value of the phase deviation at these maxima is $3\lambda/8$.

9.16.3. Pyramidal horn

This is the most widely used horn and has been flared in both the directions. Its radiation characteristics are a combination of the E and H plane sectorial horns. Pyramidal horn is shown Fig. 4.41

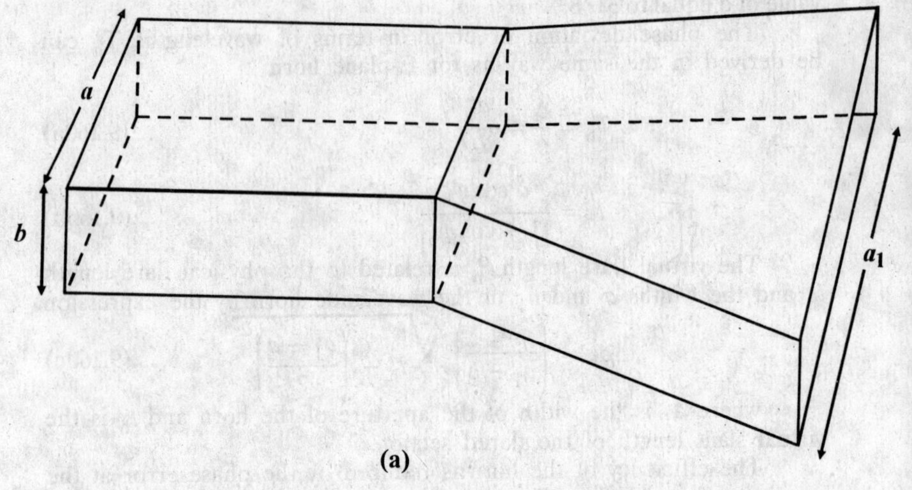

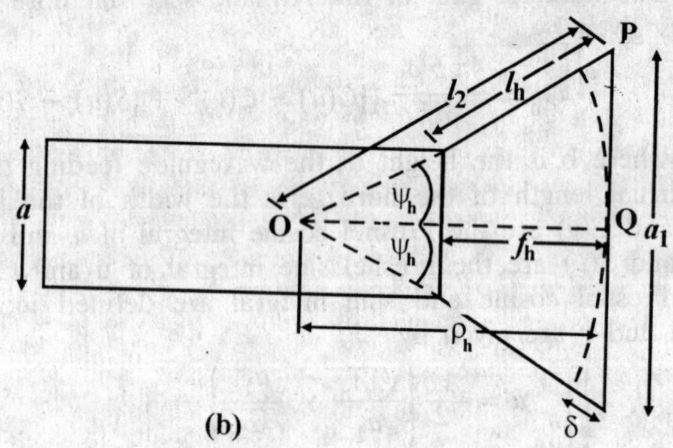

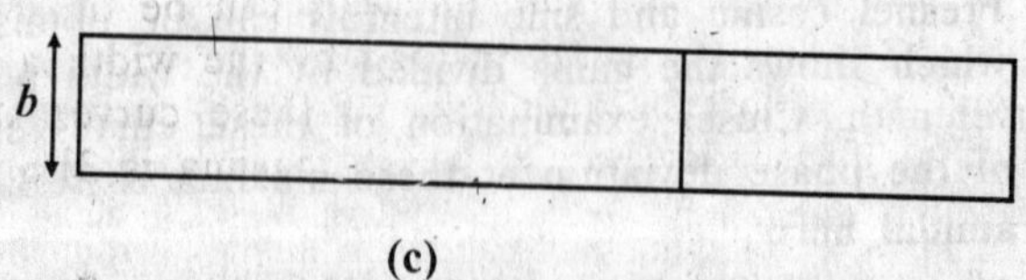

Fig. 9.40 H-plane sectoral horn (a) perspective view, (b) plan view, and (c) side view.

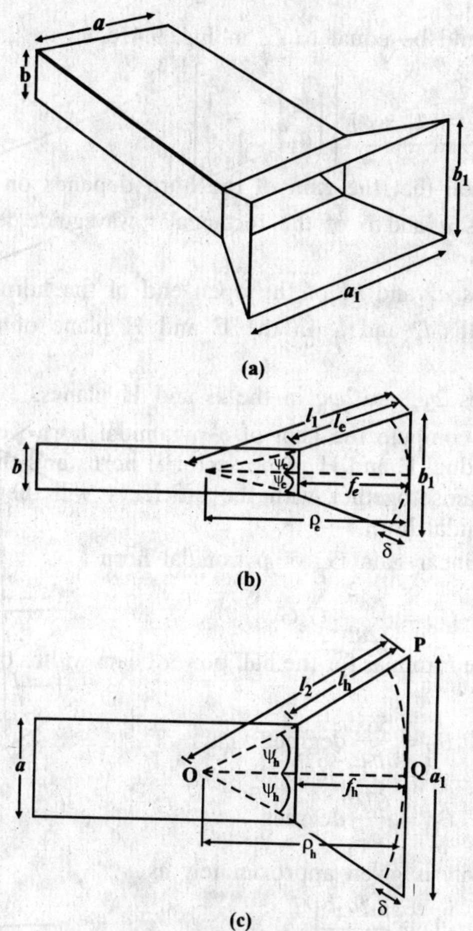

Fig. 9.41 Pyramidal horn (a) perspective view,
(b) side elevation – E plane,
(c) plan view – H plane.

To physically construct a pyramidal horn the dimension f_e in Fig. 9.41 is given as

$$f_e = (b_1 - b)\left[\left(\frac{l_1}{b_1}\right)^2 - \frac{1}{4}\right]^{1/2} \qquad \text{....(9.164)}$$

and this should be equal to f_h in Fig. 9.41c

$$f_h = (a_1 - a)\left[\left(\frac{l_2}{a_1}\right)^2 - \frac{1}{4}\right]^{1/2} \qquad \text{....(9.165)}$$

Finally, we conclude that the gain of the horn depends on

1. The dimensions a and b of the rectangular waveguide feeding the horn.
2. The dimensions a_1 and b_1 of the open end of the horn.
3. The slant lengths l_e and l_h in the E and H plane of the flared section.
4. The flare angles $2\psi_e$ and $2\psi_h$ in the E and H planes.

In order to compute the gain of a pyramidal horn we calculate the gains of individual E and H plane sectorial horns and the product of the numeric gains together with the efficiency will then give the gain of the pyramidal horn.

Hence the linear gain G_p of pyramidal horn

$$G_p = \frac{\pi\lambda^2}{32ab} G_e G_h \qquad \text{....(9.166)}$$

Approximate formulas for the half power beam widths of optimum flare horns are

$$\theta_E = \frac{56\lambda}{b_1} \text{ degrees} \qquad \text{....(9.167)}$$

$$\theta_H = \frac{67\lambda}{a_1} \text{ degrees} \qquad \text{....(9.168)}$$

The directivily is given approximately as

$$D = \frac{7.5a_1b_1}{\lambda^2} \qquad \text{....(9.169)}$$

9.17. Slot Antennas

If a narrow slot is cut in a large flat sheet of metal and properly connected to a source of rf power, it will radiate in a manner as a dipole will radiate having dimensions as that of the slot. If the conducting sheet is a plane of infinite extent, the shape of the radiation pattern will exactly correspond to that of a dipole except that now the electric and magnetic vector are interchanged. The same relationship exist between the radiation pattern of an electric dipole and small loop. The impedance properties of slot are different from that of a dipole. These complementary properties of a slot in an infinite plane conductor and a thin flat dipole of exactly the same dimensions as the slot, are predicted by an important result of electromagnetic theory known as Babinet's principle. It also relates the impedance properties of the two kinds of radiators. Figure 9.42a,b shows a slot antenna in

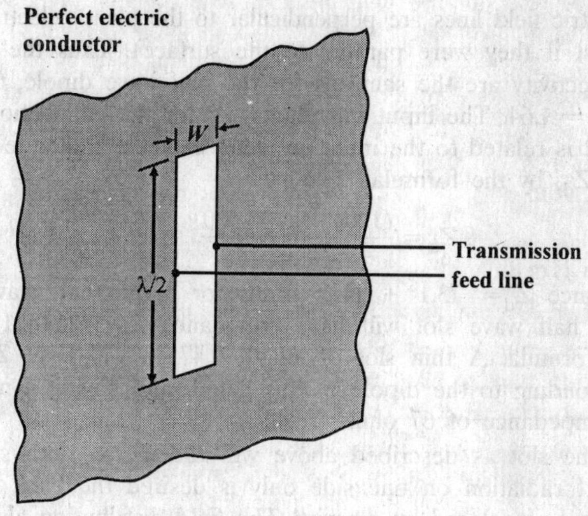

(a) λ/2 thin slot (w → o)

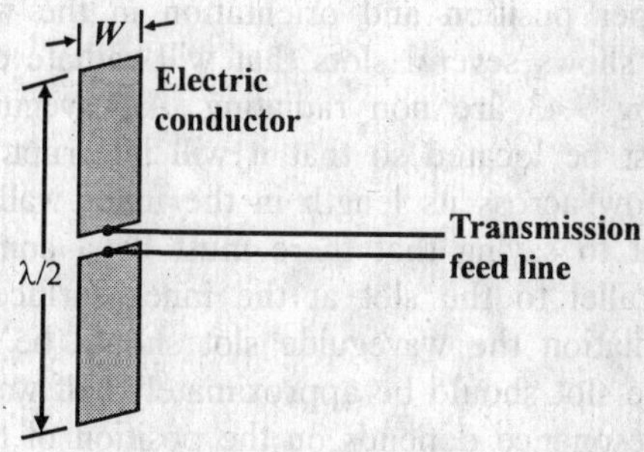

(b) λ/2 flat thin dipole (w → o)

Fig. 9.42. Half-wavelength thin slot on an electric screen and its complement.

a conducting plane and a two wire transmission line connected to it, and the complementary flat dipole antenna formed by the metal removed in making the slot. Since the E and H vectors are interchanged, the polarization is opposite to that of the corresponding dipole. It is surprising that the "doughnut" pattern exists unaffected by the presence of the conducting plane on both sides of it except for the infinitesimaly thin slice eliminated by the metal sheet. The required electric field intensity exists in the space at the surfacé of the conducting plane because the electric field lines are perpendicular to the plane (electric field will not exist if they were parallel to the surface). Thus the beamwidth and directivity are the same as for the half wave dipole, $\theta_{3dB} = 78°$ and D = 1.64. The input impedance Z_s for the connection shown in Fig 9.42 is related to the input impedance of the center fed half wave dipole Z_d, by the formula.

$$Z_s = \frac{(120\pi)^2}{4Z_d} = \frac{35{,}530}{Z_d} \qquad \text{....(9.170)}$$

Since $Z_d = 73.1 + j42.5$ ohms for a thin half wave dipole a narrow half wave slot will have impedance $Z_s = 363\text{-}j211$ from the above formula. A thin slot of length 0.475 λ will have $Z_s = 530\Omega$ corresponding to the dipole of this length and having a non reactive input impedance of 67 ohms.

The slot as described above will radiate on both sides of the sheet. If radiation on one side only is desired the back side of the slot may be enclosed by a cavity. The field distribution along the slot will then change by the dimensions of the cavity.

A unidirectional radiating slot may also be obtained by cutting it in a proper position and orientation in the wall of a waveguide. Figure 9.43 shows several slots that will radiate and two of the slots shown in Fig 9.43 are non radiating. A waveguide slot if it has to radiate, must be located so that it will interrupt currents that would otherwise flow across its length in the inner walls of the guide. This is equivalent to saying that there must be a component of magnetic field **H** parallel to the slot at the inner surface of waveguide. For efficient radiation the waveguide slot should be resonant, hence the length of the slot should be approximately half wave length. The exact length for resonance depends on the position of the slot in the guide. A waveguide slot does not radiate the total power flowing in the guide, it couples only some fraction of the waveguide power, rest continues to flow down the guide to the termination. If it encounters a short circuit it is reflected. By using proper impedance matching devices it is possible to couple all the power to the slot. General waveguide slots are not used singly, but an array of them are cut

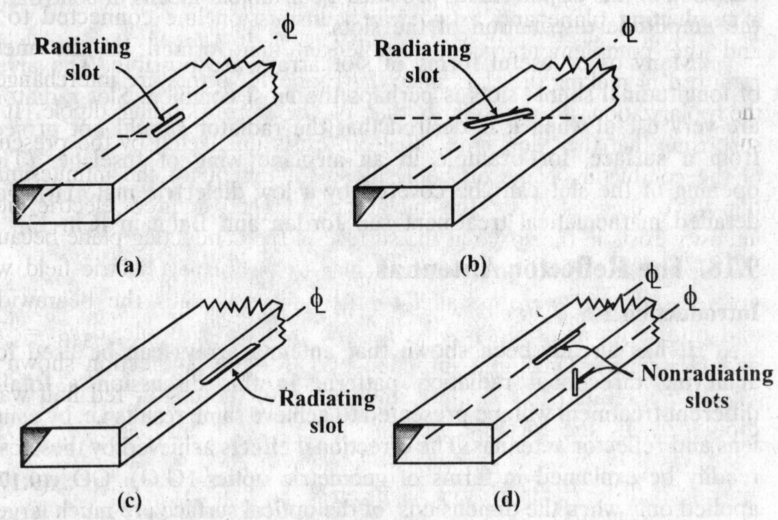

Fig. 9.43 Radiating and nonradiating waveguide slots in rectangular guide, TE_{10} mode.

along the length of the line as shown in Fig 9.44. These waveguide slot arrays are mostly used at mm wavelength where $\lambda_{g/2}$ will be in mms, the guide is operating in TE_{10} mode and the slots are spaced half guide length apart along the length of the guide. Also they alternate on opposit sides of the center line. Placing slots in this way results in in-phase broad side radiation.

The lateral displacement of the slot from the guide center line determines the coupling of the power from the waveguide. Therefore

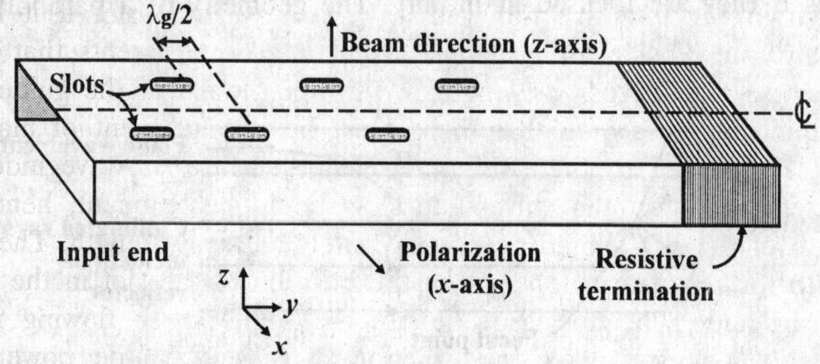

Fig. 9.44. Broadside array of longitudial shunt slots in a waveguide.

variation of this displacement provides a convenient means of controlling the amplitude distribution of the slots.

Many other useful forms of slot arrays are possible. The array of longitudinal shunt slots is perhaps the most common. Slot radiators are very useful when it is desired that the radiator should not project from a surface, for example in an airplane wing of fuselage. (The opening of the slot can be covered by a low dielectric material). For detailed mathematical treatment see Jordan and Balmain [Ch. 13].

9.18. The Reflector Antennas

Introduction

It has already been shown that antenna arrays can be used for achieving directional radiation pattern. In this discussion a totally different treatment will be presented to achieve same results i.e. by using lens and reflector antennas. The directional effects achieved by these can readily be explained in terms of geometric optics (G.O). GO can be applied only when the dimensions of the optical surface are much larger than the wavelength used. That means a reflector 3 meters in diameter would not behave in accordance with geometric optics analysis at 1 MHz where the wavelength is 300m. However it would behave well at 10 GHz as the wavelength is only 3 cm. Generally antennas based on geometric optics behave well above 1 GHz frequencies. We will describe a parabolic reflector specifically in this category of antenna.

9.18.1. Parabolic reflector

If a point source of radiation is placed at the focus of a suitably curved surface like a parabolic surface as shown in Fig 9.45a, the rays from it will be reflected in such a way that they emerge as a parallel beam. The rays that are parallel are said to be collimated or as if they are focused at infinity. The geometry of a parabola can

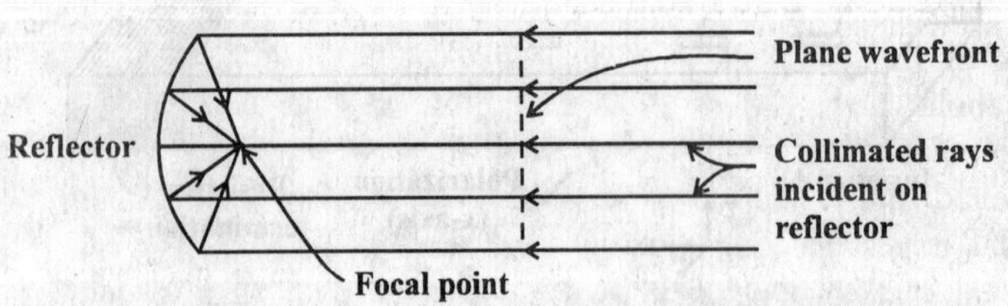

Fig. 9.45. (a) Focusing by a curved reflector.

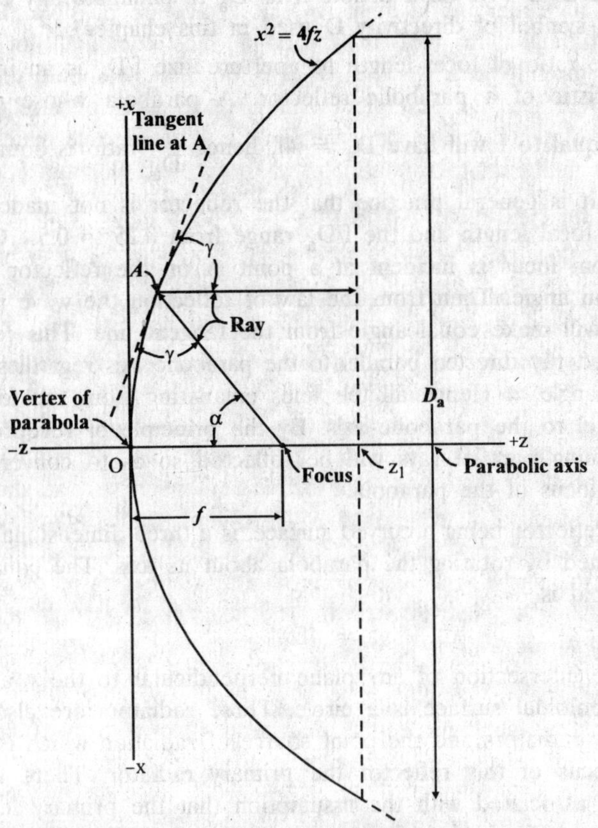

Fig. 9.45b Geometry of parabolic reflection.

be expressed from the Fig 9.45b. The horizontal axis x lies along the axis of the parabola. The point at which this axis intersects the parabolic curve is called the vertex. The second axis z passes through this point. At a distance f from this point on the z axis is a point labelled focus. The equation of parabola in terms of these coordinates and f is written as

$$x^2 = 4f\ z \qquad ....(9.171)$$

The curve defined by equation 9.171 extends to infinity in the +z direction, and consequently also in the +x and -x direction. The open mouth of the parabola is known as the aperture. Practical parabolic reflectors are of finite depth, they terminate or are "cut off" at certain distance z_1 from the vertex. The aperture dimension is labeled as D (We shall denote it as D_a to eliminate any confusion from the symbol of directivity D used in this chapter).

The ratio of focal length to aperture size f/D_a is an important characteristic of a parabolic reflector. A parabola whose depth is exactly equal to f will have $D_a = 4f$, hence $\frac{f}{D_a}$ ratio is equal to 1/4 or 0.25. It is general practice that the reflector is not made deeper than the focal length and the f/D_a range from 0.25 to 0.5. Consider a ray from focus is incident at a point A on the reflector surface, making an angle. Then from the law of reflection the wave reflected from A will make equal angle from the tangent line. This results in a reflected ray directed parallel to the parabolic axis regardless of the value of angle α. Hence all the lines emanating from the focus will be parallel to the parabolic axis. By the principle of receprocity all the incoming parallel rays will be reflected so as to converge to a point at focus of the parabola.

A reflector being a curved surface, is a three dimensional object. It is formed by rotating the parabola about its axis. The equation of a parboloid is

$$x^2 + y^2 = 4fz \qquad \text{....(9.172)}$$

The intersection of any plane perpendicular to the *y* axis with the paraboloidal surface is a circle. These radiators are also called secondary radiators and the point source of radiation which is placed at the focus of this reflector the primary radiator. There are two problems associated with the assumption that the primary feed is a point source Firstly their is no such point source in reality which is capable of illuminating the paraboloid dish. Secondly even if such a source was possible, rays escaping the reflector surface called the spill over, causes the radiation pattern to diverge. This spillover is also responsible for noise pick up when the paraboloid is used as receiving antenna. Finally the isotropic source is a disadvantage since its primary radiation along the axis of the paraboloid (called back lobe radiation) interferes destructively with the main pattern [11].

The feed radiator considered by itself, has a radiation pattern and beam width that are different from the pattern and beam width of the antenna as a whole.

The beam width of the secondary radiation pattern of the paraboloid antenna is given as

$$BW = K_1 \frac{\lambda}{D_a} \quad ....(9.173)$$

where K_1 is a constant. If the beam width is in degree and both λ and D_a expressed in same unit of length, then K_1 is of the order of 60 to 70. For example if D_a is 15 wavelength, the beamwidth will be about 4 to 4.5 degrees.

Directivity

The directivity of a reflector antenna is expressed in terms of the aperture area A.

$$D = K_2 \left(\frac{4\pi A}{\lambda^2}\right), A = \frac{\pi D_a^2}{4} \quad ....(9.174)$$

where K_2 is a constant and has a value between about 0.5 and 0.7, depending upon the shape of the aperture and the characteristics of the source of the radiation used.

9.18.2. Feed for radiators

The source of illumination to the secondary reflector should be of such nature that it illuminates the entire surface with little or no energy radiated in other directions. An isotropic radiator is a poor primary feed from this consideration. The most common choice of a feed for paraboloid reflector is a waveguide horn. Sometimes a small dipole array may also be used as a feed. Fig. 9.46b shows the reflector antenna fed by these two types of feed system [10].

Primary pattern requirements

The feed should be so designed that it fully covers the surface of the reflector and spill over from the edge is not more than necessary.

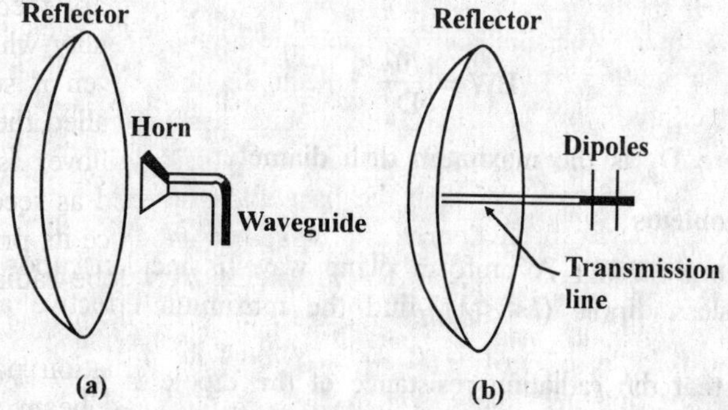

Fig. 9.46 Paraboloidal reflector fed by (a) horn radiator and (b) double-dipole endfire array.

If the feed radiators are narrowed appreciably in order to avoid spill over, the power density at the edges of the reflector will be reduced greatly compared to that at the center. This variation of the intensity of the radiation over the aperture is called the illumination taper. The edge taper is the ratio of the power density at the edge of the aperture to that at the center or a decibel equivalent of this ratio. An excessive taper causes loss of gain and widening of the beam due to inefficient use of the available reflector area. It results into a larger than necessary value of K_1 in Eq. 9.173 and a smaller value of K_2 in Eq. 9.174. Too little taper causes loss of gain due to excessive spillover and causes larger then necessary side lobes and back lobes. A compromise is required for optimized illumination, so that maximum gain and low side lobe and back lobe levels are possible [1].

It may be shown that the gain of an ideal paraboloid [*l*] with uniform illumination and no losses is given by

$$G = \left(\frac{\pi D}{\lambda}\right)^2 \qquad \text{....(9.175)}$$

If the apeture is not uniformaly illuminated, an illumination efficiency term (η) must be introduced. Eq. 9.175 becomes

$$G = \eta\left(\frac{\pi D_a}{\lambda}\right)^2 \qquad \text{....(9.176)}$$

Generally η is of the order of 60%. Hence Eq. 9.176 becomes

$$G = 6\left(\frac{D_a}{\lambda}\right)^2 \qquad \text{....(9.177)}$$

where G is the power gain ratio, not the decibel power gain.

The beam width of an ideal paraboloid uniformly illuminated is given by

$$BW = \frac{70\lambda}{D_a} \qquad \text{....(9.178)}$$

where D_a is the maximum dish diameter

Solved problems

Example 9.1. : A uniform plane wave is incident upon a very short lossless dipole ($l << \lambda$), find the maximum effective aperture assuming that the radiation resistance of the dipole is $R_r = 80\left(\frac{\pi l}{\lambda}\right)^2$, and the incident field is linearly polarized along the axis of the dipole.

Solution :

For $R_L = 0$, the maximum effective aperture reduces to

$$A_{em} = \frac{|V_T|^2}{8W_i}\left[\frac{1}{R_r}\right]$$

Since the dipole is very short, the induced current can be assumed to be constant and of uniform phase. The induced voltage is

$$V_T = El$$

Here, E and l are the electric field and length of the dipole. For a uniform plane wave, the incident power density can be written as

$$W_i = \frac{E^2}{2\eta}$$

η is the intrinsic impedance of the medium for free space and it is equal to 120π .

$$\text{Hence } A_{em} = \frac{(El)^2}{8(E^2/2\eta)\,(80\pi^2 l^2/\lambda^2)} = \frac{3\lambda^2}{8\pi} = 0.119\lambda^2$$

The above value is only valid for a lossless antenna. If loss resistance is not zero but equal to R_r, then the effective aperture is half of A_{em} calculated above. To understand the significance of the effective aperture, consider the length of the short dipole is $l = \frac{\pi}{50}$

$$\therefore \quad A_{em} = \text{length} \times \text{width} = l\,\omega_e$$

$$\text{or } 0.119\,\lambda^2 = l\,\omega_e = \frac{\lambda}{50}\,\omega_e$$

$$\text{or } \omega_e = 5.95\,\lambda.$$

Typical diameter of the wire used is $\approx \lambda/300$. Thus the maximum effective width ω_e is about 1785 times larger than its physical width.

Example 9.2. A transmitting station of 25 kW power is radiating in free space, find out the field strength 30 km away.

Sol. The fields strength at a distant point is given by

$$E_{rms} = \frac{\sqrt{90\,W}}{r}\ \text{V/m.}$$

Substituting W = Power in watts.

r = distance in metres.

E_{rms} = 50 mv/metres.

Ans = 50 mv/metres.

Exmple. 9.3. At what distance from a 50 Hz circuit is the radiation field approximately equal to the induction field.

(IETE-June 1974)

The distance at which both radiation and induction fields are equal is given by

$$r = \frac{\lambda}{2\pi} = 954 kms.$$

Example 9.4. Show that the directivity of an electric current element is 3/2.

$$G = \frac{\text{Power radiated by the current element}}{\text{Power radiated by an isotropic antenna}}$$

$$= \frac{P_r}{\frac{W_i}{4\pi r^2}} = 4\pi r^2 \frac{P_r}{W_i}$$

Power radiated by a current element is given by

$$P_{r(av)} = \frac{\eta (I_m dl \sin\theta)^2}{8\lambda^2 r^2} W/m^2 \qquad (1)$$

Power will be maximum when $\theta = \pi/2$

$$\therefore \quad P_{r(v)} = \frac{\eta (I_m dl)^2}{8\lambda^2 r^2}$$

Also power input is given by

$$W_i = 80\pi^2 \left(\frac{dl}{\lambda}\right)^2 I_{rms}^2 \qquad \therefore \text{Irms} = \frac{I_m}{\sqrt{2}}$$

$$W_i = 40\pi^2 \left(\frac{dl}{\lambda}\right) I_m^2$$

Substituting in the relation for Gain we get G = 3/2

Gain in decibels is equal to 1.761 dB.

Example 9.5. A short vertical grounded antenna is designed to radiate at 1MHz. Calculate the radiation resistance if the effective height of antenna is 30 meters.

$$R_r = \frac{160\pi^2 le^2}{\lambda^2} \Omega \approx 15.8\ \Omega$$

Exampl 9.6. An antenna has an effective height of 100 meters and the current at the base is 450 amperes (rms) at 40 KHz. What is the power radiation ? If the total resistance of the antenna circuit is 1.12 ohms, what is the efficiency of the antenna ?

Power radiated

$$W = R_r I_{rms}^2$$

$$R_r = 160\pi^2 \left(\frac{le}{\lambda}\right)^2 \approx 1576 \left(\frac{le}{\lambda}\right)^2$$

Given $l_e = 100\,m, f = 40\,KHz$

$$I_{rms} = 450$$

$$\lambda = 7500\,m$$

$$\therefore \quad R_r = 0.2807\,\Omega$$

Power Radiated (W) $= (450)^2\ (0.2807)$

$$= 56.84\,KW$$

Antenna efficiency $\eta = \dfrac{R_r}{R_r + R_i} = \dfrac{\text{Radiation Resistance}}{\text{Total Antenna CCt Resitance}}$

$$\eta\% = \frac{0.2807}{1.12} \times 100$$

$$\eta = 25.07\%$$

Example 9.7. A transmitting antenna has an effective height of 61.4 meters, fed with a current of 50 Amp (rms) at a wavelength of 625 meters. Find

(a) Radiation resistance of the antenna

(b) Power radiated

(c) Antenna efficiency for a total resistance of 500.

Sol. Given $l_e = 61.4\,m$

$$I_{rms} = 50\,A$$

$$\lambda = 625\,m$$

$$R_r = \frac{160\pi^2(61.4)^2}{(625)^2}$$

$$= 15.26\,\Omega$$

$$W = I_{rms}^2\, R_r = (50)^2 \times 15.26$$

$$= 18.15\,KW$$

$$\eta = \frac{R_r}{R_r + R_i} = \frac{15.26}{500} = 0.3052$$

$\eta = 30.52\%$ **Ans.**

Example 9.8. A grounded vertical antenna, fed at the bottom with an RF current of 32 Amperes at 1MHz, produces a fields strength of 9 milli-volt/meters at a distance of 100 km. Calculate the effective height of the antenna in meters. (UPSC, 1979)

Sol :
$$E_{rms} = \frac{120\,\pi\, le.\, I_{rms}}{\lambda r}$$

$$l_e = \frac{E_{rms}\,\lambda.r}{120\pi.\, I_{rms}}$$

References

1. Blake, L.V., **Antennas**, Wiley, New York, pp. 289.
2. Kraus, JD., Carvel, K.R., **Electromagnetics,** McGraw-Hill, New York 1973, pp. 648-650.
3. Silver, S. (ed.), **Microwave Antenna Theory and Design**, M.I.T. Radiation Labaratory series, Vol 12., McGraw-Hill New York, 1949.
4. King, R.W.P., **Theory of Line Antennas,** Harward University Press, Cambridge, Mass., 1956
5.. Kraus, J.O., **Antennas**, McGraw-Hill New York, 1950.
6. Tai, C.T., and Pereira, CS, **"An approximate formulae for calculation of the directivity of an antenna"**, IEEE Transacations of antennas and propogation, Vol. AP-24 March 1976, pp 235-236.
7. Johnson, R.C., and Jasik, H., **Antenna Engineering Hand book,** New York McGraw-Hill Book company, 1984.
8. Jordan, E.C., Balmain, K.G., **Electrmagnetic waves and Radiating systems,** Prentice-Hall of India Pvt. Ltd., 1991.
9. Schelkunaff, S.K., and Friis, N.T., **Antennas : Theory and Practice,** Wiley, New York, 1952, pp 229-244, 351-353.
10. Collin, R.E. and Zucker, F.J. (eds.), **Antenna Theory Part 2,** Chapter 23 and 24 (by Wait, J.R.) McGraw Hill, New York, 1969.
11. Lo, Y.T., Lee, S.W., **Antenna Hand Book, Van** Nostrand Reinhold. New York, 1993.
12. Ballanis, C.A. **"Antenna theory" Analysis and design,** John Wiley & Sons, 1992.
13. Monaco, F., **"Introduction to microwave technology"**, Merrill Publishing Company.
14. Macnamara, T., **"Hand book of Antennas for EMC"**, Artech House Inc., 1995.

15. Johnson and Jasik, **Antenna Engineering Hand Book,** 2nd ed., McGraw-Hill, New York, 1984.

Problems and Review Questions*

1. What is the difference between the inductance field and radiation field of an antenna ?
2. Define and illustrate beamwidth and bandwidth for an antenna.
3. Define radiation patterns and explain what information it conveys.
4. Since an antenna is a passive device how can it have gain ? Distinguish between directive and power gain.
5. Describe the important characteristics of a Yagi-Uda antenna. Why is this antenna referred to as a parasitic array ?
6. Derive expressions for power density and radiation resistance of a half wave dipole antenna.
7. What is meant by radiation resistance and directivity of an antenna? Obtain the expression for the radiated power of a half wave dipole.
8. Explain directive properties of endfire and broad side array. Explain the working of a broad side array. Draw the radiation pattern of four element broad side array.
9. Describe the construction and working of normal mode helical antenna.
10. Discuss the concept of an image antenna to find the field of an antenna in the vicinity of a perfect conductor. What determines the sense of the current flow in an image antenna relative to that in the actual antenna.
11. Obtain expressions for radiated field by an open ended rectangular wave guide in free space and hence obtain an expression for gain of such a radiator.
12. What are three basic forms of horn antennas ? Why is the horn flared?
13. What is a paraboloid antenna ? Why is it so important at microwave frequencies.
14. What is a microstrip antenna ? Discuss how the dimensions of a rectangular patch microstrip antenna could be selected ? Write advantages and disadvantages of microstrip antenna.
15. Discuss the radiation pattern from a resonant half wave slot in an infinite plane conductor.
16. A paraboloid antenna is designed to have a power gain of 5000 at a frequency of 10 GHz. What is the diameter of the paraboloid ?

* Selected from universitives examination papers

17. If the current feeding an antenna is reduced by 50%. What is the percentage change in the field intensity at a given point of reception?
18. A half wave-length dipole is placed vertically on an infinite electric ground plane. Assuming that the dipole is fed at its base, find the
   (a) radiation impedance (referred to the current maximum)
   (b) input impedance (referred to the input terminals).
   (c) VSWR when the antenna is connected to a lossless 50-ohm transimission line.
19. A horizontal $\lambda/50$ infinitesimal dipole of constant current and length l is placed parallel to the y-axis at a distance h = 0.70 above an infinite electric ground plane. Find all the nulls formed by the antenna system in the $\phi = 90°$ plane.
20. Mention various types of horn antenna and draw their structure.
21. Write short note on slot antenna.
22. (a) Discuss expression for power density and radiation resistance of a half wave dipole antenna.
   (b) Discuss the radiation pattern from a resonant half-wave slot in an infinite plane conductor.
   Explain the mechanism by which an antenna transmits or receives e.m. waves.
23. What are reflector antennas ? Explain the geometry and working of a paraboloid reflector antenna. Mention different feeding systems. Calculate the beam width between nulls and power gain of a 2 meter paraboloid reflector antenna operating at 10 GHz.
24. (a) Define antenna gain, half power beam width and efficiency in brief.
   (b) Obtain expressions for radiated field by an open ended rectangular wave guide in free space and hence obtain an expression for gain of such a radiator.
   (c) Inner dimensions of a rectangular open waveguide radiator are 2.29 cm. × 1.02 cm. It is recommended for use in dominant mode for frequency 8.2 GHz. Calculate the gain of such a radiator.
25. What is meant by radiation resistance and directivity of an antenna? Obtain the expression for the radiated power of a quarter wave monopole antenna.
   Assuming the sinusoidal current distribution

$$I = I_m \sin \beta (H - Z)$$

show that the expression for the effective length of a dipole antenna of length L = 2 H is

$$l_{\text{eff}} = \frac{\lambda (1 - \cos \beta H)}{\pi \sin \beta H}$$

26. An open end of a rectangular waveguide of dimension 0.9" × 0.4" radiates electromagnetic energy when excited. Calculate its gain at the operating frequency of 10 GHz and use that antenna is 100% efficient.

27. (a) Explain the radiation through an aperture.

    (b) Explain the properties of line arrays and give its theory.

28. Develop expression for the field radiated by a current element. Obtain an expression for the radiated power and show that radiation resistance

$$R_{\text{rd}} = 80\,\pi^2 \left(\frac{dl}{\lambda}\right)^2$$

    Find the effective area of a radiator of gain 1.5 at 5 GHz.

29. Use the method of multiplication of pattern to illustrate the radiation pattern of a four element broadside array.

30. (a) What do you mean by radiation resistance of a transmitting antenna ? Derive an expression for the field radiated by a current and hence obtain an expression for the average power radiated and the radiation resistance of a short dipole antenna.

    (b) State the relation between the directive gain G of a receiving aerial and its effective area A. The gain of a certain aerial is 1.5, the frequency being 200 MHz. Calculate the effective area of the aerial.

[illegible] principle of multiplication of pattern [illegible] array.

10

Microwave Measurements

10.1 Introduction

Microwave measurements are concerned with distributed circuit elements which are acted upon by electromagnetic waves having interdependent E and H fields. The time varying magnetic fields generate the time varying electric fields and vice versa. The electromagnetic fields produced, propagate in the free space with a velocity which approaches the velocity of light. Once the electromagnetic waves leave their source of generation, these fields are completely independent of any changes occuring at the source. The motion of an electromagnetic wave is two fold (i) a translational velocity which is outward from the source and is dependent on the medium, and (ii) an oscillatory motion in a plane perpendicular to the direction of propagation.

Microwave system which include power generation, transmission and detection are in many ways different than low frequency radio wave systems. Hence the measurement techniques and parameters measured are also different.

At microwave frequencies most important parameters to be measured are the power, impedance and the frequency. Other quantities which are measured are the phase-shift, attenuation, VSWR and the noise factor. In this chapter we shall concentrate on the measurement of above mentioned parameters.

10.2 Frequency Measurements

10.2.1 Various components of a microware bench.

The basic experimental arrangement used in the laboratories for these measurements is described below (Fig. 10.1). X-band microwave sources, detectors and components are easily available, hence X-band

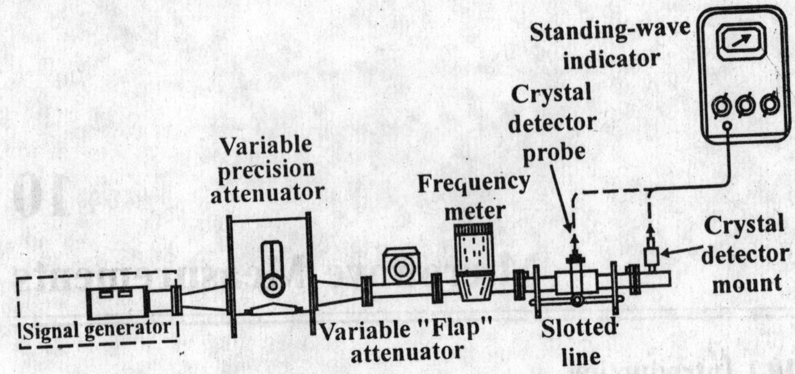

Fig. 10.1 Frequency measurement setup.

set up is generally used for teaching purposes. Figures 10.2a, b, c, d show most commonly used measurement equipments.

Fig. 10.2a. Precision attenuator.

(i) A microwave source used is either a Gunn diode oscillator or a reflex klystron, the output is of the order of few milliwatts. Signal output from these sources is generally square-wave modulated at an audio-frequency of 1 kHz. (see Fig. 10.7 in section 10.3.3).

(ii) The second component is a precision attenuator which can provide 0-50 dB attenuation above its insertion loss (Fig. 10.2a).

(iii) Then is a frequency meter in the form of a cylindrical cavity, which can be adjusted to resonance and is coupled to the waveguide through a slot Fig. 10.2b.

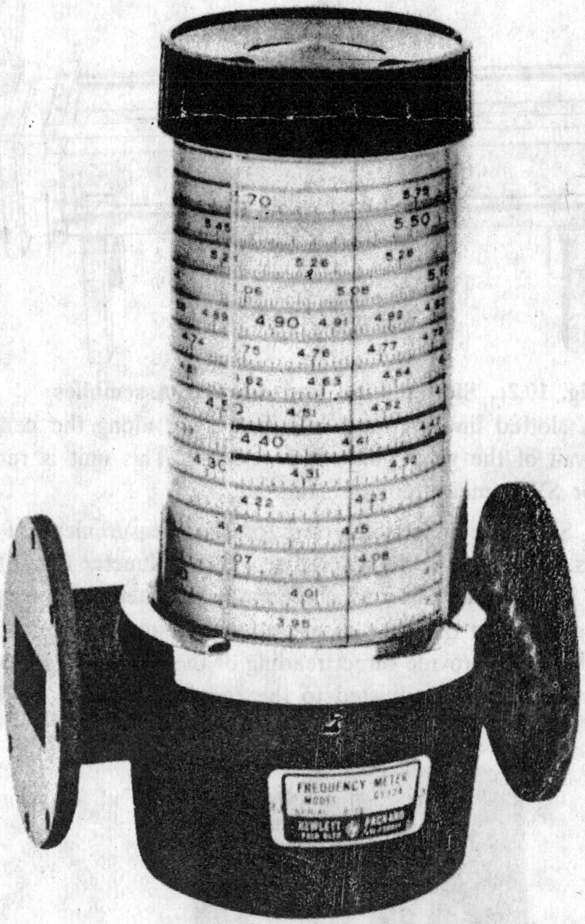

Fig. 10.2b. Resonant cavity frequency meter.

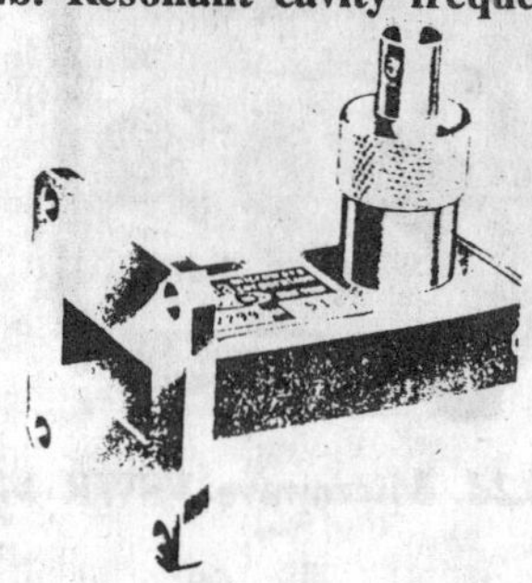

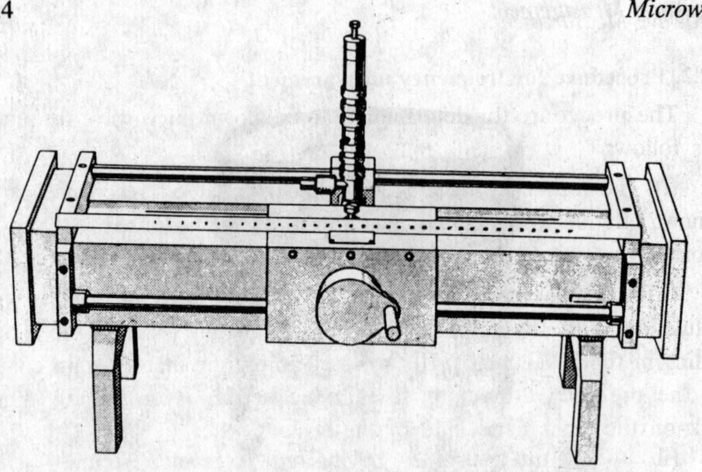

Fig. 10.2c. Slotted Line And Adapter Assemblies.

(iv) A slotted line section which has a cut along the centre of the broad wall of the wave guide is connected. This unit is required primarily for SWR measurements (Fig. 10.2a).

(v) A SWR meter is connected for the measurement of SWR directly. This meter is basically a sensitive, tuned voltmeter Fig. 10.2d. It consists of a high gain amplifier which operates at a fixed audio frequency (1 kHz). The amplifier output is measured with a square-law calibrated voltmeter which can provide direct reading of the SWR. A gain control allows the reading to be adjusted to the required value.

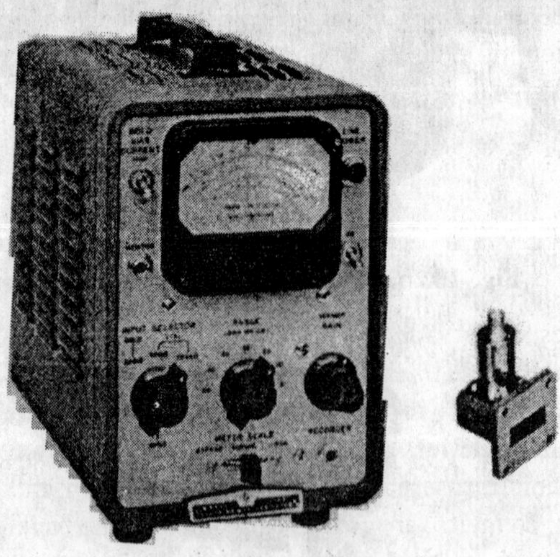

Fig. 10.2d. Microwave VSWR Meter.

10.2.2. Procedure for frequency measurement

The procedure for determining an unknown microwave frequency is as follows

(i) The frequency meter cavity should be at off resonance at the unknown frequency. The attenuator should be adjusted to provide appoximately 6-10 dB loss. The measurement setup is shown in Fig. 10.1.

(ii) Activate the microwave source and switch to square wave modulation. Vary the amplitude and the frequency (1 kHz) for a peak reading in the SWR meter. If necessary adjust the meter's gain control and the precision attenuator so that the needle is on the '0' degree mark on the right hand side of the scale.

(iii) Adjust the size of the cavity until resonance occurs. A small amount of microwave energy from the waveguide will be delivered to the cavity. An appreciable dip in the SWR meter will be indicated. The unknown frequency can then be read directly from the scale of the calibrated frequency meter. A typical Q value for the cavity is about 5000.

The basic accuracy of the cavity wavemeter is ± 1%. This value is subjected to changes in temperature and humidity. These effects can be overcome to some extent by sealing the cavity properly.

An alternative method of determining the frequency is to use a slotted line. The slotted line is terminated by a short circuit so that a standing wave pattern appears. Accurately locate the positions of two adjacent nulls by moving the probe along the slotted line, read the position of nulls in the vernier scale of the slotted line. These two positions are separated by half a guide wavelength, $\lambda_g/2$. The free space wavelength λ can be calculated by using the relationship :

$$\lambda = \lambda_g \sqrt{1 + (\lambda_g/2a)^2} \qquad \text{....(10.1)}$$

The frequency is calculated using f (GHz) = $30/\lambda$ cm. The accuracy of the result will depend partly on the measurement accuracy of the waveguides inner wide dimension a. The overall accuracy obtained is of the order of ±1%.

The methods of measuring frequency described so far depend on mechanical devices such as the cavity and the slotted line. However for precision measurement of frequency, electronic devices such as frequency counters are used to compare the unknown microwave frequency with a high order harmonic of an accurately determined lower frequency.

10.2.3. Electronic techniques for frequency measurement

These techniques are based on the comparison of the unknown frequency with a harmonic of the known standard frequency. Instruments that use null-beating technique for this comparison are known as transfer oscillators. There are automatic transfer oscillators which provide direct display of microwave frequencies. Basic principles of operation of these instruments are discussed below.

Transfer oscillator – A typical block diagram for a transfer oscillator is shown in Fig. 10.3. Signal from a stable frequency source is amplified and fed to a harmonic generator which provides a comb of frequencies in the desired microwave range. This harmonic output is mixed with the unknown signal frequency.

If the frequency of the stable frequency source is varied and the mixer output is connected through a detector to an indicator such as an oscilloscope, beat frequency output can be observed. Frequency of the stable frequency source is measured from the null beat condition. The unknown frequency is an integral multiple of this value. The value of the integral multiples can be obtained by noting the next higher frequency which produces null beat. If two frequencies are f_1 and f_2, the unknown frequency f may be found by the following equations

$$nf_1 = f \quad \text{....(10.2a)}$$

$$(n-1)f_2 = f \quad \text{....(10.2b)}$$

Eliminating n we may write

$$f = \frac{f_1 f_2}{f_2 - f_1} \quad \text{....(10.3)}$$

Since f_1 and f_2 can be measured very accurately this method provides very precise frequency measurement. In fact this method is generally used to calibrate resonant cavity type wavemeters.

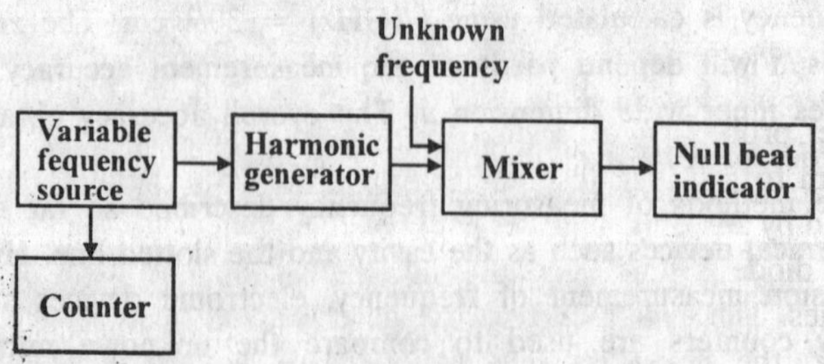

Fig. 10.3

10.3. Slotted Line Techniques For VSWR Measurment

Standing wave patterns are usually measured by means of a travelling detector which probes the electric field intensity along the axis of propagation. The whole assembly comprises of a slotted section, an electric probe and a detector. This assembly is often referred to as a standing wave detector. The slotted sections are both coaxial and waveguide type. It consists of a longitudinal slot milled along its surface. The slot is located at the place where surface current is minimum so that its presence do not change the field configuration considerably. The slot is tapered at both the ends so that a smooth impedance transfer is achieved and the discontinuity effect of the slot reduces to a minimum. The electric probe is inserted within the holder which rides above the slot as shown in Fig. 10.4.

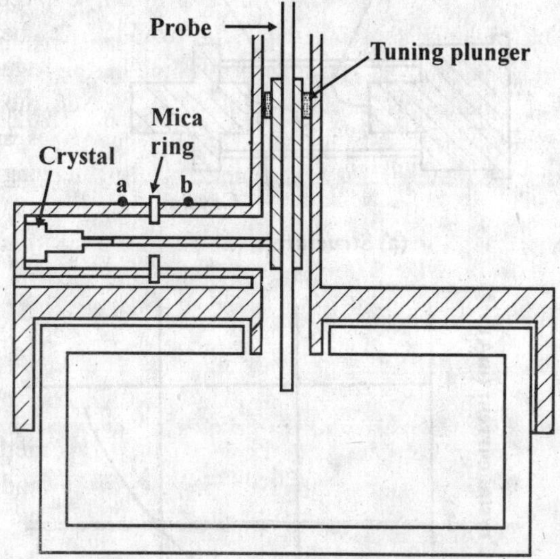

Fig. 10.4 Standing-wave crystal detector unit.

The probe length inside the guide is adjusted by a screw mechanism to provide loose coupling to the electric field. The voltage is detected by any of the devices, *viz* crystal, bolometer or thermocouple. A crystal diode is simplest of all and is generally used in the teaching laboratories. The crystal current-voltage characteristic is square law in nature *i.e.* the crystal current varies nearly square of the voltage detected.

To match the probe and crystal assembly for maximum power transfer, a tuning plunger composed of a sliding short circuit is used to introduce variable reactance. The crystal diode may be mounted in a short length of either a coaxial line or a wave guide. The voltage induced in the probe is proportional to its exposed length within the electric field. Greater sensitivity can be realized by increasing the probe insertion. However if inserted too far, the probe would load the guide and will change the original pattern.

10.3.1. Crystal detector

Most crystals used are N-type crystals and conduct more readily when the whisper is negative as shown in Fig. 10.5. These are easy to construct and quite sensitive.

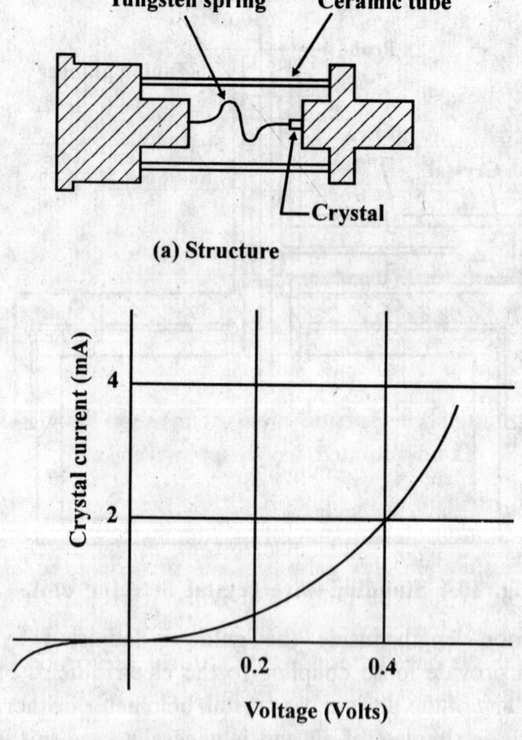

Fig. 10.5 Structure and current voltage charactristic of typical crystal diode.

10.3.2. Measurement of low VSWR

A. Unmodulated Frequency Procedure

In this case the microwave source (Reflex klystron) output is directly read by a microammeter, the experimental set up is shown in Fig. 10.6.

1. All components are mechanically aligned to avoid leakage and residual standing waves.
2. Set the microammeter shunt so that sensitivity is minimum. Even if large signal is passed through the meter it will not be damaged.
3. Switch on the reflex klystron oscillator. Vary the reflector voltage until oscillations are available on galvanometer.

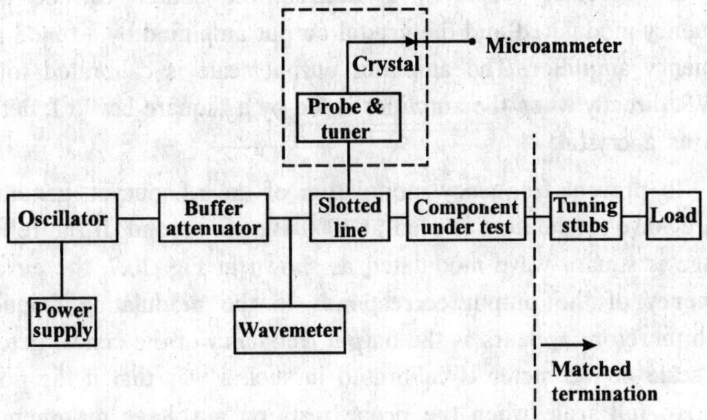

Fig. 10.6 Slotted line section measurement of VSWR-Method Unmodulated frequency method.

4. When oscillations are obtained tune the system. Vary reflector voltage and antenna stub till maximum power is indicated by the maxima on the galvanometer probe in the slotted line sections at the maximum of standing wave pattern. Now tune the probe for maximum sensitivity by adjusting the tuning plunger on the slotted section. Adjust the probe depth to a minimum, increase the galvanometer sensitivity.

5. Measure output frequency by calibrated frequency meter.

6. Remove component under test and measure standing wave pattern for matched condition.

$$VSWR = \sqrt{\frac{P_{max}}{P_{min}}} \text{ and it should be less than } \leq 1.02.$$

7. Insert the component again and note the maximum and minimum value.

$$PSWR = \frac{P_{max}}{P_{min}}$$

$$VSWR = \sqrt{PSWR}$$

10.3.3. Modutaled frequency procedure

If a greater sensitivity is desired, the source can be audio-frequency modulated and the crystal output amplified by a tuned audio frequency amplifier. The amplifier output scale is calibrated to read VSWR directly when the amplifier is fed by a "square law" r.f. detector such as a crystal.

To prevent frequency modulation of the r.f. output, generally a square wave modulation is used at 1000 Hz per second. If the reflector voltage is square wave modulated as shown in Fig. 10.7, the envelope frequency of the output corresponds to the modulation frequency, which therefore appears as the output frequency of the crystal detector. The scale of the meter is calibrated in such a way that if the pointer is set to full scale when the probe rests on a voltage maximum, the VSWR is read directly when the probe is moved to a voltage minimum.

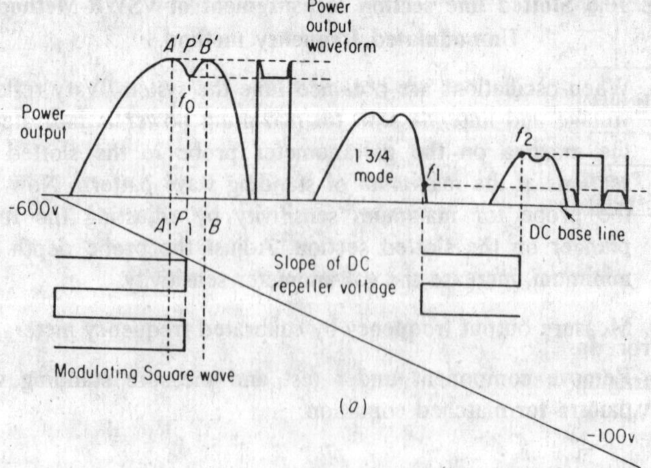

(a)

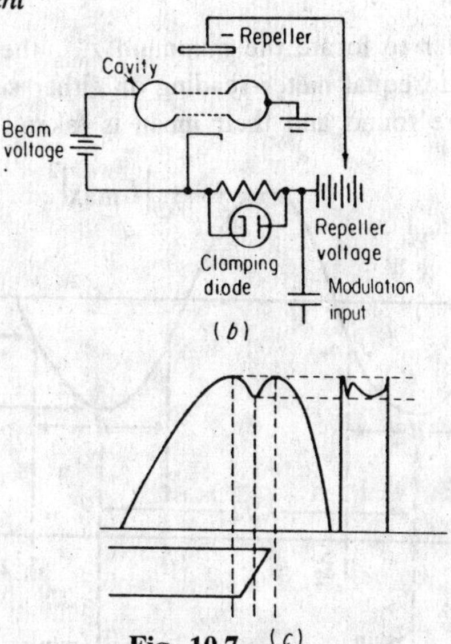

Fig. 10.7.

The set up for measuring VSWR by means of a modulated source is shown in Fig. 10.8.

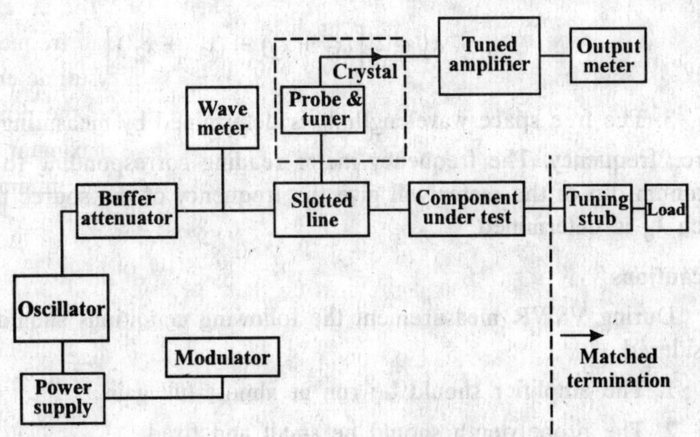

Fig. 10.8

Procedure to measure VSWR is described in the earlier section. The averaging technique of locating a VSWR is recomended whenever the VSWR is less than 2.

1. In order to locate the minimum z_{min} the positions x_1 and x_2 corresponding to equal meter reading on either side of x_{min} as shown in Fig. 10.9, are found and their mean is taken.

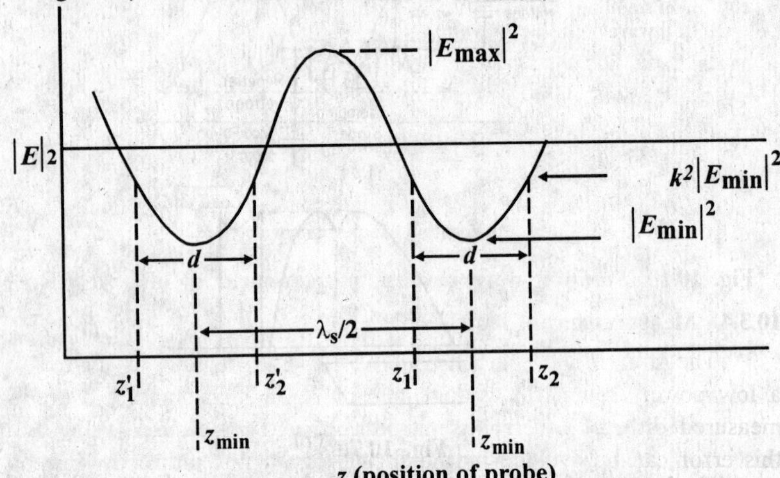

Fig. 10.9. Accurate location of Vmin.

2. The guide wavelength is obtained by finding the distance between two successive minima.

$$\lambda_g = 2\left[(x_1 + x_2) - (x_1' + x_2')\right]$$

3. The free space wavelength λ_0 is determined by measuring the source frequency. The frequency meter reading corresponding to the maximum dip of the meter will give the frequency of the source from which λ_0 is determined.

Precautions

During VSWR measurement the following conditions should be considered

1. The amplifier should be run at almost full gain.

2. The probe depth should be small and fixed.

3. The tuning stub should be adjusted for maximum power transfer.

4. The noise level of the amplifier when the source is not oscillating, should not be more than a very small fraction of the full scale reading.

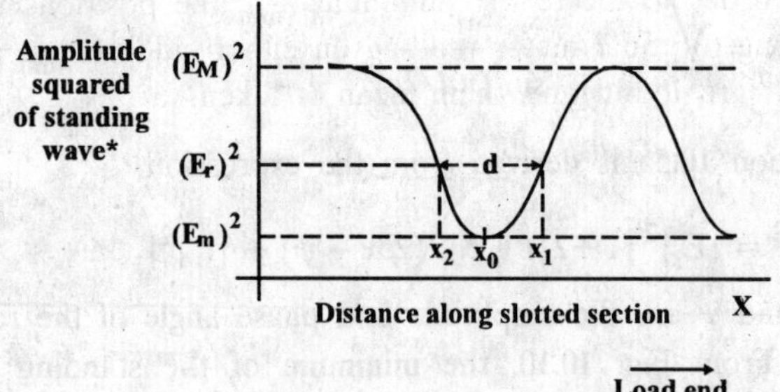

Fig. 10.10. Standing-wave pattern : measurement of high VSWR.

10.3.4. Measurement of high VSWR

The square law characteristic of a crystal detector is limited to a low power. When the voltage maxima of a high standing wave is measured directly an error is introduced in the measured value and this error can be avoided by measuring the VSWR indirectly. Instead of detecting the maximum value of the standing wave, an intermediate value which lies between the minimum and maximum amplitude is selected as shown in Fig. 10.10.

Referring to Fig. 10.10, assume that the intermediate value selected is $(E_r)^2$. Define a factor k^2 as

$$k^2 = \frac{(E_r)^2}{(E_m)^2} \qquad \text{....(10.4)}$$

d is the distance between two points one on either side of a minimum, where the $(E_r)^2$ reading occurs. The VSWR can be computed from the measured quantities κ^2, d and λ_g (the guide wavelength) by means of formula

$$\text{VSWR} = \frac{\sqrt{k^2 - \cos^2\left[\dfrac{\pi d}{\lambda_g}\right]}}{\sin\left[\dfrac{\pi d}{\lambda_g}\right]} \qquad \text{....(10.5)}$$

The value of κ^2 is generally chosen as 2, in that case Eq. 10.5 becomes

$$\text{VSWR} = \sqrt{1 + \frac{1}{\sin^2(\pi d/\lambda g)}} \qquad \text{....(10.5a)}$$

Equation 10.5a is derived from the expression

$$|E_r|^2 = |E_i|^2 [1 + 2|\Gamma| \cos(2\beta x - \psi) + |\Gamma|^2] \qquad \text{....(10.6)}$$

where $|\Gamma|$ and ψ are the amplitude and phase angle of the reflection coefficient. From Fig. 10.10, the minimum of the standing wave is given by $|E_m|^2$, and it occurs at $x = x_0$. We also know that the minimum corresponds to

$$2\beta x_0 - \psi = \pi \qquad \text{....(10.7)}$$

or

$$\psi = 2\beta x_0 - \pi$$

Equation 10.6 reduces to

$$|E_m|^2 = |E_i|^2 [1 - |\Gamma|]^2 \qquad \text{....(10.8)}$$

Now let $|E|^2 = |E_r|^2$ at $x = x_2$ in Fig. 10.10. For this condition equation 10.6 yields

$$|E_r|^2 = |E_i|^2 [1 + 2|\Gamma| . \cos(2\beta x_2 - \psi) + |\Gamma|^2] \qquad \text{....(10.9)}$$

From equation 10.7, the quantity $(2\beta x_2 - \psi)$ becomes equivalent to

$$2\beta x_2 - 2\beta x_0 + \pi = 2\beta(x_2 - x_0) + \pi \qquad \text{....(10.10)}$$

But from Fig 10.10

$$(x_2 - x_0) = \frac{d}{2} \qquad \text{....(10.11)}$$

Therefore

$$(2\beta x_2 - \psi) = \beta d + \pi \qquad \text{....(10.12)}$$

By substituting Eq. 10.12 into Eq. 10.9 $|E_r|^2$ reduces to

$$|E_r|^2 = |E_i|^2 [1 - 2|\Gamma| . \cos(\beta d) + |\Gamma|^2] \qquad \text{....(10.13)}$$

However from Eq. 10.4, for perfect square law detection

$$k^2 = \frac{(E_r)^2}{(E_m)^2} = \frac{|E_r|^2}{|E_m|^2}$$

Eqs. 10.8 and 10.13 result into

$$\text{VSWR} = \sqrt{\frac{2^{\left(\frac{1}{1 \pm \delta}\right)} - \cos^2 \pi d/\lambda_g}{\sin (\pi d/\lambda_g)}} \qquad \text{....(10.14)}$$

The quantity $|\Gamma|$ represents the magnitude of the reflection coefficient and it is related to the VSWR or S_v by the equation.

$$S_v = \frac{1 + |\Gamma|}{1 - |\Gamma|} \qquad \text{....(10.15)}$$

$$\therefore \qquad k^2 = \frac{S_v^{\,2} (1 - \cos \beta d) + (1 + \cos \beta d)}{2} \qquad \text{....(10.16)}$$

Since the phase constant $\beta = 2\pi/\lambda_g$, substitute in Eq. 10.16, the VSWR is given as

$$S_v^{\,2} = \frac{\kappa^2 - \cos^2 \left(\frac{\pi d}{\lambda_g}\right)}{\sin^2 \left(\frac{\pi d}{\lambda_g}\right)} \qquad \text{....(10.17)}$$

When $\pi d/\lambda g$ is small, Eq. 10.17 results into

$$S_v = \frac{\sqrt{k^2 - 1}}{\pi d/\lambda_g} \qquad \text{....(10.18)}$$

For the condition $k^2 = 2$, Eq. 10.18 reduces to

$$S_v = \text{VSWR} \approx \frac{\lambda_g}{\pi d}$$

The above derivation assumes perfect square law detection. As the detector response deviates from the square law characteristic, an inherent measurement error is introduced which can be evaluated once the response law is known.

The current response of the square law detector is $I = A|E|^2$ where A is a constant of proportionality and E is magnitude of electric field intensity. If the response of a non-ideal square law detector is given as

$$I = A \,.\, |E|^n \qquad \text{....(10.19)}$$

and $$n = 2\,(1 \pm \delta) \qquad \text{....(10.20)}$$

where δ is the measure of deviation,

the correct value of VSWR will be

$$k^2 = \frac{[1 - 2\,|\Gamma\,|\,\cos(\beta d) + |\Gamma\,|^2]}{[1 - |\Gamma\,|]^2} \qquad \text{....(10.21a)}$$

For small angles it reduces to

$$\text{VSWR} \approx \frac{\lambda_g}{\pi d}\left[2^{\left(\frac{1}{1 \pm \delta}\right)} - 1\right]^{\frac{1}{2}} \qquad \text{....(10.21b)}$$

In this way very high and moderate VSWR can be found out with the help of a slotted section. The slotted section method of measuring standing wave is susceptible to many errors. These are listed below.

10.3.5. Errors in standing wave measurement

Slotted section system errors

1. Error due to frequency instability—The frequency instability in the source will cause standing wave to shift while measurements are performed. They may arise mainly due to mechanical vibrations, thermal changes, too close coupling between the oscillator tube and the measuring bench or inadequate regulations of the source tube.

2. Coupling error—Coupling between the components of the measuring bench should be tight and properly aligned to avoid leakage and reflections.

3. Standing wave detector error—These are mainly due to deviation from square law behaviour, the admittance associated with the probe and the presence of the slot in the slotted section.

A. Square law detector error

Microwave crystals are usually made of germanium and silicon crystal, their characteristics are strongly dependent upon the contact between the wire and semiconductor and is subjected to defects such as uncertain response law, changes in sensitivity with temperature and r.f. impedance. When the crystal current is above one microampere then calibration of the crystal is necessary.

B. Probe error

The presence of the probe introduces a field distortion which affects the pattern of the standing wave. The distortion is more pronounced at a voltage maximum. The effect can be minimized by reducing the depth of the probe and by tuning it for optimum power pick up. The action of the probe is equivalent to a shunting admittance comprised of a conductance component G_p and a susceptance component B_p. Conductance G_p is proportional to the extracted power from the sampled field. The susceptance B_p depends upon reflections set up by the probe and is affected by probe tuning. The simplified equivalent figure is shown below Fig. 10.11a.

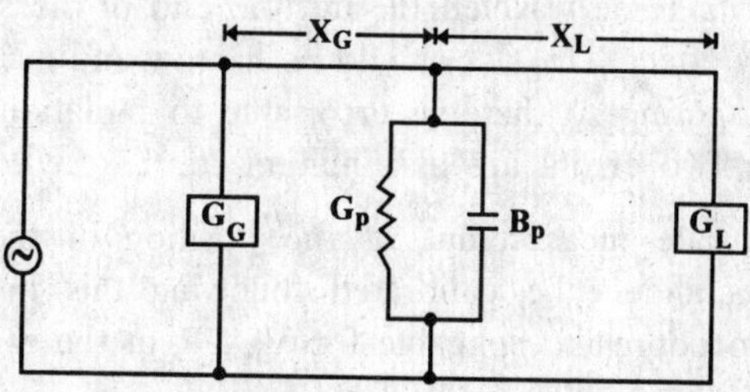

Fig. 10.11a Simplified equivalent circuit of the probe and line.

The effect of the probe is to alter the value of the standing wave pattern (S_v) and the location of maxima and minima. Let us assume that the load terminating the slotted section is real and has an equivalent conductance G_L, then the measured VSWR (S_{vm}) is normalized with respect to the correct VSWR (S_v), given by the expression

$$\frac{S_{vm}}{S_v} = \frac{1 + G_L + G_p G_L}{1 + G_L + G_p} \quad \text{....(10.22)}$$

If $G_L \leq 1$ and $B_p = 0$ which is achieved by proper tuning of the probe, under this condition the measured VSWR is less than the true VSWR. The shift in minima (Δ_{min}) and maxima (Δ_{max}) is given by

$$\frac{\Delta_{min}}{\lambda_g} = \frac{G_L^2 B_p}{(1 + G_L)^2} \quad \text{....(10.23)}$$

and

$$\frac{\Delta_{max}}{\lambda_g} = \frac{B_p}{(1 + G_L)^2} \quad \text{....(10.24)}$$

For $G_L >> 1$, expression for Δ_{min} will change to Δ_{max} and the one for Δ_{max} will change to Δ_{min}.

For $G_L = 0$ which corresponds to a terminating open circuit, the zeros do not shift but the shift in the maximum is equivalent to B_p. From the expressions 10.23 and 10.24, one concludes that shift in minimum is less than the shift in the maximum and the location of minima should be observed for all measurements using slotted section.

C. Slot error

The slot in the slotted section loads the waveguide and produces slight shift in its guide wavelength, and the end of the slot introduces a discontinuity effect. The slot should be narrow and cut symmetrically with proper tapering so that the error due to radiation is eliminated and the other two errors are also minimized.

For accurate measuremnt of the position of the minima the slotted section should be calibrated following this procedure. This calibration procedure is applicable for VSWR in the range of 1 to 5.

(1) Short circuit the slotted section end by a good short (smooth metal plate). Locate the minima nearest to the end. This is reference minimum position dr_m of the short.

(2) Remove the fixed short and connect a variable short in its place. Keeping the probe at the reference minimum position, move the variable short screw till the minimum is obtained. Read the scale attached on the variable short. This will give the reference position Sr on the short.

(3) Measure λ_g from the slotted section and λ_{gs} in the adjustable short.

(4) Vary the position s of the short and for each position of s, find the position of the voltage minimum d_{min} in the slotted section.

(5) Plot a graph $\Delta d = -(d + s\lambda_g/\lambda_{gs})$ versus d (see Fig. 10.11b), and draw a line through the average of this curve.

The correct value dc_{min} of the location of voltage minimum is obtained by finding the correction factor Δd from the calibration curve. If in an actual system, the measured VSWR and the position of voltage minimum are S_m and d_{min} respectively, the correct value S_c and d_{min} are given by

$$d_{min} = \left[d_{min} + \Delta d \left(\frac{S_m^2 + 1}{S_m^2 - 1} \right) \right] \frac{\lambda_{gs}}{\lambda_g}$$

where Δd is the correction factor obtained from Fig. 10.11b at $d_{min} - \lambda_g/8$.

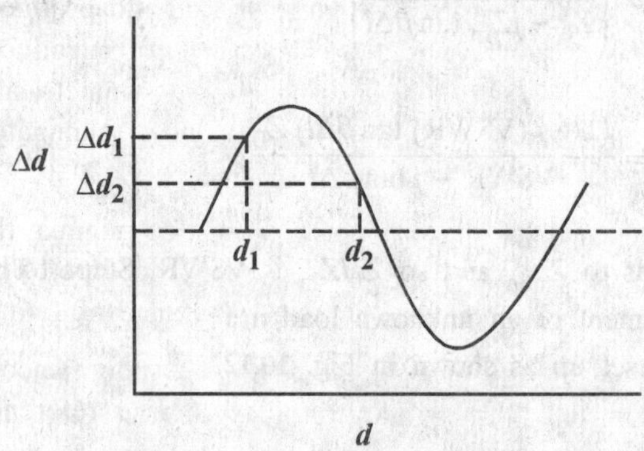

Fig. 10.11b Calibration curve for slotted section

10.3.6. Impedance measurement

An unknown load impedance can be found just by measuring the VSWR using the techniques described earlier, and finding the position of voltage minimum. The basic set up is as shown in Fig. 10.12. We know from transmission line theory that the waves incident from the generator on the load get reflected (if the load is not the characteristic impedance) and standing waves are formed between the load and generator. The magnitude and phase of the VSWR are the characteristic property of the load. The input impedance of a transmission line is given by the transmission line equation.

$$Z_{in} = \frac{V_s}{I_s} = \frac{V_L \cosh \gamma l + Z_0 I_L \sinh \gamma l}{I_L \cosh \gamma l + V_L/Z_0 \sinh \gamma l} \quad \text{....(10.25a)}$$

For a lossless line, $\gamma = \alpha + j\beta, (\alpha = 0)$

$$= j\beta$$

$$Z_{in} = Z_0 \frac{Z_L + jZ_0 \tan \beta \Delta l}{Z_0 + jZ_L \tan \beta \Delta l} \quad \text{....(10.25b)}$$

where Z_L is the load impedance (unknown impedance), Z_0 is the characteristic impedance and Z_{in} is the impedance at the input of the transmission line. $\beta\Delta l$ is the electric distance, being measured in wavelengths between position of termination and standing wave minimum. In terms of Z_L Eq. 10.25b is written as

$$Z_L = \left(\frac{Z_{in} - jZ_0 \tan \beta\Delta l}{Z_0 - jZ_{in} \tan \beta\Delta l}\right) Z_0 \qquad \text{....(10.25c)}$$

or

$$Z_R = \frac{(1 - j\,(\text{VSWR}) \tan \beta\Delta l)\, Z_0}{\text{VSWR} - j \tan \beta\Delta l} \qquad \text{....(10.26)}$$

where Z_{in} corresponds to Z_{min} and so Z_0/Z_{in} is VSWR. Steps to be followed for measurement of an unknown load are

1. Arrange the set up as shown in Fig. 10.12.

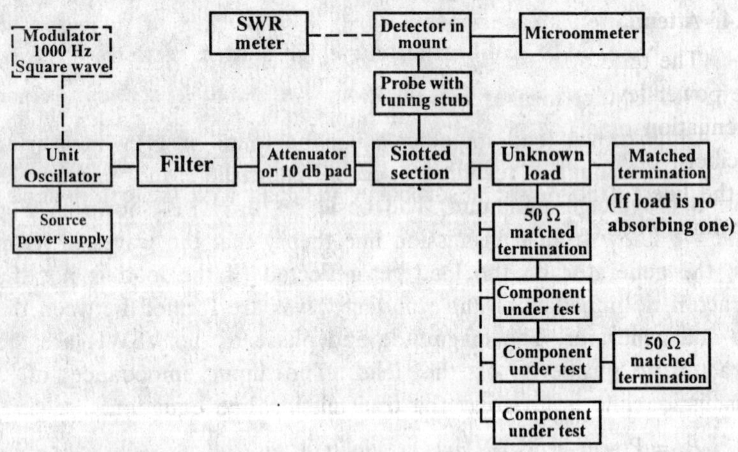

Fig. 10.12. Set-up for the measurement of VSWR at the input of the component under test.

2. Terminate the load end with the unknown impedance, measure λ the wavelength and VSWR.

3. Record the position of a minimum with the help of the probe, at around the center of slotted section. Call this reading say as x_1.

4. Replace the load by short circuited termination and move the probe carriage to new standing wave minimum and record it as the value x_2.

5. Find the shift in minimum $(x_2 - x_1)$. It will be positive if it is shifted towards load and negative if it is shifted towards generator. Convert the shift Δl in wavelength units, *i.e.* $\frac{x_2 - x_1}{\lambda}$ wavelengths.

Compute impedance using Eq. 10.26. Substituting for $\beta \Delta l$,

$$\beta \Delta l = \frac{(x_2 - x_1)}{\lambda} 2\pi \qquad \text{....(10.28)}$$

6. Unknown impedance can easily be found by using Smith chart. The only parameters to be measured are VSWR and shift in minimum position as explained in step 4.

10.4. Attenuation Measurements

The term attenuation is defined as the ratio in decibels, of either the power level or voltage level between two points in a circuit. Hence attenuation of a component under test will be the ratio expressed in decibels, of the power absorbed by the load without the component in the line to the power absorbed by the load with the component in the line, when the signal sources under load are perfectly matched.

$$\text{Attenuation A} = 10 \log_{10} \left(\frac{P_1}{P_2} \right) dB \qquad \text{....(10.29}$$

P_1 = Power absorbed by the load without the given component in the line

P_2 = Power absorbed by the load with the given component in the line.

Attenuators are generally of three types–

(i) Fixed pads

(ii) Step-adjustable

(iii) Continuously varying

Attenuation measurements are made primarily by using either the power ratio method or the RF substitution method. In its simplest form, the power ratio method involves connecting an unmodulated microwave source to a bolometer mount and a power meter. Power level is measured initially, the attenuating device is then inserted between the source and the bolometer, and the new reading is taken. The ratio of these two power readings will be the measure of the attenuation of the device. This method is normally limited to values of attenuation that range up to 20 dB.

Measurment of absolute power for determining the attenuation is not essential, since we are mostly concerned with relative power levels. A detector with a square law characteristic can be used to measure power ratio without knowing the absolute power levels. The experimental set-up is shown in Fig. 10.13.

The steps involved with this power ratio method are as follows

(i) Set the precision attenuator to approximately 20 dB and the flap attenuator to 0dB.

(ii) Energise the microwave source at the desired frequency and modulate its output with a 1 kHz square wave. Adjust the modulation for a peak reading on the SWR meter.

(iii) For the crystal detector to operate within its square law characteristics, the microwave power level at the crystal should be around 0.1 *m*W. This is achieved by switching the meter to its 30 dB range. The meter's gain control or, if necessary the precision attenuator's control can be used to bring the needle to the 0-dB mark.

(iv) Rotate the control of the flap attenuator to provide the unknown loss. The amount of this loss can then be read directly off the decibel scale of the SWR meter. If necessary the experiment can be repeated for a number of required frequencies.

In this method we have assumed that both power levels with and without the unknown attenuation are capable of operating the crystal detector within its square-law characteristics. If this is not so there will be an error in the measurement. Greater accuracy can be provided by the RF substitution method, the steps for which are as follows

(i) Assemble the set-up as shown in Fig. 10.13.

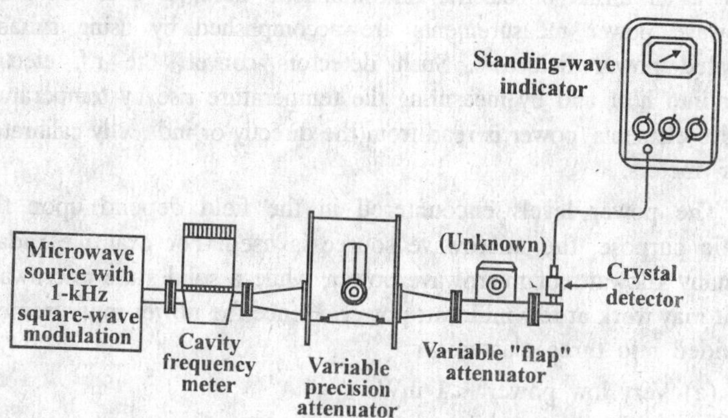

Fig. 10.13 Attenuation Measurement Set up.

(ii) Set the precision attenuator to approximately 40 dB higher than the expected attenuation of the component under test.

(iii) Energise the microwave source and repeat the second and third steps of the power ratio method described earlier and record the reading of the precision attenuator.

(iv) Rotate the control of the flap attenuator to provide the 'unknown' loss. The needle of the SWR meter will fall back but should be restored to the 0 dB mark by reducing the value of the precision attenuator. Then the difference between the new reading of the precision attenuator and its reading in step (i) is equal to the unknown attenuation.

The advantage of the substitution method is that the power level at the crystal detector is the same when taking both readings of the precision attenuator.

10.5. Power Measurement

Microwave power is one of the few fundamental quantities that can be measured directly and conveniently. It is helpful in ascertaining the proper functioning of all microwave devices and circuits.

Other electric properties can be derived by determining relative or absolute power levels of the equipments. Although microwave power is defined in the same way as power at low frequencies, that is, it is the product of rms voltage, rms current and power factor ($P_{av} = I_{rms}\ E_{rms} \cos\phi$). However at microwave frequencies measurement of current and voltage is difficult as the propagation of microwave power is in terms of electric and magnetic field [E and H]. Most microwave power measurements are accomplished by using suitable calibrated power detectors. Such detectors convert the r.f. electric power into heat and by measuring the temperature rise by temperature sensitive elements, power is read from the directly or indirectly calibrated power meters.

The power levels encountered in the field depend upon the specific purpose, the microwave source is used. For example radars use many kilowatts of microwave power, while a solid state microwave circuit may work at few milliwatt power. Hence the nower measurement is divided into three classes :

(a) Very low power <1 mW

(b) Low power <10 mW

(c) High power (10 mW to few hundreds of watts).

10.5.1. Very low power measurement

Specially designed thermocouples are used to measure low power levels below 1 mW. These thermocouples consist of thin films of antimony and bismuth deposited on thin resistive strips. When two junctions of a thermocouple are at different temperatures a thermo emf is produced. Fig. 10.14a depicts the construction of the strip-junction thermocouple element. These thermocouple, units are subjected to variation in ambient temperature over loading and aging. Some internal calibration provisions must be included in the power meters using these thermocouple elements. Fig. 10.14b shows a typical thermocouple detector and the calibration circuit.

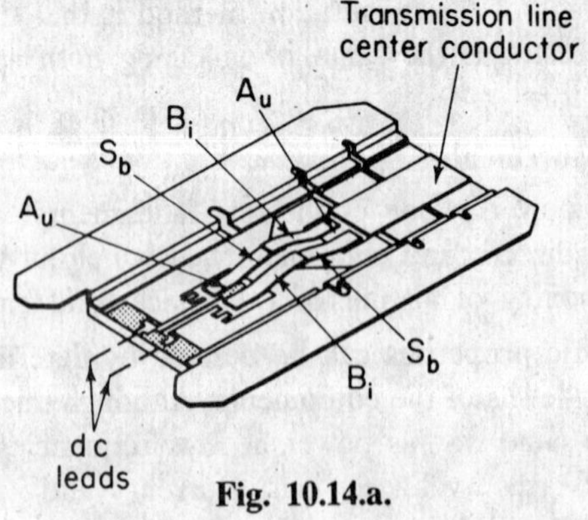

Fig. 10.14.a.

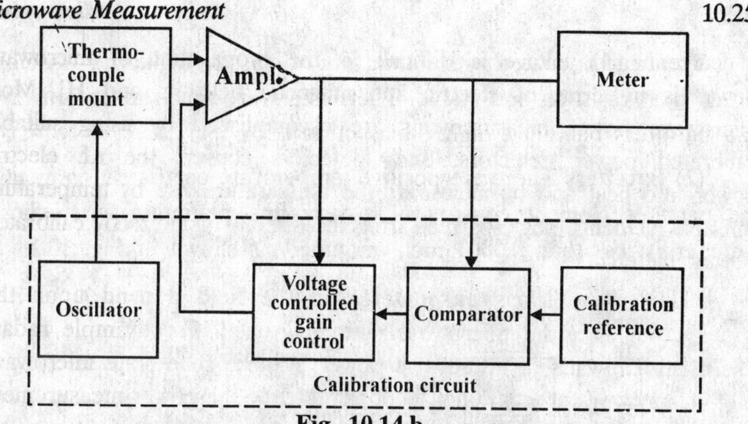

Fig. 10.14.b.

10.5.2. Low power measurement (1 to 10 mW)

The low power measurements make use of the temperature sensitive elements known as bolometers. Bolometers are microwave power detectors and operate on the property of change in its internal resistance with rise in temperature caused by heat dissipating microwave power. They are of two types :

(1) Thermisters – Thermistors are negative temperature coefficient semiconductors. It consists of a small bead of semiconducting material such as complex metallic oxide of Ni, Mn, Co, etc. supported between two wires as shown in Fig. 10.15.

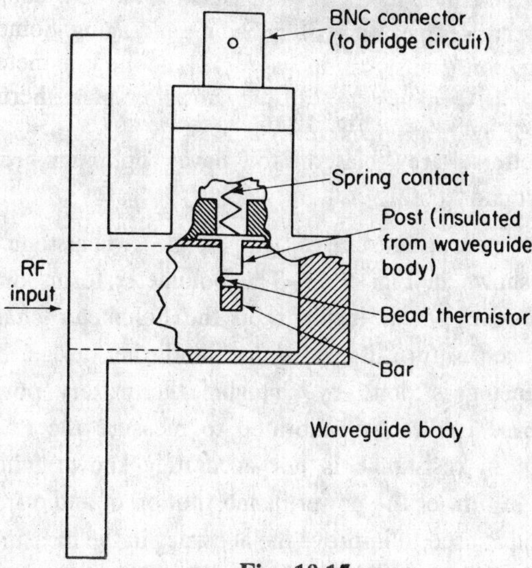

Fig. 10.15

The bead is coated with a thin film of glass to make the assembly strong, heat resistant and stable. Thermisters are much more sensitive than baratters but need higher bias current.

(2) Baretters These are positive temperature coefficient elements. The barrater element consists of a very fine platimum wire whose diameter is less than 0.0001 inch, mounted as shown in Fig. 10.16.

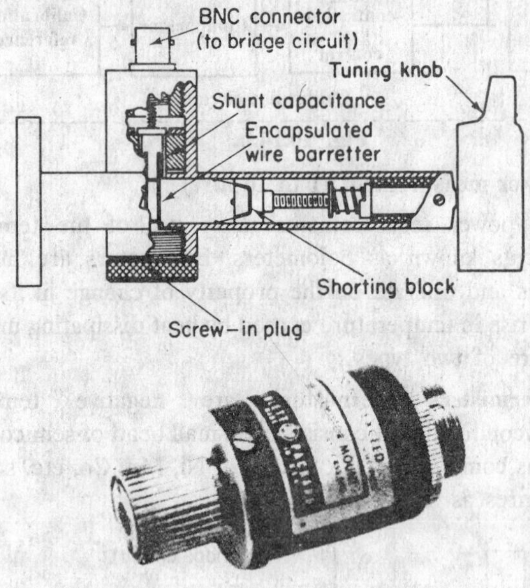

Fig. 10.16

The barretters are biased to have optimum resistance approximately around 200Ω .

The basic measuring unit is a simple wheatstone bridge arrangement as shown in Fig. 10.17. The bolometer forms one of its arms. The microwave power incident on the bolometer changes its temperature, hence in turn its resistance and the bridge becomes unstable. Rebalancing is done by changing the battery power, the amount of decrease is directly calibrated to measure the r.f. power. Since the change in resistance is not accurately known function of temperature and in turn of the power, a substitution of audio frequency (af) power method is used to improve the accuracy in the measurements. In this method the bridge is initially balanced with low frequency (af) power. When r.f. power is applied to the bolometer, low frequency power is withdrawn until the bridge is again balanced. The amount of power removed is amplified and displayed on the indicating meter and is equal to the true power substitution.

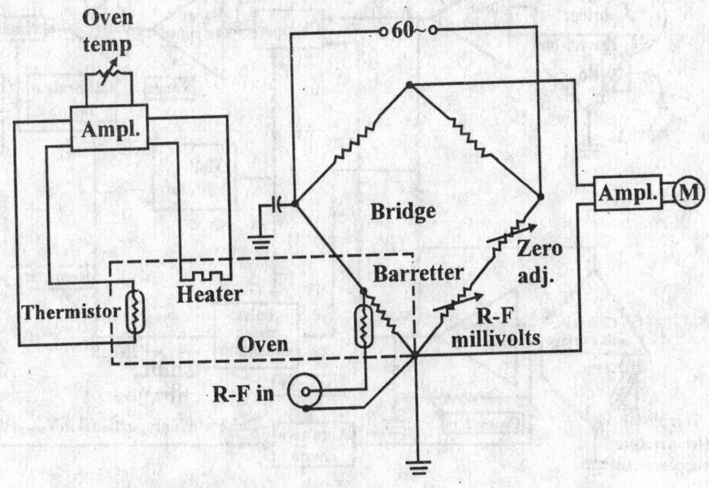

Fig. 10.17 Manually balanced bolometer bridge.

In such simple bridge arrangements the bridge can be imbalanced due to ambient temperature change from applied power, which can produce imbalance variations in highly sensitive bridge measurement. The answer to this is, use two thermister mounts placed in close thermal proximity so that both are affected equally by changes in ambient temperature and can compensate for the characteristics of each other. Hence a dual bridge arrangement, one for each bolometer is used. The second bridge is called metering bridge and performs two functions. Firstly it controls the audio frequency bias which balances the detection bridge (first bridge) under ambient temperature conditions. Secondly when microwave power is applied to the detection bridge it causes a change in dc bias of the metering (second) bridge. The change in the bias is applied to the current squaring circuit which measures the output power. Thus the meter becomes direct reading and automatic. A dual bridge circuit is shown in Fig. 10.18.

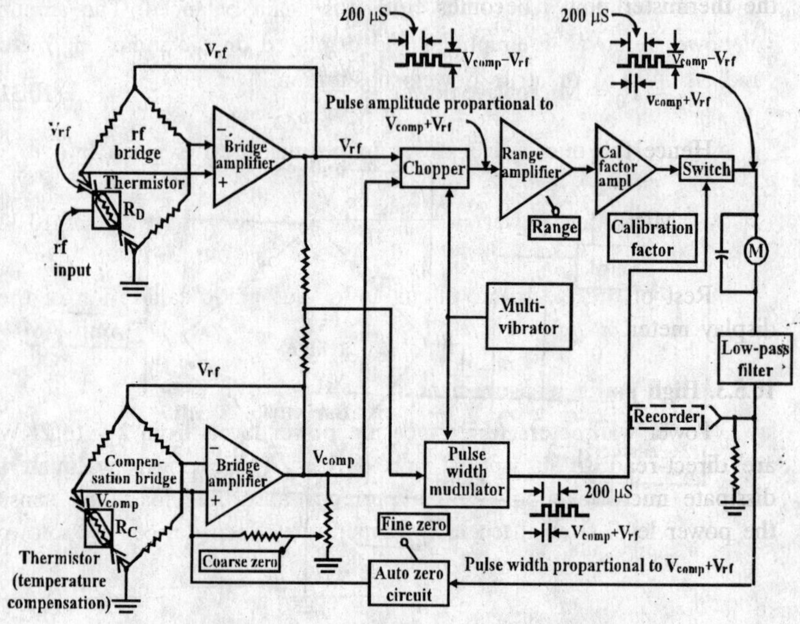

Fig. 10.18 Dual bolometer bridge circuit.

Bridge amplifiers provide proper bias to the bolometers used in the bridges so that they have the proper value of bolometer resistance. When microwave power falls on the thermister of the detecting bridge, its resistance varies and the bridge becomes imbalanced. The error voltage thus produced is amplified by the amplifier and then applied at top of the bridge to change the power dissipation in the thermister and its resistance to rebalance the bridge. The two thermisters are placed in identical physical conditions, so a change in the ambient temperature will cause an error signal in both the bridges and thereby get cancelled. Thus the rf bridge voltage V_{rf} and compensating bridge voltage contains complete information about the incident microwave power.

Initially V_{comp} is adjusted equal to V_{rf}, when no microwave power is incident on the thermister. In this case total power dissipating in the thermister is

$$P_0 = \frac{V_{comp}^2}{4R} \quad \text{....(10.30)}$$

When microwave power is applied and the bridge is rebalanced, the thermister power becomes equal to

$$P_0 = \text{Microwave power} + \frac{V_{rf}^2}{4R} \qquad ....(10.31)$$

Hence the microwave power to be measured is given by

$$\text{Microwave power} = \frac{V_{comp}^2 - V_{rf}^2}{4R} \qquad ....(10.32)$$

Rest of the electronic circuit is for automatic calibration of the display meter.

10.5.3. High power measurement

Power wattmeters which measure power levels from 2W to 2KW are direct-reading absorption type devices. These power wattmeters dissipate microwave power in a perfectly absorbing load and sense the power level from the rise in temperature. Such devices are known

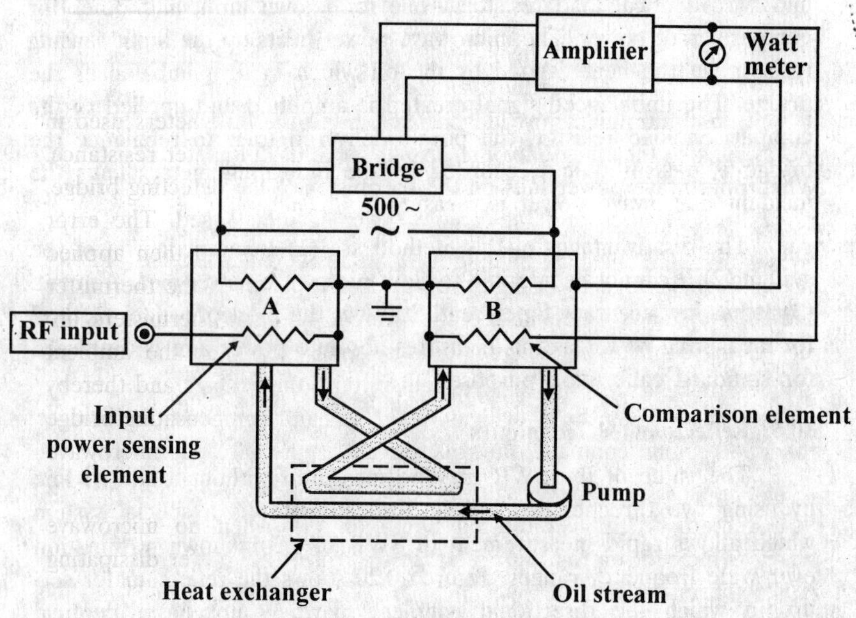

Fig. 10.19 Simplified diagram of the H.P. 434A calorimetric wattmeter.

as calorimeter wattmeters as shown in Fig. 10.19. The calorimetric methods of measuring power are based on the complete conversion of the incoming microwave energy into heat. They are classified in different ways (1) In the direct heating method the heating effect on the load that terminates the line is measured (2) In the indirect heating method the heat is transferred in whole or in part from the power absorbing medium to some other medium for measurement. True calorimetric method determines the power by the measurement of temperature, mass and time. Substitution method uses a known low frequency power to produce the same physical effect as the unknown microwave power which is to be measured. In either case the calorimetric system is either a static or circulating type. In the circulating wattmeters the load could be water, oil or ammonia gas. In the static or noncirculating type the load could be a coaxial line filled with high lossy dielectrics. Circulating type calorimeters are most commonly used and are commercially available. Fig. 10.19 shows a commercially available self balancing type wattmeter. It has two identical temperature-sensitive gauges (one in each arm), a high gain amplifier, an indicating meter and two identical load resistors – one for known input and other for comparison of power. The microwave power heats up the input sensing resistor via the heat carried by the oil which in turn imbalances the bridge. The imbalanced signal created is amplified and applied to the comparison load resistor, the power delivered to it to rebalance the bridge is measured and recorded by the indicating meter. Thus the incident microwave power is measured.

The disadvantages of this method are (1) Inherent inertia of the system (2) It cannot be adopted for low microwave power measurement. (3) It has low accuracy 5 per cent. Still it is the most prevalent method for measuring power as this measures absolute power and is thus used for standard calibration purpose.

10.6. Reflectometer Techniques

The value of the SWR may be measured without a slotted line by using two directional couplers. Reflectometer is a special system which allows rapid measurement of SWR of an unknown termination over wide frequency ranges. Figure 10.20 shows the reflectometer set-up, in which the directional couplers may/may not have identical characteristics. The forward 20 dB coupler samples incident power from detector 1, will be 20 dB down or one hundred of the power out put from the microwave source. The power coupled to the auxiliary arm is detected and applied to the incident channel of the ratiometer. The power coupled to the 10 dB reverse coupler (2) is much small and is absorbed in the internal termination of the coupler and negligible power flows to the connected detector. The remaining power impinges on the load. If the load is not a matched one, a portion of the incident power proportional to the degree of mismatch, is reflected and travels back towards the microwave source. The reverse 10 dB coupler (2), samples the reflected power, which is applied to the reflected channel of the ratiometer via tuned detector. The remaining reflected power passes through the 20 dB coupler (1) connected in reverse direction and hence the power coupled is absorbed by its internal termination. The variable attenuator is generally provided to avoid overloading of the source due to reflected power. There is no interaction between the two readings due to the directional properties of the couplers. The ratiometer measures and displays the ratio of the magnitudes of reflected and incident power, which is nothing but the reflection coefficient. Since detectors follow square law in the specified range of power we are working in, so the ratiometer is calibrated to indicate square root of detected powers. The calibration of the ratiometer is achieved by a waveguide short circuit termination which corresponds to a hundred percent reflecting load. Since any load will be less reflecting than the short, so taking reference level determined by short other reflection coefficients can be obtained in dB.

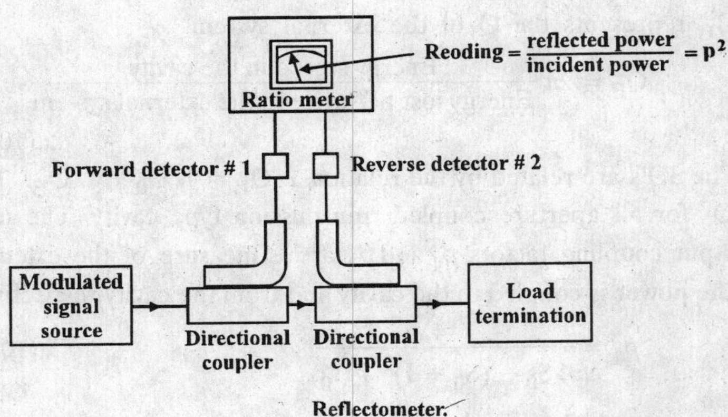

Reflectometer.

Fig. 10.20

10.7. Measurement of Cavity Q

At microwave frequencies the accurate measurement of Q for cavities having very high Q is quite difficult. This is due to the fact that the 3dB bandwidth of the cavity response curve is very small fraction of the resonance frequency. There are three different definitions of Q as given below.

(i) Unloaded Q

$$Q_0 = 2\pi \frac{\text{Energy stored in the cavity}}{\text{Energy lost per cycle in the cavity}} \quad \text{....(10.33a)}$$

Q_0 is selectivity factor of the cavity depending on the geometrical portion of the cavity.

(ii) Loaded Q

$$Q_L = 2\pi \frac{\text{Energy stored in the cavity}}{\text{Energy lost per cycle in the cavity + Energy lost per cycle in the external system}} \quad \text{....(10.33b)}$$

Q_L represents the Q of the entire system and includes all sources of energy loss. Q_L is found by the expression

$$Q_L = f_0/\Delta f$$

where f_0 = resonance frequency

Δf = 3dB bandwidth

(iii) External Q

Q_E represents the Q of the external system

$$Q_E = 2\pi \frac{\text{Energy stored in the cavity}}{\text{Energy lost per cycle in the external system}} \quad \text{....(10.33c)}$$

The 3Q's are related by the relation $1/Q_L = 1/Q_0 + 1/Q_E$. Thus $Q_L < Q_0$ for all aperture coupled transmission type cavity. The input and output coupling factors β_1 and β_2 are a measure of the extent to which the power is coupled to the cavity and from the cavity respectively.

$$\beta_1 = \frac{4}{4\,S_0 - (S_0 + 1)^2\,T\,(f_0)} \quad \text{....(10.34a)}$$

$= 1$ (critical coupling)

< 1 (under coupling)

> 1 (over coupling) ....(10.34b)

$$\beta_2 = \beta_1 S_0 - 1$$

$$Q_0 = Q_L (1 + \beta_1 + \beta_2) \quad \text{....(10.34c)}$$

Here S_0 VSWR at the resonance frequency f_0

$T(f_0) = P_{out}/P_{in}$

Transmission loss at the resonance frequency f_0.

Measurement of both the transmission loss $T(f_0)$ and VSWR S_0 at resonance gives the data needed for calculating β_1 and β_2 and unloaded detuning Q_0. There are various methods used for measurment of Q, few of them are listed below.

10.7.1. Slotted line method for measurement of Q

1. Q of a reflection type cavity can be measured by a slotted line. The measurement setup is shown in Fig. 10.21 The klystron is energised and the VSWR of the cavity is measured for several frequencies available from the generator. It should include the resonant frequency f_0 of the cavity.

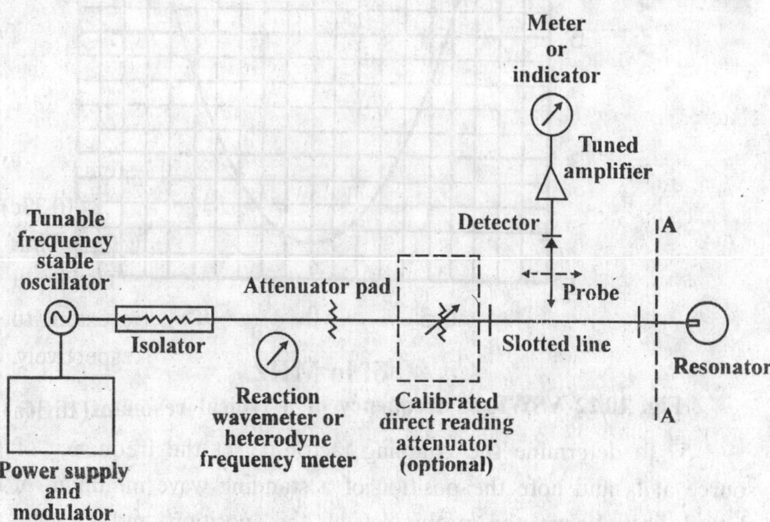

Fig. 10.21. Slotted line setup for measuring Q of a reflection type cavity

2. Repeat these measurements for frequencies above and below the resonant frequencies.

3. Plot VSWR against frequency from the above data as shown in Fig 10.22. Determine f_0 and VSWR (S_0) at resonance from the minimum point of the curve. Find the frequencies f_1 and f_2 at half power points from the figure on both sides of f_0.

4. Calculate Q_L using the equation

$$Q_L = f_0/\Delta f$$

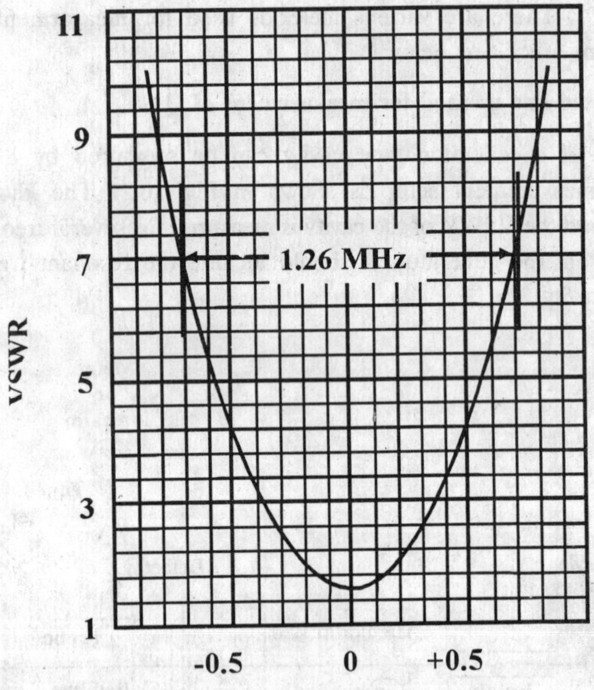

Fig. 10.22 VSWR vs frequency of a typical resonant cavity.

5. To determine the coupling factor β, set the frequency of the source at f_0 and note the position of a standing wave minimum in the slotted line. Leave the probe set at this position and change the frequency by an amount five or more times Δf. Note whether the probe is now near a standing wave maximum or minimum by moving it through

a small distance. If the minimum has been replaced by a maximum, the cavity is over coupled and $\beta = S_0$. If the minimum has shifted very little, the cavity is undercoupled and $\beta = 1/S_0$.

6. The unloaded Q is given by

$$Q_0 = (1 + \beta) Q_L$$

Q_0 is always greater than Q_L.

Other methods which can be used for finding the Q are listed below.

1. Q measurement from the shift in position of a standing wave minimum (Nodal shift method).

2. Reflectometer method for measurment of Q.

3. Measurment of Q by reflected power presented on a oscillos cope.

Ref [1] has treated the Q measurment in detail.

10.7.2. Measurment of Q for transmission type cavity by transmitted power measurement.

If the cavity is transmission type, measuring power transmitted through the cavity as a function of frequency is a simple and accurate method. The transmission method has the advantage of yielding the loaded Q directly even in the presence of coupling losses. However this method can not yield the unloaded Q without a number of additional measurements.

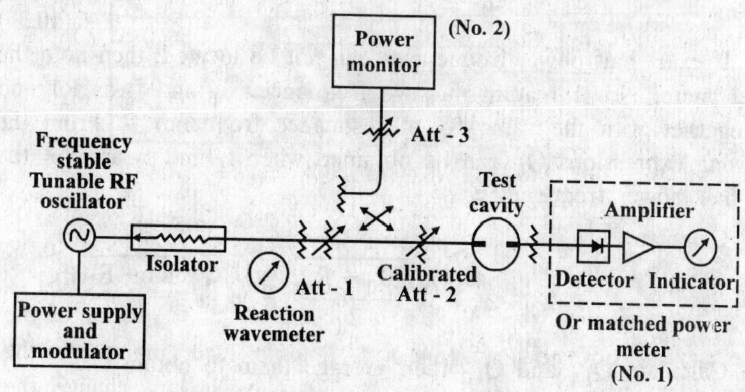

Basic arrangement for transmission method of measuring Q.

Fig. 10.23

The basic measurement setup is shown in Fig 10.23. A matched well isolated generator and a matched detector at the cavity output are required over the frequency range of measurement.

Procedure

1. Power meter 1 is used to measure transmitted power from the cavity and power meter 2, for measuring input power coupled to the directional coupler.

2. Adjust the power level in the main line with variable attenuator 1, to get a full scale reading on output power meter No 1. Similarly adjust level in the directional coupler arm to give a convenient reference reading on the power meter No. 2, using Att-3.

3. Note and record the reading at both power meters and the resonance frequency (f_0) on the wavemeter. After noting f_0 detune the wave meter sufficiently so that it does not interfere with subsequent measurements.

4. Vary the frequency of the source on either side of the resonant frequency until the reading of the output power meter (No. 1) reduces to half the reading obtained at resonance. At each of the two frequencies f_1 and f_2 where this occurs, note the reading of the monitoring power meter (No. 2). This reading should remain same as was obtained at the resonance. Adjust Att-1 for this purpose. Measure and record the half power frequencies f_1 and f_2 on either side of resonance.

5. Calculate Q_L as follows–

$$Q_L = \frac{f_0}{f_2 - f_1} \qquad \text{....(10.35)}$$

If exact half power frequencies can not be located, then note the power meter No. 1 readings at two frequencies f_1 and f_2 as R1 and R_2 together with the value R_0 at resonance frequency f_0. From the following expressions Q_L can be obtained when f_1 and f_2 are not the true half power frequencies.

Calculate

$$\alpha_1 = \sqrt{\frac{R_0 - R_1}{R_1}}, \alpha_2 = \sqrt{\frac{R_0 - R_2}{R_2}}$$

Calculate Q_{L1} and Q_{L2} then average them to obtain Q_L.

$$\text{Thus} \quad Q_{L1} = \frac{\alpha_1 f_0}{2|f_2 - f_1|}, \quad Q_{L2} = \frac{\alpha_2 f_0}{2|f_2 - f_1|}$$

$$Q_L = (Q_{L1} + Q_{L2})/2$$

10.8. Antenna Measurement

The transmission and reception of microwave power into the space and from it, is essential in microwave communication. Antenna behaves as an impedance transformer between the power source and free space. The characteristics of an antenna are expressed in terms of the antenna radiation pattern, gain, directivity and bandwidth. An open ended transmission line will act as an effective antenna if its output end is well matched to space. Horn antennas are extensions of waveguides whose ends are flared either in E or H-plane, to obtains E-plane or to H-plane sectorial horns. When flare is in both E and H-plane pyramidal horn is obtained. Conical horn is obtained when a circular waveguide is flared in a conical shape. Different type of horns are shown in Fig. 10.24.

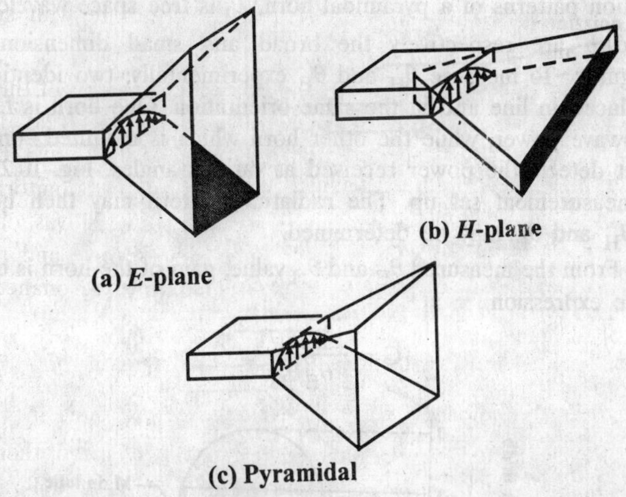

Fig. 10.24 Typical electromagnetic horn antenna configurations.

10.8.1 Radiation pattern

A short dipole radiates equal power in all the directions and is called an isotropic radiator. But a practical antenna like horn or helix does not radiate isotropically. The field strength or power intensity as a function of aspect angle at a constant distance from the radiating antenna is known as the radiation pattern of the transmitting antenna. The radiation pattern in the E and H-plane will depend upon the fact, as which field is parallel to the ground. If the receiving and transmitting antennas are identical and have same polarization, then the transmitting and receiving radiation patterns are also identical. A typical radiation pattern shown in Fig. 10.25a shows a main lobe, side lobes and a back lobe. Major portion of the radiated power is concentrated in the main lobe. An efficient antenna should radiate minimum power in side lobes and back lobe so that most of the power can be concentrated in the desired direction (main-lobe direction). The angle between the two points on the main lobe where power intensity reduces to half of the maximum, is known as 3 dB beam width. Borrow and Chu showed that beam width is inversely proportional to their respective dimensions as shown below

$$\theta_H = \frac{80\lambda_0}{a} \text{ and } \theta_E = \frac{53\lambda_0}{b} \qquad ....(10.36)$$

where θ_H and θ_E are respectively the beam widths of H and E plane radiation patterns of a pyramidal horn, λ_0 is free space wavelength and a and b are respectively the broad and small dimensions of the waveguide. To measure θ_H and θ_E experimentally, two identical horns are placed in line and in the same orientation. One horn is fed by the microwave power, while the other horn which is mounted on a rotary mount detects the power received at various angles. Fig. 10.25b shows the measurement set up. The radiation pattern may then be plotted and θ_H and θ_E may be determined.

From the measured θ_E and θ_H value, gain of the horn is calculated by the expression

$$G = \frac{13325.71}{\theta_E \theta_H} \qquad ....(10.37)$$

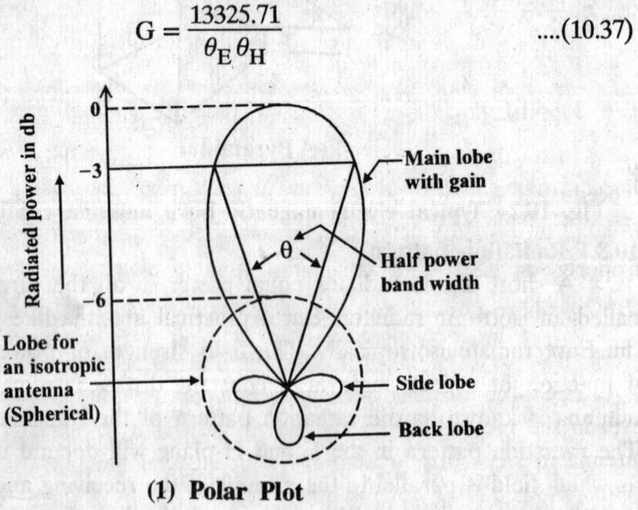

(1) Polar Plot

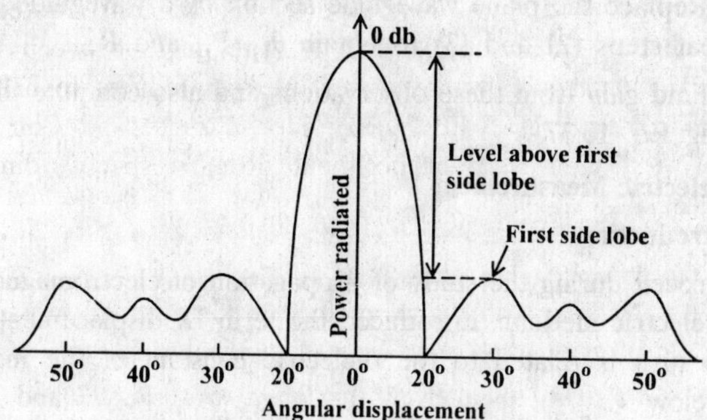

Fig. 10.25.a Antenna radiation pattern

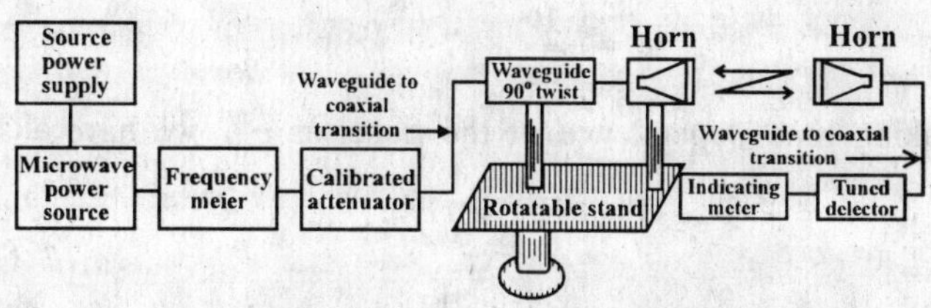

Fig. 10.25.b Set-up for measuring gain of a horn antenna (two identical horn method)

Procedure

1. Assemble the setup as shown in Fig. 10.25b with the horns properly aligned and distance between antennas greater than $2D^2/\lambda_0$, where D is the aperture of the larger dimension of the antenna. The E vector should be kept parallel to the ground.

2. Switch on the microwave source and obtain suitable power level in the meter. Record the power received. Rotate the transmitting antenna in steps of 5° on both the sides and note the power received.

3. To get E-plane radiation pattern, plot the power received versus angle on a polar graph and determine beam width θ_E. Compare it with theoretical value obtained from equation 10.36.

4. Remove the plane waveguide section horns and connect a straight waveguide section and record output power. This is the power transmitted (P_{tr}).

5. Replace the plane waveguide section by a waveguide 90° twist, and repeat steps (2) and (3) to obtain θ_H, P_{tr} and R_{rec}.

6. Find gain from these observations and also compute theoretical gain using Eq. 10.37.

10.9. Dielectric Measurement

Introduction

Maxwell during the study of propagation of electromagnetic wave in the dielectric medium, introduced the term D, displacement current, which in turn is related to the dielectric constant of the medium as shown below

$$\nabla \times H = J + \frac{\partial D}{\partial t} \quad \text{where } D = (\varepsilon E)$$

From Maxwell's relations, it is possible to show that the velocity c of an electromagnetic wave is a function of medium parameters, permeability (μ) and permittivity (ε) as

$$c = \frac{1}{\sqrt{\mu\varepsilon}}$$

Taking time dependence of the fields as $e^{j\omega t}$ we have

$$\nabla \times H = \sigma E + j\omega\varepsilon E \qquad \text{....(10.38)}$$

or

$$\nabla \times H = j\omega\left(\varepsilon - \frac{j\sigma}{\omega}\right) E = j\omega\varepsilon^* E \qquad \text{....(10.39)}$$

$\varepsilon^* = \left(\varepsilon - \dfrac{j\sigma}{\omega}\right)$ is known as complex dielectric constant.

Let ε_0 be the dielectric constant of vacuum (free space)

$$\frac{\varepsilon^*}{\varepsilon_0} = \varepsilon_r = \left(\frac{\varepsilon}{\varepsilon_0} - \frac{j\sigma}{\omega\varepsilon_0}\right) = \varepsilon' - \varepsilon'' \qquad \text{....(10.40)}$$

where ε_r is the ratio of the complex dielectric constant to the dielectric constant of vacuum and is known as the relative dielectric constant. The real part $\varepsilon' = R_e(\varepsilon^*/\varepsilon_0)$ shows the ability of the dielectric material to store electric energy, while the imaginary part $\varepsilon'' = -I_m(\varepsilon^*/\varepsilon_0)$ is associated with losses occuring in the dielectric. We can write Eq. (10.40) as

$$\varepsilon_r = \varepsilon' \left(1 + \frac{\varepsilon''}{\varepsilon'}\right) = \varepsilon' (1 + \tan \delta) \qquad ....(10.41)$$

where $\tan \delta$ is known as loss tangent of the dielectric and represents the ratio of power lost in the dielectric (ε'') to the energy stored per cycle (ε') in the dielectric.

Dielectric constant varies slowly with change in frequency and can be taken as constant over a narrow band of frequencies. The variation of $\tan \delta$ with frequency is more pronounced than that of ε'. The dielectric constant is also a function of temperature and humidity, hence these parameters should be kept constant during measurement and have to be recorded along with the result.

There are several ways in which dielectric measurements may be made. They are given below

1. Von-Hipple or Shorted waveguide method.
2. Corfield coaxial line method.
3. Two point method.

10.9.1. Two point method of measuring dielectric constant involving the solution of a transcendental equation

This method is most widely used for the measurement of dielectric constant. The accuracy of the measurement depends on the equipment used during the experiment and can be used for 'Lossless' dielectric and for dielectrics with medium losses.

Lossless dielectric

Consider Figure 10.26a showing the position of minima in a waveguide with and without a di electrtic piece. Fig. 10.26b, shows an empty short-circuited wave guide. A probe located at voltage minima is denoted as position D_R. Fig. 10.26c shows the same waveguide loaded with a sample of length l_ε and terminated by a short-circuit, touching the dielectric sample. In this case, the position of voltage minima is shown by D. Looking from the plane T_0 towards the right and the left, one can write the impedance equation

$$Z_0 \tan \beta l = - Z_\varepsilon \tan \beta_\varepsilon l_\varepsilon \qquad ....(10.42)$$

The respective distances from the short circuit are $(l + l_\varepsilon)$ and $(l_1 + l_\varepsilon)$.

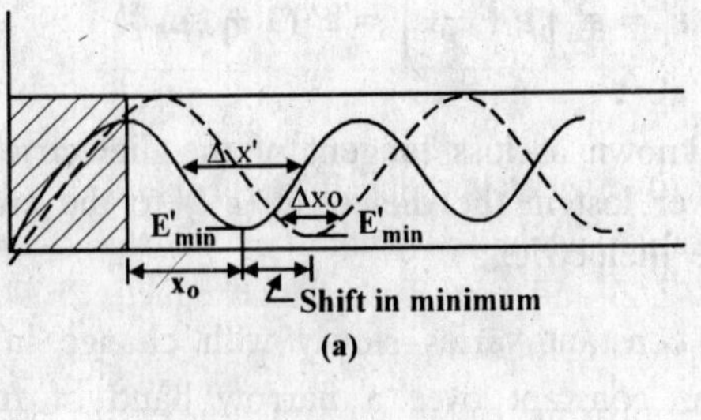

(a)

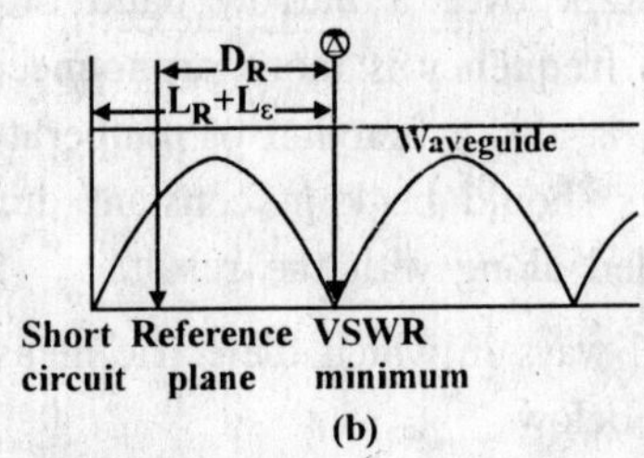

(b)

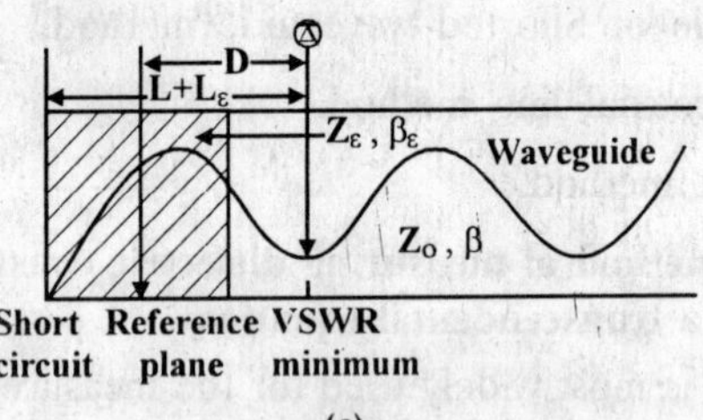

(c)

Fig. 10.26.

Similarly from Fig. 10.26b looking towards the right at the short circuit the impedance equation can be written as

$$Z_0 \tan \beta(l_R + l_\varepsilon) = 0 \qquad ....(10.43)$$

Now consider the expression

$$\tan \beta(D_R - D + l_\varepsilon) = \tan \beta[(l_R + l_\varepsilon) - (l + l_\varepsilon) + l_\varepsilon]$$

$$= \tan \beta\,[(l_R + l_\varepsilon) - l] \qquad ....(10.44)$$

Expanding the tangent relation and using Eq. 10.43 one obtains

$$Z_0 \tan \beta(D_R - D + l_\varepsilon) = Z_\varepsilon \tan \beta_\varepsilon\, l_\varepsilon \qquad ....(10.45)$$

Recalling the relation Z_0/Z_ε from Eq. 10.42, Eq. 10.34 can be written in the form

$$\frac{\tan\beta(D_R - D + l_\varepsilon)}{\beta l_\varepsilon} = \frac{\tan\beta_\varepsilon l_\varepsilon}{\beta_\varepsilon l_\varepsilon} \qquad ....(10.46)$$

Equation. 10.46 shows that all the quantities on the left hand side are measurable, while the quantities on the right hand side are of the form tan Z/Z and is a multivalued function. The correct value can be selected in the following two ways

(i) When approximate value of the dielectric constant is known, select that value say β_ε, and compute dielectric constant from the relation

$$\beta_\varepsilon = \frac{2\pi}{\lambda_0}\left\{\varepsilon_r\mu_r - \left(\frac{\lambda_0}{\lambda_c}\right)^2\right\}^{1/2} = \frac{2\pi}{\lambda_d} \qquad ....(10.47)$$

where $\lambda_c = 2a$ is cutoff wave length, λ_0 is the free space wave length, λ_d = guide wavelength when it is filled with the dielectric, ε_r is the relative permittivity or dielectric constant and μ_r is the relative permeability.

$$\varepsilon_r = \frac{\left(\frac{a}{\pi}\right)^2\left(\frac{\beta_\varepsilon l_\varepsilon}{l_\varepsilon}\right)^2 + 1}{(2a/\lambda g)^2 + 1} \qquad ....(10.48)$$

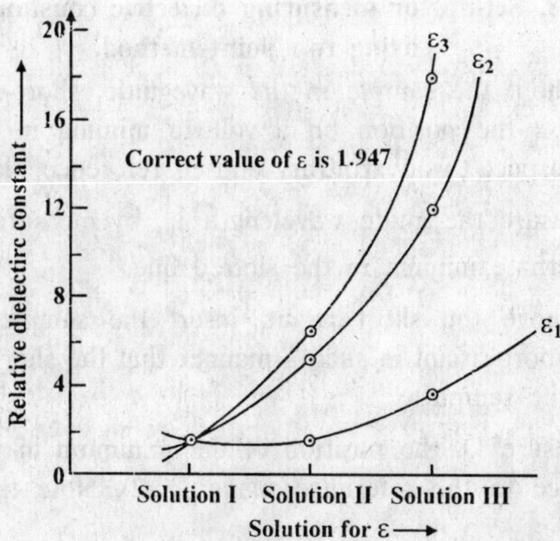

Fig. 10.27. Illustration of the graphical method for calculating dielectric constant using two point method.

If this value is close to the approximately known value then the **value** obtained is the true value, otherwise try another solution and so on.

(ii) If approximate value of the dielectric constant is not known, the identical experimental procedure is repeated with the sample of different lengths. The proper solution of the transcendental Eq. 10.46 is common to the two sets of solutions and is thus the point of intersection of the two curves drawn for each sample between dielectric constant ε and the solutions for $\beta_\varepsilon l_\varepsilon$ as shown to Fig. 10.27

The proper solution in this case is the one common to the two sets of solutions. In other words it is the intersection point as shown in Fig. 10.27.

Procedure

1. Connect the equipment as shown in Fig. 10.28.

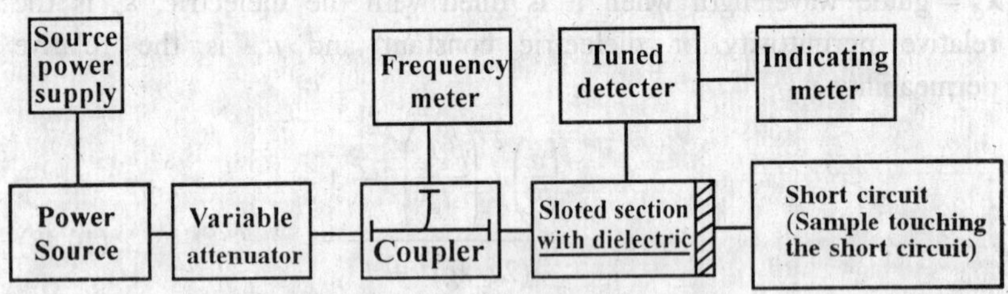

Fig. 10.28. Set-up for measuring dielectric constant of a Solid using two point method.

2. Without the sample in the waveguide, short-circuit the wave guide. Choose the position on a voltage minima in the slotted line (D_R) with respect to an arbitrary chosen reference plane ($D = 0$).

3. Measure the guide wavelength λ_g, by measuring the distance between alternate minima in the slotted line.

4. Remove the short-circuit, insert the sample dielectric and replace the short-circuit in such a manner that the short-circuit touches the end of the sample.

5. Measure D, the position of the minimum in the slotted line, with reference to the reference plane $D = 0$. Note the value of the VSWR.

If the dielectric constant of the sample is not known apriori, then identical set of measurements have to be made with the dielectric sample of different lengths. Depending upon the conditions, proper solution is carried out and from it dielectric constant ε_r is computed.

10.10. Spectrum Analyser

We know that an oscilloscope is used to display a wave in time domain, similarly a spectrum analyzer is used to display a wave in the frequency domain. There are two types of spectrum analysers (i) real time spectrum analyser (ii) swept tuned frequency spectrum analyser. Both types of analysers display periodic and random signals. Spectrum analysers do not display phase relationships on the cathode ray tube.

The most common type of spectrum analyser used at microwave frequency is the swept tuned spectrum analyser. The block diagram of a swept tuned spectrum analyzer is shown in Fig. 10.29.

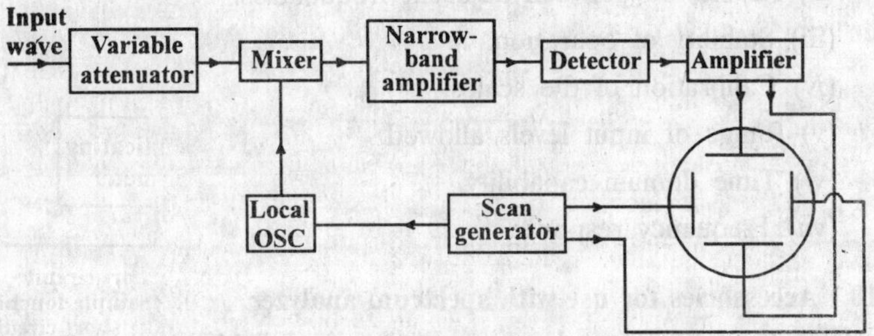

Fig. 10.29 Swept-tuned spectrum analyser.

The input signal is applied directly to the mixer through an attenuator. The input amplifier must be sensitive, it sets the limit of minimum input signal. Input signals as low as -125dB$_m$ can be selected. The local oscillator (LO) is swept through a range of frequencies in synchronization with the horizontal sweep of CRT. The input wave and LO frequency are applied to a mixer (nonlinear device) to form intermediate frequency (IF). Each input frequency will mix with the LO frequency, a different frequency at the IF bandwidth is observed detected and amplified by the IF amplifier. It is then filtered and displayed on the CRT.

The equation that governs the frequency conversion at the mixer is given by

$$f_s = f_l \pm f_{IF} \qquad \text{....(10.49)}$$

where f_s = input rf signal to spectrum analyzer, Hz.

f_l = Local oscillator frequency, Hz.

f_{IF} = IF amplifier frequency, Hz.

The range of spectrum analyzer can be extended by using harmonic frequencies generated by the local oscillator. The equation for the signal frequency would then become

$$f_s = nf_l \pm f_{IF} \qquad ....(10.50)$$

where n = harmonic number.

n = 1 for fundamental harmonic

n = 2 for second harmonic, and so on.

All types of spectrum analyzers provide two types of amplitude scales linear and logarithmic. For proper operation the spectrum analyzer depends on the following factors.

(i) Frequency range of operation.

(ii) Resolution between adjacent frequencies.

(iii) Stability of operation.

(iv) Calibration of the scales.

(v) Range of input levels allowed.

(vi) Time domain capability.

(vii) Frequency response.

10.10.1 Accessories for use with spectrum analyzer

Spectrum analyzers have a variety of available accessories that expand their operational capability. These include (1) the attenuators and limiters to avoid damage to the front end of the spectrum analyzer, (2) signal generators, function generators, comb generators and frequency counters, (3) digital multi-memory storage unit.

Operation of a spectrum analyzer

A typical spectrum analyzer (HP 8559 A) front panel with CRT and controls is shown in Fig. 10.30.

The front panel controls of the spectrum analyzer vary from unit to unit. These front panel controls are normally grouped into three categories.

(1) Display adjustments

(2) Frequency selection

(3) Amplitude controls

Since there are many controls associated with the spectrum analyzer, most analyzers have preadjustment settings to be set at the start of each use.

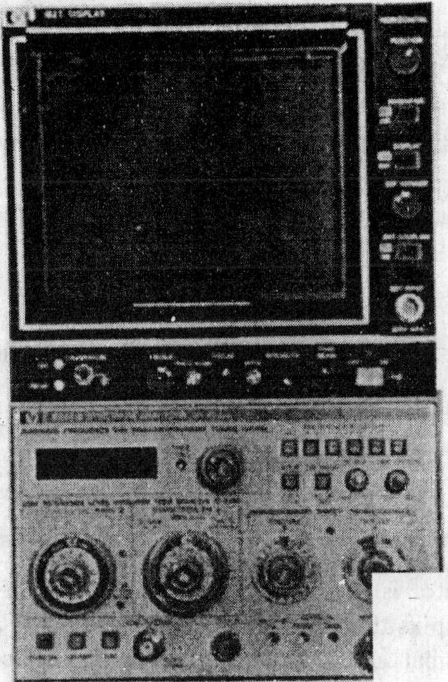

Fig. 10.30. Typical spectrum analyzer front panel.

Spectrum analyzer is used for the following purposes.

(i) Identifying frequency terms and their power level

(ii) For measuring the harmonic distortion in a wave

(iii) For determining types of wave modulation.

(iv) For measuring the signal to noise ratio.

(v) For identification of wave distortion.

(vi) For determining the frequency response of filters.

(vii) For determining the power and voltage levels of individual frequency terms.

10.11. Network Analyser (NA)

There are two types of network analysers

(i) Scalar network analyser.

(ii) Vector network analyser.

Vector network analyser are used for amplitude and phase measurements over a wide frequency range within a reasonable time while if the same measurments are done by slotted line they are very slow and time consuming. The basic measurement involves an accurate reference signal with respect to which the test signal amplitude and phase are measured. The most common network analyser available is the 8410A. The 8410A (NA) performs all functions upto 12.4 GHz and has limited capability upto 18 GHz. The latest analyser available in the market is 8510C.

Fig. 10.31 shows a schematic block diagram of HP1810 A network analyser.

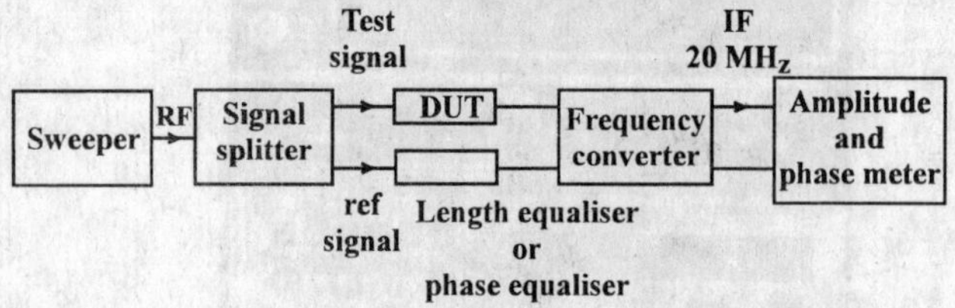

Fig. 10.31 Block diagram of a network analyser.

Sweep generator is used to generate frequencies of entire range. The signal splitter splits the input rf signal into test signal and reference signal. The test signal is transmitted through the device under test, while the reference signal passes through a phase equalising length of line. Measurment at rf frequencies is not easy hence frequency converter is used to generate IF frequency (20 MHz), at this frequency phase measurment is easy. The signal retains both amplitude and phase characteristics after conversion. The length of the phase equaliser should be such that the distance travelled by reference and test signal are equal. Details of the harmonic frequency converter are shown in Fig. 10.32.

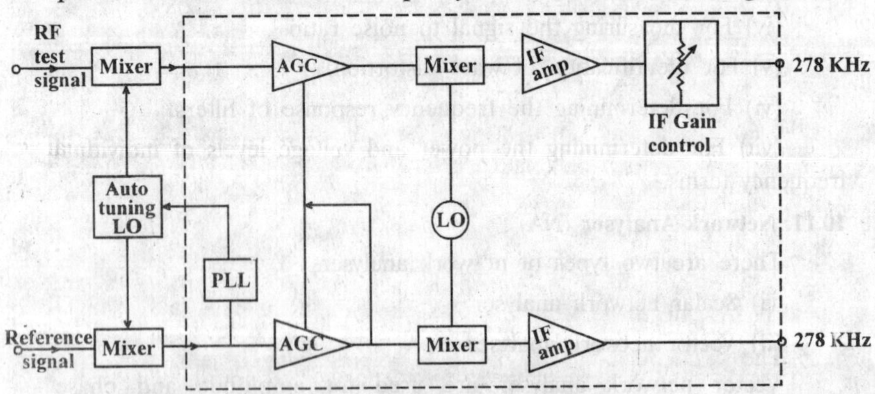

Fig. 10.32 Block diagram of the frequency converter.

The input signal is converted to a fixed IF frequency (20MHz) at which amplitude and phase can be measured. To make the system capable of swept frequency operation, the internal phase lock loop keeps the reference channel tuned to the incoming signal. This loop ensures the accuracy of test measurments. One of the two matched AGC amplifiers keep the signal level of the reference channel constant and apply an error signal to a matched amplifier in the test channel so that the later signal level does not change. The IF in MHz range is further changed into a fixed IF in the KHz range by the second mixer for the final amplitude and phase comparison.

The vector network analyser is used

(i) For transmission and reflection measurements.

(ii) For measurement of s-parameters.

(iii) For phase-magnitude display.

(iv) For phase gain indication.

10.11.1. Transmission measurement

In transmission measurements we can measure insertion loss, gain, conversion loss, attenuation and S parameters. The measurement setup for S parameters is shown below Fig. 10.33.

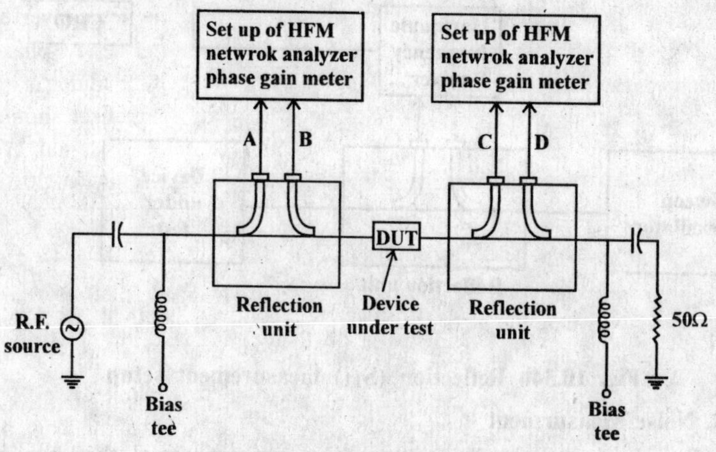

Fig. 10.33 Set up for measurement of S-parameter.

The parameters are derived using the expression

$$S_{11} = \frac{B}{A} \underline{\left| \phi_B - \phi_A \right.} \quad \text{....(10.51)}$$

$$S_{21} = \frac{C}{A} \underline{\left| \phi_c - \phi_A \right.} \quad \text{....(10.52)}$$

For the parameter S_{22} and S_{12}, we reverse the device under test.

For transmission (S_{12}) and reflection (S_{11}) parameter the setup used are given in Fig. 10.34a-b respectively.

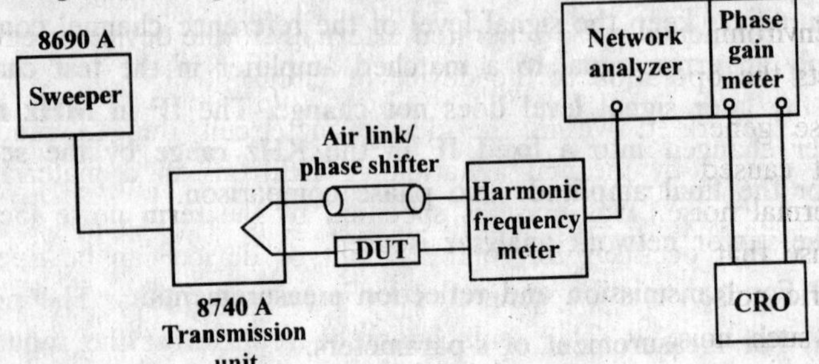

Fig. 10.34a Transmission (S_{12}) measurement setup

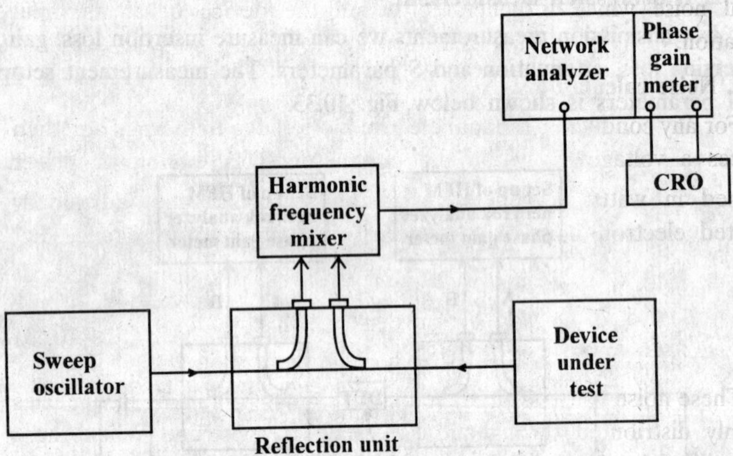

Fig. 10.34b Reflection (S_{11}) measurement setup

10.12. Noise Measurment

In microwave communications the weakest signal that can be detected is usually determined by the amount of noise added by the receiving system. Hence any decrease in the amount of noise generated in the receiving system will produce an increase in the output signal-to-noise ratio equivalent to a corresponding increase in the received signal. Noise interference within a device, amplifier, or circuit can be seperated by its source. Three general sources of noise that occur in microwave circuits are

1. Noise generated by the amplifier or device.

2. Noise generated and added to the input signal before the device.

3. Environmental noise generated externally to the device or circuit that affects the operation of the device or circuit.

Noise generated within the device or circuit due to random movement caused by thermal agitation of electrons in a material is called thermal noise. This noise is specified by the term noise factor. Signal noise that occurs prior to the circuit or device can be due to atmospheric noise or noise generated by previous circuits. The noise factor of such noise is fixed and cannot be reduced at the input to the device. Environmental noise is normally called radio frequency interference (RFI) noise or electromagnetic interference (EMI) noise.

Here we shall be dealing with only the noise measurements for thermal noise which is generated within the device or at its input termination.

10.12.1. Noise calculations

For any conductor, random electric motion due to thermal agitation produces a voltage e_n within the conductor. This motion or power expressed in watts, is generated by the square of the individually generated electron noise voltage across the generator resistance R_n. Thus

$$R_n = \frac{e_n^2}{R_n} \quad \text{....(10.53)}$$

These noise voltages produce output signals containing frequencies randomly distributed throughout the entire rf spectrum. When these are amplified by receiver of a given bandwidth B, the output will be proportional to bandwidth, absolute temperature and the value of the equivalent output resistor R.

$$e_n^2 = 4K\,TR_n\,B$$

where K = Boltzmann's constant (1.37×10^{-23} W-sec/°k)

T = Temperature in degrees absolute (kelvin scale T = 290° at ambient of 20°C)

B = bandwidth (in Hz)

If the generating resistor is matched to a load, power across it is

$$P_n = kTB$$

This input noise power is amplified and picks up noise power on its way from other resistive amplifier units. So the total noise of an amplifier output consists of (a) the minimum inherent input noise N_1 multiplied by the amplifier gain, plus (b) the internally contributed noise power.

The noise factor is defined as

$$F = \frac{S_{in}/N_{in}}{S_{out}/N_{out}} \qquad \text{....(10.54)}$$

$$= \frac{N_{out}}{N_{in}\left(\dfrac{S_{out}}{S_{in}}\right)} = \frac{N_{out}}{N_{in}\, G}$$

where G is the gain of the device. If we measure the output of given noisy amplifier, a combined power is measured. It is then compared to the minimum input noise power to obtain the noise factor

$$F = \frac{N_1}{k\,T_0\,BG} \qquad \text{....(10.55)}$$

But we want an expression for the amount of excess noise added by the receiver itself Nr. Nr is the difference between the measured noise and the calculated minimum noise.

$$N_r = N_1 - kTBG$$

$$= F\,(KTBG) - KTBG$$

$$= (F - 1)\,(KTBG) \qquad \text{....(10.56)}$$

Inherent receiver noise thus centers around a simple power-meter output measurement N_1, other contributory factors are the receiver bandwidth and gain (by measurement or specified), plus specified temperature and boltzmann's constant.

Measurement of N_1 can be made with a CW noise generator and a conventional power meter. The usual procedure is to connect the noise generator and note the noise power level with the generator turned off. Now turn on the noise generator, increase its output till the power output level is double of the initial generator "off" output level. The increase in generator power calculated from the increased microvolt level allows us to calculate the noise figure.

10.12.2. Basic excess power noise measurement

Excess noise power output measurements use input calibrated noise generator source shown in figure 10.35a. Two measurements N_1

with the excess noise source cold, and N_2 with the excess noise sources fired are noted. Noise reading under these conditions by breaking down the noise component are shown as in Fig. 10.35 b and c. The gain bandwidth factors are common at two noise temperatures hence do not enter in final calculations. The final ratio N_2/N_1 is

$$\frac{N_2}{N_1} = \frac{(\text{terminal noise} \times G) + (\text{internal receiver noise}) + (\text{signal generated excess noise} \times G)}{(\text{terminal noise} \times G) + (\text{internal receiver noise})}$$

and can be developed using Eq. 10.56

$$F = \frac{T_2 - T_0}{T_0} \frac{1}{\left(\frac{N_2}{N_1}\right) - 1} \quad \text{....(10.57)}$$

Converting in to logarithmic notation

$$F_{dB} = 10 \log \frac{T_2 - T_0}{T_0} - 10 \log \left(\frac{N_2}{N_1} - 1\right) \quad \text{....(10.58)}$$

The first term is a known quantity. For an argon discharge the excess noise ratio is 15. 2dB. Thus,

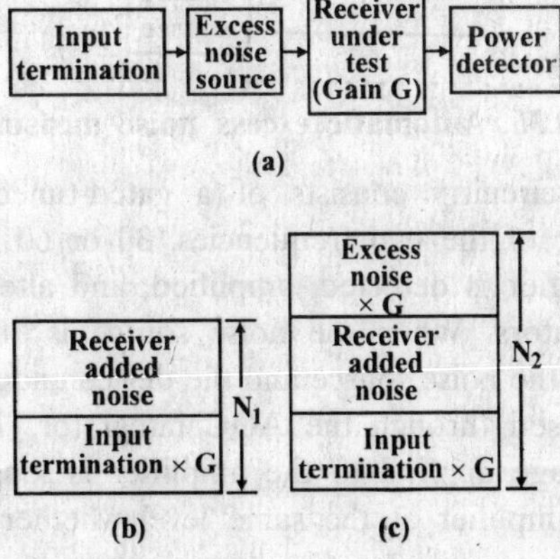

Fig. 10.35. Analysis of noise power components.

$$F_{dB} = 15.2 - 10 \log \left(\frac{N_2}{N_1} - 1\right) \text{dB} \quad \text{....(10.59)}$$

The temperature of the argon-gas source is approximately 10,000° k, $(T_2 - T_0)/T_0$ becomes a ratio of 33.3, accounting for the 15.2 dB in Eq 10.59.

10.12.3. Automatic excess noise measurments

Noise factor can be measured automatically and continuously using the basics of measuring and comparing N_1 and N_2 noise voltages. The device operates according to the layout diagram shown in Fig. 10.36.

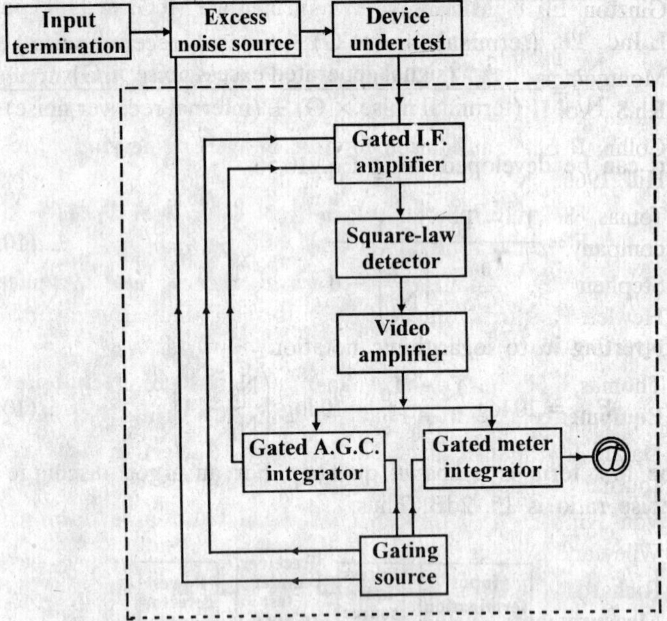

Fig. 10.36. Automatic excess noise measurement.

The input circuitry consists of a gated-tuned amplifier which operates at either of the two frequencies, 30 or 60 MHz. The output from tuned amplifier is detected, amplified, and alternately applied to two gated integrators. When the noise source is "on', the combined noise power from the noise source and the device under test is amplified, detected and passed through the AGC integrator. The time constant of the AGC voltage applied to the amplifier is long enough to hold the gain of the amplifier at the same level whether the noise source is "on" or "off".

when the noise source is turned "off", the combined noise power from the source and the device under test is amplified, detected and passed through the meter integrator and displayed on the meter. Because of the AGC action, the meter deflection is proportional to the ratio of the noise power when the source was "on" and "off" and since the noise from the noise source (excess noise) is accurately known, the meter face is calibrated to read the noise figure directly in decibels.

References

1. Sucher, M and J. fox, **"Handbook of microwave measurement"**, Vol. I and II and III.
2. Ginzton, E.L., **"Microwave Measurments"**, McGraw-Hill company L Inc., 1957.
3. Montgomery. CG., **"Technique of microwave measurements"**, Rh.S., Vol II.
4. Collin, R.E., **"Foundation for microwave Engineering"**, Mc Graw Hill, 1966.
5. Tomas S. Laverghetta, **"Practical Microwaves"**, H.W.S. and company, Indianapols., 1984.
6. Stephen F., Adam., **"Microwave theory and Application"** Hewlett-Packard company, Prentice-Hall Inc., Englewood Cliffs NJ., 1969.
7. Thomas, H.E., **"Handbook of microwave Techniques and Equipments"**, Prantice-Hall Mc, Englewood cliffs, N.J., 1962.
8. Dakin, T.W. and works, C.N., **Microwave Dielectric Measurements,** Journal of Applied Physics, Vol. 18(a), Sept 1947.
9. Von Hipple, A., **"Dielectric Materials and applications"**, John Wiley and Sons Inc., New York (1953).
10. Richard, OB., **"Laboratory Manual for Microwave Measurements"**, Vol I, Edn III, 1963.
11. Wheeler, G., **"Introduction to Microwaves"**, PHI India Pvt. Ltd, (1978).
12. Veley, V.F., **"Modern Microwave Technology"**, PH Inc., Englewood Cliffs, New Jersey (1987).
13. Svrber, Jr. WH, and Crouch, GE, Tr., **"Dielectric Measurement Methods for solid at Microwave frequencies"**, J.Appl. Physics, Vol. 19, No. 12, Dec. 1948.
14. Balanis, CA, **"Antenna Theory Analysis and Design"**, Harper and Row, Pub. New York, 1982.
15. Sigh, A, **"An improved method for the determination of Q of cavity resonator"**, IRE Trans, on Microwave Theory and Techniques, MTT-6, pp 155-160, April 1958.
16. Ginzton EL, **"Microwave Measurment in the presence of coupling Losses"**, IRE Trans. on Microwave Theory and Techniques. Vol. MTT-6, pp. 383-389, October 1958.
17. The Narda Microwave Corporation catalogue No-12.

18. The Hewlett-Packard company, Catalogue No.-10
19. Application note 150-10, Spectrum Analyser-services, "**Spectrum Analysis, Field strength Measurment**", Hewlett Packard, Palo Alto, 1976.
20. Sisodia, M.L., and G.S. Raghuvanshi, "**Basic Microwave Techniques And Laboratory Manual**", New Age International (P) Limited publishers, New Delhi, Reprint 2000.

Problems and Review Questions

1. Name five types of test equipment used to make microwave measurements.
2. Explain precautions to be taken when connecting microwave equipment to connectors and devices.
3. Explain how a series isolator reduces system mismatch to the generator.
4. Define attenuation and insertion loss. How do they differ ?
5. Explain the general method of measuring Q of a cavity
6. Name three devices that detect power.
7. Explain how bolometers are mounted in a line to detect power.
8. How does a thermo couple differ from a bolometer as a means of detecting power ?
9. Explain the operation of a calorimetric power meter.
10. How is frequency measured in a microwave system on a continuous basis using a frequency counter ?
11. Explain why an isolator and low pass filter are located after an unknown generator.
12. What types of noise can affect amplifiers ?
13. Explain how measurements are made using a noise-figure meter.
14. What is a microwave network analyzer ?
15. A 25-dB isolator is added in series at the ouput of a signal generator to reduce the possibility of frequency pulling due to an affected system VSWR mismatch of 1.75/1. If the generator power output is 234 mW, what is the value of the reflected signal received at the generator ?
16. The calibrated power from a generator, as read at the power meter is 25 mW. When a 3-dB attenuator with a VSWR of 1.30/1 is inserted between the generator and the detector what value should the power meter read ?

17. What is the average power for a periodic wave if the peak power is 1300W and the pulse width is 0.56 & ? The periodic frequency of the wave is 1500 Hz.
18. How long a slot would be required on a slotted waveguide section to measure the wavelength of a microwave whose frequency is 5.4 GHz ?
19. If the output noise power is 0.0037 pW and the gain bandwidth product is 5105 Hz, find the noise factor and the noise figure.
20. If the noise factor for an amplifier is 1.38 dB, find the amplitude of noise if the gain of the amplifier is 300 and the bandwidth is 32 kHz.
21. A slotted line is used in association with an X-band microwave source. When the line is terminated by a short circuit, adjacent nulls are found at positions which are shown as 9.27 and 11.05 cm. What is the value of the guide wavelength ?
22. An unmodulated microwave source is connected to a bolometer mount and an appropriate power meter. The microwave power level reads as 25 mW. When an attenuating device is inserted between the source and the bolometer, the power reading falls to 5mW. What is the amount of attenuation (in decibels) provided by the device ?
23. A slotted line is used to determine the SWR value of a waveguide. Adjacent null positions are located at 13.31 cm and 15.45 cm. If the seperation between the twice-mininum power points is 2mm, what is the value of the SWR ?
24. Two identical directional couplers are placed in a waveguide to sample the incident and the reflected power. The meter readings show that the power level of the reverse coupler is 10dB down from the level of the forward coupler. What is the value of the SWR on the waveguide ?

INDEX

□□□